D0105815

Tolstoy

THE ULTIMATE
RECONCILIATION

Tolstoy

THE ULTIMATE RECONCILIATION

Martine de Courcel

TRANSLATED BY PETER LEVI

Charles Scribner's Sons
NEW YORK

Collier Macmillan Publishers
LONDON

This English version of
Tolstoï: L'Impossible Coïncidence
is gratefully dedicated to Jacques Barzun.

Originally published as *Tolstoï: L'Impossible Coïncidence*

Charles Scribner's Sons
Macmillan Publishing Company
866 Third Avenue, New York, NY 10022
Collier Macmillan Canada, Inc.

Library of Congress Cataloging-in-Publication Data
Courcel, Martine de.
Tolstoy : the ultimate reconciliation.
Translation of: Tolstoï.
Bibliography: p.
Includes index.
1. Tolstoy, Leo, graf, 1828–1910. 2. Novelists, Russian—19th century—Biography. I. Title.
PG3385.C6513 1987 891.73'3[B] 87-23374
ISBN 0-684-18569-5

10 9 8 7 6 5 4 3 2 1

Printed in the United States of America

Contents

Tolstoy

THE ULTIMATE RECONCILIATION

Life and the ideal are hard to reconcile.
To try to make them follow the same path
is a life's work.

LEO TOLSTOY

INTRODUCTION

The Riddle of Tolstoy's Departure

ON MAY 31, 1856, the young Count Leo Tolstoy, his head heavy with laurels—he had already published *Childhood*, *Boyhood*, and *Sevastopol Stories* with huge success—set out on horseback from his estate, Yasnaya Polyana, for Spasskoye, some twenty kilometers away, to pay a visit to Turgenev.

Turgenev was away and Tolstoy walked about waiting for him. That evening he observed in his journal: "His house showed me his roots and threw a lot of light on him; also it reconciled him to me."

I had a similar feeling when I went to Yasnaya Polyana for the first time in April 1975,* particularly in the little room from which Tolstoy fled into the night on October 28, 1910.

It was there that the idea of writing this book came to me: I wanted to understand why a man of eighty-two who was recognized as one of the greatest writers of his time, and who was "the conscience of humanity," had abandoned everything and finally succeeded in dying as he would have wished to live.

The most generally accepted opinion is that Tolstoy fled from Yasnaya Polyana because he could no longer tolerate his wife; another view is that he wanted to retire from the world like the great sinners of the past; a

* The author was in Russia in 1972 and 1975, and again in 1978 as a guest of the Soviet Union of Writers. On this last visit she was already at work on this book and had access to certain documents first published on the one hundred and fiftieth anniversary of Tolstoy's death.

third is that when he felt the approach of death he went away to die in hiding, as certain animals do.

These are no more than fragmentary interpretations, and they take no account of the profound motives that led Tolstoy to make his decision. The departure was no mere passing accident, felt to be important because it was final, and it was not Tolstoy breaking away from his past; on the contrary, it was the outcome of his entire life.

Tolstoy left because the divided, dismembered personality he had always been had found its unity at last. Alexandra Andreyevna Tolstoy, his distant kinswoman and close friend, who with attentive kindness had followed his struggle with himself ever since his youth, said: "Like a mirror broken to pieces," Tolstoy "reflected in every one of the fragments of himself a little of that blazing light he had received from on high." It was only at the end of his life that the pieces were to come together.

He had always wanted to go away: from childhood he dreamed of becoming a "Fool of God," which already implied abandoning Yasnaya Polyana.

His whole youth was to be a painful search for his true self. This search takes place in a chaotic rhythm in which dissolute living, work, and exaltation of spirit alternate, and sometimes coexist. He sets out often, and all his departures take place in a kind of panic.

In his maturity Tolstoy experienced a brief golden age: the mutual love between himself and his wife and the fulfillment he discovered in literary creation reconciled him to himself for a time; for those ten years the idea of going away did not exist for him.

This hiatus in his anxious quest for identity closed up slowly, and his old torments returned in strength and led him into the famous crisis of his middle years, which was really not so much a new crisis as the climax of an earlier one dating from childhood, never to be resolved until his extreme old age.

In spite of this overwhelming desire in his eighties to alter life itself and to change his mode of existence, Tolstoy did not manage to become a new man: he achieved nothing but the mutilation of the man he was. He attempted every renunciation, yet he managed no more than self-denial and rejections, the most painful of which was undoubtedly his resolution to stop writing—or, more precisely, to write nothing but works on politics and religion, dedicated to the good of mankind. He "burned what he used to adore," that is, love and art, and dreamed more and more often of abandoning "the lie of his existence which fills him with shame." He wondered "where to go to save himself from others and from himself."

He fled into action and good works, but did not on that account find peace.

What Tolstoy wanted to do was to realize the "impossible coincidence" between the law of men and that of God, between what is and what should be, and even more urgently between what he was and what he wanted to be. His life was a long readjustment from refusal to consent—a laborious process, the slow pace of which resulted from the fact that his psychological conflict and his religious disturbance had roots that were twined and tangled at the very heart of his being. In the end they constitute one single problem with a double variable. Tolstoy did not manage to resolve it as long as he kept looking for two distinct solutions; there could be no separate peace, one with himself and the other with God.

By a double movement that amounts to nothing less than the effort of an entire lifetime, Tolstoy ended by accepting himself as he was within what came to seem to him God's purpose: Leo Nikolayevich Tolstoy was not sent on earth to save humanity, but to write.

Writing then takes on a very different meaning for him; it ceases to be the vice he goes back to in spite of himself; it becomes the fulfillment of the will of God.

The exaggerations of *What Is Art?* thereby fall into perspective: art is no longer a lie, "it alone can create on the ruins of our present regime of violence and constraint that Kingdom of God which appears to us all as the highest object of human existence."

What Tolstoy owed to humanity was a book: *the* book. He could not write it at Yasnaya Polyana and so he left.

Why venture this supposition? Because in the last months and even the last hours of his life one can see a pattern analogous to that which had presided over the working out of each of his novels and every one of his essays and stories.

I began this enquiry without prejudgment and without any prepared hypothesis, knowing only that to understand the death of Tolstoy one would first have to understand his life. I set out therefore like an explorer on his track and performed, as it were, the task of an archaeologist on the ground of Tolstoy's life and work. I turned over the stones along his path and the words of his books to see if a hidden answer was not to be found there.

It was only at the end of this painstaking work that a flight over the excavation revealed its structure, rather as the plan of a buried city shows up more clearly in photographs taken from the air.

I

THE DIFFICULTY OF BEING LEO TOLSTOY

ONE

Childhood

Tolstoy's journey starts from Yasnaya Polyana: he deliberately made available certain clues to the riddles of his life and left others scattered in his writing, but it always seemed to me that a good number of them lay in this, his house. My second visit to it confirmed that impression, not only because Tolstoy was born there on August 28, 1828, passed the greater part of his life there, and left there only four days before his death, but also because he loved this estate, this house, as one loves a human being, and maybe even more, because he inherited it from his mother, who died before he was two years old. He knew little about her and venerated her memory to the extent of praying for her soul in what he called "the middling period" of his adult life, a charming euphemism meaning that it was fairly dissipated. His veneration did not become less as he grew older. He had turned eighty when he wrote in his diary: "I walk in the garden and dream of my mother, my mother of whom I recollect absolutely nothing, who has remained an ideal of saintliness for me."

He had been present at her last moments, since in those days death was not concealed as it is today, and his nurse had led him howling out of the room where his mother lay dying. Being unable, it seems, to take the horror of it on himself, he was (as he tells us) to put "that piercing, terrible cry, full of such fright that if I live a hundred years, I will never forget it,"[1]* into the mouth of a little girl in his first novel, *Childhood.*

In the course of his long life, Tolstoy witnessed numerous deaths, but he was never able to come to terms with that first one: "The room was

* The numbered references are grouped as notes at the end of the book.

nearly dark. It was hot and it smelt of mint, eau de Cologne, camomile and Hoffmann drops; that smell made such an impression on me that not just when I smell it but whenever I remember it, imagination carries me back in an instant to the sombre, suffocating room, and brings back every smallest detail of that frightful minute."[2] It is not an old sensation experienced again, as it is with Proust, that has this evocative power, but the mere memory of it.

Yasnaya Polyana is the link between Tolstoy and his unknown mother, who died at thirty, and of whom not even a portrait exists, though the walls of the house are covered with family pictures. He was to know of her only through a little girl's profile: two heads facing one another in silhouette on a pale blue background, Princess Marya and her sister, shadows painted and permanent, whose blackness and stillness must for a child have added to the mystery. Yet at the end of his life Tolstoy had come to be happy that "in the representation" he entertained of his mother there was only her "spiritual face."

Princess Marya Nikolayevna Volkonsky was an only daughter, born and brought up at Yasnaya Polyana by a father who was early a widower, and by whom "she was passionately loved," with that same attention and discipline he would perhaps have brought to bear on the education of the son he never had. "Apart from Russian, which she wrote correctly, in contrast to the ignorance of that language permitted in those days to daughters of the artistocracy," Tolstoy records in his *Memoirs* that "she knew four languages: French, English, German and Italian."[3] Contrary to custom, her father* was just as demanding over the study of geography, physics, and mathematics.

At first, Tolstoy's mother was to him a dream mother, a character out of a novel, and in *Childhood* he was to write: "Beautiful as her face was, it became incomparably more so when she smiled, and everything around her appeared to rejoice with her."[4] It would take Tolstoy more than fifty years to be reconciled to the truth. In *Recollections* he writes: "My mother was ugly." Being too good an analyst not to be aware of the contradictory blend in certain of his reminiscences, he wondered whether he might not be combining "a number of different impressions in a single memory," as happens "so often in dreams."[5]

This phenomenon of fusion, or of confusion, between several levels of reality and imagination, of shuttling between reality and fiction, occurs frequently in Tolstoy's work. The mother in *Childhood* is and is not his: He came to recognize, on the one hand, that he retained no memory of

* In *War and Peace*, Prince Bolkonsky teaches mathematics to his daughter Princess Mary, and Tolstoy himself taught his older children.

her, and on the other, that it was the mother of his friends, the Islenyevs, who had served as a model for the character in his novel. This myth-mother has "a beauty spot on the neck just below the place where her little curls rested," and Anna Karenina was to have the same "short curling locks that stray down on her neck as on her temples."

Tolstoy's love for Yasnaya Polyana is linked also to the years of his childhood, which was as happy as a childhood can be for an orphan who loses his mother at two and his father at nine. Count Nikolay Ilych Tolstoy, "with eyes forever sad," was a gambler, intelligent, lively, likeable, and independent. He read a great deal, had a fine library, and would proudly state that he did not buy new books until he had read the old ones. A gentleman of the old school, he had fought for the Tsar and managed his own estates without cruelty to any of his people: his friends were like himself, "free men who had not accepted office and baited the government a little."

At twenty-four, Tolstoy exclaimed: "Happy, happy times of childhood fled for ever! These memories exalt my soul, they are the source of my purest rejoicings."[6] For the orphan's two lost parents had been replaced: by Tatyana Alexandrovna Yergolskaya, a distant cousin of his father's on his grandmother's side, and by his brother Nikolay. Tatyana was a very noble character who revealed to the child "the spiritual joy of love"; she had refused to marry Tolstoy's father when he was a widower, although she had been in love with him since her youth. At that earlier time, for lack of a dowry she had withdrawn in favor of Marya Nikolayevna Volkonskaya, who was a rich heiress. Upon his wife's death Nikolay Ilych Tolstoy wanted to give his children a mother and proposed marriage, but Tatyana turned him down, for she knew that he did not really love her.

She was the only person to whom Tolstoy ever compared his mother, who he considered to be "obviously on a higher spiritual level" than his father or his family, except, he added, for "Tatyana Alexandrovna Yergolskaya . . . a woman remarkable for her moral qualities."[7]

As soon as Leo Tolstoy took possession of Yasnaya Polyana in 1847, his first care was to install his Tante Toinette;* she lived on there to her

* Russians address or refer to people by first name and patronymic. To avoid these rather long appellations, they often use diminutives or surnames. Tolstoy's family called Tatyana Alexandrovna Yergolskaya "Tante Toinette"; Countess Alexandra Andreyevna Tolstoy was "Alexandrine." That is how I shall refer to them. It seemed preferable not to follow the formal Russian usage except in cases of ambiguity. Tolstoy's sister and his second daughter were both named Marya and called "Masha"; his sister-in-law and his eldest daughter were both Tatyana; he called his first son after his second brother, Sergey, and his third son Lev, like himself.

As for Tolstoy's wife, Sofia Andreyevna, whom he called Sonya, it seemed logical to follow the habit of most Western biographers and call her Sofia.

dying day on good terms with her nephew's wife. Her delicacy was without limits: when she felt herself close to death, she asked to be carried to another room to prevent any sad association from spoiling the happy memories bound up with her own chamber. It was to this room that Tolstoy used to come after his escapades in Tula or in Moscow to chat with his aunt hour after hour. There he opened his heart freely to her, and she poured out on him all the affection he was hungry for. "She knows," he was to write in *Recollections*, "everything that I have done, deplores it, but will never rebuke me."[8]

Leo Tolstoy's brother Nikolay, his elder by five years, "a remarkable child who went on to become a remarkable man," played the role of father to the younger boy. His influence was partly due to the fact that the whole family thought Nikolay Nikolayevich was, morally speaking, very like his mother. She had brought him up to the age of seven with the same care and the same principles she had received herself.*

Tolstoy adored these exceptional people. Writing to his aunt from Tiflis on January 6, 1852, he said: "The two worst tragedies that could happen to me would be for you and Nikolay to die: you are the two people I love more than myself."[9]

In the series of family portraits Tolstoy sketched in his *Recollections*, the one of his grandmother Pelagaya, the daughter of Prince Nikolay Ivanovich Gorchakov, is a particularly entertaining mixture of cynicism and poetry. It is also of great interest, because in the course of it Tolstoy introduces another personage who had an unmistakable influence on his vocation as a writer, a certain Leo Stepanovich, a blind serf who had been bought simply to tell stories to the old lady, and from whom Tolstoy might well have acquired his narrative skill. The children were allowed to take turns at spending the night in their grandmother's room. Here is the impression Tolstoy retained of that curious ritual. "I remember the minute when the candle was put out, and only a little lamp was left alight before the gilded icons. Grandmother, that amazing grandmother who made the miraculous soap bubbles, lay stretched out high up on her pillows, altogether white—dressed in white and covered in white, in a white nightcap—and from the window sill came the strong, tranquil voice of Leo Stepanovich. . . ."[10]

In spite of his overwhelming affection for his aunt and his brother, it is certain that Tolstoy's mother's ghost never stopped roaming within his unconscious thought and begot in it that nostalgia for pure love which

* She kept a "Journal of Nikolay's Conduct" in which she noted daily her eldest son's intellectual and moral progress. Tolstoy as a child was very curious about this sort of record, in which he probably found a living everyday picture of his mother.

was to obsess him during his youth in his periods of debauchery, and still more in his maturity, as is shown by the violence with which he reviled bodily love in *The Kreutzer Sonata*.

Tolstoy's earliest years passed by in a deeply religious atmosphere: "not only my mother but everyone of the people around me during my childhood, from my father to the coachman, figured in my mind as beings who were wholly good."[11] One has the feeling that Tolstoy as a little boy lived in a world much like that of the children's books by the Comtesse de Ségur, only less mawkish.

Yasnaya Polyana was really a sort of hospice. In addition to the numerous friends, relations, and tutors who lived there, it gathered numbers of poor wretches and wanderers, known or unknown. Charity was no empty word in that house; Tolstoy and his wife were to continue its tradition.

In *Childhood*, the mother defends Grisha, one of the "official" beggars of the house, against her husband's criticism: "It is hard to believe that a man of sixty who goes barefoot summer and winter and always wears chains under his clothes . . . lives like that merely out of laziness."[12]

The dwellers in Yasnaya Polyana did not lack originality. Tolstoy's father's sister, Countess of Osten-Saken, "Aunt Aline," had lived there ever since her husband had gone mad and tried to kill her. Failing that attempt, he got her to stick out her tongue, pretending to be interested in her health, and then tried to cut it off with a razor. The poor woman was pregnant at the time and gave birth to a stillborn baby girl. The drama concluded with a fantastic episode of substituted babies. She then came to live with her brother in edifying seclusion. This aunt, whose way of life became increasingly monastic, entertained many of the perpetual pilgrims the Russians call Fools of God. In *War and Peace* the ones whom Princess Mary assembles at Lyssya Gora (which stands for Yasnaya Polyana) reflect the fascination that Tolstoy as a child felt about these holy men as they made their way toward Kiev or some other sanctuary, propelled by the same mysterious force that would one day take him far from home. He could see them, run into them, on the road below the avenue that leads up to the house. He often merged as a child into this flow of pilgrims* that had moved for centuries around the base of Yasnaya Polyana; he came back to lose himself in it again at the time of his great crisis in the 1880s, in the hope of emerging regenerated.

* At this time, tens of thousands of pilgrims, *bogomolitzi*, moved ceaselessly across Russia from one holy place to another. They were a kind of nomadic class, who took shelter, paying according to their means, in private homes, or in religious houses, which always had a hostel attached to them.

Tolstoy himself made a number of pilgrimages,* with a sack on his back and a stick in his hand.† At least three times, he did the one hundred and ninety-six versts (one hundred and thirty miles) between Moscow and Yasnaya Polyana on foot, always in a spirit of voluntary poverty.

The deeply religious atmosphere in which Yasnaya Polyana was immersed seems to have had an influence even on the games of the little Tolstoys. Some were profane, like the one invented by their adopted half-sister Dunyechka, the natural daughter of a friend of their father's and a pensioner at Yasnaya Polyana. The trick was to spit a little copper chain into one another's mouths: in the excitement one day, one of the boys swallowed it.

But the game of the "Brother Ants"‡ was quite a different matter. Tolstoy himself thought it had played a crucial part in his spiritual development. This esoteric ritual was special to the Tolstoy children and an original element in their family folklore. It was a mixture of "playing stagecoach" and some scrap of information gleaned by Nikolay about a religious sect founded in the fifteenth century in Bohemia that preached equality and universal love. The passengers in the coach first became Moravian brethren and then gradually got transformed into Brother Ants, because the Russian word for ant, *mouravei*, sounds like "Moravian."

Nikolay, the grand master of the "Brother Ants," was also keeper of a secret. He knew where the little "green stick" was kept, the wand with spiritual rather than magic power, which could ensure the happiness of

* He went to Optina-Pustyn several times. In July 1877 (which is to say, at the beginning of his moral crisis) he first set out there to meet the Starets Ambrose, who had an enormous reputation for holiness all over Russia and served Dostoyevsky as model for Father Zossima in *The Brothers Karamazov*; at that time Tolstoy set out from Moscow with Nikolay Nikolayevich Strakhov, his friend and disciple.

He was to return there, on foot as before, from Yasnaya Polyana in June 1881 with the master of the school he had founded for the village children; on the way he spent nights with the peasants, like a real pilgrim.

He was to pay another visit in February 1890, when he went to see his sister Masha, who had retired to a convent nearby.

And it was there at Optina-Pustyn that he was to spend his first night of freedom when he left Yasnaya Polyana for the last time in October 1910.

† Tolstoy's wife, Sofia Andreyevna, had a passion for photography. She developed hundreds of snapshots herself, as people did in those days, and took a number of her husband dressed as a pilgrim.

‡ The game consisted in putting chairs together, covering them with handkerchiefs or shawls, and sitting in the "stagecoach" underneath. Once they were in this shelter or hideout, "as crammed together as possible," writes Tolstoy, "we felt a special affection for each other. Sometimes a gesture showed it, a hug, or we just cuddled up close. But that was unusual. We knew all along that closeness was not the goal, and stopped at once. Being 'brother ants,' as we used to say, meant only hiding out of everyone's sight, being away from them all and loving each other." (L. Tolstoï, *Souvenirs et récits*, Paris: Gallimard [Pléiade], 1970, p. 441)

all mankind. This double distinction enhanced his prestige with young Leo and confirmed his role as acting father to him. When Tolstoy wrote *Childhood* in 1851, he did not mention the game of Brother Ants, although it belonged to the time about which he was writing, but in 1905 in his *Recollections* he speaks of it at length, having restored his past emotions to their proper place in the hierarchy of his feelings.

Among other memories, Tolstoy tells the story of a little boy, a neighbor, who arrived one day at Yasnaya Polyana and declared, as if it were the latest news, that God did not exist. Fifty years afterward, when he was writing *A Confession*, Tolstoy was to recall that the children "received this discovery as something most interesting and quite possible," a good indication of their concern with religious matters.

The death of his mother and the Brother Ants game were thus two great events in Tolstoy's childhood. A third was associated with the day he was locked up by his French tutor, Prosper de Saint-Thomas, who is Saint-Jérôme in *Boyhood*. At the age of seventy-seven, in the preface he wrote to Biryukov's official biography of him, Tolstoy was to wonder "whether that incident might not have caused the terror and disgust I feel at violence of any kind, a disgust I have felt all my life."[13] This repulsion is rather close to what the idol of his youth, Jean-Jacques Rousseau, felt when he was unfairly accused of breaking the tooth of a comb, an episode in his life which he says at the beginning of his *Confessions* he was never able to recall "without my pulse beating faster even now, and which has remained engraved on my soul" as "my first experience of violence and injustice."

When Tolstoy wrote *Youth* between the ages of twenty-seven and twenty-eight, he sensed that he would never change: "I am convinced that if I am permitted to live to extreme old age and my story reaches that far, I shall be nursing as an old man of threescore and ten exactly the same chimerical and childish dreams as I do now."[14] His idea at that time was to write a sort of continuous mythified autobiography; in the end he replaced it with the two realities of his journal and his novels. In his mature years, for quite a while, he thought of his life as divided into two distinct parts, one before and the other after 1881, the year of his "conversion," which he called his rebirth. It was only at the age of seventy that he became newly conscious of the unity of his life and wrote that "the ideal of the Brother Ants linked to one another in affection, not under two chairs covered with handkerchiefs but under the heavenly vault that extends over all mankind, has remained for me intact."[15]

Childhood is the work of a very young man; *Recollections* is by a man over seventy-five years old; but between these two works there stands a text of five pages, *First Memories*, *Autobiographical Notes*, written in 1878 when Tolstoy was fifty and in the depths of his depression, unable to master either his psychological or his metaphysical problems. He was attempting to explore the earliest regions of his memory, seeking as far back as possible in his past the roots of his present difficulties.

These *First Memories* should bring a delighted gleam to the eye of any psychoanalyst: "I am tied, I want to get my arms free, I cannot do it . . . Two well-meaning silhouettes bend over me. It seems to them necessary that I should be tied, though I know it is useless. I want to prove it to them, and I break out in unbearable yells. What has remained in my memory is not my cries or my suffering, but the complexity, the contradiction of my sensations. I want to be free, I do not bother anybody, and I who need strength am weak."[16] The symbolism of these memories is clear: Tolstoy was to experience all his life long that feeling of captivity, of lack of freedom,* to which he refers again later in a passage of his *Recollections*.

Tolstoy's earliest memory therefore is the longing to escape the feeling of being a prisoner. "My second impression is a joyful one," he adds in these *First Memories*. "I am sitting in a basin surrounded by the new and not unpleasant smell of something being rubbed on my little body . . . for the first time I noticed and liked my body . . . [taking pleasure in] the dark, smooth basin, the maid's arms with rolled-up sleeves, and the mixture of tepid and cold water, the steam it gave off, the noise it made, and especially the sensation of the smooth wet sides of the basin when I moved my tiny hands over them."[17] The summoning up of this first awakening to life leads Tolstoy to meditate on the mystery and brevity of human existence. The questions he sets himself are the same ones that his books will take up again and again so tirelessly: "When did I begin? When did I begin to live? And why is it joyous to me to imagine myself at that time, and yet has always frightened me to imagine myself again entering that state of death of which there will be no recollections that can be expressed in words? Was I not alive when I learned to look, to listen, to understand, and to speak, when I slept, took the breast, kissed it, and laughed and gladdened my mother? I lived, and lived blissfully. . . ."[18]

This digression indicates a deep adult nostalgia for the mother and the paradise of childhood, but it also reflects the existential anguish Tolstoy

* It was only on the rear platform of the train that carried him toward the unlikely place where he was going to die, the stationmaster's house in the small town of Astopovo, that he was able to cry out, "How happy I am to be free!" (*Tolstoï vu par lui-même et ses contemporains*, Moscow: Editions du Progrès [Ouvrage Collectif], 1977)

was a prey to at the time when he was writing *First Memories*. He had already defined the short period of infancy in which the die is cast for the future human being. "Did I not acquire then everything by which I live now?—and so rapidly that in all the rest of my life I have not acquired one additional hundredth of it? From the child of five to my present self is only a step. From the newborn infant to the child of five . . . a horrifying distance. From the embryo to the newborn infant . . . an abyss. And from the non-being to the embryo, not just an abyss but something inconceivable."[19]

What Tolstoy discovers, however far he retraces his memory, is the simultaneous perception of a fundamental constraint—the prison of life—and of a joyful freedom—"the happiness of living on this earth." His whole life will be a long and painful effort to escape from the one and recover the other. Tolstoy makes it clear, and this is the important point of the utterance, that what he remembers is not so much the suffering he went through as "the contradiction of my sensations." Contradiction* is at the center of the Tolstoy problem—the contradiction between his desires and his aspirations, and that between his way of life and his convictions. Tolstoy lived the perpetual martyrdom of the conflict of body and soul.

All the same, it is not Tolstoy's contradictions that give his life and his work their impetus; it is rather—one might even say it is *on the contrary*—his ceaseless attempts to resolve them.

* The frequent occurrence of the word "contradiction" in the vocabulary of nineteenth-century Russia is striking: of course Lenin uses it, but so does Dostoyevsky, and Tolstoy himself says that in *War and Peace* he wanted to show up in Napoleon and Tsar Alexander I "the contradictions found in those that surround them and in themselves." Was it a word that was in the air, and fitted the predicament of the times, or is it possibly among the fundamental traits of the Russian character? (L. Tolstoï, *Journaux et carnets*, Paris: Gallimard [Pléiade], 1979, vol. I, p. 560)

TWO

Boyhood

Tolstoy left Yasnaya Polyana for the first time on January 10, 1837, when he was eight. The entire family went to Moscow with a dozen coaches and thirty servants. Count Nikolay Ilych Tolstoy wanted his two elder sons to go to high school to prepare for admission to the university.

Little Leo discovered for the first time that the world did not end at the boundaries of the family estate. He recalled the shock fifteen years later: "Has it ever happened to you, reader, at a certain period of your life to notice all of a sudden that your way of looking at things has changed utterly, as if every object you had ever seen suddenly appeared from a new angle you had no knowledge of? This sort of moral metamorphosis happened to me for the first time during our journey, which I regard as the beginning of my adolescence."[1]

What Tolstoy calls moral metamorphosis is rather like a kind of moulting; he was destined to go through it more than once. In a succession of wrenches and sheddings, he broke loose from a variety of cloaks: very quickly from that of young aristocratic landowner, then the pedagogue's,* then the officer's, or military observer's, half civilian, half writer, and finally the novelist's. But he was never to complete *that* shedding of an old skin, though he did manage to get rid of his preacher's carapace.

The year of the family establishment at Moscow was marked by the

* Tolstoy, who voluntarily gave up advanced study, had a passion for teaching and several times sought refuge in it when he was experiencing his worst bouts of mental disarray.

sudden death of his father in June, and of his grandmother Pelagaya less than a year later. Tolstoy, already hostile to the conventional ideas that society compels us to substitute for true feeling, reflected with disillusionment on the fact that people usually associate a person's death with their own fear of dying. He protested against "this feeling that one habitually confuses with grief."

The narrator in *Boyhood* states that toward the age of fourteen, "none of the changes that occurred in my way of seeing was so striking as my being led to think no longer of one of the chambermaids as a servant of the female sex, and to think of her as a WOMAN, on whom my peace of mind and my happiness might to a certain extent depend."[2]*

Tolstoy feels his first sexual excitement and discovers amorous jealousy. The behavior of a little girl he thinks of as "a traitress" teaches him the perfidy of women. It was at this time that he pushed little Lyubov Islenyev out of the window while they were playing, because she was paying more attention to another boy than to him. Oddly enough, the same little girl was going to be his mother-in-law at a later day.

Tolstoy's discoveries were not limited to the domain of feeling. His French "governor" is amazed at his maturity and his taste for philosophic ideas. Tolstoy was afraid he would not be believed when he told of "the most constant subjects" of his reflections during adolescence, and he added that already his "weak, childish intelligence struggled with all the ardour of inexperience to resolve those problems whose definition represents the highest level the human mind can reach. . . ."[3]

His studies bring him the revelation of stoicism: he whips himself in secret and carries heavy dictionaries at arm's length to the point of exhaustion. This is one of the first manifestations of the power of ideas on Tolstoy's behavior. Later on, his readings in skeptical philosophy led him to doubt the reality of things and reduced him for a moment to a condition close to madness.

After their father's death, Aunt Aline became the guardian of the Tolstoy children. When Pelagaya died, Nikolay Ilych's other sister, who was called "Aunt Pauline," succeeded to the same position. Tolstoy and his brothers and sisters left Moscow and went to live with their aunt at Kazan. This new family involved them in a whirlwind of parties and social high life. Leo then began his university studies, which were, to put it mildly, chaotic.

* In 1876, entirely hostile to censorship as he was, and favoring "spontaneous" education as he did, Tolstoy asked for the chapter of *Boyhood* where this passage occurs to be withdrawn from the children's edition; he extended the same act of censorship to the chapter called "The Servants' Room."

He was now an adolescent, and his face was that of a simple mujik. Though in later years he longed to look like one of his peasants and idealized them to the point of believing that their beards smelled of spring, at the time when he did look like one he suffered greatly from the resemblance. He was a gangling youth, felt awkward, and envied his brother Sergey for his ease and beauty: "I was modest, but my modesty was increased by the conviction that I was a monster." He was "sure that nothing has so decisive an influence on the character of a human being as his outward appearance, and not so much appearance as the sense of being or not being attractive."[4] He thought he was ugly and suffered from it for a long time. Yet the photographs of those years show him to be pleasant looking enough—at least according to present standards.

Tolstoy was greatly preoccupied with his appearance; he thought it an obstacle to the unconditional, universal love he wanted to inspire. Like most motherless children he felt that nobody loved him. His attention to his physique took comical forms. One day as he left his room on the way to confession he threw a glance at the mirror and brushed his hair "high up," under the impression that it gave him "a pensive air." For his university entrance examination he was careful to wear a suit from the leading tailor. He tells us that having read a hundred French novels by Eugène Sue and Alexandre Dumas that summer, he noticed that the most fascinating hero in one of them had very thick eyebrows. In order to look like him he gave his own a light shave in the hope that they might grow back in a denser growth. He performed this operation so badly that he had to use makeup and tell his family that he had burned himself. Later, in the Caucasus, he was tormented by the fact that his mustache was longer on one side than on the other.

Among the faults of adolescence that Tolstoy believed he had gradually got rid of, the one which, as he wrote afterward, was certain to do him the most harm, was his "penchant for reasoning." That obsession would dwell with him all his life; it undoubtedly helped his work as a thinker and writer, but it drove him into more than one dramatic intellectual and moral dead end.

The feeling he thought the most important at the time was "a disgust with his own person . . . intertwined with the hope of happiness." It was this disgust that later aroused in him a perfectionist compulsion that never left him. He came to envy the belt studded with nails that Pascal wore; he read and admired the *Pensées* constantly from youth to old age, but his own religious torments, burning as they were, never had the mystical fervor of Pascal's.

Tolstoy passed his examination and entered the university; "he becomes a grown-up, he is congratulated," he goes to a dance and believes he is loved. The dreams of glory that are natural at his age take on a peculiar intensity. They put him into a kind of trance and keep him "perpetually in the anxious expectation of some magical happy event." He dreams of the ideal woman who will bring him happiness, and even more of the love of love. He works out a theory* in which he distinguishes between *aesthetic love* "limited by the love of the beauty of one's feelings,"† *devoted love* "based on the joy of sacrificing oneself to the beloved," without bothering to know whether the beloved is any the better for it, and lastly what he calls *active love*, which is "the urge to satisfy the needs, the desires, and even the vices of the beloved."[5]

In spite of his precocious gift of psychological analysis, it is to be doubted whether Tolstoy conceived his theory (it foreshadows the novelist of married life) when he was only sixteen, as he claims; more likely it belongs to the period when he was writing *Youth*, toward the age of thirty.

Though dreaming of true love and trying to elucidate its mysteries, he experienced physical love first with a street girl. Nothing much is known about the episode, except that the hero of *Journal of a Scorekeeper*, written in 1855, weeps at the foot of the bed of the young prostitute who has just shown him the realities of love.

Tolstoy, then, sows his wild oats, *il fait la noce*, as it was then called in

* The way in which Tolstoy introduces this theory is ambiguous and could lead one to think it was an apologia for homosexual love. He writes: "I do not speak of the love of a young man for a young woman or vice versa . . . I suspect these fondnesses. I speak of love for the man who concentrates according to his greater or lesser powers of soul on another or others, or a great number: of filial, brotherly, and paternal love, of love for a comrade, a friend, one's country, or mankind." For this problem of Tolstoy's supposed homosexuality—a hypothesis that the catalogue of his amorous exploits and conjugal ardor renders absurd—one should recall that in 1910, at the time of the outcries caused by the will that Tolstoy executed without his wife's knowledge, she accused him of an erotic relation with his disciple, Chertkov. In support of this statement she quoted a note in Tolstoy's journal dated November 28, 1851: "Men, I often fall in love with them; my first love was the two Pushkin brothers." (He named another four or five, and said there were "many others.") He added that he had fallen for these men, "well before I had any idea of the possibility of pederasty, and that never had my imagination presented me with images of lust, on the contrary, that disgusts me terribly." Tolstoy tells of this first idyll in the most charming way in his *Childhood*: "Seeing him was enough for my happiness. I desired nothing . . . disliking my own physical appearance, I gave too much importance to superior beauty in other people." He had gone so far as to adopt a mannerism this boy had of twisting his eyebrows in a certain way. The episode of "the marriage" in *Youth* is just as ardent and as innocent. "I remember that evening I was seized with a great fondness for Dorsat's pupil and for Frost. I learnt their German song by heart and kissed their sweet lips."(L. Tolstoï, *Souvenirs et récits*, Paris: Gallimard [Pléiade], 1970, p. 342)

† Tolstoy gives an example of feelings of this kind when he speaks of "women who would have seen their love for friends, husband and children disappear instantly, if they had only been forbidden to speak of this love in French." (*Souvenirs et récits*, p. 282.) This is not a fit of xenophobia, but the reflection of a moralist, for Tolstoy, who wrote the first sixty pages of *War and Peace* in French, and justified himself at length in his article, "A Few Words about the Book *War and Peace*," had nothing against what Dostoyevsky called "second-class Russo-French, the language of high society." (Dostoïevski, *Journal d'un écrivain*, Paris: Gallimard [Pléiade], 1972, p. 632)

Russian as in French, and he retained from it "a not altogether agreeable sensation." At parties he apparently holds himself aloof, is always "waiting for it to begin. . . . Not only did it seem to me to be lacking in fun, but I was convinced that everybody else was as bored as I was. . . ."[6]

At the beginning of his university years, Tolstoy went through a crisis of religious conformity, the only one in his life, for when he attempted later to subject himself to the rules of the Orthodox Church, it was no mere sacrifice to tradition but a real attempt to submit, and one which failed.

This attack of conformity indicates a lack of self-confidence; he was trying to reassure himself by joining a group that seemed at ease in daily life. Tolstoy wanted to be *comme il faut* (he uses the French expression). There were two classes of people, those who are and those who are not *comme il faut*: a man who "pronounced French badly" was to him "a detestable being"; he thought it a matter of life and death to have long, well-cared-for fingernails; "the relation of boots to trousers revealed "a man's standing in an instant"; one should on all occasions maintain "a certain air of distinguished and disdainful boredom." Later on, in *Youth*, he was to find these ideas "the falsest and wickedest that education and society had impressed on him."[7]

Tolstoy plays around but is not playful. The discovery of his independent life affords him a passing euphoria. He is glad to own his student's sword, and thrilled to have a carriage and a coachman, but he is not really happy at Kazan, and he is bored by his work.

This disappointing and unsatisfying life melts away as soon as he goes back to Yasnaya Polyana: there he is on his own ground. In a chapter of *Youth* that he is supposed to have dictated in tears (the title chapter), Tolstoy tells how he spent his days after returning to the house where he was born: "I would get up early, I slept on the terrace in the open air and it was the slanting, glittering rays of morning sun that woke me. . . . I dressed quickly, took a towel and a French novel under my arm, and went off to bathe in the river in the shadow of the birch wood and was thrilled to feel in myself just the same life force, fresh and young, that nature was breathing all around me." But he yields again to his dreams and in spite of the bliss he imagines, he writes: "Something told me that SHE, with her bare arms and her burning embraces, was far from being the sum of happiness, and even my love for her was far from being the only good. . . . The more I looked at the full moon high in the sky, the more real beauty and true good seemed to me more elevated, purer and closer to Him . . . and tears of unsatisfied joy, disturbing tears, came to my eyes."[8]

It is curious that at this time not only did Tolstoy suffer from his likeness to the mujiks, but the sight of them anguished and confused him: "When in the course of these walks I passed peasant men or women at work, though the PEOPLE had no existence for me, I would always experience, unconsciously, a violent commotion, and I managed not to be seen by them."[9] The discomfort he was undergoing would turn into the guilt he felt all his life for being, as the Russian proverb has it, "born with a shirt." But at that time he was ignorant of the values the mujiks embodied, though one day they would be the only values he acknowledged as his own.

For the time being he observes his fellow students. Some of those he meets do not belong to the *comme it faut* category. They wear dirty cotton shirts, their fingernails are short and black, they smoke soldiers' tobacco, and they get their accents wrong in Russian as well as in French. There is, moreover, a precious affectation in the words they use, which appears to Tolstoy the height of vulgarity. While he sees "no chance of any rapprochement" with them, he notices some good in them. He envies their superior knowledge and their French, which in spite of their pronunciation is better than his. But above all he is struck by the character of their dealings with one another: they call each other "pigs and blackguards," and yet at the same time they are "extremely sensitive and reserved, as are only the very young and the very poor."[10]

Tolstoy reads hugely, mostly outside the syllabus, which bores him. He reads the Russian writers, Pushkin, Lermontov, Gogol, and Turgenev, but Sterne's *Sentimental Journey*, Rousseau's *Confessions* and *Nouvelle Héloïse*, and Schiller's *Die Räuber* as well. He does little work, and in April 1845 he fails the qualifying exam for the second year. The failure humiliates him deeply. He stays in his room for three days, weeps a lot, and for an instant considers suicide; he goes as far as to look for a pistol with which to do the deed "if he had really wanted to"; and he finds it hard to put up with his family's sympathy for "one who had already fallen very low."[11]

In a moment of "repentance and moral revival," he confides to a notebook his new "Rules of Life,"* from which he is determined never to depart, and sets off for Yasnaya Polyana. Fifty years later, the hero of *Resurrection* will speak of "launderings of one's conscience" in which he

* Between February and May 1845, Tolstoy drew up his "Rules of Life," divided into three large sections dealing with relations with the Supreme Being, with his equals, and with himself. All human activities were to be governed by these rules: rules for developing physical will and affective will; for controlling the feelings of pride, cupidity, love, love of humanity, love of country, and love of certain persons; for the development of rational will, of memory, of mental powers, of visualization, comparison, and deduction; for the organizing of deductions, etc. (L. Tolstoï; *Journaux et carnets*, Gallimard [Pléiade], vol. I, pp. 28–38)

indulged in his youth: "These were what he called the moral crises in the course of which he cleansed his soul of all the dirt that had piled up in it over a period long or short and was causing a slackening or a halt in his inner life. . . . Emerging from these crises, Nekhlyudov always established rules that he resolved never to infringe; but every time the seductions of the world would seize him, and without even noticing it, he fell back to his old level, and often to a lower one still."[12]

At Yasnaya Polyana Tante Toinette received him with open arms and offered no reproaches for his impulsive return. Tolstoy gave himself freely to the joy of homecoming, and immediately felt "the caress of that dear old house." It was more like a big colonial house than a great mansion. In *Youth* Tolstoy describes the nights he used to spend on "the terrace,* watching the light and shadows, giving an attentive ear to the silence and the sounds."[13] Like Francis of Assisi, Tolstoy is "the brother of the wind and the rain." He has no need to merge with the universe, he is already at home in it. Turgenev used to say that Tolstoy's eyes were like an animal's or a bird's, and that the man must have been a horse in a previous incarnation; otherwise he could not have described the feelings of the horse, Strider, as he had done.

After the artificial life of Kazan, Tolstoy plunged with delight into nature, losing himself in a feeling of total communion: "I, lowest of worms, already sullied by all the wretched, narrow human passions, yet gifted with a limitless power of love, I always had at such moments a sense that nature, the moon, and myself were all one being."[14]

Tolstoy reverts to this special bond in his *Recollections*, observing that "up to the age of five or six I cannot call up a single memory of what we call nature. Perhaps one must stand at a distance to see nature: and in those years I *was* nature."[15] He never ceased to be such.

As happens to every adult who returns to his childhood home, the house seemed to him "smaller, lower," yet he rediscovered with some melancholy "the same mother-love spread over all the familiar things,"[16] including the old armchair where he used to curl up in the evenings when he was little.†

Next, Tolstoy set out again for Kazan. He transfers from the faculty of oriental languages, where he had intended to prepare himself for the

* Not that of the present house with its wooden balustrade carved with portraits, which innumerable photographs have made familiar, but the pillared terrace of the big family house which had been dismantled and sold in 1854 to cover Tolstoy's gambling debts.

† Repin painted a portrait of Tolstoy sitting in this "Voltaire chair" in 1909. In 1975 the chair still had its original upholstery; it has since been replaced, very respectfully, with silk material similar to the old design.

diplomatic service, and joins the faculty of law. But more and more he follows his own whim and gets suspended for irregular attendance in the history course.

He forced himself from the beginning of the year to keep up a "Use of Daily Time" in two columns, "Future" and "Past." In the first he was supposed to note what he wanted to do and in the second what he had done: the latter rather often features "nothing" or "little," and seldom, "done." On February 3 he wrote on the left, "3 to 5 and 5 to 8 Russian history," and on the right, "read Gogol."[17]

University constraints and syllabus requirements seemed more ridiculous and more useless to him every day and without relation to his true preoccupations. In April 1847, he decided to leave the university without completing the course. The fact that by his father's will, settled on the eleventh of that month, he inherited Yasnaya Polyana (with four other villages and three hundred and thirty souls), which traditionally went to the youngest son of the family, was probably not irrelevant to his decision.

THREE

Youth

BETWEEN THE DAY HE LEFT the University of Kazan and the day he went to the Caucasus with his brother Nikolay, Tolstoy was to say of himself that "he sowed his wild oats."[1]

He had set out for Yasnaya Polyana with the best intentions in the world, after working and confiding to his journal, as usual, a plan for the two years he intended to spend there, so ambitious as to make one smile: "(1) Learn all the juridical science necessary for University finals; (2) Learn practical and some theoretical medicine; (3) Learn French, Russian, German, English, Italian, and Latin; (4) Learn Agricultural Economy, theory as well as practice; (5) Learn history, geography, and statistics; (6) Learn mathematics, the high school course; (7) Write a thesis; (8) Attain a middling level of proficiency in music and painting; (9) Draw up rules; (10) Acquire some knowledge of the natural sciences; (11) Write essays on all the subjects of study."[2]

He had conceived this program of work so as to be in a position to modernize the management of the estate of which he was now master. He came up against the indifference and occasional hostility of the mujiks and soon understood that his hope of progress for the peasants of Yasnaya Polyana was no more than a dream. Discouraged by this inertia on the part of the parents, he turned to their children and created his first school, but without much success.

Tolstoy could have said to Tante Toinette what Nekhlyudov wrote to his own aunt in *The Morning of a Landowner*:* "Is it not my strict and sacred duty to devote myself to those seven hundred souls for whom I shall have to render an account to God?" Another echo of this experience is to be found in *Anna Karenina*, where Levin in turn tries to emancipate his serfs.

Disheartened by his double failure, and feeling less indifferent than he may have wished to the fascination that great cities hold for the young, Tolstoy set out for St. Petersburg; he was twenty.

He registered in the faculty of law, and told his brother Sergey emphatically: "The main thing is that I am quite sure now that one cannot live by reflection and philosophy, one must lead a positive life, that is, be a practical man."[3]

His life was far from being as positive as he imagined: he gambled madly and lost large sums of money. He thought of leaving the university again, of doing his military service, even of enlisting: "I have come to St. Petersburg without any reason. I have accomplished nothing here except to run through a lot of money, and I am in debt.† But now I have changed my mind; I want to enroll as a noncommissioned officer in the Horse Guards."

Disturbed by this incoherence, by the changes of direction and above all by the gambling losses, Sergey made his younger brother return to his estate. But back at Yasnaya Polyana, Tolstoy continued to lead the same dissolute life. It was here he seduced Gasha, his aunt's innocent maidservant; she was fired, but found refuge with Tolstoy's sister, whose children she brought up. That exploit never vanished from his memory, and fifty years later, in *Resurrection*, Katyushka Maslova is similarly seduced by a young aristocrat, but with more tragic consequences.

Tolstoy was not unmoved by the charms of robust peasant girls, either. The days and nights he was to spend at Tula and in Moscow with the gypsies were to inspire his first work, written in 1850, *Stories of Gypsy Life*.

In this restless period, Tolstoy read largely; he borrowed a good many novels from the French bookseller Gauthier. He was equally mad about music and often played the piano with his aunt, and also with a German virtuoso named Rudolf, a great drinker of vodka, whom he had found in a Moscow tavern and brought back to Yasnaya Polyana.[4] At the same time, he toiled away at what he did not know was to be his life's work: he wrote

* Published in 1856. In Tolstoy's mind it was to be the first part of a great work, *The Story of a Russian Landowner*, which he never finished.

† Tolstoy gambled heavily until his marriage and lost substantial sums of money. Gambling, a widespread passion in the nineteenth century, was one of the few means for a young man in society to make any money.

A History of Yesterday, inspired by a brief stay with one of his girl cousins.

Tolstoy had gone back to Yasnaya Polyana determined to lead an exemplary life. Given his failure and his disposition to pass with the greatest ease from one determination to another, he was now convinced that he could mend his ways only in Moscow and decided to spend the winter there.

This availability, this wonderful capacity for surrendering to the urge of the moment, makes his roaming and his precise whereabouts difficult to follow. Each phase caused him to forget the one before: the road behind him vanishes. Tolstoy is subject to one passion after another, all exclusively absorbing: "Men are unhappy, they suffer, they die, there is no time to fool around," he was to write in 1886 in *What Then Must We Do?* Always a single idea moves him to action, a single task summons him. It is a sign of immaturity that he never got over; it gives a childlike quality to some of his adventures.

But this sense of urgency is also the sense of total commitment that he analyzed so well in a passage of *Youth*:

> It seemed to me so easy and so natural to break with my past, to change, and to forget all that had been and begin a life new in every respect, so that the past did not weigh on me or bind me. I delighted in this hatred of the past and tried to see it in even darker colours than it had worn in fact. The darker the circle of my past memories, the purer and more luminous, by contrast, the pure and luminous point of the present appeared to be, and likewise the rainbow colours of the future. Ye voices of repentance . . . , benevolent, consoling me many times over in those sad moments when the soul submits in silence to the rule of falsehood and debauchery, ye have set yourselves bravely against every imposture, ferociously unmasking the past, showing me and forcing me to love the shining point of the present moment, promising me goodness and happiness in the future. Benevolent, consoling voices! Is it possible that a day will come when you cease to make yourself heard?[5]

One finds in this text that delight Tolstoy took in blackening his character which reappears on every page of *A Confession*, as well as a fine definition of sin "when the soul submits in silence," but one sees especially the desperate optimism that never deserted him: he would always believe as he did at Kazan that "it was going to begin."

Thus, on March 8, 1851, he wrote to his aunt from Moscow: "With the springtime rebirth of nature one would wish to feel oneself reborn, one regrets the past, one repents one's weakness, and the future shines like a bright light ahead of us. . . . Ever since I began to live by myself, spring has always put me in a good mood which I persisted in for a short or long time. But winter is always a stumbling block to me—I always go astray."[6]

In Russia, the spring of every year is a cataclysm, an explosion, a true *sacre du printemps*, a transformation without gradualness from one state to another. Tolstoy was ever deeply conscious of it: the renewal of nature is a subject he was often to treat in his writings. It was no mere literary theme, but a vital one. In several of his works, such as *The Morning of a Landowner*, and in a number of his letters, including some written in old age, one can smell the grass and hear the birdsong.

In April 1858 he wrote to his other well-loved kinswoman, Countess Alexandra Andreyevna Tolstoy, called Alexandrine: "Spring has such an influence on me that at times I catch myself dreaming that I am a plant that has just come up among the others and is going to grow simply, tranquilly, joyously, in God's earth."[7]

Tolstoy returned home to spend the summer at Yasnaya Polyana, where what was left of his close family, that is, Tante Toinette, his three brothers, and his sister, were shortly to forgather. In his journal he mentions the project of writing *Four Periods of Growth*, and in July he began to compose *Childhood*.

Nikolay was on leave, and it was his turn to worry about his younger brother's instability and his follies. Paternal as always, he suggested taking Leo to the Caucasus with him, where he himself was serving as an artillery officer.

FOUR

The Caucasus and Sevastopol

SERGEY HAD HOPED to put his brother Leo back on the straight and narrow path by sending him off to manage his estate. This first attempt having failed, Nikolay tried another recipe: the army. This brotherly act appeared to Tolstoy a heavenly intervention: he saw his own "frivolous idea" of going to the Caucasus as "an inspiration from on high."

So on April 29, 1851, Tolstoy set out again with his brother. He took part as a civilian in a number of military operations; Pierre Bezukhov was to do the same at the battle of Borodino in *War and Peace*.

Tolstoy's army career falls into three parts: in the Caucasus from April 1851 to February 1854; then his transfer to headquarters in Moldavia, where he asked to go when his extremely early retirement was disallowed; and lastly in the Crimea, where he went as a volunteer and took part in the siege of Sevastopol. He did not finally shed his uniform until 1856.

During the years that he followed the flag, Tolstoy led a life that was by no means exclusively military. He sums up his strange existence as an officer in the still partly unsubdued Caucasus in a letter to Tante Toinette*: "I have spent two months with Nikolenka at Staroglad-

* Tolstoy believed that his numerous letters to Tatyana Alexandrovna Yergolskaya (Tante Toinette) constituted the best biography for this period of his life.

kovskaya. We followed there our usual ways: hunting, reading, conversation, chess."[1]

When they had said their goodbyes to Moscow and Kazan, the two brothers hired a boat and boatmen to take them down the Volga to Astrakhan, and then proceeded to Nikolay's camp by road. Tolstoy was disappointed at first by the base camp at Starogladkovskaya. Three days after getting there he wondered in his journal: "How have I landed up here? I don't know. To do what? Don't know. I should like to write a lot. . . ."[2]

But on going with his brother to the camp at Stari-Yurt, Tolstoy quickly discovered the beauty of the Caucasus and the charm of its inhabitants. It is easy to imagine how, being a disciple of Rousseau, he marveled at the grandeur of the country and the "kindly savages" who lived in it. He thought of them as "fine, strong, and free" men who "live as nature lives."[3] The moral elevation of these thieving and courageous lady-killers pleased him as much as their women thrilled him: "One must once at least have known life in all its savage beauty. One must see and understand what I see before my eyes every day: The eternal, unapproachable snows of the mountains, and women majestic in their primitive beauty—as the first woman must have been when she came from the hand of her Creator."[4] The freedom he marveled at in the men amazed him even more in their mates: "In their relations with men, women and particularly girls enjoy complete freedom."[5]

These unpolished beings, whom servitude had not debased and who were still unspoiled by the constraints of so-called civilization, attracted Tolstoy much more than did his brother officers. He lived on the outskirts of the camp and bivouacked with a peasant whose brother was to become one of the main characters in *The Cossacks*, which is based on memories of this period. For Tolstoy the contemplation of nature would always be one of the paths to God. The beauty of the Caucasus aroused heavenward stirrings in him, and the beauty of the women, fervors of a more earthly kind.*

Tolstoy was still using the "Franklin system" that he had taken up when he began to write his journal in 1847. It consisted in noting his daily shortcomings in morality, patience, chastity, or work. The choice of Benjamin Franklin—a kind of secular saint—as a spiritual mentor shows that at this time Tolstoy's preoccupations were as much moral as religious.

* Professor Nicolas Weisbein says Tolstoy walked "with his eyes on heaven" but was "held down to earth by heavy leaden soles" (*L'Evolution religieuse de Tolstoï*). He was held down much more by the invisible weight of problems whose solution he sought in vain.

Throughout his life Tolstoy loved to classify and categorize his ideas, to number the paragraphs of his letters, to itemize points in programs for action, to list moral rules, even rules for games and sports,* all these being so many vain attempts to check the abundance of his thoughts and give them an air of logic. He never lost the taste for taking inventory and auditing his failings. Saint Ignatius of Loyola has written: "The craze for keeping tabs on oneself is obsessional, not only because it is endless, but because it generates the very faults it deals with."[6] Unlike the sixteenth-century mystic, Tolstoy was never able to rid himself of that craze.

The journal naturally reflects the struggle of forces within Tolstoy: bodily forces that rivet him to the earth and spiritual forces that pull him heavenward.

> Yesterday I scarcely slept all night: wrote my Journal then began to pray to God. Sweetness of feeling I have experienced in prayer: impossible to convey. I said my usual prayers: Our Father, Hail Mary, Trinity, Mercy, Angel Guardian and stayed on praying. If you define prayer as petition or thanksgiving I wasn't praying—I desired something sublime and beautiful, but I cannot convey what; though I was clearly conscious of what I desired—I longed to be one with the Universal Being. I begged him to pardon my faults, no, I didn't beg for that, because I felt that if he granted me that happy instant, it would mean he had forgiven me. I begged and at the same time felt I had nothing to beg, could not beg, did not know how to beg. I gave thanks, yes, but not in words or in thoughts. I united everything in one feeling, prayers and thanksgiving together. The feeling of fear had completely disappeared. . . . Yes, that is what I felt yesterday—the love of God. . . . From how pure a heart I begged of God to receive me in his arms! I had no sense of flesh, I was spirit alone. But no! Not an hour passed before I heard the voice of vice and vanity again; I knew where it came from. I knew it would destroy my good state. I struggled and fell to it. I fell asleep dreaming of glory, and of women; but it's not my fault. I couldn't help it.[7]

These stirrings that stop short are a habit of Tolstoy's. They witness to his "passionate desire for perfection" and help him to be aware of himself, at times with candor. "I do not know how others dream: so far as I have heard and read, quite differently from me."[8]

Tolstoy was not yet sure of his vocation of writer, but was writing more and more, and his eye was already that of a novelist. The events of this period were going to be adapted or incorporated unchanged into his tales: the military operation he and Nikolay took part in soon after their

* In December 1850 he composed "Rules for games in Moscow to Jan. 1st" (*Journaux et carnets*, vol. I, p. 60) and in June 1851, "Rules for Gymnastics" (p. 60), and he marked the number of times he did the exercises he had set himself to do.

arrival gave him the subject of *The Raid*, which he wrote the following year. The people he met here in the Caucasus were to provide inspiration for *The Cossacks* as well: the officers whose life he shared in fact as little as possible; the old Cossack Epichka, who became Uncle Erochka with his ancestral lore; the beautiful Marenka, the model for Marion, who is passionately loved by Olenin, the young officer whose likeness to Tolstoy is that of a twin, and who wonders in the book: "Perhaps it is nature I love in her, the personification of all the beauty of nature. In loving her, I feel an indivisible part of God's whole happy universe."[9] Also like Tolstoy, the hero of *The Cossacks* will never be quite convinced by his old uncle Erochka that love is no sin and that woman "was created to be loved and to give pleasure."[10] Sado, a young Circassian who was a close kin to the Lucas of the book, devoted body and soul to Tolstoy, winning back at cards Tolstoy's IOU for a gambling debt which he, Tolstoy, had no way of paying—that Tolstoy was just as much attached to him is shown by his later refusing to leave Sado in an ambush when his own faster horse would have saved him by fleeing alone—all this became part of the fabric of *The Cossacks*.

That book, full of freshness and lyricism, which Tolstoy wanted to make "as wild and fresh as a Biblical legend," was completed after many interruptions in 1863, when Katkov,* the editor of the *Russian Herald*, bought the manuscript—thus enabling Tolstoy to settle another gambling debt.

The Notebooks of Thoughts and *Reading Notes* of the years 1851 to 1853 are those of a writer. They contain brief descriptions, criticisms of books, psychological notes, and matters for reflection. Tolstoy is beginning to speak with admiration of "the people," one of the most obsessive motifs in his writings and in his life. (He had given no sign of this in *Boyhood*.) "The simple people are so much below us, through their life of work and deprivation, that there is something ugly on our part in seeking to depict what is bad in them."[11] He had written two years earlier: "The people have no literature and never will have, until one begins to write it for them."[12]

This idea sinks out of sight for a long time, but reappears in strength, first in his educational work and, in the end, in dogmatic form in the theories of art that attempt to demonstrate that the only valid art is art accessible to all. The same idea led Tolstoy to found *The Mediator*† in

* Mikhail N. Katkov, the son of a civil servant and professor of philosophy at the University of Moscow. He had bought *The Russian Herald* in 1856 when the University dropped the chair of philosophy.

† The role that this periodical played in his literary and his private life will become more evident later on in these pages.

1884, the real ancestor of our paperbacks, with the aim of publishing great authors at modest prices.

In the high flight of love in which the young officer who is the hero of the novel dreams of turning Cossack himself and marrying the fair Marion, Tolstoy is expressing his longing to lose himself, to give up the system of established values, and to discover the true meaning of life by drowning himself in the ocean of humanity. In his later writings it was this same aspiration that brought Father Sergey in the story of that name, and Nekhlyudov, the hero of *Resurrection*, to their final escape, and it was this urge again, more than any other reason, that compelled Tolstoy himself to flee from Yasnaya Polyana.

His duties as an officer did not prevent him from keeping his journal, writing a great number of letters, and working on *Childhood*, which still had the title *Story of My Childhood.* Here is how he describes his life, on March 20, 1852: "Spent September at Starogladkovskaya, did some riding, at Groznaya and at Stari-Yurt, with some hunting expeditions. I courted Cossack women, drank, wrote a bit, and translated."[13]

The first interruption in military life was when he set out for Tiflis to regularize his position with the army. He hunted (he even went so far as to buy some hounds), wrote a great deal, and contracted an ailment about which he kept a discreet silence. "In October I went to Tiflis with my brother to join the service. I spent a month at Tiflis in indecision and a head full of stupid vain plans. . . . From the beginning of November I stayed idle at home for two whole months until the New Year. I spent that time in a wearisome but useful, tranquil way: I wrote the whole first part [of *Childhood*]. January was spent partly on journeys, February in the field. . . . At the beginning of March, I went to communion."[14]

The smallest incidents of this period supplied material for his writings; some were written up as notes, others remained in his memory. For instance the surrender of Hadji Murad, which Tolstoy spoke about to his brother in a letter of December 23, 1852, was not to be used until half a century later, when Tolstoy began to write the novel (posthumously published) that bears the name of this legendary figure of the Caucasian war. In his diary during this period he remarks: "As far as I have been able to observe myself, I think that in me three evil passions predominate: gambling, lechery, and vanity."[15]

His taste for women, toward whom he was driven by what Rousseau called a "combustible temperament," never stopped tormenting the young Tolstoy. Still haunted by the will to improve himself, he had noted in March of the same year (1852) that the best way of struggling against the flesh and the imagination is "work and being occupied, both physically—gymnastics—and morally—the task of writing." But for once he is indulgent toward himself and adds: "It's not really so. Seeing that this is a natural tendency, the satisfaction of which I find evil only because of the unnatural situation I happen to be in (a bachelor at twenty-three)."[16]

He returned for a while to the camp at Starogladkovskaya, not yet quite recovered: "I am as I always have been, of strong physique and weak health,"[17] he wrote to Tante Toinette. And the young soldier set off again to take the waters.

It was from Piatigorsk, a fashionable spa where he remained from May 15 to July 6, 1852 (and during another longer stay from July 3 to October 12, 1853), that he wrote again to his aunt: "I find my pleasure and my usefulness in work, and I am working."[18]

True enough, in spite of being pulled into an active social life by friends from Moscow, he does write a lot. On July 3, 1852, he had sent off the manuscript of *Story of My Childhood* to N. A. Nekrasov, the editor of *The Contemporary*, a review founded by Pushkin. The script was accompanied by a letter that is surprising by its professional tone, that of a writer sure of himself. Later on he delegated relations with publishers to his wife, but from the beginning he showed himself a good bargainer about his works, insisting on being paid as much as Turgenev or Ostrovsky. The alterations that were made in *Childhood* without his knowledge sent him into a fury, and when he dispatched the manuscript of *The Raid* a year later, he required not only a higher price per page but also that absolutely *nothing* in his text should be changed.

On August 28, 1852, Tolstoy was twenty-four. He wrote in his journal: "What I have done so far is nothing. But I feel it is not in vain that for eight years I have been fighting with doubts and passions. . . ."[19] Next day he got a very nice birthday present: the publisher's letter accepting *Childhood*.

Tolstoy resumed his military life. But the discipline and the constraint he had considered necessary for a period of time—he had even rejoiced "in being no longer free" at the moment of joining—began to weigh him down.

One day, having failed to take his turn of guard duty because he was playing chess, he was naturally put under arrest. He was unable to be present at the ceremony of awarding medals. Earlier, he had been put up for the Cross of Saint George, but had not been able to receive his decoration because then his military position was irregular. This second misadventure annoyed him greatly. He had exhausted the charm of the Caucasus. He was tired of the life and did not want to stay in the army:

he asked for his discharge. "Set out on the 19th for Stari-Yurt, learnt failure regarding the Cross [of Saint George]."[20]

So far, Tolstoy had kept in his journal two kinds of "audit" about himself—his expenses and his moral transgressions: laziness, gambling, lechery, drink, anger. Now he added literary precepts to rules of conduct: his journal becomes a writer's diary. He regrets having been too hasty in sending off to Nekrasov the manuscript of *Notes of a Billiard Marker*—its form has not been polished with enough care;[21] and he is working at *Boyhood*. His reading becomes critical. He reads *The Captain's Daughter* and finds that "Pushkin's prose has become dated."[22] He sets himself literary rules of increasing severity. "Every piece completed in rough ought to be revised, cutting out everything superfluous and adding nothing."[23] On January 27, 1854, he noted that he should "often remember that Thackeray prepared himself thirty years before he wrote his first novel, and Alexandre Dumas wrote two a week."[24]

Tolstoy left the Caucasus without a medal but with several manuscripts that had made substantial progress—and his head full of ideas. Military life had curbed his disordered energies at least. For the first time he had had to submit to rules other than his own, and he had ceased to be what he was when he arrived in the Caucasus—"free, as only those could be who were sons and heirs of the forties, still young and without relatives."[25]

Tolstoy came back to Yasnaya Polyana on February 2, 1854, having nearly lost his life in a storm on the journey. "Wandered all night, got the idea of writing a story."[26] It was *The Snowstorm*. He was now living through every event with a view to his work.

He was back with his brothers and Tante Toinette, whom he had not seen for three years. This stay of a month at Yasnaya Polyana was marked by family parties and receptions at neighboring houses.

Tolstoy got his next orders and set out for Moldavia, to which he had asked to be seconded. Apart from taking part in the short siege of Silitsia,* Tolstoy did not turn into a very busy nor yet a very zealous staff officer. He wrote, went out a good deal, looked after himself, and read a lot: Goethe, Lermontov, Pushkin. He felt rather depressed, as one can see from the portrait of a self-flagellating Narcissus that he draws of himself on July 7, 1854:

* In the very detailed account he gives of this event to Tante Toinette in a letter of July 4, 1854, Tolstoy expresses admiration for Prince Serge Gorchakov (a kinsman through his paternal grandmother), who had accepted without grumbling the Tsar's countermanding the siege he had organized, and had even been happy to avoid the butchery (*Tolstoï par Tolstoï*, E. Halpérine-Kaminski, Paris: L'Edition Moderne, 1912, p. 133). This commander who proved human furnished some traits for the character of Kutuzov in *War and Peace*. The rest came from General Kornilov, who commanded at the Battle of Sevastopol.

Lack of modesty! that is my big failing. What am I? One of the four sons of a retired Lt. Colonel, looked after by women and outsiders from the age of seven, without social education or instruction, and let loose at seventeen with no great fortune, without the least social position and above all without rules . . . a man who has spent the best years of his life without purpose and without pleasure, and finally exiled himself to the Caucasus to get away from his debts and still more his habits, and then . . . gets himself transferred to the army of the Danube at twenty-six as a cadet.

I am ugly, awkward, unkempt and socially uneducated. I am irritable, boring, immodest, impatient, intolerant [this word in French], and as shamefaced as a child. I am all but completely ignorant. What I do know I have learnt alone, heaven knows how, in scraps without connection, without method, and it is so little. I am incontinent, irresolute, inconstant, idiotically vain, and swept off my feet like all people with no character. I am not brave. I am negligent in my life, and so lazy that idleness has become my almost incurable habit. I am intelligent but my intelligence has never yet been put to serious proof in anything. I have no practical nor social nor active power of mind. I am good, that is I love the good, I have made it my habit to love it and when I depart from it I dislike myself and return to it with pleasure, but there are things that I love more—glory. I am so ambitious, and this feeling has been so little satisfied that I often fear between glory and virtue I would choose the first if I ever had to choose between them.[27]

It was then that to distract himself as well as out of genuine concern for the morale of the troops (and in this as elsewhere he was an innovator, since the military did not begin to worry about the problem until the end of the First World War) it occurred to Tolstoy to start, with some officer friends, a paper to be called the *Soldier's Newsletter*, in which, as he explained to his brother Sergey in a letter of November 20, 1854, "he would give the biography of the plain people, little people, the unknown people."[28]

But the Tsar did not authorize the publication of the periodical, the tone of which ran contrary to prevailing conventions about the army and about patriotism. Tolstoy felt keenly the Tsar's refusal: "This failure, I must admit, has grieved me very much and considerably altered my plans."[29] Boredom settled on him once more, he began to gamble again, and in the end he asked to be sent to the Crimean front: "I should like to get away from the Serzhputovsky headquarters which I dislike, and even more on account of patriotic feelings, feelings that I admit have come over me rather strongly."[30]

This instability, impatience, and mobility did not wholly distract him from seeking self-improvement: "What matters most to me in life is to cure myself of laziness, irritability, and lack of character. Love of all the world and distaste for oneself."[31]

* * *

Tolstoy's stay in the Caucasus had been a kind of bucolic and military diversion: it was a guerrilla war, rather like a very dangerous sport, and it did not exclude the attractions of civilian life. During his "two years of service" in the Caucasus, Tolstoy had spent some two months in Tiflis and more than four at a spa.

The siege of Sevastopol was to be quite another matter. When he arrived there, the town under siege had its ordinary look, the daily life of the garrison officers and the civilians seemed to follow its normal course: "Throng of soldiers and women in the lanes."[32] Tolstoy danced, kept on gambling, which in his case generally meant losing; and on January 28, 1855, he notes that he has lost Yasnaya Polyana. Did he have the big family house that he adored sold in April 1854, as Henri Troyat suggests, to pay this gambling debt or was the house used as a stake, as the note in his diary for January 28 asserts? The positive fact is that he lost it. For two days and two nights he had "played stoss. Upshot clear enough—lost everything, lost the house at Yasnaya Polyana. No need to write. So disgusted with myself I wish I could forget I was alive."[33]*

All the same, he wrote a great deal. On leave for a few days at Simferopol, in the suburbs of Sevastopol, he worked at *Youth* and *Notes of a Billiard Marker*. He also drew up a memorandum for army reform. "These last days I have twice spent several hours writing my plan for army reform. I progress painfully, but I am not giving up the idea."[34]

The contacts Tolstoy had made at Odessa with English and French prisoners from the battle of Alma had given him a chance of perceiving the obsolete features of the Russian army organization and increased his sense of the absurdity of war: "I spent two hours in the allied wounded room; French, English and Russians were playing cards." The radical pacifism of Tolstoy's latter years had its roots in these encounters.

But Tolstoy's most important experience in this period has no connection with any single event; it belongs to his inner life. It is the illumination that came to him at the beginning of March 1855 on the meaning of his life; he records it as follows:

> Today I took communion. Yesterday a conversation on faith and the divine led me to a great, an enormous idea, to the realization of which I think I am capable of devoting my life. This thought is to found a new religion that fits human evolution, a religion of Christ but stripped of faith and mysteries, a practical religion which does not promise future beatitude but gives beatitude on earth.—To put this idea into execution I understand needs

* The large family house was either lost or sold to a neighbor, but without the land. It was dismantled and transported piece by piece to the new owner's estate. All that remained were two small stone buildings (or pavilions) that originally stood on either side of the big house. It was in one of these that Tante Toinette continued to live.

generations consciously working to this end. One generation will bequeath this idea to the next and one day fanaticism or reason will bring it about. Conscious action to unite mankind by the help of religion: that is the foundation of an idea I hope to follow.[35]

This statement is of the highest interest, for it shows that before the age of thirty, and not after his conversion at fifty, as is generally believed, Tolstoy had already conceived the grand design that was to occupy him all his life, the design to create a new religion suited to "the present stage of humanity's evolution."

Tolstoy was possessed by a sense of urgency; he felt within "the power of transforming himself into a single desire, a single idea, of putting his head down and flinging himself into an abyss without knowing why or for whom."[36] And he was as impatient about heavenly as about earthly undertakings: one must act *now*. He had neither the wish nor the ability to await the eternal beatitudes foretold by the Church, he wanted "happiness on earth," not pagan happiness, of course, but the happiness promised by Christ: impatience for the Kingdom took possession of him and it did not leave him.

By 1855, then, Tolstoy was clearly pondering a genuine reform of Christianity, the keystone of which was to be the notion of humanity's present stage of development. This idea which he hit upon at Sevastopol is found again forty years later in a note on Pascal dated December 7, 1895, later included in *A Cycle of Reading*, a collection of famous pieces Tolstoy put together in about 1900 as a kind of secular breviary, a great book of initiation to true knowledge, which he advised his disciples to ponder upon and which he had his daughter Alexandra read to him on his deathbed.

In his commentary on the extract from Pascal, Tolstoy writes: "Men must find such answers to explain their faith as fit their intellectual and moral development according to the questions raised by Pascal."[37]

Tolstoy wants to finish the task that "God or chance" did not permit Pascal to carry to a conclusion; or it may have been the work of Christ himself he wanted to continue. He adds: "One cannot imagine the genius of Pascal, at once honest with himself and yet believing in Catholicism. He had no time to put it to a test of reason as exacting as the one he adopted to prove the necessity of religion, so in his soul Catholic dogma remained intact."[38]

For him, Pascal "died with only part of his work completed, without finishing or even beginning the rest. . . . It's quite simple, Pascal (the same is true of Gogol) believes in the Trinity, in communion; it is clear he was ill and abnormal."[39]

Though Tolstoy follows Pascal in accepting "the necessity of religion," he refuses to follow him in admitting that "man is an enigma explained only by the religion of Jesus Christ."[40] That is the precise point where their thought diverges irrevocably. Tolstoy kept looking all his life for the best "possible explanation," whereas Pascal, for whom "one reaches God only through the heart," accepts "eternity, prophecies and miracles" as parts of an explanation; a belief Tolstoy thinks a sign of madness.

This call to found a religion, to be a reformer,* is one of the most complex and interesting strands in Tolstoy's personality: would not the desire for "fame" he is always talking about find its most sublime form in a divine mission, in being the new Christ, rather than in simple military or literary glory? The seed of reform was sown, but its secret germination proved to be slow, very slow. For the moment, Tolstoy continued to drink and above all to gamble, but his debauchery did not reduce his soul to silence. He was not yet thinking of giving up his fortune, only of freeing himself from the obligations it imposed: "Today I had the idea of giving my estate in trust to my brother-in-law. I would accomplish a triple purpose: disengage myself from the worries of working it and of habits acquired in youth, limit myself and get rid of my debts."[41]

In early April 1855 Tolstoy was recalled to Sevastopol, where he took part in the stubborn defense of the famous Fourth Bastion. He saw "terrible sights that sear the soul";[42] it was there he really discovered the horrors of war: "War no longer under its brilliant exterior which is so righteous and so attractive, with music and drum-beat, flags unfurled and generals prancing, war with its real face, in the blood and suffering and death."[43] He heard the cries of the wounded and breathed the stench of the hospitals, while he was also not indifferent to the charms of the Sister of Mercy he caught sight of at the first-aid post.

The pounding was intense: "More than fifteen hundred guns firing at the town for two days,"[44] he wrote to Sergey on November 20, 1854. In spite of all this he "managed to write, although busied by events and partly by the service . . . one little formless page of *Youth*."[45] In the end he came to love the Fourth Bastion and to relish "the attraction of constant danger." As the post kept up a desperate defense under the merciless bombardment, Tolstoy wrote, just as Malraux during the Spanish Civil War composed *Man's Hope* between two flying missions.

On April 13, although he had been on duty "four days out of eight," Tolstoy wrote quite copiously and completed the first version of *Sevas-*

* It is probable that Tolstoy, like other orphans, was trying to compensate for the emptiness that was his fate; he experienced "a need to remold an order determined by a particular conception of the world that a human being entertains when he wishes, consciously or not, to be revenged for a frustrated childhood." (Dr. Pierre Rentchick, *Les orphelins et la volonté de pouvoir*, 1978)

topol Day and Night, which was to become *Sevastopol in December*. He finished the final draft on the twenty-fifth, sent it to his publisher on May 8, 1855, and wrote some pages of *Youth*.

His work was pulled about by censorship, which cut certain passages and, curiously, added others of a more conventional patriotism than the author's.* Its success was immediate and substantial. Turgenev wept as he read the first installment. The next, *Sevastopol in May*, which Tolstoy had originally called *A Spring Night at Sevastopol*, and which he completed in a week, was at the publisher's in July. It is more shocking. From the opening sentence, Tolstoy denies the very legitimacy of war. "Take your choice: either war is mad, or if men commit this madness, they are absolutely not the reasonable creatures that we conventionally believe them to be, God knows why."[46]

Tolstoy is already the man through whom scandal comes—the scandal of truthfulness. He shows himself the profaner of holy hypocrisy. His questioning of war and such descriptions as that of the ward where "doctors on their knees probe into wounds with their fingers" were not calculated to sustain morale behind the lines or to encourage enlistment. But the great undertaking of demystification had begun: he wanted to show war as it is, as in *The Cossacks* he had wanted to show his readers the true Caucasus and not a cardboard country. So, likewise, he wanted to rediscover true Christianity behind what he was later to call the most lamentable Greco-Russian heresy, meaning Orthodoxy. Even in description he detested the graces of so-called literary style, the false windows put in for symmetry; these are for him the writer's lies. Readers caught on and so did the censors and the authorities.†

Tolstoy had become suspect: the Tsar, who had refused to let the *Soldier's Newsletter* appear, now decided the *Sevastopol Stories* must be censored in their turn. These first two vexations inaugurate the long persecution‡ that was to end only at Astopovo with the measures taken by the police around the dying man.

* The original text was restored in the 1856 edition, published at St. Petersburg under the title *Military Stories of Count Tolstoy*.

† The government used censorship to persecute Tolstoy, not daring to attack him directly. His closest disciples, such as Chertkov and Biryukov, were exiled or put under house arrest again and again, and conscientious objectors who declared they were Tolstoyans were sentenced to prison or hard labor.

‡ From 1862 on, the police began to watch Tolstoy, whose educational activities aroused the suspicion that they were a cover for revolutionary plots, and the Yasnaya Polyana school paper was permitted to appear only after prolonged negotiations. A search that made poor Aunt Yergolskaya ill took place at Yasnaya Polyana during one of Tolstoy's journeys abroad; the pond was dredged and the stable floor taken up. After the publication of *A Confession* in 1882, Tolstoy

On the last page of *Sevastopol in May* Tolstoy expresses his admiration for the courage and self-denial of the soldier, but reiterates his despair at the absurdity of war. It is all the more absurd that it is waged "by people who are Christian and profess the sole great law of love."[47] Twenty years later when he came out in open struggle against Orthodoxy, the reproach he put above all others was that the Church did not oppose war but helped glorify it.

From the publication of *Sevastopol Stories*, Tolstoy shows himself to be essentially a subversive, one who overturns or threatens to overturn the established order and accepted values. He himself was sometimes gripped by a kind of fear about his work, asking himself whether he was right to stir up the dregs of war as he did, knowing that one must not stir up "the dregs of wine lest it be spoilt."[48]

But this unease was soon swept away. What does it matter if the passion is dangerous; he acknowledges its power and he utters the famous declaration: "The hero of my story, the hero I love with all the strength of my soul, the hero I have striven to represent in all his beauty, is and for ever will be worthy of admiration and his name is truth."[49] It is positive that at that moment, and in the end at any moment whatsoever, given the alternatives that Dostoyevsky evoked in a letter from Siberia—"If there were a conflict between Christ and the truth I would rather remain on the side of Christ than of truth"—Tolstoy would make the opposite choice. He could not be a Fool of God; he would be a "fool of truth."

Legend maintains that the Tsar was so overwhelmed by *Sevastopol in December* that Tolstoy was removed from the front lines on the order of the sovereign, out of concern for the life of a young writer so full of promise.* The transfer took place seventeen days before the book appeared, as Tolstoy makes plain in his journal: "I was chosen on May 5th to command a battery of mountain artillery, and I have gone to camp on the Belbek, twenty versts from Sevastopol."[50] There Tolstoy underwent what he called "a great seizure of sloth," which was perhaps an

---

was suspected of contacts with sectarians. In 1883 police reports mention subversive interviews with peasants at Samara, and commemorations of Turgenev's death were postponed *sine die* when it became known that Tolstoy intended to take part. In 1884 the authorities confiscated *What Is My Faith?* which thereafter circulated secretly.

In 1887, although Alexander III had liked *The Power of Darkness* when he had it read to him by his Grand Chamberlain, and the Imperial Theatre at St. Petersburg had begun its production, it was forbidden by the Tsar under pressure from Pobedonostsev, the Tsar's former tutor and now minister to the Holy Synod, and the public sale of the text was prohibited. In August of the same year *The Mediator* was not allowed to publish the *Popular Tales*. By the turn of the century most of Tolstoy's works were being published in Geneva or England by Chertkov.

* The work was read to Alexander II, who issued orders for its immediate translation into French—which gave Tolstoy enormous pleasure.

attack of fatigue after the grueling days he had spent in the Bastion. To relax he read *Faust*, which he finished "at eleven in the evening, May 31st," and then went on to Thackeray. He read *Henry Esmond*. "Lazy! Lazy! Lazy!"[51] he writes on June 5. Three days earlier he had been angry with his battery servant "for bringing him infected girls."[52]

Tolstoy's worst trial is something else: the role of officer was stifling, it depressed him, and he was irritable. He had hated corporal punishment from childhood, yet he got so worked up that he found himself striking some of the "men he was drilling," and he remarks: "My service in Russia is beginning to drive me beside myself, as in the Caucasus."

In the partial inactivity of the Belbek camp, he starts gambling again, so he draws up some very complicated rules in his journal, with stake limits and percentages to be observed, and no more adheres to these than to his other "rules of life." At the same time he discovers and admires more and more the virtues of the private soldiers, "mujiks in uniform," as he was to call them later, and becomes convinced that "the epic of Sevastopol, whose hero was the Russian people, will leave traces in Russia for a long time."[53]

He is more and more preoccupied by the problems of serfs; he wants to represent them in *The Story of a Russian Landowner*, the principal idea of which is to be as follows: "It is impossible for a landed proprietor of today who has an education to lead a right life with serfdom."[54] That remark is dated August 1, 1855; the one dated August 10 takes a different tack: "Summer at Bakhtchi-sarai, I have bought a horse, used up my time and fornicated; in general, behaved badly, to say nothing of the idleness I have yet to conquer."[55]*

Sevastopol fell on August 28, 1855, on Tolstoy's birthday: he was twenty-seven. He wept when he saw the town on fire and the French flags flying on the bastions. This Russian disaster overwhelmed him. He recalled the desolate sight of the ruined town when he came to describe the burning of Moscow in *War and Peace*. He mastered his grief and took up his pen: "Today worked well at writing the description."[56] He wrote his *Sevastopol Stories* with passion, but he also had to perform another task that inspired him much less: to make a synthesis of twenty reports handed in by bastion commanders. It may be that this thankless labor, which resulted, according to him, in "a naive and necessary lie," was the origin of his theory that there is no genuine History, only various stories. The twenty versions of the siege of Sevastopol may have helped him to

* Biryukov's translation is more blunt: "Bought a horse, fornicated, generally behaved very badly, to say nothing of the laziness I couldn't manage to overcome." (*Journal intime de la jeunesse*. Paris: Guérin, 1921).

hammer out the technique he used for the battle of Borodino in *War and Peace*, which is not viewed through the eyes of a single Fabrice at Waterloo, as in Stendhal's *Charterhouse of Parma*, but through the eyes of a hundred Fabrices dotted around the battlefield like so many cameras.

Tolstoy's moulting season was nearing its final stage: "It is necessary to get out of the rut of military life which is harmful to me: my purpose is literary fame. The good I can do through my writings."[57] His desire to write was already aiming at a moral purpose, but just a few words later, with an enthusiasm free of ulterior motive, he adds: "My career is literature. Write! Write! Starting tomorrow I work my whole life through—or else I send everything packing—rules, religion, proprieties, everything."[58]

Tolstoy's diaries and intimate letters, from his departure for the Caucasus to his return from the Crimea, afford the opportunity to follow his development as a writer and as a reformer. He gave up his journal, a chronicle of his inner life that goes beyond ordinary introspection and takes on at times the fascination of a true self-analysis, as in his period of happiness and creativity during the years 1865 to 1878. He took it up again at moments of great anguish. In the last months of his life, starting in July 1910, he even kept two diaries, a main journal and the *Diary for Myself Alone*, the writing of which was to be his final literary activity.

As for his letters, a kind of diary in parallel, some sentences from them are found word for word in the essentially autobiographical works of this period, and he kept up this practice throughout his life. What notion did Tolstoy himself entertain about his years of apprenticeship? He commented on them on two occasions, the first time in a letter to Alexandrine Tolstoy written in May 1859, four years after returning to civilian life, a period that included his meteoric passage through St. Petersburg literary society, two journeys to Western Europe, and months of experience as a schoolteacher: "As a child I believed fervently, sentimentally and unthinkingly. Then at about fourteen I began to think about life in general, I clashed with a religion that would not lend itself to my theories, and it goes without saying I think it meritorious to destroy it. I have lived without it very peacefully for a dozen years. To my eyes all was clear, all was logical, all was classified, and there was no room for religion. The moment had come when everything was laid open before me, when there was no more mystery, while life itself began to lose its meaning for me."[59]

A reader of the journal and the letters finds that things were not as simple in Tolstoy's adolescence and youth as he came to believe later. On the contrary, what he says in the same letter to Alexandrine about his first two years in the army confirms what his writings of the period have made plain: "Then I was living in the Caucasus, alone and unhappy. I began to think with all the strength a man can think with for once in his life. Never before or after have I attained such intensity of thought, and never have I attempted to penetrate the beyond as I did in those two years. I found an old and simple thing I know like knowing a person: I found there is immortality, there is love, and one must live for others in order to be happy eternally."[60]

Twenty years after that letter, in *A Confession*, Tolstoy was to make a second, quite different, analysis of the same period of his life: "At the age of sixteen I had ceased to pray, I had ceased going to church of my own free will, and making my devotions. . . . But I believed in something. My true belief then was my faith in perfectionism. Moral perfectionism was soon replaced by perfectionism in general . . . [a] desire to make myself better in the eyes of other men. . . . With all my soul I desired to be good, but I was young. I had passions, and I was alone, absolutely alone in search of good."[61]

He felt frightfully alone; not even wonderful Tante Toinette was of any help; she belonged to the system that he had rejected because he felt like an alien in it. As he saw it, she was part of the "conspiracy of hypocrisy," encouraging him to give himself to "base passions," going so far as to advise him, as others did, to form a liaison with a woman "in good society." This cynical advice, coming from a person whose high moral demands he knew, so overwhelmed him that he recalled it when he wrote *Anna Karenina* and gave old Countess Vronsky the same words to say: "Nothing educates a young man so well as a liaison with someone in good society."[62]

In the recollection of this period, Tolstoy sets down a confession within *A Confession* such as would have condemned anyone less well known to hard labor: "I cannot recall those years without horror and disgust. I killed men in war, I challenged a man to a duel in order to kill, I lost vast sums gambling, I squandered the produce of peasant labour. I punished them, I committed adultery. I deceived. Lying, theft, cupidity in all its forms, drunkenness, violence, murder, there is no crime I have not committed . . . and for all that I was praised and respected."[63]

If this picture is as somber, as extreme, as overloaded as it sounds, it is because between 1878 and 1881, when he was writing *A Confession*, Tolstoy had an even greater need to expiate his sins than to confess them. There is no real falsification of the facts but an exaggeration, an inflation of the past, which produces the distortion required by that present need. Exhibitionism plays a part in this urge to confess in public; there is still the same self-complacency under an outward self-castigation, the same narcissistic fascination with his faults, an equilibrium between self-disgust and a kind of self-satisfying wallow in baseness, a certain delectation in the act of avowal. But behind this showing off of the ego in its goodness and its evil lies a sincere desire for purification, such as may be found also in Nikita, the tragic hero of *The Power of Darkness*, obsessed with a longing to confess his crime, and in Nekhlyudov, who at the end of *Resurrection* seeks by means of total renunciation to expiate his past sins—a procedure akin to Tolstoy's.

FIVE

Literary Life and Travels

On reaching St. Petersburg on November 19, 1855, Tolstoy went to see Turgenev. The two writers had never met, but no matter: Turgenev at once invited him to stay with him.

Such was the beginning of a "difficult" friendship, made up of storms and misunderstandings. Turgenev was first of all a man of letters and did not catch fire like his visitor did about causes alien to literature. One of their quarrels nearly ended in a duel and led to a break of seventeen years. Yet on his deathbed in 1883 Turgenev solemnly implored Tolstoy to return to literature.

In 1855, Tolstoy did not lose a minute before succumbing once again to the temptations of the big city. Turgenev wrote to the poet Fet, one of their friends in common: "He is just back from Sevastopol and his battery, has stopped here, and is painting the town red! Orgies, gypsy dance halls, cards all night, and then he sleeps like the dead until two o'clock."

At the same time, the young author quickly became a favorite of the literary crowd, as well as of high and not so high society in St. Petersburg. He brought them all a sense of freshness, of innocence, and also of heroic experience in war, whose multiple realities those circles knew nothing of. After the austerities of the Caucasus and the real danger he had undergone in the Crimea, Tolstoy was so taken with St. Petersburg life that, amid the fever of his pleasures and social rounds, he felt the death of his brother Dimitri as a mere vexation—it stopped his going to a Court ball! It was probably to exorcise his remorse for that lack of feeling that he made his brother live again, and in particular made him die again, long afterward, in *Anna Karenina*, as Levin's brother Nikolay.

But he soon tired of the Russian "republic of letters." The quarrels between Westernizers and Slavophiles exasperated him; he found the outlook of these last "too narrow and not sufficiently to the point."[1] For him, the real problem lay in another realm; it was not to be found in the pointless discussions of this Vanity Fair.

A dissipated life and the self-disgust it brought did not prevent the young literary lion, the writer of the moment, from writing, publishing, and strengthening his reputation. This was the time when, according to him, he set himself to write "from vanity, pride and covetousness."[2] *Sevastopol in August* came out in June 1855, *Notes of a Billiard Marker* two months later, and *The Morning of a Landowner* in December.

The view Tolstoy took at fifty, in *A Confession*, of his life as student and as army officer is that of a repentant sinner. His judgment of the years that followed his return to civilian life was even more severe. "They received me as one of themselves and flattered me. And before I had time to look round I had adopted the views on life of the set of authors I had come among, and these views completely obliterated all my former strivings to improve. . . ."[3]

But "although it was very pleasant and profitable to be one of these high priests," Tolstoy thought them "very inferior in character" to "people he had met in military life." The intrigues between coteries did not amuse him. His intense, feverish, almost crazed activity at this period was not enough to overcome or even to mask his gnawing dissatisfaction. Unable to bear for very long the artificialities of an existence he thought dangerous to what was best in him, he withdrew from it, resolved to become useful by devoting himself to the enlightenment of his "souls," that is, his peasants, and the material improvement of their lives.

On May 26 he stopped on the way at his friends', the Behrs. The servants of the house having gone to church, dinner was served by the children; six years later he was to marry the middle one of the three daughters.

Now for the first time he was going to put his theories to the test of reality, and all his life thereafter he tried again and again to fit his actions to his convictions. But he was soon disappointed. His attempt to free his serfs ahead of the rest was a failure: "They don't want their freedom."[4]

In *Anna Karenina*, Levin's brother Sergey makes fun of him affectionately: "They don't approve of your working in the fields . . . the peasantry have very definite ideas as to what the gentry should and should not do."[5] As for Levin himself, he saw a "stumbling block [in the] insurmountable distrust of the peasants."[6]

The angry young man who wanted to reform the world had other interests as well. When he was twenty-three he had already considered his bachelor status unnatural, and for a long time he had been thinking of marriage. He fixed on a young country neighbor, Valeriya Arsenyevna. The correspondence that resulted is interesting for its playful, gossipy tone, unusual for Tolstoy. Some years later it was to inspire his story *Family Happiness*.

In a letter to this young woman he paints his own portrait at twenty-eight in a realistic way, not very encouraging for the potential partner in the marriage. He depicts himself under the imaginary name of Khrapovitsky, "a man morally old, who did many foolish things in his youth for which he has paid with the happiness of the best years of his life, and who has now found for himself both a purpose and a vocation—literature—at heart despises society, adores a peaceful, moral, family life and fears nothing in the world so much as a dissipated social life, in which all good, honest, pure thoughts and feelings perish and in which you become the slave of social conventions and creditors."[7]

In another letter Tolstoy describes the relatively modest standard of living the Khrapovitskys will have to adopt, given their small income: no chef, but a cook, and a rented carriage. There follows a veritable treatise on the ethics of marriage in seven pages, praising the advantages of the simple country life and listing the foes of domestic happiness—jealousy, flirting, idle pleasure, concealment, anger, sloth, lack of order, and dissipation. This lesson in the matrimonial virtues may surprise in a suitor, but Tolstoy never let up in his passion to educate. The protective, didactic attitude may be better understood when one remembers that on the death of Vladimir Arsenyev, Tolstoy had become guardian to Arsenyev's three daughters.

The diary notes of the summer and autumn of 1856 and early 1857 show clearly that he wanted to be married for the sake of being married, rather than from any feeling toward the young Arsenyevna. Once again, he was trying to combine the demands of his heart with those of his reason, hoping to transform a marriage of convenience into a love match. He failed, after dancing a sort of hesitation waltz with the girl: on June 21 he writes: "The more effect she has on me, the less I could speak to her,"[8] but three days later, "Valeriya was awfully bad and I've quite calmed down."[9] On June 30 he says she was an excellent little girl "but I definitely don't like her." In early July their relations are "easy and pleasant,"[10] and he is happy she has "put her hair behind her ears"[11] as she knew it would give him pleasure. Tolstoy seems really involved: "I'm beginning to like Valeriya as a woman, whereas before it was just as a woman that she repelled me."[12] Three days later, no trace of this remains: "V. is apparently just stupid."[13] Yet two weeks later, they spoke of marriage: "She's not stupid, and is exceptionally kind."[14]

Tolstoy thereupon paid a short visit to Moscow; it seems clear to him there that she is "unfitted for either a practical or an intellectual life"; she is no more than "an unpleasant memory."[15] Ten days later he sees her again. "She's grown terribly stout and I definitely have no feeling for her."[16]

A week goes by; Tolstoy admires her at a ball. "Valeriya was charming, I almost fell in love with her."[17] He shows her this note in his diary and she tears out the page. Next day he finds her hairstyle "terrible," dislikes her purple dress; "I felt hurt and ashamed. . . ."[18]

Tolstoy noticed that little by little he had become "quite involuntarily . . . a sort of fiancé."[19] He confessed to his brother Nikolay that he felt "remorse with [himself] for having gone so far" and that he did not know how to break off these relations "that weigh down on [him] terribly."[20] He wrote to Tante Toinette: "I am more than indifferent towards her, and feel that I can't deceive either myself or her any more."[21]

Between the uncertainties of this pseudo-engagement, daily workouts in a gymnasium, dinners in town, literary conversations, and some casual affairs, Tolstoy had done a great deal of work* and much reading: Pushkin, Gogol, "a stupid novel by Eugène Sue," and also: *Werther*, *Pickwick Papers*, Mérimée's *Carmen* (which he found "weak"), and (with admiration) *Pole Star*, a journal published in London by Herzen that circulated secretly in Russia. He also read a few plays, including Shakespeare's *Henry IV*, for he was writing a play, *A Practical Person*, whose hero he visualized as crying out, "clamouring a great protest against everything."[22]

As everyone at Tula, in Moscow, and in his family kept carping at him, he decided to set out for Western Europe. Tolstoy was running away not only from Valeriya Arsenyevna but also from the excessively social and perpetually debauched life he had relapsed into in Moscow, and still more from the literary crowd, with whom he was increasingly disappointed. Of these, Turgenev was first and foremost: "He's definitely an uncongenial, cold, and difficult person . . . I'll never get on with him."[23]

Oh, to be free of all that! "The literary atmosphere disgusts me to a

* On December 17 Tolstoy got the proofs of *Youth*, "completely messed up by the Church censorship." (*Souvenirs et récits*, p. 376)

greater extent than anything ever before!"[24] he exclaims on November 22, 1856. And the next day he notes: "[I want to] write in the way in which I am now beginning to think about art—a terribly pure and exalted way."[25]

After a ten-day journey that took him through Warsaw and Berlin, Tolstoy arrived at the Gare du Nord in Paris on February 21, 1857. He did not feel out of his element, speaking fluent French as he did, and he was taken up at once by the Russian society of the city—intellectuals such as Nekrasov or Turgenev, who lived there in a liaison with the singer Pauline Viardot. Russian aristocrats often lived or spent long periods in Paris. He wrote to Tante Toinette: "In every family there are girls who are, it appears, my cousins."[26]

He stayed at the Hôtel Meurice, later moving to 206 rue de Rivoli, and then to 11 rue de l'Arcade. On arriving he had noted in his journal "that above all" he wanted to work for at least four hours a day, but nearly every evening he dined with some Russians, went to a ball or to the theater. Though accusing himself of laziness as usual, Tolstoy showed his usual vitality: he took lessons in English and Italian, explored the treasures of Paris and its environs, and gave himself up to whatever temptations the city had to offer.

To initiate him into Parisian life, Turgenev took his friend to the Opéra ball the first night he arrived. Tolstoy thereafter went to the theater incessantly: "Les Précieuses ridicules, l'Avare, 'excellent.' "[27] The next day he saw a production of Marivaux's *Les Fausses Confidences*, "a miracle of elegance." He saw *Le Malade imaginaire*, "wonderfully acted." He read Balzac's *Honorine*, "an immense talent." He went to the Sorbonne no less than to public dances. He was at a play by Alexandre Dumas, *A Money Matter*.[28] Some days later he was attending "lectures on political economy by Baudrillard"[29] at the Collège de France. The next day he went to the Musée de Cluny and records that he was "solicited." On the third, he had already been "picked up on the street." On the eighth he was off to Fontainebleau and his only comment is: "the forest,"[30] which obviously impressed him more than the château. He spent some days with Turgenev at Dijon and looked at churches. Back in Paris on March 16, he went to the Louvre in the afternoon and to the Opéra Comique in the evening for *La Fille du Régiment*. Tolstoy seems indefatigable though he complains of his health. The day after, he visited the Invalides to see Napoleon's tomb: "Deification of a villain; it's terrible," and he adds that soldiers are "animals trained to bite everyone." He visited Notre Dame: "Dijon cathedral is better." But his mood was dismal: "Terribly sad, spent a pile of money."[31] All the same, that evening found him at *Le Barbier de Séville*. He ran away from Turgenev, who got on his nerves. The following day he was at the Stock Exchange: "Dreadful!"[32]

Then suddenly, for no apparent reason, his anxiety gets worse: "Last night I was tormented by sudden doubts about everything. And now although they don't torment me, they are still with me. Why? And what am I? More than once it seemed to me that I was solving these questions, but no, my life has provided me with no confirmation of that."[33] Thus on March 19.

Still, the mood had no influence on his occupations: he visited the Sainte Chapelle and went to see Racine's *Les Plaideurs*. The day after, Bobino music hall and an evening with Russian officers, "so-called jolly supper and brothel."[34] Tolstoy pursues his discovery of Paris: the law courts, the Bibliothèque Nationale, the Académie Française. On March 27 he went to Versailles, where he felt "his lack of knowledge."[35] His "incoherent life" weighed him down, he was unable to work. His brother Sergey was in Paris, and Tolstoy notes that, although he loves him dearly, their "development has been so different that [they] can't live together."[36] On April 5 he spent the day at the races, but felt "a boredom he cannot shake off."[37]

It was in that state of mind, or rather it may be because he was in that state, that Tolstoy had the strange idea of attending a public execution due to take place at dawn the next morning. The abominable sight* made him literally ill: "The impression it made was a strong one and not wasted on me. . . . The guillotine kept me awake a long time and made me reflect."[38]

He had gone to spend a fashionable evening with the Trubetskoys to cheer himself up, but Turgenev was there and got on his nerves: "He does not talk, he chatters." Next day he got up late, "felt unwell . . . and suddenly a simple, sensible idea occurred to me—to leave Paris."[39]

A letter to the literary critic Botkin, begun on March 24 and finished on April 7, 1857, shows how Tolstoy's opinion of Paris and the French was turned upside down by the sight of the execution. In the first part of the letter he had written: "I've been living in Paris for nearly two months now, and I can't foresee the time when the city will have lost its interest for me . . . I'm a complete ignoramus; nowhere have I felt this so keenly as here. Consequently for that reason alone I can be happy and content

* The fact that Tolstoy mentions this episode in *A Confession* shows its importance to him, because he records in that work only the salient events of his life: "When I saw the head part from the body and how they thumped separately into the box, I understood . . . that no theory of the reasonableness of our present progress could justify this deed." (*A Confession*, p. 12)

with my life here, the more so since I also feel that my ignorance is not beyond redemption here." He planned then to settle for at least two more months near Paris. But the second paragraph begins like this: "I wrote this yesterday and was interrupted. I was stupid enough to go and see an execution." Of course in the Caucasus and the Crimea he had witnessed atrocities, but they were not this "cold, refined calculation . . . a convenient way of murder." He adds: "The law of man—what nonsense! The truth is that the state is a conspiracy designed not only to exploit, but above all to corrupt its citizens. . . . More people will be killed too before long, but from today I will certainly never go and see such a thing again, and I will never serve any government anywhere."[40]

He took the train to Ambérieu and continued his journey by coach to Geneva. Traveling by moonlight, Tolstoy noted: "For the first time in a long while I sincerely thanked God again that I was alive."[41]

Geneva had not been chosen at random; he knew that among the members of the Russian colony there he would find Alexandra Andreyevna Tolstoya, his beloved "Alexandrine."* He had met her on his return from the Crimea and felt a somewhat amorous and—since she was his kinswoman—mildly incestuous friendship for this spinster who was eleven years his senior. This ambiguous feeling eventually turned into a spiritual intimacy that often was a great consolation to Tolstoy. On the practical level, Alexandrine Tolstoya, who held an official position at Court, was to help extricate him more than once from the predicaments that his anti-government declarations were always getting him into.

Tolstoy reached Geneva on the day before Easter, and went to confession on April 17: "a good deed in any case."[42] But his anxiety persisted: "Slept badly as though afraid of being late somewhere."[43]

He went about here and there in Switzerland, often on foot, and in that way came to the Saint Bernard Pass, where he found "a monastically unctuous welcome."[44]

He stayed three months at Clarens, which moved him because of its links with the *Héloïse* of Rousseau; he shared the social life of Russians on holiday. He was also working at *The Cossacks* and *A Lost Man* (later to be called *Albert*) and dreamed of what might have been "if Alexandrine had only been ten years younger."

At Lucerne he was shocked by the rude behavior of the guests at a luxury hotel toward a musician whom they had previously listened to with pleasure. To teach them a lesson, he invited this unhappy guitarist to have a drink with him, but in this move the attitude of the hotel staff

* Alexandrine's portrait in the Tolstoy Museum in Moscow shows a certain likeness between her and Sofia Tolstoy.

shocked him even more. The incident inspired him on the spot with a story, *Lucerne*, which was published that September.

At Geneva he fell into dissipation "in the urban manner." He had conversations about freemasonry, got interested in "the 'Grand Orient' in France and 'Alpina' in Switzerland,"* and noted and underlined "Rousseau was a freemason."[45]

He continued his journey, passed through Schaffhausen and set out for Stuttgart. On July 23 he noted in his diary: "Very important—the idea occurred to me, clearly and forcibly, of starting a school in the country for the whole neighbourhood, and of general activity of that kind."[46]

At Baden-Baden he was ill, and went gambling. He was still unhappy, unfulfilled, "ill at ease: filth, these people. And above all, filth, myself."[47] He borrowed money to pay a gambling debt, gambled that, and lost it: a hopeless situation. In the end it was Turgenev who was alerted and got him out of it. Next, off again, in the Tolstoy manner. He was depressed and weary of the wandering life. Besides, he loved the summer at Yasnaya Polyana, and most of all, he was afraid if he stayed he would continue gambling. The news of his sister's divorce staggered him and he decided to go home at once. Once more, his departure was like a flight.

Home from his first journey abroad, Tolstoy felt contradictory emotions: first, the joy of getting back to his native soil. The Russians are perhaps more organically tied to their own land than are any other people in the world—whence the importance of the theme of homesickness in their literature.

On July 31, 1857, he was in ecstasies about: "The blue-grey morning, the drenched and dewy earth, with birches—Russian—wonderful."[48] At the same time he felt an immense sadness, anger almost, when he compared the style of life in his own country with that of the European nations he had just visited. After Western Europe, Tolstoy was shocked to see that the steward at Yasnaya Polyana did nothing but "beat and whip," and he was staggered by the "poverty of the people and the sufferings of the animals. . . ." On August 6 he noted: "Russia is disgusting—I simply don't like it."[49]

As he confided to Alexandrine in a letter of August 18:

> If you had seen, as I did one week, how a lady in the street beat her maid with a stick, how the district police officer got me to say I would send him a cartload of hay before he would provide my man with a legal permit, how,

* Names of the national Freemason ruling bodies.

> before my eyes, an official almost beat a sick old man of seventy to death because the official had got tangled up with him . . . if you had seen all this, and a whole lot more besides, you would believe me that life in Russia is a continuous, unending struggle with one's feelings. Happily, there is one salvation—the moral world, the world of the arts, poetry, and one's affections.[50]

His return to the double reality of Russia, to the blue-grey mornings and the whip, overwhelmed him. But to this suffering from visible causes there was superadded, or rather there underlay, a depressive condition which increasingly beset him: "Sensuality torments me; laziness again, boredom, and sadness. Everything seems stupid. . . . And soon, eternal night."[51]

As always, Tolstoy lost no time and by August 13 he reports: "Started allowing the domestic serfs to buy their freedom."[52] But the peasants still suspected some trickery on his part: "Not many of the peasants want to transfer to quit-rent."[53]

Happily, Tante Toinette is there to love and understand him: "Aunty is wonderful. All her advice is golden truth, whatever strange flat-footed form it may take."[54] He wants to make her one of the chief characters in a novel he is thinking about.

The day after his twenty-ninth birthday he read the Gospels, which "he had not done for a long time," and wondered (after reading *The Iliad*), "How could Homer not have known that goodness is love?"[55]

He plants trees from morning to night, he sees old friends, the Arsenyevs and the Behrs. Still, everything bores him, he has "no taste for anything." He questions himself deeper and deeper about the meaning of life: "What is strange is not that God ordained that a piece of bread should be His Son's flesh; what is 100,000 times more strange is that we live and don't know why. . . ."[56]

He worked at *Albert*, and was upset to notice that his "reputation has fallen, or is just about surviving," admitting to himself that this made him feel very much "saddened at heart."[57]

Tolstoy dragged his boredom from Yasnaya Polyana to Moscow and St. Petersburg; he went in heavily for physical exercise, as if by the exercise of his bodily strength he wanted to reassure himself about feeling his moral and intellectual strength declining.

Eighteen fifty-seven ended sadly. He made a trip to Yasnaya Polyana, "where the farming is going very badly."[58] Early 1858 did not begin cheerfully either. He worked at *The Cossacks*, a veritable Penelope's web among his works of fiction. He revised *Albert* "definitively" (or so he thought). He sought refuge in music, and founded a Musical Society which was later to become the Russian Conservatory, but its beginnings were difficult.

Even Alexandrine, who on October 22 was still "charming—a joy and a comfort,"[59] grew old and "ceased to be a woman" for him.[60] Still, he kept writing to her, without reserve. On April 14 he noted that he had "just written [her] a stupid letter,"[61] no doubt because it was too lyrical and too sincere. It was the famous letter on spring ("Spring has such an influence on me that at times I catch myself dreaming that I am a plant. . .") quoted at the end of chapter three. He told her of his conflicting feelings, "How these are reconciled I don't know and can't explain"; what is clear is that "dogs and cats do lie in the same shed."[62] Tolstoy never painted his own portrait better. During this stay at Yasnaya Polyana he suffered from what in *The Devil* he was to call "that important drawback to country life—enforced [sexual] self-restraint."[63]

By way of remedy he had recourse to "the Zassieke* Soldier"[64]† of whom he wrote in his diary for April 26, 1858. This man arranged a rendezvous for him in the woods with a young woman of twenty-two, Aksinya Sakhorov; she was married to Bazykin, a peasant from a village a few versts' distance from Yasnaya Polyana, but from all accounts Bazykin was a complaisant type who was no more faithful to his wife than was she to him.

On May 4 Tolstoy noted: "I have been in love all day."[65] The affair seems to have eased his anxiety and restored his taste for life, for he remarks: "Aunty and I are living splendidly together, as we were before."[66] The description of his encounters with the peasant girl "in that hazel and maple thicket, bathed in bright sunlight,"[67] or in the orangery, inspired a number of scenes in *The Devil* that have the lyrical power and bathe in the same sensuality as the erotic episodes in Lawrence's *Lady Chatterley's Lover*. Tolstoy was all at once very much smitten. By May 13 he noted: "Caught a glimpse of Aksinya. She's very pretty. I've been waiting for her these last few days in vain. . . . Her neck is red from the sun. . . . I'm in love as never before in my life. I've no other thoughts. I'm tormented."[68] The affair lasted three years. Aksinya had a son, Timofey, who forty years later became coachman to Tolstoy's own son Andrey, and then manager of his stud farm. According to some of the gossip of the time, Andrey Lvovich and his coachman may have been half-brothers.

* The estate forest.

† In *The Devil* the hero's procurer would be Danilo, an old gamekeeper.

Consciously or not, Tolstoy perhaps wanted to put his daily life in harmony with his amour, for he worked a great deal on the estate: "All day in the fields"[69] on May 15 and the same on the sixteenth. On the nineteenth, "I'm not writing, not reading, and not thinking. I'm wholly absorbed in the estate."[70]

After the haymaking he left for Moscow. When he got there he discovered that he had "aged terribly, and grown tired of life this summer. . . . There's no possibility of happiness in life; on the other hand, it's easier to be an out-and-out spiritual being, 'a dweller on earth, but devoid of physical needs.' "[71] The Moscow routine caught him up again—going out, the club, literary conversations—"Dined at the Behrses'. What sweet girls!"[72]

He tired of Moscow quickly and began now to think that he could work only at Yasnaya Polyana. He went back, but found that he felt just as bad: "I've let myself go so much that it's impossible."[73] So once again to Moscow at the end of December, where he was pained by the lack of "public interest" in him. "Literature, which I had a sniff of yesterday at Fet's, disgusts me: i.e., I think that since I began my literary career in the most flattering conditions of general praise, sustained for two years, during which I occupied almost the first place—without such conditions I don't want to know literature, i.e., literature for the public—and thank God! I must write quietly and calmly, without the aim of publishing." That is what he is doing, for he adds: "Wrote a note about the gentry problem, and burned it without showing it to anyone."[74]

Tolstoy's existence continued to lack a fixed center. He went from place to place, from one person to another. One day, taking part in a bear hunt organized by Fet, he escaped by a miracle from a she-bear that he had wounded; its hide now lies under the piano in the Tolstoy house in Moscow.

In early 1859, he was made a member of the Society of Devotees of Russian Literature, and on February 4 delivered his reception speech. In it, he raised the question of what was then called the "literature of accusation" and declared that "however great may be the importance of a political literature that reflects the temporary interests of society, there is another literature that reflects eternal and universal interests, the dearest and deepest feelings of the people, a literature accessible to men of all peoples and all times, a literature without which no people has ever developed that had sap and strength."[75]

Oddly enough, after many variations of attitude toward literature, it was to this idea of a universal literature that he came back at the end, in his very last thoughts on art. During the early part of this year 1859, he worked on *Anna*, which became *Family Happiness.* Its appearance in May plunged him into despair, for he found it a bad novel and wrote to Botkin: "I'm now dead and buried as a writer and as a man."[76]

But his attention was by no means exclusively focused on fame, as is shown in a letter to Alexandrine written the same day: "With me it isn't religion that makes life, but life that makes religion. When I lead a good life, I'm closer to it . . . but when I lead a bad life, I feel there's no need for it. Just now . . . I feel such self-disgust, my heart feels so arid, that it's dreadful and horrible, and the need for religion is all the more apparent. . . . You laugh at nature and the nightingales. For me nature is religion's guide. Each soul has its own path. . . ."[77]

Even Aksinya, when he met her again, could no longer give him the old peace of mind, and he remembered "with revulsion—her shoulders."[78] In his diary, still on the same day, he gives vent to his dismay: "A week in the country already. Things are going badly on the estate, and I'm fed up with it. Received *Family Happiness.* It's a shameful abomination. . . . My heart simply doesn't respond to anything this year. I don't even feel sorrow. Only the need to work and forget—what? There's nothing to forget. Forget that I'm alive. I prayed today and want to force myself to work regularly and do so little that it is bound to be good."[79]

During five months the diary is silent; he takes it up again on October 2 with a laconic summary of the gap: "A summer of work on the estate, melancholy, disorder, irritability and laziness."[80] His moral state is "worse and worse every day—almost back in summer rut."[81] "Continue to see Aksinya exclusively."[82] And next day, "nausea at myself, vexation."[83]

Early 1860 finds Tolstoy organizing a school in his own house, on the third floor. But the peasants are as distrustful of the young master who wants to share his knowledge as they were when he wanted to share his land: "The schoolboy Andrey told me he had not come for his day's work because his father was afraid that if I taught him I would give him no more money. This infuriated me."[84]

Twenty years later, in *A Confession*, Tolstoy remembered his pleasure in this new occupation: "I had not to face the falsity which had become obvious to me and stared me in the face when I had tried to teach people by literary means. . . . In reality, I was turning round and round one and the same insoluble problem, which was: How to teach without knowing what to teach . . . I thought to evade this difficulty by letting [the children] learn what they liked."[85]

In his listless mood Tolstoy kept on working at *The Cossacks.** It was probably his own vague desire to take Aksinya away from her husband Bazykin and marry her himself that made him give his hero Olenin the intention of marrying the Circassian girl he loved.

While working away at his novel, Tolstoy was tormented by religious difficulties rather than literary ones: "But pray to whom? What sort of God is it that can be imagined so clearly that one can ask Him for things, communicate with Him? And if I imagine Him to be like that, He loses all grandeur for me. A God one can petition and whom it is possible to serve is an expression of weakness of mind. He is God precisely because I can't imagine to myself His whole being. Therefore He is not a being; He is law and might. Let this page stand as a memorial to my conviction of the power of Mind."[86]

He was still in love with Aksinya and on May 26, 1860, he noted: "She was nowhere about. I looked for her. It's no longer the feeling of a stag (for a doe), but of a husband for a wife. . . . I try to awaken my former feeling of surfeit, and I can't."[87] That remark turns up again nearly word for word in *The Devil:* "From the time I had her I experienced a new feeling, the real feeling of a husband. Yes, I ought to have lived with her."[88]

His love for this peasant girl, whose initial does not appear more than a dozen times in his journal, was certainly an experience of great importance in Tolstoy's life. At the age of eighty-one he could still write: "I looked at my bare feet and remembered Aksinya."[89] It was perhaps the intensity of that memory that led him to take up again the manuscript of *The Devil*, which he had abandoned for twenty years. Meanwhile, the affair preyed on his mind; he was depressed; summer had put an end to his educational efforts, the pupils having gone back to the fields, like their master.

Tolstoy's brother Nikolay Nikolayevich was still seeking to be cured of his tuberculosis at Soden, a little German spa town, but the news was bad. His sister Marya ("Masha") was also ailing. Tolstoy left on July 27, 1860, to visit the sick man with Marya and her husband and children.

Tolstoy was now most concerned with education, and this second stay abroad turned into a serious survey of teaching methods in Germany, Switzerland, France, and England. Tolstoy's view of this enterprise

* A. Efremov, in his study of "the popular element in the language" of this novel, maintains that the Cossack dialect in this book was gradually replaced by the dialect of the Tula area. (V. Shklovsky, *Lev Tolstoy*, Moscow: Progress Publishers, 1978)

verged on sarcasm: "I went abroad a second time to discover how to teach others while myself knowing nothing."[90]

In Berlin, on the first leg of the journey, he attended evening classes, meetings of workingmen, and public lectures. He went to Dresden to meet the novelist Berthold Auerbach, about whom he said later to Biryukov: "It is to this writer that I am indebted for the setting up of a school for my peasants, and for becoming interested in educating the people."[91] After meeting him he wondered, "What is Auerbach's place?" The answer is: "An intermediary between the people and the educated classes."[92] No doubt Tolstoy dreamed of occupying the same position. Yet he was disappointed by what he saw in Germany. The day before meeting Auerbach, he had visited a school he very much disliked: "Terrible. A prayer for the king, beatings, everything by heart, frightened, morally crippled children."[93]

Tolstoy was not content with merely visiting schools; he went in for theory and noted in haste: "Read a history of pedagogy. Francis Bacon, founder of materialism, Luther, a reformer in religion: back to the sources . . . Riehl in politics. Met Fröbel. An aristocrat and a liberal."[94] Two days later, he read Montaigne, who for him was "the first to express clearly the idea of freedom in education."[95]

Tolstoy traveled energetically, carrying on his educational research at Höchst, Frankfurt, and Geneva. In the castle of Wartburg he meditated in the room where Luther had translated the Bible. Much later in life, Tolstoy was to learn Greek and Hebrew so as to go back to the Scriptures himself and do his own translation of the texts.

His brother Nikolay's condition was no better. The whole family moved to Hyères, in the south of France, where the climate was supposed to work miracles for the sick man: he died on September 20, at the age of thirty-seven, "literally"[96] in his brother's arms. Tolstoy gave a very precise description of the scene in two long letters, one to Fet, the other to his brother Sergey; but it is his diary for October 13 that best shows how deeply moved he was. "It will soon be a month since Nikolenka died. This event cut me off from life terribly. Once again the question: why? It's not long now before I travel there. But where? Nowhere. . . . I can't ascribe to work the importance I need so as to have the strength and patience to work . . . Nikolenka's death is the strongest impression of my life."[97]

Clearly it is the riddle of death, of his own death, that Tolstoy was at this moment unable to bear, as *A Confession* confirms: "Not understanding why he had lived and still less why he had to die, no theories could give me, or him, any reply to these questions during his slow and painful dying."[98]

In the state of intense intellectual receptiveness that often follows an emotional shock, Tolstoy experienced a new revelation, which extended his vision of March 1855 as to the idea of a "practical religion." The "reformer" heard his second call to action: "During the funeral itself the idea occurred to me to write a materialist Gospel, a life of a materialist Christ."[99]

It is an enigmatic utterance if ever there was one, but it shows that well before what Tolstoy called for convenience his "conversion," he was questioning certain aspects of Christianity and rejecting the supernatural nature of Christ. He conceived his plan for a "materialist" gospel at the very moment when Ernest Renan in France was giving it expression by writing his later world-famous *Life of Jesus*.*

Deeply stirred by his brother's death, Tolstoy stayed on at Hyères. He had "loved and esteemed him more than anything in the world,"[100] and the crowd of sick people dragging out their tuberculosis there gave him a sense of still living in Nikolay's world.

He went on excursions with his nephews and other children of the Russian colony. He took them to Porquerolles and organized their games. He turned himself into a schoolmaster once more (always a remedy of his at difficult times) and got his little pupils to write stories. He encouraged them with colored pencils† bought in Marseilles, where he had gone to visit the "people's schools." These he found bad, and made a quick note: "School is not in the schools, but in the streets and the cafés."[101] He

* The position of the two writers may seem similar, both seeing Christ as "an incomparable man" and both considering themselves believers, though the Church thought them atheists. Actually, their attitudes differ greatly. After reading *The Life of Jesus*, then forbidden in Russia, in 1878, Tolstoy wondered in a letter to Strakhov: "I asked myself 'well, what new thing have I learned from these historical details? Think hard and admit NOTHING, absolutely NOTHING.' " (*Tolstoy's Letters*, New York: Scribners, 1978, vol. I, p. 323.) For him Renan's idea "that if Christ's teaching exists, then some man or other existed, and this man certainly sweated and went to the lavatory," was of no interest. "The Christian truth—i.e., the highest expression of absolute good—is outside the framework of time, etc. But the Renans confuse its absolute expression with its expression in history, and reduce it to a temporal manifestation and then discuss it. If Christian truth is elevated and profound, it is only because it is subjectively absolute. But if one looks at its objective manifestation, it is on a level with the Code Napoleon." He thinks Renan's approach "childish and superficial." He admits that "moral truth can and should be studied," but he thinks the study should "proceed inwards, as it does with religious people." In 1891 Tolstoy went even further in criticism, on reading *The Future of Science*: "Renan is just the sort of eunuch with his moral testicles cut off, as [are] all the scholars of our time." (*Tolstoy's Letters*, vol. II, p. 473)

† As reported by Sergey Plaxin in his memoirs published in Moscow in 1902 under the title of *Tolstoy and Children*. Plaxin had been nine years old and one of those children in 1860.

admired the level of knowledge of the Marseillais, which he attributed to easy access to "books, newspapers, *cafés-chantants*, comedies, and little plays" that together made up "an unconscious education many times stronger than the compulsory one."[102]

Tolstoy finally left Hyères, still to pursue his round of schools. He went about so rapidly that it would be hard to describe his jaunts. He summed them up in his diary under date of April 1–13, 1861: "It's difficult to write down now what has happened these last four months—Italy, Nice, Florence, Livorno. An attempt to write of Aks[inya], Naples. The first vivid impression of nature and antiquity—Rome (back to art)—Hyères—Paris—reconciliation with Turgenev—London—not too bad—a loathing for civilisation. Brussels . . . Eisenach—the journey—thoughts about God and immortality. God has been restored—hope of immortality . . . Weimar, a wench . . ."[103]

In London, Tolstoy had attended a session of the House of Commons and heard a lecture on education by Dickens. He thought highly of him and kept a large portrait of him in his writing room at Yasnaya Polyana. The English writer's descriptions of poverty in London did not differ much from those Tolstoy had given of the slums of Moscow, and Dickens' ideas about popular education interested him greatly. Tolstoy met Matthew Arnold,* then professor of poetry at Oxford, who gave him introductions to a number of English schools.

He stayed two weeks in London and saw Herzen† several times. Herzen bore him no grudge (or perhaps he never knew about it) concerning Tolstoy's shameful indecision and plea of ignorance over customs procedures as an excuse for not daring to bring Herzen the documents that their common friend Kolbasin had wanted taken to him back in 1857.

If Turgenev's concerns had been too purely literary for Tolstoy, Herzen's were too political for any genuine understanding to exist between them. Nor was Herzen without reservations of his own toward Tolstoy; he wrote to Turgenev: "He is obstinate and says silly things, but he is a good and an innocent man. Why can he not think instead of acting as if he were still at Sevastopol, taking the position by assault?"[104]

All the same, Tolstoy and Herzen both felt that in Russia "the ice was

* Matthew Arnold in a fine article on *Anna Karenina* in 1889 wondered whether the religious writings of Tolstoy at that time "do more for the cause of religion and the teaching of the true spirit and message of Christ than what Count Tolstoy implied by telling in *Anna Karenina* the mental history of Levin." (*Essays in Criticism*)

† Alexander I. Herzen, author and revolutionary leader, had left Russia voluntarily in 1847, considering it impossible to express his ideas there in complete freedom. After traveling in Germany, France, and Italy, he settled in London in 1852 and published two émigré periodicals: *The Bell* and *The Pole Star*. Through these, he had a lasting influence on Russian intellectuals and revolutionaries, and on European ones as well.

cracking and breaking," and they knew they had a lot to say to each other. In a letter from Brussels dated March 14, 1861, Tolstoy argues: "You say I don't know Russia. No, I know my own subjective Russia."[105] He was curious about Herzen's opinions* and asked him what he thought of the official Manifesto on the Liberation of the Serfs. He himself was convinced that "the peasants won't understand a word and won't believe a word." In the same letter he thanks Herzen for the special number of *The Pole Star* on the Decembrists, which had especially interested him: "About four months ago I began a novel, of which the hero is to be a Decembrist returning from exile. I wanted to have a talk with you about it. . . . Please tell what you think about the propriety and the opportuneness of such a subject. Turgenev, to whom I read the beginning, liked the first chapters."[106]

From London Tolstoy went to Brussels. Herzen had given him two letters of introduction, one to the Polish revolutionary Joachim Lelewel, who was living there in destitution, and whose idealism won Tolstoy's admiration; and the other to Proudhon, exiled by Napoleon III. What was the conversation like between the man who had proclaimed that *Property Is Theft* and the man who thought it was a sin?

Tolstoy records that when he said to Proudhon, "As far as one can judge from a distance, awareness has now dawned in Russian society that without public instruction no kind of organized State can be solid," Proudhon had answered, "If that is true, then the future belongs to you Russians."[107]

Tolstoy proceeded on his journey of investigation, he "tore himself away from the laces of Brabant" to make for Warsaw by way of Dresden and Jena. From Frankfurt-on-Main, he wrote to Herzen to express regret that he was unable to attend a banquet Herzen was organizing to

* Tolstoy's opinion of Herzen changed several times. In London he was visibly under the spell of Herzen's intellectual charm. But when he organized his second school at Yasnaya Polyana on his return from Europe, he discouraged the students he took on as teachers from reading Herzen. Isaiah Berlin says in his preface to Herzen's memoirs that "at this time Tolstoy had declared his hostility to faith in liberal reform and improvement of human life by legal or institutional change—Herzen fell under this general ban." (A. Herzen, *My Past and Thoughts*, London: Chatto & Windus, 1979, p. xxxvi.) And yet in 1888, in the most committed time of his life, Tolstoy wrote to his friend, the painter Nicholas Gay: "Lately I've been reading Herzen, and still am . . . What a wonderful writer! Our Russian life for the last 20 years would have been different if this writer hadn't been hidden from the young generation. As it is, a very important organ was violently wrenched out of the organism of Russian society." (*Tolstoy's Letters*, vol. II, p. 437)

But in 1896 he asks himself, "What has Herzen said that is of the slightest use? As for the argument that the generation of the forties could not say what it wanted to say because of the rigid Russian censorship, Herzen wrote in perfect freedom in Paris, and yet managed to say nothing useful." It was only in 1908 that Tolstoy finally expressed the opinion that fundamentally he had always held: "Herzen was a narrow socialist, even if he was head and shoulders above the other politicians of his age and ours." (*My Past and Thoughts*, p. xxxvi) celebrate the serfs' emancipation. He had meant to attend with Turgenev, but Turgenev broke his promise, so Tolstoy gave up the idea. He thanked Herzen for another issue of *The Bell*, in which he had read an extract from the *Memoirs* of Ugarov and decided that "without knowing a single Decembrist," he had discovered "the mysticism peculiar to these people."[108]

At Jena he met a young student named Keller, who seemed to him "a very good worker." He thought Keller would make a perfect teacher of natural science for his school at Yasnaya Polyana and decided to take him home to Russia.

In spite of, or perhaps because of all this agitation, Tolstoy was still in a deplorable state of mind and suffered from a nagging sense of discontent[109] with himself. He continued his educational inquiries for a while longer, then set out again for Russia, where the abolition of serfdom had been decreed on March 19, 1861.

Tolstoy reached Yasnaya Polyana in April. On May 6 he stopped at the Behrs' and was clearly still considering settling down, possibly with the eldest girl: ". . . pleasant day at the Behrses', but I daren't marry Liza."[110]

Turgenev having invited Tolstoy to stay with him at Spasskoye, the latter arrived there on May 23. The next day, the two friends went over to Fet's at Stieponovka; on the morning of the twenty-seventh, an altercation broke out between them. Turgenev was congratulating himself in front of Tolstoy and the Fet family on the excellent education an English governess was giving his natural daughter, who was being brought up in Paris by his companion, Pauline Viardot. He was delighted that Miss Hinnis had not only asked for a sum of money to be allowed to the teenage girl for almsgiving, but even more because the governess got her to mend poor people's clothes. This display of fine feeling was the last straw:* Tolstoy was annoyed and ill-disposed toward Turgenev to begin with, because for some time the latter had courted his sister Masha, who was separated from her husband, and in Tolstoy's view had behaved badly toward her. He exploded.

Tolstoy related this episode, the most dramatic in a stormy friendship, to his wife in January 1877, and she put it in "Various Notes to Serve as Documentation": "Leo Nikolayevich says one should not choose [one's poor] in the English manner and leave them a small fixed fraction of one's

* Tolstoy's annoyance was an old story; when he came home from Sevastopol he had accused Turgenev of deliberately promenading "his democratic rump" in front of him, and on his first stay in Paris in the spring of 1857, he had "run after him from all directions in order to be friends with him, but it's impossible." (*Tolstoy's Diaries*, New York: Scribners, vol. I, p. 131)

income."[111] According to Fet, he added: "And I think that a richly dressed girl who manipulates dirty, ill-smelling rags is acting a false and theatrical farce."[112]

Voices were raised, and things went so far that, as Sofia tells the story, Turgenev grew enraged and shouted, "If you go on speaking in that tone I will punch your ugly mug."[113] He might not have been so irritable perhaps if Tolstoy, on the day of his arrival at Spasskoye, had not fallen asleep over *Fathers and Sons,* which Turgenev had lent him to read and comment on.

After this violent quarrel, the two writers left Stieponovka immediately. Tolstoy went off to see his friend I. P. Borisov at Novosalky, and from there sent off to Turgenev at Spasskoye a mounted messenger with a biting missive: "I hope that your conscience has already told you how badly you behaved toward me, especially in front of Fet and his wife. Therefore, write me a letter which I can send to the Fets. If you find my demand unjust, let me know. I shall wait at Bogoslov."[114]

Complication number one: Turgenev had his reply delivered to I. P. Borisov at Novosalky, presuming Tolstoy was still there, and not to the post office at Bogoslov. Receiving no reply from Turgenev, Tolstoy sent him a second letter, challenging him to a duel. A month later Tolstoy wrote in his diary: "A remarkable quarrel with Turgenev, a final one—he's an absolute scoundrel—but I think that in time I'll relent and forgive him."[115]

And indeed, by October 23 Tolstoy had written him a conciliatory letter.

Complication number two: The Davydov bookshop, where Tolstoy left this new missive for Turgenev, did not deliver it until early January 1863. So not knowing that any appeasing message was on its way, Turgenev wrote to Tolstoy, as we learn from the latter's diary: "Yesterday I received a letter from Turgenev in which he accused me of telling people that he's a coward and of distributing copies of my letter to him."[116] Turgenev suggested that they should fight a duel on his return from Paris. In reply, on the same day, Tolstoy's magnanimity was equal to his insolence: "Dear Sir, in your letter you call my conduct dishonourable, and furthermore you said to me personally that you would punch me in the face, but I ask your pardon, acknowledge myself to blame and decline the challenge."[117]

They remained enemies for seventeen years. In time, as he had foreseen, Tolstoy forgave and broke the silence that had reigned between them. In a letter of April 6, 1878, he urged: "Let us extend our hands to each other."[118]

At about the time of this quarrel, Tolstoy had been appointed "commissioner of the peace" in his district, in spite of opposition from the Marshal of the Peerage, who was expressing the hostility of numerous landowners in the area; in their view, Tolstoy figured as a dangerous liberal. He had himself been aware since 1858 that he had become "the enemy of our province."[119]

It was the duty of these commissioners to bring together the landowners and the former serfs to settle problems arising from the latter's emancipation. Tolstoy performed his task with authority, but the landowners were suspicious of his objective judgment;* they could not understand, for example, how he could take the side of a servant who wanted to leave his master when the master wanted to keep him. Tolstoy's comment on his role expressed disillusionment: "My work as an arbiter hasn't provided me with much material and has made me quarrel with all the landowners for good, and has ruined my health."[120]

He had written, just before leaving Europe: "One purpose alone—the education of the people."[121] So now he decided to reopen his school of 1849. Its plan was highly original; at one time, it is said, a placard hung over the door bearing the words: "Enter and leave when you want." Fundamentally what Tolstoy was after was a Russian solution to the problem of public instruction. What he had seen in Europe had shown him what mistakes not to make. And he thought that children, like the mass of the Russian people, being uncorrupted by bad teaching methods, were still intellectually "noble savages" with whom his own methods would work miracles.

There is no gainsaying that his educational ideas and the practical application he attempted were new: the classrooms were painted pink or blue; the shelves were stocked with shells and minerals and very few books, and the walls were hung with maps and pictures. It was a "progressive" (or "action" as it was called in Russian) school already at that early date—no reprimands, no homework, team work for storytelling, walks in the countryside for studying natural history, and plenty of handicrafts.

Tolstoy believed in "unconscious instruction," and he had seized on the importance of motivation. As "coercion in teaching is, by conviction and by temperament, hateful to me, I put no constraints on them, and when I noticed that they did not accept certain things voluntarily I never insisted; I looked for another line." His view of education was perpetual

* Tolstoy was twice summoned to court over his decisions, but both times his arbitration was judged correct, and the case was dismissed. (*Tolstoy's Letters*, vol. I, p. 160)

research: "When every school is so to speak a 'laboratory of education,' only then will it not fall behind general progress."[122]

His responsibilities as schoolmaster did not stop his going to Moscow, for he was still thinking of marriage with the eldest daughter of the Behrs': "Liza Behrs tempts me, but nothing will come of it. Mere calculation isn't enough and there's no feeling."[123]

During this stretch of time, Tolstoy devoted all his energies to his role as commissioner and to education. "School and arbitration business are going well. . . . Yesterday I opened a third school, which won't be a success."[124] He set up more than a hundred in his district.

Later, the apparent tranquillity of this period of his life amazed him and he disclosed its hidden cracks in *A Confession*: "Things appeared to be going well, but I felt I was not quite sound mentally and that matters could not long continue in that way."[125]

He tried to stifle his uneasy thoughts by distractions in Moscow. He gambled, he lost, and returned to writing *The Cossacks*, begun in the Caucasus in order to settle a gambling debt. Tolstoy was nervously exhausted, and on the advice of Doctor Behrs went to take a cure of *kumys* (mare's milk) at Samara. "So hard is my struggle as Arbiter, so obscure the results of my activities in the schools, so repulsive my shuffling in the magazine (which always amounted to one and the same thing: a desire to teach everybody and to hide the fact that I didn't know what to teach), that I fell ill, mentally rather than physically, threw up everything and went away to the Bashkirs in the Steppes, to breathe fresh air, drink kumys, and live a merely animal life."[126]

It was during this absence that the police, probably acting on information laid against him, carried out a search of Yasnaya Polyana. Tolstoy was indignant and wrote to Alexandrine when he got back to Moscow. He speaks of "three troikas galloping up to the house at Yasnaya, with bells ringing and full of armed gendarmes."[127] He admits that he had "all the charming proclamations of Herzen and *The Bell*, but only for a week: I simply returned them without reading them. I find it boring, I know it all, and I quite genuinely despise [these publications] with all my heart."[128]

Back home at Yasnaya Polyana, he heard from Tante Toinette ("so ill she cannot get up") the story "of the police raid." He was beside himself with fury. He insisted on public amends from the Tsar. He wrote a second time to Alexandrine, still more vehemently. He feared that all his endeavors would founder—"this school which was my whole life; it has been my monastery, my church, in which I sought and found a refuge from all the anxieties, doubts, and temptations of life." He affirmed that the twelve students he had taken on as masters for his schools "had arrived with manuscripts of Herzen in their trunks and revolutionary ideas in their heads, and all but one burned his manuscripts within a week." He even considered for a moment leaving Russia with "a bang, [but] not to go to Herzen—he has his way and I have mine."[129]

He wrote to the Tsar on August 22. His petition, and perhaps even more, Alexandrine's influence at Court, had a swift result: on September 5 the governor of Tula was informed by courier that "his Majesty has been pleased to decide that the action taken should entail no consequences for Count Tolstoy personally."

But the harm had been done, and Tolstoy was well aware of it. In the peasants' eyes, the police search was frightening: it discouraged them from sending their children to the school. "The police visitation has altogether ruined the people's opinion of me, which I value, which I have earned over the years, and which is essential to me in my chosen occupation—the founding of [more and more] schools for the people."[130]

II

THE TWO DROPS OF HONEY: LOVE AND ART

SIX

Engagement and Marriage

TOLSTOY'S TRAVELS, his educational activity, and his work as arbiter had left him unsatisfied; they had brought him no certitude in his religious quest, and no stability in his mental life. He was alone, more alone than ever, and he gave himself up to a sort of endless drifting, carried forward by the "mortal illness of the spirit" that was already chronic, but not diagnosed by him until seventeen years later in *A Confession*.[1]

The Behrs house was a refuge: Doctor Behrs' wife was that same Lyubov Islenyev whose family lived near Yasnaya Polyana, and had furnished Tolstoy with many traits for the family in *Childhood*. With them, he found as Levin did with the Scherbatskys, the "home life . . . of which he had been deprived by the death of his own father and mother."[2] He fell under the spell of the three daughters of the house, and once again like the hero of *Anna Karenina*, "he seemed to feel that he had to be in love with one of the sisters, only he was not sure with which."[3]

Everyone, himself included, believed he was in love with the eldest. Sofia alone had always known that it was for her that he visited, and undoubtedly she knew it by the age of ten, when she tied a ribbon on the armchair where Tolstoy as a young officer was sitting when he came to say goodbye to Doctor Behrs and his family before joining the Danube army.

In the first few days of August 1862 the Behrs ladies stopped at

Yasnaya Polyana on their way to grandfather Islenyev's house. Mother and daughters spent the night in the Vaulted Room.*

They were short of a bed. Tolstoy had the idea of improvising one by putting together a big square stool and a large armchair.† "I'll make up your bed for you," he said to young Sofia. She "felt embarrassed, but there was something lovely and intimate about making up the beds together,"[4] and she remembered later that when she was in bed, "my heart was singing with joy as I remembered Lev Nikolayevich arranging my bed for me."[5]

Sofia has also told us that in the course of a picnic Tolstoy encouraged her to ride a horse he had obviously saddled for her and took her along with him, after persuading her that a yellow dress with buttons and a black velvet belt made a perfectly suitable outfit for a gallop with him in the woods: "There will be no one but the birds and the trees to see you."[6]

Mother and daughters having gone on their way to Ivitsi, Tolstoy finds he cannot bear their absence more than two days: ". . . toothless old fool that I am, I've fallen in love,"[7] he wrote to Alexandrine on September 17, 1862. He turned up unannounced on his white horse, to everyone's delight, and attended, though without dancing, as he is "too old for that,"[8] an improvised ball to celebrate the girls' arrival at their grandfather's. It was after this ball that Tolstoy made Sofia a strange declaration of love, in a manner no less strange.

In the notes at the beginning of her diary, under the heading "Marriage to L. N. Tolstoy" in the chapter "What the Chalk Wrote," Sofia relates that when the guests were retiring, Tolstoy made a sign bidding her to stay and began to scribble in chalk on the green baize top of a card table, telling her: "I'm only going to write the initials—you must guess the words."[9] He then wrote: "y.y.a.n.f.h.t.v.r.m.o.m.a.a.i.f.h." Sofia insists in her diary: "I read the initials rapidly, without a second's hesitation. . . . 'Your youth and need for happiness too vividly remind me of my age and incapacity for happiness.' "[10] Sofia adds that she then telepathically read a second group of initials as well, this one stating: "Your family has the wrong idea about me and your sister Liza. You and your sister Tanechka must protect me."[11]

Tolstoy's diary contains little on this brief period of courtship. He realized not without some alarm that it was the young, the too young Sofia (she was eighteen and he thirty-four) who attracted him: "What if this is the desire for love, and not love? I try to look only at her weak sides, but nevertheless, a child! It could be!"[12]

Although she was nearly engaged to a young officer, Sofia had long

* This room became the writer's study after his marriage.

† Both pieces of furniture are still in the Vaulted Room.

been disturbed by Tolstoy's visits, "the dear poetic Count, with his wonderful, deep, bright gaze."[13] She wrote a story, *Natasha*, which shows her perplexity: its four characters are her sister Liza, her young admirer, herself, and Tolstoy, whom she calls Prince Dublitsky.

When he read Sofia's story, Tolstoy noted in his diary for August 26, 1862, that the "unusually unattractive appearance and fickleness of opinion" that she gives the Prince "touched [him] on the raw."[14]

Her words made him feel his age, and on August 28, 1862, his birthday, he wrote: "You ugly mug, don't think about marriage; your vocation is something else, and for that you have been highly gifted."[15] In the same note he goes on: ". . . worked a bit; wasted my time writing to Sonya [i.e., Sofia] in initial letters."[16]

Tolstoy visited the Behrs nearly every day. Frightened by the feelings Sofia aroused in him, he shifted even more rapidly than usual from happiness to anguish: "Every day I think that it's impossible to suffer more and at the same time be happy, and every day I become more demented."[17]

On September 3, 1862, he wrote: "Never has my future life with a wife presented itself to me so clearly, joyfully and calmly."[18] But on the seventh he addresses himself by the name Sofia had given him in her story: "Dublitsky, don't intrude where youth, poetry, beauty, and love are."[19] He gets drunk and thinks of entering a monastery. But he cannot flee from his passion as easily as that. Tolstoy now had the feeling that everything he did was for Sofia: "My diary is insincere. *Arrière-pensée* [haunting thought] that she is with me, and will sit beside me and read and . . . this is for her."[20]

Nor did the two other sisters cease to disturb him. He was responsive to their chitchat and had invented a term to define it—*Behrsage*. In fact, the second daughter, Tatyana Behrs, appealed to Tolstoy a great deal, and he depicted something of her physical presence and character in the Natasha of *War and Peace*. As for Liza, he told himself as he looked at her, "How beautifully unhappy she would be if she were my wife." Sofia "draws [him] irresistibly."[21]

On September 9 he could not bring himself to work; "instead, I wrote her a letter which I won't send."[22] This is the letter on which Shklovsky based his theory that Sofia had *not* guessed the message in chalk.* But the fact that Tolstoy did not send it seems rather to indicate that the meaning

* Shklovsky among other critics interprets this sentence and part of a letter to Sofia of September 9, 1862, in which Tolstoy gives the solution to the sentence written only in initials as proof that the young girl had not originally been able to read it. They think that Sofia, who wrote the account of the episode only in 1912, was influenced much more by a similar scene in *Anna Karenina* than by what had actually happened in September 1862. But what does it matter today whether the telepathic miracle occurred in life or in the novel?

of the initials had been sufficiently understood by Sonia to make further explanation unnecessary.

Tolstoy can no longer sleep: "dreamed and suffered agonies like a sixteen-year-old boy."[23] On the eleventh he dare not go and visit. On the twelfth he admits that he is madly in love, and uses almost the same words as he did about his love for the peasant girl Aksinya: "I'm in love as I never believed it possible to love. I'm mad, I'll shoot myself if it goes on like this. . . . She's charming in every respect. But I'm the repulsive Dublitsky."[24]

On September 14, after another night of insomnia, he writes at dawn: "My God, how afraid I am of dying! Happiness, and such happiness, seems to me impossible."[25]

The next day, writing up his diary, he has the same strange feeling once again: "I can't write for myself alone. It seems to me, in fact I'm sure, that soon there won't be any secrets for me alone, but secrets for two; she will read everything."[26]

After these four days of hesitation and mad anguish, Tolstoy decided at last to propose marriage. The Behrs parents were outraged; they wanted their eldest to be the first married, as custom dictated. Tolstoy sent Sofia a letter in which he begged her: "Tell me, as an honest person, do you want to be my wife?"[27] She agreed and he noted, at a loss: "She said—yes. She's like a winged bird. There's nothing to write. All this can't be forgotten and can't be written down."[28]

As always when Tolstoy made up his mind, he could brook no delay. The marriage must take place as soon as possible. Madame Behrs objected: "What about the trousseau?" "No trousseau," replied the impatient fiancé. The marriage occurred within a week, on September 23, 1862.

On the morning of the wedding, Tolstoy was prey to "fear, distrust and the desire to run away,"[29] and he went over to Sofia, torturing her with his doubts. At six that evening she had to wait for an hour, in dire anxiety, for the best man to come and tell her that her future husband was at last ready for her in the church. This delay was not due to renewed worrying but to the fact that his wedding shirt had been packed by mistake in the luggage to be taken to Yasnaya Polyana; he had been searching for it in vain.*

It had all happened so quickly that the wedding was rather like a kidnapping. Immediately after the ceremony, Tolstoy took his young bride to Yasnaya Polyana.

* Tolstoy used the incidents of his own marriage for Kitty and Levin's in *Anna Karenina*.

A period of wild happiness began. It was the time when "the two drops of honey—my love of family and of writing—which diverted my eyes from the cruel truth longer than the rest"[30] were sweet to him. Tolstoy, as it were, put up two screens between himself and his anxieties—his love for Sofia and hers for him. To these he would soon add a third—artistic creation.

Tolstoy and Sonia had each kept a journal before their marriage. They went on doing so, with a few interruptions. What was more dangerous, they gave them to each other to read. The step itself was ambiguous: at first it was a proof of mutual confidence, but it soon became a twofold self-scrutiny and confession, turning at times into mutual accusation. The perilous device by which each opens up to the other the secret garden often becomes an attack upon the other's inmost self. Tolstoy was soon its victim; he wrote on June 18, 1863, "I don't write anything for her that is untrue, but, from a choice of many things, something I wouldn't have written for myself alone."[31]

During their brief engagement Tolstoy had let Sofia read the journal of his youth.* The innocent girl had wept all night as she read the list of horrors her fiancé had been guilty of. It was to be the diaries of those early years that became the center of the drama played out fifty years later between Tolstoy, his wife, and his secretary and disciple Chertkov. At Tolstoy's own wish, Chertkov and the publisher censored these diaries, and we have them only in an expurgated form. In January 1912, at a lunch with Charles Salomon and Romain Rolland, Tolstoy's friend and French translator Michael Stakhovich, who had had access to the original, told Rolland much about their contents: "He confirmed to me [writes Rolland] the appalling frankness of certain passages. In particular, during the Caucasus period, there is a scene of rape by Tolstoy, told in the cruelest manner. It drove his wife to distraction; she begged him to destroy it. But he always refused; he said it was an expiation. If he became well known later, these things about him ought also to be known. He said one never knew a man if one did not know his relations with women. Sexual relations are the key to character, if not to life. In that diary, one finds Tolstoy listed his various daily expenses, such as: '1 horse—20 or 50 rubles; 1 woman—1 ruble 20.' "[32]

Reading these pages written in the Caucasus and those describing his

* The diabolical idea of hiding nothing was virtually a Tolstoyan dogma; it was what the couple had done in *Family Happiness*; Levin gave his diary to Kitty in *Anna Karenina*; Nekhlyudov had his read by Katyushka in *Resurrection*; and Tolstoy had already shown his own to Valeriya Arsenyevna. In real life, Tatyana Behrs, Sofia's sister, turned hers over to her fiancé, just as Tatyana Lvovna, Tolstoy's own daughter, was to do.

affair with Aksinya had plunged Sofia into despair. When she got to Yasnaya Polyana, the day after her wedding, she found that her husband's former mistress was still living in a nearby village and came occasionally to do household tasks in the house. In addition to jealousy, Sofia now had to suffer the humiliation of being the successor to "that fat, pale peasant woman."[33]

Tolstoy, in his violent, passionate love, felt gnawings of jealousy over his young wife's past, innocent though it was. And by a kind of projection into the future, he grew also jealous of what might happen,* while Sofia suffered from what had already been. Actually, when she read Tolstoy's journals she should have been more disturbed by her husband's yearnings for heaven than by any catalogue of his debauches. Tolstoy was probably never unfaithful to her, although there is a note dated January 6, 1889, when he was sixty, in which he says: "Went to see Petrushka; failed at the brothel."[34] (The Russian edition of the journal reads only: "Failed at b.") But it was not women, it was his spiritual development that took him away from her. Sofia felt it; "I am always jealously following him—his thoughts and his actions,"[35] she wrote on October 17, 1863, commenting on his friendship with Alexandrine.

She should also have read *Family Happiness* more attentively (it had appeared in May 1859); then she would have learned what puritan ideas Tolstoy had of marriage and of life in general, in spite of the excesses of his youth.

* Tolstoy suffered agonies later during the pathetic, platonic, and one-sided love that Taneyev, the musician, aroused in Sofia in 1895.

SEVEN

Married Life

THE HOUSE where Leo and Sofia Tolstoy began their married life was one of the two "wings," or pavilions, that remained of the old family mansion, the main part of which had been sold by Tolstoy in 1854 to pay a gambling debt. This pavilion was a small stone building that Tolstoy already knew quite well, for it was here that he had settled in with Tante Toinette in 1856, on his return to civilian life. Its five front windows make up the central facade of the house of Yasnaya Polyana as it stands today.

This main dwelling was to grow bit by bit as the family increased. The first alteration came in 1866, after the birth of Ilya, the third child; it was enough then to extend the house on the right by adding a small outbuilding that, before it was moved here, had served for some time as a neighborhood tavern. In 1871, after the birth of the fifth child, Masha, Tolstoy built an addition of two rooms on the ground floor, this time on the left, where he made his study, with one long room above it that became "the big room." It was used by turns as a dining room, reception room, and a theater and music room. The two pianos played on by Tolstoy,* his wife, and some of the children, as well as a number of composers and virtuosi of the time, are still there.

* Music overwhelmed Tolstoy and often made him weep. His son Sergey said he had "known no one as deeply moved by music as my father." (*Tolstoï vu par lui-même*, pp. 153–60.) Sergey says that in the seventies Tolstoy spent three or four hours a day at the piano, alone (sonatas by Mozart, Weber, the early Beethoven, Chopin, and Schumann) or with his wife (Haydn and

The big covered terrace made famous by a number of photographs was not built until 1892. The last alteration was made in 1894, at the request of Tolstoy's two eldest daughters, Tatyana and Masha, still unmarried at the time. The wooden annex of 1866 was replaced by a stone building of two stories, with two rooms on the ground floor and two on the second, one of these being taken by Sofia in 1897.

So it was quite a small house that Sofia took charge of when she came to Yasnaya Polyana. It was simply furnished, with bits of the furniture from the original big house, and other pieces made on the spot for it.* Tante Toinette was already living there with her companion, Natalya Petrovna. Sergey Nikolayevich, Tolstoy's elder brother, came to stay to help her welcome the young couple. It was Toinette who held the icon for them to kiss and gave them the traditional bread and salt. On that evening, September 24, 1862, Tolstoy noted in his diary: "Aunty is already preparing for trouble."[1] He was wrong; there was never any conflict between the old lady and the young wife; Sofia's real "wicked mother-in-law" was to be Chertkov.

Tolstoy gave up the room where he had got used to working since his return to Yasnaya Polyana, and took the Vaulted Room. He left that in 1864, soon after the birth of his daughter Tatyana: "Sonya and the two children are moving into my old study."[2] In 1866 he moved into the new annex, then in 1871 into one of the rooms in the second new building, where he wrote until 1902, when he reoccupied the study he had had before his marriage, and which he kept until his death.

Whatever room Tolstoy wrote in, two pieces of furniture always went with him: a big writing desk with three drawers that had belonged to his father and the famous black leather couch, which is now reupholstered

---

Mozart). They often played until one or two in the morning. In youth Tolstoy was fond of gypsy music and Cossack songs. He loved the songs of the Yasnaya Polyana village; his daughters Tatyana and Masha often sang them for him, accompanied by his son Mikhail or his brother-in-law Kuzminsky playing the balalaika. At times, Sergey also played the piano at Tolstoy's request.

According to his son's account, Tolstoy had a good sense of rhythm and expression, but a weak technique; he would "bend and breathe hard" to overcome a certain clumsiness of the fingers.

From the 1880s onward, Tolstoy rejected a whole realm of music—Wagner and the late Beethoven, who he thought had begun the decadence of music, and even Chopin, whom he admitted liking, because (as he said) "my taste is already spoiled."

In spite of this attitude, musicmaking continued at the Tolstoys'; in Moscow, where Chaliapin came to sing in 1900, as well as at Yasnaya Polyana, where Wanda Landowska came to play, bringing her clavichord with her in 1907.

* Most of these pieces still exist. At the time of the German invasion the curators at Yasnaya Polyana evacuated them and saved them from looting and from the outbreak of fire that followed the departure of the German troops. Yasnaya Polyana was occupied from October 29, 1941, to May 24, 1942. (N. Puzin, *Yasnaïa Poliana*, Moscow: 1964)

with imitation leather. The couch appears like a talisman in nearly all his books;* Tolstoy and his three brothers and his sister were all born on it. When a birth was due, the couch was moved to the room where the child was to be born, and such was the way in which Sofia gave birth to nine of their thirteen children.

Tolstoy records in his diary the birth of his eldest son, Sergey, on June 27, 1863: "I ran about and kept busy having the couch I was born on set up in the bedroom."[3] The drawers in the base of the piece held the paraphernalia (basins, towels, etc.) used at the time of births; toward the end of his life Tolstoy kept in them the manuscripts he most valued.

In the evening of the first day of their life together, September 25, 1862, Tolstoy took up his journal again. He had abandoned it for just a week. After a short casual note he writes that "she laughed too suddenly," a thought that shows a very critical man who cannot for an instant cease being an observer. But disquiet swiftly gives way to wonder: "Unbelievable happiness. Again she is writing beside me. It is not possible that this will end simply with life."[4]

What he writes on the following days lets one glimpse his tumultuous discovery of happiness. "I do not recognize myself. All my errors are clear to me. I love her as much as ever, if not more. I cannot work. Today there was a scene. I was sad that everything should be with us as it is with others. Said so to her, she wounded me in my feeling for her. I wept. She is a delight. I love her still more. But isn't there something false?"[5]

These shadows proved fugitive, and Tolstoy shared his enchantment with Alexandrine, the confidante of his joys and sorrows: "As I write I can hear upstairs the voice of my wife, whom I love more than anything in the world, talking to my brother. I've lived to the age of 34 not knowing that it was possible to be so much in love and so happy."[6]

Silent since her wedding, Sofia did not wait much longer to take up her own diary. On October 8 she writes: "The last two weeks my relations with him, with my husband, have seemed simple, at least my life has been easy. It's Lyovochka† who has been my diary, I had nothing to hide from him."[7] But now "her soul is heavy" and anxiety forces her to return to her old habit of noting her impressions nearly every day: "Yesterday when he told me he did not believe in my love, I was frightened."[8]

These remarks consigned by the two of them to their journals so soon after their wedding are interesting for what they tell us about this period, but even more for the light they cast on the future. As Tolstoy's early

* In *Childhood*, *The Morning of a Landowner*, *Family Happiness*, *War and Peace*, *Anna Karenina*, and even the *Memoirs*.

† One of Sofia's diminutives for Leo.

years throw light on his whole life, the first months he spent with Sofia at Yasnaya Polyana—a kind of childhood of their married life—form a prologue to the drama that marked the end of it.

In each of them one finds a clear-sightedness about themselves, a kind of self-disgust, which at the same time is not free of a certain enjoyment close to exhibitionism. This mixture of uncompromising demands and considerateness shows Tolstoy and his wife starting out in married life on a very high level of emotional intensity. She is afraid that they must "become settled and reasonable people":[9] they never did, they always lived their life without the benefit of a safety net.

The note of October 8 with which Sofia took up her diary again corresponds to one of Tolstoy's dated October 2–14: "We have had two clashes: one because I was rude and the other on account of her [word illegible] . . . I love her more and more all the time, though with a different love. There have been painful moments. Today I am writing because I am breathless with happiness. Everything is coming clear, the inspection review and other business."[10]

But the next day he writes that he is tired of being busy only with "practical tasks": "I am constantly dissatisfied with my life and even with her. I simply must work."[11]

The diaries show their individual difficulties in adjusting to married life together: she to a man for whom she is not the only interest in life, whose preoccupation comes from a twofold "elsewhere"—that of art, and still more difficult to understand, that of the soul; and he to a woman for whom by contrast he is the *only* interest.

As soon as he fell in love with Sofia, even before their engagement, Tolstoy had the feeling that he would never be writing for himself alone, and he felt happy about it; the crazy gesture of giving Sofia his diary to read was an expression of that longing to be at one, fused with the beloved, which is present in all lovers. But he soon notes: "the thought that she is there reading over my shoulder diminishes and distorts my truthfulness."[12]

Both were shortly to feel that although these diaries convey a reflection of themselves, this reflection is distorted to the extent that they are partly written for someone else to read, however special that reader might be through his love for the other: the confidant turns into an informer.

These diaries, chronicles of the life of a couple, were kept up until their deaths, with a few interruptions at times of extreme happiness or extreme misery. No doubt the journals of many other marriages would resemble Tolstoy's and Sofia's, and sound perhaps even worse, if they were written with the same sincerity.

Sofia was madly in love, tormented, jealous. There are "moments when it hurt her to look at him and hear him."[13] She broods on Tolstoy's past: "so terrible that I doubt whether I shall ever become reconciled to it." But passion sweeps her away at once. "When I caught sight of him I was invaded by an extraordinary feeling of power and love. . . . I would have liked to go up to him, but I thought if I approached, it would no longer feel so right."[14] In this state of passionate excitement, it is not surprising that she had a premonition of the future: "Little by little I will grow in on myself and poison his existence . . . today I felt that he and I were going each his own way."

Tolstoy's way was the way of creation. He began working again, wrote for his educational review, *Yasnaya Polyana*,* and finally finished the first part† of *The Cossacks*. "Another month of happiness," he noted on December 18, 1863.[15]

For Sofia things were very different: "I was the only one to understand that he was infatuated but did not love me."[16] She thinks that he "does not let me enter into his inner world."[17] Her journal betrays a permanent anguish and dissatisfaction. She "thinks only of him," but acknowledges that although she loves him "passionately" she is "very little under his influence."[18] She cannot avoid feeling a deep melancholy, and like many young wives goes through bouts of homesickness for her family.

The spiritual communion she expected from marriage did not take place. Physical union does not seem to fulfill her any better. "All these carnal relations repel me,"[19] she wrote‡ on October 9, 1862. She often complained of being nothing but an object of pleasure to her husband, and all her life long their frequent reconciliations in bed never ceased to sadden her: "the physical side of love plays a large part in his life, and none with me."[20]

Isolated in Yasnaya Polyana, Tolstoy and his wife seemed to have lost all sense of time; they refer to their married life as if it had lasted a long while when in fact it was only a few weeks. They both had the impression that a certain lethargy had taken hold of them. Tolstoy speaks of "a strange dream-like feeling"[21] and Sofia "hesitates between past and

* Intended to spread Tolstoy's ideas on education and information about other education experiments in progress, in Russia or abroad. Tolstoy's ideas were strongly opposed to those of the Tsarist government, and the review was frequently censored and finally suppressed. (Cf. D. Maroger, *Les Idées pédagogiques de Tolstoï*, Lausanne: Editions l'âge d'homme, 1974)

† The last one published in his lifetime.

‡ Simone de Beauvoir says of Sofia: "She always detested making love with her husband." (*Vieillesse*, 1970, p. 376.) Other interpreters, on the contrary, maintain that it was just when Tolstoy showed less ardor for his wife that their relationship deteriorated utterly.

present" and writes: "I shall wake up and both of us, Lyovochka and I, will be pleased with me."[22]

But hardly two months after their wedding, the secret rift opened that would never cease to widen between them. On November 23, 1862, all of Sofia's resentment and anguish explode: "He disgusts me with his 'people'!" It is a terrible cry of selfishness and ferocity, which sounds also like a pathetic call for help from a woman shorn of defenses, or rather, armed only with her love, and whose rival will soon be the whole suffering human race. "I feel he must choose between the family which I personify and 'the people' whom he loves so violently." She puts Tolstoy's eternal problem with extraordinary lucidity—she who is eighteen and has lived with him only a few weeks—but Tolstoy will never make his choice. Then comes the essential feminine—or feminist—demand: "If I do not interest him, if I am nothing to him but a DOLL, a 'woman,' and not a human being, I cannot and will not continue to live like this."[23]

It is a strange complaint, because in his letter proposing marriage, Tolstoy had begged her to answer "as a man of honor," and he had just written on October 5 to his special confidante, Alexandrine Tolstoy: "She immediately strikes one as being 'a man of honor'—literally so, both honorable and a man."[24]

At this time Tolstoy was quite certainly less tormented than Sofia, and he proclaims his happiness in a number of letters. "Here I am fifteen days married and happy, a new man, completely new,"[25] he wrote to his friend the poet Fet on October 9.

The pair spent the Christmas holidays in Moscow. Tolstoy seems to have had a little revival of ardor for his sister-in-law Tatyana: "I watch her constantly."[26] This watching was to continue for years, and Natasha Rostova in *War and Peace* owes to it a great part of her charm. Sofia for a moment took umbrage at this admiration, but her sister remained her most intimate confidante, and Sofia always opened her heart to her without restraint.

At Yasnaya Polyana Sofia had longed to return to Moscow, but when she got there she was unhappy. She loved her husband "to the point of being ill,"[27] and she guessed that he was unhappy with her when he compared her with other women, that he was almost "regretting."[28] She let him go alone into society. She missed the intimate tête-à-têtes that were later to weigh on her so heavily: "Let us return quickly to Yasnaya Polyana, where Lyovochka lives more with me and for me . . . where I am alone with Auntie and with him."[29]

Apart from him she has no need of anyone or anything, but she knows it is not the same for her husband. On January 29, 1863, while she is writing in her diary that Lyovochka has made her feel "it was impossible to be content with a husband, a wife, and family life; besides all these, one must have other occupations," Tolstoy sits down beside her as if to play a duet, and adds* in his own writing: "I need nobody and nothing but you. Lyovochka is a liar."[30]

They stayed in Moscow six weeks. "Family happiness absorbs me utterly—but it is not possible to do nothing." Though the simple joys are not enough for Tolstoy, he does not adore his wife any the less for that, and the same note of bliss suddenly modulates to a litany of love.

> I love her night or morning when I wake and I see her looking at me and loving me . . . I love her when she sits close to me and we know we love each other as much as we can . . . I love her when we are alone a long time and I say What shall we do? Sonya, what shall we do? and she laughs . . . I love her when she is angry with me . . . I love her when she doesn't see me and doesn't know it and I love her in my way . . . I love her when she is a little girl in a yellow dress and pushes out her lower jaw and her tongue . . . I love her when I see her head thrown back and her face serious and scared and childish and passionate, I love her when. . . .[31]

Not only is Tolstoy in love, but he is well aware of his wife's exceptional qualities: a young wife, almost a child, for whom nothing counts but ideal love, unstable and swept by doubts, yes, but wonderfully lucid, and she will never really lose that clear-sightedness. Unlike her husband, Sofia is not strong on humor. Her intelligence is practical rather than abstract, and Tolstoy mentions this to her a year later: "What a clever woman you are in everything you want to think about—for that reason I say you are indifferent to intellectual interests, but so far from being narrow-minded you are intelligent, very intelligent."[32]

They returned to Yasnaya Polyana at the beginning of February. There, Sofia is just as bored as she was in Moscow. As for Tolstoy, he does not remember ever "feeling such a strong urge, a peaceful, assured urge to write,"[33] and he is not over-troubled by the state of mind of his wife. He has recovered his usual energy: he is enthusiastic about *Les Misérables*, finishes an article on education, *The Progress and the Definition of Teaching*, and he begins *Strider, the Story of a Horse*.[34]

Sofia becomes difficult, very nervous in her first pregnancy, as she was to be in all the others. They quarrel over nothing, a dress, the refurbishing of her room. Tolstoy falls in with her moods: "With my wife

* Not only did Tolstoy and his wife give each other their diaries to read, they often read the letters that one or the other wrote, sometimes even adding a few lines.

the best of relations. Ebb and flow do not surprise nor frighten me." But above all he is at peace: "What joy! She pleases everybody."[35]

Sofia felt that she was no longer the sole object of his concern; it makes her gloomy: "If only someone could understand how slowly time is passing."[36] Relations between them were really less good than Tolstoy wants to admit. In late March he wrote two curious letters to his attractive sister-in-law Tatyana; they are couched in a fantastic, slightly mad style, quite unusual in Tolstoy, and they lead one to think that things are not so clear between man and wife. The first letter begins: "O younger sister of the wife of her husband!"* Then he tells her a dream he has had: "Two doves were riding in a carriage; a third—more like an officer than a dove—was smoking cigarettes—oil, not smoke, was issuing from the cigarette, and this oil was love."[37] It is clear that the two doves are the Behrs sisters and the third is Tolstoy. The dream goes on to become more and more mad and incoherent, as does the tone of the letter.

So it is no wonder that Sofia should write to her sister on that same day, March 23, that she "did not understand a blessed word of Lyovochka's letter." Tolstoy snatches the pen out of her hand, and in the same bizarre mood as earlier begins to tell his sister-in-law a second dream—how suddenly at ten in the evening on March 21, 1863, Sofia turned into a little china doll. The story that follows is rather long, and as unrestrained as it is symbolic; the Behrs family took it for a simple and charming literary joke. Tolstoy makes it clear that the coldness of the porcelain was like marble, the touch of his fingers could not warm it, and in the end he hid the doll under his beard and went to sleep with the doll in the cradle of a dent he made in the pillow with his fist. He says he got up in the morning without daring to look at her. But the marvel was that Sofia's transformation into a china doll took place only when Tolstoy was alone with her. When others were present, all was normal. In the end he ordered a wooden box that shut with a hook, but just as he was going to put the tiny figure into it, Natalya Petrovna, Tante Toinette's companion, dropped it, and one of the legs of the little figure broke. A valet told them that one could glue it back with egg white. Tolstoy ends his account by asking Tatyana whether "they knew the recipe for that glue in Moscow."[38]

This story of a china woman is strange, but it did not prevent Tolstoy

* The editor of these letters in English says he has consulted the best Tolstoy specialists in Russia, and neither they nor his own reading of the diary of Tatyana Behrs have been able to throw any light on the strange and absurd elements in this letter and the one (originally begun by Sofia) that followed it.

from writing on April 11: "Read one or two of her diaries—excellent. She is particularly happy at the moment."[39]

Expecting a child was for Sofia "physically and morally unbearable."[40] She would hereafter live in constant terror of pregnancy, a justified terror, since it occurred thirteen times. Now she feared that her husband took an interest in her only from pity. "To sit all day needle in hand or to play the piano"[41] seemed to her real slavery. But on other days she "feels he loves me and my love for him just grows and grows."[42]

Tolstoy cannot have been easy to live with or to understand, no more so at that time than at many later periods. He did not now ask himself—as he had done before and would do often again: "Who am I?" but "Where is my self, the self I loved and knew, which arose at times entire for my own delight and terror? I am petty and worthless. And what is worse [crossed out] I am so since I married my wife whom I love."[43]

This anguish over his identity and the coherence of the self in him led his thoughts deeper. He worked his way from introspection to religion, including theology and metaphysics, in a fashion that soon became with him a habit. He asked himself "whether the same law of gravitation of matter towards the earth exists also for what we call spirit and draws it towards the spiritual sun."[44] Well aware of his own happy state, he knew at the same time that it could never be enough to give meaning to his life: "There can be wife, children, health, etc., but happiness is not there. Lord have mercy and help me."[45]

At the end of June the birth of Sergey, his first child, surprised him more than it pleased him. He was moved by the "serious, honest, brave beauty of his wife,"[46] but after her delivery he was exasperated by her sudden changes of mood and her whims. The breast-feeding of the newborn babe led to a serious quarrel that was to weigh heavily on the relations of husband and wife. As a disciple of Rousseau, Tolstoy thought it was "monstrous not to suckle one's child"[47] and he accused Sofia of being a bad mother, whereas it was an ordinary inflammation that made it impossible for her to breast-feed the baby.

Tatyana Lvovna Tolstoy was to write in her memoirs: "Taking on a wet nurse seemed a crime to my parents."[48] It is not likely that her mother, who went through such frightful pain, shared this opinion. Tolstoy's desire to respect the laws of nature was genuine enough, but the fierceness and the kind of fanaticism he put into his belief show how early he became a prisoner of his doctrines.

He finally came to see his cruelty and the injustice he had committed, and he expressed his remorse in a few lines in Sofia's own diary: "I was rude and callous—and to whom? To the one creature who has given me the best happiness in life and who alone loves me."[49] But a few minutes later, in another fit of irritation, he crossed out these few words of affection.

Poor Sofia! On August 17 she was thinking "of the nights of madness"[50] before her engagement only a year before. She was depressed, although she loved Tolstoy with "honest, pure and faithful love,"[51] and she makes mild fun of his jealousy over Erlenwein, one of the young students who taught in Tolstoy's school.

The two people who emerge from this year of apprenticeship were both aware of the dangers that their passion for each other exposed them to. Sometimes the very intensity of their experience made them afraid: "We have felt for some time that our happiness is frightening. Death, and all is over. Really over? God. We prayed."[52]

The wounds they had inflicted on each other and on themselves were in some sense initiations that changed them greatly in a short time. Sofia seemed anxious, full of violent and contradictory impulses, very sensitive and lucid—a woman capable of passion and psychologically infinitely more frail than she appeared, very far from being the dumpy *bourgeoise* exclusively preoccupied with domestic practicalities, which was the impression she gave others for most of her life.

The wonder is that although Sofia was virtually a child when she married Tolstoy, and he already a mature man of thirty-four, she was less altered by marriage than he. When less than six months married, Tolstoy wrote: "She does not know and will never imagine to what extent she has altered me, far more than I have her."[53] He quickly came to perceive his wife's unchangeable nature and the dynamism of his own personality. In one of the last letters he was ever to write to her, he would still be reproaching her about it. "I have nothing to forgive you for, you were what your mother made you . . . and stayed like that, didn't want to work on yourself, to progress towards goodness and truth."[54]

Married happiness seems to have had on Tolstoy a settling effect for a time; he was more appreciative than Sofia of the sweetness of "the honeyed life." In this period of his marriage, it was close to matching the perfect love he had dreamed of since writing *Boyhood*, and had described to Tante Toinette on his way to the Caucasus: "After an unspecified number of years I [see myself] at Yasnaya, neither young nor old—my affairs are in order, I have no anxieties, no worries, and you still live at Yasnaya. . . . It's a beautiful dream, but it's still not all that I allow myself to dream of. I [also see myself] married—my wife is a sweet, good affectionate person; she loves you in the same way as I do."[55]

Suddenly, a melodramatic act shatters the tranquil life of Yasnaya Polyana: on September 22, 1863, Tolstoy decides he wants to enlist; troubles in Poland make him fear the outbreak of war. This fervor was rather surprising in a man who was a pacifist ten years earlier, and who later saw in conscientious objection the universal remedy for the evils of modern society. At first Sofia thought it "a joke," and in spite of her anger at the recklessness and levity of her husband, "the father of her son," she cried out: "The worst thing is I love him. When I see him look unhappy, my soul is overwhelmed."[56] Tolstoy finally gave up his plan—for the simple reason that war did not break out. But Sofia remained anxious and decided that their "lives were drifting apart more and more"; she admitted: "I feel incapable of really understanding him, which is why I spy on him so jealously."[57]

From that time forward, Sofia never ceased keeping watch on her husband; it irritated Tolstoy so much during the last year of his life that it was one of the "immediate causes" of his leaving home. One can accept the fact more easily if one thinks of it as a kind of loving vigilance.

From the beginning of that year, Tolstoy complained of being unable to work: "The Piebald Gelding," as he sometimes refers to *Strider, the Story of a Horse*, "was written laboriously," he had noted in March; in October, Sofia rejoiced that he was absorbed by "the story of 1812."[58]* He had mentioned this idea earlier in a letter to Alexandrine Tolstoy written between October 17 and 31.[59] He gave her good news about the family, and added: "I've never felt my intellectual powers, and even all my spiritual powers, so free, and so capable of work. . . . This work is a novel of the 1810's and 1820's, which has been occupying me fully since the autumn." He also confided to her that his "views on life, on the PEOPLE and on SOCIETY were now quite different," and that he could hardly understand "how he can have loved them so deeply." He stated emphatically: "Now I am a writer with ALL the strength of my soul." These confidences about his deepest concerns seem to have made him nostalgic for his old friendship with Alexandrine and for their spiritual intimacy; after some effusions akin to a outright declaration of love, he closes his letter with a request that she tear it up.

The letter is an echo of the last lines of the journal for 1863 in which a few days earlier he wrote: "I am happy through her: but I am terribly unhappy with myself. . . . I roll and roll down the deathward slope and can scarcely feel the strength to stop myself. . . . The choice is made, and long ago: Literature, art, education and family."[60]

* The preparatory work for *War and Peace* had begun.

EIGHT

War and Peace

AFTER A HONEYMOON in which the cooing of lovers was sometimes drowned out by scenes and arguments, while their discovery of each other took place in mingled wonder and exasperation, a new phase begins, as harmonious in Tolstoy's life as in his work.

Isolated from the world, because Yasnaya Polyana is far from anywhere, and shut off even more in the world of their love, Leo and Sofia Tolstoy came to see their life, their desires, and their dreams tending toward a single purpose: the work to be written.

Tolstoy discovers his wife's talents as lady of the house. He would remember his amazement ten years later when writing *Anna Karenina*: "Great was his surprise to see the exquisite and poetical Kitty thinking from the earliest days of their life together about furniture and bedding and linen and table laying and the cook."[1]

Sofia had been quick to grasp the fact that her husband was not managing Yasnaya Polyana very efficiently: "Lyova is tiresome, he is incapable of looking after the estate."[2] Tolstoy must have come to agree with her, since he took on an estate manager in 1866.

Sofia was to spend more and more of her time running the place and doing the accounts in order to free Tolstoy from anything that might disturb his work. But she was possessive, and taking charge of the management was at the same time a way of keeping her husband dependent on her. In the end Tolstoy unloaded all his practical duties onto Sofia, ostensibly because they took up too much of his time, but mainly because they forever reminded him that he was far from living according to the principles which he professed. Their youngest daughter, Alexandra, tells us in *My Life with My Father* (published in England and the U.S. under the title *The Tragedy of Tolstoy*) that "he wanted to chat with the peasants of Yasnaya Polyana about their lives, their needs, their beliefs, but he seldom managed to do so. The mujiks insisted on changing the subject, talking about estate business, or they complained and beseeched. 'All right, all right,' my father would say, 'I'll talk about it to Sofia Andreyevna.' "[3]

During this period, Tolstoy was too taken up with his work to keep up his journal regularly: for 1864 there is only one page; 1865 begins on March 7 and ends on November 9; most of the entries are less than twenty lines long, often only four or five. In the end he gave up altogether, and began again for a short time in 1873. Then, finally, in 1878, he wrote an almost continuous diary down to November 3, 1910, two days before his death.

Sofia attended to her diary irregularly also. It is "covered with dust" and has only four entries for 1864. Relations between them were good, and Tolstoy only once said to her, "You are in a bad temper, go write your diary."

Toward the end of 1864 Tolstoy broke an arm in a fall from his horse. He had to go to Moscow to be operated on, the fracture having been badly mended by a doctor from nearby Tula. Sofia was deeply upset by the accident: "In such a happy little group, a continual fear and anguish and the thought of Lyova dying never leaves me, a feeling born on the day he broke his arm."[4] This fear was to haunt her constantly.

It is their first separation since their wedding. Nearly every day Sofia and Leo Tolstoy write each other letters full of prosaic details about their daily lives but also full of declarations of love: "Oh, Sonya, won't these 5 days hurry up and pass."[5] He waits for her letters as impatiently as any young lover.

During this stay he did research for the novel he had started: *1805*. He consulted archives, read history books on the period, and tried to find surviving eyewitnesses of the battles. But nearly all the years it took to produce *War and Peace* Tolstoy spent at Yasnaya Polyana; he paid just one other visit to Moscow, in 1866, to see to the publication of part of the novel, and in 1867 he went to visit the battlefield of Borodino. The single diary entry for 1864, dated September 16, is an indication: "This is a good year. Relations with Sonya are strengthened and consolidated. We love each other, that is, we are more dear to each other than all other human beings, and we stare serenely at one another. . . . Since I set to work at my novel, have written about ten printed pages and am at present in the stage of crossing out and revision. It is painful. . . ."[6]

Tolstoy was completely taken up by the enormous amount of work required for his book. He still thought he was going to write a novel, when in fact he was going to create a *world:* even so, he was seized with vertigo at the "enormous dimensions of the task that lay before him."[7]

In 1865 Sofia opened her diary hardly more than a dozen times. On February 25 she notes, first, that she is not pregnant, but that she is frightened of being so often in that condition;* next, that her husband's mood has changed. "He hardly ever has the fits of gaiety he used to have, and he is often irritated with me, his work engrosses him, but gives him no joy."[8] Her own sadness did not cloud her judgment: "His will is strong and I sense an intense life in him."[9] She had taken up her diary because she was again depressed. She saw everything looking black, even flowers appeared to her "out of place," but Tolstoy comes home from hunting, and "scarcely was he home when everything was light and easy for me, he smelt of fresh air, and he himself gave me the sense of fresh air."[10] All the same, she was at once seized by another attack of jealousy, wondering whether Tolstoy had not in fact been to see his old mistress, the peasant Aksinya.

Work was a bond tying them together and she forgets all her resentments: "At times he lets me see his plans." While he was hunting she had spent "all the morning copying."[11] "I copy for him and am happy to be useful to him."† She was his first reader. "Lyovochka recites the military scenes of his novel; they are passages I do not like."[12]

They must have often spoken about this dislike, because Tolstoy had already written to her from Moscow in 1864: "I remember your saying that all the military and historical side over which I am taking such pains will turn out‡ badly, but that the rest—the family life, the characters, the psychology—will be good."[13] Thus at that time they felt very close to each other. One evening, Lyovochka played Chopin's preludes and she noted that her relations with him had become simple and pleasant again. So good indeed that Sofia no longer felt the need to read her husband's

* A second child, Tatyana, had been born on October 4, 1864.

† This working intimacy never really ceased until the last months of their life together. Even then, collaboration continued, without intimacy. In 1890 she copied *The Kreutzer Sonata*, although she viewed it as an insult to her and to their love. In the 1900s, when their relations were more than strained, she helped him correct *Resurrection*. Sofia was involved in the composition of *Hadji Murad* between 1897 and 1904, as she points out in her daily journal, as well as in its course of publication in Moscow, and in 1910 she was working on a new edition of the *Complete Works*.

‡ Some of these passages were suppressed in the 1873 edition and restored by Sofia and Strakhov in 1886.

daily notes: "I hear him, he too is doubtless writing his journal, I hardly read it any more. As soon as we read each other, we cease to be sincere, and for some time I have been so sincere that life has become light and pleasant to me."[14]

On that evening Tolstoy was not writing his journal, but he had made some brief entries on the preceding days and added others just as terse on the days that followed. March 23: "Wrote little in the evening, but decent stuff. I can. I absolutely must write every day. . . . Tomorrow I shall try the portrait of Bilibin."[15] (The reference is to a character in the diplomatic service who appears in Book Two of *War and Peace.*) Tolstoy's diary contains as it were only working notes. On March 25 his brother came and they talk about his novel: "Told Seryozha Napoleon. No writing. Read Ragusa."[16]* On March 28 he complained of writing laboriously, with difficulty: "I am writing badly, must cut." There followed a last note on April 10, before the long interruption till September: "I love Sonya very much, and we are so very all right, she and I! For three days writing with great effort, but still make [little] progress. We have decided to go abroad.† This morning noted various things about education."[17]

Beginning in 1865 Tolstoy, while continuing to write his diary, acquired the habit of putting certain thoughts, merely numbered, in notebooks.‡ Under the date of August 13, one finds a long dissertation on Proudhon's maxim, which he reproduces in French: *la propriété c'est le vol.*§ He thought this was "the absolute truth. . . . This truth is conceived in the same way by the educated Russian and the Cossack," a clinch to Tolstoy, since only that which was intelligible to the masses was valid: "This truth is not a myth, it is a fact" which finds its best expression in peasant communities, "in Cossack communities." That was doubtless what made these communities so close to his heart. And he added: "This idea belongs to the future."[18] Such preoccupations were far indeed from his literary work, but they never really left him.

Many of these notes are undated; in some he says clearly "for the novel": they constitute a potpourri of thoughts on philosophy, morality, and psychology: "Alexander a weeping child; a diplomat; the very young man alone with himself at the mirror; a joker; the girl at the evening

* Marmont, Duke of Ragusa, appointed governor of Dalmatia by Napoleon in 1806, left memoirs that Tolstoy often consulted.

† This travel plan was not carried out. After 1861 Tolstoy never left Russia again. He thought of doing so at the time when his relations with his wife were beginning to be extremely bad, in 1884. Later on he considered political exile.

‡ He always carried a notebook when he went out riding or on foot.

§ "Property is theft."

party—she dances, dances, and when she can takes refuge in a quiet room to be alone" (as Natasha does at the ball in *War and Peace*). Others are more explicit: "Pierre is tormented by fear of death before the duel."[19]

In February 1865 were published the first eighteen chapters of *The Year 1805*, which became *War and Peace*; the next ten chapters came out in May. Reactions were restrained. Turgenev's judgment was severe: "The second part is weak. How small and artificial it all is," he wrote on June 26, 1865. He joined the majority of the historians who were hostile: "Tolstoy's novel is bad . . . the author has studied nothing, knows nothing, and under the names of Kutuzov and Bagration he parades little modern generals whom he portrays with servile accuracy."[20]

The publication of the book was already far advanced before Turgenev understood, as did many others, the magnitude and importance of the work. It was then he wrote to Fet (June 12, 1869): "I have just finished the fourth volume of *War and Peace.* Some parts are intolerable and some amazing, and these predominate; they are so marvellous that no one in our country has ever written anything better, and I doubt whether anything as good has ever been written. The third volume is almost entirely a masterpiece."[21]

Critics from the left thought the book reactionary; those from the right thought it revolutionary. The lay public saw in *War and Peace* only a *roman à clef*, and people close to Tolstoy were not far from thinking the same. Tatyana Behrs in a letter to Polivanov, Sofia's rejected fiancé, wrote that in early 1864 Tolstoy had read the first chapters of *War and Peace* to her family and some friends, after which a game began that consisted in guessing who the models were for all the main characters. Shklovsky also tells how during a reading aloud of *War and Peace* at a Tula landowner's house, an old woman servant had called out, "This is so-and-so, that's so-and-so."[22]

The likeness that exists between certain members of Tolstoy's family and circle and many of the characters in his novels has given rise to numerous interpretations that critics have conveniently linked together under the "prototype theory." Not only do some Tolstoy heroes appear to be simple copies of real people, but some have the gift of ubiquity and move from book to book. His grandmother Gorchakov, after figuring in *Childhood*, became Countess Rostov in *War and Peace*; his own father also appeared in that first book, *Childhood*, and so did his brother Sergey, who was renamed Volodya; Lyubov Alexandrovna Islenyev, a friend of the young Tolstoys and of the children in the same novel, achieved a curious reentry into reality by becoming in real life Tolstoy's mother-in-law;* the

* See p. 71.

hero in *Albert* is the violinist Kilevetter, whom Tolstoy knew well, and Tolstoy's near engagement to Valeriya Arsenyevna inspired *Family Happiness*; Tante Toinette is recognizable in the Sonya of *War and Peace*, and although Tolstoy knew almost nothing about his mother, he gave the qualities he had always endowed her with to Princess Mary in that same novel; in *Anna Karenina*, Levin's brother was to die as Tolstoy's own brother Dimitri had died, and in the courtship and marital scenes Tolstoy used the circumstances of his own engagement and wedded life; one can see that his sister-in-law Tatyana lent many of her traits to Natasha in *War and Peace*, and that her unhappy involvement with Tolstoy's brother Sergey inspired some of the complications that characterize Levin's marriage to Kitty in *Anna Karenina*.

While the characters of *War and Peace* belong to both of Tolstoy's worlds, his own and that of the novel, the places* where they live are also the places where he has lived: the Rostov house is the original old pillared house at Yasnaya Polyana where Tolstoy was born, and the town house where Natasha finds Prince Andrey wounded is modeled on that of Count Laputin, which Tolstoy often visited when he was in Moscow. (The house is now the Literary Museum.)

The names† of characters are also not untouched by these borrowings from the real: Tolstoy contented himself with changing only the first letter of his mother's name Volkonsky to Bolkonsky before giving it to a family in *War and Peace*; in the same way, Trubetskoy became Drubetskoy in the novel.

The people of Tolstoy's world and those of his novels live in the same surroundings and use the same objects. Thus a little bronze dog on a marble base that had belonged to Tante Toinette and was employed by Tolstoy as a paperweight—it is still on his desk at Yasnaya Polyana—figures in *Childhood*, in *Anna Karenina*, and even in *Resurrection*. As for the famous black divan, it is part of the furniture of nearly all his novels.

Princess Louisa Ivanovna Volkonskaya, the wife of a first cousin of Tolstoy's, added her voice to those of the critics and wrote to Tolstoy asking for further details about one of the heroes of *War and Peace*, Prince Andrey Bolkonsky. She had in fact some right to wonder what models Tolstoy had been using; first, because she bore the name Volkonsky, one of those he had transmogrified, and also because he had given in *A History*

* The setting of *Family Happiness* is Yasnaya Polyana, which Tolstoy outfitted on his return to civilian life in 1856.

† In 1888, in an article entitled "A Few Words Apropos of *War and Peace*," Tolstoy justified his use of well-known Russian names, changing them only slightly: "I could not invent for my characters names that did not sound Russian to my ears."

of Yesterday the story of a visit he had paid her in the country in 1851. It is highly probable that Tolstoy portrayed her in *War and Peace* under the guise of the "little princess" Lisa Bolkonskaya.*

In his reply he tries to justify the novelist's right to borrow characters from reality and transform them as he likes. "Andrey Bolkonsky is nobody, like any character by a novelist as opposed to a writer of personalities or memoirs." Tolstoy goes on to explain to her the genesis of Prince Andrey: "I needed a brilliant young man to be killed at the battle of Austerlitz, later to be described." He decided to tie the young man to the novel by making him the son of old Bolkonsky. "Then he began to interest me: I imagined a part for him to play in the further course of the novel, and I took pity on him, wounding him seriously instead of killing him. So there you have, dear princess, a completely truthful, although for that very reason unclear, explanation of who Bolkonsky is. . . ."[23]

This theory of prototypes, over which so much ink has flowed, is not really of great importance. It is a game that can be played with nearly all novels. The one prototype in all of Tolstoy is Tolstoy himself. It is in that sense that people from the real world appear in the novels. There are resonances, echoes, and bridges between Tolstoy's imaginary world and the one he lived in: every being, every place, every thing has as it were its double in the world he created. Tolstoy loved truth too much to make up his characters out of whole cloth. If he can be said to have invented them, it is in the sense of making a discovery, as one finds a treasure; his heroes existed, but it was Tolstoy who unearthed them. Tolstoy's realism is to make reality look real.

Some light is cast on his relation to his character drawing from his correspondence with the painter M. S. Bashilov. Only five letters have survived. He commissioned from Bashilov illustrations for *War and Peace*, and the letters show that Tolstoy attached enormous importance to the physical reality of his heroes. He did not want them to be two-dimensional like those of a romance, but to have thickness, a material body of their own, recognizable to other people.

In one of these letters Tolstoy says: "Pierre's face is good; you must add just one thing to his forehead to suggest a greater disposition towards philosophizing—a wrinkle or some bulges above the eyebrows; but his body is too small—he should be broader, taller, stouter."[24] Six months later—the illustration followed the slow rhythm of the writing—Tolstoy was asking him if "he could not model Natasha on Tanichka Behrs—there is a picture of her at 13—and not make Boris so stiff." He ends by

* According to Shklovsky, Sofia was the "priestess of the dogma of prototypes." She wrote on the back of the portrait of Louisa Volkonskaya that she was "the model of Lisa Bolkonskaya, the wife of Andrey Bolkonsky."

saying "but I am sure that you, as an artist, having seen a daguerrotype of Tanya when she was 12, then her picture in a white blouse when she was 16 and then her big portrait last year, won't fail to make use of this model and its stages of development which are so very close to those of my model."[25] Although Tatyana Behrs was Tolstoy's model for the physical aspects of Natasha Rostov, he liked to say that he had got Natasha by mixing Tatyana and Sofia in a test tube: did he perhaps say so in order to spare his wife's jealous feelings?

Another time he pointed out to the illustrator that Bagration, commander of the Russian Army, should have "much coarser features," and in particular that he ought not to wear "a fur hat but an astrakhan cap—which was the dress of the time."[26]

Tolstoy was very careful about the features of the face and the details of clothing and still more about the bearing of his characters. He added, in the same letter about Bagration, that "his seat, as a Georgian, should be relaxed—slightly to one side, with his feet not down hard on the stirrups."

This concern for details—"Natasha's small upper lip," "Karenin's long ears," or "the tip of Alexander's boot"—got badly on Turgenev's nerves. He maintained that Tolstoy wanted to make the reader "believe he knew all about everything, he stoops to such futilities, whereas such futilities are the only things he knows."[27] This technique made Shklovsky say Tolstoy employed a metonymic method, that is, "took a detail to make the reader see the whole, as in reality. He copied this procedure from human vision which sees details first."[28]

Turgenev on the contrary thought that Tolstoy observed things and people "like a bird or an animal." Everyone who met him, even if only once, and his intimate friends, too, spoke of his glance; Bunin said he had "wolf's eyes, which struck everybody by their strangeness: they were not aggressive but watchful like a wild beast's."[29] Perhaps he should have said like those of certain insects, whose eyes are multifaceted and made up of multitudes of small elementary eyes that see what man cannot see. As for Gorky, he spoke of "Tolstoy's thousand glances."

The art of Tolstoy is akin to that of the cinema* and not merely

* When Tolstoy viewed a film for the first time he had long since given up literature in favor of human salvation, and thought sadly that he could have seen his father and mother if they had been filmed. But above all he thought of the possibilities for mass education. When Dukov came to make a film at Yasnaya Polyana in 1908, on Tolstoy's eightieth birthday, the old man was tired and fed up with the celebrations and showed himself reticent and difficult. But he thought at once of filming peasant scenes, and the myth reported by Levaninsky (*Tolstoï et le Cinéma*, in *Lettres Soviétiques*, n. 236) is that Tolstoy wrote a scenario on the spot, *The Peasant Wedding*, and thought out the setting himself. What is certain is that a film was made during one of Tolstoy's visits to Kochety, the country estate of his son-in-law Sukhotin and daughter Tanya (who were married in 1899).

through the use of the close-up. Already when he described the siege of Sevastopol, he had in a sense employed a number of cameras at different angles. Later, he used them to *track*, as only the camera can, in numerous battle scenes or crowd movements in the Moscow slums.

Tolstoy worked immensely hard at the preparation of his novels. In 1867 he made location studies by visiting the battlefield of Borodino; in 1898, when he was writing *Resurrection*, he joined a column of prisoners being taken to the station on the way to Siberia. He searched for exact particulars, going to the Fortress of Saint Peter and Saint Paul to look at the leg-irons the Decembrist prisoners had worn. This minuteness is the aesthetic expression of his love of truth. Every scene is thoroughly worked over, the paragraphs becoming so many sequences. Tolstoy even gives stage directions including pantomime and intonation.

Take, for example, the scene where after the fighting at the siege of Sevastopol, a little boy walks in the devastated town:

> But look at this little boy of twelve with an old helmet on his head, no doubt his father's: feet bare in his shoes, with nasty cotton pants held up by broken braces . . . he has gathered pale blue wild flowers, the valley is covered with them . . . he has stopped by a pile of bodies that have been carried there, and he has stared a long time at a frightfully headless body which was near him. After staying motionless for quite a long time, he has gone forward and touched the rigid stretched-out arm of the corpse with his foot. The arm rocked slightly. He touches it again, harder. The arm rocks again and returns to its position. The boy suddenly utters a cry, hides his face in his flowers, and begins running full speed towards the fortress.[30]

In *Anna Karenina*, the transformation of Nikolay's sickroom by his sister-in-law Kitty is a further illustration of the cinematic quality of Tolstoy's novels; quite as in an animated cartoon played at high speed, one watches a ballet of objects: the simultaneous arrivals of the medicine, the aromatic vinegar, new lamps, fresh sheets, a decent shirt for the sick man.[31] These devices, which are familiar to modern readers, no doubt disconcerted Tolstoy's contemporaries: *The Year 1805* had a tepid reception. Tolstoy was evidently disappointed by it, but it did not affect his certainty that he had something important to say: "Everything is clear, but the amount of work still to do terrifies me. It's good to set limits to one's future work. Then, in view of the important things to come, you don't stop and revise trivial things endlessly."[32]

He read a great deal—Goethe and, as always, Ragusa. In his youth he had known "spiritual bliss"; now he speaks to Alexandrine of the "bliss of thought."[33] He works with complete assurance: "I have been suddenly carried away by a cloud of joy and a feeling of certainty that I can add something great to the history of thought by writing the psychological story . . . of [Tsar] Alexander [I] and Napoleon. All the baseness, every phrase, all the madness, all the contradictions of the people who surrounded them and of themselves too."[34]

As always at the approach of summer, Tolstoy is in "no mood to write." Tatyana Behrs came to Yasnaya Polyana, hunting and riding began again, and so did Sofia's jealousy—only the characters in her husband's novels seemed to escape it (and yet Sofia was jealous of Anna Karenina). Sofia now thinks that Tanya "insinuates herself too much into Lyovochka's life. They are never apart."[35] But her fears were unjustified, her sister had fallen in love with Tolstoy's brother Sergey Nikolayevich. After hesitating for a long time, they had decided to marry, but alas, Sergey had been living with a gypsy who had borne him four children: he could not in the end make up his mind to abandon her, so he renounced marriage to sweet Tatyana, who slumped into despairing gloom.

In September, after a summer disturbed by the break between his brother and sister-in-law, Tolstoy began working again. He kept on reading a great deal—Trollope, Guizot, Montaigne, Dickens, Joseph de Maistre. His journal contains almost nothing but notes for his work. "Must add to Nikolay's love of life and fear of death on the bridge"—which ought to be easy for Tolstoy since he is himself possessed by both those feelings—"and to Andrey memories of the battle of Brünn."[36] Two days later: "Sonya and I have come home. We are so happy together, as perhaps one man in a million is."[37]

But alas, poor Sofia is expecting a child again, and as always it puts her in a bad temper. Tolstoy is philosophical: "With Sonya yesterday—explanation. It is no kind of use—she is pregnant."[38]

Only his work matters. "Yesterday overflow and vigour of mind. Wrote what comes before the battle and all that will follow it. Today decided not to publish until I complete the entire novel."[39]* Next day he writes: "Nearly finished the third part. Much is becoming quite clear. Killed two hares in half an hour."[40]

He closed thirteen years of journal writing with these words.

For the two years following, Tolstoy worked at nothing but *War and Peace*. The further he advanced, the more aware he became that he was writing much more than a novel. He tells his publisher: "I am writing this in order to ask you not to call my work a novel in the table of contents, or perhaps in the advertisement either. This is very important, and I particularly request that you do so."[41] (January 3, 1865.)

It is so important that the idea still preoccupies him in 1888, when in

* He tells Alexandrine of this decision: "Only a third part of my novel is written, and I won't publish it until I have written two further parts, and then in about five years time—I'll publish the whole lot as a separate work." (*Tolstoy's Letters*, vol. I, p. 199)

an article entitled "A Few Words Apropos of *War and Peace*" he gives the answer: "It is not a novel, even less is it a poem, and still less an historical chronicle. *War and Peace* is what the author wished and managed to express in the form in which it now exists."[42] This phrase suggests that Tolstoy was in some way compelled to do this work, which is not a novel, not by a simple desire to write, but by a kind of pressure, a sense of obligation. He had referred in his journal to the "task" that was assigned to him; when he embarked on *Anna Karenina* he spoke of "the field he was *compelled* [Tolstoy's italics] to sow."[43]

Tolstoy had begun *War and Peace* as a family chronicle in the form of a novel; he had consciously or unconsciously refashioned a world—that of his childhood, his family, his friends, and his background—and set it in the framework of history. But after two years' work a change to a different dimension took place in the book. His characters made him enter into something much vaster than a novel: through telling their story, he was brought face to face with the human condition.

The whole machinery he had designed and built suddenly began to move: it was an enormously complex machine, and it called for amazing concentration from its inventor, because at any moment the machine could seize up. Each character is a cogwheel that controls another and is in turn controlled by a third, like the works of a clock. The mutual influences of the characters on one another would be hard enough to control if they were inside a closed universe, inside a clock case, but they move about in a space and a time that belong to history.

The novel ceases to be a set of gear wheels and becomes a planetary system, in which all the principal characters gravitate in a four-dimensional world (the three dimensions of space and that of time), and there exists between the planets a whole network of mass interactions, deriving not from simple mechanics but from the movement of the spheres.

At this time Tolstoy achieves a state of equilibrium that is unique for him. He owes it to the harmony of his married life and the flowering of his creative gifts: "I am very happy with my farming, very pleased with my family life and enormously pleased with my work,"[44] he wrote to Fet in the spring of 1866.

He was nearly thirty-eight, he was happy with Sofia, and he continued to be amazed by his felicity: "Do you remember I once wrote to you that people are mistaken if they expect the kind of happiness where there are no labours, no deceptions, no sorrows, but where everything goes smoothly and happily—I was mistaken myself then—there is such a happiness, and I have been living with it for over two years now—And each day it becomes smoother and deeper,"[45] he wrote to Alexandrine at the beginning of the same year.

His trade of writer suits him, and his notion of the novel is purely literary, not very different from that which he had expounded to the Society of Friends of Russian Literature in 1859: "There is another literature which reflects eternal and universal interests: the dearest and deepest feelings of humanity, a literature accessible to men of all nations and all times."[46] This was an aesthetic ideal as remote from art for art's sake as it was from the more socially conscious conception of an art that edifies and teaches which he would later adopt.

What he wanted just then as a novelist was to make his readers share his love of life and the happiness he was experiencing. His idea was not to give his readers a moral lesson: "If I were to be told that I could write a novel whereby I might irrefutably establish what seemed to me the correct point of view on all social problems, I would not even devote two hours' work to such a novel, but if I were to be told that what I should write would be read in about 20 years' time by those who are now children, and that they would laugh and cry over it and love life, I would devote all my own life and all my energies to it."[47]

At the beginning of 1866 Tolstoy was not well; suffering from stomach troubles and a humming in his ears, he went to Moscow with his wife and two children to undergo treatment. "Began a severe cure under Dr. Zakharin, and most important, I am having my novel printed."[48]

He divided his time between sculpture and gymnastics. Sofia, on her side, pondered the fragility of things: "Everyone envies our happiness, and this makes me wonder what makes us happy and what that happiness really means."[49]

In Moscow Tolstoy showed jealousy of Mitrofan Polivanov, Sofia's handsome one-time suitor, with whom she undoubtedly flirted. When they got back to Yasnaya Polyana it was Sofia's turn to be jealous: "We have a new bailiff here, with his wife. She is an attractive young woman and a 'nihilist.' She and Lyova have endless lively discussions . . . they may be flattering for her but for me they are a complete torture."[50] Three days later she notes: "The very thought is driving me insane."[51] A brief return to public life took Tolstoy away from his book. A billeting sergeant had struck his captain in the face, and Tolstoy wanted to help his defense in court. Alas, Sergeant Chabunin was shot, despite the intervention of Alexandrine, whom Tolstoy always called on to help when he wanted to influence authority.

Life at Yasnaya Polyana continued to be gay and lively, with as many guests as ever. The children grew, a second son called Ilya was born in

May, the house proved too small, so they added the old *isba* (outbuilding) that had served as a neighborhood tavern and Tolstoy occupied it. As usual, he had his furniture moved there, particularly "the old-fashioned leather couch which had always stood in the study."[52]

Summer was delightful. On September 17, 1866, Sofia's name day, Tolstoy, who later grew hostile to all forms of entertainment, secretly imported a regimental band that was encamped in the neighborhood. There was dancing, and of that evening Sofia later observed in rapture: "To my surprise and delight, a band struck up a tune for me just as we were eating dinner, and there was dearest Lyova gazing at me so tenderly. That evening we sat out on the verandah, which was lit by lanterns and candles. . . . I do not believe any two people could be closer than we are. We are terribly fortunate, in every way—in our children, our relationship, our life."[53]

It was during this improvised ball that Tatyana Behrs performed a shawl dance. In *War and Peace* at an impromptu musical evening at Lyssya Gora Natasha is shown doing the same dance, and the old servant, Anisya Fedorovna, weeps tears of joy "as she watched the slender, graceful countess, reared in silks and velvets, in another world than hers, who was yet able to understand all that was in Anisya and in Anisya's father and mother and aunt, and in every man and woman."[54]

Leo and Sofia Tolstoy were happy. Their union in those days was sealed not only by love and the joy they felt in their children, but even more by *War and Peace*.

The working relation forged at this time between Tolstoy and his wife, which was to last when every other form of intimacy between them had vanished, is difficult to define, for one should not exaggerate it by speaking of collaboration or joint effort. Rather, Sofia turned out to be the "guardian" of his works.

Maxim Gorky, who admitted "never having taken Countess Tolstoy to his heart," was nevertheless so indignant after her death, when Chertkov brought out his "diatribe . . . for the exclusive purpose of sullying the name of the late Sofia Andreyevna Tolstoy," that he wrote some fine pages in defense of her memory. He threw clear light on her role: she was "the woman who over the whole course of [Tolstoy's] life was his only true friend and the active helper in his work." He put it even better and more clearly still: "She was also his intimate, his faithful, and I think his only friend,"[55] using the masculine form of *friend* to make the point.

Sofia's help was not the mere labor of copying, as her detractors would have had us, or still would have us, believe. She was much more than an amanuensis; until Chertkov's intrusion she was Tolstoy's literary agent and editor; she had his works printed, saw to reprintings, personally involved herself in the necessary dealings with censorship, and went as far as asking the Tsar for an audience to get the authorization to publish *The Kreutzer Sonata*—which she detested—in the *Complete Works*.

Once again Gorky tells us: "While not forgetting the superhuman insight of genius, I none the less believe that certain feminine traits noted in his great novel cannot but have come from a woman's mind and that the author got them from her."[56] In so saying, he himself showed remarkable powers of clairvoyance, as he could not have seen the manuscript page of *War and Peace* where Tolstoy describes the preparations for the ball, which includes in Sofia's hand the description of Natasha's dress. Tolstoy had asked his wife to dress Natasha for this scene, and it was she who had also insisted that Anna Karenina should be beautiful, which she was not at the beginning of the first part of the novel.

In the last entry in her diary for the year 1866 (Tolstoy was in Moscow, where he had gone with Tatyana Behrs, still sunk in depression over her break with Sergey Nikolayevich), Sofia explains the happiness she feels in playing her particular role in her husband's life: "I now spend most of my time copying out Lyova's novel (which I am reading for the first time). . . . Nothing touches me so deeply as his ideas, his genius. This has only been so recently. Whether it is because I have changed or because this novel really is extraordinarily good, I do not know. . . . He and I often talk about the novel together, and for some reason he listens to what I have to say (which makes me very proud) and trusts my opinions."[57]

Sofia was intelligent, and by the standards of her circle, cultivated. She spoke fluent French, of course, and adequate English, and she had studied to become a teacher. She loved literature and had already written an autobiographical story that she got Tolstoy to read at the time of their engagement; many a page of her diary bears witness to a true writer's qualities of insight and psychological observation.

Tolstoy, entirely absorbed in his novel, was on the point of drifting away from her: he is "irritable and excited, often with tears in his eyes,"[58] she observes. The sparse pages of Sofia's diary are gloomy: "I am angry because I do love him so intensely, so humbly . . ."[59] and she thinks sadly about her last birthday.

Soon the history books and memoirs no longer suffice for Tolstoy; he needs to tread the ground of Borodino himself, and breathe its air, and he sets out with his brother-in-law Stepan Behrs, then twelve years old. The local guardian was an old soldier who had taken part in the battle, and

Tolstoy was keen to question him. Unfortunately, he had just died, but his dog was still there, and Stepan played with him. It may have been this dog who survived his master that gave Tolstoy the idea of making Pierre Bezukhov inherit the peasant soldier Platon Karatayev's dog.

On his way home Tolstoy stopped in Moscow, where on September 27, 1867, he wrote to Sofia: "If God gives me health and peace and quiet, I'll write a battle of Borodino the like of which there has never been before."[60] This letter sounds a note of Tolstoy's demanding yet often disappointed affection for his wife: "But the main thing is that your letters make me feel good at heart, because there is YOU in them. And you put all the best of you into your letters and your thoughts about me. But in daily life this is often stifled by sickness and quarrelsome feelings. I know it."[61]

As soon as he got home Tolstoy went back to work. The first three volumes of *War and Peace* came out on May 15, 1868; a second edition in four volumes appeared the following October. That same year, whether from happiness or too much to do, Sofia wrote in her diary only once, on July 31, to draw up the balance sheet for her first six years of marriage:

> It makes me laugh to read my diary. What a lot of contradictions—as though I were the unhappiest of women! But who could be happier? Could any marriage be more happy and harmonious than ours? When I am alone in the room I sometimes laugh for joy and cross myself. . . . I always write my diary when we quarrel. There are still days when we quarrel, but this is because of various subtle emotional reasons, and we wouldn't quarrel if we didn't love one another. I have been married for six years now, and I love him more and more. He often says it isn't really love, but that we have grown so used to one another that now we cannot be separated. But I still love him with the same passionate, poetic, fevered, jealous love, and his composure occasionally irritates me.[62]

Meanwhile, Tolstoy felt exhausted by this period of intense hard work. In a letter to Alexandrine* he analyzed the feeling he began to have of being a stranger in the world, a feeling that was soon to possess him altogether:

> The two of us travel on by different paths that sometimes cross, and that is how we met, at one of those crossings. All the same you and I have already gone a long way. . . . In summer I always think a lot and seriously, but never so much as this summer, and how the road of the spirit leads always in the same direction when one is thinking seriously. Then I think more and more about death "*et toujours avec un nouveau plaisir*." [Tolstoy writes this

* This letter is not in the Centenary Edition. Halperin-Kaminsky, one of Tolstoy's translators, got it from Alexandrine Tolstoy.

phrase in French] . . . Now I feel not only that I could swim and do gymnastics but the most difficult feat in life as well, do the dive down.[63]

Death will become the principal theme of Tolstoy's meditations, or to put it more precisely, the idea of death will never leave him alone.

It appears that at the time when he left the place where he had led a kind of double life with his characters, his work began to take on a new breadth. Until then he had entertained the curious notion of publishing his whole novel under a title that seems more suitable for a drawing-room comedy, *All's Well That Ends Well.* This is what he changed to *War and Peace*.

It is generally thought that Tolstoy borrowed this title, consciously or not, from the work of Proudhon, which the latter had doubtless discussed with him, since he was just finishing it when Tolstoy visited him in Brussels in 1861; the book was published in Russia three years later, just before Tolstoy changed his title. But according to Shklovsky[64] it is possible that Tolstoy's title was inspired by a long article of Herzen's which was also called "War and Peace." The two words, which together make up what Proudhon called a correlative expression, offer a perfect summary of the fundamental and irreducible conflict that was tearing Tolstoy apart and which he expressed in his work.

In proportion as "the vast universe which had not existed before him"[65] became more complex, its creator entered a period of gestation that grew more painful every day. The cosmology of *War and Peace* fell into place, but every character had to be set precisely in its orbit, and its course controlled in relation to the courses of all the others. Tolstoy found himself at the center of a universe he had created but which he found harder and harder to control. He confided to his friend Fet: "Apart from my conception of the characters and their movement . . . I have another, historical conception which complicates my work in an extraordinary way and which I'm evidently not coping with."[66] He found it very hard to make audible what in 1901 he would refer to as "the complex music of the characters."*

For ever since the Caucasus, and still more since Sevastopol, Tolstoy had known that things are not told by historians or by novelists in the way they really happen. The first distortion of reality, perhaps involun-

* Paul Claudel was particularly conscious of this music. In 1941 he reread *War and Peace*, which had "bored him greatly" at eighteen. He was astounded by "the bitter psychological dissections, which precede and go beyond Proust. His characters of young men and girls, children and old men are wonderful. How much better than *Anna Karenina*! But what one discovers in all the characters who are more or less the author's mouthpieces is religious anguish, the frightful feeling of the vanity and insufficiency of this world." (P. Claudel, *Journal*, tome 2. Paris: Gallimard [Pléiade], 1969, p. 384)

tary and inevitable, resulted (in his opinion) from the fact that those who take part in an action on the spot, however incoherent it may have been and however fragmentary their impression of it, are bound to give a what they consider *logical* account of it. The account his superiors had made him edit after the siege of Sevastopol, synthesizing the twenty reports sent in by the bastion commanders, seemed to him "the best example of the naive, inevitable, military falsehoods from which reports are made."[67]

If the immediate evidence of those who have taken part in an action or been present at an event is scarcely trustworthy, the evidence of hindsight is still less so. Thus Tolstoy was much struck when he walked on the field of Borodino, and again when he questioned in Moscow those who had taken part in the battle, by the fact that they all told him "one and the same thing, all in accord with the false accounts of Mikhaylovski-Danilevski, Glinka and others,"[68] and none of what they themselves had seen.

In addition to this inevitable distortion, which arises from the impossibility of total objective knowledge, there exists another, deliberate distortion, which was shocking to Tolstoy, the worshipper of the goddess of truth, for it arose from an attempt to justify errors on the part of those who committed them: "And so the battle of Borodino was not fought at all as the historians describe, in their efforts to gloss over the mistakes of our leaders . . . [it] was not fought on a carefully picked and fortified position. . . ."[69]

Tolstoy considers that history cannot be known by its makers for a still more fundamental reason: "The course of earthly things is predetermined from on high, and depends on the combined volition of all who participate in those events, and . . . the influence of a Napoleon on the course of those events is purely extrinsic and illusory."[70] Men cannot accept the idea that the influence they have on reality is so slight, so that "when a battle has been won, the most dubious plans seem inherently excellent. . . ."[71]

In underlining the errors of historians, and even more the contradictions among them, Tolstoy brings the very idea of history into question: "History is like a deaf man answering questions no one has put to him."[72] Likewise, it was the contradictions among the various churches and their internal contradictions that led him later in life to a rejection of all religion.

"Historians writing their histories have described the noble sentiments and fine speeches of various generals, instead of giving us a history of the facts,"[73] and worse still "they interpret the facts as they choose, according as they are Bonapartists or Republicans."[74]

The historians Tolstoy calls "specialist" give only "fragmentary analyses, biographies and national histories and special accounts that are a kind of paper money, that passes current only so long as no question is raised as to their conversion into gold";[75] that is to say, as long as one does not try to put them into circulation in general history.

Still, in Tolstoy's view, the "general" historians are no better, for "when the thing fits their theory, they say power is the result of events, and when they want to prove something, they say it was the power that produced the events." As for "historians of culture," Tolstoy finds them ridiculous: "They go so far as to believe that littérateurs and ladies who hold salons are the forces that produce events."[76]

These events, even if one rules out the intervention of God, transcend the power of human free will: for instance, according to Tolstoy, Napoleon never decided to undertake his Russian campaign; what he wanted to do was invade England, and it was only in consequence of "a series of events"[77] that he wound up finding himself at the gates of Moscow.

In view of the failures of the special, general, and cultural historians, Tolstoy proposes *another* kind of history, as he has already called for *another* kind of literature, and will later preach *another* kind of religion and proclaim *another* kind of revolution. His ideas about education foreshadowed modern pedagogy, and his ideas about history correspond to a quite new tendency in contemporary historical research: "To elicit the laws of history we must leave aside kings, ministers and generals, and select for study the homogeneous, infinitesimal elements which influence the masses."[78]

History as it is written is unsuited to give an account of reality because "the presence of the problem of man's free will, though unexpressed, is felt at every step in history;"[79] it is also to be found on every page of *War and Peace*.*

"The fundamental question that history raises is the question of how man's consciousness of freedom is to be reconciled with the law of necessity to which he is subject."[80] In the face of the mystery of the meaning of life, the scope of history is limited, since it "examines the manifestations of man's free will in connection with the external world in time and in dependence on cause; that is, it defines this freedom by the laws of reason. And so history is a science only in so far as this free will is defined by those laws."[81] But freedom is not always subject to these laws.

* George Steiner points out in *Tolstoy or Dostoevsky* (New York: Knopf, 1959, p. 14) that "Tolstoy composed on a vast canvas commensurate to the breadth of his being and suggestive of the links between the time structure of the novel and the flow of time through history."

That is why Tolstoy rejects this blind alley and proposes a new idea of history: "[As] it was necessary to surmount the sensation of an unreal immobility in space and to recognize a motion we did not feel . . . it is similarly necessary to renounce a freedom that does not exist and to recognize a dependence of which we are not personally conscious."[82]

The human condition could be described as a system that draws its energy from the dialectic between freedom and a more or less constraining necessity. It is this dialectic which animates *War and Peace.*

It has seemed to many readers, including Turgenev, that the "Epilogue" in which Tolstoy indulges in this long meditation on history is in a way foreign to the work—it seems to them something tacked on; they find themselves suddenly faced with a short treatise on the philosophy of history, perhaps a metaphysics of history. But this Epilogue really belongs to the novel. Tolstoy is not sticking a gratuitous ethics onto his work, he endows it with a moral of his own, which is that only when each character has run his course in life within "the welter of phenomena governed by liberty and necessity,"[83] that the character finds his or her true integrity—his or her "truth" in the Tolstoyan sense of the word. For what happens to each of these characters in the novel becomes the story of the single struggle by which he finds his own freedom within the grip of necessity; each actor in the great drama is as it were saved by reconciling, however briefly, his freedom and the constraints the world imposes on him. Prince Andrey had already glimpsed this inner freedom, which he found at the moment of death, when, lying wounded on the field of Austerlitz, eyes turned to the sky, he suddenly thought: "How quiet, peaceful and solemn. . . . Quite different from us running and shouting and fighting. . . . How differently do these clouds float across that lofty, limitless sky. And how happy I am to have found it at last!"[84] He had a second moment of illumination when he recognized in the young officer whose leg had just been cut off and who was groaning in heart-rending fashion his old rival for Natasha, Anatole Kuragin. Andrey understood then in a flash that "sympathy, love of our brothers, for those who love us and for those who hate us, love of our enemies . . . is what remained for me had I lived."[85] Earlier, it was only after rediscovering Natasha that he succeeded in "slowly waking to a new life."[86] The death of Prince Andrey in turn brings Natasha one of those "spiritual wounds"[87] that arise from an overwhelming shock to the inner self and mark one forever. Natasha herself is to be saved, humanly speaking, only by the love of Pierre Bezukhov, another case of miraculous healing through suffering.

The strange Pierre Bezukhov, who wandered around among the

soldiers at Borodino "in search of the battle," when it had been going on for quite a while, a civilian lost and at first suspect, but so odd with his white hat that he became a kind of mascot to the fighting men—this wealthy man, who "by being ruined has become much richer,"[88] had his eyes opened by a simple peasant soldier, Platon Karatayev, the embodiment of popular wisdom and faith, "the very personification of all that was Russian, warm-hearted, and 'round.' "[89] Pierre, who had searched for the meaning of life in the philosophers and especially the Freemasons, "suddenly during his captivity . . . had learnt, not through words or arguments, but by direct feeling, what his old nurse had told him long ago; that God is here and everywhere. In his captivity he had come to see that God in Karatayev was grander, more infinite and unfathomable than in the Architect of the Universe recognized by the Masons."[90]

In the last chapters of *War and Peace* one witnesses not only the reconciliation of every character with himself but also the reconciliation of all mankind with one another. Tolstoy had already shown the Russian and French soldiers fraternizing after the fighting at Sevastopol; now an officer of Napoleon's army says to Pierre: "If all Russians are in the least like you . . . it is a sacrilege to wage war on such a people."[91]

Kutuzov, the old one-eyed sage, who is superior to any of the great strategists or geniuses of the general staff, because "he knows that there is something stronger and more important than his own will—the inevitable march of events,"[92] also plans a general reconciliation. After the battle he proves extremely generous to the French soldiers; on one occasion he says to his men: "They are human beings too, isn't that so, lads?" though it does not prevent him from adding a little later: "But after all, who asked them to come here?"[93]

It is only in the light of its epilogue that the novel *War and Peace* takes on its whole meaning and appears as a long variation on the theme of freedom, for in the end it is through the experience of the suffering brought on by war, in its most spectacular or its most commonplace form, that every character finds his own peace.

NINE

After War and Peace

WHEN TOLSTOY WAS YOUNG, his journal had enabled him to give expression to many of his problems: *War and Peace** played the same role. In the novel his obsessions are declared indirectly, but for that very reason perhaps more freely.

The deeply anguished man who arrived at Yasnaya Polyana the day after his wedding was to find solace with Sofia and maybe still more with the characters he invented; they were just as real to him though they were the fruits of his imagination. He was living in two worlds, his own and theirs, but the first was made bearable only by the second.

More than any other work, *War and Peace* is an externalizing and a reactivation of its author's past; when he finished it, Tolstoy was not cured, his self-analysis was not over. The writer arose from his novel in the fragile emotional state of a young woman after childbirth, vulnerable to depression and even to madness: the feeling he experienced was more that of emptiness than of liberation.

Tolstoy compels us to use the metaphor of childbirth, for when lamenting the virtually universal incomprehension that greeted the end of the novel, he wrote to Fet on May 10, 1869: "The epilogue wasn't made up by me, but painfully torn from my insides."[1]

* *War and Peace* can be considered a sort of multiple psychoanalytic cure, the mechanism of which was not based on the exclusive transfer to the analyst but on the multitude of transfers to each of the characters, functioning as what Freud calls "the partial selves," and into which Tolstoy could place the antagonistic tendencies of his personality.

Once the links that bound Tolstoy to every one of his heroes were broken, the creator found himself once again at grips with the questions unanswered in his book: his characters had left him, bequeathing their problems.

After the immense task, Tolstoy was truly on holiday, and also "out of work" for the first time in seven years. He used his newfound freedom to work in the fields, to walk, to swim—in short, to merge himself with nature. He was never really cut off from it anyway, since he hunted or rode every day and wrote very little in summer. But now he turned especially to reflecting on human destiny and to the study of philosophy. Sofia, who wrote only nine lines in her diary for July 5, 1870, to record that she had weaned her latest born "Liovushka"* with sorrow and was afraid she was pregnant again, had noted on February 14 in a notebook captioned "Various Notes for Future Reference": "He spent the whole of last summer reading and studying philosophy. . . . He engaged in long and painful meditation. . . . He often said . . . that he was finished and it was time for him to die. . . ."[2]

The thoughts on freedom and the will that had taken precedence over the characters at the end of *War and Peace* continued to torment him: "Do you know what this summer has meant for me? Constant raptures over Schopenhauer and a whole series of spiritual delights which I've never experienced before. . . . I've sent for all his works and I'm reading them (I've also read Kant)."[3]

In the postscript of this letter to Fet, he let him know of his intention to go to the government of Penza and buy an estate in that remote province. It was on this trip in September 1869 that one of the most important episodes in Tolstoy's life took place: the night at Arzamas, when, in the inn where they stopped, he was overcome by a strange agony that brought him to the verge of madness.

It is another sign of his sense of intimacy with his wife that the next day but one he wrote to tell her about his startling adventure:

> How are you and the children? Has anything happened? For two days now I've been tormented with anxiety. The day before yesterday I spent the night at Arzamas, and something extraordinary happened to me. It was two o'clock in the morning, I was terribly tired, I wanted to go to sleep and I felt perfectly well. But suddenly I was overcome by despair, fear and terror, the like of which I have never experienced before. I'll tell you the details of that feeling later: but I have never experienced such an agonizing feeling before and may God preserve anyone else from experiencing it. I jumped up and ordered the horses to be harnessed. . . . Today I feel well and happy, in so

* Lev Lvovich, Tolstoy's third son and fourth child, born in 1869.

> far as I can be, away from the family. During this journey I felt for the first time how much I have grown together with you and the children. I can remain alone doing a regular job, as I do in Moscow, but when I have nothing to do, as now, I definitely feel I can't be alone. . . .[4]

Did he tell his wife in more detail about what happened to him? What is certain is that fifteen years later in 1884 he recorded it in an unfinished piece twenty pages long, which he never published; it appears in the *Posthumous Works* under the title, *Memoirs of a Madman*.

Like a psychiatrist Tolstoy describes an attack, or rather several bouts, of anguish. In 1905, in some autobiographical sketches that were eventually published as *Last Words*, he returned to this event and tried to throw light on the problems he struggled with at the time by seeking their roots in his childhood; but in 1884, in describing the night at Arzamas, he asked himself whether his inexplicable "sobbing and despair as a child were not the first onset"[5] of his present state. Perhaps he was right, though the two instances of childish terror[6] he mentions in *Memoirs of a Madman* do not seem pathological and are common enough in sensitive and imaginative little boys.

Biographers and critics have attached great importance to the night at Arzamas, sometimes going so far as to compare it to Pascal's "fiery night" when the eternal silence of infinite space so terrified the seventeenth-century mathematician. Their interest arises from the precise dating of this episode in Tolstoy's life and from the literary quality of his account, which gives it a place in the great genre of the fantastic. They are much less interested in the other two bouts described in *Memoirs of a Madman*, yet those are just as significant: the hero records his anxiety in a Moscow hotel where he spent the night, and the agony he went through one day when he was lost in a forest.*

If Tolstoy gave his night at Arzamas a prominent place within a series of such episodes, it was because he had by then gone through several himself: one day Sofia found him wandering in a corridor at Yasnaya Polyana; he had woken up and did not know where he was. These more or less spectacular fits of anguish were linked with the idea of death, and the gut fear that it aroused in him gives the measure of his love of life.

When he wrote *Memoirs of a Madman* Tolstoy was fifty-six,† and it seemed odd to him not to have had a bout since childhood. He was wrong about that, for although he may have had no conspicuous fit of the sort,

* At this time Tolstoy occasionally stayed at a hotel when he visited the capital and got lost several times in the snowstorms.

† On the night at Arzamas Tolstoy was only forty-one, and the narrator of *Memoirs of a Madman* was to be thirty-five.

all through his adolescence and youth he experienced states of mind very close to critical. His journal bears witness to what in those days were called neurasthenic tendencies. It is clear that at Kazan, in the Caucasus, particularly during his time at Tiflis (and even at Sevastopol), as well as often in his European travels, Tolstoy went through deep depressions.

His flight from Paris, the day after his watching a public execution, was not so much a reaction of fear at physical death—he had courageously confronted it in battle—as an existential terror at the ineluctable nature of death.

In the room of the inn at Arzamas, as in the hotel in Moscow, the narrator feels claustrophobia linked with fear of the grave. ("This is silly," he tells himself. "Why am I so depressed? What am I afraid of?" And Death answers: "You are afraid of me. I am here."[7]) Speaking of that earlier room in Arzamas the narrator remarks, "I remember that it tormented me that it should be so square"[8] and in Moscow it was "the narrow dimensions of the room" that was painful to him. "And suddenly I was seized with an attack of the same horror as in Arzamas."[9] "I had suffered all night unbearably. . . . Again my soul and body were being painfully torn asunder."[10]

The account of the night at Arzamas in the little village inn is probably the best description any man could give who had known such horror. "A fit of spleen seized me—spleen such as the feeling before one is sick, but spiritual spleen."[11] How better to describe the physical revulsion caused by intense psychic suffering? Then the anguish returns in a second wave: "Always the same horror: red, white and square. Something tearing within that yet could not be torn apart. A painful, painfully dry and spiteful feeling, no atom of kindliness, but just a dull and steady spitefulness towards myself and towards that which made me."[12] Metaphysical follows physical terror—a surge of rebellion against the Creator—and Tolstoy adds: "I realized that something new and heavy had come into my life and would poison my whole existence."[13]

He was not unaware that "the apathy that often seized him" was not of physical origin, and he was to suffer for the rest of his life from "the tearing within that yet could not be torn apart." He knew all this in 1884 when he wrote *Memoirs of a Madman*, but did he already know it at Arzamas? For it does look as if in 1869 Tolstoy was seized by an animal panic in the face of physical death rather than by anguish at confronting its metaphysical meaning.

The great writing block and deep restlessness that Tolstoy experienced between writing *War and Peace* and starting *Anna Karenina* had its roots in this remote corner of Penza: like the hero of his story he no longer could work, and he took refuge in "reading magazines, newspapers, and novels, and playing cards for small stakes. The leftovers of his energy went into hunting."[14]* And it was precisely while out hunting that he had another attack of his anguish: "I . . . was seized with the same horror as in Arzamas and Moscow, but a hundred times worse. My heart palpitated, my arms and legs shook as if with cold. I was expecting I know not what."[15]

Having experienced the strange splitting of the self that the severely depressed undergo, the narrator felt that his "continued momentum followed rails already laid down without beginning anything new. . . . His wife noticed it, and never stopped nagging him about it."[16]

In real life, Sofia also expressed her concern at her husband's nervous condition, which was close to semiprostration. "All this inactivity (which I would rather call mental rest) has been a strain for him. He is ashamed of his idleness, not only in front of me but in front of the servants too and everyone else. There are moments when he thinks his inspiration is returning and that makes him glad. At other times (but only when he is away from home and family) he imagines that he is going mad, and so great is his fear of madness that I am terrified whenever he talks about it."[17]

Puzzled by this new behavior, Sofia tried to find a reassuring explanation. Once again biography and fiction intermingle. In *Memoirs of a Madman* the hero says his wife "pretended that my religious scruples arose from my illness." But he himself was quite sure that the true explanation lay elsewhere. "I knew that my weakness and ill health were the effect of the unsolved question within me."[18]

It was indeed very likely at that time, or rather in those times, that the great split in Tolstoy's life history occurred. "What had formerly constituted my life was now nothing to me."[19]

The sight of wretched poverty had always been to Tolstoy a source of suffering. In childhood he could not accept that a child taken in by his father (she had been the illegitimate daughter of one of Count Nikolay's bachelor neighbors) might not lead the same life as his own sister just because she was poor and not a blood relation. In youth he had suffered at the sight of the physical and intellectual destitution of his peasants, as in maturity he was to suffer when he saw the condition of the Moscow working class. In old age the misery of the whole world became more and more unbearable to him.

After Arzamas this burden took on a new dimension. Tolstoy had gone to Penza to buy land there. The "madman" in the tale traveled for the

* During the bout of depression that followed the publication of *Anna Karenina*, Tolstoy hunted every day.

same reason: it was at the very moment when he had got home and was telling his wife all the advantages that came from acquiring the property that he suddenly felt he no longer wanted their wealth to be "based on the misfortune of others."[20] Like so many Tolstoyan heroes, he had instants of illumination that each time cast fleetingly a new light into the author's mind.* "As I said this I suddenly realized the truth of what I was saying—the chief truth, that the peasants are men like myself, have a right to life, that they are my brothers and the sons of the Father as the Gospels say."[21] From then on he never wanted to possess anything anymore. "And there at the church door I gave away to the beggars all I had with me . . . and went home on foot talking with the peasants."[22] His behavior became so strange that he finally consulted alienists, who declared him of sound mind though he was convinced that the opposite was true.[23]

The sentence in *Memoirs of a Madman* in which the hero declares, "I know I am mad," was considered by literary critic Lev Chestov the most important confession Tolstoy ever made. He argued from it that "Tolstoy was even more frightened of his madness than he was of his death," though he admits some lines later that "Tolstoy was not always in this mad condition. . . . The fits were temporary."[24]

It is absurd to maintain that Tolstoy was really mad: the problems he was trying to deal with are those that every human being faces or refuses to face. What makes Tolstoy's conflict special is not its nature but its scale.

The universality of Tolstoy's problems is the cause of the fascination his writings continue to exert on readers of whatever age, nation, or culture. He is like the rest of us, but at a different height, not superhuman but the most human of mankind. Tolstoy is a genius whose originality lies precisely in its extreme of ordinariness; his writings are an apotheosis of ordinariness.

It would seem that his very unusual physical constitution† was matched not by a powerful psychic constitution but by a kind of psychological gigantism. If one uses the psychoanalytic chart to decipher his personality, it seems that the three divisions‡ of the self in him were

* Tolstoy's own illumination came later, because two years afterward he bought another property, this time in Samara, but ultimately he was always trying to get rid of his possessions.

† He continued to cultivate his natural vigor by gymnastics: at eighty-two he nearly killed himself by pulling down a cupboard on top of himself; at Samara he wrestled with the Bashkirs, who were well-built toughs, and won; he rode nearly every day until the year of his death, and his daughter Tatyana says that till the end of his life she found it hard to keep up with him, which amused him greatly.

‡ In most people one of the three (id, ego, and superego) dominates the other two or at least one of them: in Tolstoy they appear to have been not only of unusual strength but also of equal force.

all disproportionate. Paradoxically it was their great individual strength that rendered him so vulnerable.

On one side, extremely strong life impulses,* on the other, a rare intelligence and creative power that led to great achievements on the plane of the organized ego, and finally an idealized ego bordering on spiritual megalomania—these carry out among them a permanent and devastating conflict. This colossus incapable of mastering his urges had a fragile ego—like a rock on which the slightest touch leaves a deep mark.

In his periods of literary creation or intense activity, these forces had an outlet; when Tolstoy had finished *War and Peace* they relapsed into their conflict. Emerging from a world that was reassuring because he created it—a world he may have created in order to be reassured—Tolstoy once again rediscovered the problems he had dragged with him since childhood.

But the love between him and his wife, a happy family life, and above all the longing to undertake a new work—his only chance and sign of recovery—still held him back from the edge of the abyss. Abandoned by the characters of *War and Peace*, Tolstoy now wanders in search of other protectors.

He takes refuge in reading but gives up the philosophers. "He was a great admirer of Schopenhauer, but thought Hegel merely a collection of empty phrases. . . . He began to read Russian folk tales and popular epics";[25] he thinks of writing an ABC for children. "He has been reading a whole series of plays—Molière, Shakespeare and Pushkin's 'Boris Godunov' (which he dislikes and doesn't think much of)."† He plans to write a play, but Sofia is sure that "it is not really serious work."[26] They talk together about Goethe and Shakespeare; one morning, passing by his desk, she finds that "he is reading Ustryalov's history of Peter the Great. . . . He is searching history for a good subject for a play and taking notes on anything that seems suitable."[27] On February 24, 1870, she notes in her diary that after long hesitation her husband has decided to write a novel on Peter the Great, since that will give him more scope than a play, and then adds in passing: "Last evening he told me he had had the vision of a married woman of noble birth who became the cause

* Stefan Zweig goes so far as to say that "it does not take much insight to make out in Tolstoy a sensuality of monstrous proportions." (S. Zweig, "The Great God Pan," *Europe*, No. 67, July 15, 1928, p. 325.) Tolstoy did confide in Gorky that he had been a tireless fornicator. M. Gorky, *Reminscences of Tolstoy, Chekhov and Andreev*, London: Hogarth, 1934, p. 23)

† Changeable Tolstoy! Three years later it was "thanks to the divine Pushkin" (*Tolstoy's Letters*, vol. I, p. 261) that he experienced a kind of intellectual transport and wrote the first pages of *Anna Karenina*.

of her own ruin. The difficulty was to represent this woman not as culpable but as worthy of pity. . . ."[28] Tolstoy did not think of that again for three years.

He lives in a sort of lethargy: "All winter I've been enjoying simply lying on my back, going to sleep, playing bezique, skating,* and most of all lying in bed (ill); it is then that the characters in a drama or comedy begin to act. And they perform very well."[29] Is he pretending to believe that the heroes of the remote time of Peter the Great are going to be as docile, so to speak, as those of his own life and his own past had been?

In the spring, Tolstoy was always very active on the estate: he describes himself "coming home from work, covered with sweat, with axe and spade, and consequently 11,000 versts away from whatever is art and especially from our own writings."[30]

Summer and its pleasures pass; Tolstoy returns to what he calls his "winter work," literature. He thinks he has begun another *War and Peace* and continues writing to Fet, to whom he is very close at this time: "I am depressed and am writing nothing, but am working painfully—You can't imagine how difficult I find this preparatory work of ploughing deeply the field which I am *compelled* to sow. It's terribly difficult to think over and rethink everything that might happen to all the future people in a work to come, and a very big one, and to think over millions of possible combinations in order to choose 1/1,000,000 of them. And that is what I am busy doing."[31] He is busy, true enough, but not wholly absorbed by the task. He took it into his head to teach Greek, which he did not know, to his eldest son, and decided therefore to learn it at the age of forty-two. "Since December, Lyovochka has been persevering with his Greek";[32] and to the amazement of his Hellenist friends he was very soon able to read the classics in the original. He found in the Greek authors one of those *voluptés* of the spirit that he loved, and at the same time a concrete task to distract him from his deep agonies. What is more, he thought secretly of writing "on a subject drawn from life in old Russia" and longed to create "a book that would be as pure, elegant and devoid of excess as classical Greek literature, or Greek art."[33]

But Greek is an insufficient distraction for a man sunk in the profound distress of which he complains to his friend Urusov.† "I have never experienced such a depression in my life. I have no desire to go on living."[34] A month later he tells Fet "of an extreme weakness in which

* Sofia said he adored figure skating and acrobatics on the ice.

† Alexander I. Urusov, lawyer and author, but also a theoretician whose ideas on the application of mathematics to military science thrilled Tolstoy and even inspired him with a plan for army reform—a strange concern for an antimilitarist like Tolstoy.

one longs for nothing but the calm one cannot attain,"[35] and he says that Sofia is sending him off along with her young brother Stepan to drink mare's milk in Samara. She was more and more alarmed at her husband's condition: "Since last winter, he has become completely indifferent to living and to everything that used to interest him. Something—a shadow—seems to have come between us and separated us . . . he drags me with him into his state of melancholy and despair."[36]

When he recalled this time in *A Confession*, he wrote: "The life of our circle, the rich and learned, not merely became distasteful to me but lost all meaning."[37]

The letter he sent Sofia the day after his arrival at Samara is an excellent description of nervous depression:

> At 6 o'clock every evening, I begin to feel a kind of physical anguish like a fever; it seems as if soul and body were parting company. . . . I have been worse in the three days I've been here. The main thing is weakness, depression and wanting to play the woman and weep, and it's embarrassing, whether with the Bashkirs or with Styopa.* . . . There are no intellectual pleasures, especially poetic ones. I look at everything as though I were dead—the very thing for which I used to dislike many people—and now I myself can only see what exists; I understand and grasp it; but I can't see through it, as I used to, with love.[38]

Tolstoy knows the highs and the lows of the depressed: five days later he writes to her that he feels fine.

This region, where Tolstoy found again the rustic, patriarchal society which at bottom was always his social ideal, pleased and soothed him as it had done since his first visit in 1862. He decided to buy an estate there; he arranged the purchase† on the spot and concluded the deal on August 25, 1871, as soon as he was back at Yasnaya Polyana.

His mood was unstable, yet he remained in the steppes for nearly two months. Like the Bashkir nomads, he lived in a felt tent, a kibitka. In his notebook for the year 1871 he made numerous entries on landscapes, camp organization, customs, and breeding methods of the inhabitants of the Karalyk region.[39] Though a prey to gloomy thoughts, he read Herodotus with delight and discovered that the Greek historian "accurately described these same Scythian lactophagi"[40] whose primitive life he had now come to share.

Back at Yasnaya, he has no heart for writing and envies his friend

* Stepan Behrs, his sixteen-year-old brother-in-law.

† In 1871 Tolstoy had lost the uncompromising generosity about property that he showed in his youth; his ideas were very different from those he gave to the hero of *Memoirs of a Madman* in 1884, and still more so from the attitude he professed at the end of his life.

Strakhov,* his favorite correspondent of the 1870s, for being in a creative period and enjoying the feeling he himself had known, of awareness of self and of one's powers "like a man exhausted after a hot bath."[41]

A fifth child, a second daughter, "Masha," was born in February 1871, and once again the house was too small, and once again was added to. "Everything goes well with me, you will not recognize the house. We have added on a new building. Another matter: I have re-opened the school, and my wife and children and all of us teach, and we are very happy."[42] This time the school is in the house itself, it numbers thirty-five pupils, and the teachers are really Tolstoy, Sofia, Sergey, who is eight, and Tatyana, who is seven.

Tolstoy's feelings about his children were complex. He did not like babies, or rather he was frightened of them. He once explained this attitude, which is common enough with fathers, to Alexandrine: "There are two sorts of men—those who don't hunt and like little children and can pick them up in their arms, and those who hunt and have a feeling of fear, disgust and pity for babies." He adds dogmatically: "I don't know of any exception to this rule."[43] Tolstoy belongs to the second category. In fact, he wrote to his sister-in-law Tatyana: "I do not like holding a live bird in my hands; it gives me a kind of shiver,"[44] and like many men he became more interested in his children as they grew up. In November 1872 he drew for Alexandrine a very detailed picture of each of them. The most charming of the six portraits is perhaps that of his second daughter, Masha. "[Almost] two years old . . . large, strange blue eyes—strange by virtue of their deep serious expression—very clever and not good looking. She's going to be an enigma—she'll suffer and search and find nothing; but she'll go on searching for ever for what is most unattainable."[45] It is hard not to see a portrait of the father in the one he paints of his daughter.

Tolstoy concerned himself a good deal with the older children. He often went walking with them, to pick violets or mushrooms; he read to them Jules Verne and Dumas. One time at Christmas he dressed up as a goat. He invented a game in which one of the children was shut in a linen basket which was then carried all over the house, and the victim had to

* Nicholas N. Strakhov, trained in science, taught mathematics and physics and later served as librarian at St. Petersburg, 1863–65. Coedited the periodical *Time* published by Dostoyevsky. An article praising *War and Peace* led to his friendship with Tolstoy. He came to Yasnaya Polyana every year, and the children had christened one of their father's favorite walks "Strakhov Alley." Tolstoy not only used to appeal to him for books, but discussed his own literary and religious works with him, and asked Strakhov as a friend to correct the proofs of *Anna Karenina*. Between 1870 and 1880 they exchanged more than 300 letters. Tolstoy always retained his friendship for him, but later drifted away, finding that Strakhov had grown too reactionary.

guess which room he was in. The family was wild about another game called Numidian Cavalry. In a burst of joy or in order to react against a fit of sadness, Tolstoy would start running around the furniture like a galloping horse, the children would fall into step with him, and the whole cavalcade careered all over the house. Certain particularly pompous or solemn guests might also occasion one of these outbursts of high spirits.

Tolstoy not only played with his children, he gave them lessons as well. "He is giving Seryozha mathematics lessons," Sofia writes. "He sometimes loses his temper with him, but always asks to be told when he gets too angry."[46] Tolstoy was therefore in no way an absentee father, and nothing at that time suggested the lack of interest in his children he was to show in later life. That estrangement was certainly one of his greatest griefs, for he never ceased to love them, as one can see from the emotional and intellectual intimacy he shared with his daughters as adults, or the joy he expressed when his son Sergey came to see him at Astopovo.

He drew away from them because he wanted them to be brought up according to his new principles*—the boys to wear simple cotton shirts and the girls, grey dresses; yet he saw them gradually transforming themselves into elegant, social, urban aristocrats, the thing he detested most in the world.

As a fulfilled husband, father, and landowner, he told Alexandrine of his "brainless joys," "teaching the peasant children to read and write, breaking in a young horse, admiring a large room newly furnished, computing the future income from a newly purchased estate." He tells her also about his "great joys": his "frightening happiness, being terribly fortunate—children who are all fit and well, and I am almost certain intelligent; then my projects—last year it was the study of Greek, this year it's been the Primer and now I am beginning a big new work. . . . I am starting work joyfully, timidly and apprehensively, as I did the first time. . . ."[47]

Yet this idyllic family life could no longer afford him protection from his inner torments. On September 13, 1871, he wrote to his dear Strakhov: "We don't know who we are and why and how we live and where we are going."[48]

Tolstoy's "frightening happiness" was solely objective; he felt the

* In the education of his children Tolstoy does not escape from the usual contradiction between his principles and reality: he would have liked them to have no toys, because they prevent the imagination from developing freely, but every time he went to Moscow he brought some back for them.

despair of the man "who has everything to make him happy," which Levin suffered in *Anna Karenina*.

Ten years later, Tolstoy in *A Confession* threw direct light on this paradoxical state, without a fictional character as intermediary: "I, a healthy, fortunate man, felt I could no longer live."[49] The words he had written Strakhov found here an almost exact echo: "Something very strange began to occur in me. At first it was moments of perplexity and arrest of life. . . . They were always expressed by the same questions: Why? What about it? And afterward, what?"[50]

And as always when he grapples with problems of knowledge, Tolstoy seeks refuge in those of learning, of education. An American method for teaching children to read that he had looked at gave him the idea of writing a primer. He hurled himself passionately into this task, which he actually thought of as the keystone of a future reform of all Russian education. Besides reading exercises and little stories, this manual included an arithmetic course for teachers. "All my time and energies are taken up with the Primer,"[51] he told Strakhov, and Sofia says in her diary that they worked together on it till four in the morning.[52]

Like all depressives, Tolstoy tended to exaggerate the difficulties that he ran into. For a while he had been held responsible for the accidental death of a young shepherd who worked on the estate, and he expressed indignation to Alexandrine that he had "been kept under observation."[53] He complained that the law deprived him of his security instead of guaranteeing it. For the first time he thinks of leaving Russia for good and settling in England. But this resolve, though it would have been a radical step, did not seem to cause him much concern: Sofia Andreyevna "loves everything English." His only worry was how to marry off his daughters, the eldest of whom was then only eight! And he counts on Alexandrine's connections to open to them the doors of "some good aristocratic families."[54]

He was disappointed, "angry and upset,"[55] to see the *Primer*, into which he had put so much of himself, ill-received by the official educational authorities. All the more so because for a time he had hoped to get state aid; the comparison between a group of children taught to read by the method he supported and a group taught traditionally had shown his reader was the better. Tolstoy was convinced that with "this alphabet" he had erected to himself "an intangible monument."[56] He was right, because although rejected by the hidebound officials of the time, this primer is still in use today in the Soviet schools.

"He is reading material about Peter the Great period. . . . He jots down in various little notebooks anything that might come in useful for an accurate description of the manners, customs, clothes, houses and the general way of life in this period—particularly that of the peasants and those far from the court and the Tsar,"[57] writes Sofia. Tolstoy worked with persistent energy. "He has written about ten different opening chapters, but isn't happy with any of them."[58]

While he was passionately studying Greek, he had hoped to find in the age of Peter the Great a theme for a Russian *Iliad* and *Odyssey*. But writing a book on this subject did not mean only a wish to write the epic of a crucial period in Russian history, it meant also a return to the sources of the quarrel that still divided Russian intellectuals into Slavophiles and Westernizers. It meant trying to put into contemporary terms the question that Dostoyevsky called "Russianism"; it meant trying to discover whether what the Russians saw through "the window opened on Europe" by Peter the Great was or was not superior to the contents of their own house.[59]

Tolstoy had no liking for either the character or the period: "I have piled up around me works on Peter the Great and his period. I read, take notes, have every wish to write, and cannot,"[60] he complains to Strakhov on November 12, 1872.

If he cannot manage to write, it is no doubt because he is absorbed and lost in religious and metaphysical reflections, which he sums up in January in a very long letter to Strakhov "on the search for faith." This letter is of high importance, for it foreshadows Tolstoy's later criticism of dogmatic theology. He already sees religion as the sum of "billions of vague responses of equal significance, which had the result of making these responses more precise." And he formulates the principle that was to dominate his religious activity, as well as his thought, for the rest of his life: "The only test to which I subject and always shall subject tradition is to see if the answers that tradition gives are in accord with the vague and personal reply written in the depths of my conscience."[61] This accord was found less and less often, until it finally turned into complete discord.

Tolstoy worked with furious energy. He kept on having books* sent from Moscow by his friend P. D. Golokhvastov, an historian specializing in early Russian history who came to see him several times at Yasnaya Polyana.

To Sofia on January 2, 1873, Tolstoy said: "The machine is all ready,

* *The Domestic Life of the Tsars* and *A Study of Russian Antiquity* by Zabelin; *Journey of an Englishman in Russia*; *Peter the Great's Private Office*; and *Studies of Dissidents*, which is by Essipov, an eighteenth-century historian of Russia. (*Tolstoï par Tolstoï*, pp. 237–38)

it only remains to make it go."[62] The truth is, it was never going to start.

On the evening of March 17, 1873, Sergey Lvovich, who was nearly ten, wanted to read to his great-aunt Toinette. Sofia chose *The Tales of Belkin*. The old lady fell asleep. Sofia "couldn't be bothered to put the book back on the shelf." The next morning Tolstoy found it "on the drawing room windowsill." He read it and reread it. "He went into ecstasies. 'What things I am learning from Pushkin!' He is my father; one must always be guided by him.' "[63]

The next day Tolstoy began *Anna Karenina*.

TEN

Anna Karenina

TOLSTOY ABANDONED for a woman the monument he had begun to raise with such care to Peter the Great.

Like a shadow in search of flesh and blood, she had moved through his imagination three years earlier, but only in a hut at Yassenki station,* that had been taken over as a morgue, did he find her a Christian name and a bodily form. The body was that of a young woman of the neighborhood called Anna Stepanovna, who in January 1872 threw herself under a train, from heartbreak over a love affair. The body lay exposed to indifferent eyes, "completely undressed, dissected and her skull visible."†

So it was at the station closest to Yasnaya Polyana that Tolstoy discovered the physical reality of Anna Karenina. He had explained her symbolic reality to Sofia as early as March 1870, when he imparted his wish to write the story of a guilty woman who was to be pitied, not despised. Her sociological reality he probably came across when he overheard some society people talking on a boat trip on the Volga about a married woman whose behavior was creating a scandal in Moscow.[1]

Tolstoy borrowed from passing events, from stories he was told, or

* Yassenki or Yassenka according to the spelling of Countess Tolstoy's diary.

† In twenty lines entitled "Why he has given Karenina the Christian name of Anna, and where he got the idea of such a suicide," Sofia says clearly that the scene made "a deep and terrible" impression on her husband, and that Anna Stepanovna had "grey eyes." (*Journal de la comtesse Léon Tolstoï*, Paris: Plon, 1930)

from people he knew or who were close to him, the substance of his characters. This habit did not, of course, come from lack of imagination, but from his passion for truth. In his writings, the situations and people are seldom complete inventions: life had to offer him a block of stone that he could chisel.

Like all great novelists, Tolstoy collected authentic details to deck out an imaginary character. This concern for the truth he carried very far: "Would you kindly ask your brother Sasha," he wrote on March 22, 1874, to Tatyana Behrs-Kuzminskaya (in 1867 his adored sister-in-law had forgotten brother Sergey enough to marry a young magistrate, Alexander Kuzminsky), "whether I can include in the novel I am writing the story he told me about the officers who rushed into a married woman's room instead of a 'mademoiselle's' and how the husband threw them out."[2] This story occurs in chapter five of the second part of *Anna Karenina*.

Similarly, Tolstoy was greatly vexed at not having made Levin arrive at the church before Kitty on their wedding day, that being the custom in the Orthodox ceremony. He wrote twice to Strakhov about this (what may seem) futile matter[3] and let him know in the second letter that he meant to correct the error when the novel, which was then a serial, was published as a book.

Tolstoy wrote the first version of *Anna Karenina* in less than two months, between mid-March and the end of May 1873, and felt considerable satisfaction: "I am writing a novel which has no connection at all with Peter the Great. I have been writing it for more than a month now and have finished it in draft form. This novel—I mean a novel, the first in my life*—is very dear to my heart, and I'm quite absorbed by it. But in spite of that, philosophical problems have been occupying me very much this spring."[4]

He had doubtless forgotten that already on March 25 he had told Strakhov to keep it a great secret that thanks to his son Sergey he had "reread Pushkin probably for the seventh time," and had somehow, unwittingly, not knowing what would come of it, "thought up characters and events" that had resulted in "a very lively, impassioned and accomplished novel," which he was "very much pleased with and which will be finished in 2 weeks' time."[5]

Tolstoy spent the summer with his whole family at Samara, as he was to do for seven years. But down there he had other things to think about than writing books. Famine was raging in that arid region, and he began a campaign in the press for help to be sent; he posted an article to the

* So Tolstoy still thought *War and Peace* was not a novel.

Moscow Gazette. The Empress was the first to subscribe, and Tolstoy had soon amassed two million rubles, which meant the distribution of ninety thousand pounds of bread.

Back at Yasnaya Polyana he was "polishing, revising and continuing with the novel,"[6] but he began serious work on it again only in December, then once more he put it aside quite quickly.

When Tolstoy finished *War and Peace*, the concerns that he expressed through his characters had not ceased to haunt him. After the first draft of *Anna Karenina*, he experienced a similarly disturbed state; this time the osmosis between his life and his writings was even more obvious.

In *War and Peace* Tolstoy had created a resonance between History at large and the history of his family; in *Anna Karenina*, the resonance is between his own life and contemporary society. The real meaning of certain episodes in the novel can only be revealed by events in the life of its author; at other times, on the contrary, it is the novel that casts the light on his life. At the end of *War and Peace* certain issues remain open; in *Anna Karenina* they are all closed: the heroine cannot escape from her situation except by death, Vronsky's departure for the war is like a suicide; as for Levin, he keeps on looking for reasons to live, and so does Tolstoy.

Once again he took refuge in education. In 1874 he did virtually no work on his book; all his energy was concentrated on problems of teaching. He got down to a new ABC book and composed four *Russian Primers*, which appeared at the same time as *Anna Karenina*. In January he went to meetings of the Committee for Literacy and succeeded in having new experiments made with his reading method. In the end it was turned down, but the controversy that followed in the press gave Tolstoy the opportunity to vent his ideas in a number of articles. At the same time he was trying to create a Teachers' Training College for Peasants.[7]

Tolstoy had always refused to allow himself to be painted, but when he got back from Samara he finally agreed that the famous Kramskoy should do his portrait. What chiefly persuaded him was that Sofia, who was always clever at negotiation, had got the artist to agree to do two pictures, one for the Tetryakov Gallery and the other to be kept at Yasnaya Polyana, where it still is. In that copy, Tolstoy appears at the height of his maturity, with an abundant but well-cut beard, his hair at half length and carefully combed. He wears a blue-grey smock, not that of his last years which is familiar from photographs; this one is more an artist's smock than a mujik's. Tolstoy looks elegant in it. He always conveys the same impression of ease when he wears a smock, whereas in the photograph Dyaguchenko took of him in Moscow in 1876, where he wears a frock coat, he has a somewhat cramped and Sunday look. In the painting, the facial expression is serious and meditative, the pose is natural; the portrait creates an impression of power and energy, though not free of disquiet.

Kramskoy painted while Tolstoy wrote. They exchanged ideas about art and about religion; in *Anna Karenina* the painter Mikhailov holds roughly the same views as those Kramskoy recorded in his memoirs.

Tolstoy now experienced the greatest difficulty in composing. It was probably as he observed Kramskoy at work that the explanation of this impotence, about which he told Strakhov, came to him: "As a painter needs light for the finishing touch so I need inner light, of which I always feel the lack in autumn."[8]

The distress into which he was gradually sinking was aggravated by a succession of bereavements. He writes to Fet of the death of his youngest son, adding: "This is the first death in our family."[9] Here is how Tolstoy recalled these unhappy events to Alexandrine in 1876:

> The sixth was a sturdy little lad, Petya, whom my wife loved very much. At one year of age, he took ill in the evening, and in the morning, just after my wife had left him, I was sent for—he had died of croup.* After him a charming little boy (his wonderfully nice nature was obvious when he was only a few months old) also one year old, fell ill with dropsy of the brain. It still pains me, pains me terribly to remember that awful week of his dying.† This winter my wife was ill and close to death. It started with whooping cough. And she was pregnant too. She nearly died and gave premature birth to a daughter [on October 30, 1875] who lived only a few hours.[10]

Two other children in the family had already died in 1873; Sergey Nikolayevich Tolstoy had lost a son and Tatyana Behrs-Kuzminskaya a little girl, Dasha, Tolstoy's favorite. Her death had hit him hard.[11]

Delightful Tante Toinette died in June 1874 at the age of seventy-nine, Tolstoy sending the news to Alexandrine: "I lived with her all my life and I feel frightened without her. . . . I have stopped publishing my novel and I want to give it up, I dislike it so much. Instead I am occupied with practical things. With pedagogy actually. I am organizing schools, writing projects, and battling with the St. Petersburg pedagogues."

Aunt Pauline, who had moved to Yasnaya Polyana the previous year, died on December 22, 1875, and Tolstoy writes once again to Alexandrine: "The death of this eighty-year-old woman upset me as no other

* November 9, 1873.
† February 20, 1875.

death. I was sorry to lose her, sorry about this last memory of the departed generation of my parents . . . there was something else about her death which I cannot describe to you, but will tell you about sometime."[13]

These partings greatly distressed Sofia, too. Every time she lost a child, she plunged the depths of despair: "When I think of the future I see none for myself," she wrote after Petya's death.[14] Many years later, in 1895, the death of Ivan, their last and particularly dear son, was to cause her such psychological disintegration that she could no longer face the difficulties that confronted her, and she sank into that nearly hysterical condition in which she lived the last years of her married life.

Sofia was a passionate wife, but also a passionate mother, and was sometimes worried by the violence of her feelings: "I love my children with a passion that is often painful."[15] Perhaps Tolstoy would not have described the love of Anna Karenina for her son Sergey so well if he had not had under his eyes the example of Sofia's love for her children. The mother-and-child reunion scene would probably be less overwhelming (it made Turgenev weep) if one did not feel the almost carnal passion with which the child is "wriggling about in her arms so that all of him should feel the contact."[16]

The alternation of deaths and births does not seem to have slackened Sofia's rhythm of working, since in March 1874 the first part of *Anna Karenina* was sent off to the publisher, and she began at once to copy the second part. For Tolstoy, things did not follow suit. The pace of composition for *Anna Karenina* was very different from that of *War and Peace*; it was slower and notably more intermittent. Apart from the interruptions that correspond to Tolstoy's seasonal rhythm of creation, he had written *War and Peace* in a single stretch of seven years. *Anna Karenina* went otherwise; at times it even seems as if the making of the novel interrupted Tolstoy's educational activities and philosophic meditations rather than vice versa.

As for Sofia, she proceeded regularly with her work of copying. She was to say later that she worked as a mujik goes to a tavern. She spent whole days and many nights in Tante Toinette's old room, which had become her study, sitting at a mahogany desk that survives to this day in the Moscow house, to which she had it moved when they settled there in 1881.

The first fourteen chapters of *Anna Karenina* appeared in January 1875; then the end of the first part, the whole second part, and the first ten chapters of the third, between February and May, as a serial in Katkov's *Russian Herald*.

Its success was immediate, and Tolstoy expressed his amazement in a letter to Strakhov: "I am surprised that something so commonplace and trifling should please the public."[17] Later he would say, "Anna Karenina is nothing—just a woman in love with an officer and who kills herself." His friend replied that "only a battle or a speech by Bismarck could cause as much excitement in the press as does each new installment of *Anna Karenina*."[18]

Society people went wild over a novel in which the characters resembled themselves. They tore the *Russian Herald* from each other's hands and sent for every number as soon as it was announced. Bunin records that when the one in which Anna Karenina dies appeared, many members of Moscow society were as cast down as if one of themselves had perished.

A large number of these readers went on to wonder, and others are still wondering to this day, why in this novel Tolstoy had also told the life story of Levin and not contented himself solely with that of his heroine. It is, in fact, easily possible to read each of the stories separately. Such a reading brings two surprises; first, that *Konstantin Levin* would be a longer novel than *Anna Karenina*, and second and infinitely more important, the fact that both plots, both melodic curves, lose much of their weight, become flat when separated; the fullness of each narrative appears only through its contrapuntal relation with the other.

In *Anna Karenina* Tolstoy was not making a collage of two alternating plots with nothing in common except their subject and the period in which they are set. Possibly that is the plan he started out with when he originally intended to call the novel *The Story of Two Marriages*, but what he actually wrote is the story of marriage itself, its vicissitudes highlighted by the outbreak of passionate love in Anna Karenina's life and by the fulfilling love in Levin's, which far from helping him solve his problems only masks them. In this regard he is indeed Tolstoy's twin, who could not regard marriage as a mere literary theme and proclaimed this fact in the motto of the fifth version of *Anna Karenina*: "For some, marriage is the most difficult and important undertaking in life; for others it is a pleasant pastime."[19]

The true mortar in which all the characters of the book are set is the fundamental question that recurs obsessively again and again: "Why? Whence do we come? Where are we going?" Tolstoy had been haunted by this question all his life; every birth and every death repeated it with renewed stringency, and it resounds throughout the novel. "The sight of his brother and the presence of death revived in Levin that sense of horror in the face of the enigma,"[20] much like Tolstoy's feelings when his own brother Nikolay died in Hyères in 1860. Birth is "another mystery, equally unfathomable."[21] Facing his firstborn, Levin wonders, "Why this baby? Whence, wherefore had it come, and who was it?"[22]

It was also Anna Karenina's last question before throwing herself under the wheels of the train: "Where am I? What am I doing? Why?"[23] She finds her answer in death, but Levin desperately continues to search for his. "All that day, while talking to the bailiff and the peasants, at home with his wife, with [their daughter] Dolly . . . Levin's thoughts were busy with the one and only subject that interested him at this time: What am I? Where am I? And why am I here?"[24]

The other bonding factor of the novel is, as it already was in *War and Peace*, that hidden light of which the characters are occasionally allowed a brief glimpse. Even Karenin has his moment of illumination, although he quickly forgets what it so fleetingly reveals. It is all the brighter for shining on this prisoner of convention and appearance, caught in the web woven around him by his clear conscience. In that moment he reached the depths of humiliation and anguish. At the bedside of his dying wife, who had just given birth to her lover's child, he felt the change within her and was moved by her open remorse. She had ceased to see in him that stiff, cold man "whose ears were too long," and she cried out in her delirium, "He is good, he doesn't know himself how good he is. . . . No one knows him, I'm the only one. . . . Now I understand it all . . . I see it all."[25] Suddenly, this man, who had never known anything but the letter of religious teachings, is overwhelmed by the spirit of compassion: "A glad feeling of love and forgiveness for his enemies filled his heart . . . he sobbed like a child."[26] Perhaps he also cried at seeing laid bare "the depths of her soul," which he had thought "were now closed against him."[27]

In the end, it is Anna Karenina herself who is least saved, most punished, punished for her genuine but culpable love, through which she experiences the agony of forbidden happiness. She was a victim of that fatal passion which carried her irresistibly toward Vronsky. She strove to defend herself against this "little officer" and had tried to escape him by leaving Moscow, but at the first station, there he was on the platform, saying "what her heart longed to hear, though she feared it with her reason. . . . 'I have come to be where you are . . . I can't help myself.' "[28]

That night Anna was at home alone with her thoughts and "her face shone with a vivid glow; but it was not a joyous glow—it suggested the terrible glow of a fire on a dark night."[29] She already had a premonition of what she understood only when she walked to her death: "I am the cause of his unhappiness and he of mine."[30] But on that earlier day she had smiled and murmured "too late." Anna Karenina was not to be the Russian *Princesse de Cleves.**

This "terrible glow" lighted Anna's path all the way to Obiralovka station; it surrounded the lovers when "that which for nearly a year had been the one absorbing desire of Vronsky's life . . . that which for Anna had been an impossible, terrible, but all the more bewitching dream of bliss, had come to pass."[31]

A strong sensual feeling emanates from this scene, even though it is written with a kind of modesty. Anna Karenina is driven to despair by what she calls her "spiritual nakedness," and Vronsky tries to calm her: "As the murderer throws himself upon the body and hacks at it, so he covered her face and shoulders with kisses."[32]

This glow gave her that strange charm which was to act so fast on Levin when, reluctantly, he called on her. "He, who had hitherto judged her so severely, now . . . thought only how to exonerate her. At the same time he was sorry for her, and began to fear Vronsky did not fully understand her."[33] It is this same somber radiance which made the audience at the opera "forget la Patti for her."[34] She is enveloped in this same light when "her beauty though it attracted [Vronsky] even more than before, gave him, now, a sense of injury."[35]

Pathetic and admirable Anna, thus Tolstoy wished her to be, torn between a lover and a son, incompatible parts of her life: "I love . . . equally, I think, but both more than myself, these two beings. . . ."[36] This rift was made all the worse by the social isolation to which her affair condemned her. She bore it impatiently, as is shown by that gesture of defiant despair with which she braved Moscow society at the opera.

Anna Karenina's love not only banned her from the "salons," it also divorced her from reality. Her last few hours were spent in a state of utter confusion, merging the past with the present, and mistaking her daughter for her son. She arrived as if in a trance at Obiralovka station, where she hoped to find a message from Vronsky. At that point the break with reality is absolute; she throws herself under the train.

The tragedy of passion fell upon Anna Karenina's life; that of death hovered over Tolstoy's and, for several years, darkened the atmosphere of Yasnaya Polyana. Tolstoy's third son Lev Lvovich wrote in 1923 in his memoirs: "I was a child, four to six years old, when death struck our

* The heroine of Madame de la Fayette's famous novel, *La Princesse de Clèves* (1678), though passionately in love with the young Duc de Nemours, remains faithful to her husband. Stendhal considered the work "unsurpassable."

family five times during the years 1873–1875. I vividly remember my father's terrible black moods during these calamities, his face stern and distraught, his voice harsh and sounding as if he were accusing someone."[37]

Both Sofia and Tolstoy were miserable, but they were not yet isolated each in his own unhappiness as they were to be later on. By early 1873 Sofia had begun to be bored by country life; before her wedding she had only visited there briefly, and perhaps she had imagined that as a married woman she would live at Yasnaya Polyana as if in perpetual holiday. "I want gaiety, smart clothes and chatter"; she wanted to lead the life of "normal people. . . to curl her hair and put ribbons in it."[38]

In October 1875, a few days before the birth of the little girl who was not to live, Sofia wrote: "This isolated country life is becoming intolerable. Dismal apathy, indifference to everything. . . . Besides, I am not on my own, I am tied to Lyovochka . . . and I feel it is mainly because of him that I am sinking into this depression. . . . It's painful for me to see him when he is like this, despondent and disaffected for days and weeks on end, neither working nor writing. . . . It's a kind of emotional death."[39] Yet Sofia should have been happy copying out the manuscript of *Anna Karenina*, for the story of Levin and his wife Kitty strangely resembles those "blissfully happy years" she shared with Tolstoy at the beginning of their marriage and which were to continue for a little while longer. Legend has it that Sofia copied out *Anna Karenina* twenty times; could it be that she did it for her own pleasure?

Levin's life as a bachelor and newly married man is illuminated by a very different light from that of the fire that gradually destroyed Anna Karenina and her world. It is a glow whose intensity and cheerfulness bring out even more painfully the torments of the fulfilled young husband. Many things that Sofia might have found incomprehensible in the early years of her marriage must have become clear as her copy work progressed. Understanding had also come to Tolstoy as he wrote the book. The novel clarified and exorcised their past.

The account of Levin and Kitty's engagement must have enchanted Sofia: Tolstoy, too, had proposed by writing with a piece of chalk on a card table. Equally, she must have been delighted by the story of the wedding, which told of the bridegroom's last-minute doubts and of the shirt packed by mistake.

More than these reminiscences, one particular short sentence must have moved her: "He saw in her sweet, pitiful, tear-stained face the irremediable sorrow he had caused . . . and was appalled at what he had done."[40] This passage of *Anna Karenina* showed Sofia that Tolstoy himself had not realized "the effect the confession might have on her"[41] when, during their engagement, he had given her his diary to read. It showed her that he understood too late that sincerity is a murky passion which encourages every sort of crime. She must have been touched also by the incident of "the raspberry jam made without water,"[42] a Behrs family secret mentioned in the book. Nor could she have read without emotion the scene of Nikolay's death, in which Kitty and old Agatha Mikhailovna (like Natasha and Princess Mary at Prince Andrey's bedside in *War and Peace*) play the principal part; for women, like "the people," know the "science of life"[43] and are initiated in the mysteries of death. "Different as those two women were . . . both knew without a shadow of doubt, what sort of thing was life and what death was, and though neither of them could have answered, or even comprehended the questions that presented themselves to Levin, they had no doubt of the significance of this event, and were precisely alike in their way of looking at it—a way they shared not only with each other but with millions of other people."[44] Above all, it must have been wonderful for Sofia to discover that Levin knew that only "love saved him from despair."

But these events were long past and Tolstoy was "now depressed and dejected." He was closer to Levin than he had been or would ever be to any of his other characters. In the novel as in the author's life, religious preoccupations were about to smother happiness. Levin's life became almost schizophrenic. Obsessed as he was by the question of "why and wherefore?"[45] he "looked at his watch all the same, to reckon how much the farm workers could thresh in an hour. . . . So he lived, not knowing and not seeing any chance of knowing what he was and for what purpose he had been placed in the world. He was tormented by this ignorance to the extent of fearing suicide, yet at the same time was resolutely cutting his own individual and definite path through life."[46]

Tolstoy was in the same state of mind and found it more and more difficult to devote himself to literature, which he really regarded as "trifling."[47] He wrote to Fet on August 26, 1875: "Now I'm settling down again to dull, commonplace *Anna Karenina* . . . , to get it off my hands as quickly as possible in order to clear a space [for something else] . . . not for pedagogical activities, I love my pedagogical activities just as much, but I want to force myself not to pursue them."[48] They "take up too much time," and the "something else" proved to be his articles on religion. In November he started assembling the notes he was to use in *A Confession*.

The novel continued to be serialized. Between February and May 1876 the *Russian Herald* published the end of part three, the whole of part four, and the first nineteen chapters of part five. But Tolstoy was already deep in his great moral crisis; he had written to his friend in the same letter: "I think ceaselessly about the problems of the meaning of life and death. . . . I desire with all my heart to find solutions to the problems that torment me."[49]

Anna Karenina dragged on. He wrote to Alexandrine on May 8, 1876: "I am fed up with my Anna, sick and tired; I am dealing with her as with a pupil who has turned out to be unmanageable; but don't say nasty things about her or, if you must, at least do so *avec ménagement* [in French in the original], since she has been adopted nevertheless."[50] A month earlier he had already confided to his spiritual mate: "I cannot at the moment apply my mind to anything except the novel. . . . I need to concentrate completely to work on something so trivial. . . . During the summer I shall devote myself to my work on philosophy and religion, which is not for publication but for myself."[51] He then imparts the source of his problem to this dearest of friends: he believes in nothing, "not in anything that religion teaches us; but at the same time I . . . hate and despise unbelief."[52] This confession of unfaith, which is at the same time a sort of negative act of faith, could not have been made by the young Caucasian officer who dreamed of a "new religion"—a prime example of Tolstoy's progression, which comes in bouts of contradiction rather than by an accumulation of certainties.

Tolstoy analyzes his need to believe and his inability to accept the church's teachings in a manner both graphic and poetic: "With the demands of my mind and the answers given by the Christian religion I find myself in the position as it were of two hands endeavouring to clasp each other while the fingers resist."[53] This image gives a good idea of the almost physical suffering that intense metaphysical anguish can cause. If the sacred connotation that "incarnation" bears in the Christian faiths is abstracted from the word, Tolstoy could be said to have experienced incarnation intensely; that is, he felt the torment of his soul in his body*—hence the power of conviction in all his books. They do not read simply as fiction, but as a confession and a slice of life. Tolstoy himself said that "whenever one dipped one's pen in the ink pot one should bring out a piece of flesh."[54]

With him philosophic thought was never purely speculative; he was driven to it by his own problems, which he then tried to resolve in his books. Haunted by the enigma of death, he wrote to his ailing friend Fet

* Tolstoy went to Moscow several times to consult his physician, Dr. Zakharin, at the beginning of 1877 and during the following years. He complained of migraine and stomach trouble, which seem to have been psychosomatic.

on April 29, 1876: "You are ill and thinking about death—while I am well and never cease to think about the same thing and to prepare for it. . . . I have tried to express much of what I thought in the last chapter of the April issue of the *Russian Herald*,"[55]—in other words, in *Anna Karenina*.

Tolstoy's struggles were indeed echoed in Levin's; they took place along that ill-defined border between physical and spiritual anguish. Levin briefly turned toward God: "At the time of his wife's confinement an extraordinary thing had happened to him. He, an unbeliever, had prayed and prayed with a sincere faith."[56] Trying to recapture that fleeting sense of certainty Levin immersed himself in the very books Tolstoy had taken up after finishing *War and Peace*. "He became convinced that he would get no answer from the materialists, and so went back to Plato, Spinoza, Kant, Schelling, Hegel, and Schopenhauer, thereby falling into the subtle verbal mesh—devoid of solidity." When reading Schopenhauer one day, Levin substituted "the word love for the word will," and for a day or two this new philosophy cheered him.[57] But after a few days he saw in it nothing but "a muslin garment with no warmth in it."[58]

On November 30, 1875, in a long letter to Strakhov Tolstoy reviews the links between science, religion, and philosophy. He challenged the "Idealists and Spiritualists, the Positivists, Plato and Schopenhauer," and told his friend that he was working "on the introduction to a philosophical work."[59] This later became *A Confession*. He also began to draw up a balance sheet of his life as he used to do in his youth.

> I am 47. . . . And so I have reached old age, that inner spiritual condition in which nothing from the outer world has any interest, in which there are no desires and one sees nothing but death ahead of one. Life really is a stupid and empty joke . . . and so I began to search for a view of life that could do away with its apparent senselessness. . . . That is the aim and contents of what I am writing at present. . . . I would like to expound this whole mass of religious and scientific views of our time, to show the gaps and—forgive my boldness—without denying anything, to fill in these gaps.[60]

Like Levin, Tolstoy found no peace of mind in meditating on the mysteries of life and studying the philosophers. "All that spring he was not himself, and experienced some terrible moments."[61] And Levin: "A happy father and husband, in perfect health, [he] was several times so near suicide that he had to hide a rope lest he be tempted to hang himself, and would not go out with a gun for fear of shooting himself."[62] In *A Confession* Tolstoy almost repeats Levin's words—he admits that he, "the fortunate man," had to hide the rope "lest I should hang myself from the crosspiece of the partition in my room* . . . and I ceased to go out shooting with a gun."[63] This obsession with suicide pervades *Anna Karenina*. Not only does the heroine eventually throw herself under a train, but Vronsky attempts to take his life after Anna's illness, and Levin hides bits of string in order not to give way to the urge to kill himself. This state of deep depression, however, went side by side with an "objective happiness" and the business of everyday life. Tolstoy likewise was far from rejecting the inherited values of his ancestors. He wished to keep "the patrimony in such a condition that when his son inherited it he would thank his father, as Levin had thanked his grandfather."[64]† He could find peace only by working in the fields with the peasants and day laborers of Yasnaya Polyana. Like Levin he experienced "moments of oblivion, when it was possible not to think of what one was doing. The scythe cut of itself. Those were happy moments."[65]

In *War and Peace* the humble Platon Karateyev had been the instrument of Pierre Bezukhov's revelation; in *Anna Karenina* the angel of the visitation wears the "perspiring face, black with dust,"[66] of Fyodor the thresher. Levin, overseeing the harvest, starts a very prosaic conversation with him about the rent of a field. Fyodor describes the respective merits of two potential tenants and makes a rather commonplace remark: "Folks are different. One man lives for his own wants and nothing else, [another] thinks of his soul. He does not forget God."[67]‡ As soon as he hears these words, Levin runs off like a thief with his loot or a beggar with his piece of bread. "At the peasant's words about . . . living for his soul, rightly in God's way, dim but important thoughts crowded into his mind, as if they had broken loose from some place where they had been locked up and . . . whirled in his head blinding him with their light."[68]

Levin, exhausted, lay on the thick grass and wondered: "What makes me so happy? What have I discovered?" and realized that "he had been living . . . on those spiritual truths that he had imbibed with his

* Lev Tolstoy later reported: "The beam between the wardrobes in his room, on which he wanted to hang himself, struck us with terror, for we knew everything that went on in the family." (L. L. Tolstoy, *The Truth About My Father*, London: John Murray, 1924.) The son was then ten years old.

† Tolstoy never stopped adding to it, as shown by his purchases of land between 1863 and 1870.

‡ In *A Confession* he records a similar experience: "I listened to an illiterate peasant, a pilgrim, telling about God, life, and faith and it was to me a revelation."

mother's milk, yet in thinking he had not only refused to acknowledge these truths but had studiously ignored them."[69] Like Prince Andrey at Borodino: "Lying on his back, he was now gazing high up into the cloudless sky. . . . Levin ceased thinking and, as it were, only hearkened to mystic voices that seemed to be joyfully and earnestly conferring among themselves. . . . Can this be faith? he wondered, . . . gulping down the sobs that rose within him and with both hands brushing away the tears that filled his eyes."[70]

True, on the way back, Levin lost his temper with the groom; barely home he wrangled with his brother about the unrest in Serbia; after which he quarreled with his wife for taking the baby out when a storm threatened; but in spite of all this, after his revelation a feeling of certitude stayed with him. "This new feeling has not changed me, has not made me happy and enlightened all of a sudden as I dreamed it would. . . . Be it faith or not—I don't know what it is—through suffering this feeling has crept imperceptibly into my heart and has lodged itself firmly there."[71]

This meditation brings the author to the last lines of his novel, or to be more precise, of the story of Konstantin Levin, which ends on a declaration: "My life now . . . every minute of it is no longer meaningless as it was before, but has a positive meaning of goodness with which I have the power to invest it."[72] This exclamation repeats in a different key the famous line in *Sevastopol in May*: "The hero of my tale . . . is truth."

Levin may have found his "inner truth" but Tolstoy remained very far from *his* certitude. He was still mired in his difficulties, but believed he was on the right track. He wrote to Alexandrine on April 15, 1876: "I know that this work (my search for a comprehensive vision of human existence) and this suffering are better than anything else I have done in my life."[73]

Despite these torments or possibly because of them, Tolstoy resumed writing. Sofia notes it in her diary on November 20, 1876: "All this autumn he kept saying, 'My brain is asleep.' But suddenly about a week ago, something within him seemed to blossom and he started working cheerfully again—and he seems quite satisfied with his efforts too . . . revising the chapter dealing with Anna's arrival in St. Petersburg."[74] She imparts this good news to her sister Tatyana: "We are at last writing *Anna Karenina* as we should, that is to say without interruption. I am copying night and day."[75]

That Tolstoy and Sofia were close is shown by the "we are writing" of this letter. They are linked by *Anna Karenina* as they had been by *War and Peace*. Tolstoy, though already studying the map, has not yet set sail on his long solitary journey.

Sofia was as much in love as she had been fourteen years earlier. Tolstoy had gone to Samara for a few days. As it was her birthday and she was alone, she had "Lyovochka's papers" brought to her. She read them with deep emotion but feared that she would not be capable of writing her husband's biography, as she had undertaken to do, for "she could never be impartial."[76] She was disheartened and tired, but when handed a telegram from Tolstoy announcing his return, suddenly "the house was all happiness and light."[77]

On September 4, 1876, on his way back he had written to her from Moscow: "You are constantly in my thoughts for I love you so much. I am carried back into the past, I see Pokrovskoye [the Behrs' estate] again, your purple dress and a tender feeling makes my heart beat faster."[78] Not only does he open his heart to his wife but he tells her of his most intimate concerns. Several days after his return, Sofia consigns to her diary, under the heading "Notes on Remarks Made by L. N. Tolstoy on His Writing," that her husband, coming back from a walk, had cried out, " 'How happy I am!' 'What makes you happy?' I asked him. 'First of all you do, and secondly my religion.' " He tried to explain to her that he had not been converted to Christianity by devout people such as his beloved Alexandrine, the Countess Alexandra Andreyevna Tolstoya, but by Dr. Zakharin the materialist, whom he had seen in Moscow, and also by the historian Levitsky, who had stayed with them at Yasnaya Polyana, "with those stories he read us, which deal with Russian history in such a splendidly original and religious manner."[79] Tolstoy's anguish seemed to have been appeased, and Sofia writes of his admitting "that he couldn't endure much more of this terrible religious conflict with which he had been struggling these past two years."[80]

But the lull was short-lived. Religious preoccupations were about to swamp everything—his life, his novel, and his correspondence, in which the major themes of *A Confession* can already be found.

A month earlier he had sent a cry for help to Alexandrine—but that was before his last stay in Moscow, when he found that she was somewhat bigoted: "It's not a question of who can argue better, but of how not to be drowned."[81] He was in a paradoxical situation, for even though religion seemed to be his life-saving raft, it was precisely when he clutched at it that he thought he was going down with it, whereas "somehow or other *je surnage* [in French] as long as I don't seize hold of it."[82] In the same letter he told Alexandrine of his plan to go to

Optina-Pustyn with Strakhov, who was also "convinced that philosophy has nothing to offer and that it's impossible to live without religion,"[83] but who, like himself, could not find faith. Tolstoy went ahead with his plan, and according to Sofia it was a success: "On July 26 [1877] he visited the Optina-Pustyn Monastery and was much impressed by the monks' wisdom, culture, and way of life."[84]

However beguiling the monks of the Optina desert, Tolstoy knew he would not find the answers to his questions in the confines of a monastery. He described his most private desire to Strakhov: "If I were alone I would not be a monk, I would be a jourodivi, a Fool in Christ, i.e., I would not value anything and would not do anybody any harm."[85] But he was far from being alone: he had a wife and five children. A great reader of Pascal, he followed the French mystic's advice[86] and started to practice again. Sofia noted: "His religious faith is becoming more firmly established with every day that passes. He says his prayers every day now as he did when he was a child, and on every holy day he goes to matins . . . on Wednesdays and Fridays he fasts, he speaks constantly of the spirit of humility."[87]

But the more he wanted to believe, the more he became revolted by the church: "his hands would not clasp each other." He attended catechism lessons and declared them "monstrous." "It was all so disgraceful. The clever children . . . can't help despising [the priest's words]. . . . I wanted to try to expound in catechism form what I believe in, and I've tried to do so. The attempt showed me how difficult it was for me, and I fear, impossible."[88]*

The turmoil of the Russo-Turkish war came to increase Tolstoy's personal anguish. A fresh set of inhibitions grew within him, caused by these public events. Sofia wrote on December 13, 1877: "The anxiety caused by the incoherence of the Serbian Movement" sent him to Moscow "simply to get news of the war." Tolstoy's loathing for this outburst of Slav nationalism comes out in the epilogue of *Anna Karenina*,† in which Levin calls "the best representatives of the people a 'restless crew.' "[89]

Tolstoy's pacifism, latent in *Sevastopol* and in *War and Peace*, is now

* In 1884 Tolstoy achieved this purpose in *What I Believe*, and in 1907 he composed a résumé of the Gospels for children.

† Readers of *Anna Karenina* are often as much taken aback by this epilogue as were those of *War and Peace* by the concluding digression on the meaning of History. Neither group sees how well integrated with the novels those final portions are: "Book VIII of *Anna Karenina*, with its unpremeditated polemic and its tractarian intent, is not an accretion adhering clumsily to the main structure of the novel. It expands and clarifies that structure." (G. Steiner, *Tolstoy or Dostoevsky*, p. 104)

openly expressed in a manner more religious than humanitarian. He took his children to visit Turkish prisoners and was greatly impressed to see the Koran in their kit. He thought that "war is such a bestial, cruel, dreadful affair that no man—to say nothing of a Christian—can take upon himself personally the responsibility of beginning a war."[90] This stand was a source of indignation, particularly for Dostoyevsky, who, in the April 1877 installment of his *Diary of a Writer*, had rejoiced that "when the Tsar's Manifesto was being read the people were crossing themselves."[91] Dostoyevesky firmly believed that the war would "clear the air which we breathe,"[92] and that "with war and victory the new word will be uttered."[93]

For a long time the author of *The House of the Dead* had seen nothing more in *Anna Karenina* than "the same old story of a Russian noble family, although the plot [is] different."[94] Yet, as he read further installments of the book in the *Russian Herald*, he had begun to marvel "at finding in the novel both a great eternal truth" and "pages of genuine topics of the day." Considering that "the current or essential Russian interests"[95] were brilliantly illustrated in the debate between two Russian aristocrats such as Levin and his brother-in-law, he had even entitled his article in *The Diary of a Writer*: "One of the Most Important Questions of Our Time."

Feeling betrayed, Dostoyevsky now gave vent to his fury in a series of long and very contentious articles, these also published in *The Diary of a Writer* (July and August 1877 installments). He found Tolstoy's "desertion of the great All-Russian cause"[96] and the "apostasy" of a writer of his caliber intolerable. He even caricatured it by stating that Tolstoy would "let them put out children's eyes rather than risk killing a Turk."[97] This is how he explained Tolstoy's "desertion" in his analysis of part seven of *Anna Karenina*: "Levin likes to call himself the people because he knows how to yoke horses to a cart and that fresh cucumbers are served with honey. All the same, hard as he may try, he will always remain the son of a nobleman and an aristocrat. With all his love of country he is shaky on 'particularism.' "[98]*

The troubles in Serbia and the Russo-Turkish war that broke out in April 1877 not only caused Tolstoy deep anguish and supplied a theme he dealt with at the end of his novel, they also had practical consequences: Katkov refused to publish the epilogue to *Anna Karenina* in his

* In March 1876, in an article entitled "Lord Radstock" published in *The Diary of a Writer*, Dostoyevsky had defined what he meant by "particularism": "The fact that we are cut off from the soil, the nation. . . . As the intellectual class in our society, we are a small separate nation, now and forever." Lord Radstock was a spiritualist and theosophist popular in the high society of Moscow at that time.

Russian Herald. Tolstoy had to bring it out himself, separately from the novel. The editor's rejection infuriated him, yet he should not have been surprised: his publisher "was campaigning for armed intervention in the Near East crisis, in the face of which the Tsar still hesitated."[99]

Instead of the epilogue, Katkov published in the fifth issue of his journal a brief paragraph summing up the end of the book.* Tolstoy, irritated, wondered why "for three years the editor of the *Russian Herald* gave so much space in his journal to this novel. With the same gracefulness and laconism he could have recounted the whole novel in no more than ten lines."[100]

Tolstoy was becoming increasingly morose and, like Levin, "was glad to get away . . . especially on a shooting expedition, which always served as the best solace in all his troubles."[101] He wanted to start working again and toyed once more with the idea of writing *The Decembrists* but failed. In a letter to Strakhov on August 10, 1877, he explained: "Whether I am in a good or bad frame of mind, the thought of war overclouds everything for me."[102] This is confirmed by Sofia. "L. N. says: I can't write anything while there's a war going on."[103] She also wrote on the day after Christmas 1877:

> At three in the morning on December 6 our son Andrey was born.† This seemed to release L. N.'s mind from its mental shackles, and a week ago he started writing some new religious philosophical work in a large bound volume. . . . Today he was saying to my brother Styopa: "The purpose of the work I'm writing in the large book is to demonstrate the absolute necessity for religion!" . . . L. N.'s mood has changed greatly over the years. After a long struggle between lack of faith and the longing for faith, he has suddenly become much calmer. . . . The perpetual struggle for self-perfection, which he began when he was young, is now being crowned with success.[104]

Who, on reading these lines, can say that Sofia did not understand her husband? She was just being overoptimistic. Tolstoy's victory was far more dubious than she thought. At the end of *Anna Karenina* Levin is saved: "He felt with joy that something new and important had happened to him."[105] Not so for Tolstoy.

* The note by Katkov was indeed an insult: "In the previous issue, the words 'to be continued' appeared at the end of the *Anna Karenina* installment. But with the death of the heroine the novel really comes to an end. The author had planned an epilogue of a few pages, in which we learn that Vronsky, distraught and grieving, left for Serbia as a volunteer in the army. The other characters are all well, but Levin, in his country retreat, remains hostile to the volunteers and the Slavophiles. Perhaps the author will add chapters to this effect in a special edition of his novel." (R. F. Christian, ed., *Tolstoy's Letters*, New York: Scribners, 1978, p. 305.) These offensive words were a means of disconnecting the editor from Tolstoy and his hero's attitude.

† Andrey was Tolstoy's sixth son and the ninth child that Sofia bore. Three children—Petya, Nicholas, and the little girl who lived only a half hour—were already dead by this time.

The epilogue to *Anna Karenina* was but the prologue to the crisis which, looming at the end of *War and Peace*, now overwhelms Tolstoy. Sofia, along with the characters of both novels, had over the years formed a protective wall around him; this now begins to crack under the pressure of metaphysical demons.

III

THE GREAT UNSETTLING

ELEVEN

Moral Crisis or Rebirth? A Confession

I

THE END of *Anna Karenina* marks the close of the long interval within which Tolstoy's contentment in marriage and his almost exclusively literary activities are to be found: happiness did not reconcile him with himself. He felt the same burning indignation at the human condition and still refused to accept its contradictions, just as he was unresigned to his own; there was no real movement into maturity, but on the contrary a regression toward adolescence and youth. He had not got over his deep-seated anxieties, and his sense of guilt was as strong as ever; neither Sofia nor his novels had brought him the existential security he had sought since childhood. He was as alone among his numerous family as he had been in the Caucasus. At the worst of his religious crisis, he was to know the feeling of being "a man cast away on the high seas."

His fame was universal; he was read in Germany, France, England, Japan, and the United States. His life gave every appearance of happiness, and he himself wrote to Alexandrine in August 1879: "With us everything is as it has been, I am happy with my wife and not unhappy about my children."[1] But success did not bring peace. The returning tide of questions that love and art are not enough to stem swamps him; the old fear of death is the breach in the dyke; he had cemented the crack by writing, but now it opened up again.

Tolstoy lived for a while on the stimulus of *Anna Karenina* and then came the breakdown; it had already been on the point of occurring after *War and Peace;* he had avoided it only by flinging himself headlong into work and, when his novel was finished, by immediately undertaking research for a book on Peter the Great and his times. When *Anna Karenina* was over, he proceeded to do the same thing: "L.N. has been busily reading up on Nikolai Pavlovich [Tsar Nicholas I]. He is fascinated mainly by the history of the Decembrists* and is totally immersed in his studies. He went to Moscow and brought back a huge pile of books."[2]

He did not just go to bookshops. He had several conversations with the nonconformists† which inspired the "Kremlin Debates on Faith" that he wrote on his return to Yasnaya Polyana, but did not publish.[3] During this period, he wrote a series of articles on religious questions, *Church and State: What a Christian Is Permitted and Not Permitted,*[4] though still without the intention of publishing.

Just as he had gone to Borodino, Tolstoy went to visit the fortress of Saint Peter and Saint Paul in St. Petersburg. He wanted to collect on the spot details of the living conditions endured by the Decembrists who had been imprisoned there. He used them only long afterward in *Resurrection.* In a letter of January 27, 1878, he asks Alexandrine for information about General Perovsky, a Decembrist of whom she had firsthand knowledge. He ended up with so much information that he felt like "a cook (a bad one) who has gone to a rich market and after looking over all the vegetables, meat, and fish at his disposal, dreams of what a dinner he could make! I know how often I've had splendid dreams and then spoiled the dinner or done nothing."[5]

In a letter to Strakhov, written probably on the same day, he revealed quite other concerns: "I seek answers to questions which in essence are beyond reason yet I require that they be expressed in words, the instrument of reason, and I am then taken aback because they do not satisfy my reason . . . there are answers, it is only by these answers that

* Tolstoy was back at the novel begun in late 1860 during his European travels. The Decembrist Revolution interested Tolstoy enormously because it was led by members of the Russian aristocracy against Nicholas I in 1825. He saw it as the possible reconciliation of nobility and people of which he always dreamed. The idea of "a revolutionary noble or simply a good noble" pleased him greatly. (V. Shklovsky, *Lev Tolstoy*, Moscow: Progress Publishers, 1978)

† The nonconformists, or *reskolniki*, were several million strong in old Russia; the number nine million was estimated in 1890. These schismatics were violently persecuted down to Peter the Great, then deprived of civil rights. In Tolstoy's day, the chief sects were the Wanderers, the Stranglers (who murdered the dying in the belief that one must die by violence to enter paradise), the Infanticides, the Jumpers (who lived in total promiscuity), the Seekers (for Christ), the Dukhobors or Wrestlers of the Spirit (who wanted to put gospel teaching into practice without the intervention of priests or sacraments), and the Molokans or milk-drinkers, who were opposed to baptism. In the most committed period of his life Tolstoy was greatly interested in these last two sects.

people live and have lived, and that you yourself live . . . answers are required not to questions posed by reason, but to other questions—I call them questions of the heart."[6] The same sentences turn up again word for word in *A Confession*.[7]

Tolstoy departs from Orthodoxy, though perhaps not so far as he imagines, since he does not reject the notions of awakening, of second birth, and of faith inwardly revealed, which are part of Russian Orthodox teaching. And the word "heart" means for him as it does in the Eastern Christian tradition, "the center of the human person."

While he worked on his historical research, Tolstoy carried on his religious meditations, prolonging those Levin records at the end of *Anna Karenina*. Tolstoy takes up a comparison he had used five years earlier in a letter to Strakhov, and confides to Sofia that "just as a pattern needed a background, he too needed a background, and this would be his present religious ideas . . . for instance, one should observe the December 14 revolt without condemning anyone. . . ."[8]

Sofia wrote down a conversation she had on January 31, 1881, with Yuriev, the editor of *Russian Thought*, who was visiting Yasnaya Polyana. He wanted to know why "Lev Nikolayevich had abandoned work on *The Decembrists*."[9] She explained that after amassing documents for a whole year her husband had begun in early summer to take long walks on the Kiev road, which was crowded with pilgrims: "Feeling that his knowledge of the Russian language was far from perfect, L.N. decided to set himself the task of studying the language of the people. . . . [He] jotted down in his notebook all the popular words, proverbs, and expressions he was hearing for the first time. But it had some quite unexpected results."[10] Sofia did notice what was peculiar about finding faith when one was looking for words.

She never seriously misinterpreted her husband's thoughts, and she gives a good analysis of his spiritual revolution. "Until about 1877 L.N.'s religious feelings were vague, or rather indifferent. He was never an outright unbeliever, nor was he a very committed believer. This caused L.N. terrible torments . . . from close contact with the people, the holy wanderers and pilgrims, he was deeply impressed by their lucid, unshakable faith, and terrified by his own lack of it. And suddenly he resolved wholeheartedly to follow the same path as the people. He started going to church, keeping the fasts, saying his prayers, and observing the laws of the Church. This continued for some time."[11]

It is certain that at this time Tolstoy showed excessive and quasi-obsessional obedience to the rules of the Church, seeking to appease his fits of anguish with a ritual fervor that went so far as to worry his doctor.

In the end, the doctor forbade him to fast on Wednesdays and Fridays, attributing his migraines to indigestion brought on by such a regimen. Sofia goes on to reveal that "little by little L.N. saw to his horror what a discrepancy there was between Christianity and the Church. He saw that the Church, hand in hand with the Government, had conspired against Christianity."[12] The fact that she speaks of terror, and a little earlier of fright, shows that Sofia understood her husband's torments. He would probably not have altered a word of this passage: "This is L.N.'s current preoccupation. He has begun to study, translate, and interpret the Gospels. He's been working on this for two years now. . . . His soul is now happy, he says. He has seen the light (in his words), and this light has illuminated his whole view of the world. . . . He now has millions of men as his brothers. Before, his wealth and his estate were his own—now if a poor man asks for something he must have it." She notices he is thinner and paler. "He does not appear to be as happy as I should wish, and has become quiet, meditative, and taciturn. We almost never see those cheerful exuberant moods of his now, which used to enchant us all so much. . . . His soul is undoubtedly in a state of calm clarity, but he suffers deeply for all the human misery and poverty he sees about him . . . for all the hatred, injustice, and oppression in the world. . . ."[13]

This description of the different stages of Tolstoy's conversion is in perfect agreement with the account he himself will give in *A Confession*. It is all there: suffering from uncertain faith, desire to believe, discovery of authentic faith among the people, new conception of the world, rejection of the Church, consciousness of fraternity among mankind, and finally a new attitude to property thereby required.

It is curious, all the same, that having supposedly so clearly observed the causes and nature of the crisis her husband was going through, Sofia took so badly the changes that such a conversion was bound to bring in Tolstoy's way of life. One possible explanation is that Sofia revised and corrected a great part of her notes and her journal after her husband's death, and may have seen his progression more clearly then; for in a letter of 1879 to her sister Tatyana, speaking of the work that absorbed him, she wrote: "May he finish it as quickly as possible and may it pass like a fever," adding that there would not be "a dozen persons in Russia interested in such a book."

Life at Yasnaya Polyana had not changed and it went badly with Tolstoy's state of mind. At the age of fifty, he had not yet begun the kind of inward exile that he achieved later within the family circle—fleeing the world and his own world in particular—to find an absolute refuge in God. He simply retired into a log cabin not far from the main house to write.

He often went hunting with those of his sons who were old enough. "Lyovochka and Seryozha [Sergey] off with their guns and the hounds,"[14] Sofia noted on September 24, 1878. The day before, he had gone with Ilya; he also hunted with greyhounds; one day he brought home a woodcock; the next day five hares. Tolstoy was always a keen huntsman, and hunting was one of the pleasures he found hardest to renounce. But even though at this time he went out every day, he also went to Mass every morning, which was something new.

The house was nearly always full. Besides the numerous children and their various teachers and tutors, there were always a crowd of visiting friends and relations. They played croquet and went on picnics; horses and donkeys were brought over from the estate in Samara. There was music and dancing. On September 25, 1878, Tolstoy, accompanied by the novelist Grigorovich, played Beethoven's "Kreutzer Sonata."[15]

Turgenev was among the guests. He stayed once at Yasnaya Polyana on his return from Paris early in August 1878, and again at the end of the following month just before returning to France. In his desire for universal reconciliation Tolstoy had written to Turgenev in June, suggesting that they forget their quarrel. The guest's demonstration of the French cancan to the enthralled children annoyed Tolstoy. He was always grateful to Turgenev for being his literary godfather, but he never thought him serious, never committed enough; in fact, he thought him too much a man of letters.

"Everyone here, including the children, is in a tense state,"[16] wrote Sofia on December 18, 1878. There were frequent arguments. One day a terrible quarrel flared up over their property at Samara, and Sofia confided to her diary: "I still don't think I've done anything wrong, but I hate everything: myself, my life, my so-called happiness."[17] The idea of leaving Yasnaya Polyana took hold of her. "I also wish I were prettier and keep thinking of clothes and other silly things. I long to go to Moscow with the children."[18] Tolstoy withdrew more and more into himself. "Lyovochka returned, with four hares and one fox. He is lethargic, silent and lost in thought; he does nothing but read."

The children were gay and noisy, they played jokes and stole caviar; their father was "bilious, inactive," but Sofia noted that they were "still friends and happy." They worked at a biographical sketch of Tolstoy for the *Dictionary of Russian Writers.** In the evening, "the two of us went over Lyovochka's entire life for his biography, and took notes while we talked."[19]

In spite of his inner distress and the activity around him, Tolstoy

* It appeared only in 1921.

worked at *The Decembrists*, and found himself in exactly the situation that had occurred with the projected novel on Peter the Great. He wrote the opening ten times, and made the same remarks to Sofia that he had uttered five years earlier: "All the characters and events and ideas are here in my head."[20] *Anna Karenina* had distracted him from Peter the Great, and his encounter with God now made him forget *The Decembrists*.

Tolstoy still took part in family life but grew more and more interested in current events. He became passionate about the trial of Vera Zasulich, a young revolutionary who escaped conviction though she had in fact wounded General Trepov, the St. Petersburg commissioner of police. Once again the writer was in contradiction with himself; he who believed that no one ought to be condemned was now worried by the clemency of the judges. He wrote to Strakhov on April 8, 1878: "The Zasulich affair is no joke—it's an absurdity, a madness that overtakes people, and not for nothing. These people are the first terms in a series we don't understand, but it's a madness that matters—the Slavonic business was the precursor of war; this could be the precursor of revolution."[21] He was tormented by the trial. Two days earlier in a letter to another favored correspondent of those days, Alexandrine, he had said: "All this heralds much misfortune and much sinfulness."[22]

But Tolstoy had other preoccupations. On a visit to Fet on June 11 he made a pilgrimage to the Lavra (Laura) of Kiev and there met the Starets Antony, who brought no relief to his torments. Nor did he find appeasement with the Metropolitan of Moscow when he went to see him to try and clear up certain points of doctrine he found particularly disturbing;* nor with the Bishop of Tula, with whom he brought up the subject of taking holy orders; the Bishop discouraged him and said it was a "dangerous path."

Literary work, family obligations, and increasing interest in what was going on in the world did not thwart the inner search that Tolstoy was conducting through meditation and ritual and that resulted in *A Confession*.

* The Greek word *Laura* was used in the early days of Eastern Christianity for a little hamlet of hermits living alone but meeting once a week: by extension, it means monastery. The one at Kiev, the most ancient sanctuary in Russia (ninth century), consisted of the Cathedral of the Assumption, monastery, hospital, grotto of Saint Antony, and that of Saint Theodore—a classic example of a holy place in Russia. The memory of the struggles of the people of Kiev, first against the Tartars and then the Polish Catholics, was part of it, and people came from all over Russia to worship the numerous relics of saints and hermits assembled there.

A *starets* in the Eastern Orthodoxy is a revered teacher and moral counselor, not necessarily an ordained priest, who lives apart from the world. The Starets Antony was sought by many plagued with religious doubts, like Tolstoy, for he was considered the holiest man in Kiev, a city noted for holy men.

A *metropolitan* in the Orthodox Eastern Church is a bishop, ranking just below a Patriarch.

II

In writing *A Confession* Tolstoy yielded to a double compulsion that corresponded to the two meanings of the word in the French language:* he admitted his sins and proclaimed his faith.

The first two chapters of the book, the descriptions of his anguish and depression, indicate how Tolstoy viewed the various stages of his life. The next two throw light on the character of Levin in *Anna Karenina* and thereby on Tolstoy himself. From the fourth chapter onward, he is no longer speaking of the past but of the present. The book contains one of those self-portraits that punctuate Tolstoy's work and mark the beginning of each new period of his life:

> I was not yet fifty; I had a good wife who loved me and whom I loved, good children, and a large estate which without much effort on my part improved and increased. I was respected by my relations and acquaintances more than at any previous time. I was praised by others and without much self-deception could consider that my name was famous. And far from being insane or mentally diseased, I enjoyed on the contrary a strength of mind and body such as I have seldom met with among men of my kind; physically I could keep up with the peasants at mowing, and mentally I could work for eight and ten hours at a stretch without experiencing any ill results from such exertion.[23]

Tolstoy thinks one cannot live unless one is "intoxicated with life."[24] And now not only has he lost this intoxication but he records that "the two drops of honey which diverted my eyes from the cruel truth longer than the rest, my love of family and of writing—art as I called it—were no longer sweet to me."[25] So long as he had the reassurance of his physical and intellectual vigor, he had believed in a kind of infinite growth which contained its own legitimate goal. When he came to the dead center that precedes old age, the questions that life had held back returned in strength, and it was only after several attempts at stating them—"What will come of my whole life? Why should I live?"—that he summed them up in a single question, the one he had already put to himself at Arzamas: "Is there anything in my life that the inevitable death awaiting me will not destroy?"[26] He knew that if he were to live he must answer the question; once asked, it would never leave him at peace again; nothing would retain its value, not work, not family, not fame. He began to search "painfully and persistently day and night";[27] he plunged into "the forest of the human sciences and the dark pit of the experimental

* In French, *confession de foi* means what *profession of faith* means in English.

sciences."[28] But just as in *War and Peace* History had answered questions that nobody had postulated, all Tolstoy got from men of science was "an infinite number of exact replies concerning matters about which I had not asked."[29]

His insatiable hunger for reading was like Levin's. He writes to Strakhov on November 26, 1877, asking him to send books: "I need books, only not philosophical ones—books on religion. . . . Is there in philosophy any definition of religion and faith other than that it is a prejudice? . . . And what is the form of the purest Christianity? These in vague form, are the two questions which I would like to find answers to in books."[30]

Disappointed by philosophy, he turned in his second phase to his fellow humans and found them as mute as philosophers and scientists, also seeking refuge in "false solutions." He distinguished four of these: ignorance; hedonism; then, the energy of strength—but this third leads the bravest to suicide, and in increasing numbers;* the last is the weakness of those who tolerate their intolerable position. That was the attitude Tolstoy himself seems to have adopted hitherto, but unlike "the majority of people of [his] circle,"[31] he could not forget the thing that kept Buddha from sleeping: like Hamlet, Tolstoy did not shrink from asking questions that lead to madness or questions no man dares put in words.

He was not infected by what Wilhelm Reich calls "the emotional plague," that is, the refusal to look the problems of life in the face.[32] Tolstoy's detractors, like his admirers, reproach him for preaching, but what actually upsets them is *what* he preaches.

His questions are those that only children put, for children have not yet joined the universal conspiracy of lying. Tolstoy was part of it only very briefly, in his "proper" period; he had left it forever behind at Sevastopol. He had chosen Truth as his hero, a choice that implied the asking of questions, pleasant or not. This will to tell the truth at any price, to push to the end one's demands, is perhaps what has struck certain readers as the most dangerous thing in Tolstoy's doctrine. Not Romain Rolland,† though, who inscribed a copy of *Jean Christophe* to Tolstoy in these terms: "To Lev Tolstoy, who gave us the example

* Dostoyevsky said Russia was "a land of suicides."

† Romain Rolland (1866–1944). Nobel Prize for Literature. Great humanist and internationalist. Much influenced by Nietzsche and Tolstoy. Friend of Gandhi, he succeeded in reconciling Indian thought with Communism. His life of Tolstoy is generally agreed by Tolstoy's family to be the best ever written. Rolland is also the author of a life of Beethoven and one of Charles Péguy, of numerous polemical works, *Above the Battle*, and of an important ten-volume novel, *Jean Christophe*.

of telling the truth, cost what it may, to everybody, including ourselves."*

The diary, taken up again in 1879, betrays weariness and exhaustion, but Tolstoy continued to believe that the problem of the meaning of life can be solved like a problem in mathematics. With disarming ingenuity and obstinacy he was ready to redo his sums again and again, wondering whether he hadn't perhaps forgotten in his addition to "carry one." " 'There is something wrong,' said I to myself, 'I have blundered somewhere.' But it was a long time before I could find out where the mistake was."[33]

Indefatigably, he tries to understand why he has not killed himself, does not kill himself. He decides that it is the "consciousness of living," what we would more simply call the instinct of self-preservation, that alone held him back from it. But he observes, sweet dreamer (in Dostoyevsky's phrase) that he is, that a lot of people are alive, hence a lot of survivors, and that fact worries him. The statistical argument convinces him that if "millions have lived and are living"[34] there must be some meaning to their existence. Mass consensus seems always to have had for Tolstoy a force against which one could not argue. Having failed to find answers among "people of his own circle," he made in his third phase an attempt to seek answers from the disinherited. "Thanks perhaps to the strange physical affection I have for the real labouring people, [I felt] that I was compelled to understand them and to see that they are not so stupid as we suppose."[35]

He concludes that only the people have "a knowledge of the meaning of life,"[36] but finds it hard to admit that they owe it to faith: "God, One in Three; the creation in six days . . . and all the rest that I cannot accept as long as I retain my reason."[37] His "position is terrible": he cannot accept the terms of the choice he has to make between alternatives; science for him means denial of life, and faith means denial of reason. He experiences the acme of all frustration, the desire for God. Sartre in our day had no need of God to construct his system for representing the world, but Tolstoy needs God to consolidate his. It was only much later that for him God as an explanation gave place to love of God.

The literary critic Nicolas Wiesbein sums up Tolstoy's progression by saying that he was trying to distinguish knowledge by faith from knowledge by reason.[38] But did he not try to reconcile them rather than to distinguish them? It may be possible to resolve this question by inverting its terms. Tolstoy says his reason cannot accept his faith. But

* Dated 1908. The book is in the literary museum at Yasnaya Polyana.

one may wonder whether it was not his faith that refused to accept his reason, whether he was not struggling against a kind of "instinct toward faith": he believed against his own reason, and his anguish arose from that very contradiction. Into his rational construction a doubt about doubt gradually insinuated itself, and doubt about doubt is perhaps one definition of faith. He began to ask himself whether reason was so very reasonable after all, and if unreason was so unreasonable. "The line of reasoning is correct, but results in the answer that a equals a, or x equals x, or 0 equals 0."[39] On the other hand, "faith [gives] a meaning to life and [makes] life possible. Without faith [one] cannot live."[40]

Tolstoy saw a proof of the existence of God in the fact that belief in Him helps men to live. God exists because He is necessary. And he adds that it is not because faith is true that it is good, but that it is true because it is good. Later, by a similar inversion, he would say that Christ preaches the truth not because He is God, but that He is God because what He preaches is the truth.

Having discovered the necessity of faith, Tolstoy directed his research to the study of religions, declaring himself "ready to accept any faith if only it did not demand of me a direct denial of reason."[41] He made nearly all of them run the gauntlet of his reason, including Buddhism and Islam, while concentrating especially on Christianity. Hope yielded swiftly to despair, because the inconsistency between the lives of Christians and their faith revolted him. "[They] lived just as badly as, if not worse than, the unbelievers," and he thinks that for them faith is "but an epicurean consolation in life."[42]

Failing to find the answers he was looking for in what was really a rather superficial study of religions, he turned to those who practice a religion or, rather, who live it: "Convinced that they have a real faith . . . I began to draw near to the believers among the poor, simple, unlettered folk; pilgrims, monks, sectarians, and peasants."[43]

It is easy to recognize here the period when his walks on the Kiev road were his substitute for reading the Gospels. What he found edifying was that these simple people, unlike the privileged class, had no fear of dying: "A troubled, rebellious, and unhappy death is the rarest exception among the people."[44] At this juncture, it seems, Tolstoy sought the company of "pure hearts," not so much from love of them as because they possessed the secret of the meaning of life and death. He thought that by mixing with them he would in the end seize upon that great answer, which was not in books nor among the rich, the philosophers, or the scientists.

He even wondered whether he might not have to become one of the poor to penetrate the mystery of human existence. In contact with them, "the life of our circle, the rich and learned, not merely became distasteful to me, but lost all meaning in my eyes."[45] It had never had much meaning for him anyway; he had always been a solitary, whether in the university, the army, or the literary circles. Now the break with these was complete, and it led slowly to the break with his own family.

Tolstoy himself summed up this period: "So I went on for about two years, and a change took place in me which had long been preparing and the promise of which had always been in me." That change revealed to him (and this was his true discovery) that "it was not an error in my thought that had hid the truth from me so much as my life itself." So at last he understood the words of the Gospel, " 'that men loved darkness rather than light, for their works were evil.' "[46] He now saw that "the meaning of human life lies in supporting it," and if the poor believe, it is because "they live well." His whole earlier life suddenly seemed "senseless and evil."[47] This conviction lies at the root of the contempt for literature that he later professed. "Art is a misdeed that gives the leisured the illusion of work,"[48] as he would say in 1897.

Tolstoy, then, had looked for signs of the Deity among the learned and the privileged like himself; he found it only among the poor, whose secret he finally unearthed. "All that time, together with the course of thought and observation about which I have spoken, my heart was oppressed with a painful feeling, which I can only describe as a search for God. I say that that search for God was not reasoning, but a feeling, because the search proceeded not from the course of my thoughts—it was even directly contrary to them—but proceeded from the heart."[49] Always closer than he imagined to the Orthodox Russian tradition, Tolstoy was but following the advice of one of the *Stories of a Russian Pilgrim*:* "It is enough to sink oneself silently into one's own heart; at once, one sees an inner light in whose effulgence appear some of the mysteries of the kingdom of God."[50]

Tolstoy confusedly knew that his varied attempts at finding an answer from others were vain. He needed the greater courage to search within himself and not resist going down to the deepest level of his being: "If I exist, there must be some cause for it, and a cause of causes. And that first cause of all is what men have called 'God.' "[51] Thus he grew ready for the great initiation, for the painful act of giving birth to oneself, which is the

* Published for the first time in Russia about 1870. *The Stories of a Russian Pilgrim*, whose author has remained unknown, is a work in the contemplative tradition which goes back to the early centuries of Eastern Christianity.

mystery of all conversions. He was living with "a feeling of being orphaned, isolation in a strange land, and a hope of help from some one."[52]

That was why he prayed to the God in whom he did not believe. "The more I prayed the more apparent it became to me that He did not hear me, and that there was no one to whom to address myself."[53] It was one such prayer that he wrote down in March 1879, not in his diary, but on a stray piece of paper:

> What am I doing here thrown among the people of the world? To whom shall I turn? To men? They do not know. They laugh, they do not want to know—they say: those are trifles. Don't think about it. Here is the world and its comforts. Look. But they do not deceive me. I know they do not believe what they are saying. Just as I do, they torment themselves and suffer from fear of death, from fear of themselves, and of Thee, Lord, whom they will not name. I too was a long time before I named Thee. . . . How terrible is the fire of despair hidden in the heart of the man who will not name Thee. However much water floods in, it will consume their inmost being just as it consumed mine. But Lord, I have named Thee, and my sufferings are at an end.[54]

He had also written, "I have called on Thine aid," but then crossed it out. In this state of spiritual destitution, of dereliction, of absolute void, there slowly emerged from the depths of his being that certainty without proof which constitutes faith:

> Again and again . . . I returned to the same conclusion that I could not have come into the world without any cause or reason or meaning; I could not be such a fledgling fallen from the nest as I felt myself to be. Or granted that I be such, lying on my back crying in the high grass, even then I cry because I know that a mother has borne me within her, has hatched me, warmed me, fed me, and loved me. Where is she—that mother? If I have been deserted, who has deserted me? I cannot hide from myself that someone bore me, loving me. Who was that someone? Again "God"?[55]

These lines describe the very instant of the fusion between his psychological self and his spiritual self, the instant when the existential void is filled, and Tolstoy rediscovered his wholeness, however fleeting. It is significant that at the moment of what he called his second birth he pronounced the word "mother." She who had deserted him by dying, three weeks before his second birthday. . . .

But the devil of argumentative reason was not lulled, and "not twice or three times, but tens and hundreds of times, I reached those conditions, first of joy and animation, and then of despair and consciousness of the impossibility of living."[56] Tolstoy was unable to believe that this rediscovered God was the three-personed creator whose existence he had been already unable to admit in his early youth in the Caucasus: "And again that God, detached from the world and from me, melted like a block of ice. . . ."[57]

Even so, in this swing between hope and despair which became habitual, something new emerged, and he wondered: " 'What more do you seek?'. . . This is He, He is that without which one cannot live. To know God and to live is one and the same thing. God is life. Live seeking God. . . . the light did not again abandon me." After this tumult, everything fell into place. "I quite returned to what belonged to my earliest childhood and youth. . . . I returned to a belief in God, in moral perfection, and in a tradition transmitting the meaning of life. There was only this difference, that then all this was accepted unconsciously, while now I knew that without it I could not live."[58] The sought-for goal is a return to the starting point.

He compared himself to an inexperienced oarsman, left alone in a boat to follow other boats whose happy crews assure him that he is moving in the right direction. Suddenly he hears the noise of water on the rocks where his boat is certainly about to founder, so he looks back and discovers a throng of rowers struggling against the current. This "looking back" is his conversion. That is how Tolstoy interprets the allegory: "That shore was God; that direction was tradition; the oars were the freedom given me to pull for the shore and unite with God."[59]

He was always impatient to apply his new theories. For him "the Christian truths are not only for conversation,"[60] as he wrote not long afterward to Tsar Alexander III. They now replaced the "rules of conduct" he had set for himself since childhood. It proved easy for him to renounce the world, which to him had never been more than a "semblance of existence." Abandoning the pleasures of life, working, humbling himself, suffering, performing good deeds, were all equally feasible, and Tolstoy's feelings of guilt favored this attempt to become detached. The real difficulties arose when it came to resuming the practices of religion. "At first my reason did not resist anything," he writes; and in this he was helped by his wish to "be in a position to mingle with the people, fulfilling the ritual side of their religion."[61] He gets up early, goes to Mass, fasts, performs many genuflections (the children admire his agility), and tries not to hear in the service what he always thought pointless verbalizing and to heed only the essential words: "Let us love one another in conformity."[62]

But although in this phase "it was . . . necessary for [him] to believe in order to live,"[63] what seemed to him "contradictions and obscurities"[64] could not remain hidden for long. Baptism and communion soon appear "not incomprehensible but fully comprehensible doings" that he considers "scandalous," and he is faced with a dilemma: "whether to lie or to reject them."[65] All rebellion is forbidden him: "Apart from faith, I had found nothing, certainly nothing, except destruction; therefore to throw away that faith was impossible, and [so] I submitted."[66]

He found comfort in listening to peasants and pilgrims; their sayings reveal faith to him "more and more," whereas when he had approached the learned believers, it seemed to him that he was walking toward the abyss.[67]

Tolstoy submitted for three years. He ended by being no longer able to accept the mysteries of religion. "When I approached the altar gates, and the priest made me say that I believed that what I was about to swallow was truly flesh and blood, I felt a pain in my heart."[68] Here again one can assign a date to this passage in *A Confession*: Tolstoy took communion for the last time in March 1879.

He was to rationalize his refusal, maintaining that it was not so much because of particular dogmas that he was obliged "to renounce communion with Orthodoxy as impossible," but because the Church's solutions to the "questions of life"[69] seemed to him contrary to the essence of religion. According to Tolstoy, what made him leave the Church was, in the first place, his disgust with the sectarian rivalry of different Christian churches—he was already dreaming of ecumenism—and second, the Church's approving stand on the death penalty, though the Bible unequivocally states: "Thou shalt not kill." Last, it was the Church's tolerance of war or active complicity in it. Already in Sevastopol he had felt indignation that Christians could slaughter one another, and the epilogue to *Anna Karenina* reflected his growing pacifism.

The peculiar self-contradicting gait of Tolstoy's dialectic is apparent again in this religious crisis: the closer he comes to faith, the further he moves from religion. As his faith strengthens, so his disgust with the Church increases, and the fact that true and false are mingled in the Church's teaching becomes more and more unbearable to him. So he has to go back to the sources: "And whether I liked it or not, I was brought to the study and investigation of these writings and traditions—which till now I had been so afraid to investigate."[70]

If he had feared to undertake the study, it was because he knew that "on this teaching religious doctrine rests, or at least with it the only knowledge of the meaning of life that I have found is inseparably connected,"[71] and he was frightened of disturbing this certainty. So he began to work with prudence. His ambition was limited, he wanted everything "inexplicable" to remain so, "not because the demands of my reason are wrong . . . but because I recognize the limits of my intellect. I wish to understand in such a way that everything that is inexplicable shall present itself to me as being necessarily inexplicable, and not as something I am under an arbitrary obligation to believe."[72] That was an ingenious and fallacious verbal sleight of hand, which did not of course let him dispose of the supernatural so easily. To be sure, he did not deny that truth resides in the teachings, but it seemed to him just as much beyond argument that those teachings included an element of untruth; it was therefore his duty to find out "what is true and what is false and disentangle the one from the other."[73]

The identity he had won through literary creation was suddenly brought into question again by this crisis of his maturity. At the end of *Anna Karenina*, under the shell of the writer, which was becoming looser and looser, the skin of the reformer was beginning to show; it toughened with *A Confession*, and Tolstoy did not really slough it off until shortly before his death.

The second mutation (the first made a writer out of a soldier) was now complete. But it was always Tolstoy who split himself off, and that meant schism: the young Tolstoy's very precise vision in the Caucasus of founding a new Christianity without Christ was being taken up by Tolstoy at fifty. Would he succeed?

III

A Confession, the chronicle of a conversion, shows that what is generally called, for convenience, "Tolstoy's crisis" was in actuality only a peak in a "crisis" that went back to his adolescence, and that was never resolved until the final months of his life. Nonetheless it marks a radical change of direction. Tolstoy himself was to say ten years later in, of all places, his preface to the works of Maupassant: "That time [1881] was for me a period of most ardent inner reconstruction of my whole outlook on life."[74]

From that moment on, he devoted all his intellectual energy to problems of religion, before dedicating himself, in a second phase, to establishing in the world his rediscovered faith. He embarked on a study of the Gospels by asking his usual provider, Strakhov, to send him a German translation of the New Testament that he thought the best. But at the same time, Tolstoy began to write *A Criticism of Dogmatic Theology*, to which *A Confession* was intended to be the preface. He did not undertake profound, systematic work—he would have been incapable of it at the time—but contented himself with "clarifying a certain number of ideas that arose after a reading of the *Manual of Theology* by Mgr. Macaire,"[75] this in the course of a few weeks. The *Criticism* circulated clandestinely in Russia, like most of what are called Tolstoy's "religious" works, and was published abroad by Chertkov, first in Geneva in 1891, then in London in 1903.

Three hundred and seventy years earlier, Luther had nailed his Ninety-five Theses to the door of the chapel of Wittenberg Castle; Tolstoy could have posted his *Criticism of Dogmatic Theology* under the church porch at Yasnaya Polyana, for his work is certainly a general refutation. He rejects the three-personed God and the divinity of Christ, treats the hierarchical church as a usurper, maintains that Christ did not institute the sacraments in the form in which we receive them and, of course, denies the Resurrection and the Ascension. He ends by proclaiming that salvation cannot be achieved through the sacraments, which strip man of his very liberty, but only through deeds. In thus abandoning the dogmas of the Church, he thought he was freeing himself; in fact, he was about to become captive to the dogmas of his own making.

Though his spiritual crisis had given a new direction to his intellectual life, it had not yet had any noticeable influence on Tolstoy's daily round at Yasnaya Polyana. Country house life went on. In June 1880 Turgenev appeared in person to lay siege to Tolstoy, to persuade him to take part in the Pushkin centenary celebrations; he met with a refusal. Still, the two writers went shooting together, and Tolstoy flattered himself that he had convinced Turgenev, ten years his senior, of the seriousness and usefulness of the work that was presently absorbing him.[76]

Tolstoy's "conversion" caused a stir in Moscow and in St. Petersburg, in society as well as in the political and intellectual world. On one of his visits to St. Petersburg, in January 1880, Tolstoy had a violent argument with Alexandrine: he rebuked her for not living according to her faith and not dropping her official responsibilities, even though just a year before he had written to her that "her cross was the Court, as his was the labour of thought."[77] In the years that followed, they were to exchange letters shot through with regret over their doctrinal disagreements. But they both held steadfast to their positions.

In January 1881 Dostoyevsky died at the age of sixty, and Tolstoy wrote to Strakhov: "I never saw the man and never had any direct relations with him, and suddenly when he died, I realized that he was the very closest, dearest and most necessary man for me. . . . When I read that he was dead, some support gave way under me. I was overcome; but then it became clear how precious he was to me, and I cried and am still crying."[78]* These words were not mere sentiments appropriate to the occasion. Tolstoy may rarely have spoken of Dostoyevsky, but he was nonetheless aware of his importance.† One must bear in mind that Tolstoy was reading *The Brothers Karamazov* when he left Yasnaya Polyana in October 1910 and that he had in a way paid homage in advance of Dostoyevsky's death in a letter to Strakhov dated September 1880: "I have just re-read *The House of the Dead*. I don't know a better book in all modern literature, Pushkin included. Not the tone, but the point of view is astonishing—sincere, natural, and Christian."[79]

A document that points to Tolstoy's real preoccupations and makes one understand better why perhaps he felt close for the first time to Dostoyevsky is his long letter to Tsar Alexander III,[80] after the assassination of his father Alexander II. He explained to the Tsar that if one considered the measures to be taken with the regicides "from a material point of view, there are [only two and] no other ways—either firm measures of excision or liberal weakness." But there was a third, and it was clearly the one he advocated: "One should without more ado no longer call the application of God's will to political affairs a daydream or madness; it is the more necessary to forgive because punishment would be a new murder."

What matters is not to wipe out the revolutionaries, because others will take their place, but that since "they are people who hate the existing order of things, to fight against them one must fight spiritually. . . . One must oppose their ideal with another ideal which will be superior to, and will include their ideal. Only one word of forgiveness and Christian love, spoken and fulfilled from the height of the throne, and the path of Christian rule which is there for you to tread, can destroy the evil gnawing away at Russia."[81]

Tolstoy took infinite pains to see that his petition got to the Tsar. He entrusted to Strakhov the task of handing it over to the Procurator of the Holy Synod, Pobedonostsev.‡ It was an odd notion to put this ideological bomb into the hands of one of the worst reactionaries of the age, a man who opposed on principle the publication of Tolstoy's philosophic works,

* This letter is oddly like the one that Gorky wrote at the time of Tolstoy's own death: "And now I feel an orphan. I write weeping. Never in my life have I wept so inconsolably, so despairingly, so bitterly." (*Reminiscences of Tolstoy, Chekhov and Andreev.*) Gorky was certainly no less reticent about Tolstoy, whom he loved and understood (as his marvelous pages on their Crimean conversations show), than Tolstoy was about Dostoyevsky in his lifetime.

† George Steiner says that Tolstoy (and Dostoyevsky) "afford the historian of ideas and the literary critic a unique conjunction, as of neighboring planets, equal in magnitude and perturbed by each other's orbit." (*Tolstoy or Dostoevsky*, p. 12)

‡ Konstantin Petrovich Pobedonostsev (1827–1906), Procurator of the Holy Synod of the Orthodox Russian Church (1880–95), tutor of Alexander III, and later Councilor to him and to his son Nicholas II. Favored the death penalty and general repression.

The Kreutzer Sonata, and the production of some of his plays. He was in fact one of the chief contrivers of Tolstoy's excommunication. Pobedonostsev was obviously unwilling to pass on the message. Sofia had foreseen the refusal and added a postscript to Tolstoy's letter to Strakhov in her own hand, expressing her anxiety about the consequences of this intervention on her husband's future.

It was not only the petition that alarmed Sofia; she saw that her husband's conversion complicated life instead of simplifying it, and in the long run would make it dangerous; and still it did not seem to have brought him peace. She tells him in a letter dated August 3, 1881: "I am beginning to think that when a happy man suddenly notices that life is horrible in every direction and shuts his eyes to the good in it, that is because he is ill. . . . You had already suffered from this state of boredom for a long time, you used to say: 'for lack of faith I would like to hang myself.' Well then, now that you have faith, why are you unhappy?"[82]

Tolstoy's petition finally did get to Alexander III through one of his brothers, the Grand Duke Sergey. Had Tolstoy for one second believed that the Tsar would listen to him? He was deeply saddened by the failure of his action. With his zeal as a convert he had hoped that here he had hold of the idea that might bring about *the* great change in world affairs; he had dreamed of seeing it transform human relations. He had thought that if the Christian example came from high up—"from the highest"—it could not fail to be followed.

By writing his letter to Alexander III Tolstoy opened a new period of his life. He had not found his inner unity through love or through art and had only glimpsed it at his own conversion; now he would try to realize it by means of the world outside him. It was in this dream that Tolstoy and Dostoyevsky, so distant in their origins, their religion, their political and aesthetic ideas, joined hands, and Tolstoy knew it. They both sought for "the solution to the problem."[83] Dostoyevsky, like Tolstoy, had wanted Russia to be the land that spoke "the new word to the world"[84] and showed "to the miseries of Europe the solution that the Russian soul could offer, a universally human and unifying solution, making room in that soul for all our brothers in brotherly love, and finally perhaps uttering the final word of universal harmony, of irrevocable brotherly agreement by the evangelical law of Christ."[85]

From now on Tolstoy would ascribe his deepest preoccupations to all of mankind, just as he had projected them in the past upon the characters of his novels. He knew that he would find himself only through complete self-transformation. Generalizing this conviction, he concluded that the whole world could only achieve its salvation through radical change. He was going to undertake the establishment of the Kingdom of God on earth.

Nineteen years later Tolstoy wrote: "It seems to me that just as there is a critical sexual age . . . so there is a critical spiritual age—about fifty—when a person begins to think seriously about life and [tries] to solve the problem of its meaning. . . ."[86] This midlife crisis, which most human beings pass through, was particularly dramatic in Tolstoy's case. First he had turned his destructive impulses on himself, with ceaseless self-reproach and the infliction of punishments, and finally going so far as to consider the ultimate self-punishment: suicide. For a time he had sublimated these urges in artistic creation; henceforth he would turn them outward. It was no longer a matter of substituting for the world a fiction, but of changing it. That was to be his great quarrel—with the Church, the Tsar, justice, love, and, in the end, art. He now saw everything as a fraud.

Tolstoy wanted not only to transform the living conditions of men, which means revolution; he wanted also to remodel the relations of man with God, to reforge the link that the churches had broken, by founding his own "direct" religion. He was convinced that mankind can be happy only after the restoration of its true bond with God. The message was not quite clear, not even to Tolstoy at first, and still less to those to whom he addressed it. They were sure only of one thing: he was attacking both spiritual and temporal authority at the same time. The guardians of the faith felt threatened and so did the guardians of law and order. And in Tsarist Russia the two were one.

The Tsar remained deaf to his pleading, and Tolstoy was disappointed in this rejection of his great design. He sought consolation for the lack of understanding of the great of this world by drawing closer to the ignorant people, the repository of true knowledge. He visited Tula prison on June 15, 1881, and decided to go to the monastery at Optina-Pustyn accompanied by the village schoolmaster of Yasnaya Polyana and his own valet. On his return he wrote to Turgenev (June 26): "My pilgrimage was a great success. I could count up some five years of my life which I would exchange for those ten days."[87] These pilgrimages, which he later called "praying with one's legs,"[88] have often been criticized; some have thought that taking a servant along proved that his devotion was a sham.

Though Tolstoy was a born organizer, he was also extremely haphazard. Sofia says that when he undertook any small job, he was "always clumsy and crude about it. Yesterday . . . he singed his beard with a candle."[89] He was well aware of this lack of dexterity, and his feeling of inferiority about it led him to overvalue manual labor, which he invested with a restorative and redeeming virtue. Like many people who have always had servants, he was baffled when faced with a pair of boots to clean; he had after all led on the material plane a very protected life. Even as a youth at Kazan he had had his valet and his coachman; during his childhood every little Tolstoy had a serf of his own, as well as a nanny or a tutor. Tatyana Lvovna recalled that there were still thirteen or fourteen servants* at Yasnaya Polyana in the 1880s. Just as a young girl in those days could not go out unchaperoned, so a Russian nobleman, even on a pilgrimage, could not travel without his valet.†

The religious motive that impelled Tolstoy to undertake these pilgrimages was strong, but not entirely free of an element of childishness: being a pilgrim fulfilled one of his childhood dreams. Some members of the upper orders are attracted by the lower depths of great cities; Tolstoy's yearning, on the other hand, was for the high places of piety, but in making for them he was also exploring forbidden territory: a world of purity, integrity, and poverty that ordinarily was denied him.

When he got home from Optina, he started with almost equal fervor on another pilgrimage, this time to the purest sources of nature: he went off to spend several weeks at Samara with a few friends. There he led the simple life that suited him: he had always loved the patriarchal habits of the people of this region. He played at being a Bashkir and drank mare's milk. He also visited the sectarians who lived nearby, which did not fail to confirm the suspicions of the authorities toward him.

Meanwhile Sofia was in Moscow, renting a house where the Tolstoy family would soon settle.

What difference had the "crisis" made? Only the lights and shadows changed; the world was different under the new light, but Tolstoy remained the same; he was still prisoner of himself, of "the old man." Conversion did not narrow the split in the self, but practically made it worse. Something was preventing the "unveiling" Tolstoy was waiting for. The "change . . . which had long been preparing and the promise of which had always been in me is foreshadowed but not brought about."[90]

Tolstoy was confusing salvation with rejection of the world. He

* Tolstoy's eldest daughter Tatyana notes on November 18, 1878, when she was fourteen, that she had a governess, Mlle. Gachet, and her sister Masha had Annie, who was English; the three older boys had M. Nieff; and little Andrey, who was only a year old, had his own nanny. "We also have a Russian teacher, Basil Alexeyevich, and teachers of drawing, Greek, music, and German, who live outside." (T. Tolstoy, *The Tolstoy Home*, London: Harvill Press, 1950, p. 1)

† Later in life Tolstoy learned to do without servants and vainly encouraged his family to do the same; but this was certainly not easy for him—no doubt the reason why he speaks of the problem so often.

wanted to let himself go, but resisted his own urge—there is no acceptance in him. He believed himself more Christian than the Church, and "accepts it in his own way," taking on a huge part of Christianity, but not the essential: the divinity of Christ. He distills from the Gospels "the materialist Christ" whom he envisioned in the Caucasus, but it is a hollow and empty Christ.

That is why he was with God, yet not *in* God, for he refused the mediation of Christ. He wrote in 1887 in the essay "On Life" that he was "obliged to make real all the truth in his own life and in the world's for himself, not by the mediation of another." He still thought the same in 1901, and wrote to a French Protestant minister that "the principal meaning of Christian doctrine is to establish a direct communication between God and man."[91] Such is the meaning it had for him, but certainly not for the Christian churches; for them communion comes through the sacraments that Christ instituted, while for Tolstoy "every man who takes this role [of priest or mediator] upon him prevents whomsoever he seeks to guide from communicating with God."[92]

It was not *diabolical pride*, as it was in Father Sergey (in Tolstoy's story of the same name), that prevented Tolstoy from "throwing himself on God."[93] It was the fact of being possessed by the need and not the love of God. One day in the Crimea, Tolstoy let Gorky read his diary. When Gorky returned it, he asked for an explanation of the phrase "God is my desire," which had struck him. Tolstoy demurred. "He began to laugh, and rolling up the book into a tube, he put it in the big pocket of his blouse."[94]

He had to wait more than a decade to discover that "the achievement of doctrine lies in the movement of the self towards God," and that the Christian practices are a working on the self to the point where they restore "in man the primitive awareness of the self, not in his animal self but in his divine self, of the divine spark."[95] For the time being the progression was only from psychological to metaphysical narcissism.

Tolstoy passes into a kind of autistic spiritual state; for him, "salvation is within you" means it is *in oneself*, so that the real proof of God's existence for Tolstoy is the fact that he *believes* in Him. His absorbing religious quest has become self-originating, and it takes on a character at once theosophist and gnostic. It is theosophist because he believes he can find God by deepening his inner life; but this extreme subjectivity also enhances his receptiveness, which in turn brings him from theosophy to gnosticism.*

* Gnosticism, from *gnosis* (knowledge), is the belief that positive knowledge in spiritual matters comes through intuition and openness to ideas.

Tolstoy makes no pretense of reconciling the various religions; he moves from one to the other like Don Juan from one woman to the next. He plucks flowers of wisdom from Buddhism, Taoism, and Islam, to make of them *his* truth and to go beyond them; that is, of course, what he has done in all his writings.

This phase of gnosticism goes with his aspiration toward a cosmic existence. Tolstoy felt that he belonged among "those who know": he had *gnosis*. As early as 1873 he had already held toward religion a "globalizing" outlook, considering that "millions of vague but synonymous answers have given definition to these answers. These answers constitute religion."[96]

There is no direct reference to the ancient Gnosis in his writings. Did he know it existed, had he any links with it beyond a casual interest in Freemasonry? Tolstoy's gnosis seems rather to be a spontaneous, natural attitude: he is the one who will provide a solution for everything, his answer is going to be *the* answer.

Tolstoy is a gnostic in taking his own understanding as the unique point of reference; he is a gnostic also in denouncing authority, the rich, the powers that be, and in preaching to the governed the duty to *disobey*. His vocabulary is in truth that of the Gnostics: awakening, exile, wandering, the nothingness of (worldly) knowledge. His ideas on love resemble those of the Cathari of the Middle Ages: like the Perfect,* Tolstoy would wish men to renounce procreation so as to give themselves utterly to the service of the Spirit.

Tolstoy stayed within the Christian ideology, which was acceptable to his reason and founded on reason, but he did not dwell within the faith, which is founded on revelation and tradition. He came within that realm only when his self had been, as he put it, "spiritualized," when he had freed himself from the shackles of his narcissism to attain, as his sister said after his death, that "spiritual humility he did not yet possess, though he was not far from it in his last days."[97]

Tolstoy went through his conversion by negatives: it consisted in death to the world in *Ivan Ilych*, denial of love in *The Kreutzer Sonata*, and finally rejection of literature in *What Is Art?*

* The hierarch of the Cathari, a group of antisacerdotal heretics in southern France during the twelfth and thirteenth centuries. They believed in sexual abstinence as a means of achieving enlightenment.

TWELVE

Moscow

I

NEARLY TEN YEARS EARLIER, Tolstoy had written to Alexandrine that he had decided never to go back to Moscow and that he looked with terror to the day when his daughters would be of an age to go out in society.[1] After *A Confession*, he abandoned the vanities of the world forever, but Sofia stayed in the world and even dug herself deeper in it. At Yasnaya Polyana the whole family lived in a sheltered and reassuring universe; in Moscow they had to face not only their own special difficulties but the threats of a great city and the realities of modern life.

From very early in his marriage, Tolstoy tended to load Sofia with the management of Yasnaya Polyana; still, he took an interest in his children's education, gave lessons to the older ones, and with skill and judgment saw through the press *War and Peace* and *Anna Karenina*. It was only little by little that he turned over all such duties to his wife. This gradual abdication was bound to upset, bit by bit, the equilibrium of their marriage: the wife assumed nearly all the responsibilities and the husband made full use of his freedom to engage in activities that lay outside the marital orbit. The common territory was broken up, each fragment drifting away out of control; love was not strong enough to prevent this disintegration.

So long as Tolstoy was writing, Sofia had not only accepted this transfer of duties, she had encouraged it, for her energy and intellectual ambitions found satisfaction in the real part she played in her husband's work, though she may have exaggerated its importance. She now began to think that the new sort of endeavor which engrossed Tolstoy was irresponsible: by devoting himself to the study of religion, he was on the wrong track and wasting his gifts. She behaved like a woman betrayed and made all the false moves of a neglected wife. Trying to "hold" her husband, she rebuked him for the spiritual "escapade" in which she neither could nor would follow him. The actual escape and desertion did not take place until thirty years later, in 1910, but in one sense Tolstoy did leave his wife and Yasnaya Polyana at the time of his conversion.

Sofia was thirty-seven. She was thrilled to be back in Moscow, for which she always entertained a certain longing, now bound up with the feeling that her youth is over. She is still a city woman, delighting to go into society with her daughter, and not indifferent to her own success there. She is happy in the Orthodox religion, bringing up her children in the tradition she herself inherited. She runs the house efficiently, manages the estate with competence and authority, proves a good accountant, an excellent businesswoman, and takes more and more responsibility for the publication of her husband's writings.

She felt neither guilty nor useless. In short, she was a woman of exceptional energy and organizing ability. She not only carried out all the tasks cited above, but she also made her husband's shirts (it is said that he refused to wear any others),* mended his socks, cut out and embroidered her children's dresses, and knitted numerous woolen coverlets that are still visible on beds at Yasnaya Polyana and in the Moscow house. She developed the large number of photographs that she took herself, and as Gorky put it, "what is more, she was Tolstoy's wife."

Although Sofia was not far from what Tolstoy had dreamed of as a wife before his marriage, she now represented everything he hated: social success and money. Money, which was becoming more and more important to her and the children, had turned for Tolstoy into something repulsive. To avoid the contamination he felt in anyone who had it, Tolstoy gave his wife power of attorney over all his possessions in May 1883. No one was really fooled by this false renunciation, least of all himself. On December 3, 1885, he wrote to Chertkov that he was afraid of seeming "a fraud writing against property and then, under my wife's name, squeezing as much money as possible out of people through my

* It is rather puzzling to see at Yasnaya Polyana, in a glass-fronted dresser, among clothes and boots that belonged to Tolstoy, a "Russian shirt" labeled inside the collar: "Au Carnaval de Venise, Avenue de l'Opéra, Paris." On hangers in a wardrobe one can still see the big, lined dressing gown made by Sofia as well as the overcoat Tolstoy purchased with some of his *Anna Karenina* money. He also bought his wife a ruby ring with the same money "to thank her for copying out the manuscript three times." (S. Tolstoy, *Tolstoy Remembered*, London: Weidenfeld & Nicolson, 1961)

writings."[2] As for the peasants, they never understood why Tolstoy had contented himself with this stratagem.

By 1891 Tolstoy thought the power of attorney inadequate and he decided to take another step toward poverty by dividing his property among her and the children, besides giving up all his rights to books published since 1881, the year of his "rebirth." Later still, in 1910, he tried to leave his works in toto "to the Russian people," thereby causing a complicated legal problem.

During the last years that Leo and Sofia Tolstoy lived principally at Yasnaya Polyana, their relations had become more and more difficult. From the moment they settled in Moscow, chronic discord prevailed; it led to the acute crisis of 1910 and the dramas that ensued.

Sofia had become the scapegoat for Tolstoy's failure to reconcile his principles and his life. He accused her of preventing him from living in the state of poverty he desired, and of forcing him to share the opulent life she and her children wallowed in—as he put it. She is luxury incarnate and will soon be lust incarnate, as *The Kreutzer Sonata* will virtually announce to the world.

As for Sofia, she had married a successful writer and in Moscow finds herself with a mujik who is a dissident and a prophet. For her, Tolstoy is a renegade who has betrayed everything—love, art, family, religion. For indeed he rejects the love of his wife, writes no more novels, does not play his part as a father, and ceases to practice his religion—even repudiates it. Sofia nurses an even more serious grievance against him: she resents the numerous and frequent pregnancies he has imposed on her, and lives in terror of having another child.*

Misunderstanding became endemic: both of them thought in all good faith that they were the innocent victim of the other's behavior, without the slightest notion that they might be partly responsible for provoking it. Scenes grew more and more frequent. Domestic peace returned only when some external event wrenched them out of their daily routine—the death of Alexey of croup in 1886 at the age of four, and still more so when Ivan ("Vanichka"), aged seven, succumbed to scarlet fever in 1895; during the period when the entire family took part in the fight against famine in 1891; at the time of Tolstoy's serious illness in 1901; and after Sofia's operation for a stomach tumor in 1906.

* On December 20, 1879, a tenth child (and seventh son), Mikhail, had been born. Before the eleventh child, Alexey, was born on October 31, 1881, Sofia wrote: "The thought of this new baby fills me with gloom." (*The Diaries of Sofia Tolstoy*, p. 69.) If one is to believe the story of Alexandra's "niania," Sofia even went so far, when she was expecting her last daughter, as to visit the midwife of Tula, who refused the nobleman's wife what she would have granted easily enough to any peasant woman. Alexandra Lvova was born on June 18, 1884. (C. Asquith, *Married to Tolstoy*, London: Hutchinson, 1960)

In Moscow, Leo and Sofia lived in complete disapproval and absolute intolerance of each other. Their spiritual separation was manifest, but their bonds of feeling were never broken, even in their final conflicts. Sofia suffered from this slow tearing apart and understood its true causes: "It is he who has made himself a stranger to us, not so much through his daily life as through his writings, his sermons to mankind, and the rules of conduct he lays down for them."[3]

From that time forward, Tolstoy's family is too much for him and his exasperation grows endlessly. He ends up blaming his sons for going out hunting and his daughters for wanting to marry, Sergey for playing the piano and even Alexandrine Tolstoy for not holding to her beliefs.[4]

While it is true that after they settled in Moscow, Tolstoy, to his wife's distress, lost interest in the children, the reason was not so much selfishness, as she thought, but his feeling that they were brought up in privilege, whereas he had envisioned for them a "natural education," virtually that of a "family commune." They on their side found it hard to bear that this killjoy, whose own childhood had been so comfortable, indeed spoiled, and whose youth had been more or less one of debauchery, should preach to them the hatred of luxury and the virtue of asceticism. The boys expressed the habits and ambitions of their milieu: Sergey was attending the University, and the younger boys were to go to the Gymnasium. On this point, Tolstoy provided a typical example of the ridiculous situations into which his unbending principles constantly betrayed him. Before a boy could enter the Gymnasium, his father had to give a written certificate of the boy's future good conduct: Tolstoy refused to sign any such document. He argued in the name of freedom that one man could not make a moral commitment on behalf of another. This refusal meant that Tolstoy had to send his sons to a private school where no moral sponsorship was demanded. The result was in flat contradiction with his other principles, since he wanted his children to receive a democratic education and be brought up like everybody else.

Apart from Leo Lvovich, who suffered the long aftereffects of this "Tolstoy disease,"* Tolstoy's sons always remained rather unreceptive to "father's ideas." He was unhappy at this "lack of communication" and

* Tolstoy's third son wanted to be a doctor for humanitarian reasons, though his father thought doctors "the most repulsive class in our society." When the time came for his military service, he considered refusing to do it, "being a convert to Tolstoyan ideas," but resigned himself to it in the end. Lev notes that his father then grew more interested in what regiment he was to serve in than in his religious notions. Later, during the Russian-Japanese war, Lev wrote pro-war articles which saddened Tolstoy much more than his short story "The Chopin Prelude," written in reply to *The Kreutzer Sonata*. (L. Tolstoy, *The Truth About My Father*, London: John Murray, 1924)

wept happy tears when Ilya, then twenty-two and on the verge of marriage, confessed to his father that he was still a virgin; at the time father and son were speaking on each side of a screen, so as to lessen their mutual embarrassment.

The daughters were reconciled with their father rather quickly. They were often more "Tolstoyan" than he was himself. Masha was the first to work with him, Tatyana understood him better than anyone else, and Alexandra was in on the secret when he finally left home.

These family relations naturally grew more and more painful and difficult; Tolstoy shared in none of their pleasures, and to him their enjoyment seemed futile, absurd, shocking. His need to be loved was great and his feeling of being deserted consequently terrible. His family seemed a hostile coalition arising out of a social system he had escaped from and was at war with. He once said to Sofia at a later time, but referring to this period, that if she had been unable to share his beliefs, she should at least have "given in to them out of love"[5]—an odd argument from a man who saw himself as the champion of individual liberty and truth.

The futile life of his wife and children made him still more sensitive to the misery in Moscow: it annihilated him, it seemed so infinite, so bottomless. Three years later he would write to Sofia from Yasnaya Polyana that he always found poverty and suffering everywhere but that "they are easier to see in the country. You can see them all here from start to finish. And you can see both the cause and the remedy."[6] In Moscow he could find no remedy.

Tolstoy sums up for Alexeyev* the extent to which his discovery of life in the capital city, where until then he had only made short visits, devastated him. "It is very hard for me in Moscow. I've been living here for more than two months and it's still just as hard. . . . The mass of evil overwhelms me, depresses me and makes me incredulous. It's astonishing, but how is it nobody sees it? . . . I'm hot-tempered, angry, irritable and dissatisfied with myself."[7] He was so overborne by the depth of urban poverty that he lacked even the urge to help combat it: he gives up trying to empty the sea with a bucket. All the same, one day he did pull a woman out of the gutter when he saw her collapse in the sight of her own child. Another time, he tried to save a laundry woman unjustly thrown out of her house but she died of exhaustion anyway.

* B. A. Alexeyev, a Tolstoyan, left in 1875 to found an agricultural commune in the United States; he returned in 1877 and became tutor to Tolstoy's oldest son, Sergey. He had to quit Yasnaya Polyana in 1881 after a quarrel with Sofia.

Inwardly he despaired seeing the frightful sufferings of the poor, yet he knew no way of giving them practical help.

Tolstoy was about to dive even deeper into "real life" by taking part in the census of the Moscow population in January 1882. For three days he lived in the hell of poverty, ignorance, overcrowding, and physical and moral corruption. He immediately wrote an article entitled "On the Moscow Census" by which he hoped to rouse the well-to-do out of their inertia. The same experience was also the inspiration of a more important work, *What Then Must We Do?*, which absorbed him from February 1882 to January 1885, and in which he considered "economic and social problems, pauperism, social slavery, no longer on the temporal but on the spiritual plane."[8]

He would go home to Yashaya Polyana as often as possible, and on any pretext, writing from there very affectionate letters to Sofia. Distance reduced their daily disagreements to proper size, and when they were separated, the accumulated venom of their clashes would dissipate somewhat. In a letter of March 1882 he asks her not to worry about him and above all not to blame herself for anything; he forgave her long ago; besides, life in Moscow has taught him much and showed him more clearly the work he ought to do; so, in the end, it has brought him closer to her.[9] Eight days later he admitted to Strakhov that he was tired and feeling feeble, that he often longed for death, and that his "death would be useful for his cause."[10]

Sofia was pleased with her new life, but very much aware of her husband's state of mind. "We have been in Moscow since September 15, 1881. We are staying in Prince Volkonsky's house.* . . . Our life in Moscow would be quite delightful if only it did not make Lyovochka so unhappy. He is too sensitive to survive the city, and his Christian disposition cannot reconcile all this idle luxury with people's struggling lives here."[11]

He would see some few friends "who think like him," particularly the peasant Syutayev, a member of the Old Believers sect, whom he regarded as one of his masters. Tolstoy said of this friend that, although illiterate, "his influence on people, on our intelligentsia, is greater and more significant than all the Russian scholars and writers. . . ."[12] Syutayev preached the joys of communal living. Everything must be shared: land, goods, food, work, even women.

"Festivities, indifference, proprieties, and the habitual presence of evil and deceit"[13] were unbearable, and when he had been working at one of

* Sofia had kept the best room in the house for her husband to make into his study; Tolstoy could not stomach its opulence and rented two rooms somewhere in the city to work in.

his "philosophical-religious" writings, as Sofia would say condescendingly, Tolstoy would cross Moscow to cut wood on the Sparrow Hills. "There you see real life and plunge into it at least sporadically and come out refreshed."[14] How pathetic is the sight of this man, world-renowned and admired as a writer and thinker, slipping furtively out of his house, disguised as a mujik, and going to the neighboring woods to work with real peasants!

II

21 Khamovnichesky Street

The family went back home to Yasnaya Polyana for the summer. Tolstoy knew that a permanent residence in Moscow was now unavoidable, but he no longer wanted to return to the Volkonsky palace; he decided to buy a house. If he could not live where and how he wanted, he could at least consider his own convenience, and he made a point of not leaving the choice to his wife.

In September 1882 he left everybody in the country and alone in Moscow began house hunting. He chose a rather large wooden edifice of sixteen rooms, with three-fourths of an acre of garden "as thick as the taiga [pine forests]" at 21 Khamovnichesky Street, a nearly suburban district at the time, in the middle of factories and workshops.

Tolstoy was looking for the countryside within the city. The garden delighted him more than the walls. He needed space, trees, and grass. Not only did he want as bucolic a setting as possible, but consciously or not, he hoped to reproduce the atmosphere of Yasnaya Polyana.

That September he supervised the rather important alterations himself—raising one story, which entailed the construction of a staircase. And he bought the furniture, most of it secondhand: he did not want a rich man's house. If the Moscow house is like Yasnaya Polyana, that is largely because he meant to live in it the same kind of life. The writer's study was on the second floor, with direct access to the garden so that he could go down early in the morning without disturbing anyone. In a small adjoining room he set up a sort of workshop with his cobbler's bench and tools.*

One can still see the divan in this study, very like the one at Yasnaya Polyana, on which Tolstoy sometimes lay down to write after a walk, and

* Apart from the tools and dumbbells, it now displays his English bicycle. Tolstoy began to ride a bicycle in 1895 at the age of sixty-seven.

a kind of lectern where he could work standing up. At the desk,* which he went to buy at the maker's warehouse, is a chair from which he sawed the feet himself: Tolstoy was short-sighted and hated glasses, and sitting very low enabled him to do without them. In this room he worked for nearly twenty years. It contains no useless or decorative object. Its furnishings consist of a glass-fronted wardrobe and some shelves for books, a few chairs for visitors, a table, and a side table on which there still lies a folder, inscribed in Sofia's writing: "File used by Leo Nikolayevich for the Census." Those two second-floor rooms were Tolstoy's private world.

As at Yasnaya Polyana, the whole life of the house centered on "the big room," which was approximately two hundred square feet in size, with three great windows giving onto the garden. No pictures on the walls, only sixteen sconces, "no carpets or soft chairs," as Leonid Pasternak was to note. Little furniture, except for the enormous table brought from Yasnaya Polyana, called the centipede, with a samovar on it. In the country, there had been two pianos, of half and quarter size, but here there was only one, standing on a bearskin.† Rimsky-Korsakov, Tchaikovsky, and Rubinstein played on it. It was in this room on certain evenings that classical or popular music soirées were given. Chaliapin came there to sing in 1890, but Tolstoy, although a great lover of Chopin and Beethoven, preferred gypsy or Caucasian songs to operatic arias.

On a table was a chessboard. When Tolstoy played, he attacked all the time, showing his combative nature. Lev Lvovich says his father's moves "were full of risks, which is why he won so seldom."[15] Tolstoy hated losing and gave up chess toward the end of his life: he always finished the game hating whomever he played with, which was inconsistent with his principle of brotherly love.

The great room was not kept just for musical evenings; it was also used at times for literary meetings. Tolstoy loved reading his works to his friends and collecting opinions from the very mixed lot of guests, among whom were writers such as Chekhov, Korolenko, Leskov, and Gorky after 1900. It was there that the first reading of *Resurrection* took place. In fact everything took place there, fancy dress balls,‡ children's parties, and amateur theatricals.§ Tolstoy also organized scientific meetings: the

* At that desk, between 1882 and 1901, Tolstoy wrote more than one hundred of his works, among them: *A Confession*, *What I Believe*, *The Kreutzer Sonata*, *The Death of Ivan Ilych*, *The Power of Darkness*, *The Living Corpse*, as well as numerous polemical and religious articles. The last piece he wrote in Moscow was *A Reply to the Synod's Edict of Excommunication*, composed in 1901.

† From the bear that wounded Tolstoy in 1858.

‡ One day the philosopher Lev Lopatin came as Tolstoy, to Tolstoy's great amusement.

§ Daughter Tatyana Lvovna sometimes illustrated the programs.

scientist Preobazhensky demonstrated optical illusions of color and light, and Tsinger the physicist, who was still a student, gave a lecture with a demonstration about liquefied air.

The painter Leonid Pasternak, who was Tolstoy's friend and father of the author of *Doctor Zhivago*, records that there were "soirées at regular intervals," characterized by an atmosphere of the old aristocratic hospitality. In an unbelievable way there mingled with all the rest, and on good terms, a number of strange Tolstoyans who were completely opposed in their ideas and their whole life-style to that kind of thing. Famous Moscow artists, composers, performers, professors of painting, and learned men, distinguished foreigners, not just from Europe but from America and Australia even, ladies-in-waiting from St. Petersburg, officials, governors, Crown prosecutors, plus the young swains and admirers of his daughters and his sons' friends—all came to that house. Next to a general of the Tsar's retinue, a friend of Tolstoy's youth, one might see revolutionary socialists due maybe for exile in Siberia or just back from there, and disciples of Tolstoy's who had suffered for their principles. Everything that seemed incompatible in life and even in imagination came peaceably together at that large table laid for tea. This assembly of all incompatibles was possible nowhere else. It even had a special name: The Tolstoy Style.

Off the great room is the drawing room. Tolstoy disliked it, no doubt because it was too conventional and cozy for him;* he called it "the boring room." For the same reasons, Sofia loved it best. She would settle down there to do the household accounts and handle the business details arising from the publication of Tolstoy's works. Sitting there she could watch the entrance to her husband's study. It was on the divan which stands against the wall of this room, draped with some embroidery by Sofia, that Tolstoy spent his last night in Moscow in 1909.

Still on the second floor there is a little sitting room which served as Tolstoy's and Sofia's room from 1882 to 1888; their last child, Ivan ("Vanichka"), was born in it. Then it became Tatyana's room, then the boys' room, and it was there that the married sons used to stay when they came with their wives to see their parents. All these rooms give onto the garden and are separated from the front rooms on the street by a long corridor that habitual visitors called "the catacombs." It is narrow and dark and leads to a few steps down to Tolstoy's study; it also leads to the servants' quarters and to Masha's room.

On the ground floor was the dining room: English china, portraits of

* Copies of portraits of various members of the Tolstoy family hang on its walls. The originals are at Yasnaya Polyana.

daughters Masha and Tatyana; the kitchen was outside, to avoid risk of fire and bad smells. Then came the corner room, occupied in turn by the eldest sons and by the tutors of the youngest children. Tolstoy's sister or friends of the family occasionally stayed there.

Still on the ground floor—Tatyana's room. Being a painter, she often entertained artists there, and Tolstoy sometimes came down with his own guests to round off the evening. Next, the schoolroom, dominated by an armchair that Sofia had embroidered; the servants' rooms; and Vanichka's room. He died in it at the age of seven, in 1895, and his toys are kept there—a sort of small museum within the big one. Finally, the room that was Sofia's and Leo's from 1888 onward, divided into two by a screen that he bought secondhand. On one side is Sofia's "salon," where she entertained her closest friends; above a sofa with a wooden back in the Russian manner stands a copy done by Nicholas Gay in 1886 of a portrait by Zakharov of Sofia holding Alexandra in her arms. The most moving piece of furniture is the small desk on which Sofia copied and recopied *War and Peace* and *Anna Karenina*; she brought it with her when they first settled in Moscow. On the same desk she likewise copied out *The Kreutzer Sonata* and *Resurrection*. On the other side of the screen are two narrow mahogany beds.

Tolstoy organized his days on a pattern that remained the same throughout his numerous winters in Moscow. He got up at the sound of the factory sirens. With his longing to be one with "the people," he loved being summoned to work at the same time as the workers, "his brothers and sisters." He did his appointed household jobs—carrying in wood and water for the whole house (six baskets and ten buckets). He often made his own coffee and wanted it the way the poor had it—without much coffee in it. These domestic jobs, like the work in the fields, which from youth on he attacked with a passion at Yasnaya Polyana, had a touch of the frivolity of Marie Antoinette playing dairymaid in the Petit Trianon at Versailles: he may have cleaned his own chamber, but his personal manservant always lived in a little room close by.

Tolstoy took ever more frugal meals with his family and worked until three or four in the afternoon; then he would go out walking or woodcutting, to be "in touch with the people." In the evening after dinner he "entertained." His friends were not his wife's friends, they were disciples—poor people, army officers, revolutionists, writers, artists, friends of his sons and daughters, and—provided they shared his ideas—aristocrats. Everyone argued, even the children took part in the conversation. The study was often too small for the variegated group, which might number up to fifty people; some of the guests had to sit on the staircase.

Tolstoy was working on articles explaining his social and religious philosophies, but more especially he was studying the Bible, the Gospels. In November 1882, at the age of fifty-four, he decided to learn Hebrew. Just as he had wanted to read the *Iliad* in the original, now he expected to read the Old and New Testaments without a translation, which he said was always "the wrong side of the cloth." His aim was the same old one of disentangling the texts from the lies that the priests of all religions had hidden them under.

The study of Hebrew did not have the same therapeutic effect that Greek had on him after he finished *Anna Karenina*. He wrote in a letter to Alexeyev on November 7, 1882: "I'm quite calm, but sad—often because of the exultant, self-assured madness of the life of the people around me"—the people who are, to his distress, every day more alien to him. "We just stand opposite one another without understanding each other, being astonished, and condemning each other." And he adds the detail: "All this time I've been studying Hebrew very intensively. . . . I'm taught by a local Rabbi [named] Minor."[16]

In a letter five thousand words long, written between December 20, 1882, and January 1883 to Engelhardt, then in exile for taking part in student commotions, Tolstoy makes clear his present religious position:

> The importance of Christianity is the indication of the possibility and the happiness of fulfilling the law of love. . . . In the Sermon on the Mount Christ expounds the simplest, easiest, most understandable rules for loving God, one's neighbor, and life, without the recognition and fulfillment of which it is impossible to speak of Christianity. And no matter how strange it is to say this after 1800 years, it was my lot to discover these rules as if they were something new. Only when I understood these rules—only then did I understand the significance of Christ's teachings. . . . But this clear expression of Christ's teaching was hidden from people. . . .[17]

Tolstoy's mission was to reveal it.

This letter, which circulated undercover for a long time, shows not only Tolstoy's religious position at the time, but what he had to suffer by leading the same life as before: "I can reason admirably and be sincere, but no one will ever believe me as long as they see that I live in mansions and get through in a day with my family the cost of a year's food for a poor family."[18]

He was perfectly well aware of his weakness and always would be, but like so many others he refused to see that his inability to follow his own doctrine proved it wrong: "Accuse me—I do this myself—but accuse ME and not the path I follow, and which I show to those who ask me where it is in my opinion. If I know the road home and walk along it drunk, staggering from side to side, does that make the path I follow the wrong one?"[19]

Sofia's diary has only three entries for the year 1882. The second one, for August 26, is important for its information on the stormy relations then prevailing between the two of them, and even more for its first mention of Tolstoy's longing to go away: "Today he shouted at the top of his voice that his dearest wish was to leave his family."[20] She tells us that they argued "about trivialities." She had reproached him once again for taking no interest in the children, and when she was through blaming him, he had uttered the terrible threat which from that moment on hung over Sofia's head.*

The quarrel was so violent that "for the first time in my life Lyovochka has run off to sleep in the study." He stayed there only twenty-four hours, and then they forgave each other. "We both cried, and I realized to my joy that his love for me, which I had mourned all through the night, was not dead."[21]

Sofia was still full of romance and remained so to her dying day. After that night of reconciliation, she was in a sort of transport of love and went to bathe at dawn in icy water. "I sat for a long time in the icy water, hoping to catch a chill and die. But I did not catch cold. I returned home to feed Andreyechka, who smiled with joy at seeing me."[22]†

After this crisis their relations appear to have improved. On their return to Moscow, Sofia noted on March 5, 1883: "Our life at home, away from the crowded city, is much easier and happier than it was last year. Lyovochka is calmer and more cheerful; he does sometimes get in a rage and blame me for everything, but it doesn't last so long now and doesn't happen so often. He is becoming nicer every day, in fact."[23]

In May 1883 Tolstoy gave Sofia a power of attorney to manage the estate; it simply formalized the arrangement that already existed, but it allowed him finally to rid himself of the responsibility—and, partly, of the sin—of property. A selfish independence was far from being the sole motive of the gesture: Tolstoy was really haunted by a longing for

* Until then Sofia had lived in constant terror of expecting another child; from now on she would live in fear of being abandoned by Tolstoy: these two obsessions ended by shattering her nerves.

† Sofia must be making a mistake: Andrey was born in December 1877; she must have meant the ten-month-old Alexey, born on October 31, 1881, the first child not to be born at Yasnaya Polyana. (The English edition gives the correct *Alyoshka*.)

poverty and for sloughing off his possessions; it was in the same spirit that a few months later he sold some of his land at Samara.

He doubtless considered his family not quite so lost as he had feared when he took the trouble to set down a "plan of life." This plan is an example of the naïveté of so intelligent a man when the reformer in him had the floor. The scheme was first of all to make everyone live at Yasnaya Polyana, to give away the income from the Samara and Nikolskoye estates to the poor and to the schools, and to keep only the income from Yasnaya Polyana: "Give the elder ones the choice, to take for themselves the part of the Samara and Nikolskoye money intended for the poor, or they can live with us and help us. To educate the small ones in a way to make them ask less of life. . . . To keep no servants except as far as is necessary to help us alter ourselves and teach us, and that for a short time, while we learn to do without them. All live together: men in one room and women and girls in another. . . . Seeing we are spoilt, another separate room for the weak." One must also sell or give away "pianos, furniture, carriages. As for arts and sciences, to devote oneself only to those one can share with everybody."[24] A program, in fact, that Rousseau himself might have found somewhat draconian.

Dreaming of nothing but evangelical poverty, Tolstoy had acquired almost in spite of himself a reputation not only as a writer but also as *the* leader of the opposition to the regime. When Turgenev died in August 1883, this notoriety had reached such a pitch that the authorities, hearing that Tolstoy intended to take part in the official tributes to the novelist, postponed the ceremony *sine die*. It was a strange epilogue to a friendship that remained paradoxical even beyond the grave.

People from all ranks were now coming to ask for Tolstoy's advice on "how to live." This celebrity weighed on him more than it pleased him, but he was glad of these requests, which gave him an opportunity to preach the good word; he gave the benefit of it even to apprentice writers who came to ask him the recipe for success.

Tolstoy's visitors, in Moscow as at Yasnaya Polyana, were mostly peasants, sectarian or other, students of more or less revolutionary tendency, and men of letters—all of them, for different reasons, dissatisfied with the state of the world. Among these, Vladimir Grigoryevich Chertkov, a former Guards officer and the son of a general commanding one of the Tsar's crack regiments, seemed out of place. He was rich, handsome, and wellborn, and the conversion of such a man of the world to Tolstoyism astounded Petersburg society. Sofia viewed his advent favorably, because he was "normal" and made a change from the peculiar breed that flocked around her husband. She could not know that in welcoming him she was opening her arms to the man whose influence over them both would help turn the latter days of their married life into a tragedy.

When Chertkov discovered Tolstoy's ideas, "his own torments ceased," and when he met Tolstoy he gave up everything to follow him. Once persuaded of the significance of his mentor's ideas, he envisioned spreading them worldwide; in that mission, which he, much more than Tolstoy, assigned himself, he was to prove successful.

In 1883, when they first met, Tolstoy was fifty-five and his good-looking and charming admirer thirty years old. Chertkov brought what Tolstoy had always longed for, and what Sofia had not been able to give him—unconditional love. In one sense, Tolstoy's spiritual isolation ceased with Chertkov's arrival. At the end of his life, when writing his secret will, Tolstoy finally recognized that his friend had led him into wrongdoing, but for years Vladimir Grigoryevich was to be the master's beloved disciple.

THIRTEEN

A New Way of Seeing

THE SPIRITUAL DISSENT that Tolstoy espoused after his conversion utterly altered his way of looking at things. To borrow the expression he used about Dostoyevsky, one may say that he too "achieved a spiritual change of foot."

Gide considered that Tolstoy's conversion explained "his end as an artist; it dried up the springs of his imagination more than did the process of aging."[1] As a matter of fact conversion did not dry up inspiration but only deflected its course. Sofia talked about "artistic suicide," but "suicide as an artist" would have been closer to the truth.

Tolstoy's decision to give up writing has in it an element of penance. It came at the time when Tolstoy was trying to cut loose from all his old pleasures—wine, hunting, tobacco, and finally sensual indulgence. But another reason why he abandoned literature was that it no longer had meaning for him. True, "it had been pleasant to look at life in the mirror of art."[2] That mirror—an image he borrowed from Stendhal*—had become "useless, superfluous, ridiculous, unbearable,"[3] because it no longer served his new purpose—to put "the law of God" into practice. This renunciation filled Sofia with despair and Turgenev with consternation; they both wanted Tolstoy to be a writer, and not a man exclusively bent on his own and the world's salvation.

Settling in Moscow went with a kind of scattering of his creative

* "A novel is a mirror that one parades along a public road." (Saint-Réal, quoted by Stendhal in *The Red and the Black*, book I, chapter 13)

energies, quite different from the concentration that had presided over the birth of *War and Peace* and *Anna Karenina*: his work now split into fragments forming a kind of dust cloud—religious writings, polemical articles, tales and stories, long and short, and pieces for the theater. Yet the scattering is more apparent than real, because every piece of writing grows out of Tolstoy's one obsession: to save his soul and particularly the souls of others, and to serve the people.

Unity of life breaks up at the same time as unity of work. Tolstoy and Sofia had spent the "eighteen happiest years of their life"[4] almost uninterruptedly at Yasnaya Polyana. From 1881 onward it was quite the opposite. Tolstoy came and went continually between town and country, and in 1891 he left to fight the famine in the Kazan district, where he remained until 1893. After his return, the comings and goings did not stop; and as the years passed he lived less and less in Khamovnichesky Street; from 1901 to 1909 he never went there at all.

At Yasnaya Polyana Tolstoy had first lived a kind of double duet, playing one with Sofia and the other with his novels. Little by little the cast had grown larger, and when the family settled in Moscow, the children ceased to be just part of the scenery to become full-scale actors in the drama. Then in 1883 Chertkov made his entry as well. The file on the Tolstoy case begins to build up. To Tolstoy's and Sofia's diaries, notes by the children, the secretaries, the disciples, and the close friends begin to be added. This accumulation of reports and comments made Tolstoy say that the documents about him constituted "a pyramid with its top downwards and the base upwards; very little biographical material for the beginning of his life and too much later on."[5]

The memoirs of Sergey, Tatyana, Ilya, Lev Lvovich, and Alexandra show that their father was less indifferent to the children than Sofia made out, but they especially revealed what close bonds united the family in every aspect. Tatyana was to say, "I had the good fortune to grow up among creatures who loved one another and who loved me"; and it is true that down to 1881 the Tolstoys' history was like that of those "happy families" mentioned in the first sentence of *Anna Karenina*.

All the same, these tight bonds were not without harm: they made every member of the family extremely dependent on the others and created tensions and rivalries within a space that was after all a closed world—and this in spite of the spreading circle of Tolstoy's influence.

The great number of works in progress, the increasing number of residences, and the growing number of confidants surrounding the two main characters created an atmosphere of turbulence from which Tolstoy suffered and tried more and more to escape.

* * *

From 1884 on Tolstoy stayed as often as he could at Yasnaya Polyana. During these separations the pair exchanged a great many letters. They are not without tenderness and express the constant hope that their next coming together will find them once again as one.

Sofia tried to analyze what it was that kept them apart: "Yes, we walk different roads from our childhoods: you love the country and peasant children and the primitive manners you left to marry me. Myself, I am urban, and in spite of all my attempts to convince myself, and longing to love the country and the people, I am not capable of loving them with all my heart."[6] Tolstoy was worried about his wife's condition; at the end of March he wrote in his diary: "She is very seriously ill mentally. And the crux of it all is her pregnancy. A very great sin and shame."[7] On June 18, 1884, Alexandra (Sasha), their twelfth child, was born. In his final days, she was to become her father's confidante—and her mother's nemesis.

The two outer worlds they moved in were as different as their inner worlds. Sofia went about the salons, and Tolstoy the slums. When he was in Moscow he would get up at seven and go to bed as early in the evening as nine. He made boots and shoes. He put manual labor on the same level as intellectual work, if not higher, and undoubtedly found happiness in "creating" anything at all, in expending energy with concrete results. But it was also a way of becoming the equal of the workers to perform tasks just like theirs. He wrote to Sofia on December 13, 1884: "There is no real pleasure except what follows from making something."[8]

He was intellectually active besides. At the beginning of the year he wrote *What I Believe*, a work that ran into the usual difficulties with the censors. In April he began *The Fruits of Enlightenment*, and nearly finished *Ivan Ilych*, which he gave Sofia for her birthday. On March 30, he noted: "Thought of writing 'Notes of a Not-Madman' in reply to Gogol's *Notes of a Madman*."[9] (This eventually became the never finished short story, twenty pages long, that was published posthumously as *Memoirs of a Madman*.) On April 13, he "worked at the Gospel," that is to say, at *The Translation and Harmony of the Four Gospels*, begun in 1880.

The night before, he had written: "Atmosphere at home not very friendly." He consoled himself by reading extensively in Confucius; he believed that "without him and Lao-tzu the Gospels are not complete"; he read Erasmus on March 22, seven chapters of the Gospel in Hebrew on March 26, and Michelet and Montaigne in September. There is mention for the first time of the idea of a *Cycle of Reading*. He did not put it together until 1903, but he already knew what texts should go into it: Epictetus, Marcus Aurelius, Lao-tzu, Buddha, Pascal, and the Gospels.[10]

He obtained his documentation by field work: at the end of March he visited a nearby stocking factory, and took down the working hours of women and children—information to be used in *What Then Must We Do?* which he began on April 2.

The diary for 1884 mentions a number of quarrels. They were more or less serious, and generally followed by loving reconciliations. On April 2 Tolstoy notes: "Drank tea. Was alone with her . . . I was unfortunate and cruel enough to touch her pride, and it all started." But the next day he noted: "She is gentler now without a grudge"; and the day after: "still gentler, morbid and submissive."[11]

Tolstoy went through "torments of the soul," feeling so misunderstood by his family that he wanted to die. He writes on August 25: "I long for true death, I wish to live, not to survive." He could not find a way to endure the lack of communication with his nearest and dearest. "Why can't I talk to the children; to Tanya? Seryozha [son Sergey, then twenty-one] is impossibly obtuse. The same castrated mind that his mother has. If you two should ever read this, forgive me; it hurts me terribly."[12] In an entry of May 4 to 16 he complains that his children are "crude." Something new: he now rarely calls Sofia "Sonya," but just "she," and he records: "They don't see and they don't know my sufferings."[13]

Every day of that summer Tolstoy groaned under what he calls "the weight of futility."[14] His French translator Halperin, who stayed a short time at Yasnaya Polyana, tells us that "he [Tolstoy] worked in the fields mowing and reaping for whole days with the mujiks," and that when he got home in the evening "he was discontented with his family."[15]

Tolstoy kept on making shoes as he had done in Moscow, and taking care of widows and orphans in the village, for "one has only to go into a worker's cottage and one's soul blossoms forth."[16] Every morning he received a throng of petitioners under the "tree of the poor,"* and suffered from his inability to do much for them.[17] He went to Telyatinki to see what he could arrange in behalf of some people in jail. On June 11 he jotted down: "My drifting apart from my wife goes on getting worse."[18] Quarrels took place almost daily, and after a few days the situation explodes into drama. Thirteen years later, Sofia would recall that on June 18, 1884, "He completely lost his temper with me . . . and

* This big tree behind the house, where those who wanted to see Tolstoy assembled, is now dead: the trunk is kept in the garden like a relic of the True Cross.

putting some things into a linen bag, he said he was leaving for good, possibly for America."[19] He changed his mind: "Her pregnancy made me turn back half-way to Tula,"[20] but from that time on Sofia's fear of his going away never left her; it became her obsession.

The children were grieved by the scenes they witnessed and at the same time consumed with curiosity. When she was writing *My Father's Death* in 1928, Tatyana said that she could "still see him disappearing down the alley between the birches"[21] and her mother "sitting in front of the house under the trees . . . she was due to have another child and could already feel the first pains. The hour was nearly midnight. It was Ilya who carefully brought her indoors and put her to bed."[22]

The "summary" of June 1884 that Tolstoy put in his diary is laconic: "Break with my wife one can no longer say worse, just bad but complete." He added that he no longer drinks wine at all, eats no meat, and still smokes, but less. As for the July summing up, it begins with a phrase that defines the situation: "Struggle with the family."[23]

In this period his friendship with Chertkov was of great help. Tolstoy talked over his worries with him with complete trust, going so far as to admit that he had set up a rendezvous for himself with a woman, but that God had protected him: he had passed by one of his sons' rooms and remembered he had promised him a lesson. He saw the boy through the window and decided to stay at home. In the same letter he also tells his friend that recently, "lying in bed beside his still wakeful wife," he had suffered "feelings of loneliness in the midst of his family" because of his principles. He was sure that those close to him saw the truth but turned away from it. All the same, he wondered whether he had ever "expressed his thoughts to Sofia Andreyevna lovingly and gently."[24]

Soon, in addition to a spiritual and intellectual bond between master and disciple, the relation of co-workers was established. Together they founded Posrednik Editions: *The Mediator*. "Their aim is to publish what is accessible, comprehensible, and necessary to everbody, and not to a small circle of people"; and of course, "it has a moral content in accord with the spirit of Christ's teaching."[25] This enterprise proved unquestionably Tolstoy's greatest educational success. He published the great writers of antiquity, some popular works, and a number of his own books. In 1905 he declared: "In the ten years of my management, Posrednik Editions sold an average of three million items a year. In round numbers, fifty million in twenty years."[26]

Sofia for her part had organized in Khamovnichesky Street the Office for the Publication of the Complete Works of Tolstoy. It was to distribute her husband's books for the sole, acknowledged purpose of making money. So the wife and the disciple were fated to quarrel not only over Tolstoy but also over his works.

No doubt it was not so much weakness as the fact that leaving his wife and children would have been an act of violence repugnant to Tolstoy that kept him from resolving to do so; but for staying away from Moscow he found every excuse. He did spend a couple of winter months there in 1885, and he returned in March for another factory tour, before leaving for the Crimea with his friend Alexander Urusov, who was dying of tuberculosis and thus seeking a less rigorous climate.*

During his first visit to Moscow, Tolstoy was much absorbed by the launching of *The Mediator*. This strenuous effort, the revision of *Strider, the Story of a Horse* (which dated from 1863), and the writing of *The Death of Ivan Ilych* in no way lessened the deep sadness he felt about the chasm existing between him and his family. Still and all, it seems extraordinary that Tolstoy, who thought only of the salvation of the world, should have been so broken up by the conflict between himself and his near ones, or to be exact, between his principles and theirs. He could never accept the idea of living in a world separate from that of his wife and children, nor that they should belong to a class whose life "is entirely arranged for the sake of living for oneself and is entirely based on pride, cruelty, violence and evil."[27] Dostoyevsky had been struck by Tolstoy's tendency to hide his problems from himself and accused him of "making landowner's literature." But the point is not to decide whether Tolstoy was right or wrong; what matters is the reality of his sufferings.

He wrote to Chertkov early in June that he was witnessing "the systematic corruption of the children"; then he mentioned his longing for death and his "plans to run away."[28] Tolstoy was captive in the prison of privilege, and his fellow prisoners are the well-to-do who, like all who are mad, do not know that they are: he alone knows it. The language of his letters and his diary is that of the world of prisons and torture: he says of Sofia that to her dying day "she will remain a millstone round my neck and round the children's."[29] In his letter to Chertkov he speaks "of a cannonball" that shackles him, and of "the immoral mad-house" in which he is "condemned to suffer every hour." And he confides that his "desire to set the vertical and the horizontal arms of the cross at right angles† is a

* Near Sevastopol they passed "by the place where nearly thirty years before during the war, Lyova had opened fire on the enemy. . . . He suddenly jumped out of the carriage . . . to pick up a cannonball he thought must have been fired by his battery," as Sofia writes in her journal in the only entry for 1885. (*Journal de la comtesse Léon Tolstoï*, Paris: Plon, 1930, p. 185)

† This is symbolic. The longer upright of the cross means God's will, and the smaller crossbar is man's will.

dissatisfaction with the conditions" in which God has placed him, "a failure to do what he was sent to do."

In holiday times at Yasnaya Polyana, he feels that when his family joins in work in the fields it is only an amusement for them, one entertainment among others, not a kind of prayer as it is for him, a communion with God's creation and with men. Tolstoy knows that if he cannot manage to communicate "the light of life" he has glimpsed to his nearest and dearest, he will never be able to impart it to humanity. This failure torments him. "I am in a difficult and complicated position now as an envoy, and I sometimes don't know how best to do the will of Him who sent me—I shall wait for elucidation—He has never refused it and has always given it in good time."*

Since no one would listen to him at home, he would write for the destitute who had need of his word, who thirsted for it—hence the wonderful popular tales into which Tolstoy put all his artistry, abating none of its power and beauty, for the benefit of the common people: poetic tales as simple and clear as the verses of the Bible.

He had hoped to "find brothers and sisters in his own family,"[30] but they became strangers to him. Happily there lived one creature on earth who understood him. Tolstoy wrote to Chertkov on December 9, 1885: "Nobody loves the good that there is in me as much as you."[31]

It is Sofia he blames the most for not following his lead. Had she done so, what would have happened? Did Tolstoy ever think seriously about it? True enough, repentant sinners who become hermits seldom have nine (living) children and do not have to face questions of this kind. It was nearly impossible for Sofia, even if she had been thoroughly convinced that it was her duty (which was far from being the case) to undertake at her age a return to the land such as Tolstoy favored, or to alter the mode of education for her children without taking risks that a mother as conscious of her responsibilities as she was could not run. But she *could* have become poor in spirit, and that she did not do; quite the contrary. Indeed, instead of seeing money as a necessary evil, she thought of it more and more as an indispensable good.

It must have annoyed the whole family, and her in particular, to hear this preacher continually expounding to them that they lived in luxury, on filthy lucre, although the Tolstoys' mode of life was in fact well below that of people equal to them in rank and fortune.† Tolstoy was indeed

* It is interesting to note that it was in a letter to Chertkov, to whom he writes without reserve, that Tolstoy refers to himself as "sent"—an envoy. (*Tolstoy's Letters*, vol. II, p. 384)

† The attendant at Yasnaya Polyana told me that she had several times heard young Soviet Russians express amazement that the house was so modest and its furniture so simple, and remark that today's State rest centers were far more luxurious.

infuriated by his sons' behavior: "They overeat and amuse themselves by buying with money the fruits of the labours of other people for their own pleasure."[32] Oh, forgetful old man, not to remember how he used to haunt the best restaurants of Moscow and St. Petersburg, and how he ordered his suits from the best tailors! But Tolstoy had the intolerance of the prophets: he commits to the flames what he used to worship and wants others to take part in the holy bonfire. The one "meagre consolation" he has left, so he says, are his daughters, who "love him for what deserves to be loved. . . ."[33]

Things went on worsening, until they became so bad that according to a letter from Sofia to her sister Tatyana, Tolstoy came to her one evening and shouted: "I've come to tell you that I want a separation. I can't live like this. I am leaving for Paris, or America." Astounded, she asked, " 'What's happened?'—'Nothing, but you can only go on loading things onto the cart for so long. When the horse can't pull it any more, the cart stops.' " A violent scene followed, in which Tolstoy cried out: "Wherever you are the air is poisoned."[34] Sofia in despair sent for her trunk, but at her children's entreaties, she stayed.

Oldest daughter Tatyana Lvovna later wrote: "I remember that terrible winter night. There were nine of us children then. I can still see us older ones down in the hall, sitting on chairs, just waiting. Every now and then we would go over to the bottom of the stairs and listen to the sound of our parents arguing upstairs." She added what is surely the best analysis ever made of the conflict between Tolstoy and his wife: "Both were defending something more important to them than their lives; she the well-being of her children, and what she regarded as their happiness; he, his very soul."[35] After that dramatic scene, Tolstoy did go away, but only "to regain his peace of mind, to think." Tatyana took her father "in the little two-seater sleigh to the Olsufyevs', about ten miles out of Moscow."

In September Tolstoy stayed at Yasnaya Polyana to work. When he rejoined his family in early November he was visibly so unhappy that Sofia herself encouraged him to go and stay a few days with her sister Tatyana. Before going off, he left his wife a letter* of a dozen pages; it constitutes a formal step for reconciliation between a couple on the point of splitting up. He told her that there could be "no agreement and no loving life between them" until she came "either from love . . . or from conviction to the view of life" he now held, and that *he* would never return to that "lost world" which had once driven him "to the brink of

* In the margin are the following words in Sofia's handwriting: "Letter from Leo Nikoleyevich to his wife never given or sent to her." (*Tolstoy's Letters*, vol. II, p. 393.) So she knew nothing about it until her husband's death.

suicide." He acknowledges that she has "assiduously" published his writings, that she "has taken so much trouble in St. Petersburg," and "has hotly defended his articles which were banned." But what *was* in those articles? "My works, which have been nothing more nor less than my life, have been, and are of so little interest to you that when you come across them you read them out of curiosity, like works of literature; while the children are not even interested in reading them at all." He blames her for forgetting that they are "written with blood and tears," and for treating his convictions as "eccentric and inconsequential ideas." He deplores that "this fundamental revolution which has changed his life" should be to her "a morbid and abnormal phenomenon," and that she treats him "as a man mentally ill." Then he threatens to "resort to force to give up his property" or abandon his family. But he has second thoughts, not wanting "to break God's commandment," and he finally proposes to "continue to live" as before, but with the aim of developing in himself "the strength to fight against evil, lovingly and gently." Having accused Sofia of being the "unwitting, unintentional cause" of his sufferings, Tolstoy goes on to suggest concrete measures of a touching candor: "You look for the cause: look for the remedy. The children can stop overeating (vegetarianism). . . . They can do their rooms, stop going to the theatre, feel sorry for the peasants, start reading serious books—I shall be happy and cheerful. . . . But no, you obstinately and deliberately refuse." The last paragraph of the letter is somewhat enigmatic: "A struggle to the death is going on between us. Either God's work or not God's work. And since God is within you . . ."[36]*

Distance had the usual and wished-for result, and after this verbal and epistolary violence, it was a letter full of good feeling that Tolstoy addressed to Sofia from the Olsufyevs': "How grieved I am that you torment yourself so much. . . . I rejoice that I am again in such a normal state that I shall not distress you as I have lately done."[37]

Was Tolstoy sincere? This question, which occurs apropos of every act of his life and every sentence in his writings, arises here with all its implications. For if ultimately he was not sincere, he was a monstrous destroyer† who laid waste everything out of sheer pride: he undermined his own world and his family's, and he shook the world in which he lived

* The dots lead one to assume it was unfinished, and got no further than a first draft. This makes it even more interesting than a revised and corrected text.

† On November 29, 1851, Tolstoy had written in his diary: "I observe in myself a tendency to squander which expressed itself in my youth in the destruction of everything that came to hand; it expresses itself now in the destruction of Vanyushka's peace and quiet" (he is referring to having asked his valet to bring him a pipe he had no wish to smoke, solely for the pleasure of disturbing him) "and the squandering of money without any cause or pleasure." (*Tolstoy's Diaries*. vol. I, p. 39)

by attacking the State in all its institutions and the Church in all its doctrines.

The problem of Tolstoy's sincerity is closely connected with that of his self-contradictions, which in turn have their source in his love of truth. In October 1877 he wrote to Romain Rolland: "I will never believe in the sincerity of anyone's Christian convictions, philosophic or humanitarian, who has his chamber pot emptied by a servant." It is just as hard to believe in the sincerity of a man who rebukes the Church for "interpreting" holy scripture, and himself writes a summary of the Gospels,* who seeks to found a Christianity without Christ, who advises others to renounce their possessions but contents himself with "distributing" his own to his wife and children, shrugging off the burden of culpability, while continuing to benefit from the comforts that money buys.† It is also hard to believe in the sincerity of a man who draws up a profession of faith the day after he has decided to give up Communion; who announces his devotion to Christ and maintains that recognizing Him as the son of God is blasphemous; who learns to make boots no one can wear from a cobbler who comes to teach him at home, like a girls' dancing master; who preaches love of one's neighbor and makes his wife and children miserable; who preaches chastity in marriage and fathers thirteen children; who denies laws but relies on them when he makes his will; who rejects Orthodoxy yet seeks refuge in a convent on the occasion of his flight and who even thinks of retiring there altogether.

From youth onward Tolstoy's progress was through spurts of self-contradiction. He brought everything into question, knocked everything over. All he accomplished was to restate old problems in new terms without resolving any. He tore down without reconstructing. By the challenges he flings in all directions, this fabulous destroyer gives the impression of a man with all the answers, but his "ratiocinative mania" prevented him from admitting the power of the irrational, let alone the supernatural—an impossible position for a Christian such as he claimed to be, and was. This mania led him only to negative beliefs.

The utopian reconciliation of "cat and dog," the impossible "harmony"

* Lenin points out that with Tolstoy "the struggle with the Church strangely coexists with a new religious mission." (S. Lafitte, *Léon Tolstoï et ses contemporains*, Paris: Seghers, 1960, p. 245)

† Like many rich people, Tolstoy was not fully aware of those advantages that his wealth brought with it. His biographers and Tolstoy himself speak of "footmen in white gloves," but what one ought to consider more seriously is his ability to manage Yasnaya Polyana at his whim, to have *War and Peace* illustrated at his own expense, to finance his various schools and teachers (he brought Keller from Germany), to feed all the Tolstoyans he took in, and to be able to work as long as he chose on a novel without having to send his publisher a manuscript he was not satisfied with simply in order to earn his bread, as Dostoyevsky often had to do.

that he tried for by main force, has its origins in the passion that Tolstoy felt for what he called "truth," but which really was rather a longing for purity. He wanted to restore things to their primal innocence (hence his passion for the Caucasus, and for virgin nature in general). He wanted to disentangle religion, politics, art, and love from the accretions under which society and the Church had buried them. He wanted to recover the splendor of naked truth. Tolstoy fought pharisaism and hypocrisy of every kind, imposture and profanation in every guise.

This purifying flame consumes everything in its path; it also burns the hand that carries it, and the burn is undeniable proof of Tolstoy's sincerity. His suffering validates his destructive undertakings, for he really was deeply unhappy.*

Levin in *Anna Karenina* speaks after his conversion of "a new feeling that had crept into my heart through suffering":[38] it also invaded Tolstoy's. It is this feeling that gave his life authenticity in spite of the contradictions he failed to resolve, of the compromises he accepted; and it was this same feeling that gave his writings their power to convince. "Works of art, like artesian wells, rise the higher, the more deeply suffering has scarred the heart,"[39] as Proust said in *Le Temps Retrouvé*.

It was Tolstoy's suffering that allowed him to call himself a Christian. He was on the cross with Christ, and that is how he achieved a kind of sanctity—for he did take upon himself the misery of mankind.

* Simone Weil said, "Through suffering I burn away sin."

FOURTEEN

The Death of Ivan Ilych

On January 18, 1886, Alexey (Alyoshka), the youngest son of Leo and Sofia Tolstoy, was suddenly carried off by croup. As he died he sat up in his bed, "his shining eyes open wide and in them a look of delighted astonishment. 'I see . . . I see . . .' he said, and fell back dead."[1] The words were as if spoken by some Tolstoyan hero.

The death of this little boy of four, by—as it were—breaking the hellish circle within which the couple moved, improved Tolstoy's relations with his wife. When this drama was over, life slowly resumed its even tenor at Yasnaya Polyana. Visitors thronged, as they did every summer. Among them came an unusual traveler, Paul Déroulède.* He was on a special mission in Moscow and wanted to see the sage of Yasnaya Polyana. Tolstoy asked him, "So you go on dreaming of revenge?" Déroulède answered, "I don't dream of it, I'm preparing it." The two men evidently liked each other, but between the one who preached nonresistance to evil, and the other, who wished to destroy it by force, no true communication of ideas was possible. But the visit of this famous nationalist poet and parliamentarian shows how wide an audience Tolstoy had at that time, not only as a writer but also as a

* Paul Déroulède (1846–1914), founder and president of the ultra-nationalist League of Patriots. He was a French deputy who in 1899 tried unsuccessfully to rouse the army against the parliamentary Republic.

political thinker. His teachings were beginning to be known, and Tolstoyan colonies were coming into being all over the world. These communes, founded with enthusiasm in Russia as well as in the rest of Europe and the United States (and later even in India), enjoyed the brief existence of utopian societies.

Tolstoy took up again *The Power of Darkness*, a terrible peasant drama inspired by a murder committed by a certain Koloskov, who in 1880 had smothered the child he had had by his own stepdaughter, aged sixteen. On the day of the stepdaughter's wedding he had publicly confessed his crime and tried to kill his own six-year-old daughter to spare her the shame of having a murderer for a father. Davydov, the prosecuting attorney at Tula, had told the story to Tolstoy, who went twice to visit Koloskov in prison.

In September 1886 Tolstoy injured his leg while he was carting hay for a peasant woman at Yasnaya Polyana. The wound became infected and the festering sore had to be drained. He was stuck in bed for nine weeks. This mishap brought him closer to Sofia, who looked after him lovingly, and probably inspired in part (only in part, because the problem goes far beyond the event) his remarkable account in *Ivan Ilych** of the state of mind of a sick man isolated in the bosom of his family. Tolstoy now completed this long story, begun in 1882 and once more taken up in 1884, and published it. The original title was *Death of a Judge*; his plot was based on the death in July 1881 of the magistrate Ivan Ilyich Mechnikov.

Although Tolstoy was now in the period when religious or philosophic meditations were to count for more and more, he revealed himself perhaps more fully in this piece of fiction than in any expository work. The story throws light on his changed attitude toward death; it is an allegory of his own "death to the world," and it expresses his ideas more clearly than his theoretical works.

In effect, *The Death of Ivan Ilych* is the epilogue to *A Confession* and the prologue to *The Kreutzer Sonata*. By a kind of "literary equivalence," the moral sickness unto death from which Tolstoy suffered while he was writing *A Confession* became an organic disease, the cancer from which the hero of the story died. The ill that gnaws at the body of Ivan Ilych is the anguish that was doing the same to Tolstoy as he wrote: the incomprehension of those close to Ivan Ilych is what the writer's own family showed toward him and, in particular, what his religious crisis aroused in

* In the Centenary Edition, volume 15, the last name is transliterated as *Ilych*; but in the Penguin Classics translation, from which the quotations in this chapter are taken, the name is given as *Ilyich*. For consistency, the patronymic has been spelled "Ilych" (as in the definitive Centenary Edition) throughout these pages.

his wife. The refusal to understand her husband which Praskovya Fedorovna, the wife of Ivan Ilych, wrapped herself in is like Sofia's, and it gives a foretaste of the questioning of love and marriage that Tolstoy was to undertake in *The Kreutzer Sonata*. In *Ivan Ilych* two themes are intertwined—the discovery of true life and rejection of the old (the subject of the earlier *A Confession*) and the breakdown of marriage and family that Tolstoy had observed at the time of his crisis (the subject of the later *Kreutzer Sonata*).

The parallels between the story and Tolstoy's life at the time are numerous and obvious: Ivan Ilych's wife groans incessantly about her lot. After her husband's death she explains how distressing his pain was for her: "At the last he screamed, not for minutes, but for hours on end. It was unendurable."[2]

Like Tolstoy, Ivan Ilych had "to fence off a world for himself outside his family life . . . he retreated into his other world of official duties, and there found satisfaction."[3] It was for reassurance that he haunted doctors and specialists, hoping to hear words of comfort from their lips; for the same purpose, Tolstoy had gone to see doctors of the soul. The cancer victim had a weakness for listening to everything people said about his illness, and relating it to himself,[4] just as Tolstoy wrongly expected answers to his questions from the Starets Ambrose and Antony, from the Metropolitan of Moscow, and from books. Ivan Ilych's "principal occupation became the exact observance of the doctor's prescriptions regarding hygiene and the taking of medicine,"[5] thinking it would cure him, as Tolstoy had hoped to find peace for his anguish in ritual practices and the acceptance of dogma.

But both Tolstoy and the hero of his story were disappointed in their quest; they encountered nothing but lack of understanding. Those closest to them wanted above all to keep to their familiar routine: a dying man interferes with the course of normal life; Tolstoy, dying to life in the world, likewise disturbs his family. Ivan Ilych's wife and daughter think only of balls, fuss over a possible suitor, go to the theater to see Sarah Bernhardt.[6] Blind to the painful reality under their eyes, "those about him did not understand, or refused to understand."[7]

Tolstoy, too, had the feeling of being the only seeing creature in a world of the blind. Like Ivan Ilych he would have liked his wife and daughter to give up pretty dresses, going out in society and to the theater; he even went so far as to wish that Tatyana Lvovna would refuse to marry. Novelist and hero alike are strangers in their own homes; Ivan Ilych's wife thought he "was himself to blame, and she was lovingly reproaching him for this";[8] even his daughter could not understand. " 'Why are we to blame?' said Liza to her mother."[9] By an odd coincidence, Sofia used almost the identical words in her diary for September of the same year: "I often wonder why Lyovochka is always blaming me, when I'm not guilty of anything?"[10]

Nor can Tolstoy and Ivan Ilych expect any better from their friends; Ilych remarks that his own family "would begin to rally him in an amiable way about his nervous fears, as though that nightmare thing that was going on inside him . . . were the pleasantest subject in the world for raillery."[11] What he would have liked was "to weep and to have someone cry" over him.[12]

The only one who understood the sick man was his valet, Gerassim; he was of the people and did not lie. For him death was a simple, natural thing. He took no stock in hypocritical make-believe and offered no deceiving words: he holds up the dying man's feet to lessen his pain. In the same way, Chertkov knew how to assuage Tolstoy's moral pain.

But as had happened before Tolstoy's religious crisis, so before Ilych's illness misunderstanding had already crept between husband and wife. "There remained only those rare periods of amorousness which still came to them at times but which did not last. These were islets at which they put in for a while, only to embark again upon that ocean of concealed hostility. . . ."[13] It was on this sea that Tolstoy and Sofia had been sailing ever since the end of *Anna Karenina*.

For Tolstoy and for Ivan Ilych, resettling in Moscow was a trial. When he mentions it in his story, Tolstoy writes: "This was in 1880, the hardest year" of Ivan Ilych's life.[14] He could have added, "and of my own." The author and his hero were close indeed: Tolstoy had insisted on altering and furnishing himself the house in Khamovnichesky Street, and Ivan Ilych himself "superintended the arrangements, selected the wallpaper, bought more furniture."[15]

The story became autobiography; the quarrels that mark the daily life of the Tolstoys turn up again in the book: "Most of the conversations between husband and wife, especially those concerning the children's education, led to topics recalling previous disputes, so that quarrels were apt to flare up at any moment."[16] Ivan Ilych "had to live thus on the edge of the precipice alone, without a single soul to understand and feel for him."[17] So had Tolstoy lived over the abyss at the bottom of which the dragon awaited him in *A Confession*.

To the great question that Levin had already put and that Tolstoy had used as a lever to upset the old world of conventions so as to rediscover the true life among the ruins of the old, Ivan Ilych gives a reply: "He searched for his former habitual fear of death and did not find it. 'Where is it? What death?' There was no fear because there was no death either."

Peace comes to him. "In place of death there was light. 'So that's what it is!' he suddenly exclaimed aloud. 'What joy!' "[18]

Was it this victory over death at the close of the story that led Tolstoy to change the title of the philosophical essay he was working on at the same time, calling it "On Life and Death"?* Sofia noted in her diary for August 4, 1887: "He . . . deleted the word Death, since after he had finished it he decided that 'there is no death.' "[19] Or was it, in reverse, his spiritual experiences of that time that inspired Tolstoy's climax in *Ivan Ilych*? Once again, as with *War and Peace* and *Anna Karenina*, it is hard to say whether life influenced art or art, life. This very uncertainty enables one to detect the secret impulse behind Tolstoy's progression; a double motion gives his writings, multiple and contradictory as they are, their unity and power, and gives his life its dramatic resonance.

The death of Alexey and Tolstoy's illness had brought man and wife closer, but as early as September Sofia's mood darkened again. She too felt herself a prisoner. Perhaps she entertained the wish to follow the path to which Tolstoy was committed. "I can't do what my husband wants (so he says), without breaking all the practical and emotional chains that have bound me to my family."[20] She saw that, as soon as he had recovered, he was escaping from her again. "Although the last two months, when Lev Nikolayevich was ill, were an agonising time for me, strangely enough they were also a very happy time for me."[21] She was tired of her family chores and the role in which Tolstoy confined her. "I shall . . . have business meetings with publishers, get some money for Lev Nikolayevich, who constantly comes up to me with that air of indifference, malevolence and even hatred, and demands that I give him more money to give to all his minions and paupers."[22]

Her children reproached her for "holding views opposed to their father's," and she felt that some of them were ready to swing over to Tolstoy's side, particularly the two older girls, who acted more and more of the time as his secretaries. He had asked Tatyana to look for popular sayings and proverbs that he wanted to use in the dialogue of "a new play about peasant life"[23] just begun.

Sofia was happy to see her husband resume literary work; she was glad to copy the first act of *The Power of Darkness* on October 27 and the second on October 30, but she did not understand why he was as "unhappy as ever now that he has faith"[24]—so "incompletely saved," as Nietzsche would have put it.

* Published under the title "On Life."

FIFTEEN

The Power of Darkness

"WE HAD a peaceful and happy winter," Sofia writes on March 3, 1887, and she notes that Tolstoy stays in Moscow more willingly: "He joins in games of vint [Russian whist], sits down at the piano again, and is no longer driven to despair by life in the city."[1]

Tolstoy was very sensitive to music; certain compositions are known to have moved him to tears, and he often sought an escape in music—that is, until his utter rejection of it at the end of his life. It may be because he was feeling more in a prison than ever that he went back to cards and the piano, for two days before his wife wrote her optimistic note, Tolstoy had wondered in a letter to Biryukov: "Where could I go to get away from myself and from people?"[2]

On January 27, 1887, Alexander Stakhovich had read the manuscript of *The Power of Darkness* before the Tsar and the Grand Dukes, and Alexander III had exclaimed, "It's a wonderful play." The Imperial Theatre at once undertook to produce it, but on March 14 Sofia got news from St. Petersburg which she records: "It was not yet certain whether or not they would allow the play to be performed. But rehearsals have started and they are going ahead. I can't decide whether to attend the dress rehearsal!"[3]

Tolstoy took an active part in the rehearsals. His instructions to Svobodin, the actor, on his interpretation are like those to the illustrator of *War and Peace* in their exact and concrete detail: "Akim stutters, he doesn't splutter. One should exploit the contrast between his comic, incoherent babbling and the ardent, and at times solemn delivery of the words which 'issue forth' from him."[4]

Unfortunately Pobedonostsev* succeeded in utterly reversing the Tsar's opinion, so that Alexander now declared, "It is important to put an end to the scandal caused by Leo Tolstoy. He is nothing short of a nihilist and an atheist. It would even be desirable to forbid the sale of his plays."[5] On March 24, with the costumes already completed, all the Imperial theaters were suddenly ordered to remove *The Power of Darkness* from their programs. Still, its publication was permitted and it had a notable success: two hundred and fifty thousand copies were sold in three days. Tolstoy wrote to Biryukov: "If I had known it was going to be so popular I would have taken the trouble to write it better."[6]

The number of Tolstoyans was steadily increasing. They approached the master to ask for his rules of life and he was generous with advice. He explained to Zheltkov, a member of the Molokan sect,† that he was delighted to see that he was writing, first, because he was a peasant, and second, because he was "free from the false teaching of the Church which conceals from the people the meaning of Christ's teaching."[7] He answered a young man asking for advice about marriage that he must "certainly not marry 'for love' but 'from calculation,' "[8] though he failed to add that these were to be spiritual mathematics. A Moscow schoolteacher who criticized some liberties Tolstoy had taken with the Gospel was told: "I wanted as far as possible to depolarize, like a magnet, words of an ecclesiastical interpretation which had acquired an uncharacteristic polarity."[9]

He replied at length in French to Romain Rolland, then a young student at the Ecole Normale in Paris, two of whose letters he had read "with tears in my eyes," and he defined for him one of his fundamental attitudes by means of the famous sally on the "sincerity of Christian convictions" already quoted.[10]‡ Tolstoy also explained the significance he attributed to manual work. He saw in it the means of "repairing the prejudice that our depraved society—a society of so-called civilised people—has provoked in the people by burdening them with this type of work for which they receive no compensation."[11] He added that the true vocation of a prophet can only be tested by the sacrifices a man is

* See page 159.

† The Molokans, or Milk-Drinkers, rejected Orthodoxy and refused to have their children baptized, thereby incurring the penalty of the law. Under it, the authorities could take the children forcibly away from their parents. Not until 1901 were the Molokans allowed to emigrate to California and Mexico.

‡ See page 188.

prepared to make.[12] Lastly, he proclaimed that he would brave anything or anybody to follow the dictates of his reason.[13] Thus in spite of "his call," it was to the power of reason and not God that Tolstoy was ready to sacrifice everything.

The disciples did not content themselves with consulting Tolstoy by letter; on any and every pretext they betook themselves to the oracle in person. "He maintains equally strange relations and correspondence with people who have the most frightful reputation, people generally regarded as downright criminals."[14] Sofia viewed these visitors with a suspicious eye; they signify danger to herself. "All these so-called friends of his . . . are trying desperately to set him against me—and not always unsuccessfully either,"[15] but she thought they were an even more serious threat to Tolstoy's writing. "Now he has become entangled with all those 'new Christians' again . . . he began pining for the country and his creativity was smothered."[16] Many of these Tolstoyans were what today would be called dropouts. She judged them severely: "There is not one among them who is normal. And most of the women are hysterics."[17] She names as an example (ill-chosen) Marya Alexandrovna Schmidt,* who left her post as *dame de classe* at the Moscow Girl Foundlings' Institute to settle near Yasnaya Polyana: "In the old days she would have been a nun—now she is an ecstatic admirer of Lev Nikolayevich's ideas."[18] She devoted herself entirely to copying out Tolstoy's forbidden works and led a life of privation and sanctity. Sofia thought the behavior of a certain Feinermann particularly reprehensible. "He has left his pregnant wife and his child somewhere—and has come to us . . ."[19] On June 17 it was a "medical student and revolutionary fanatic" who turned up at Yasnaya Polyana: "Lev Nikolayevich tried to convince [him] of the error of his ways. Whether he was successful I do not know. . . ."[20] On July 19 came a young man who was "dark, one-eyed, and very silent . . . he wears blue-tinted spectacles." He was Anatol Stepanovic Butkevich, the son of a landowner of Tula, who had been to prison twice for revolutionary activities; Tolstoy had met him when he returned from exile in Siberia in 1886.

Sofia's first enthusiasm for Chertkov had already withered. She had read a letter in which he congratulated himself on having a wife who was a spiritual companion and pitied Tolstoy for lacking the same good

* She was a remarkably good and disinterested woman who always tried to calm down the troubles of Tolstoy with his wife. In 1897 Sofia wrote a second portrait of this eminently Tolstoyan character: "She simply lives for L., whom she worships fanatically. She used to be an extreme adherent of the Orthodox faith, but then she read all Lev Nikolayevich's articles, took down her lamps and icons, and hung up portraits of Lev Nikolayevich in their place. Now she possesses a complete edition of his banned works, and earns her living copying them out and selling them." (*The Diaries of Sofia Tolstoy*, London: Jonathan Cape, 1985, p. 196)

fortune. She now thought him "sly, malicious, obtuse and narrow minded,"[21] and she began to fear his influence.

Tolstoy was still engrossed in his article "On Life." On March 14 he had read it before the Psychological Society (it was the second time he had read it at the university) and he kept Sofia continually busy copying it out. "No sooner do I copy it out than he covers it with scribbles and it has to be done all over again."[22] There was for her one fresh source of satisfaction: her husband's fame had reached America. Both rejoiced, but for different reasons. "He is delighted by his success, or rather by the favourable response to him in America—although fame and success generally have very little effect on him."[23]

Life at Yasnaya Polyana is still much as it was before 1880. One evening in June, Tolstoy "played the piano accompaniment to some violin sonatas by Mozart, Weber and Haydn . . . and clearly enjoyed himself immensely."[24] Peace seems to reign between husband and wife. On the evening of July 2, Sergey was playing the piano and Tolstoy invited Sofia to dance. "We danced, to the delight of all the young folk."[25] The next day the eldest son and his teacher, Liassotta, a pupil at the Moscow conservatory, were going to play Beethoven's Kreutzer Sonata. Tolstoy was happy; he alternated between intellectual activity and physical exercise. "Lyovochka is busy with the mowing and spends 3 hours a day writing his article. It is almost finished now."[26]

The happiness of these summer months made Sofia imagine her husband "cured" and concealed from her the real evolution of his mind. Tolstoy was all the time moving farther along the road to asceticism, eating no meat, trying to give up smoking, drinking no alcohol,* and attempting to enlist everyone else in his renunciations.†

It seems that in the summer of 1887 visitors to Yasnaya Polyana were even more numerous than usual. Strakhov spent several days in early July and took long philosophizing walks with his host. Alexandrine Tolstoy stayed from July 25 to August 4, and Biryukov went back to Moscow with "On Life" completed at last. These friendly presences—that of Repin, who was to paint two portraits of Tolstoy,‡ that of his two

* At the end of 1887 Tolstoy founded the Union Against Drunkenness. He edited for *The Mediator* the works of Doctor Alexeyev, a pioneer in the fight against alcohol, and thought of writing on the same problem himself. He did so, but not until 1909, in an edifying piece, *All Virtues Come from It*. But he instructed the artist Repin as early as February 1, 1888, asking for illustrations "as terrible as possible" for this piece.

† In April 1888, in the same spirit of poverty, Tolstoy walked the one hundred and thirty miles from Moscow to Yasnaya Polyana with the son of the painter Gay after the birth of his own last child, Ivan. (It took them five days.)

‡ One shows Tolstoy writing in the Vaulted Room, sitting on a bench with one leg folded back underneath him, a position he often assumed. In the other picture he is sitting in the pink wing chair in the salon.

older sons from Moscow, and that of Sofia's brother Stepan and his wife—compensated Sofia for her displeasure at "the peculiar and disagreeable people that flocked around Lyovochka."[27]

Sofia knew the exceptional importance of the intellectual, spiritual, and literary adventure she was witnessing, and for the first time she had the idea of collecting all the notebooks, manuscripts, stray papers, and portraits of Tolstoy so as to send them ("I am only being sensible, but for some reason it makes me sad"[28]) to the Rumantsyev Museum. It was all the more admirable of her to think of this gift now that she was pregnant again, and to her this was still "a torment, physically and emotionally."

One evening the actor Andreyev-Burlak, who was passing through Yasnaya Polyana, told Tolstoy and Repin how on a train journey he had received the strange confidences of a man he did not know, who had killed his wife from jealousy. The subject interested Tolstoy, and he suggested writing the man's story; Repin could illustrate it, and then Andreyev-Burlak, whose principal talent was as a monologuist, could do readings of it in a theater. Only the writer was to carry out this plan,* the actor's tale having apparently been a catalyst for Tolstoy's thoughts on marriage. In October he began the first version of *The Kreutzer Sonata*.

* Andreyev-Burlak died less than a year later in May 1888.

SIXTEEN

The Kreutzer Sonata

EIGHTEEN EIGHTY-NINE was the year of *The Kreutzer Sonata.* By a paradox, the relations between man and wife seemed to be rather better—which did not prevent Tolstoy from writing: "She suffers and causes me pain like a toothache, and I don't know how to help her, but I'm looking for ways."[1]

In early winter he saw many people in Moscow and talked to them about art, marriage, and religion, but he was dissipating his energies and found it hard to work. He read extensively, his syllabus eclectic: Voltaire's *Zadig* in February; Ruskin in March, because he had begun to write about art. Later on, he read a French book on Saint-Simonism, Fourierism, and the communes,* and also Lamennais.† The summer found him deep in Schopenhauer's *Aesthetics.* "What frivolity and lack of clarity!" is Tolstoy's verdict. He was interested in American religious movements, and in October he read articles on Universalists, Unitarians, and Quakers.‡ In November *The Disciple* by Bourget made him exclaim: "How vile!"[2] But in December he found Maupassant's *Fort comme la mort* (*Strong as Death*) "a beautifully written novel . . . though the theme is

* *Saint-Simon, sa vie et ses travaux*, G. Hubbarb, Paris, 1857.

† Félicité Robert de Lamennais (1782–1854), a Roman Catholic apologist and liberal, was ordained a priest in 1817 but excommunicated in 1831 because of his unorthodox beliefs. Several volumes of his works, annotated in Tolstoy's hand, are in the library at Yasnaya Polyana.

‡ Tolstoy received Christian Science publications, and through them kept up with religion in America.

sordid."[3] Tolstoy did not want to be "a maker of books"; his business was quite other: "I must say what I know, it is that which consumes my heart. For I'm old and could die today or tomorrow without having said what God has put it in me to say."[4]

At the end of March he went seeking peace and quiet to visit the Urusovs at Spasskoye where he stayed a fortnight. He took with him the *Sonata*, the work "On Art," and a sketch for a play, *The Fruits of Enlightenment*. But as was his habit, he did not spend his time just on literature: he went to see the local cobbler—"a colleague"—and wrung from him a promise to join the Temperance Society.[5] The next day he visited a factory newly set up in the district.

From Spasskoye he wrote to Sofia on March 29, 1889: "I never cease to sympathise with your spiritual life. . . . I am convinced that it will manifest itself in you more and more vigorously, and will deliver you from your sufferings and give you the happiness which you sometimes seem not to believe in but which I constantly experience, and the more keenly, the nearer I approach my physical end. . . ."[6] It was an odd worry for a man about to give his wife a moral stab to the heart. On April 6, he read *The Kreutzer Sonata* to his host: "Urusov liked it very much. Yes, it's true that it's new and powerful."[7]

He went back to Moscow two days later with a much developed manuscript. He found in his mail books from America on the teachings of the Shakers: "Very fine. Complete sexual abstinence. How strange that it should be now, while I am occupied with these matters that I receive it."[8] He saw it as a sign and an encouragement and took up his tale again. Moscow was really unbearable, the city was "a moral monstrosity."[9] He needed to purify himself, to go back to his sources of truth, to find again the pilgrim road; so he set out for Yasnaya Polyana on foot. At dawn on May 2 he left with Yevgeny Ivanovich Popov; the hike took them seven days; they spent their nights in houses along the way. "Everywhere the scourge of alcohol."[10] Tolstoy handed out pamphlets and spoke out against war to soldiers and peasant women: "They understood"; and he preached abstinence.

Settled once more at Yasnaya Polyana, he kept delivering his message as often as he could. On May 15 he recorded that he had "read the Gospel to mujiks magnificently."[11] He spent the summer working in the fields and on *The Sonata*. In July he cut the hay as usual and took advantage of being among peasants to impart to them the good news. "I spoke to them of the sin of sleeping with one's wife," he says, "and they agreed."[12] But there was always some zealous follower who reproached Tolstoy for the life he led: S. D. Romanov, a member of a Tolstoyan commune, was indignant that "sixteen servants are looking after twelve ladies and gentlemen."[13]

Tolstoy was working hard at *The Kreutzer Sonata*. He jotted down variants in his diary.* Poor Sofia copies and recopies. "She's upset," writes Tolstoy, who seems surprised. On July 4: "She talked last night about the disillusionment of a young woman, the sensuality of men, alien to her at first. . . ."[14] This conversation, painful for the wife trying to defend herself against her husband's implicit reproaches, was useful to Tolstoy: "The whole drama of the story, which I haven't been successful with all this time, is now clear in my head. He cultivated her sensuality."[15] Three weeks later he records: "Finished it in rough. I realize now how I must reorganize it all, bringing in love and compassion for her."[16] Was he thinking of Sofia?

His relations with his children continued to sadden him, if one can rely on a letter written in August to Alexeyev: "Of my children, only Masha is close to me in spirit. The others, poor things, are only oppressed by the fact that I'm always around, reminding them of what their conscience demands of them."[17] Some days earlier he had observed that between him and Lyova (his son Lev), "mutual animosity leapt forth like a wild animal that had broken loose from its chain";[18] and as for his youngest sons, Andrey and Mikhail, he found them "amazingly underdeveloped."[19]

He was not satisfied with *The Sonata*. If he had thought of it purely as a work of literature, not a work of piety, he would surely not have published it "as is"; he would probably have put it aside and taken it up again later, as he did with so many of his other writings. He could not see his way to finishing, and on September 21 he noted: "Finally decided to revise it; there's no need for the murder."[20] On October 6 he recast chapter 20, and four days later records: "looked through and revised everything from the beginning."[21]

He had already written on August 29: "Thought about the fact that I'm fussing over my writing of *The Kreutzer Sonata* out of vanity; I don't want to appear in public as not fully finished, clumsy, even poor. . . . A perfectly finished story won't make my arguments more convincing. I must be a holy fool in my writing too."[22] So he proved to be, since a version of the story circulated under cover beginning in October 1889. It was only after many vicissitudes that the censors authorized its publication in June 1891.†

* Sixteen manuscripts of it are extant in the Tolstoy Museum and in the Tolstoy archives in the Lenin Library.

† From that time forward, many of Tolstoy's writings appeared first abroad. Three editions of *The Sonata* were published in Berlin in 1890, and the definitive one by Elphidine in Geneva in the same year. *The Kreutzer Sonata* shocked puritan America, where the post office banned it.

* * *

Ivan Ilych had been the expression of Tolstoy's break with the vanities of this world; *The Kreutzer Sonata* was that of his resolve to detach himself from the shackles of the flesh. The effort was part of his scheme of general renunciation, of which it is the conclusion: tobacco, meat, alcohol, and finally sexual desire.

When Poznychev, the hero of the story, killed his wife thinking her unfaithful, the murder was not premeditated; but the symbolic murder of his own wife that Tolstoy perpetrated by writing *The Sonata* was. Indeed, the book has remote origins. For a long time Tolstoy had been thinking of a story he wanted to call *The Man Who Murdered His Wife*; he had noted down the plot on two half-sheets of notepaper folded twice. These sheets, according to Shklovsky, established through "paper, heading, and watermark that the sketch dates from the second half of the 1860s."[23] Its ultimate origin may even be earlier, for Tolstoy's hatred of his own sexuality always coexisted with the excesses to which it drove him. The feeling goes back to the young man's disgust with himself over his debauches at Kazan, and maybe to what he very clearly names in *The Sonata*: "impure solitude"[24] in his boyhood, an account of which he kept in his journal.

The Kreutzer Sonata begins with fresh confessions, in which Tolstoy takes up two themes already present in *Anna Karenina* and rehandled later in *Resurrection*. Their persistence in Tolstoy's novels indicates the importance they assumed in his own life: the hero of *The Sonata* was encouraged as a young man, just as Tolstoy had been by Tante Toinette, to have an affair with a married woman. Also like Tolstoy, he showed his fiancée his diary, "from which she could learn something, if but a little, of my past, especially about my last liaison."[25]*

A direct echo of the conversation Tolstoy had with Sofia in July is to be found in the opening pages of the story: the husband is going to pervert this "innocent girl, sold to a profligate . . . the sale accompanied by certain formalities."[26]† He will initiate her in a pleasure akin to that of smoking: "Pleasure from smoking just as from that, if it comes at all, comes later. The husband must cultivate that vice in his wife in order to derive pleasure from it himself."[27]

Tolstoy was not such a misogynist as he has been thought. In *The Sonata* the wife is perverted by her husband; as early as 1884 he had

* Tolstoy was well aware of the wound that reading his youthful diary had inflicted on Sofia, and once again he was trying to exonerate himself by justifying the gesture.

† On November 8, 1889, Tolstoy wrote in one of his notebooks that marriage is "the acquisition of the right to 'own' a woman." In this he gives perhaps one of the deepest reasons for his hostility to marriage—he sees it as the most humiliating form of property. (*Journaux et carnets*, vol. I, p. 1112)

ended *What Then Must We Do?* with an impressive "Appeal to Women," in which he was already proclaiming that "woman [is] depraved by man and descend[s] to his level."[28] That book, which was about poverty and wealth, ended with a lyrical outburst: "Women—mothers . . . in your hands alone is the salvation of the men of our world."[29] In 1905, in his Afterword to Chekhov's story *The Darling*, he was to say that "men cannot do what is loftiest, best, and brings man nearest to God—the work of loving, of complete devotion to the beloved. . . ." That is why Tolstoy condemned not women but "the fashionable woman's movement," founded on the refusal to admit that "the ideal of perfection for a woman cannot be the same as the ideal for a man."[30]

The Kreutzer Sonata is not an anti-feminist book, it is a pamphlet against marriage. The hero is in the same impossible situation as Tolstoy, for Christian union is only "lust legalized—an apish occupation,"[31] as he says elsewhere. Sooner or later "all husbands must either live dissolutely . . . or kill their wives as I have done."[32] There remains a third possibility, which tempted Tolstoy and which Poznychev considered, that of flight: "I think of running away from her, hiding myself, going to America."[33]

In real life Tolstoy chose a variant of the solution he had conceived for his hero. Like him, he would kill Sofia, but the murder would be lived out on the level of fantasy. *The Kreutzer Sonata* would be the most abominable letter of breaking off ever written to a woman and the most perfect crime without a corpse. In the novel, life in common or what is left of it—"a period of love—then a period of animosity; an energetic period of love, then a long period of animosity; a weaker manifestation of love, and a shorter period of animosity"[34]—leads the husband irresistibly to murder his wife. Just so, ever since the early eighties, Tolstoy's relations with Sofia, now passionate and now antagonistic, led him with the same inevitability to write *The Kreutzer Sonata*, the wife who ought to have been the path to God being in fact an obstacle that must be removed. And human love has to be murdered because it is a rival to the love of God: "One must cease to think of bodily love as something particularly noble" and understand that "love and union with love's object (whatever efforts may be made in verse or prose to show the contrary) never assist the pursuit of an end worthy of man, but make it even more difficult."[35]

The Sonata is an outlandish device for systematic destruction, in which the monstrous steamroller of rationalist logic relentlessly crushes love, reducing it in the end to an "animal condition degrading to human beings," far indeed from the "elevated and poetic condition that people generally try to see in it."[36]

Tolstoy had written pamphlets against alcoholism; here he pens propaganda against love. No holds are barred—aggression, invective, exaggeration, and virulence. Yet the will to edify and the bombast of the preacher that weigh down *The Sonata* do not utterly blot out the art of the writer; the scene of the husband murdering the wife is possibly one of the finest he ever wrote.

Tolstoy's private conflict, like Poznychev's, had coincided with his settling in Moscow. His moral isolation, his panic in the face of urban poverty, and the provocative absurdity of the life of the rich had become intolerable. The hero of *The Sonata* is in the same situation; when his wrath against Eve breaks out, Poznychev kills his wife; symbolically Tolstoy does it as well: he writes *The Kreutzer Sonata*. He wants to "settle accounts" with the flesh once and for all; and perhaps, while he is at it, with music also, because music arouses in him amorous feelings (he cannot hear it without weeping) and inclines him toward tenderness. He has his hero say: "Music makes me forget myself, my real position; it transports me to some other position not my own."[37]

Tolstoy condemns music because he is musical and sensuality because he is sensual. Maybe his hostility to wealth comes from being wealthy, to violence because he is violent, precisely as, contrariwise, he favored manual labor because he was clumsy and reason because he was unreasonable.

It is only when the husband-turned-killer looks at the face of his dead wife, "bruised and disfigured," that he forgets "himself, his rights, his pride, and for the first time discovers a human being in her."[38] The invisible bruises and wounds with which *The Kreutzer Sonata* had scarred Sofia's heart forever did not become evident to Tolstoy until long afterward. In April 1891 he confided to Chertkov: "There was something ill-natured about *The Kreutzer Sonata* . . . something bad about the motives that led me to write it, and so much bitterness has come from it." He added: "Any mention of it is terribly painful to me."[39]

The manuscript in its eighth version was finally read at the Kuzminskys' by Koni, the district attorney, and a second reading was given the next day at *The Mediator*. Three days later eight hundred lithographed copies circulated in St. Petersburg.[40] Tatyana Behrs-Kuzminskaya wrote to let her sister know of the success of the reading, and Sofia showed the letter to Tolstoy. "It is making an impression—good, I am delighted," says he in his journal for November 2.[41]

The furor created by *The Kreutzer Sonata* was indeed great. The reactions of critics and readers, whether enthusiastic, scandalized, or merely petrified, were numerous and in every case impassioned. Reviews in newspapers and even in book form appeared instantly, some before the work was printed.

To calm people down, and even more because of pressure from Chertkov, indeed almost under his constraint, for Chertkov wanted the "sexual teaching" of the Tolstoyans to be clear, Tolstoy wrote an Afterword to *The Kreutzer Sonata* indicating the conclusions that could be drawn from it. This Afterword is even more violent, more schematic, more brutal than the book itself. Perhaps Chertkov's dogmatizing influence is to be seen in this piece of a few pages, which Tolstoy wrote very swiftly, for he was already engrossed in a new project. On December 6 he had "looked through the whole of *The Kreutzer Sonata*, made deletions, corrections, and additions," and he had noted at the same time: "I'm having clearer and clearer thoughts about Koni's story. In general I've been in a state of inspiration for two days now."[42] What this means is that Tolstoy had just begun *Resurrection*, for that is the title he ultimately gave to "Koni's story."

Chertkov pressed him for a longer piece for the Afterword, but Tolstoy replied with some annoyance: "Although I've started writing an afterword, I probably won't finish it, and so the passage about the ideal of mankind being not fertility but the fulfilling of the law for achieving the Kingdom of Heaven, which coincides with purity and continence, will have to be left as it is."[43]

The "conclusions" Tolstoy suggests to his readers are, properly speaking, raving mad, in spite of their presentation in the numbered form so dear to Tolstoy. The second preaches that "violation of the promise of fidelity given in marriage should suffer the penalty of public opinion at least as much as the non-payment of a debt, or as commercial fraud"; the third states that "continence, an essential condition of human dignity outside marriage, is still more necessary within marriage."[44] A year later, in a letter dated September 16, 1890, Tolstoy was to take a more conciliatory line, and admit that "a man ought not to set himself the task of chastity, but only the approach towards chastity." The main thing was "the inner recognition of the superiority of chastity over dissoluteness, and the preferability of greater purity over lesser."[45]

Certain pages of *The Kreutzer Sonata* have about them a touch of caricature that makes one forget the fine peroration. Tolstoy builds his whole argument on the teaching of Christ, according to which celibacy, because it enables one to be wholly at God's disposal, is preferable to marriage. If he had not relied so much on invective but had tempered his own resentment against Sofia with a more reasoned treatise on married morality, the reader might have understood more easily that Tolstoy is against marriage because it distracts man from God, reduces "his range of action,"[46] and prevents him from going ever onward "towards new horizons."[47] He had already expressed the same idea much more clearly in October 1887, when he was trying to dissuade his twenty-one-year-old son Ilya from marrying: "Marriage and the birth of children offer so many joyful things to look forward to that it seems as if these things actually constituted life itself, but that is a dangerous delusion. . . . The most selfish and wicked life is the life of two people united in order to enjoy life, and the highest calling is that of people who live in order to serve God by bringing good into the world, and uniting with each other for that purpose."[48]

Instead of transmitting this message clearly, *The Kreutzer Sonata*, by preaching the absolute rejection of sexuality, gives the impression of expounding a sort of psychological self-castration.

Once again Tolstoy refutes the teaching of the Church in the name of Christ's word, and it is by invoking the Gospel that he brings into question the whole theology of marriage. But there is a violence in his preachment, a vindictiveness against the flesh, and finally an exacerbated sensuality, which are far from the true Christian attitude. The flesh is there, muzzled and conquered, but still not accepted, and once more Tolstoy's doctrine is one of negation.

SEVENTEEN

The Aftereffects of The Kreutzer

AT THE REQUEST of his daughter Tatyana, who wanted to put on a play at Yasnaya Polyana with friends and neighbors for the year-end celebrations, Tolstoy had, in November 1889, resumed work on *The Fruits of Enlightenment*, begun in 1886. It was a satire on the fad of spiritualism* which had originated among the Anglo-American peoples and was raging in Russia at the time. In addition, the play gave Tolstoy another chance at contrasting the frivolity of a landowning family with the seriousness of their peasants and servants. "They're performing my play, and really I think it's having an effect on them and that in the bottom of their hearts they are all conscience-stricken and therefore dejected."[1]

In the early months of 1890 Tolstoy was continually revising his play. He explains to Chertkov with a kind of shame that he has worked on it for ten days without stopping,[2] and he records in his diary that he cannot stop thinking up "new details for the comedy."[3] "A work of art must be sharpened for it to penetrate," he remarks, with Gogol's *Inspector General* in mind.[4]

Tolstoy felt himself growing older. He has stomach pains, of the kind he was already complaining of at the Urusovs' the previous year. He speaks of the "wasting of the muscles of the arms and legs";[5] and in March he thinks he has jaundice. He who was so proud of his physical strength sees in its decline the coming of a kind of inner renewal. "Fine misfortune

* Tolstoy had already described in *Anna Karenina* a spiritualist séance at the Countess Lydia's.

if I die carnally . . . love is this aspiration to be done with what perishes in one's personality."[6] He thinks physical decay unimportant and even productive of a certain enrichment. "My intellectual vigour does not enter into the awareness of my spiritual self. This consciousness consists in something else (in humility, devotion to the love of God), in that to which most of the time intellectual and physical vigour are an obstacle."[7]

Tolstoy at sixty-one was still putting questions to himself about his identity, but he was beginning to do so in new terms. He wondered what he was to be after death. "Shall I be myself? Myself?"[8] And he has a hunch that he will not be able to answer that question—to him so fundamental that he has been asking it since boyhood—until he has "clear knowledge" of what he means by self, until he stops thinking of self as "something quite material: which drinks and eats and breathes."[9] Though his physical powers were diminishing, his intellectual vigor was still intact.

On February 3, after a conversation with "the good Marya Mikhaylovna,* Tolstoy notes that he "told her the story of the saint's life and the music teacher," and then adds: "It would be good to write it up."[10] The story was that of Father Sergey, a holy hermit who was tempted by pride, then by love, to which he fell. In this story, begun in 1891 and finished seven years later, Tolstoy treated the problem of lust in a much more interesting way than he had done in *The Kreutzer Sonata*: the themes of flight and atonement foretell his own attitude on the eve of his death. In the story, just as in *The Devil*, the first sketch of which he wrote in ten days in 1889† and finished in 1898, Tolstoy, by limiting himself to a description of the power of sexual desire on men, proved more convincing than he had been in his diatribe against the flesh in *The Kreutzer Sonata*. At that same time he had an idea for a play that would treat "the despair of a man who has seen the light and has brought his light into the darkness of life . . . and suddenly the darkness becomes darker still."[11]‡

When a problem or a stray event struck him, Tolstoy sometimes noted it only in his memory and seemed to forget it for years on end. He himself observed in November 1889: "When I'm in a self-assured mood, I think that the themes of my writing are like bottles of Kefir; one bottle gets drunk—the writing gets done—and the others go sour."[12]

* The gypsy woman whom his brother Sergey finally married after she had borne him four children.

† On November 10, 1889, Tolstoy had noted: "After dinner I unexpectedly began to write the story of Friedrichs"; and on the nineteenth: "Wrote all morning, finished Friedrichs more or less." (*Tolstoy's Diaries*, vol. I, pp. 269, 270)

‡ This is the subject of *And the Light Shineth in the Darkness*, which he began in 1896.

Some days later he enters in his diary the fact that he has thought a great deal about Koni's story: *Resurrection* has already ousted *The Fruits of Enlightenment*. Meanwhile, he kept working on the Afterword and the final revision of *The Kreutzer Sonata* until April 24.

All the same, intense literary activity did not interrupt Tolstoy's religious quest. At the end of February 1890 he went again to Optina-Pustyn. This monastery, founded in 1821, seems to have been for many Russians a spiritual watering place where they went to take the waters of the spirit. It was his third pilgrimage.* He stayed from February 27 to March 1. Life in a convent struck him as mere "spiritual sybaritism."[13] But he was "touched" by Boris, a young monk who was a cousin of Sofia's; "Amvrosy, on the contrary, is pathetic, impossibly pathetic with his temptations."[14]

Back at Yasnaya Polyana, Tolstoy wrote to his friend Professor Wagner on March 25, 1890,† that he had been struck to see "people there burning with true love for God and mankind, and at the same time considering it necessary to stand for several hours a day in church, take communion, and give and receive blessings, thereby paralyzing the active power of life in themselves."[15]

Tolstoy was now getting letters from all over the world. People of many different kinds wrote to consult him on literary, political, and, most particularly, religious questions. He used the exchange of letters as a platform to expound his ideas. In a letter of April 1890 he discusses the confinement of lunatics, telling his correspondent that "if people were to refuse for their own safety, to lock up . . . madmen and so-called criminals, they could concern themselves with seeing to it that more madmen and criminals are not created. . . ."[16]

Writing to E. B. Getz, a correspondent for several foreign newspapers who came to Yasnaya Polyana in May to get clarification on anti-Semitism, Tolstoy agrees that the persecution of the Jews will go on, "just as in America the persecution of better, cheaper, and more industrious workers than the Americans—the Chinese—will not cease." Even so, he thinks that everybody should give up the law of an "eye for an eye and assimilate the true Christian principles of life."[17]

Although overworked, Tolstoy kept up his interest in *The Mediator* and suggested to L. P. Nikiforov, who was helping him at the time, the

* He had been there in 1877 and in 1881.

† N. P. Wagner was professor of zoology at St. Petersburg University and a spiritualist; he feared that Tolstoy had taken him as a model for the professor in *The Fruits of Enlightenment* and was "vexed" by it. (*Journaux et carnets*, Paris: Gallimard [Pléiade], tome II, p. 29)

translation and publication of a "little book by a very original and courageous poet called Walt Whitman."[18]*

Both Tolstoy and Whitman had prophets' faces and athletes' bodies. And the likeness between them went beyond simple physical resemblance. Of course, Long Island, even in the early nineteenth century, differed greatly from Yasnaya Polyana, but each at his end of the world led the same free life close to nature, which set them (as the poet put it) "in concord with the soil of the earth, the trees, and the wind." The Front Street terminal of the Brooklyn ferry may not have been exactly like the Kiev road, but it was there that Whitman as a child got to know coachmen and bus drivers, just as Tolstoy had discovered "the people" by mixing from childhood with pilgrims and working with peasants. Both men glorified manual labor: Whitman went from farmhand to typographer before becoming a journalist, and Tolstoy turned the making of boots into a spiritual exercise. At seventeen, the American poet was a teacher on Long Island, as the Russian novelist was at Yasnaya Polyana; a school-master as odd as Tolstoy, he preferred chatting and playing with his pupils to traditional instruction. Every summer Tolstoy joined in haymaking; Whitman went home to his island at harvest time, working just enough to make the little money he needed to live: Tolstoy would have liked to be a Fool of God, Whitman's tramp existence made him a fool of humanity. Tolstoy dressed like a mujik, Whitman took care always to look like an American laborer.

Just as Turgenev, the established writer, had introduced Tolstoy to literary circles, so did the famous philosopher Emerson for Whitman. The American was an abolitionist, the Russian denounced serfdom. Tolstoy hated war and, like Whitman, became a pacifist from seeing battlefields and campaign hospitals—though the siege of Sevastopol was nothing like the battle of Fredericksburg.

Whitman was to a certain degree hostile to progress and considered "science the whore of war and industrialization," a dictum Tolstoy himself might have uttered. Both, moreover, were singers of "the self";

* In February 1889 Tolstoy noted in his journal that G. Stewart, Whitman's friend, "a real eccentric Englishman," had come to see him. In June, Stewart sent him a copy of the English 1887 edition of *Leaves of Grass*, which is now in the Yasnaya Polyana library, heavily annotated. Tolstoy had then recorded: "Got books. Whitman, stupid verses." His suggestion a year later of publishing Whitman's poems in *The Mediator* shows that Tolstoy quickly revised his opinion. In 1900 he wrote to Edward Garnett, whose wife, Constance, was a great authority on Slav literature and did as much to introduce the Russian novel to England as Melchior de Vogüé did in France, that he ranked Whitman with Emerson, Ballou, and Thoreau "in a bright constellation, such as is rarely found in the literatures of the world." (*Tolstoy's Letters*, vol. II, p. 588)

and of these two great individualists, while one exalted comradeship between men, the other did the same for universal love. They both thirsted for a new religion and believed the era of priesthood was past. But Tolstoy belonged to a dying world and Whitman to a world in the making, and their grand designs were utterly different: one wanted to establish the kingdom of God on earth, the other the kingdom of men.

Tolstoy not only kept up a worldwide political and literary correspondence, but in that decade he often wrote to his sons, preaching sermons to them that are not without humor: "What is incumbent upon us in our privileged situation," he wrote to Sergey on May 8, 1890, "is to get off the backs of the people we're sitting on."[19] In November he replied with severity to Lev Lvovich who had sent him two stories turned down by his publisher: "You have, I think, something very ordinary called talent. . . . In these two stories I find no sign of a genuine inner need to express yourself, or else you haven't found a sincere and genuine form of expression."[20]

During Tolstoy's visit to his brother Sergey in early May, it finally turned out that it was not jaundice but an "inflamed duodenum" that Tolstoy was suffering from. He became so ill that he was unable to write in his diary and had to dictate to Sofia. In one of these notes he explained that his letters were an opportunity to teach and those he received were a sourcc of inspiration. "Many of the ideas which I've been expressing recently don't belong to me but to people who . . . turn to me with their problems, quandaries, ideas and plans."[21] Thus Tolstoy reveals that "the basic idea," or better, the sentiments in *The Kreutzer Sonata*, "belonged to a certain woman, a Slav, who wrote me a letter, comical in its language but remarkable in its contents, about the oppression of women through sexual demands."[22]

Work in the fields began again on April 5 and alternated with literary work. On June 2 he began *Father Sergey* and continued revising his preface to a book on nonresistance by the American Universalist clergyman Adin Ballou. He did not on that account give up manual labor, and on July 15 he began on a new pair of boots.

During the summer there was always the same coming and going at Yasnaya Polyana. "The table was set for thirty people," he records on July 10. The comfort, a kind of opulence,* and the frivolity that pervade the house are most painful to him, but he remains free of illusions. He had long said that without his wife and children he would live the "life of a saint: I have reproached them for preventing me . . . and this

* Under date of June 25, 1890: "I ought to write a book, GLUTTONY." (The capital letters are Tolstoy's own.)

prevention is myself."[23] On that day, September 3, 1890, his notebook goes even further: "I am angry with my wife and children because they will not let me live as I want: I made them what they are. They are my sins."[24]

Strange people continue to come and see him—a cook deceived by his wife and "obviously on the verge of mental illness" made the trip to Yasnaya Polyana on the advice of a Moscow physician, to ask Tolstoy how to behave.[25]

"*Father Sergey* grips me more and more strongly," he had noted in April: what interests him is the problem of "the temptation of worldly fame and celebrity—i.e., a delusion for the purpose of concealing one's faith."[26] As always, he is himself close to his hero, for in spite of his longing for saintliness, Tolstoy was not immune to the temptations either of pride or of the flesh. He noted again on August 19, 1890, "I remember my ignoble acts: Fyodor's wife—the pool, mirror,"[27] and in the notebook of the same date: "lust in the water."[28] He believed one ought to write about these "ignoble acts," but wondered whether it would be useful or harmful: "useful to know we are all alike, harmful that nothing is unclean."[29] Some days earlier he had written in the notebook: "For *Father Sergey*. Happiness of the man who has lost all and who can lean on nothing but God. He has recognized this support and solidity for the first time."[30]*

Tolstoy's reading was always extensive and varied. He was curious about everything; he read Sienkiewicz[31] as well as magazines from the United States, developing through these an interest in American political ideas. He finishes at last his preface to Adin Ballou's *Catechism of Non-resistance*, which became the essay *The Kingdom of God Is Within You*. During the summer Thoreau's *Civil Disobedience* interested him, and so did the ideas of William Lloyd Garrison about the blacks; they were close to his own.[32] On April 20 he "read Ibsen's *Wilde Ente* [*The Wild Duck*] in German. Not good,"[33] and next day another play, "*Rosmersholm*. Not bad so far." He was to read more Ibsen when work in the fields was over. In November he took up Rousseau's *Emile*, Coleridge, and a treatise on early Church history; then Albert de Broglie's book on the Church and the Roman Empire in the fourth century and a story by Maupassant in translation—"wonderful."[34] He read the *Odyssey* with the girls[35] and discovered in Renan's *Future of Science* an idea that appealed to him: "for

* By now, Tolstoy jotted down more and more often in his *Notebooks* ideas that he later took up in his *Diary*. The first mention is often more striking than the later elaboration. "For *Father Sergey*, I must describe the new state of happiness . . . of a man who has lost everything and can't lean on anything but God. For the first time he gets to know how secure that support is." (*Tolstoy's Diaries*, vol. I, p. 291)

mankind before the scientific view of things, the supernatural was the natural."[36]

Every morning before starting to write, Tolstoy went for a walk during which he prayed: "Prayer continues to fortify me and get me going."[37] Some days later he adds: "I pray always with the same delight; it is not for men, but for Thee and in Thy presence that I work."[38]

But Tolstoy's endeavors would not be complete if he did not devote part of his time to some victims of injustice. At the end of November he spent two days at Krapivna with his daughter Masha and his Kuzminskaya niece, Vera, Tanya's daughter, to attend the trial of four mujiks accused of killing a fifth. Tolstoy's presence always inclined the judges to mercy, so the sentences were less heavy than they might have been. He took notes on the trial, the judges, the court, and the procedure.[39]

Chertkov was beginning to lay his hands on his master's works. On June 20 he sent M. N. Chistiakov to Yasnaya Polyana as his representative to take possession of all Tolstoy's diaries. "It would give offence" (to Sofia, of course, as Tolstoy notes), and he contents himself with having certain marked passages copied out by Masha.[40] But Chertkov was already holding a good many manuscripts; at the end of December he sent back the one titled "On Art" for Tolstoy to rework.[41]

Sofia was shackled to *The Kreutzer Sonata.* In a letter of January 15, 1889, Tolstoy let Chertkov know that she was finishing the fair copy of the final version in order to send it to Danish and American translators and to Melchior de Vogüé for a French edition.

Sofia was facing total failure and tried to account for it. "I have done everything in my power to achieve a slightly deeper and more spiritual intimacy with him—it's what I want more than anything else in the world." She had exerted all her strength to that end and read his diary in secret "in the hope of discovering how I could help him, and myself, understand how best we might be reunited." But reading him only "reduced [her] to even greater despair."[42] Silence reigned between them, and she resented it. "Days, weeks, months pass when we say not so much as a word to one another."[43] This was true but not wholly true, since in August Tolstoy wrote: "Drank coffee and talked frankly with Sonya for almost the first time [in] many years. She spoke about prayer sincerely and intelligently. . . ."[44]

The Tolstoyans she can stand less and less. "To think that these are the great man's disciples!—these wretched specimens of human society, windbags with nothing to do, wastrels with no education."[45] Tolstoy was slowly drifting away from her. Ultimate act of desertion, he entrusted the copying of all his manuscripts to his daughters. Sofia thought of "killing herself," of "running away," and even of "falling in love."[46] She was so jealous of Masha that "sometimes she feels like letting [her] go."[47] And she wonders why—though she disapproves of the idea—she should not let Masha marry Tolstoy's secretary Biryukov as she wants to do: "Let her go with Biryukov!"[48]

Wandering around Yasnaya Polyana like a beaten dog, Sofia would half-heartedly set the children to work. One evening in the late winter when Sofia was playing the piano with Tatyana, Tolstoy took his daughter's place. "We didn't get it right at first, and he went for me peevishly."[49] Though she nagged her husband, he was not indifferent to her, but he saw her as "a woman without convictions, weak, but *journalière*, fickle, and exhausted by the unnecessary cares [she] takes upon herself."[50]

It is true that she wound up as the one responsible for everything. Peasants from a village near Yasnaya Polyana had stolen some birch trees: Tolstoy and Sofia decided to teach them a lesson by first suing them and then forgiving them, but the machinery of the law took its course without their knowledge; the offense was criminal and the mujiks were sentenced to "6 weeks in jail and a 27-ruble fine."[51]

The verdict appalled Tolstoy: "Lyovochka was in despair at the thought of Yasnaya peasants going to prison. . . ."[52] Although he had agreed to the arrangement for dealing with them, he now held her to blame for consequences that neither of them had foreseen, and it was Sofia who had to meet the offenders when they came to beg for mercy.[53]

She thought that "being expected to manage the estate and the household 'in a Christian spirit' " was "a heavy cross to bear"; she felt she was losing her judgment in "this chaos of innumerable petty worries"; she believed it was "driving [her] insane."[54]

Since *The Sonata*, she had lost her inner security, already badly shaken, and she fretted about everything: the education of the youngest children; Tolstoy's physical and moral health; the older children's debts; the sale of the Samara estate; "the new edition and Volume 13, which contains the banned *Kreutzer Sonata*"; insurance, taxes, servants' passports; the balancing of accounts. To this already long list she adds: "Misha's nightshirts and Andryusha's boots and sheets . . . for all this I am directly, inescapably responsible, as well as for the copying of manuscripts."[55]

Tolstoy regretfully observes that "Sonya is overcome by requests for money from her sons," and he worries about it. Surely "it would be better if she were to give up her literary property rights at least. How restful for her, how morally good for her sons and how joyful for me, how useful to men and pleasing to God."[56]

"She's ill all the time and afraid of being pregnant,"[57] he notes early in July, but two weeks later he remarks that she still refuses "to sleep separately."[58] To Sofia's regular terrors is now added that of not being loved and of appearing ridiculous in everybody's eyes. This fear led her to pursue a course of self-justification that lasted the rest of her life. As soon as *The Sonata* was published, she wrote an afterword of her own—*Who Is to Blame?*—a novel in which she took up Tolstoy's themes from a woman's point of view. Her family had a hard time to stop her from publishing it. After Tolstoy's death she wrote *My Life* to answer Chertkov's attacks, in a last attempt to prove her innocence.

For the time being she takes on "the daily task," regardless of all her other duties, of copying ten pages of the diaries of Tolstoy's youth. As a matter of fact, this chore is the only thing that interests her: she is looking in the past for an explanation of her present unhappiness and finding food for her jealousy. "I have been copying out his diaries in a frenzy, drunk with jealousy and agitation whenever I read anything to do with women."[59] Being thoroughly honest, she tries in vain to understand her husband, and she is struck by the fact that "along with all the debauchery, he actually seeks out opportunities to 'do a good deed' every day."[60]

The year's end sees them reconciled, but Sofia was almost outraged that her husband should return to her. Her disillusionment gets worse as she copies from the diary such sentences as: "There is no such thing as love, only the need for intercourse and the practical need for a life companion." Having Tolstoy return to her arms seems almost to depress her. "The coldness and severity melted, and the end was the same as always."[61]

A degree of gaiety around her could not distract her from her obsession about being pregnant again or from her fear of ridicule. "I am ashamed at the thought that everyone will know and people will mechanically repeat the joke circulating in Moscow society: 'there goes the real epilogue to *The Kreutzer Sonata*.' "[62]

The Christmas holidays were at their peak: "In the evening the servants all came in dressed as mummers and danced to the harmonica and piano." But her mood was sad. "These rowdy parties always make me depressed."[63] Tolstoy and Sofia were perhaps more at one than they knew, for on the same day Tolstoy wrote in his diary: "dancing in the evening . . . unceasing moral depression."[64]

Yasnaya Polyana was now to Tolstoy more and more of a gilded prison; to Sofia, an inn whose guests she disliked.

In January 1891, Sofia corrected the last proofs of *The Kreutzer Sonata*, "without being as depressed as she has been," remarks Tolstoy. Copying out her husband's diary she is overwhelmed by the "coarse, cynical lechery" described on a page torn out from "Lyovochka's diaries about the Crimean war and Sevastopol." She was equally struck by the "connecting thread between Lyovochka's old diaries and his *Kreutzer Sonata*."[65] This link was not merely in her imagination; it really was remorse at the memory of his soldierlike debauchery, which weighed on his conscience, that Tolstoy was trying to exorcise by the denial of sexuality proclaimed in *The Sonata*.

As soon as Tolstoy's journals were fair-copied by his wife, he reread them: "And it hurt me. And I began to talk to her irritably and infected her with my anger."[66] The next day he concluded by forbidding her "to copy out his diaries."[67]

Sofia thought that *The Sonata* had been aimed at her and had "destroyed the last vestige of love between [them]." She tried to put off the track all those who were at one in pitying her, "from the Tsar himself down to Lev Nikolayevich's brother and his best friend [and childhood companion Dimitry] Dyakov."[68] With this in mind she went so far as to appeal to the Tsar. She obtained an audience on April 13, 1891, and begged Alexander III for permission to publish the banned novel in the thirteenth volume of the *Complete Works*. This move was intended to make people discount the idea that she had been her husband's model for the heroine. She also hoped to prevent Tolstoy from giving *The Sonata* to *The Mediator*, as he thought of doing, for she did not want Chertkov to make use of the work, either as a rival for Tolstoy's heart or as a publisher.

Tolstoy was furious at this intervention. "Her seeking the good graces of the Sovereign has been disagreeable for me," he noted in the diary for April 13, and the next day he wrote to Chertkov: "My wife returned from St. Petersburg yesterday where she saw the Emperor. . . . He promised to allow *The Kreutzer Sonata* to be published, which doesn't please me at all; there was something bad about the motives which led me to write it."[69] He felt that Sofia's reasons for acting as she did were not wholly self-interested, and he recognized that "she is impulsive, but well-disposed towards me."[70]

A month earlier she had spoken to him about this plan to publish the book, "not understanding how this depressed [him]."[71] The next day, to cut the ground from under her feet, Tolstoy had said "with difficulty and with trepidation" that he was going to announce "that everyone would have the right to print [his] writings."[72] This caused another battle. Sofia argued that Tolstoy must not dispose of "copyrights which belong to [his] children."[73] All the same, she felt "material considerations" to be "paltry compared to the pain of our estrangement."[74] She asked forgiveness for her impatience and they wept together. "After dinner she came up to me, started to kiss me, saying she would do nothing to oppose me. . . . I was very, very glad."[75]

After these troubles over the publication of *The Sonata* there came a rapprochement like those which took place between the hero and heroine of the novel: "outbursts of passion . . . followed by periods of prolonged coldness."[76] But these patchings-up were marred for Sofia by melancholy as she reflected: "If only people who read *The Kreutzer Sonata* so reverently had an inkling of the love-life that he leads. . . ."[77]

Tolstoy was then correcting and transcribing "On Non-resistance."[78] He was "writing abundantly" but complained of "advancing slowly." He feared that he had "dug too deep" for his essay "On Art."[79] Sofia, as observant as ever, had noted: "It is hard for him, as an artist, to write these weighty articles, but he cannot do his own artistic work."[80]

He went on "teaching." Sofia said he was "writing sermons which masquerade as articles";[81] some of his letters are in fact real manifestos. Thus he answered Hamilton Campbell, a minister of the Church of Scotland, who had asked him about some points of his doctrine: Miracles? "Faith in the miracle excludes faith in the teaching." The divinity of Christ? "If he is a man, the chief purpose of his advent is his teaching . . . but if he is God, his teaching is only a small part of his significance."[82]

Tolstoy was full of go; he thought his "first, early novels were unconscious creations. Since *Anna Karenina* . . . I've been dissecting, separating, analysing; now I know what's what and I can mix it all together again and work in this mixture."[83]

He was reading Pascal again and observed that "some of the *Provincial Letters* written with such love are superfluous, but the *Pensées* are works of God."[84] He thinks Montaigne "old."[85] He read Ibsen, as well as Heine or Plato, in French translations.[86]

Tolstoy was soon to give another proof of his determination to purify himself of the sin of property. He was hurt more than he liked to admit by the criticisms that reached him, some of them insulting letters.* In

* In August 1890 he had already noted "insulting anonymous letters—the article in *Le Temps* copied out (and sent)." (*Journaux et carnets*, tome II, p. 214)

February he took note of a Chicago paper that had exhibited him and Booth, the founder of the Salvation Army, "as examples of pharisaism—saying one thing and doing another."[87]

In April, accordingly, he decided to practice what he preached and to distribute his possessions among his heirs. To do this he had to sign a deed of gift, and thereby "to acknowledge the right of property," which "humiliated him in his principles."[88]

After some discussion the division of the estate took place. "Masha refuses hers, naturally."[89]* She had of course renounced her share out of Tolstoyan conviction. Sofia, practical as ever, had her daughter's portion kept in reserve, and the latter was thrilled to get it back later, when she married a penniless young aristocrat in 1897. Yasnaya Polyana was left to Sofia and the youngest son, Ivan.† The Nikolskoye estate, Samara, various pieces of land, and the Moscow house were divided among the eight other children. All this talk of business and property displeased Tolstoy. He had "evil thoughts of going away"[90] and comforted himself by going to visit a prison and a slaughterhouse, and by mowing hay.

Visitors came with the summer. Sofia noted that "a German from Berlin" has come to see Tolstoy.[91] Another of the guests was Repin, who came to paint a portrait of Tolstoy praying, and a second showing him in the vaulted room. The sculptor Ginzburg arrived to make a bust and a statuette of him standing.[92] As usual, Alexandrine spent a few days in July, and Charles Richet, the French psychologist, was there in August.[93]

A bad harvest caused a shortage. "Everyone is talking about a famine . . . how disgusting it is."[94] Social chitchat about human suffering Tolstoy always found intolerable. (The reader will recall how that very thing occasioned his break with Turgenev.) Tolstoy thought that true charity should never be a source of entertainment for rich people, and that they should not "begin to do good because of some particular event."[95]

Tolstoy was still working away at his piece "On Non-resistance," but with famine and its problems at hand, he wanted again to write about "gorging" and did in fact compose an article that he first called "Gluttony" but which he eventually published as *The First Step*; he was outraged to see the rich wasting food while peasants went starving.

Out of the same urge to dissociate himself from everything connected

* At the time of the final signature of the deed, the following summer, Tolstoy remarked: "Tanya and Lyova [Lev] were suggesting to" Masha that she was committing "a low action" by refusing her property. (*Tolstoy's Diaries*, vol. I, p. 318)

† Tolstoy himself had inherited it by virtue of being the youngest son.

with wealth and ownership, Tolstoy returned to his idea of giving up author's rights in all his writings subsequent to 1881, the year of his "conversion." On July 14 he noted: "a talk with my wife, still on the same subject of renouncing the copyright of my works."[96] The nineteen lines that follow are crossed out: no doubt they were about the scene that ensued.

Sofia, though, records it at length in her own diary. When, earlier, Tolstoy had told her what he intended, she had seen only the legal aspect of the question. Now that he wanted to publish his decision in the press, she suddenly saw the psychological implications and understood for the first time that this renunciation was "another way of publicising his dissatisfaction with his wife and family."[97]

Enraged by this remark, Tolstoy at the climax of the scene shouted "Get out! Get out!" Sofia ran into the garden like one demented and was bent on throwing herself under a train. She was brought back to reason and to the house by the Kuzminsky brother-in-law, who happened by the purest chance to be in her path, having been diverted from his own route by "a swarm of flying ants."[98] But she set out again at once, this time toward the river to drown herself. On the way she saw a dog that she thought was a wolf, grew frightened, and turned homeward.

That day shook Sofia's already tightly strung system. She told her husband she "could no longer live with him as his wife."[99] This he accepted, happy surely to be able to conform to his own teaching in *The Sonata*. But a few days later, early in the morning, "Lyovochka woke [her] with passionate kisses."[100] Not only did she yield, but she confesses: "His passion dominates me too, but I do not want it, my whole moral being cried out against it."[101]

Tolstoy then left to spend a week with his brother at Pirogovo. He did not want to go back to Moscow. Once again Sofia was faced with the dilemma of leaving her sons by themselves, for they had their studies to carry on, or of being separated from husband and daughters, for "if Lyovochka is moved to Moscow he will only be angry and fretful."[102]

She went to Moscow to see Andrey and Mikhail and came back after two weeks to Yasnaya Polyana. There she found Tolstoy much disturbed by the publication without his permission of parts of a letter of his, written in early July to the writer Leskov. In it he had criticized those who were organizing the famine relief:

> I think that good deeds ought not to be done suddenly on the occasion of a famine, but that whoever does good, did it yesterday and the day before, and will do it tomorrow and the day after, and during a famine and not

> during a famine. . . . I am writing this for people who assert that to collect money or to obtain it and hand it round is a good deed, not realising that a good deed is only a deed of love, and a deed of love is always a deed of sacrifice. . . . The most effective remedy against the famine is to write something which might touch the hearts of the rich.[103]

Which is what he had attempted himself by writing "Gluttony."

If Tolstoy was greatly put out by the publication of this letter, it was because he was now in a quite different state of mind. On September 18 he says: "didn't get to sleep till 4 o'clock, still thinking about the famine."[104] He could no longer contain himself: the famine had taken on the proportions of a national disaster. He wanted to go and see on the spot what was happening and what he could do. On September 19 he went back to his brother's at Pirogovo, which was a badly stricken region. Before leaving he said to Sofia that "he was tormented by thoughts of the famine; we should organise canteens where the hungry could be fed . . . but above all people should take some personal initiatives," and he added "he hoped [she] would donate money."[105]

During two whole days he visited villages with Tatyana and his brother's eldest daughter and called on a number of mayors. Back at Yasnaya Polyana, he found Sofia "unwell and out of sorts. . . . I said there was work to do here, feeding the starving. . . . A scene began."[106]

Amid this agitation, in spite of all the comings and goings, Tolstoy managed to work. At his brother's he reread *Father Sergey*: "to my surprise, not bad as it is."[107] In a following phrase, he observed that he had written a little "on non-resistance." He had made up his mind to write an article "On the Famine," but found it difficult, and thinking of the "invective" it would earn him, he was annoyed that he felt upset about it.

As early as September 25, Tolstoy decided to move in with his friend Rayevsky at Begichevka, in the middle of the region most afflicted. And he daydreamed: "It would be good if Sonya doesn't object."[108]

During the first half of October, Tolstoy worked on his famine article and also jotted down literary subjects. "What a good type for a work of fiction—a weak, corrupt, but kindly person."[109] This person was later to become the main character in his play *The Living Corpse.* He thought about him again in February 1894,[110] but did not write the play until 1900.

On October 26, 1891, two months after denouncing the organizers of famine relief in his letter to Leskov, Tolstoy set out with his daughter Masha and his niece Vera to spend the winter on the famine front.

IV

IMPATIENCE FOR THE KINGDOM OF GOD

EIGHTEEN

Famine

FAMINE opened the way to the flight so long dreamed of, and it promised at the same time the immersion in misery he had so much desired. Tolstoy did not become aware of the ambiguity of his own motives until some years later, when on April 29, 1898, he wrote: "I accepted money and undertook to use it only in order to have a pretext for getting away from Moscow. And I acted badly."[1]

During Tolstoy's journey with Tatyana, in early autumn 1891, to the region where famine was raging, he had taken part in the registration of famine victims and "discussed how best to go about setting up canteens. There and then Lyovochka decided what to do so he and his two daughters would have to move to the Rayevskys' for the winter."[2] In the event, he spent the greater part of two winters there, and did not return to Yasnaya Polyana until after the good harvest of 1893, which brought the territory back to normal.

The temptation to leave home and the longing to live and share in poverty had triumphed (for a time) over his reluctance to engage in private charity: "I don't myself know how I was dragged into this work of feeding the starving, this abominable work, because it isn't for me to feed those by whom I'm fed. . . . I now find myself distributing the vomit sicked up by the rich. I feel this is abominable and disgusting, but I can't stand aside; not that I don't consider it necessary—I consider I ought to stand aside—but I haven't the strength."[3] This to Feinermann from Begichevka in November 1891.

The life he was leading was rough and dangerous; there were typhus epidemics. Physical conditions were unsatisfactory and not comfortable; one had to be tough to survive them: Rayevsky died of pleurisy on November 26. "I loved him very much,"[4] Tolstoy records.

The relative isolation in which he now found himself favored the flowering of his inner life: he prayed more and more frequently, and on February 3, 1892, he observes: "If prayer is not the most important business in the world . . . then it is not prayer but the mere repetition of words."[5]

Tolstoy may have been caught up in this charitable enterprise by his natural generosity, but he still thought it a bad thing because it was contrary to his principles. For him the real problem was not to fill a void that one had helped to create, but to write according to one's own principles. So while he was organizing canteens and soup kitchens, Tolstoy produced "A Terrible Question," in which he explained that the "people are hungry because we eat too much"[6] and suggested that the government bring in grain from abroad. These words earned the *Russian Gazette*, which published his article on November 6, 1891, a warning growl from the Ministry of the Interior. Tolstoy had sent his pamphlet to Sofia from Begichevka on November 2,[7] begging her to oversee the corrections he had entrusted to Alexey Mitrofamovich Novikov.* The article was extremely violent ("There is no eloquence in it, and no place for it"), but Tolstoy thought it contained "something necessary and disturbing to everybody."[8]

His missionary spirit pulled his nearest family in its wake. Lev Lvovich went out to the province of Samara, and Tolstoy mentioned this, not without a certain pride, to the English publisher Fisher Unwin, who had offered to raise funds in England for the famine victims: "One of my sons is working for the same purpose in the eastern provinces, of which Samara is in the worst condition."[9]

Sofia, bored and anxious, had stayed in Moscow with Andrey, Mikhail, Alexandra, and Ivan. One fine morning she "jumped out of bed" and wrote a letter that she took by hand to the offices of the *Russian Gazette*.[10] In less than a week she had collected nine thousand rubles.

In early December 1891, Tolstoy, Masha, and Tatyana arrived in Moscow and spent ten days. Tolstoy noted on his return: "Joy. Relations with Sonya have never been so cordial. I thank Thee, Father. This is what I asked for,"[11] and he added that he was "in full health."

The father and his two daughters made a second stay, of three weeks,

* In 1889 and 1890 Novikov had been tutor to Tolstoy's children; he helped Tolstoy in the work of famine relief.

in early January 1892. On that occasion, Sofia could not resist her longing to leave with her husband, and she entrusted her four youngest children to Tatyana for a few days.

The trip was spoiled by the fact that "someone brought us an article in the *Moscow Gazette*. They had paraphrased Lyovochka's article 'On the Famine.' "[12] The magazine, unlike the *Russian Gazette*, was subservient to the government and had used "A Terrible Question" against Tolstoy: "They had treated [the article] as a proclamation and declared Lev Nikolayevich to be a revolutionary."[13]

Sofia stayed at Begichevka ten days. She lived "in one room"[14] with her husband and displayed her usual efficiency. She put the accounts in order and spent her mornings cutting some twenty "new coats and fur jackets"[15] for the most deprived. Yet Tolstoy in his diary says: "Sonya left today. I'm sorry for her. Relations with the people are very bad."[16]

Back in Moscow, she realized the seriousness of the press campaign against her husband. The hostile faction redoubled their efforts when the authorities learned that an English translation of the article, entitled "Letter on the Means for Helping the Famine-stricken Population," had appeared in the London *Daily Mail* on January 14 and 26, 1892. Sofia appreciated the danger: "I even had letters from St. Petersburg saying they had threatened to send us into exile, and urging me to go there immediately and do something about it."[17] It had also been rumored that Tolstoy might be arrested and shut up in the Suzdal Monastery.

She made move after move, wrote to the Minister of the Interior and to friends in favor at Court, and alerted Alexandrine Tolstoy, who spoke to the Tsar about the case. The Tsar reassured her: the authorities had no wish to turn the Red Count into a martyr. All the same, Sofia grew panicky about her family and wrote to her husband: "You will be the ruin of all of us with your provocative letters; where's the love and non-resistance in them? And you have no right with a family of 9 children to endanger me and them."[18]

Tolstoy continued to fight hunger, but that did not mean he had given up his real battle, that of "the word." In August 1893, he finished *The Kingdom of God Is Within You*, which had occupied him for two years and which now bore the subtitle, "Christianity not as a mystical doctrine but as a new understanding of life."[19] The formula sums up rather well his attitude toward religion at this period in his life. The piece is even more vehement than the preceding one. The apostle of nonviolence was no practitioner of it in the realm of letters. "Between the Churches and Christianity, not only is there nothing in common except the name, but they are two quite opposite and opposing principles. The one represents pride, violence, self-assertion, immobility, and death: the other humility, penitence, meekness, progress, and life."[20] Such an article was obviously not going to be published in Russia, but it was immediately translated in France, England, Germany, and the United States.

When extracts from chapter twelve of *The Kingdom* began to arrive in Russia, his account of the repressive acts of the Governor of Orel against a rebellious village was challenged by several persons, who pointed out that he had made things blacker than they were by charging that the executions had been carried out in front of the rebels' families. Tolstoy thereupon sent telegrams "asking all the translators to stop publication."[21]

To his indignation at the behavior of the powerful was added his deep disappointment in the local population: "Their interests are food, clothes, housing . . . and getting more money,"[22] he wrote his friend Prince Khilkov, then in exile in the Caucasus among the Dukhobors. The prince in turn was alarmed by certain aspects of the Dukhobors' behavior. Tolstoy was similarly grieved to discover, when some Quakers came to work at Begichevka, that "they tie themselves down to a belief in certain church dogmas, such as the resurrection and the divinity of Christ." He lamented that "they [hadn't] drawn the inescapable conclusion" of the negation of the state which should logically follow "from their position of non-resistance."[23]

He encountered disillusion everywhere. During one of his short stays at Yasnaya Polyana* he wrote on May 26, 1892: "More depressing relations than ever with the 'dark people'† . . . The childishness and vanity of their Christianity, the lack of sincerity."[24] He came back again in August, and the futility of his family's way of life pained him anew, in spite of the company of such old friends as Strakhov and Repin. It was then he put to himself the question that was to haunt him for the next eighteen years: "This isn't a thought, but on 13 August I made a note that it had become clear to me—not in a moment of anger but in a very peaceful moment—that I might, and probably will have to leave home."[25]

Tolstoy left the territory of the Riazan provincial government in July 1893. His life in the famine-stricken areas suited him in many ways; it enabled him to spend his energy without feeling that he was an

* He arrived on May 25, left on June 2, and came back for a stay from July 9 to 16 to sign the deed of gift. He then remained at Begichevka until July 29 to close down most of the food kitchens. He paid a last brief visit there on September 15 to write his draft report and conclusion. (*Tolstoy's Diaries*, vol. I, p. 320)

† "The Dark Ones" is what Sofia called the modest and unknown Tolstoyans; the expression was adopted by the whole family. They often used the French "Les Obscurs" as well.

accomplice of the rich. Even so, he gives a somewhat disillusioned summary of the period when he writes to N. N. Strakhov that this "stupid work which has been going on for two years" is finally coming to an end. He admits that "as always when you do work like this, you become sad, and unable to understand how people of our circle can live calmly, knowing that they have ruined and are completing the ruin of a whole people and, having sucked out of them all they can and sucking the last remnants now, can argue about God, the good, justice, science and art."[26] He added gloomily: "I've finished my article. It's being translated. . . . While I was writing it, I thought it would change the world."

This referred to his *Final Report on Help for the Famine-stricken*, which was published only outside Russia.* It was a cry of genuine indignation and an appeal for universal solidarity. Once again, Tolstoy was proposing the "so very simple" solution that mankind stubbornly refuses: "love need only increase to produce the same miracle as happened at the distribution of the five loaves; then everyone will eat their fill and there will even be something left over."[27]

Tolstoy detailed the results obtained by the end of 1891 and the reasons why he had chosen to organize soup kitchens rather than hand out food, which promotes trading. In February 1892 two hundred new canteens were feeding from ten to thirteen thousand people daily, and a hundred and twenty-four nurseries were taking care of three thousand children. Both types of institution functioned thanks to Russian donors and the many gift packages received from the rest of Europe as well as from the United States, which had made a notable contribution of seven shiploads of sweet corn.

Tolstoy was far from satisfied with these remarkable results. He had always felt the hollowness of "good works"; the doer of them seemed to him in "a situation as paradoxical as that of a parasite that seeks to nourish the plant that nourishes it."[28] His reservations about private charity were long established, dating back to his quarrel of 1861 with Turgenev. Tolstoy always goes to the heart of the matter: it is not symptoms but causes that he wants to cure, and for him the cause of all evils is simple—lack of love. He underlines yet again the "uselessness of the efforts of those who, without changing their relationship with the people, wish to come to their aid by handing out to them the wealth they have taken from them."[29]

When he came back to Moscow for good, in December 1893, he could

* It appeared in France under the title *La Famine* (*Vendu au profit des réfectoires gratuits du Comte Tolstoï*). (Published by Perrin, 1893.) The French subtitle refers to the fact that the book was sold throughout the world on behalf of the free canteens set up by Tolstoy.

stand the horrors of the city and its day-to-day mediocrity even less than before: "I want to do something heroic. I want to devote the rest of my life to the service of God. But He doesn't want me. Or doesn't want me to go the way I want to."[30]

He speaks of luxury, of moral foulness, of selling his books, of useless agitation, and he bursts out: "I can't overcome my melancholy. The main thing is I want to suffer, I want to shout out the truth which is burning me."[31]

NINETEEN

Master and Man

HOME ONCE MORE at Yasnaya Polyana, Tolstoy was glad to be back in his study; he began to write an epilogue to *The Kingdom of God*, and prepared an introduction to Amiel's *Journal*, which he was translating with Masha, and one to a Russian collection of some novels and short stories by Maupassant.*

In January 1894 he went to Moscow and wrote there but one article called "Toulon"[1] "on the hypnotic power of patriotism."[2] The Russian fleet had come into the harbor of Toulon in August 1893, and the political exploitation of this visit prompted an article by Tolstoy that appeared in Russian in Geneva under the title "Christianity and Patriotism." He rejects the idea that peace is ensured by preparing for war and deplores the "revanche" sentiments of the French. The article had a worldwide success; Tatyana mentions in her journal under date of March 14, 1894, the arrival of "an Editor of *Le Temps* . . . to ask about Papa's article. . . ."[3]

Tolstoy wondered anxiously whether he would have strength enough to carry out all his projects, and in January 1894 he asked Strakhov to tell him frankly "whether his talent has declined or not."[4] Although he agreed with Pushkin that "writing is the writer's business," he was more than ever convinced that "if a man doesn't strive with all his might to do what he says, he will never be good at saying what ought to be done; he

* The novels *Bel-Ami*, and *Mont-Oriol* and the short stories "Un Feu" and "Sur l'eau," according to a notebook entry of March 1894.

will never infect others"[5]—as he puts it to Maupassant's translator Nikiforov. He was ready to resume his crusade and tell mankind how to live; he hoped to "bring them all around to the same mood" by his new view of art, which he believed communicates and "infects people."[6]

He was also thinking of setting up an *International Mediator* in Switzerland, to be published in four languages: Russian, German, French, and English. He wants to help "elucidate the meaning of life, indicate the lack of correspondence between the forms of life and its meaning, and indicate means of establishing such a correspondence not by revolution or by the state, but by every individual person changing his own life": this for the benefit of "groups of people who are springing up in England . . . in Budapest . . . in Stuttgart . . . and in Finland."[7]

"The weight of the empty, luxurious and false Moscow life"[8] was always a terrible burden for Tolstoy, and the Sonya he found on his return was no longer the Sonya who had come to see him at Begichevka, she is the Sonya he had run away from in 1891. Her condition now was even worse: "the difficult, or rather nonexistent relations with my wife [have] been particularly burdensome to me."[9] Yet seeing her with Andrushka and Misha he exclaims: "What a wonderful mother and wife she is in a certain sense!"[10]

Tolstoy felt more than ever imprisoned. "I can't tear apart all these nasty cobwebs which hold me fast. And not because I haven't the strength, but because I'm morally unable to; I'm sorry for the spiders which have spun these threads."[11] How far all this from "the web of love" in which as a young man he dreamed of catching people! He was so alone within his family that he sometimes thought "we lose people who are not dead . . . they are worse than dead,"[12] and he was in such despair that he implored heaven: "Lord, receive me, teach me, enter into me. Be me or annihilate me. . . ."[13]

He was obsessed by the problem of art. His aesthetics, like the rest of his thoughts, was becoming more and more part of his religion: "Art is only true art when the inner striving coincides with the awareness of fulfilling the work of God."[14]

Summer came round again—he worked at the haymaking with Tanya and Masha; the other children must also have been somewhere in the fields, for on July 19 Tolstoy notes: "A difficult conversation with Sonya. He, Andryusha, had been telling her that the peasants in the hayfield . . . told him that Timofey was my son."[15]*

* Timofey was the son of Aksinya Bazykin, the peasant girl with whom Tolstoy had a prolonged affair before his marriage. Timofey was born to Aksinaya during this affair and thus his paternity has often been ascribed to Tolstoy, especially since he physically resembled the writer.

Visitors thronged as always: "a very interesting doctor, a Slav," arrived on August 22. This was Dushan Makovitsky, Tolstoy's Slovak translator. He came again in 1897 and 1901, and from 1904 onward was Tolstoy's physician.

As the numbers of the Tolstoyan faithful increased, their persecution intensified: F. A. Strakhov, who was in charge of the *Tolstoy Archives* (the clandestine publication of letters and articles by Tolstoy), found himself subjected to a police search. A woman doctor in Tula was imprisoned: she had already been arrested in November 1893 for propagating Tolstoy's ideas, and set free in January 1894 through the intervention of his friend Koni; now she was exiled to Astrakhan.

Tolstoy's principles made progress, little by little, even inside his own family. In September 1894 Tatyana gave away an estate of 180 hectares (450 acres) that she had inherited in the village of Ovsiannikovo. Tolstoy was pleased by this gesture, though his daughter kept the house and garden. He noted: "A strange thing . . . I have an unpleasant, uncomfortable feeling,"[16] but that did not stop him from going the next day to Tula to buy Tatyana some apple trees and help her to plant them. All the same, he remained very much alone and found "the spiritual wall that grows up between people frightening."[17] At the beginning of September he writes: "I thought up . . . a very vivid story about a master and his man."[18] A week later he goes to work: "In the evening took my pen and wrote the story of the snow storm." The story *Master and Man* is the wonderful parable of a rich merchant imprisoned by his possessions ("his money . . . his buying and selling")[19] who ends up sacrificing his life for his coachman and thus attains the inward liberty that Tolstoy was beginning to imagine. At the instant of death the hero of the story "felt himself free and that nothing could hold him back any longer."[20] Tolstoy finished this first version at the end of December, but gave it its final form only in June 1895.

Back in December 1893, longing to be persecuted for his ideas, he had admitted to his friend Rusanov what he called his weakness: "If I were to be put in prison and given pen and paper, how glad I should be to write something creative."[21] With *Master and Man* Tolstoy had yielded once again to his desire to write, but he now began an unremitting struggle against this temptation. Having tried to detach himself from the things of the world and from love, he now wanted to reject and demystify art as well; the outcome of this conflict, as of the other two, remained doubtful.

His new mission obsessed him; in a letter to Sofia of October 20, 1893, he began by worrying about what Dr. Zakharin had said about his son Lev's health, then suddenly plunged into a digression about literature attacking Chekhov, Zola, and Maupassant: "[they] don't even know what is good and what is bad, for the most part they consider what is bad to be good, and under the guise of art entertain the public with it and corrupt them."[22]

He also wrote to Lev Lvovich and Tatyana in Paris:* "Problems of the theory of art worry me incessantly . . . I am reading Knight's *Philosophy of the Beautiful*, and Guyon's *L'Art du Point de Vue Sociologique*, because one has to begin at the beginning." He lamented that Gay's picture *The Crucifixion*—in his view one of the high achievements in the history of painting—had been taken down on the ground of its being "a butchery that destroys pleasure."

Two days later he wrote to Gay that he was delighted his picture had finally been withdrawn from "The Wanderers' Exhibition,"† and that the word *butchery* had been used. "These words tell everything: one has to represent an execution . . . in such a way that it should be as nice to look at as a bunch of flowers. The fate of Christianity is astonishing! It's been made a domestic, pocketsize affair." According to Tolstoy, what had frightened people in this Crucifixion was its treatment, "which made the very story of Christ's life and death suddenly acquire its true accusatory importance."[23] This was the very thing that had so much moved him in the canvas.‡

At the end of 1894, husband and wife were on good terms: "Sonya arrived on September 25. Something thrillingly good. Mutual."[24] Perhaps his prayer a few days earlier had been granted: "Help me O Lord to establish love with the person who is closest to me."[25] Nonetheless, Sofia complains of her sick nerves [26] and of the many tasks that are hers:

> My husband . . . has loaded absolutely everything on to my shoulders, absolutely everything; the children, the estate, the house, his books, and then, with selfish, critical indifference, he despises me for doing all this. And what about his life? He walks and rides, writes a little, does whatever he pleases, never lifts a finger for his family, and exploits everything to his own advantage; the services of his daughters, the comforts of life, the flattery of others, my submissiveness, my labours.

Even so, she ends this lamentation by adding, "Lyovochka and I have been on friendly terms for some time. . . ."[27]

* Tatyana, answering her sick brother's call, had joined Lev in Paris in the spring.

† Thirteen of the more "social" artists had formed a group that organized a kind of salon which traveled from city to city.

‡ When Gay died in June 1894, Tolstoy was very much grieved. By way of funeral oration he wrote five days later to Tretyakov, the founder and director of the famous Moscow gallery of the same name, urging him to buy his friend's *oeuvre*, not just because he loved him, but because he thought him "the best painter in the history of Russian painting." (*Journaux et carnets*, vol. II, p. 398.) Tolstoy admired Gay's rather academic style, because for him the subject was more important than the treatment.

These are ancient grievances; now Sofia has other things to worry about. She is much concerned about the health of her son Lev; he had gone to Paris for treatment, and Tatyana had gone to fetch him back in March. Lev Lvovich was to say later that his trouble had been psychosomatic—his "illness was Tolstoyism." But Sofia was even more worried about her young son Ivan, the late-born little boy whom she loved passionately and whose ill health was to her a torture during every waking moment; Tolstoy thought the child tubercular. It was her love that sustained "poor darling little Vanichka with hardly a flicker of life in him."[28]

A fresh and grave cause of anxiety: Sofia had known since the summer of 1893 that Chertkov was holding on to "most of Lev Nikolayevich's manuscripts,"[29] and in November, when Tolstoy returned to Yasnaya Polyana, she had noted that "the man I love is being taken over by evil spirits."[30]

Nor was she the only one to fear the growing influence of the disciple on the master. The previous year, Tatyana, though at that time she like everyone else was under Chertkov's spell, had entered in her diary for April 2, 1894, that the Chertkovs intended to spend the summer close to Yasnaya Polyana, and she was both pleased and frightened. "Chertkov always likes interfering in Papa's work and in our life."[31]

Sofia's family burdens and practical duties became insuperable, and she put the blame for these conditions on "Lyovochka's indifference." She felt caught in an intricate net that was nothing new. "Just so long as the children don't blame me, for no one will ever be able to understand our marital relations."[32] Overtaxed as never before, she has to bear the weight of family duties alone. She writes with annoyance on January 26: "It's now 2 in the morning, Lyovochka has gone off to some meeting* . . . The lamps are still burning, the servant is waiting up."[33] It was she who early next morning had to get up and take Ivan's temperature while "Lev Nikolayevich sleeps on. Then he'll go and draw his water from the well, without even asking whether his child is any better or whether his wife is exhausted." More clearly than anyone else she saw to what extent her husband's renunciations and his charity often remained on the surface, just like his chastity. In this regard she shared, curiously enough, the opinion of many Tolstoyans.†

* This was the meeting Tolstoy mentions in his diary for January 29, 1895, a protest against a speech by Nicholas II exalting "the autocratic principle." Tolstoy began an article, which he decided not to publish, called "Crazy Dreams," a title borrowed from a sentence of the Tsar's.

† In 1908 when one of them, amazed to see Tolstoy living at Yasnaya Polyana like any other landed proprietor, asked him why he had not renounced his possessions, Tolstoy laughed and, turning to his wife, said: "I couldn't give them away again. I've already given them to her."

In spite of a certain tension, the couple's relationship appeared to continue on a fairly even keel. On January 26 Sofia played a piano duet with her husband; then she and Masha began correcting the proofs of *Master and Man*. Sofia, who longed so much to see her husband give up his "childish occupations" and come back to serious matters, that is to say, to literature, should have been delighted that he had done this piece of work. But some days later Tolstoy noted: "An unfortunate story, it was the cause of a terrible storm on Sonya's part that broke out yesterday."[34]

Sofia wanted to publish *Master and Man* in the fourteenth volume of her husband's *Collected Works* and was hastening to read proof, but Tolstoy had already promised it to Lyubov Gurevich, the woman editor-in-chief of *The Northern Herald*, and refused to take it away from her.* Sofia begged and cried, but Tolstoy was adamant. She suddenly remembered that a friend had said to her, "Gurevich must have bewitched the count,"[35] and she accused Tolstoy of being taken with that "scheming half-Jewess" Gurevich woman.[36] Whereupon, she records, "Lyovochka . . . put on his clothes and said he was leaving home for ever and wouldn't be returning."[37] Mad with jealousy, quite sure her husband wanted to abandon her for "that Gurevich woman," she decided it was she who was going to leave. She ran out into the streets in dressing gown and slippers, howling and sobbing and falling in the snow. Tolstoy brought her home by force.

But next day she repeated her request: "I'll take a copy now, if I may."[38] Another scene. Another flight. This time she put on her fur coat, her hat, and her galoshes: she was bent on dying of cold in the snow, like the hero of *Master and Man*, because in the story she had "liked the idea that Vasily Andreyevich had frozen to death."[39] Her daughter Masha recaptured her. After two days of despair, she ran away once more. Jumping into a cab, she drove to the Kursk Station. This time Sergey helped his sister to persuade their mother to come home.

Tolstoy tore out the page of his journal in which he recorded this drama. He left in what he wrote on February 15: "The following days things got worse. She was decidedly close to suicide, the children followed her on foot and by vehicle, and brought her back home. She was suffering terribly."[40]

Sofia really was in a condition bordering on insanity. "Anybody Lyovochka touched was doomed to perish,"[41] she would say. Doctors were called in; the entire family was in commotion. Tolstoy went into

* Tolstoy had sent the manuscript to Lyubov Gurevich from the Olsufyevs' house, where he stayed January 1–18, 1895.

her room, knelt before her, and bowed down, begging her to forgive him.[42] The children decided that they must separate these two terrifying people. "Lyova* has left for Droganovich sanatorium," Sofia jots down distractedly. All the same, she has achieved her purpose: "The story has been given to both me and *The Mediator*. But at what a price!"[43]

She went back to correcting proof. "I feel very humble and happy to be involved in this great work, which often brings tears of joy to my eyes."[44]

As Tolstoy was on the point of sending the proofs to St. Petersburg, he noted that "Sonya is very agitated. Poor woman, I'm sorry for her and love her, the more so now that I know about her illness."[45]

The epilogue to this drama was that Tolstoy asked Strakhov to organize a triple publication of *Master and Man*: in *The Northern Herald*, as intended; in Volume Fourteen of the *Collected Works*, "published under the aegis of Countess Tolstoy"; and also in *The Mediator*. Tolstoy's letter closed with the words: "My story has caused a great deal of unhappiness . . . Sophya Andreyevna was close to suicide."[46]

Sofia on her side had recorded this lamentable episode in a six-page note dated February 21, 1895. On the twenty-second, three lines indicate that Ivan has scarlet fever, and on the twenty-third she writes only: "My darling little Vanichka died this evening at 11 o'clock. My God, and I am still alive."[47] She was not to open her journal again for two and a half years.

The death of this seven-year-old child, whom both parents loved passionately, finally destroyed Sofia's always precarious nervous balance and intensified the dramatic character of the relations between husband and wife. Tolstoy believed that his youngest son had been "exceptionally endowed, both spiritually and emotionally";[48] he had invented games for him; for Ivan, being sickly, often had to stay in bed. Tolstoy had carried him in a big basket, like his elder brothers earlier, for "walks" around the Moscow house.

Ivan was not only adored, he was without doubt the most remarkable of all Tolstoy's children. The scientist Mechnikov used to say of him, "The first time I ever saw him, I knew that he would either die or become a greater genius than his father."[49] The third daughter, Alexandra, was to write that her young brother had "a kind of inner likeness"[50] to her father and that he was "the only consolation" of her mother. "He was her whole life. . . . Her [older] sons wanted a life of their own, and her daughters

* Their third son, Lev, who was still quite ill.

leaned toward their father's side."[51] Tolstoy thought his wife "used to take refuge from everything in life that was painful to her . . . in her love, her passionate and reciprocated love for this boy."[52]

Sofia broke down completely. "Everyone feared for her,"[53] according to Alexandra, and Tolstoy even more than the rest of the family. "I have never felt either in Sonya or myself such a need for love and such an aversion towards disunity and evil. I have never loved Sonya as much as I do now. And I feel glad because of it."[54] He confided this to Alexandrine in a letter which Sofia had begun but had not had the strength to continue. As in the days of their honeymoon in Yasnaya Polyana, Tolstoy finished it for her. For him, "the death of Vanichka was . . . like the death of Nikolenka*—though to a far greater degree—a manifestation of God, a drawing of me towards him."[55]

The road the young Tolstoy had taken to go and see his fiancée thirty years before was the road that husband and wife now took to bury their son. Back from the graveyard, Tolstoy wrote: "We've buried Vanichka. A terrible—no, not a terrible, but a great spiritual event. I thank Thee, Father. I thank Thee."[56]

His new way of "looking at death now that life itself has put the question"[57] to him shows the distance he has traveled since the death of his brother Nikolay and the night at Arzamas. In the loss of the adored child, he now sees only "a merciful event, coming from God, disentangling the lies of life. . . ."[58]

If this drama brought the couple closer together in feeling, on another level it only drove them further apart. "Sonya can't see it that way. For her the pain—almost physical—of separation conceals the spiritual importance of the event. But she astonishes me. The pain of separation immediately released her from all that was darkening her soul."[59] And he wrote to Alexandrine Tolstoy that "something great is taking place in her soul."[60]

By March 12, 1895, he seemed to have found some solution for his own misery: "Felt like writing something literary today,"[61] and he drew up a list of the work he had in hand: "Koni's Story, Who Is Right? [on the famine], The Coupon, Notes of a Mother, Alexander I, The Light Shineth in the Darkness, and the Catechism."

If Tolstoy's first reaction was to try to compensate for the child's death by a return to creative work, his second was to consider his own mortality. He consigned his wishes to his diary, requesting that this note of March 27, 1895, be taken as his last will and testament—"until I write another." Naturally, he wanted no flowers or speeches or even a notice in

* Nikolay Nikolayevich Tolstoy, his brother, who died in 1860 at the age of thirty-seven.

the papers;* Tolstoy entrusts to Sofia, Chertkov, and Strakhov "all [his] papers to be looked through and sorted out." He had added Tanya and Masha, but then crossed out their names. As for his sons, though he "loved them more and more in recent times," he considered that they were "not fully aware of [his] thoughts, have not followed their course," and thus were unable to take part in that task.[62] He also asked Chertkov to strike out in his diaries "everything which . . . might be unpleasant for anybody." But a page later he takes this back: "Let my diaries stay as they are. At least they will show that despite all the triviality and worthlessness of my youth, I was still not abandoned by God."[63] As for his heirs renouncing their monetary rights to his works, this was worded simply as a "request" on his part.

Life in Khamovnichesky Street returned to its usual routine. Tolstoy soon observes that Sofia "has started to adopt her former irritable and domineering tone—I was sorry to see the loss of that loving mood which was apparent after Vanichka's death."[64] He started bicycling again and confided ingenuously to Chertkov: "When I am carting water, I always feel glad when people see me, but when they see me on a bicycle I feel ashamed."[65] Some of his disciples found this exercise unworthy of their great man, but he defended himself by saying it was a harmless amusement.[66]

He did have more serious occupations, at once useful and edifying; he attended sessions of the Moscow district court as a mute defender of those in the dock; he took abundant notes that he later used in *Resurrection*, and his diary became more and more studded with prayers or the thoughts they aroused. "I am passionately pulled to prayer without any external impetus; at this moment as I write I struggle to hold back tears of religious emotion."[67] One evening in September, on the way back from riding, he was praying and "taking pride in his submission to God," when suddenly this struck him as so odd that he "burst out laughing: I felt very well in my soul," he added.[68]

The desire to write took hold of him again. Sofia had gone to spend a few days with her sister in Kiev. He thought of her grief, and the idea of the *Notes of a Mother* recurred to him. He decided that in the story one would have to explain that after her children have gone—into life or death—after having given her entire soul to them, she "lacks even the strength for a spiritual life."[69]

* Tolstoy's tomb is a long and narrow mound, covered throughout the summer with wild flowers and in winter studded with evergreen twigs. By his wish, he was buried in the woods of Yasnaya Polyana, several hundred yards from the house, near the ditch where his brother Nikolay used to make believe that the "green wand" was hidden, the magic stick that could bring about happiness to all mankind.

On June 15 he began "Koni's Story," the first version of which he finished on July 4. He worked as usual in the fields, but not a great deal. On August 8, he read *Resurrection* to Anton Chekhov, who had come to visit him at Yasnaya Polyana. Chekhov loved the book but noticed a factual mistake, which he pointed out to Tolstoy, always a stickler for accuracy. The fact is that convicts doing forced labor had to serve four years and not two and a half, as the heroine did in the first version of the novel.

The persecution of the Dukhobors* continued to arouse Tolstoy's indignation. He believed that they were offering to the world "a model for the possibility of non-violent government,"[70] and he admired the members of the sect for putting into practice the Gospel teaching about charity and chastity. He praised them even more for their pacifist principles, which made them refuse military service and finally caused them to burn their weapons on the night of St. Peter and St. Paul in 1894. That gesture drew upon them fearful reprisals—men shot or driven from their homes, women raped, villages sacked.

Tolstoy had sent Biryukov to the Caucasus to investigate on the spot. It seems that the Dukhobors were not the "anarchist Christians" Tolstoy liked to see in them, but sectarians who believed that their chief, Pyotr Verigin, was a reincarnation of God, and who subjected themselves to the very strict rules that he imposed.[71] Tolstoy corresponded with Verigin, who on his return from Siberia came to Yasnaya Polyana.

On the strength of Biryukov's report, Tolstoy wrote a very violent piece, "Carthago delenda est," which could not be published in Russia, but appeared in *The Times* of London in October, under the title "The Persecution of Christians in Russia in 1895." By means of this article, Tolstoy sought to defend before "the court of public opinion" the cause "of more than 450 families . . . ruined and driven out of their homes only because they were not willing to act contrary to their religious beliefs."[72] It was a court before which Tolstoy was to plead more and more frequently.

He was not happy with *Resurrection*. "My writing has become repugnant to me."[73] He complained to Strakhov: "It's pointless, vulgar,

* The Dukhobors, who also called themselves "free Christians" or "spiritual Christians," had refused to conform to the Orthodox Church in a number of Russian provinces since the early eighteenth century. Under Alexander I, they had been forced to live in Tauris; then Nicholas II had given them five years to resettle beyond the Caucasus. It was in 1902, thanks principally to Tolstoy, who had raised the money for the journey, that they were allowed to emigrate to Canada. But the Dukhobors, true rebels, refused in 1906 to take the oath of allegiance to Edward VII of England and were expelled from the Dominion, though they were allowed to settle in British Columbia.

and above all sickening to write for the good-for-nothing parasitic intelligentsia, from whom nothing but vanity has ever come or will ever come."[74]

In a letter of October 28, 1895,* he explains that for him there are two ways of writing: "One kind is legitimate and divine—writing written by a man in order to clarify his own thoughts—. . . the other sort is diabolical . . . writing written in order to obscure and confuse the truth for oneself and others. . . ."[75]

He was most attentive to Sofia's condition, which continued to disturb him, sensing as he did that "something has been distressing her." The truth is, she was more and more afraid that certain passages of her husband's journal would give posterity a bad likeness of her. She must have asked him to suppress them, for on November 5 Tolstoy says: "In fulfilment of a promise to Sonya I read through all my diaries for seven years."[76] This note explains the page torn out after the Gurevich episode and probably the seventeen lines crossed out on October 6 as well.[77] The next day he received from Kiev "a cheerful letter from Sonya.† Will there really be complete spiritual unity? Help me, Father."[78]

Tolstoy was worried not only about his wife: an epidemic of marital fever had attacked his family, and he had to write two severe letters to his youngest sons. Andrey, only eighteen, was smitten with a peasant girl from the village. (O father, once again forgetful of his own youth!) Tolstoy tells him: "The misapprehension which I am talking about consists in your taking my words that in my opinion it's exactly the same whether one marries a princess or a peasant girl . . . to mean my agreement to your marriage to Akulina Makarova." He adjured the boy to recast his thoughts before deciding to marry, which is "the most important thing in life."[79]

Ten days later Tolstoy composed another letter, five pages long, addressed to his son Mikhail, who was sixteen; he too wanted to marry a peasant girl. After rebuking him for not having even glanced at any of his father's books, except the novels, though the serious books are "the most precise and clear, applicable and necessary guides for the behavior of just such young people as himself," Tolstoy harked back to the themes of *The Kreutzer Sonata*, stressing that "being in love is only lust disguised by the imagination," and maintaining that "love is given to us, as you know,

* To Sopotsky, a medical student, who had worked with Tolstoy during the famine.

† She wrote in this letter: "The basis of our relationship, an inner feeling for one another, is still serious, strong and harmonious. . . . And the eyes of both of us are turned in the same direction—towards the exit door of life, and neither of us fears it." (C. Asquith, *Married to Tolstoy*, p. 174)

for the continuation of the species, and certainly not for pleasure." These theoretical considerations were followed by practical advice for the young man's improvement: "Carry what you can carry and clean yourself, travel on foot instead of riding." He adjured him above all things to respect his own reason. "Reason is the highest spiritual force in man, it is a particle of God within us. . . ."[80]

The following year Tolstoy had to make the same points for the benefit of his daughter Masha. After being infatuated with Biryukov, she was now in love with Prince Nicholas Obolensky, whom both Sofia and Tolstoy thought too much of a nonentity for her. Tolstoy insisted afresh on the fact "that apart from death there is no single act so important, so clearcut, so all-transforming and so irreversible as marriage."[81]*

Tolstoy was firing off spiritual directives to his children largely because he himself had been more and more intent on "living for God. How to attain to living for God? . . . It is not force of argument, not even a commanding feeling that gives firmness of conviction—it is the meaninglessness, tested by experience and incontestable, of every other way of life."[82]

Meanwhile, he was steadily hard at work. Back in Moscow for the end of the year, he attended rehearsals of *The Power of Darkness* in November. When he went to see the play in performance, he was at first refused admission to the little theater, the Malinky, because in his mujik outfit he was taken for a poor peasant.† When he was recognized, he asked to be allowed to watch from the wings, for fear his presence might cause a disturbance.

He read the aphorisms of Schopenhauer and, once again, Pascal's *Pensées*, finding that "this superb book proves beyond argument to mankind the necessity of religion." But whatever he does now, he does in a new spirit, in an unaccustomed serenity. "I have longed to lean simply on faith in God and the indestructible nature of my soul, and to my amazement I have felt a certainty (so firm and so tranquil) such as I had never before experienced."[83]

* The marriage took place all the same on June 2, 1897.

† Tolstoy, who detested uniforms, wore all his life that of the Russian peasant. This garb meant the rejection of all the habits of luxury and elegance of his class; but more particularly, in adopting it he had "taken the cloth." To the peasants, though, he remained an eccentric landowner who dressed as a mujik and ate oatmeal gruel.

TWENTY

What Is Art?

AFTER THE SUCCESS of his play, Tolstoy took a renewed interest in the theater: he read the preface to Corneille's *Le Menteur*, and soon began work on *And the Light Shineth in the Darkness.**

Tolstoy's relation to dramatic art was anything but simple. After attending performances of *King Lear* and *Hamlet*, which disgusted him, he gave Strakhov his impressions in the course of January 1896: "What a crude, vulgar, and senseless work *Hamlet* is."[1] He confided to Sofia that if he writes on Shakespeare it is to rid people of the need to pretend they like him. Being in revolt against the conventions of art as against the prevailing opinions of his age, Tolstoy took the view that "nothing confuses concepts about art so much as the acceptance of authorities."[2]

Wagner made him as indignant as Shakespeare did. Tatyana remarked in her diary for April 29, 1896: "Yesterday I went to *Siegfried*, Mamma, I, Sukhotin, Taneyev, Sergey and Micky in one box; Papa next to us in the Stolypins' box . . . . Papa could not stick the second act out, but made off out of the theatre, spouting abuse, which is still going on this evening."[3]

Tolstoy's daughter did not exaggerate. Tolstoy thundered and lightened against the opera. He uttered some of his indignation to his brother

* He never finished the play, which was not published until 1926. It is certainly the most autobiographical of Tolstoy's works. The principal character is an old man who refuses Orthodoxy through fidelity to the Sermon on the Mount and endlessly repeats, "One must get rid of this corrupting luxury." It is easy to recognize Chertkov in the heroic conscientious objector and Tolstoy's own children in the other characters; they mistrust their father, or so he believes, and lead a worldly existence. As for his wife, she does not understand him. . . .

Sergey: "Yesterday evening I went to the theatre and heard Wagner's famous modern music, *Siegfried*, the opera. I couldn't even sit through one act, and rushed out like a madman, and I can't talk about it calmly, even now. It is a stupid farce, not worthy of a child of 7. . . ."[4]

Every work of art now bore the appearance that his new perspective conferred upon it, and was judged by the criterion that art is religious in the broadest sense: "Art is one of the manifestations of man's spiritual life."[5] For Tolstoy, life takes on a new dimension that he hoped to express in his play: "The meaning of life reveals itself to man when he recognizes his own divine essence within himself."[6] That is just what Tolstoy reproaches those close to him for refusing to see. "If you have transferred your ego into your spiritual being you will feel the same pain—having done violence to love—as you feel when you do violence to the well-being of your body."[7] Tolstoy always rejected the mystical experience; his passion for reason turned him away from it; yet it seems that he did experience the bodily suffering which arises from the torments of the soul, and which Saint Teresa of Avila often speaks of. His relation to God is more and more direct, personal, freed from all ritual forms. He remarks that the Orthodox prayer says: "Come and dwell in us and purify us of all stain," and he inverts the formula; one should say: "On the contrary, purify your own soul of all stain and He will come and enter you. That is all He is waiting for. He flows into you like water to the extent that you make room for Him."[8]

Under such a definition of life, the artist can no longer be an entertainer; for Tolstoy the essential purpose of art from now on is "to manifest and express the truth about man's soul, to express those secrets which can't be expressed in simple words."[9] Tolstoy had borne these ideas within him since youth: he had long been exasperated by the futility of the literary circles in St. Petersburg. Now he believed that all elitist art was bad and decadent: "Church music [is] beautiful because it [is] accessible to the masses. Only that which is accessible to everyone is undeniably good. And so it's true to say that the more accessible the better."[10] He still allows the artist the privilege of being the only one who can focus "a microscope . . . on the secrets of his soul [which] shows to people the secrets [that] are common to all."[11]

He struggled over his work and made no headway;[12] he thought that he was having great difficulty in writing *Resurrection* because "Koni's story wasn't born inside."[13]* Six months earlier he had offered a different explanation; on November 5, 1895, he had written: "I clearly understood

* The subject of the novel was inspired by a story told him by his friend Koni, state prosecutor at Tula.

why I'm not getting on with *Resurrection*; it was because the novel opened with the description of Nekhlyudov, whereas it should begin with the peasants: They are . . . the positive element, while the rest is shadow, the negative element. . . . *Resurrection* I must begin with her,"[14] that is, with the victim.

When by the end of May he was back at Yasnaya Polyana to take up his summer quarters, Tolstoy was dispirited by the escapades in the village of his sons Andryusha and Misha.[15] He also felt hopeless about the scheme he had offered his family fifteen years before, "to give away the greater part of my property and live in four rooms," as yet unrealized.

On the other hand, he was still close to Sofia and had not yet forgotten what she revealed of herself at the time of Ivan's death. During that period he had accepted their differences and disharmonies and had written to her: "Strange is this new feeling now binding us together, it is only occasionally that the clouds of our failure to understand one another obscure the light. But I hope that before nightfall these clouds will disperse, and that our sunset will be quite clear and limpid."[16]

Things went otherwise. Nervous as she was, irritable, and wounded forever by the death of her child, Sofia began to be seen everywhere with the musician Sergey Ivanovich Taneyev, who had become a constant visitor in Moscow as well as at Yasnaya Polyana. With his high-pitched voice and effeminate airs, the chubby forty-year-old pianist disgusted Tolstoy by his "aesthetic obtuseness (real, not outward) and his *coq du village* situation in our house." When Sofia traveled to Stockholm with Tatyana and Mikhail for Lev Lvovich's wedding, the pianist went along. Tolstoy, however, tried to think of Taneyev's role in his wife's life as a test of his own feelings for her: "It's an examination for me. I'm trying not to fail." On the same day as this note he recorded the visit of "a worker from Tula, intelligent and, I think, a revolutionary [and a] pathetic seminarist"[17]—as always, Tolstoy sought comfort in the people and found it there. At Pirogovo, after a bout of depression, he went to see the village saddler and came away mightily cheered up.

Tatyana, who loved her parents equally, was saddened to see disagreement become permanent between them, and found herself increasingly perplexed by them as a couple: "What a strange combination those two! It is rarely one could find two people so different, yet at the same time so profoundly attached to one another."[18]

In the midst of Tolstoy's moral desert, one experience heartened him. On July 19 he went with Tatyana and Chertkov to Pirogovo to see his brother who was seriously ill and decided that "a spiritual revolution has certainly taken place in Seryozha; he admits it himself, saying that he was born a few months ago."[19] These words strengthened Tolstoy's belief that death opens the way to true life. That is no doubt why he always watched with an anxious curiosity the effect of death upon those closest to him. This might seem shocking if one did not understand that Tolstoy was beholding a spiritual spectacle, looking for a soul to be born, or reborn.

Every time he left his family behind, he had the feeling that he prayed better, an activity that had become essential to him. "What is prayer? A communion with God, the awareness of one's relation with him, a higher state of soul. . . . The state of prayer can be attained only for rare, exceptional minutes, . . . not in the tempest but in a gentle breath of wind. . . ."[20] And a week later: "Didn't sleep all night . . . I continue to suffer and can't surrender myself to God. One thing; I've overcome lust, but—what is worse—I haven't overcome pride and indignation, and my heart aches incessantly. . . . One thing comforts me . . . I'm not alone, but with God, and therefore, however painful it is, I feel that something is being achieved."[21]

That state of mind and the desire for renunciation made him feel even more the contradiction between his inner and his daily life; for he was more than ever convinced (so he writes to a member of the old St. Petersburg Literary Committee) that "only a man living in accordance with his conscience can have a good influence on people."[22]

On July 30, home from Pirogovo, he went to a village near Yasnaya Polyana and was overcome by the misery that reigned there—an old man of eighty forced to cultivate his field alone, a widow whose husband had died of cold and who has lived ever since in utter destitution, a whole family without one overcoat to share among them: ". . . and we [spend our time idly discussing] . . . Beethoven! . . . I prayed that He would release me from this life. And I pray again, and cry with pain. I've lost my way, I'm stuck, I can't do anything, but I hate myself and my life."[23]

While he was at his brother's, Tolstoy saw by the roadside, in the course of a walk, a tuft of starry thistles covered with dust. "It reminded me of Hadji Murat.* I'd like to write about it. It fights for life till the end, and alone in the middle of the whole field."[24] At the same time as he was longing to write, the futility of art seemed more and more obvious to him. He leafed through the works of his friend Fet and thought the novel form had become obsolete: "stories about nasty love affairs . . . boredom [while] the whole of life is seething with its own problems about food,

* The Centenary Edition spells the last name *Murad*. For consistency, in all *non-quoted* material we have opted for the Centenary Edition spelling.

accommodation, work, belief, relations between people."[25] For Tolstoy art had become something altogether different: "Help me, Father, to serve Thee by showing up this life."[26]

Such an attitude was far from setting Tolstoy apart from his contemporaries. Indeed, the Russian intelligentsia saw itself as doubly privileged—it had both money *and* education. "What in other countries is talk of careless dilettantism, in ours takes a different shape . . . a novelette becomes either useless trash or the voice of a new mind for the whole Empire."[27]*

When Tolstoy returned to his family he felt thoroughly isolated once more. The feeling of loneliness that had plagued him since childhood returned. "I can hear them playing tennis and laughing. . . . Everyone is well, but I feel depressed and can't control myself. It's like the feeling I had when [my childhood tutor Prosper de] St. Thomas locked me in and from my dungeon I could hear everyone enjoying themselves and laughing."[28] Between August 1 and September 14 he wrote nothing except during the few days when he and Sofia went to visit his sister Masha in the convent of Sharmardino; there he worked hard on *Hadji Murad* from August 11 to 14.

Everything was going badly; the children not living as he would like,† Sofia still infatuated with Taneyev, the Tolstoyans more than ever persecuted, Mikhail Petrovich Novikov (who had reformed his life after reading Tolstoy's books) under arrest. Tolstoy wrote vehement letters to the Ministers of the Interior and of Justice to get Novikov released, begging them to "transfer" their persecutions to him and away from his disciples.[29] He was himself under police surveillance. "The day before yesterday there was a police-spy here . . ." The spy was also an agent provocateur. He had come a few days earlier to borrow books, but reading them had obviously converted him to the love of truth, for he "admitted that he had been sent to keep an eye on me. It was both pleasant and nasty."[30] Another cause of worry was an alarming letter from Pyotr Verigin, the Dukhobor spiritual leader in exile in Siberia.[31] Only Tatyana and Masha brought a little joy into Tolstoy's life, as they always had. "I'm alone with my daughters. . . . It's a warm bath for the feelings."[32]

Amid all his worries Tolstoy "thinks continually of art and the

* This occurs in a letter from Druzhinin, head of a circulating library, and is quoted by Biryukov in his biography of Tolstoy.

† He was still concerned about his son Mikhail's marriage plans; in a letter to Sofia he regrets having added to her own anxiety and assures her he needed to express his grief, "and to whom closer than you?" (*Tolstoy's Letters*, vol. II, p. 549)

temptations or seductions that darken the spirit."[33] He writes the eighteen-page introduction to "On Art"[34] and goes back to "Carthago delenda est" once again.

In Moscow for his usual stay at the end of the year, Tolstoy became more and more exasperated with Taneyev, whose presence at Yasnaya Polyana he had already found hard to bear in the summer. At Pirogovo with his brother, he had jotted down two news items: the suicide of an old man and a story of substituted children. Now he noted down a subject for a novel: "A wife's betrayal of her passionate, jealous husband; his sufferings, struggle, and the pleasure of forgiveness."[35] It was his own situation. "There was a row or rather an annoyance with Sonya. And pity and love for her have conquered everything and it has become all right."[36] This is easy to believe when one reads the letter he wrote her twelve days earlier.

> You ask whether I still love you. My feelings for you now are such that I think they can never change, because they contain everything that can possibly bind people together. No, not everything. We lack outward agreement in our beliefs—I say outward, because I think the disagreement is only outward, and I'm always certain it will be eliminated. We are bound together by the past, and the children, and the awareness of our faults, and compassion, and an irresistible attraction. In a word, we are wrapped up and tied together well and truly. And I'm glad.[37]

Nevertheless, Tolstoy continued to be tortured by jealousy: "my devil still won't leave me."[38] He is bent on seeing this trial as a gift of God—a "test of humility . . . an entirely unexpected, exceptional humiliation."[39] He felt truly pitiable: "My hands are cold, I want to cry and love. Over dinner my sons' rudeness hurt me very much."[40] But his summing up at the end of the year remained positive: "The chief thing, understood my being a son of God—brotherhood and relations with the whole world have altered."[41]

Eighteen ninety-seven began badly. "The devil [of jealousy] won't go away. *Resurrection* is untrue, made-up and weak." Moscow life overwhelmed Tolstoy more than ever: "Despondency, disgust, everything repels me about this life they are living around me."[42]

He had written on January 12 to Masha, "who alone understands and appreciates [him] fully"[43] and to Chertkov. The two letters were marked "to be read alone," and they expressed in identical phrases his resentment at not being allowed to spend his old age "peacefully and not shamefully" (this to his daughter) and "away from the falsehood in which I not only live, but take part and drown" (to his friend).[44]

His distress kept him from sleeping. He prayed unceasingly. Sofia's ridiculous behavior was intolerable to him—this "senile flirtation" of hers was "revolting.[45] On January 31 Tolstoy could not stand it any longer. He took refuge once again with his friend Olsufyev. From Nikolskoye he writes to his wife in the hope of "waking her from her sleep-walking,"[46] and also to thank her for taking him to the station because she had sensed his sadness.

> I know that nothing will come now of the fact that you are going, but you can't help toying with it, and exciting yourself; and my attitude to it also excites you. . . . This game is terribly painful to me. . . . And it is happening just at the end of our life—a life spent well and purely—just at the time when we have been drawing closer and closer together in spite of everything that could divide us. This rapprochement began long ago, even before Vanichka's death. . . . Instead of a natural, good and joyful conclusion to 35 years of life together, there is this repulsive vileness which has left its terrible imprint on everything. I know you are miserable and you are suffering too, because you love me and want to be good, but so far can't, and I'm terribly sorry for you because I love you with the best kind of love—not of the body or the mind, but of the soul.[47]

He had scarcely been away three days when he learned that in his absence Sofia had read his diary and found in it signs of the resentment and anguish that her absurd infatuation for Taneyev aroused in him. "[She] is very distressed that people might afterwards conclude from it that she was a bad wife. I tried to console her—our whole life and my attitude to her of late will show what sort of wife she was."[48]* Tolstoy added that she could read his diary and make of it what she wished, but that he refused to write "with her or subsequent readers in mind, or write a reference for her, as it were." He also recorded: "Last night I vividly imagined that she would die before me, and I became terribly afraid for myself."[49]

Tolstoy showed great understanding indeed, although he could not gauge the degree of devastation that reading his diary produced in the mind of a woman already so morally and nervously afflicted. It was he who should have read Sofia's diary: "Now that I've learnt from his diaries

* According to Tolstoy's French translator E. Halperin-Kaminsky, Tolstoy had cut out this note from his diary and Chertkov restored it, saying, "As a biographer I take the liberty of lifting the veil, for in this particular case I think my indiscretion cannot fail to increase the reader's deep respect for Tolstoy and his wife." (E. Halpérine-Kaminski, *La tragédie de Tolstoï et de sa femme*, Paris: Fayard, 1931, p. 281)

what his true attitude to me is, I am merely touched by this kindness in his old age—for I'll never again abandon myself to those paroxysms of love, those outbursts of happiness and despair, as I did before reading his diaries. One day I must tell the story of those diaries, which have completely transformed my emotional life."[50]

A very different anxiety came abruptly to interrupt this new chapter in the tale of their marriage. Chertkov and Biryukov had written together an article on the Dukhobors. It was called "Help!" and included an epilogue by Tolstoy. After it appeared, Chertkov's house was searched. Tolstoy mentions this in his diary and says that he set off for St. Petersburg with his wife the very next day; she had joined him at Nikolskoye the night before. Chertkov was forced to emigrate to England, and Biryukov was sent to Courland in Latvia. Tolstoy returned to the Olsufyevs' on February 16.

The persecution of his disciples only spurred his reforming zeal. He thought of writing "An Appeal," which would be a manifesto against *all* impostures, of which he drew up a list: "The first fraud is that of land; the second fraud is that of taxes and customs; the third fraud is that of patriotism, defence; and finally . . . the worst of all is the [religious] fraud . . . of two sorts: (a) that of the church and (b) atheism."[51] This meditation led Tolstoy to his customary conclusion: the solution of men's problems lies within them, not in the world where they look for it in vain. "Release from all agitation . . . lies in destroying in oneself the illusion of the union of one's spiritual and physical I."[52] Earlier in the year, in Moscow, he had already written that "it is God and that particle of God, limited one knows not why, that constitutes our real self."[53]

The solitary life devoted to work and thought that he led at Nikolskoye was also favorable to the advent of a new inner experience which surprised him: "Walking yesterday, I prayed and had an astonishing feeling. Probably like those the mystics arouse in themselves by spiritual exercises. I felt completely spiritual, free, linked to the body only by illusion."[54] At the same time he was conscious of a great decline in energy and could not manage to write his "Appeal." He decided to get down to letter writing.* He not only found a great source of inspiration in his correspondence† but it held a special significance for him: in it, "demands were disclosed and one could perform one's task."[55]

A week later he went back to work and seemed satisfied with it.

* Many of the letters that Tolstoy wrote or received were opened by the censor. He was not indignant but loving toward his enemies: "I understood that one must pity them and I do pity them." (*Journaux et carnets*, vol. II, p. 582)

† See p. 212.

"Reread the first draft of 'On art,' not bad."[56] He read *Aristotle's Aesthetics* by Charles Bernard—"very important." On March 3 he went to Moscow, where he spent no more than a month. He invariably felt *de trop* in his own house. Sofia was forever going to concerts; somewhat later he accused her of having become a *dame de conservatoire.*[57] They lived like a pair of strangers: "We meet on the staircase, she tells me why she has not followed my ideas. So passes our thirty-fifth year together, and never the time to talk seriously."[58] Yet again he turned and sought peace at Yasnaya Polyana; on May 2 he set off with his daughter Tatyana.

The persecution of his friends continued. Aylmer Maude, his English translator, who had lived in Russia for ten years, was forced to return to England. Arrests multiplied; Trigubov, another of his disciples, was exiled to Courland after a police search of his house. In August, it was Paul Boulanger's turn to run into trouble for the help he had given Tolstoy in his campaign in behalf of the Dukhobors.[59]

Some Molokans, likewise protégés of Tolstoy's, came from Samara on May 9, 1897, to ask him to persuade the Tsar to return their children who had been taken away from them because they had refused to have them baptized. Tolstoy wrote at once to Alexandrine and other people friendly to him and close to the Tsar. The peasants themselves took the letter addressed to the Grand Duke Georgy Mikhaylovich to his palace, but they were frightened off by his servants and threw it on a "dungheap"[60] and came back disappointed. Tolstoy made another copy of the letter and entrusted it to Boulanger, who was passing through Yasnaya Polyana.

In the middle of this disturbing business, Sofia stayed for a short time at Yasnaya Polyana. As soon as she had left, Tolstoy sent her a note on May 12 to show his affection and his confidence in her judgment: "My waking up and your being there was one of the strongest, most joyful impressions I have ever experienced: and that at the age of 69, from a woman of 53." He assured her that he had cut out the passage she thought "risky" in his letter on the Molokans.[61] Alas, three days later he had a few lines from her: they announced Taneyev's arrival. "Didn't sleep all night. Never have my sufferings reached such intensity,"[62] Tolstoy noted that evening; and three days later: "I think I've come to a decision, it will be difficult to carry out, but I can't and mustn't do otherwise."[63] The decision, naturally, was to leave Sofia.

The next morning he wrote his wife a letter very different from the previous one. "My dear, darling Sonya, your intimacy with Taneyev is not merely unpleasant to me, but dreadfully agonising." He goes on to say that he had not been able to work for a year, had lived in torment and tried everything, both anger and gentleness, and was now reduced to silence. When he got her letter he "first made up his mind to go away," but in the end he thought of her own grief more than his, and would not leave without her consent; meanwhile every hour of the day he was "capable of breaking loose and doing something bad."[64]* He suggested that she should choose among "five solutions": she could break with Taneyev; he himself could go abroad; they could both go; they could accept the status quo—actually, the worst of the solutions; or, finally, they could "persuade themselves that it will pass," which he thought beyond his strength. He reminded her of how much she had suffered at the time of the Gurevich episode† "in spite of the fact that the feeling you associate with her had no semblance of a foundation and lasted only a few days." He added that he was off to Pirogovo, so that he could think things over in complete freedom; above all, there should be no "relapse into anger or false reconciliation."[65]

But he never sent the letter, resigning himself instead to Taneyev's presence. Tolstoy, impatient as he was, inclined to anger and violently jealous, was suddenly giving proof of amazing patience concerning poor Sofia's somewhat ridiculous passion for a slightly portly pianist who, if the truth were told, did not much care for women.

The children, too, began to worry about their mother's behavior. She noted on July 21: "Masha told me that Ilya was mortified to discover that my intimacy with S.I. [Sergei Ivanovich Taneyev] was the talk of Kiev—he said they were all talking about it at my sister Tanya's and at the Filosofovs."[66] The "attachment" of Sofia to Taneyev had something morbid about it: hardly had he left Yasnaya Polyana on June 5 when she ran into "the garden to talk to Vanichka‡ in the watch-tower. I asked him whether there was anything wicked in my feelings for Sergei Ivanovich [Taneyev]." In her desolation she believed that her son "wanted to draw me away from [Taneyev], probably out of compassion for his father," but she knew that he could not condemn her, "for it was he who sent him to me in the first place."[67]

Sofia had visions of a love as chaste and pure as the one she felt for her son and thought she had found it in her attachment to Taneyev; and she

* Tolstoy feared his own violence. Some critics, including Professor Makachin, with whom the author had several conversations during a stay in Moscow in 1978, go so far as to think that Tolstoy was afraid he might kill his wife.

† In February 1895 Sofia had suspected her husband of being in love with Lyubov Gurevich, to whom he had given *Master and Man* to be published. (See p. 236.)

‡ Her son, Ivan Lvovich Tolstoy, who had died on February 23, 1895, not quite seven years old.

resented being for her husband only an object of "insanely jealous physical passion, which drives all other attachments out of my heart."[68]

In the mind of this woman who had been wounded by the message of *The Kreutzer Sonata* and bruised to the depths of her being by her son's death, Taneyev and the memory of her child fused into a single being: one night she would dream of one and the next of the other.[69] That was perhaps the key to this strange passion. The musician was engulfed in spite of himself by the great void that Ivan's death had left in his mother's heart. When Taneyev came to notice the passionate excess of Sofia's feelings for him, he ran away. Perhaps also she found in this adventure a means of revenging herself for *The Sonata*; it enabled her to see what enormous power she still exercised over her husband, in spite of the detachment he professed.

Sofia was perfectly well aware of the complexity of her infatuation with Taneyev: "They all think I am in love with him! How quick they are to cheapen one's feelings."[70]

She was at the end of her strength, and after a fresh altercation with her husband she fled: "I ran out of the house intending to kill myself . . . not to be tormented by any more insane jealous scenes, like the day before yesterday, any more cruel mutual recriminations, like today. . . . This evening we made it up without explanations . . . Lev Nikolayevich spoke to me so kindly, and said it was time for us to stop loving and quarrelling so passionately."[71]

Some days later she wrote: "Lev Nikolayevich is cheerful and happy."[72] Sad and obsessed with the image of her lost son, she ended up "talking to him in her thoughts."[73] None the less, she made strenuous efforts to take heart and sometimes imagined that she was succeeding. But she noted: "My husband is not my friend; he has been my passionate lover at times, and especially as he grows older, but all my life I have felt lonely with him."[74] Things did not get any better; on July 3, she records: "Today I left the room in which I have slept for almost 35 years and moved into Masha's old room."[75]

Four days later Taneyev turns up. The next day Tolstoy writes the famous farewell letter, which betrays a radical alteration in his attitude toward his wife. Very likely, he was hurt by the absurd and humiliating Taneyev episode in just the degree to which he had felt between himself and Sofia what he called a rapprochement.

Although Tolstoy was addressing Sofia, the first three paragraphs of his letter were meant for the whole family; he does not speak directly to his wife until the second part.

Dear Sonya, for a long time now the disparity between my life and my beliefs has been causing me distress. I have been unable to make you change either the way of life or the habits that I myself trained you to adopt. Nor have I been able to leave you until now, since I thought that my going away would deprive the children, while still young, of the influence, however weak, I might exercise over them, and that it would cause you pain. However, I cannot continue to live as I have lived for these past sixteen years, sometimes in conflict with you and angering you, at other times succumbing myself to the influences and temptations that surround me and to which I have become accustomed. And today I have resolved to do what I have been inwardly proposing to do for a long while: to go away. . . . First because . . . this life becomes more and more distressing, and because I long more and more for solitude; secondly, because the children are grown now, so that my influence is no longer necessary to them, and because all of you have your own interests in life, so that my absence will not be greatly noticed by any of you.

But the main reason is this; just as the Hindus, when they reach the age of sixty, go off into the wilds, just as every aging and religious man desires to devote the last years of his life to God and not to table talk, to puns, to gossip, to lawn tennis, so I having reached my seventieth year, long with all the strength of my soul for calm, for solitude, and if not for perfect harmony at least for something other than this flagrant disharmony between my life and my beliefs and conscience.

If I had left openly, the result would have been supplications, explanations, arguments; I might perhaps have weakened and been unable to carry out my decision. And it must be carried out. I beg you therefore to forgive me in your hearts if my act saddens you. And you above all, Sonya, let me go, do not look for me, do not distress yourself on my account, and do not blame me.

The fact that I have left you does not mean that I am displeased with you. I know that you were unable—literally unable—and are unable, to see things and to think as I do; that is why you could not and cannot change your life by making a sacrifice to something you do not accept. And so I do not blame you in the slightest; on the contrary, I remember with love and gratitude the thirty-five long years of our life together, and above all the earlier half, when with the renunciation inherent in your mother's heart you were able to bear so valiantly all the burdens of what you saw as your vocation. You have given me, and given the world, what you could give: so much motherly love and self-abnegation, it is impossible not to value you on that account. But during the more recent period of our life, during the past fifteen years, our paths have diverged. I cannot believe that it is my fault, for I know that if I have changed it has not been for my own sake, nor for that of mankind, but because it was imposible for me to do otherwise. How can I accuse you in any way for not having followed me, so I thank you, and I recall, I shall always recall, with love, what you have given me. Goodbye, my dear Sonya. Your affectionate Leo Tolstoy.[76]

Why did he not hand this letter to Sofia?* And why didn't he even go away? The shock might have brought home to her how grave the situation was. She would have made a scene and shouted—something Tolstoy detested†—but the situation would have been clearer. His daughter Tatyana's remark on the letter is: "This departure did not take place. He waited another thirteen years."[77] Even so, one is entitled to wonder whether in a certain sense Tolstoy did not leave Yasnaya Polyana on July 8, 1897. . . .

During this critical period, Tolstoy seldom kept up his diary—only twice in April and five times in May. On May 17 he wrote: "And that is another test that I've failed. Instead of love within me I feel blame and spite."[78] Two months later, on July 16, he takes up the journal again, and an entry headed "end of May 1897" reads: "Torn out and burnt what I had written in rage."[79] Looking backward he notes that during that stretch of time he had worked "on my article on art, and the further I got, the better." His words on Masha's wedding to Nicholas Obolensky, whom she finally married on June 2, are less cheerful. "I was sorry for her as one is sorry for a thoroughbred horse that is made to cart water." He thinks up a subject that seems linked to his present situation: "a passionate young man in love with a mentally sick woman."[80] And he mentions some of the numerous summer visitors: Aylmer Maude, his English translator; Boulanger; the pianist Alexander Goldenweiser; a silly little Frenchman whom he does not name; Novikov; the sculptor Ginzburg; and Cesare Lombroso, who came on August 11 from a conference on criminology held in Moscow, a "naive, bald-headed, little old man."[81]

Tolstoy was revolted[82] by the decisions of the Missionary Congress held at Kazan, which confirmed the right of the Orthodox Church to take children away from the sectarians and educate them as it chose. His own mission as defender of the persecuted now took on even more importance in his eyes—and in the world's. His zeal for the cause of the Dukhobors and of the Molokans redoubled. On August 16 rumor reached him that the Nobel Committee were thinking of giving him the Peace Prize, whereupon he wrote to the Swedish papers on September 19 suggesting

* Neither did Tolstoy send the letter. He hid it in the stuffing of an armchair and told his daughter Masha of its existence when he became seriously ill in 1901. In 1907 Sofia Tolstoy was having the chair recovered, so Tolstoy entrusted the paper to his son-in-law Nicholas Obolensky, along with a second letter, asking Obolensky to hand them both to Sofia after his death.

† On June 6 of the same year, he had said: "How sweet and feminine your voice is tonight. How I hate it when you shout." (*The Diaries of Sofia Tolstoy*, p. 196)

that it should be awarded to the Dukhobors: "Sonya is afraid. I'm very sorry, but I can't help doing it."[83]

More Molokans came from Samara to ask again for his support. First, he wrote "a very cutting letter"* to be published abroad. Then, on second thought, he decided to address the Tsar and those of his correspondents whom he had already alerted early in the summer, and he sent Masha to call on the Tsar's representative to the Holy Synod, Konstantin Petrovich Pobedonostsev. The sectarians' children were returned to their parents early in 1898.

Sofia returned to Moscow alone, saw Taneyev again, and spent a disappointing evening with him. "And as for my incomparably more gifted husband! What extraordinary understanding of people's psychology in his writings, and what incomprehension and indifference to the lives of those closest to him! Me, the children, the servants, his friends—he doesn't know or understand them."[84] She was being terribly unfair, particularly at this time, when Tolstoy was showing a great deal of patience over her infatuation with Taneyev and was writing his children letters full of affection and understanding.

She came back to Yasnaya Polyana, Tolstoy recording her arrival on September 22: "Sonya came today. Thought during the night about the separation of lust from love, and about the fact that either is an extra-sensory notion. . . ."[85] In her diary she softened toward him for a moment on the day of their wedding anniversary: "We have been married 35 years . . . I thank God that we have remained faithful to one another, and now live peacefully, even affectionately, together."[86]†

Then she was off to Moscow again. Her husband "said goodbye . . . affectionately, almost shyly."[87] All the same, three days later, she spent another evening with Taneyev. "I didn't feel happy with him, in fact I felt awkward and even uncomfortable at times."[88]

She was back at Yasnaya Polyana from October 12 to 18, Tolstoy delighting in this visit: "It's the third day since Sonya arrived. I'm alone with her. She's doing some copying. She helps me very much. I'm still writing about art."[89] Sofia herself remembered only "the cold bleak

* On August 30 Sofia wrote that in principle she had no objection to the letter, but thought her husband was attacking the Russian government "in the most crude and provocative terms imaginable," and for her part always feared that he would "write something truly desperate and evil against the government, and get us all deported." She added: "He was touched by my despair. . . . decided to send a modified version of [the letter]." (*The Diaries of Sofia Tolstoy*, p. 236)

† It is rather remarkable that Sofia uses virtually the same words that he had written that same year in his letter of January 31. (See p. 249.)

house, the two filthy rooms where [she] lived with Lev Nikolayevich . . . writing, writing, morning, noon, and night."[90]

She was in a morbid state of mind and knew it: "I feel unbalanced, unhinged. Today I felt so melancholy I could have killed myself or done something truly absurd."[91] In her distress it was to Tolstoy that she turned in the end. "I long to see Lev Nikolayevich, I have missed him all day."[92] As for Tolstoy, his worries did not prevent him from working indefatigably. He stored up many notes for *Hadji Murad* and finished *What Is Art?* With the autumn drawing to a close, he was alone, quite alone at Yasnaya Polyana, for his daughters had not stayed with him as they usually did. Periods of solitude favor meditation, and for Tolstoy they always turned into spiritual retreats. On October 21, the everlasting question springs up again, "Who am I? Why am I?" For the first time he was able to write: "The answer came on its own and so clearly: Whoever and whatever I am, I have been sent by someone to do something. Then go to it, do it!" And he added: "I have so well and with such joy felt my fusion with the will of God. It is the second time I have had the lively consciousness of God."[93] He had in mind his experience while out walking at Nikolskoye the previous February.

On October 30 Tolstoy and his wife came together again at Sergey Nikolayevich's in Pirogovo and then returned home together* to Yasnaya Polyana. "We sat cheerfully together and drank tea. Lyovochka made the bed himself, and after his ride of thirty-five versts [23 miles] he still had sap enough to prove his passion to me. . . . I record this as proof of his remarkable vigour, he is seventy."[94] No matter, he scarcely longed to join her in Khamovnichesky Street; he was quietly ensconced at Yasnaya Polyana; she had sent him "an unpleasant letter" and he thought of "the journey to Moscow with horror."[95]

Dr. Dushan Makovitsky came to Yasnaya Polyana on November 25; Tolstoy found him "good, amiable, modest and pure."[96] The thirty-one-year-old Czechoslovakian physician had just set up a *Slavonic Mediator*† on the model of the publishing house founded by Tolstoy and Chertkov. Makovitsky, who was to attend Tolstoy during the final ten years of his life and be the companion of his last days, was already established in his patient's affections. Conversations with him gave Tolstoy an opportunity to define what he himself thought of Tolstoyism. "There is no Tol-

* So says Sofia's diary. In his, Tolstoy writes on the contrary that his wife went direct to Moscow from Pirogovo.

† With his *Slavonic Mediator*, he constitutes the "center of a small but I think godly enterprise." (*Tolstoy's Diaries*, vol. II, p. 451)

stoyanism or teaching of mine; there is only one eternal, universal, world-wide teaching of the truth as expressed particularly clearly for me and for us all in the Gospels. This doctrine calls on man to recognize his kinship with God."[97] This sense of kinship he felt more and more frequently. The longing to return to the Father haunts him: "You want to swim in a direction of your own, but beside us, ceaselessly, very close to each one of us, runs the divine infinite torrent of love, always in the one same eternal direction. . . . Throw yourself into this torrent."[98]

The return to Moscow proved less unpleasant in the end than it had been on other occasions.* But things were going badly. Sofia had repeatedly written "very painful letters" and was so enraged with Tolstoy for wanting to publish another piece in Lyubov Gurevich's magazine† that she had withdrawn to Trinity Saint-Sergey, so as not to be at home when her husband arrived. Tatyana Lvovna went to look for her mother, managed to calm her down, and persuaded her to come home. Against all expectations, according to Tolstoy's diary, the reunion was serene. "Talked more and more yesterday, and I heard from Sonya something I'd never heard before: an admission of guilt. . . . Whatever should happen in the future,‡ this has already happened, and it is a great good. . . ."[99]

He made plans, drawing up a list of thirteen subjects "worth the trouble of working out and which I could handle as they demand."[100]§ He knew now how he wanted to write. When he had finished *What Is Art?* Tolstoy had noted that the work had "cleared up many things" for him: "If God bids me write works of fiction, they will be entirely different ones. . . ."[101]

By December 1897 Tolstoy had indeed finished *What Is Art?* begun in the previous autumn. The question itself, he had been asking himself for

* On the way Tolstoy and his daughters made a stopover at Dolgoye, where the big wooden family house that had served as the main building at Yashaya Polyana had been moved to and rebuilt after being dismantled. He was seeing it for the first time since he had lost it gambling in 1854. "The tumbledown house made a very moving impression on me, a swarm of memories." (*Tolstoy's Diaries*, vol. II, p. 452.) His daughters said later that they recognized the house from *War and Peace*.

† He wanted to give *The Northern Herald* the important introduction he had written for the English poet Edward Carpenter.

‡ The notebook jottings are not dated exactly. We have no idea whether it was before or after this conversation that Tolstoy wrote in late December, "I complain that she does not love my soul and she lacks the machinery to understand it." (*Journaux et carnets*, vol. II, p. 632)

§ He dealt with several of these: *Father Sergey*; *The Forged Coupon*; *Hadji Murad*; "a drama of the Christian renaissance," which became *And the Light Shineth in the Darkness*; and *Resurrection*. Other projects were not carried out, such as *The Mother* (though several times he expressed his wish to deal with the subject) and *The Execution*, which would have told the story of those young people hanged at Odessa for trying to assassinate Tsar Alexander II.

a much longer time, as his journal and letters show. That selfsame query goes back to his literary beginnings, when he already held art in no very high esteem. In a letter to Fet from Hyères in the south of France on October 17, 1860, soon after the death of his brother Nikolay, he wrote: "To speak the truth, it's the one thing that I'll go on doing, only not in the form of your art. Art is a lie, and I can no longer love a beautiful lie."[102]

Tolstoy never took himself very seriously as a writer, except perhaps in the Caucasus, and maybe not even then, but he did respect his vocation as a man with a mission. His nearest and dearest, on the other hand, and particularly Sofia and Turgenev, saw only the artist in him and regarded his "moral transformation" as a betrayal; for them it was as if Leonardo da Vinci had given up painting to devote himself exclusively to mechanical invention.

Ever since 1889 Tolstoy had got Strakhov to send him treatises on aesthetics and works on art. "What is there on art and on the history of this concept? Before saying my own say, I need to know [how] the quintessence of educated people regard this matter."[103] He did not really read in order to learn. In his wide reading he never encountered a master, except perhaps Rousseau. He found only people to argue with, and one day he confided to Gussev that he read in order to "see how far the others had been and to go further."[104] He was not a man for dialogue but for assertion, and still more for contradiction; in this regard he shows himself an autodidact.* Tolstoy never adopted any system, he was neither a Slavophile nor a Westernizer and no more a devotee of art for art's sake than of social art. His condition of autodidact was one aspect of his intellectual narcissism; inclined to believe that he was the only bearer of essential truths, he could derive his knowledge from no one but himself.

Tolstoy did not find answers to his questions in books any more than he had discovered God in them when he was writing *A Confession*. So he undertook to decipher "the enigma of beauty" all by himself. "It is necessary first of all to cease to consider [art] as a means to pleasure,"[105] and to think of it as "one of the means of intercourse between man and man." It thus becomes one of the "most important things, as important as the activity of speech itself."[106]

This attempt to define art as a means of communication is very modern. He explodes the narrow conception of fine art: "All human life," he declares, "is filled with works of art of every kind."[107] Man is bathed in art as he is in language, and language is not confined to books and

* Romain Rolland said of Tolstoy's thought that it is "crudely cut from pieces of shopworn materials picked at random in the course of his self-education and sewn together again with large, awkward fingers." (*Monsieur le comte*, Paris: Albin Michel, 1978, p. 10)

speeches, either; it has no value in itself. For Tolstoy art is not entertainment, it has a social role; and in his vocabulary the word *social* means "spiritual." He points out that in the past art has always been linked to "the values that man gave to life at a given time or place. For the Jews it was divine law; for the Greeks, joy and vital energy; for the Romans, national greatness; for the Chinese, the cult of ancestors; for the Buddhists, elevation of the soul."[108] Among the Christians of the early centuries, there was only the love of Christ, and all pagan art was condemned. But alongside this authentic Christianity there soon appeared the "imposture" that Tolstoy calls "Church Christianity," which developed cults and images and so created a "new paganism."[109] From being no longer religious, art ceased to be popular; it cut itself off from the people, just as the churches turned men away from Christianity. The various schools of art have taught the artists the "counterfeiting" of art.

In the Renaissance, the old medieval values attached to faith were replaced by those of beauty and pleasure, and these were no longer accessible to all as were the values of faith. Malraux has called this the disappearance of the sacred. Art, having become non-Christian and serving only to unite some few people, changed into an elitist art which sinks into the *recherché* and the obscure.

Among the upholders of this "perverted"[110] art Tolstoy named such poets as Baudelaire, Verlaine, and Mallarmé, writers like Kipling, and the Impressionist painters.* He attacked the critics who give forth the opinions of cliques and perpetuate their errors. Wagner gets a whole chapter to himself as the perfect representative of depraved art, and Shakespeare earns an entire book, mostly written at the same time as *What Is Art?* but not published until 1904.

At the same time, Tolstoy acknowledges that "it is difficult to distinguish real art from its counterfeit,"[111] because "the external quality of the work in false productions is not only no worse, but often better"[112] than in authentic art. Only one man in a hundred knows how "to distinguish between true emotion and the diversion or nervous excitement that can be substituted for it."[113]

The reason Tolstoy wanted to "put paid" to art so harshly and vehemently is that for him it represented a lie, the acme of artificiality, the most dangerous thing that man has contrived in order to distract

* His son Lev, himself a man of letters and a sculptor who worked with Rodin in Paris, writes in *Léon Tolstoï vu par son fils* (Nouvelle Revue Critique 1931, p. 68): "His reflections on art reveal with striking clarity his imperfect knowledge of the subject." He explains this by the fact that his father had lived "in a deprived artistic environment all his life, rarely leaving his Russian countryside and his house, where apart from two pianos, some books, and some family portraits, there was nothing else by way of art."

himself from God: the supreme diversion. In *The Kreutzer Sonata* Tolstoy had wanted to clip the wings of love and of his own love; in *What Is Art?* he does the same thing: he wants to crush the artist's hand, to condemn art in general and his own art at one and the same time.* In truth, this essay marked another stage in self-detachment. The book is ultimately an attempt to rationalize and so justify this new mutilation: it is the refusal of "the second drop of honey."† But what will the criterion of beauty be in the new aesthetics? Tolstoy accepts only one, " 'the infectiousness of art': If a man . . . on reading, hearing, or seeing another man's work experiences a mental condition which unites him with that man and with others who are also affected by that work,‡ the stronger the infection the better the art."[114] Contagion alone restores communion among men and reunites separated souls. The all-important thing is that the reader or beholder should feel "as if the work were his own and not some one else's—as if what it expresses were just what he had been longing to express."[115]

Tolstoy thought that in this conception of beauty he had discovered an original definition of art, linked to the new meaning he attributed to life. "The religious perception of our time . . . is the consciousness that our well-being, both material and spiritual, individual and collective . . . lies in the growth of brotherhood among men—in their loving harmony with one another."[116] As for "perverted" art, it only separates people from each other.

The social point of view was never more for Tolstoy than a springboard by means of which he reached the spiritual plane where the true end of art was clearly revealed to him. It was "to arouse in all men the awareness of their relationship with God and with one another."[117] In the art that he called Christian he discerned two currents: the religious and the universal.[118]

Of the twenty thousand books or so in the Yasnaya Polyana library, Tolstoy places very few in the "universal" category—they would all fit on one shelf. *Les Misérables* and *Les Pauvres Gens*, by Victor Hugo; Dostoyevsky's works, particularly *The House of the Dead*; *A Tale of Two Cities*, by Dickens; *Uncle Tom's Cabin*; George Eliot's *Adam Bede*; *Don*

* Lubomir Radoyce collected Tolstoy's critical writings under the title *On Art*, but one may well ask whether *Against Art* would not be a more suitable title.

† In *A Confession* Tolstoy wrote: "The two drops of honey which diverted my eyes from the cruel truth longer than the rest, my love of family and of writing—art as I called it—were no longer sweet to me." (See p. 149.)

‡ Freud said nearly the same thing concerning Michelangelo's Moses: The state of passion, of psychic motion, which aroused the creative urge in the artist, must be reproduced in us. (*Essais de psychologie appliquée*, Paris: Gallimard [Idées], 1976, p. 10)

Quixote; Molière's comedies; *The Pickwick Papers*; the stories of Gogol, of Pushkin, of Maupassant; the novels of the elder Dumas.[119]

Tolstoy was no more indulgent when it came to his own works; he deems *War and Peace* and *Anna Karenina* worthless, to which no one else would deny a place in what he calls universal art. "I consign my own artistic productions to the category of bad art, excepting the story 'God Sees the Truth but Waits,' which seeks a place in the first class [religious art], and 'Captive in the Caucasus,' which belongs to the second."[120]

In painting he grudgingly admits that the three necessary conditions for creation are more often to be found in mediocre painters than in good ones. Among the latter he allows only one exception: Millet's *Angelus* is one of those rare works that satisfy his artistic judgment. André Suarès used to say that Tolstoy talked about art "like a pure-minded peasant [who had somehow] strayed into a museum."[121]

Although he loves their music, he also condemns Beethoven, Schumann, Berlioz, Liszt, and, of course, Wagner: "accessible only to people who have developed in themselves an unhealthy nervous irritation. . . . 'What! [Beethoven's] Ninth Symphony not a good work of art' I hear exclaimed by indignant voices. And I reply: Most certainly it is not."[122]* Tolstoy had affirmed in December 1896: "Belief in authorities causes the mistakes of the authorities to be accepted as models."[123] In systematically opposing the respectful attitude and making edifying contents the sole aesthetic criterion, Tolstoy was in danger of bringing art down to the deadly level of sacristy sculpture or social realism.

He was an ecologist before his time, and never ceased to alert and warn opinion against the misdeeds of industrialization and the dangers of technology. Yet he pinned his hopes on the "construction of means of communication—telegraphs, telephones, the press and the ever-increasing attainability of material well-being for every one."[124] And he dreamed of the day when "artistic activity will be accessible to all men," because art will be taught in primary school and "all the artists of genius now hidden among the masses" will be discovered.[125]

This new conception of art also changed the way Tolstoy saw the artist's role in society. His task being defined as the "transmission to others of the emotions he has experienced,"[126] the artist must not shut

* These exaggerations made Tolstoy's contemporary Sar Péladan say that Tolstoy, "with a superior morality and a pure and simple heart, came to burn down the Museum [at Alexandria] all over again. This Savonarola wrote the craziest indictments against art," and proposed that a mujik be assigned to every museum from now on "so that we may be guided, not by study, reason and tradition, but by this new animal, the aesthetic pig, the truffle-hunter of art, the aesthetic mujik." (Sar Péladan, *La Décadence esthétique*, Paris: Chamuel, 1898)

himself up in an ivory tower, but live like other men and have a trade. It is rather like the philosophy of the priest-worker.

By reinstating artistic work among the general activities of mankind, Tolstoy found that art and science were "as closely bound together as the lungs and the heart" and could not be separated.[127] Having condemned art for art's sake, he was no more tolerant of science for science's sake; learning should not "give preponderance to political economy or experimental science; its mission is to study religious, moral and social truths." It is on this premise that research will in future be able "to fashion a new ideal of man." Only when the new art and the new science, directed by religious awareness, have led to a genuine union of men—one brought about "by peaceful cooperation and not by the police power and the law courts"[128]—will that art finally be able to "set up, in place of the existing reign of force," the Kingdom of God.[129]

Leo Tolstoy did not become chaste after writing *The Kreutzer Sonata*. Nor did *What Is Art?* reduce him to artistic silence. Almost in spite of himself, he still was to write two admirable works—*Resurrection* and *Hadji-Murad*.

TWENTY-ONE

Resurrection

IN THE CLOSING YEARS of the century, Tolstoy's diaries and letters were no longer filled with reflections on art but with thoughts on current events and politics, viewed of course like everything else from the point of view of spirituality. Tolstoy disagreed with the socialists, who wanted to "raise the intellectual and physical level of the workers. This can only be done by religious education, but they don't recognize this, and so all their work is in vain."[1]

In the summer of 1898 he was absorbed by *Resurrection*, but was not so busy as to overlook that "the mistake of the Marxists (and not only theirs but of the whole materialistic school) is that they don't see that the life of mankind is advanced by the growth of consciousness, the advancement of religion, and a more and more clear and general understanding of life which provides a satisfactory answer to all problems, and not by economic causes."[2]

Though increasingly "engaged" in contemporary issues, Tolstoy was none the less nursing ideas of flight and liberation. Numerous colonies on Tolstoyan lines had been founded in England, in Holland, and in the United States, and on March 11, 1898, he wrote to Gibson, a member of an American group, that ". . . every man who can free himself from the conditions of worldly life without breaking the ties of love—love the main principle in the name of which he seeks new forms of life—I think such a man not only must, but naturally will join people who have the same beliefs and who try to live up to them. If I were free I would immediately, even at my age, join such a colony. . . ."[3]

As defender of the oppressed and a star of first magnitude on the international scene, Tolstoy kept up his end of a sizable correspondence. It earned him reinforced police observation at the same time as warnings from extreme reactionaries. Toward the end of December 1897 an anonymous letter had threatened him with death;[4] others followed in the ensuing days.

On March 19, 1898, Tolstoy jots down in the diary: "permission [given] for the Dukhobors to emigrate."[5] On April 19 he sent the foreign press* a letter about their persecution; it was published in England at once in the *Daily Chronicle* and ten days later in *The Times*. In it he describes the barbarities inflicted on the Dukhobors and offers "his mediation to people who wish to help them."[6] Meantime he had approached twenty Russian plutocrats in hopes of raising money for his Dukhobors. He loathed having to take such steps as much as the things he had to do in the famine of 1891, and some of the purists among his disciples blamed him accordingly.

Still, Tolstoy was living through a comparatively serene period, with literary work (he had gone back to *Resurrection*) balancing work for the good of his fellow men (Dukhobors and Molokans). In St. Petersburg Tatyana had finally disentangled the complicated situation that the members of the latter sect had got into by refusing to bring up their children in Orthodoxy.†

During early spring, famine had been declared in the region where his son Ilya lived, and in April Tolstoy settled in with him at Grimyovka. He soon saw that "the famine disaster isn't nearly as great as it was in 1891."[7] He loved the life: "I ride, every day I open a food kitchen somewhere."[8]‡ He was also deep in Boccaccio, and on June 12 he noted down: "today, quite unexpectedly, I started to finish 'Sergey.' "[9]

Active though he was in so many directions, Tolstoy was feeling old and weak. He was nearly seventy, and his "attempts at gymnastics" had convinced him that he "must completely give up physical exercise."[10] Yet in a letter to Sofia some days earlier, his vitality had seemed intact: "I

* Publishing his articles in Russia had become almost impossible. Anyone who tried it ran serious risks. "The *Russian Gazette* has been banned because of the Dukhobors and me. . . ." (*Tolstoy's Diaries*, vol. II, p. 457)

† "Got a telegram from Papa: 'Samara Molokans leaving for Petersburg. Remain and help.' " (Tatiana Tolstoï, *Journal*, Paris: Plon, 1953, p. 251)

‡ This second fight against famine inspired an article, "Famine or Not," in which he spoke of the "chronic undernourishment of a whole population." It was published in England in Chertkov's magazine *Free Thought*.

rode back through the woods of Turgenev's Spasskoye in the evening light: fresh greenery in the woods and underfoot, stars in the sky. . . ." The smells and sounds of the forest bewitched him. He felt at one with the universe, relishing "the pleasant, vigorous movement of the horse" beneath him. As he felt in youth, "the purest joy of all is the joy of nature."[11] But communion with nature did not exclude other enthusiasms. "A joy to have positively discovered with age a new state of great and indestructible felicity."[12] His new freedom led Tolstoy to the discovery that "nothing can save humanity from the deception in which it has been trapped by power. Only religious feeling can resist and conquer."[13]

Although some well-known people such as Tretyakov refused to contribute, Tolstoy's appeal for the Dukhobors had been heard, and a great deal of money had come in, though not enough to finance their migration to Canada. On July 17, 1898, he decided to let "*Resurrection* and *Father Sergey* be published for the benefit of the Dukhobors."[14] It was contrary to the principle of giving up his royalties, but as in 1891, when he set off to relieve the famine, the urgency of the task justified the contradiction.

The duty of collecting funds for the Dukhobors was both an incitement and an excuse to return to literature. Having entered a note on his decision, Tolstoy added without a break: "Sonya has gone to Kiev. An inner struggle. I don't much believe in God. I don't rejoice at the examination."[15] This "examination" consisted in finding out whether he could show "that increase of love" he recognized "as the end of life,"[16] which he continued to profess despite his wife's behavior, she being still love-struck with Taneyev. He had "no sleep at night," would get up early, and noted that he had prayed a lot.

Sofia had gone to Kiev to visit her sister. She stopped on the way, first at her daughter Masha's, and then at her friends', the Maslovs, where she was to meet her musician.

Tolstoy was miserable during his wife's absence. On July 20 he had a letter from her and one from Masha that did nothing to assuage his anguish. "I still cannot sleep."[17] There is no mention of Sofia's return on July 22; the argument that ensued at once must have been dramatic, as one can see from a few pages that Tolstoy wrote for his sister-in-law Tatyana and that fell into Sofia's hands. She sent them on with other papers to Masha, who in turn handed them to Chertkov. Chertkov dated them July 28/9, 1898. He read them as proofs of the misunderstanding subsisting between the Tolstoys, at the very time when they were showing a strong desire to make concessions.

What emerges from these pages, which Tolstoy brought together under the title of "Dialogue," is that the essential thing for him—and he repeated it many times—was Sofia's view of her own feelings. He accused her of not possessing "the moral judge" that would enable her to pass such a judgment. Her defense is simple: she protests that she loves her husband and that her feeling for Taneyev "is so unimportant that it can't be bad." Tolstoy replies, though the two characters of the "Dialogue" are called He and She, that "the feeling of an old, married woman for another man is a bad feeling."[18] "She" admits that she ought not to have gone on the journey since it made "him" feel hurt. Sofia acknowledges the truth of this. But "He," just like Tolstoy, always harps on the same idea: seeing the man or not, receiving him or not is not the question, "what is important . . . is your attitude towards your feeling."[19]

Tolstoy notes in his diary that his wife cannot give up her attachment to Taneyev, and that perhaps "it will gradually disappear of its own accord in that special way women have which is incomprehensible to me." He would like to show her compassion, but she has "reached a state of semi-hysteria" in which she screams out, "You have tormented me, for two hours you have been using the same phrase over and over again, exclusive, exclusive feeling, good or bad, good or bad."[20] She calls him crazy, pharisaical; she threatens suicide and curses him and his daughters, and ends up in a nervous fit. Tolstoy calms her down and she goes to sleep. He tells himself there is no "way out of this madness . . . since she won't acknowledge it to be bad, she can't be rescued from it, and will go on taking actions provoked by this feeling, actions which it is painful for me and the children to see."[21]

Two days later Tolstoy went to his brother's at Pirogovo. There he picks up *Resurrection* and *Father Sergey*, which he had been working on now and again for months. On July 14, 1898, he had asked Chertkov to try to "sell them on the most profitable terms to English or American newspapers (newspapers it seems are most profitable)" and to publish them now, without waiting for his death, so as to get money for the resettlement of the Dukhobors. He added that he was not really satisfied with the pieces as they stood, but was obliged to send them off to be published as they were (*tels quels*, he says in French), just as he had done when he sold *The Cossacks* to pay a gambling debt. What annoyed him particularly was that these stories were "composed in his old manner": all the same, "even if they do not satisfy my present requirements of art—they are not accessible to everyone in form—they are not harmful in content, and might even be useful to people."[22]

Chertkov had become the efficient go-between whom Tolstoy could no longer do without. It was he who now took on the task of getting all the new writings published, in Geneva and London, since their violence against authority made their publication at home well-nigh impossible.* Sofia, not only because she was possessive by nature but even more because she had an eye to the future (her children's more than her own), was pained by Chertkov's influence and his control over her husband's works: "Cherktov," she exclaims, "has Lev Nikolayevich completely in his power again, even from England!"[23]

Already before *Resurrection* appeared abroad, Tolstoy himself was rather irritated by the domineering behavior of his disciple, and let his feeling break out here and there in his letters. In one written on October 15, 1898, he stresses the fact that "being closer to the scene of action, here in Russia," he knows "better what is needed and when." Tolstoy seems at this time to have gone through a spell of discouragement in other ways; he began to wonder if it was worth giving himself "so much trouble" and "so many departures from the demands of Christianity" in order to transfer "the Dukhobors from one cruel and heartless master to another." He found it "offensive" that Chertkov suggested sending advance "outlines" to Anglo-American publishers: they are "inconceivable"—he was not about to "display his wares." He begged Chertkov, if nothing final had been concluded, to leave things alone and let him take up the business himself: "I think I shall do it better and at least I shan't be annoyed with anyone," a point that mattered to him a great deal. He asked his friend to forgive him for letting his bad temper show, explaining that his indignation over "outlines" was not pride but was part of the ideal he conceived "of the writer's vocation which cannot subordinate the spiritual activity of writing to any practical considerations."[24]

The next day again he begged his friend "to spread a veil of love over all that is bad" in his first letter. Actually, he rather aggravated the offense:

> You are very proud of your efficiency, but frankly I don't trust it. I do not say I'm right; I am only expressing my opinion. It seems to me you always take on too much work, more than you are capable of, and the work does not progress for that reason. Because of an exaggerated thoroughness you are slow and dilatory . . . and then you take a lofty, grand seigneur view of everything, and fail to see a number of things on that account. Besides, for psychological reasons your mood is changeable . . . you are a very valuable coadjutor, but when on your own—an inefficient worker.[25]

* Chertkov shared this role with Biryukov, who had joined him in London. They were Tolstoy's antennae in the Western world and did much to disseminate his work internationally, much of it through their review *Free Thought*.

Tolstoy was now giving all his time to finishing his novel: "I'm saving water and only using it for *Resurrection*."[26]* He went to the prison at Orel for background in September, and in October sent the publisher Alfred Marx the first seventy chapters of the novel. The family had been drafted to make a fair copy of these pages of *Resurrection* as Tolstoy wrote them. Alexandra Lvovna remembered later in her memoirs: "In the dining-room of our house in Moscow the whole table was flooded with manuscripts and proofs. Everybody was copying pages, Tanya, Mama, friends. My father would come down from his study from time to time to give us instructions."[27]

The publication of Tolstoy's works entailed great difficulties: his Russian publisher feared "leaks" as much as censorship. To bring out *Resurrection*, the editors of *The Niva* made use of a stratagem: they had the novel printed under the title of *Expectation*, by Vladimir Korolenko, a novelist of the angry younger generation of Russian writers, and gave the real title and true author only on publication day.[28] Even so, the book was badly mutilated; in 1928 Marya Schmidt maintained that censorship had made "490 cuts and whole chapters had been suppressed."[29] Indeed, according to her, things were no brighter abroad, "the English eliminating what shocked them, the French what went against military service, and the Germans what was against the Kaiser." She thought the least bad edition was the one published in London† in Russian by Chertkov.

After the enormous, exacting effort of trying to complete *Resurrection*, the celebrations planned for Tolstoy's seventieth birthday, which he had so much apprehended, now seemed acceptable: "The jubilee was not so repulsive and depressing as I expected."[30]

The year 1899 was entirely devoted to finishing and publishing *Resurrection*. As in the time of *War and Peace* and *Anna Karenina*, Tolstoy wrote very little in his diary that year. He dropped it on February 22 and returned to it on June 26, to pass judgment on his work: "There's a lot in it that isn't bad, things for whose sake it is being written."[31]

For four months he had worked intensively: the last chapters were written in April, the first having been published in March. Tolstoy made no mention of the visit to Yasnaya Polyana of Rilke with Lou Andreas

* "Water" is here a metaphor for energy, inspiration.

† This judgment is questionable, for Alexandra says that when Marx "had sent final proofs," her father "took them upstairs and rewrote it all over again." She adds that they had to send telegrams and stop the presses, but "the corrections did not arrive in time for the foreign edition." (A. Tolstoï, *Ma vie avec mon père*, Paris: Rieder, 1933, p. 59.) The definitive edition was published in Moscow in 1935, edited by Chertkov, in volume 32, and the documents in volume 33 of the *Complete Works*.

Salomé and her husband. The poet, on the other hand, who had translated *War and Peace* into German, recorded his visit at length in a letter of May 20, 1900, to Sophya Nikolayevna Schill. In it he speaks of "the old man whom one always approaches like a son." Like others, he had been struck by Tolstoy's eyes. "That clear unshadowed look which meets his visitors', which deliberately plumbs them, and unconsciously blesses them with some ineffable blessing, seemed independent of the old man's body."

Tolstoy was beginning to lose interest in political affairs. In January, students had gone on strike and he noted: "They keep trying to involve me." But at the time he was too wrapped up in his novel, and he advised them "to behave passively."[32] His reticence may have had deeper causes, which he expressed on the occasion of the university troubles in Kiev and at St. Petersburg in 1901: it is wrong, he thought, "to ascribe importance to student riots, they are really strife between oppressors, between fully fledged oppressors and those who still only want to be such."[33]

His brother's health was worrying him, but he must finish *Resurrection* and cannot leave Yasnaya Polyana to go and see him. Tolstoy himself was more and more often ailing—rheumatism and stomach trouble—and he experienced "more days sick than well."[34] Death had become for him "more than natural, almost desirable."[35] All the same, he managed to finish his novcl and was not happy with it: ". . . It's not good. Not revised. Too hurried, but I'm free of it and it doesn't interest me any more."[36] No matter: the emigration of the Dukhobors was assured.

It was hard for Tolstoy not to write. Even during the militant periods of his life, he always had some literary work in hand. Of course, the feeling of guilt* that he suffered whenever he yielded to the temptation of giving himself over to what he called "artistic work" grew worse after he had published *What Is Art?*; but the cause of the Dukhobors had given him an excuse.

When, almost in spite of himself, he took up his instrument again, Tolstoy had drawn from it the tragic alleluia of *Resurrection*. The subject had been given him in 1887 by his friend Koni, the state prosecutor of Tula: at the start of a court trial, one of the jury recognizes the accused as a young woman he had debauched and abandoned in his youth. Tolstoy could have found himself in the same situation: in the course of a brief stay at Yasnaya Polyana, when he was in the army, he had slept with a servant girl and had left the next morning to rejoin his regiment in the Caucasus. In 1905 he mentioned this episode to Biryukov in unam-

* "It was Tolstoy's peculiar tragedy that he should have come to regard his poetic genius as corrupt and as an agent of betrayal." (George Steiner, *Tolstoy or Dostoevsky*, p. 246)

biguous terms: "Gasha, a young maidservant who lived in my Aunt's house. She was a virgin and I seduced her. She was sent away and after that was totally ruined."[37]

It was one of the grave sins of his youth that haunted Tolstoy and that for a long time only Sofia knew about.[38] His friend's story therefore revived in him his old remorse, so that when he wrote in his diary for June 1896, "Koni's story wasn't born inside me. That's why it's going so slowly,"[39] one wonders whether he was lying to himself or whether the memory of his misdeed had been completely pushed down into his unconscious.

In 1888 Tolstoy had asked Koni "to transfer to him" the "rights" to the story. Preoccupied by *The Kreutzer Sonata* and *What Is Art?*, it was not until two years later that he sketched in his diary the detailed plan of what he then kept calling "Koneva" or "Koni's story."[40] He worked at it with great difficulty for six months. On June 13, 1890, he observes: "Wanted to write. It doesn't go," and the next day: "Wrote a bit of Koni's story. It doesn't attract me."[41] He finally gave up, to resume work five years later, after visiting prisons in May 1895 with one of his magistrate friends, Davydov, president of the Moscow District Court. Tolstoy wanted to know precisely "the law governing the marriage of a convict," "the appeal procedure," "the prison regulations," "the clothing" worn in prison, and "the daily schedule." He also wanted to know how and when prisoners were flogged, how convicts were assigned to the "Black Marias," and whether they wore "handcuffs during transfer."[42]

On July 1, 1895, the draft version was complete; in August Tolstoy read it to his family and some friends at Yasnaya Polyana. That first version was rediscovered only in 1934.* It is about eighty pages long, whereas the novel is nearly five hundred. In the description of young Nekhlyudov, Tolstoy seems to be depicting himself at the time of his seducing Gasha; it is one of his most successful self-portraits:

> A man with a double personality, in fact a being in whom at different times two personalities expressed themselves that were often diametrically opposite—the first that of a man who is strong, passionate, and blind, who sees nothing beyond the satisfaction of his instincts, a man full of life, who sacrifices everything unthinkingly to whatever passion reigns in him at the moment; the second a man severe towards himself, exacting, and as a believer in the possibility of moral perfection, striving toward that perfection, a man who is careful about his own personality and those of others.[43]

* Published in the U.S.S.R. under the title *First Version of Resurrection* in the volume *Unpublished Pieces* of the Centenary Edition, and published in France under the title *Un Cas de conscience* (Stock 1935) and reissued in 1979. It also appears in *Dossier de Résurrection* (*Anna Karénine*, Paris: Gallimard [Pléiade], 1951).

In the final version this description is cut down to a few lines: "In Nekhlyudov, as in all of us, there were two men. One was the spiritual being, seeking only the kind of happiness that means happiness for others too, and also the animal man, out only for his own pleasure, and ready to sacrifice to it the rest of the world."[44] It is not surprising that the hero of *Resurrection* bears the name Tolstoy had already given to the first of his alter egos in 1856, the landowner in *The Morning of a Landowner*, since the new protagonist is a reincarnation of the earlier. He was a boy of very noble nature; society had destroyed his ideal, for when he was serious, they made fun of him and called him "my dear philosophe"; when he was chaste, his virtuous mother worried about his health; when he gave his lands to the peasants, they called him "a dreamer."[45]*

In the first version, Nekhlyudov ended up marrying Katyushka, which meant the repentance of a man snatching a woman from the horrors of the depths into which he had flung her. In the second version the conclusion is quite different. They take different paths: Nekhlyudov is no longer the instrument of Katyushka's rehabilitation, but it is she who compasses his spiritual liberation. Katyushka throws a pitiless floodlight on Nekhlyudov's world. He and his friends are shadows.[46] Tolstoy goes out of his way to paint their world as dark as possible: the president of the Court frequents the same brothel "where Maslova† had been until six months before."[47] He attacks the "brilliant advocate" who had stripped an old woman of all her goods and got ten thousand rubles for his fee;[48] he attacks the courts, the officer corps, even the Tsar. The passage where "military service [which] always corrupts a man" is described as "legalized violence and murder, [to which] is added the corruption by wealth and intimacy with the Imperial family,"[49] was of course censored.

But the high point of the book is the famous description of the religious service in prison.‡ This bravura passage was to be brought up later as one of the reasons for Tolstoy's excommunication: he had called the consecration of the host a conjuring trick, the priest's vestment "a brocaded bag," said that transubstantiation takes place in "a cup and saucer," and claimed that the priest licked his mustache after Communion.

Katyushka on her side was meant to supply what Tolstoy called the "positive" element.§ Toothless, handcuffed to the police, she meets the eyes of the passersby with the air of a queen. The dove of the Holy Spirit

* Tolstoy and Levin in *Anna Karenina* had both endured the same trial as young men.

† Katyushka's family name, which was also the one she was known by as a prostitute.

‡ Chapter 39. It should be compared with the poetical description of the Easter Mass that Nekhlyudov attends in the village before seducing Katyushka (chapter one).

§ See p. 245.

seems to brush by her as she makes her entrance into the novel. "The blue-grey bird fluttered up and flew past her ear, fanning her with its wings. The prisoner smiled, then heaved a deep sigh as she recalled her present circumstances."[50]

That does not mean *Resurrection* is a sentimental novel: it is a violent, brutal, challenging book; Maslova is no saint, far from it; stubborn and rebellious, she has lost none of the habits she picked up as a prostitute. She is vulgar and aggressive, gets drunk, and insults spring easily to her lips. But she is clear-minded and she understands that having had physical pleasure with her, Nekhlyudov now expects from her spiritual pleasure. She treats him with familiarity and taunts him: "You took your fun at my expense in this world, and now you want your salvation from me in the world to come."[51] She derides him and his fine feelings and his repentance. "You're feeling your guilt!" she keeps harping uncharitably. "You didn't feel it then, but shoved a hundred rubles at me."[52] She was not mistaken: at one point Nekhlyudov had been tempted to get rid of her again and be free of his debt by giving her money—not a hundred rubles that time, but *all* his money; for he had discovered to his despair that "Katyushka existed no more—there was only Maslova!"[53] and that his own punishment would be precisely his inability to save her. But quickly he had had second thoughts, and felt that "he must awaken her soul."[54] Now "he did not want anything from her for himself. All he wanted was that . . . she should awaken and become what she had been before."[55] Nekhlyudov gives the real proof of his purity of intention by forgiving Katyushka an affair with one of the hospital staff; and she had been wrongly accused of it anyway. "Let her have a fling with the medical orderly—that was her business; he loved her not selfishly but for her own sake and for God's."[56] Katyushka "continued to persuade herself that she had not forgiven him and that she hated him . . . but the truth was that she really loved him again."[57] Nekhlyudov followed the way of the cross with her, as it led toward Siberia: he was an impotent spectator of the young woman's sufferings, a witness to the brutality, the barbarism, the diseases, and the death that preyed on the pitiable convoy. "All the horrible evil . . . ruled triumphant, and he could discern no possibility of conquering it or of knowing how to conquer it."[58]

On the journey she, on her side, found brotherhood with the political prisoners, among whom Nekhlyudov had managed to get her transferred. "She understood the motive that moved these creatures. . . ." The friendship she felt for Maria Palovna the revolutionary, and the love she awakened in Simonson the idealist, brought her heart back to life: "Nekhlyudov's offer of marriage was due to generosity and what had happened in the past, but Simonson loved her as she was now, and loved her simply because he loved her."[59]

Nekhlyudov was not able to complete his intended sacrifice; while it "freed him from the self-imposed obligation which had seemed hard and strange to him in moments of weakness," Simonson's decision left him "with a disagreeable, even painful sensation."[60] The man had stolen his atonement, because Simonson's wanting to marry Katyushka showed that "his own sacrifice could not have been so great after all. Plain jealousy entered into it also, perhaps."[61]

The mystery that hovers over the last encounter of the two characters demonstrates Tolstoy's mastery as a novelist. " 'It's one thing or the other,' thought Nekhlyudov. 'Either she loves Simonson and has no use for the sacrifice I imagined I was making; or she still loves me and is refusing me for my own sake. . . .' "[62]

The gentleness of this scene is in contrast with the brutality that pervades the whole novel. "You have suffered enough," says Katyushka, and Nekhlyudov answers, "I am the last person you should thank." She goes on: " 'What's the use of trying to weigh up what we owe one another? God will make up our accounts.'. . . By her peculiar squinting look, her pathetic smile and the tone of her voice when she said, not 'Good-bye' but 'Forgive me,' Nekhlyudov understood that his second supposition as to the cause of her decision was the real one; she loved him [and] by staying with Simonson she was setting Nekhlyudov free."[63]

The story of Nekhlyudov and Katyushka ends there, but for Tolstoy that could not be the end of the book. He wanted to apply his new theory of art, and to "infect" people, not by means of a "religious tract" but by a "universal" one. Being pushed for time,* he was unable to write a new version, the tenth, as he wished. So, fearing that he had not managed to convey his message (although the superb, even if imperfect work that he let go with regret carries in it the implicit hope of redemption), Tolstoy decided quite simply to be explicit about it by including in the last chapter the actual words of the Sermon on the Mount. A strange Englishman,† a prison visitor, puts the Gospel in Nekhlyudov's hands, "open by chance" just at the page of the Beatitudes. "He saw in it today for the first time, not beautiful abstract thoughts, presenting for the most part exaggerated and impossible demands, but simple, clear, practical

* He said to Victor Lebrun, "In *Resurrection* there are rhetorical passages and some artistic passages, and taken on their own both are good. But putting them together in one book was a dreadful thing to do; I decided to print the thing only because of the urgent need to help the Dukhobors." ("Tolstoï vu par un témoin," *Europe*, no. 397–80, 1960, p. 126)

† His model might have been the same "eccentric Englishman" who brought him Whitman's poems in 1889.

commandments, which if obeyed (and this was quite feasible) would establish a completely new order of human society in which . . . the greatest blessing man can hope for—the Kingdom of heaven on earth—would be attained."[64]

It is odd that a novel should end with a commentary on St. Matthew, quoted in full and followed by exegesis. Like those who had seen in *War and Peace* only a historical novel, and those who had taken *Anna Karenina* for a mere story of love, the readers of *Resurrection* were disoriented by "this open-ended conclusion," which resembles all Tolstoy's other epilogues.

After finishing *Anna*, Tolstoy had made Levin's resolution his own—to devote himself to the good of mankind. Likewise after *Resurrection*, being convinced as Nekhlyudov was that the Gospel teachings had "simple, clear, and practical applications," Tolstoy went on to adopt the Sermon on the Mount as the platform of his political purpose.

With *Resurrection* published, Tolstoy returned with fervor to preaching. He grew more and more interested in the conditions of the working class and visited several factories. Near his house in Moscow, there was a silk factory employing 300 women and 700 men; his visits there inspired a long article called *The Slavery of Our Times*. This essay, begun in January 1900, as "The 36-hour Day,"[65] is much more anarchist than revolutionary; it attacks everything, even the revolution. Instead of pitting force against force, as urged by the revolutionaries, Tolstoy favored universal, nonviolent rebellion. He sees the new slavery as arising from artificial needs,* encouraged by governments that issue laws "whose essence is organized violence." He went on to ask himself with implacable logic, "How then can we destroy governments?" The answers he offered to this question proclaim the great Tolstoyan utopia: "First, by taking no part in any act of government (neither under duress nor voluntarily); second, by paying no tax, direct or indirect; third, by not looking to the government to guarantee one's property or security." Though the actions of men in power are clearly evil, those of farmers and businessmen are just as bad, and so are those of revolutionaries, socialists, and anarchists: "Only moral and spiritual action is good; a wave that brings all to chaos and inaction."[66]

During this period, in parallel with his increasingly radical involvement in the war of ideas, Tolstoy began in May to write act one of *The*

* In the article Tolstoy included railways among artificial needs, declaring that "enlightened men will always prefer horses." Anyway, he detested this kind of locomotion, and said that "the railway is to travel what the brothel is to love—a convenience."

Living Corpse. Tolstoy was starting on a new play in order to define himself in contrast with another writer. Chekhov, who later became his friend, was just then his bête noire, not because he lacked talent, but precisely because he had so much and was, in Tolstoy's view, vulgarizing it. On January 16, 1900, Tolstoy had read Chekhov's *The Lady with the Little Dog*, and said: "It's all Nietzsche* . . . people who haven't worked out for themselves a clear philosophy of life . . . now think they are beyond good and evil, but remain on this side. . . ."[67] Some days later he went to see *Uncle Vanya*: "Was shocked. Wanted to write my drama, *The Corpse*, and sketched out a draft."[68]

This play is one of the most autobiographical chapters in a body of literary work that was never anything else. Once again, the subject was drawn from a news item—the story of a debauched, gambling husband who faked his own death to let his wife change her life and remarry.

Though the hero's motives in the play are unlike Tolstoy's, their purpose is the same as his—to die to the world. Here, as in *Resurrection*, the trial scenes in *The Living Corpse* offered the writer a new opportunity to deride human justice, which he calls "public injustice." "Looking at the guilty," he wrote, "one gets the impression that it's not they who are on trial but those who judge others."[69]

Everything that happened was now an occasion for Tolstoy to take a public stand. In March 1900 he criticized the Hague Peace Conference which had taken place in April 1899. It had proved to him that "nothing can be expected from the powers that be. . . . This terrible, menacing situation can only be sorted out, if at all, by the efforts of private individuals."[70] When the King of Italy, Umberto I, was assassinated on July 29, 1900, Tolstoy wrote "Who Is to Blame?" which was published in London in *Free Thought* under the title "Thou Shalt Not Kill." Then in December, he wrote "A Letter to the Monarch," to ask the Tsar to allow the Dukhobor women who had stayed in Russia to join their husbands in Canada.

Every reminder of injustice strengthened his awareness of the privileges of wealth. For example, the trepanning of his daughter Tatyana (Tolstoy was present at the end of this operation to remove a frontal abscess and nearly fainted) revealed to him the inequality of human beings in the face of illness. His attitude is unambiguous as he explains it to his daughter Masha: "A man oughtn't to be cured privately for 50 or 500 or 5000 roubles [while] other people die without help."[71] On the

* Tolstoy loathed Nietzsche and believed him to be really mad. In January 1901 he wrote to his brother Sergey: "I read Nietzsche to stimulate my bile. It's worth reading him to be horrified by what people admire." (*Tolstoy's Letters*, vol. II, p. 590)

spiritual level, such a state of things shocked him even more: people must be allowed to die because "we shall all die. . . . If we recover from one thing we shall fall ill with another."[72] This attitude, which is not far from that of Christian Science, was already evident in his Sevastopol days, and he came to feel likewise about the illness of his son Lev, and Sofia's in 1906; he still felt the same at the time of his own death.

In May Tolstoy stayed with Tatyana, who had survived her "terrible operation."[73] "I spent a wonderful fifteen days. Finished *Slavery* and wrote two acts." He had complained in April of "still doing the same work"—polemical articles—"which has stood in the way of my literary work, and I long for literary work."[74] When he returned to Yasnaya Polyana he still experienced a fierce longing "to write something literary, not dramatic, but epic—a continuation of *Resurrection*: Nekhlyudov's life as a peasant."[75]

Once again Tolstoy struggled with his desires and felt tortured at not understanding "what is the will of Him that sent me." But he also nurses a new feeling: "Having raised myself to the supreme point of my reason, I am identified with God."[76] It is by praying that Tolstoy seeks to attain this "identity": "I recall very often the prayer of every hour."[77]* He looks then, he says, to what there is in him of "divine and eternal and loving—and it hears me and replies to me."[78] He rereads the Sermon on the Mount† . . . and wonders "how people fail to understand that what has been said there should be said in the future for everyone."[79]

In August "the old temptation"—that of leaving forever—attacked him again.[80] As in every summer, most of the family had assembled at Yasnaya Polyana, the children and the grandchildren too. Tolstoy felt more and more an outsider in this world of idleness and frivolity. "They may love me, but I'm of no use to them," and he adds in French: "I'm an *encombrant* [an encumbrance]."[81]

In the autumn, there are still "a lot of visitors," says Tolstoy, "all literary." Among them was the director of the Moscow Arts Theatre, who wanted to put on *The Living Corpse*, but Tolstoy refused. Maxim Gorky visited on October 8, and Sofia took a photograph of the two men together. When Gorky had come to Khamovnichesky Street for the first time earlier that year, Tolstoy had seen in him a "real man of the people"

* This "perpetual prayer" or "continual prayer" is one of the teachings of the Philokalia. Tolstoy defines it in *La Vraie Vie*: "The prayer of every hour is the permanent certainty of the presence of God, and temporary prayer is the passing elevation of man to a higher degree of his moral life." (*Journal intime de Tolstoï, 1895–99*, Geneva: Jeheber, 1917)

† Tolstoy read the Gospels in a Dutch edition he had been told was the best; he must have begun to learn Dutch in the winter of 1898. He already spoke French, English, and German, had studied Greek and Hebrew, and at the end of his life tried to learn Japanese.

and a few days after the visit had written to him: "I have always liked your books but I found you better than them."[82] The next year in the Crimea, they saw a great deal of each other.

Tolstoy knew that what he wanted to express was more than a doctrine. Being opposed to all dogma, he rejected the idea of being a Tolstoyan in the sense that his disciples gave to the word: "I don't need to write out a system; my view of the world will become clear from what I write down here, and if any people need it, they will make use of it."[83] All systematization was so repugnant to him that he declared: "the two most terrible plagues of our time are dogmatic Christianity and historical materialism."[84]

To compensate for the vulgarities of Church religion, he read "the Buddhist Sutras," and found them "very good."[85] He entered in the notebooks: "Christian truth is dynamite."[86] Tolstoy had also gone back to *The Chinese Classics* (in English), which had been in his library for twenty years: "very important."

In November, unwell again, he was "studying Confucius," and everything else seemed to him "worthless."[87] In his diary he drew up a short summary of the teachings of the Chinese philosopher under a title borrowed from him, "The Doctrine of the Middle Way." Confucianism always attracted Tolstoy. In 1884 he had found in it the idea that "power need not be oppression when it is recognised as morally and rationally superior."[88] But what interested him even more now was the rules of life he might derive: "Confucius' teaching about paying particular attention to oneself when one is alone continues to bear fruit."[89]

He spent the tail end of the year in Moscow as usual. Passing a bookshop window that displayed *The Kreutzer Sonata* and *The Power of Darkness*, he said to himself, "I wrote [them] without any thought of preaching to people, of being of use to them, and yet all of them, especially *The Kreutzer Sonata*, have been of great use."[90] This was to discover, late in the day, that he did more good morally when he was not trying to do any, and had more influence on men through his writings as a novelist than through his philosophizing.

Tolstoy was just then equally engrossed in art and in religion. His literary notes often end in religious meditations, and at times it is the other way round. A by-product of his reflections was his note giving one of the best definitions of his own genius: "An artist, in order to produce an effect on other people, must be a seeker, his work must be a search. If he has found everything and knows everything and teaches or deliberately amuses, he produces no effect. Only if he is seeking does the spectator, the listener, or the reader join with him in his search."[91]

TWENTY-TWO

Excommunication

IN THE END, Tolstoy's intransigent confrontation exacted its penalty. The "Pastoral Letter of the most Holy Synod to the faithful children of the Greco-Russian Orthodox Church in what concerns Count Leo Tolstoy" was made public on February 22, 1901. That document put the faithful on guard against "a new false teacher, Count Leo Tolstoy, known as a writer throughout the world, a Russian by birth and Orthodox by baptism and education." It charged him with having "raised himself up insolently and audaciously against God, against Christ, and against his heritage . . ." and "with showing his dissidence" by the ill-use he made of "the talent God had given him." The Church "does not recognize him as a member, and in taking note of his dereliction, prays God for his repentance."[1]

The most surprising thing about this excommunication is that it had not occurred sooner. Tolstoy's religious writings, *A Confession* and *A Criticism of Dogmatic Theology*, were sufficiently heretical, and his polemical articles sufficiently blasphemous, to justify such a measure. Tolstoy's astonishing impunity so far was due to the fear he inspired in the Church and in the government.

When *The Kreutzer Sonata* was published, Anton Chekhov expressed amazement at the indulgence with which Tolstoy was treated. Chekhov compared him to "Diogenes spitting in people's faces, knowing he had nothing to fear in so doing"; and he added: "Tolstoy shows insolence over great problems because he knows no one can drag him to the police station."[2]

Since the early nineties, Tolstoy had indeed reached extremes of audacity and held more and more violent opinions; he practiced a sort of verbal terrorism that was in contradiction with his call for nonviolence. In 1891, the end of the "Famine" article had enjoined the overthrow of the present system; in 1893 in *The Kingdom of God Is Within You*, Tolstoy had declared that "Christianity in its true meaning destroys the state";[3] among his pacifist essays, "Carthago delenda est" contains probably the crudest piece of red-hot incitement to sedition: "Awake brethren! Do not listen to those villains who, from your childhood, infect you with the diabolical spirit of patriotism . . . [which] exists only in order to deprive you of your property, your freedom, and your human dignity."[4]

The article "On Refusing Military Service" is no less emphatic; Tolstoy accuses all governments of "defending themselves as much as they can against all manifestations of the spiritual forces on which their salvation or damnation depends."[5] He criticizes international organizations just as much; in January 1899, he says of the Peace Conference on Disarmament that it will be of no use at all; "the only solution is to refuse to serve."[6] In *The Slavery of Our Times*, he had given precise directions for destroying existing institutions.

Tolstoy went so far as to issue a direct challenge. The wife of a Tula doctor had been subjected to police harassment for having copied one of his prohibited works, *What I Believe*, so Tolstoy called down on his own head all the thunderbolts of power: "The least unreasonable thing the government could do would be to turn all its rigours against the one in whom it finds the source of all evil, against me; and this, with all the more reason, since I declare in advance that I will not cease to my dying day from doing what according to the government is evil, but according to me is my sacred duty before God."[7]

Oddly enough, it was not Tolstoy's polemical writings but the novel *Resurrection* that had proved the last straw and made the authorities decide to take action against him. In a country as religious as Tsarist Russia, excommunication had much greater force than any civil penalty whatever. It was therefore adroit to focus on the man, not the work, and to make Tolstoy a pawn of Satan "with spirit full of pride,"[8] in the actual wording of the Pastoral Letter.

According to Tolstoy's son Lev, his father's moral and religious influence was "far less than his social and political influence."[9] And thus in condemning him on the religious plane, the Holy Synod was threatening his prestige and diminishing his influence on public opinion. The Church in her wisdom had understood that, in Tolstoy's case, it was the fame of the novelist that ensured the power of the preacher.

The excommunication was therefore a clever move, but some of its side effects were the opposite of what the Orthodox hierarchy expected. On the very day the Letter was published, Tolstoy was spotted in the street and surrounded by an applauding throng of students and workmen. The next day, his portrait by Repin in "The Wanderers' Exhibition" was the rallying point of a demonstration. Letters and telegrams in great number came to the house in Moscow; censorship forbade their publication in the press. On March 31 Tolstoy noted in his diary: "Continue to receive greetings and abuse."[10] He replied in an open letter to those who had expressed their sympathy.

Sofia recorded "a strange atmosphere of celebration" in the house—visitors "filing in from morn to night. Whole crowds." She, by the way, had taken her husband's side energetically and written in vehement terms to Mgr. Anthonyi, the Metropolitan of St. Petersburg. In her letter, "which was reproduced around the world," Sofia predicted that the reading of the Church proclamation would not win "adherence, but raise indignation."[11] In a very Tolstoyan tone, she condemned "wearers of mitres and decorations thick with diamonds, punishing and excommunicating pastors,"[12] who put themselves outside the Church by making themselves "butchers of the soul to those who will indisputably be graced by God for their life full of humility, of renunciation of worldly goods, of love and charity."[13] After having endlessly deplored her husband's religious attitudes, herself being a practicing and believing Orthodox, she now took on his defense with courage and eloquence.

The letter circulated under cover and had a considerable effect. The Metropolitan Anthonyi, president of the Holy Synod, felt it necessary to make public his answer to Countess Tolstoy. "The Pastoral Letter was, on the contrary, an act of love, an appeal to your husband to return to the Church, and an invitation to the faithful to pray for him."[14]

Tolstoy took longer than his wife to react to what he calls in his diary his "strange excommunication from the Church";[15] he made no move for two months. He did not want to engage in a debate as much as make use of the forum the Holy Synod had thus opened to him to proclaim his faith and refute the false interpretations given of it.

From March 19 on, he had been composing a statement entitled "To the Tsar and His Aides," which was published in full only by *Free Thought*.[16] Tolstoy sent "A Reply to the Holy Synod's Edict" on April 4,

1901.* It begins by suggesting that priests, instead of bowing before icons, prostrate themselves before the people to ask their pardon for deceiving them; he then turns to the "illegal" and "equivocal" character of the edict, "which can have no other purpose than to pass for an excommunication without really being one."†

Tolstoy deplored the reactions of hatred that the text had provoked. He had in fact received threatening letters in which he was called an "old demon" whom people hoped would "die like a dog."[17]

In his letter to the Holy Synod Tolstoy clearly expounded the articles of his faith‡ and retorted item by item to the charge. He was accused of denying "the God of three persons . . . the miraculous conception of Christ and his divine creation, and life beyond the grave."[18] He replied: "That I deny the incomprehensible Trinity; the fable, which is altogether meaningless in our time, of the fall of the first man; the blasphemous story of a God born of a virgin to redeem the human race—is perfectly true."[19] He declared he could not "consider Christ as God without committing the greatest sacrilege." He rejected the accusation of "denying all the sacraments and not fearing to direct his mockery against the holiest of all, the Eucharist,"[20] by saying that "in the baptism of infants§ I see a palpable perversion of the whole meaning which might be

* "So that is what is true and what is untrue in the Synod's edict about me: It is true I do not believe in what they say they believe in. But I believe in what they wish to persuade people that I disbelieve in. I believe in this: I believe in God, whom I understand as Spirit, as Love, as the Source of all . . . I believe that the will of God is most clearly and intelligibly expressed in the teaching of the man Jesus, whom to consider God and pray to, I esteem the greatest blasphemy . . . I believe that [God's] will is that men should love one another . . . of which it is said in the Gospels that this is the law and the prophets. I believe, therefore, that the meaning of the life of every man is to be found only in increasing the love that is in him; that this increase of love . . . helps more than anything towards the establishment of the Kindgom of God on earth; that is, to the establishment of an order of life in which the discord, deception, and violence that now rule will be replaced by free accord, by truth, and by the brotherly love of one for another . . . I believe that to obtain progress in love there is only one means: prayer—not public prayer . . . but private prayer.

"Whether or not these beliefs of mine offend, grieve, or prove a stumbling block to anyone, or hinder anything, or give displeasure to anybody, I can as little change them as I can change my body. . . . I began by loving my Orthodox faith more than my peace, then I loved Christianity more than my Church, and now I love truth more than anything in the world. And up to now truth for me corresponds with Christianity as I understand it. And I hold to this Christianity, and to the degree in which I hold to it I live peacefully and happily, and peacefully and happily approach death." (*On Life*, p. 224)

† Professor Nicolas Weisbein also points out that "the word *excommunication* is not used by the hierarchy." (*Evolution religieuse de Tolstoï*, Paris: Librairie des cinq continents, 1960, p. 228)

‡ It had been a great concern of Tolstoy's for a long time, and two weeks after the publication of the edict he noted that he wanted "to begin an article on lack of religion," going on to give a definition of religion: "It is the establishment by man of relations with the infinite, such that by them is determined the purpose of his life." (*Journaux et carnets*, vol. II, p. 835)

§ Here again Tolstoy comes close to a tendency of contemporary theology to oppose the baptism of infants.

attached to the baptism of adults. . . . In the Sacrament I see a deification of the flesh and a perversion of Christian teaching."[21]

There is on the whole a marked continuity in Tolstoy's religious attitudes. As early as *A Confession* he thought baptism and Communion were "scandalous acts,"[22] and fifty years after proclaiming at Sevastopol that the truth was "the hero of my tale, whom I love with all the power of my soul,"[23] he resorts practically to the same words in his reply to the Holy Synod: "I love truth more than anything in the world."[24]

But it was a strange resolve to want to keep the name of Christianity for a religion that rejected its essential dogmas and that came closer to Gnosticism. In this ambiguous outlook the supernatural creeps in all the same, and one great difference between the new creed and the one Tolstoy professed in 1884 in *What I Believe* is that he now accepts the immortality of the soul—or at least what he calls "a new form of life."[25] This credo, expressed on many pages of his diary, explains the slow evolution that took place in Tolstoy's relation with death.

The Metropolitan Anthonyi in his turn took his time before answering the "false doctor." He waited until June 30, 1901; his letter, like Tolstoy's, was not polemical. After taking note of the remarks made "by certain great persons"* who were indignant at "the fortunate and exceptional situation of this writer in what concerned the impunity permitted him by the authorities," the prelate contented himself with a theological refutation of Tolstoy's credo, rebuked him for wiping out all Christianity at a stroke by denying the Incarnation of Christ and His redemption of mankind, and finally expressed indignation at hearing Tolstoy declare that if he were left free to publish his religious works in Russia "it would not take long for the Orthodox Church to be reduced to ruins." Msgr. Anthonyi winds up comparing Tolstoy to Julian the Apostate, "who wished to wipe Christ's doctrine from the face of the earth."[26] This was to distort completely Tolstoy's ideas. He had, on the contrary, stated explicitly in his reply to the Holy Synod, "If I have denied the Church it was not because I rebelled against the Lord; on the contrary, I denied it because I wished with all the strength of my soul to serve Him."[27]

Anthonyi ends his missive with the declaration: "To deny Christ His divine essence, and to maintain that it is blasphemous to recognize it, amounts in fact to pronouncing an anathema against Christ."[28] The holy

* Even among the people opinions were not all favorable to Tolstoy, and the Holy Synod won on some points. As early as the days of the Yasnaya Polyana school, some mujiks under the influence of local priests had refused to send their children to Tolstoy, while in the famine of 1891 some peasants were unwilling to accept food from an apostate.

man was probably right. Still, though Tolstoy was against the Church, he was not against Christ and, inverting the situation, the anathematized utters the anathema and proclaims himself, he, Leo Tolstoy, defender of the faith *against* the Church!

The Holy Synod's Letter had the paradoxical result of making Tolstoy the spiritual leader of many Russians and others in foreign countries; and it certainly did nothing to calm Tolstoy's prophetic ardor. For him, Christians were now infidels, and in order to recover the message of Christ in its purity, he embarked on a crusade against religion.

TWENTY-THREE

The Crimea

THE AUTHORITIES had not dared go so far as to banish Tolstoy: it was illness that drove him away from Yasnaya Polyana. In June 1901, he had an attack of angina pectoris and almost certainly malaria, and came close to death. In July and August he seldom got out of bed, yet in later days he looked back on this period with amazing pleasure: "My illness was one long spiritual holiday; heightened spirituality and calmness at the approach of death and expressions of love from all sides. . . ."[1] In October he agreed to go and convalesce on the Russian Riviera, the Crimea.

Tolstoy felt so ill when he got to the station that for a moment he thought of giving up the trip, but did not, for fear he might be too ill to get home again. He traveled in a special carriage.* The devoted Boulanger, who worked at the Ministry of Roads and Transport, had even arranged for the fittings to include a piano. The Ministry of the Interior also expressed solicitude and laid down "a series of steps to be taken in case of death." The train stopped at Kharkov, Tolstoy was cheered by a crowd of students, and at the stopover in Sevastopol found enough strength to go and revisit the scenes of his military exploits as a young man.

The end of the journey was Gaspra, near Yalta, where Countess Panin

* "The cook . . . ; the valet; and mother's seamstress . . . were to follow on another train." (A. Tolstoy, *The Tragedy of Tolstoy*, London: George Allen and Unwin, 1933, p. 44)

had put her magnificent mansion at the disposal of Tolstoy and his family. It resembled the illustration of a Gothic castle one might find in *Les Enfants du Capitaine Grant* by Jules Verne. To one of his sons, Tolstoy wrote, "So much for the simple life I was looking for! . . . two turrets and a chapel";[2] and to Chertkov: it "is the height of comfort and luxury, such as I've never known in my life."[3] A path led directly to the sea, and the beauty of the landscape made him forget the sumptuousness of the house. The patriarch rapidly recovered his health; a fortnight later, he was riding.

Not long after Tolstoy's arrival, Chekhov* came to visit him and wrote to Gorky: "The Crimea gives him wonderful pleasure; it brings out in him sheer childish enjoyment." A little later, Gorky was finally allowed to settle at Yalta and often came over to see the convalescent.† They took long walks together, the memory of which inspired Gorky with the most beautiful pages ever written about Tolstoy.‡ Chekhov occasionally joined them.

The truth is that for different reasons Tolstoy did not really like what Gorky and Chekhov were writing, but both belonged to the only nobility that counted in his eyes: they were born poor. Gorky was for him "a true man of the people," and he forgave Chekhov for his "bad art" because he was a serf's grandson and had known poverty—which did not prevent Tolstoy from wondering, "In the name of what is he writing?"[4]

Through the end of November 1901, Tolstoy was too weak to write. When he took up his pen again, it was to set down in his diary a last wish: "When I am dying, I would like to be asked whether I continue to understand life as I used to understand it, as a growing nearer to God, an expansion of love. If I'm unable to speak, I'll close my eyes if the answer is yes, and raise them upwards if it's no."[5]

Tolstoy's remoteness from the center of things and his precarious state of health did not make him any the less alarming to the authorities. More seditious than ever, he took up the "Appeals," on which he had been working before he fell ill. In his "Notes for Soldiers," he urged them "to

* Chekhov had tuberculosis and lived at Aoutka, not far from Yalta. He had gone like so many others to see Tolstoy at Yasnaya Polyana in 1895, and Tolstoy had visited him at the Ostrumov clinic in 1897. Chekhov said he had "never loved any man" so much as Tolstoy. Tolstoy thought he had a girlish air and teased him a great deal: "Shakespeare's plays are bad enough, but yours are worse . . . your characters, where do they take you? From the divan where they sit to the lumber room." (*Tolstoï et ses contemporains*, p. 220)

† Tolstoy had intervened in May that year with Prince Svajatopolk-Mirsky, Vice-Minister of the Interior, to have Gorky let out of the prison of Nijni-Novgorod on the grounds of consumption. "Keeping him in prison would be equivalent to killing him, before trial or without trial." (*Tolstoy's Letters*, vol. II, p. 597)

‡ M. Gorky, *Reminiscences of Tolstoy, Chekhov and Andreev*, London: Hogarth Press, 1934.

listen only to their conscience, which can only be within them, not in their sergeant, captain, colonel, or anyone else."[6] He accused the military of being "murderers as much as the thief who kills a rich man in order to rob him." He exhorts them to refuse to serve, even at the cost of "bearing all suffering and even death."[7]

He did not content himself with trying to suborn simply the troops. A little later, he wrote "Notes for Officers," and as he had already done with the priests, he invited them to assemble "the men of whom [they] are in command . . . asking their pardon for all the evil [they] have done them by deception,"[8] and to give up the career of soldier.

Going all the way up the hierarchy, Tolstoy ends by addressing the supreme head, the Tsar. The Panins' residence was close to the summer palaces of several members of the imperial family, and Tolstoy on July 16, 1901, entrusted the Grand Duke Nikolay Mikhailovich, uncle of Nicholas II, with a letter for his nephew. Tolstoy addresses the Tsar as "Dear Brother" and tells him that "autocracy is an obsolete form of government which may suit the needs of a people somewhere in Central Africa . . . but not the needs of the Russian people, who are becoming more and more enlightened thanks to the knowledge now common to the whole world."[9] He does not think that the solutions adopted by Western countries would be valid for Russia, "where an enormous part of the population lives on the land. . . . For the Russian people such liberation can be achieved only by abolishing the private ownership of land. . . ." Tolstoy denounces it "as an injustice as flagrant as serfdom."[10] He adjures the monarch not to listen to his counselors but to "think about this . . . in the presence of God" and to obey what He says, that is, "your conscience." Tolstoy of course signs himself "Your brother."[11]

Tolstoy sent several letters to the Grand Duke Nikolay, including one about the "single tax" devised by the American economist Henry George.* The simplicity of the theory had captivated Tolstoy, according to whom "it is only in Russia that it can be carried out, thanks to autocracy";[12] in freer countries landowners would not accept it.

Being increasingly convinced that Russia was heading toward major upheavals, he wrote to Chertkov, who was still in exile, that two things seemed important: "that the Russian people, and even the peasantry . . .

* George was opposed to property for ethical reasons; the system he favored changed the landholder into a simple renter of land. Tolstoy had happily devoured the American economist's books: "The reading of every one of your books makes clear to me things which were not so before." In the same letter (March 27–April 8, 1869, *Tolstoy's Letters*, vol. II, p. 537), he goes on to express pleasure at his correspondent's having twice mentioned "the life to come" and delight at soon making his acquaintance. But Henry George died before carrying out his plan to go to Russia.

are waking up . . . and that the government is withdrawing deeper and deeper into its shell," wanting to keep things as they are and even "go back to an earlier and more backward [state of affairs]."[13]

At the beginning of 1902, Tolstoy fell seriously ill again: he had pneumonia. "A priest sat in ambush in the chapel,"[14]* and on January 29, the Director General of the Press requested that in the event of Tolstoy's death, all journalists should observe "the necessary objectivity and decency."[15] The police were also on the watch. Gorky reported that "the Panin estate where the Tolstoys lived was surrounded by spies; they prowled in the park, and Leopold Sulerjitsky† kept chasing them out like pigs out of a vegetable garden."[16] For her part, Alexandra tells how she and her friends succeeded in shaking off a policeman who was following them, and began trailing him instead: "this occurrence became the talk of the town."[17]

Nearly the entire family was together at Gaspra: "the house is a real hospital, Papa is ill, Masha and Olga [Andrey's wife] are not well either," says Tatyana Lvovna, and adds that "all our intellectual and physical strength seems mustered for the preservation of our bodies."[18] During the night when Tolstoy nearly died, his daughter-in-law gave birth to a stillborn child. Sofia made herself over into a head nurse; Gorky marveled at her "tireless labors."[19] Ever since Tolstoy had become seriously ill, he was at Sofia's mercy, and in spite of her anxiety, she was happy to be able to prove her love by unremitting devotion. Alexandra Lvovna later wrote that her mother, "suffering from the inner discord between him and herself . . . emphasized the external care for his well-being."[20]

Hardly out of danger with pneumonia, Tolstoy caught typhoid fever. He was once again in mortal peril, but recovered against all expectations. During the critical period he could not write, but he dictated either to Masha or to Nikolay Gay, the painter's son, who had become an intimate, or at times to Sofia. Taken together, these notes are like a long meditation on death. Tolstoy defined it first as the "annihilation of the self";[21] but some days later, returning to the same idea, he says: "It seems that the self has disappeared, when [in reality] it has only entered into a new combination."[22]

* When Tolstoy had a relapse, the Metropolitan Anthonyi tried a new approach to Sofia. Tolstoy noted: "They say 'Return to the Church.' But haven't I seen in the Church a gross and obvious deceit?" He compares himself to a mujik who no longer wants any flour that he knows to be "mixed with lime." (*Journaux et carnets*, vol. II, p. 894)

† Sulerjitsky was educated at the Moscow School of Fine Arts at the same time as Tatyana Lvovna. On account of his Tolstoyan convictions he refused to do his National Service and was arrested for starting in Russia a Social-Democratic magazine.

Tolstoy had come a long way since Arzamas, but his detachment was not complete. "There is in me an ambiguous relationship with the death I await."[23] At seventy-four, he was still asking himself the same question about himself, but no longer solely from the psychological point of view. "The clarification of my spiritual awareness, the transport of our self into spiritual awareness, takes place, expresses itself, in love."[24] When he had recovered, Tolstoy wrote: "I felt the pangs of death, i.e., of a new life."[25] Reflecting on the experience a month later, he added: "My last illness has been a hard lying-in."[26]

Tolstoy was impatient to return to Yasnaya Polyana. In order not to tire the patient unduly, the journey was made by water. On June 25 he drove as far as Yalta in the Yussupovs' carriage. A crowd on the dock cheered him. Gorky went on board with him. Again, the writer traveled like a monarch, surrounded by his family, his new doctor Nukitin, and the faithful Boulanger.

Photographs taken at that time show Tolstoy frail, wasted, ravaged; only his eyes have kept their amazing life. He was so weak that he spent his days in the huge wheelchair he had brought back from the Crimea.

Almost as soon as he was home, Tolstoy went back to work, in spite of the presence of numerous visitors.* He began to collect passages from his favorite writers and thinkers and the holy books of various religions, with the purpose of making them "more accessible to the masses."[27] He grouped them under the title "Thoughts of Wise People for Every Day," published in *The Mediator* in 1903. At the end of the year, he jotted down two plans for his play *And the Light Shineth in the Darkness*; in the second he makes it clear that the central character "does everything for [his] soul with no thought for the consequences,"[28] which is just what he himself seemed to be doing.

He also worked on *Hadji Murad*, but with difficulty. He had made a note in 1898 with this novel in mind: "How good it would be to write a work of art in which one could clearly express the shifting nature of man; the fact that one and the same man is now a villain, now an angel, now a

* Throughout 1902 there would always be many: Tolstoyans home from exile, like Abrikossov, with news from other exiles; Tolstoy's children and grandchildren; tourists who came out of curiosity. "The usual Swedes," says the journal for August 5, and on the sixteenth: "the artists of the new theatre came and went"; Miss Walsh arrived to teach Alexandra Lvovna English; Paul Boyer, the Behrs, Halperin-Kaminsky (who wrote *La Tragédie de Tolstoï et de sa femme*), English translator Aylmer Maude, the younger Gay, Goldenweiser, who often played the piano for Tolstoy, and yet others. In October, "some Tula socialists and Molokans" on the first. Gorky came on the nineteenth with a friend with whom he wanted to found a journal of popularized science—he wished to draw on Tolstoy's *Mediator* experience. Pyotr Verigin, chief of the Dukhobors, called before leaving for Canada (October 30). (*Journaux et carnets*, vol. II, pp. 956–62)

wise man, now an idiot, now a strong man, now the most impotent of creatures." He refers to "an English toy called a 'peepshow,' " based on the principle of the stereoscope, which gives the illusion of depth and relief to flat images: "That is the way to show Hadji Murat—as a husband, a fanatic, etc."[29] But his hero eludes him, and when one evening Sofia caught her husband playing patience,[30] it was to her the sign that some decision to be made in his novel bothered him. She knew that being in love with reason as he was, Tolstoy considered the game of patience as a sort of tool of his trade. When he could not decide on the fate of one of his characters, he would leave the decision to the fall of the cards. That is what he had done in *War and Peace* when he was hesitating over Prince Andrey's death at the battle of Borodino.

None the less, he also used more direct means—documentary sources; he asked the Grand Duke Nikolay Mikhailovich if he could let him see some of the archives kept at Tiflis, which Tolstoy "needed for an episode from Caucasian history that he was writing,"[31] In the same letter, he told the Grand Duke that he had just finished an important study on the abolition of private property: "To The Working People," begun at Gaspra in June. Chertkov was about to publish it in Switzerland and Tolstoy asked that a copy be sent to the Grand Duke.

Being always keen on exact documentation, Tolstoy asked Stasov* to copy for him some pages of the *Imperial Court Journal* for late 1851 through early 1852.[32] He also wrote to the widow of the officer who had been in command over Hadji Murad when he rallied the Russian troops, and asked her a number of questions: "Did he speak even a little Russian? Whose were the horses on which he tried to escape? . . . Did he limp noticeably? . . ."[33]

He also turned to Alexandrine Tolstoy, whose position at Court made her an inexhaustible source of information. He asked her for details of what he calls *la petite histoire* [backstairs history]. He begged her not to think ill of him "for occupying myself with such trifles when I really do have one foot in the grave. These trifles . . . afford me respite from the real, serious thoughts with which my soul is overfull."[34]

In early 1903 Tolstoy was still very weak. Like this letter to Alexandrine, he dictated all his mail, Masha serving as amanuensis. This physical weakness seemed to set free his inward strength, and, as he wrote to the president of the Manchester Tolstoy Society on Feb-

* V. V. Stasov, historian of art and literature, was head of the Fine Arts Department of the St. Petersburg Public Library. He admired the novelist unreservedly but severely criticized Tolstoy's religious positions. They exchanged some hundred letters over a period of thirty years.

ruary 23, he was convinced that "the changes in our life must come from the impossibility to live otherwise than accordingly" [*sic*—the letter is in English] "to the demands of our conscience but not from our mental resolution to try a new form of life."[35]

"The firm belief that the world will be reconstructed not from the outside but from the inside"[36] grows in him. In that year 1903 Tolstoy intervened only once in a public event—the pogrom at Kishinyov in April.* He signed a petition to the mayor "expressing our feelings about this terrible affair"[37] and decided to compose a piece for a collection to be published in aid of the victims. After some hesitation, he wrote *After the Ball*, based on an episode during his youthful sojourn in Kazan.[38] He explained this kind of "disengagement": "The mistake is to ask me for the work of a publicist while I am entirely absorbed by one very stark question: the religious question and its application to life."[39]

Once more, back to work: "I'm still dawdling about with Shakespeare *et je ne démords pas de mon idée* [I stick to my guns]. . . . I had to express what has been cooped up in me for half a century."[40] (This to Stasov.) But Tolstoy was not satisfied with his work, knowing very well how extreme it was; indeed, it was only under pressure from Chertkov that he published the piece, with the title "Shakespeare and the Drama." His violent critique of Shakespeare is not aesthetic but moral. He was fighting the "pernicious influence" of the dramatist whose works, he felt, make the reader lose "the capacity to distinguish between good and evil,"[41] convinced as he is that Shakespeare's plays do not aim at "the elucidation and confirmation in man of the highest degree of religious consciousness."[42] Thus he is bent on proving that "Shakespeare cannot be admitted to be either a writer of great genius or even an average one."[43] Tolstoy uses the technique of denigration that he had already used in *Resurrection* to describe the Mass. He paraphrases Shakespeare's tragedies in the words of everyday life, his idea being to prove that the plays consist of thoughts "born of words or of contrasts," which explains why the characters "utter whatever comes to hand and as it comes to hand. . . . All his characters speak not a language of their own but always one and the same Shakespearean . . . language."[44] In Tolstoy's view, Falstaff alone "speaks in a manner proper to himself," because the Shakespearean speech "is quite in harmony with the boastful, distorted, perverted character of the drunken Falstaff."[45] He thinks Shakespeare not serious—he plays with words—as opposed to Homer, who "believes in what he says and speaks seriously of what he describes."[46] For Tolstoy, the cult of

* Of course, he continued to follow the fate of the Dukhobors and Molokans.

Shakespeare is one of the great pretenses of the modern world; it was brought into fashion by Goethe, "partly from a wish to destroy the prestige of the worthier French art, partly from a wish to give freer scope to his own dramatic work, but chiefly because his view of life agreed with Shakespeare's."[47]* He means to prove that Shakespeare was not a real artist at all. To knock him off his throne is thus a duty in pursuance of public health: "The sooner people emancipate themselves from this false worship of Shakespeare, the better for all."[48]

Gradually Tolstoy recovered his strength. On October 20, Tatyana Lvovna observed: "Mamma is nervy and full of complaints. . . . I found Papa extraordinarily cheerful, and fatter. He goes riding a lot. . . . Yesterday evening he read us his article against Shakespeare."[49] His intellectual vigor was also returning. In July he drew up a fresh list of a dozen literary subjects, among them *The Wife's Betrayal*, a novel he had already thought about in the terrible summer of 1896; *Alexander I*, based on the legend that this monarch had lived many years in Siberia under an assumed name; *The Living Corpse*, begun in 1900; "my play," that is, *And the Light Shineth in the Darkness*; *The Story of a Mother*, sketched in April 1891[50] and a fragment of which appeared in 1898 in aid of the Dukhobors. Tolstoy was eager to write on motherly love, for he never lost his great admiration for Sofia as a mother or his yearning for his own mother. The list also includes *Notes of a Madman*, *Samara*, *The Bashkirs and the Colonists*—another subject he had always wanted to treat; and *The Ball*, which became *After the Ball*.

Biryukov had begun to write the master's biography, and Tolstoy wanted to give him help "with all his heart," as he writes on November 21, 1903. So he rounds up his memories,† gives him a list of his amours: "first, Sonichka Koloshina (the model for Sonichka Volokhina in *Childhood*), then Zinaida Molostvova. That love existed in my imagination, she hardly knew anything about it." (She was a friend of his sister's whom he met as a student at Kazan.) Next, the Cossack girl described in *The Cossacks*. "Then a worldly attachment for Shcherbatova-Uvarova. She hardly knew anything about it either. . . . The main and most serious

* Tolstoy may have hated Shakespeare, but he had a passion for Dickens. As he got ready to demolish Shakespeare, he was writing to one of the founders of the Dickens Society of Bristol: "I think Charles Dickens is the greatest novel writer of the 19th century, and that his works, impressed with the true Christian spirit, have done and will continue to do a great deal of good to mankind." (Original in English.) (*Tolstoy's Letters*, vol. II, p. 637)

† He dictated a note to Alexandra on January 6, 1904: "I'm recalling all the nastiness of my early life; . . . these memories won't leave me and are poisoning my life." (*Tolstoy's Diaries*, vol. II, p. 506)

one was for Valeriya Arsenyevna . . . I have a great bundle of letters to her that I've asked Tanya to copy out for you and will send them."[51]

As for the diaries, he explains to Biryukov that this will be more complicated, because he cannot entrust them "to just anybody to copy"* because "their vileness is too awful"—which does not prevent their being "particularly interesting" so far "as amidst the abyss of filth there are signs of a yearning for clean air." He promises to send them "without fail."[52]

At the end of the year, Alexandrine Tolstoy was dying. He wrote to her that he almost envies her "the enlightenment that illness gives" and assures her that she is "mistaken in thinking—if you do think—that you and I are separated by our faith; my faith and your faith and the faith of all good people . . . are one and the same thing; faith in God the Father, who sent us into this world to do His will."[53] He ends by thanking her for all she has given him during their half-century of friendship.

She answered on December 27: "Dear Lev, whom I have loved so long, your tender, friendly letter was all the more gratifying to me because I felt in it that very, very sincere note which always rang out between us during the days of our youth."[54] She died in the spring of 1904 at the age of eighty-six, and Tolstoy noted simply on April 5, "Alexandra Andreyevna has died. How simple and good it is."[55] It was "good" because Tolstoy was more and more seeing death as an "awakening"[56] and a liberation. To make this idea sharper, he had begun early in 1903 to write "A Definition of Life."† As always when starting a new work, Tolstoy had read a great deal, to see what others had said: Anatole France, who "like all orthodox socialists and devotees of science . . . says that there is no need for mercy or love, only for justice,"[57] and Thoreau, by whom he was "mentally uplifted."[58] By the beginning of February, Tolstoy has framed a first definition: "Life is awareness of being a spiritual being enclosed within limits";[59] a few days later he enunciates a second one: "Life is the awareness of the modifications of the limits of the spiritual being."[60] In July he harks back to modify this definition. "I said and thought previously that life was awareness." Not so: life is what awareness discovers: "the cause of love is awareness of our spirituality."[61] When Sergey Nikolayevich's cancerous condition got worse, Tolstoy went to Pirogovo to see him and wrote: "Was very glad to be with my brother. He is disintegrating bodily, like me, and, like me, growing

* In June, he had given them to his son Mikhail, who very quickly decided not to copy them. (*Tolstoy's Diaries*, vol. II, p. 509)

† Published by Chertkov in October 1903 in *Free Thought*.

spiritually."[62] Nine months later Tolstoy returned to Pirogovo a week before Sergey's death but was saddened then by finding him "absorbed in material things."[63] Sergey died in August 1904 at the age of seventy-eight.

The Japanese attack on Port Arthur took place on January 27, 1904. It meant war. Tolstoy felt the deepest pain at this act of violence; it was unbearable to him that men were killing one another instead of loving one another. He wrote to A. Taube, professor of International Law at the University of St. Petersburg, some of whose articles on the concept of peace in various religions had been published in *The Mediator*, that there is no "problem of peace," but only "the possibility and necessity of establishing on earth the Kingdom of God—i.e., universal good, which embraces the concept of universal peace."[64]

Tolstoy expressed his pacifism in interviews with foreign correspondents who badgered him and in statements for newspapers throughout the world, which clamored for articles from him. He replied to a Philadelphia daily: "I am neither for Russia nor for Japan but for the workers of both countries who are deceived by their governments and made to take part in a war which is against their well-being, against their conscience, and against their religion."[65]

Tolstoy said what he thought about the Russo-Japanese war in his famous article "Bethink Yourselves!"* which he began the day after hostilities opened, and finished on April 30: "I'm writing about war."[66] His piece opens with a kind of biblical curse. "Your iniquities have caused the breach between you and your God."[67] He belabors the Buddhists, "professing a law of brotherhood and love"[68] and the officers† who shed blood "to add another little star, decoration, or ribbon to their ridiculous and ostentatious dress."[69] He nursed the mad hope that he could separate the combatants by his sole word as Moses separated the waters. Yet Tolstoy himself was not entirely free of the patriotism from which he wished to free others. Once again, something happened to make him gauge the precariousness of his own inward peace, for he knew that in spite of what he was writing and saying, he wanted Russia to win. On

* This article, which is sometimes translated in French as *Ravisez-Vous!* ("Change Your Mind!") was published by *Le Mercure de France* in 1905 in the collection *Dernières Paroles*. Tolstoy had told the Grand Duke Nikolay of its imminent appearance in Russia in a letter of June 1, 1904 (Tolstoy's *Letters*, vol. II, p. 644). He added that he had become so much *persona non grata* that it would be better for the Grand Duke not to come and see him, much as Tolstoy would regret it.

† On May 8, 1904, Tolstoy notes in his diary that he had had a letter from a sailor from Port Arthur asking him: "Is it God's will or not that the authorities should compel us to kill?" (*Tolstoy's Diaries*, vol. II, p. 520)

December 31, 1904, at the end of the war, he noted in his diary: "The surrender of Port Arthur caused me grief and pain. That's bad." He was under no illusion about the source of this sentiment: "It's patriotism. I was brought up in it, and am just as much a slave to it as I am to personal egoism, family egoism, even aristocratic egoism." As Tolstoy acknowledges, "all these egoisms are alive in me," but he kept hoping that the "awareness of the divine law" in him, which keeps these egoisms in check, would overcome, so that "bit by bit these egoisms are becoming atrophied."[70]

In spite of the war—Andrey Lvovich was called up for service in August—life at Yasnaya Polyana took its usual course. Visitors continued to parade through—"the new general in command at Tula"; then "Davydov, an Irish nationalist," according to Tolstoy, on June 9. In July it was a peasant disabled in a mining accident; a soldier's wife who asks him to write a letter to get her husband back; "a lady from Tiflis" to consult him about religious education.[71] Tolstoy did not keep all his advice for the humble; in February 1903 he commented adversely to an English journalist about the behavior of the Princess of Saxony, who had left her husband and children to go live in Zurich with their tutor. But Tolstoy was very much displeased when the letter was published without his consent.[72]

Contrary to what happened during the Serbian incidents, Tolstoy worked hard during the Russo-Japanese war: "The war disturbs me, but less so now," he noted on August 2, "because all my efforts have gone into my work."[73] In December he managed to finish *Hadji Murad* and began a second collection in the manner of "Thoughts of Wise People for Every Day," which he called *A New Cycle of Reading*, and he went on drafting his recollections.

This return toward his distant past made him think more and more of his near future—death. He asked himself about "the self in the past and the self in the present," the problem of personal awareness, and "the fluidity of the self." "I would say: The Self, uniting in it the child, the young man, the old man, and something else that existed before the child—that is the answer."[74] The idea of death did not leave him, but he thought of it now with a "joyful tranquillity."[75] At the beginning of January he had wondered if he was frightened, and had concluded that he felt the same emotion about it as he would about a new means of travel.[76] In May, he wrote Chertkov a letter that was to replace the diary note of March 27, 1895, serving until now as a Last Will. He stated that he put great importance on the diaries of his recent years, because they contained ideas he would perhaps not have time to develop before he died. To this letter, a page of very detailed questions is attached, typed by Chertkov and containing Tolstoy's handwritten replies.

First, he maintains his abandonment of the rights to those of his works written since 1881; second, his posthumous works are to be published by "his wife and Vladimir Grigoryevich Chertkov" (it is noteworthy that in this document, which is his literary testament, Tolstoy mentions Sofia first); third, foreign publication will continue to be managed by Chertkov; and fourth (this clause being by far the most important, since it is the germ of the later "affair of the wills"), he authorizes Chertkov to keep the manuscripts already in his hands, but does not leave it to him to choose the next trustee if Chertkov himself should die. Tolstoy clearly says that, in such an event, these papers must be returned to his wife, and not to some Russian institution. Still, the disciple did have the right, which he had expressly asked for, to see and copy any manuscript that was found in Sofia's hands or in those of any other member of the family.[77]

To the degree that he detached himself from the world, Tolstoy was prompted to arrange the disposal of what he still owned, because life seemed to him more and more "like a daydream, like a dream."[78] Dreaming was a feature of psychological life that had always fascinated him. He records several of his dreams in the diaries, and the characters in his novels often have dreams.* Now he believed that "what you find out about yourself when you are asleep is far more true than what you think about yourself when you are awake," and he tells of one of his quite recent dreams: "myself as a soldier . . . being unfaithful to my wife . . . writing only for my own pleasure. . . ."[79] That persistent urge—to write as he pleased—never left him; ten days later he noted again: "Oh, how I would like to write a second part of Nekhlyudov."[80]†

But the writer's role was beginning to have for him quite another meaning: "the artist lifts a curtain on the future—shows what it ought to be."[81] And "what ought to be," Tolstoy wants to pin down. Like Paul Valéry, though not so often, he sometimes made sketches in the margins of his notebooks and often resorted to geometry to explain or illustrate his ideas. He remarked that it was impossible to describe "a regular circle

* In August 1860 he had dreamed that he was dressed as a peasant and that his mother had not known him. (*Tolstoy's Diaries*, vol. I, p. 158.) He records at length the dream of the china doll that he had toward the beginning of his marriage. Prince Andrey dreams that death is trying to break down his door. Anna Karenina often saw in her dreams a frightful little mujik carrying something in a bag that squirmed, and she also dreamed that she was married to both her husband and her lover at the same time.

† That is, to the life of the hero of *Resurrection*.

starting from the circumference"—only by starting from the center; "it is the same with relationships with the world. . . . Find only centres. Make centres coincide and everything will coincide." He discovered that there is only one center around which everything can fall into place. "Establish your relation with God and all your relations with the world, and especially with men, will follow."[82]

TWENTY-FOUR

Tolstoy and the Revolutionaries

I

In 1905 Tolstoy had an enormous audience both in Russia and abroad. To this public at large he was a revolutionary; actually, he was a perpetual dissenter—he even opposed revolution. Yet Stefan Zweig is nevertheless right to say that "no nineteenth-century Russian revolutionary did so much to clear the way for Lenin and for Trotsky as the anti-revolutionary Count."[1]

Still, Tolstoy saw the importance of what was at stake in the uprising of 1905, and as early as July 6, 1905, he wrote (in English) to one of his American correspondents, Ernest Crosby: "The crimes and cruelties which are committed in Russia are dreadful"; but: "I am firmly convinced that this Revolution will have greater and more beneficent results for humanity than the great French Revolution had."[2]* He expressed the same idea to Masha in October: "I think, and truly believe, that this is the beginning, not of a political revolution, but of the great inner one which I'm writing about in *The End of an Age*."[3]

He was indeed observing and pondering the revolution, full of hope. But external events, however important, did not preoccupy him utterly;

* At the end of 1904, a demand for representative institutions led to meetings and protests in January 1905. These continued through the year, culminating in the spontaneous general strike of the whole country in October. In December the Moscow workers rioted, with much bloodshed. In May 1906, an edict established the first Russian assembly or Duma to be elected. Two more were chosen before 1912 but unrest continued until the beginning of war in 1914.

the same thing had happened during the Serbian troubles: the great thing that mattered now was his "new apprehension of God . . . the highest spiritual thing which alone exists, and with which we can enter into contact through awareness of it in ourselves."[4]

Tolstoy marched up to the very gates of revolution: he did not open them because they did not lead where he wanted to go:* his political ideas remained religious ideas. When he had become aware of his reformer's vocation he had decided (on March 5, 1855) that his purpose from then on would be "conscious action to unite mankind by the help of religion."[5] He still dreamed of that goal half a century later.

Tolstoy's attitude toward the Russian revolutionaries varied little. His reservations were rooted in his fundamental rejection of violence. In March 1881, shortly after his conversion, he had written to Alexander III calling on him to exercise clemency: "What are the revolutionaries? They are people who hate the existing order of things, find it evil, and envisage the foundations of a future, better order of things . . . to fight against them one must fight spiritually . . . one must oppose their ideal with another ideal which will be superior to, and will include their ideal."[6] Again, on May 8, 1886, he had explained to Chertkov that the revolutionaries were attacking "the Government externally, while Christianity does not attack it at all, but saps the foundations of the State from within."[7] The Christians should have been the revolutionaries' fifth column. What Tolstoy wanted was a religious and moral revolution, of which the result would be a political change, not the other way around.

And yet he had called for this change with all his might: "It seems to me that it can't go on like this, and that there must be a revolution."[8] So he had said in 1892 to his friend Prince Khilkov, who was persecuted for refusing to have his children baptized. But in October 1905 he asserts that "the contradiction comes as always from wanting to cut the throat of violence by violence"; what he wanted was a "revolution of souls and not of fists."[9]

Tolstoy had already enjoined the priests to prostrate themselves before the people,† so that the Church of pretense should cease to be, for lack of priests or faithful; and he had adjured the army officers to ask forgiveness from their men so that the military would wither away for lack of commanders and soldiers. He believed that as soon as souls had been

* Lenin stigmatized this attitude of watchful waiting in the opening sentences of an article he wrote in 1908 on the occasion of Tolstoy's eightieth birthday. He rebuked Tolstoy for having held himself "conspicuously" apart from the Revolution.

† In the Russian Orthodox service, the priest bows down before "the people" on the Sunday preceding the start of Lent.

transformed, the rich man would give away his possessions, the artist would devote himself to the moral uplift of humanity, and as he had already desired in the epilogue to *The Kreutzer Sonata*, "the lion would lie down beside the lamb."[10]

Just before the 1905 Revolution, he had clearly explained his attitude toward the socialists* in a letter written in English (December 1904) to Iso Abe, the editor of a Japanese socialist journal. "I do not approve of socialism. . . . It has for its aim the satisfaction of the lowest part of human nature; its material well-being; and by the means it proposes can never attain it." He saw the only effective method in "religion," by which he understood the "reasonable belief in a . . . law of God."[11] He therefore could not but remain outside the revolution. Immediately after the manifesto on freedom of conscience (which left him skeptical) was published in October 1905, he wrote to Stasov: "Throughout this revolution I occupy the status, gladly and voluntarily assumed by me, of advocate for the 100 million people who work on the land. I rejoice at everything that makes, or might make, for their good. . . . But I look with loathing on all acts of violence and all murders, on whatever side they happen. So far there is more cause to grieve than to rejoice."[12]

The peasants, though, always saw Tolstoy as a landowner; they could not understand why he had not really given up his possessions as he preached that others should do; hence they never acknowledged him as one of their own. They were wrong, because in 1905 Tolstoy had really become one of them. Lenin was the first to proclaim the fact, and Gorky thought that Tolstoy's so-called anarchism was only an expression of the old "Slav anti-statism."[13] That deeply rooted conviction in Tolstoy was linked to his firm belief that the Christian should give obedience only to God. He had already declared in 1893 in *The Kingdom of God Is Within You* that "the promise of submission to any government whatever is the absolute negation of Christianity . . . it is to betray the one divine law of love."[14]

What Tolstoy was seeking, what had always been at the center of his activism and remained there to the end, was to bring about the impossible identification of the law of God with the law of Man. He knew that the revolution that would realize that fusion was not the revolution occurring before his eyes. He therefore issued an appeal for a general revolt against authority, which will happen, so he thinks, through rebellion within the

* Tolstoy was no more gentle with the liberals. He had noted early in the year: "the government is a band of robbers"; and he added that "one shouldn't do what the liberals are now doing: recognize that the government is necessary and fight it with its own weapons. That's a childish game." (*Tolstoy's Diaries*, vol. II, p. 516)

army. "The only means of overcoming the government is now this: that the army, which is formed from the people, having understood the injustice and the harm the government causes them, should cease to support it."[15]

Under whatever monarch, "Louis XVI, Napoleon, the Mikado or the Sultan, there is always oppression of some by others."[16] To overthrow this oppression, Tolstoy puts his hopes for a moment in the anarchists, because, like him, "they recognize the spiritual arm as the only means of destroying authority."[17] But sticking to "a materialist, not religious conception of the world," they cannot in fact command that spiritual arm, and they "limit themselves to dreams that give the defenders of violence a way of denying its true basis."[18] For Tolstoy, the secret weapon is the "religious conception of life." It is the only armament that can overthrow authority.[19]

He returned to this theme in "The Russian Revolution: Its World Aspect": "The anarchist theorists know nothing of divine law"[20] and have not understood that for humanity to be good, every individual must be good. He ends his article, as he had ended "Bethink Yourselves!" and many others, with an appeal to the individual conscience.

In Tolstoy's eyes those who serve the state and those who fight it are accomplices. It is between these two kinds of violence that the true revolution should lie; if it is merely political, it is doomed to deadlock; for governments, like revolutionaries, have but the one purpose of keeping or taking power. As early as August 3, 1898, he had noted in his diary:

> Even if what Marx predicts were to happen, then the only thing that would happen would be that despotism would be transferred. Now the capitalists are in power, [whereas then] the workers' bosses would be in power. . . . The mistake of the Marxists (and not only theirs, but of the whole materialistic school) is that they don't see that the life of mankind is advanced by the growth of consciousness, the advancement of religion, and a more and more clear and general understanding of life, which provides a satisfactory answer to all problems—and not by economic causes.[21]

True, Tolstoy believed like the Marxists that property was at the root of all evil. But he preached love, which alone can unite mankind, and not class war. His certainty on this point led him to issue his "Appeal to Leaders" and "Appeal to Followers" at the same time, to persuade oppressors and oppressed together to follow this same path; and he laments that "no one wants to begin."[22]

He came back to the idea in February 1905, the day after "Bloody Sunday," in the introduction to a book by Chertkov, later republished as

"On the Revolution" in *Last Words.* His "Masks Off!," which Lenin admired, is addressed to everyone: "The revolutionaries understand by the word *liberty* the same thing as the government with which they struggle."[23] Tolstoy refuses to take part in this system; he does not want a "society in which things are demanded or forbidden."[24] He is more attached than ever to his theory of passive resistance. "While revolutionaries try to annihilate one violence with another,"[25] Tolstoy refuses to compromise over any form of violence; he wants the energies of men of good will, on each side of the struggle, to be spent on spiritual tasks.

He judged the current revolution to be anti-revolutionary, because it delayed the revolution he wanted to see. In September 1906 he wrote to Stasov: "I rejoice in the revolution, but grieve for those who, imagining that they are making it, are destroying it."[26] He had developed this thought in "The Present Events in Russia"* written in February 1905.

He despaired when he thought of "the bloody events at St. Petersburg, where men come face to face who at times are from the same village," and some of whom wear the "grey military cloak" and others the peasants' "black wool overcoat."[27] He denounced political agitation as the "pernicious illusion of social improvement by changing external forms," which "turns men away from that unique activity, the moral perfection of individuals."[28] This essay enabled him to explain to the world his own conception of revolution. He saw in what he called these "local" troubles much more than a "proof of the special wickedness of the despotic Russian government";[29] he saw "the uselessness not of such and such a government, but of all governments; that is, of any group of men able to subject the majority of the people to their will."[30] That certainty had been rooted in his mind ever since he had seen the severed head of François Richeux fall into a basket on the Place de la Roquette in Paris in 1857.

Any government seemed to him a complicated machine, "hallowed by tradition and custom for committing the most shocking crimes."[31] The absolute revolution that Tolstoy called for was not to replace one form of power with another but to eliminate all power. Violence will never bring that about: "To get rid of governments one must not fight them with external means, one must simply take no part in them, not support them,

* It was a way for Tolstoy to reply to several requests for articles from France and England, and to indignant letters he had received on the Moscow publication of an article written two months earlier for an American paper that had requested his opinion on the importance and likely consequences of the disturbances.

Tolstoy had replied that its purpose was "to limit despotism and set up representative government," but whether it succeeded or not the result would be the same, since it meant only "the postponement of real social improvement, which is obtained only through the religious and moral perfection of the individual." (L. N. Tolstoï, *Dernières Paroles*, Paris: Mercure de France, 1905, p. 319) and then they will be abolished."[32] He is convinced that "the firm, stubborn refusal of military service and taxes shatters them a thousand times more surely than the longest strike."[33] Tolstoy's doctrine of nonresistance, which was supposed to bring down the army and the Church from within, is now reformulated: "The important thing is to remove what disunites men and replace it with what unites them"; that is, "their relation to God, . . . because God is one God for all men, and the relation of men to God is one relation."[34]

But these men who must unite belong to different groups. So Tolstoy now gives up appealing to leaders or led, soldiers or officers, he launches an *Appeal to the Russian People*—to all the Russians. He summons the government to proceed with the "agrarian reform" that was "under study" and that seemed to him the road toward the abolition of private property. He explains to the revolutionaries that they cannot understand a people of a hundred million agricultural workers; he "adjures the workers to bend all their efforts to resume a rural existence."[35] Finally, he warns "the whole Russian people, . . . whose work feeds the country—that healthy body over which two parasites are fighting"[36]—that it will have to struggle "against two powers instead of one, and that it should take no part in anti-Christian actions," whether those of revolutionaries or of the government.[37]

The theme of union between men Tolstoy developed in a book that appeared in France in 1907, *La Révolution russe, sa portée mondiale*. In it he explained to the world that Russia was about to accomplish a great feat, one which Dostoyevsky had defined in other times and other terms: "to show wretched Europe the solution offered by the universally humane, universally unifying Russian soul."[38]

Tolstoy's analysis of the conditions in which the 1905 Revolution occurred is very incomplete, because in his view the "Russian people" means only the peasants. His visits to factories and workshops at the time of writing *The Slavery of Our Times* had left him with the impression that industrial workers were merely peasants in disguise, uprooted by capitalism. In reality, the Russian proletariat was an organized force that played a main role in the revolutionary struggle. Nor did Tolstoy understand, as Lenin was to point out some years later in *Peasant Reform and the Revolution*, that at that very moment the fighting role of terrorists and "isolated revolutionaries"* was over, and the struggle of the "revolutionary classes" had begun.[39]

Tolstoy thought that three factors favored the success of a real revolution, one brought about by love and by the peasants: first, the

* These were the revolutionaries Tolstoy had met and described in *Resurrection*.

deplorable example of the "parliamentary regimes that oppress western peoples; next, the fact that Russia was a great agricultural nation; finally, the deep religious feeling rooted in the people."[40]*

A year after the revolution, he wrote to his daughter Masha in Italy, to "make use of everything [she could] take from Europe," but went on: "This European life is very clean materially, but terribly dirty spiritually." He wondered if it was really necessary for Russia to go through the various stages of what he called "a sort of debauchery . . . parties, preelection campaigns, blocs, etc." and reach the dead end to which Western nations have come. He did not want to be one of those earlier opponents of progress who try to go backwards or stand still. On the contrary, "We must go forward, only not in the direction you are going, because that will lead you backwards . . . go boldly forward toward emancipation from authority."[41]

He continued to think that these "100 million agricultural workers"—a mass that may be taken as "the whole Russian people—has no need of any protective government";[42] it should "oppose power with passive resistance," cease "taking part in the old government," and not "fight it just to set up another equally oppressive."[43] For him, "going back to the land"[44] has the virtue of an economic and spiritual model; it means going back into the great order of divine grace, in which men can rediscover the law of God.

Anarchist theorists fail in their enterprise, according to Tolstoy, "because they do not recognize divine law; for one cannot liberate oneself from human law except by recognizing the divine law common to all men."[45] By these words he removes himself more than ever from political events. He thinks that once a revolution has taken place, the revolutionaries to some extent cease *de facto* to be revolutionaries and become an integral element of power, which is as harmful as ever. In order to have no part in that, Tolstoy puts himself outside the revolution. He believes, nonetheless, as he writes again to his American correspondent Crosby in April 1906, that the "present disturbances are only the precursors of the great revolution" which he hopes "will begin at once everywhere and will consist in the annihilation of state power."[46]

Tolstoy was well aware that the real Revolution had not taken place. He turned his eyes to the future, writing on December 31, 1908: "We are

* The factors that seemed to Tolstoy so favorable to the success of the revolution were precisely those denounced by Lenin in 1898 in *What Heritage Do We Deny?* as useless survivals of "Herzen-style populism": they proclaim the originality of the Russian regime, consider the peasant community superior to capitalism, and want to avoid "the dangers of the path taken by old Europe." Above all they declare that "the arrested past of Russia is her good fortune," and they congratulate themselves on being "called to reveal to the world new modes of economic management." (V. Lénine, *Sur l'art et la littérature*, vol. 2, Paris: Gallimard [Collection 10/18], 1975, pp. 208, 217)

on the eve of a great upheaval. . . ."; there are only "two paths: bombs or love." He has made his choice. He had believed for a long time that he could be a "worker for God" among men, but after 1905 he doubted it more and more. The true Revolution was not to be the creation of a new world, but the return to original innocence, to the world before sin; hence his rejection of industrial civilization and his denial of the meaning of history. His ideal was that form of Russian populism, patriarchal and essentially "reactionary, that arrested condition of Russia regarded as a blessing," that made Lenin grind his teeth.

Tolstoy kept on writing highly subversive pieces, which could not of course see the light of day in Russia. In "Genghis Khan et le téléphone," published in Paris, he asserts that the "horde of savage killers has been replaced by well-brought-up, polite killers,"[47] and he imagines with horror what the Mongol conqueror could have accomplished with modern means of communication. He then fancies with hope what good use could be made of them: "Do the railways, the telegraph and the press, which would be powerful armaments in the hands of Genghis Khan, not serve at the same time to unify the consciences of all men?"[48]

Tolstoy continued hoping for a sort of natural revolution, which would undermine "that abominable edifice called the Russian Government, which for so long has not met the demands of man, and which will crumble of itself."[49] It will happen when the populace, which "becomes more and more aware of the uncontrolled despotism of power . . . stops submitting to the authorities and collaborating with them."[50]

Tolstoy's religion lay beyond the dogmas of the Church, and his Revolution beyond the dogmas of the revolution. At the end of his life his utterances may have been intended to be political, but they were in fact utopian and religious; Tolstoy takes no account of reality; for him reality is elsewhere; he is a citizen of another world, a world to come. As such, he experienced afresh "this superabundance of thought that demands expression."[51] The lack of it had caused him great anguish in January 1901; now he was all "movement, growth, belief."[52] He continued to choose texts for his *Cycle of Reading*. He now prefers Pascal to Spinoza: "he is very fine, he writes with his heart's blood."[53] That was the ink that Tolstoy also used.

II

The revolutionaries' attitude toward Tolstoy was no less complex than his own toward them. Lenin, for one, did not minimize Tolstoy's influence on the 1905 Revolution. Indeed, he all but attributed its failure to that influence, saying in 1908 that "Tolstoyan non-resistance to evil . . . was a most serious cause of the defeat of the first revolutionary campaign."[54] First and last, he thought it desirable to devote six articles to placing Tolstoy in relation to the Revolution—the first on the occasion of the Tolstoy Jubilee in 1908, the next four in the six weeks following Tolstoy's death, and the last in June 1911.

Tolstoy and his "preaching" embarrassed Lenin. His first article, "Leo Tolstoy as The Mirror of the Russian Revolution" (September 1908), is an open letter to the writer, who no more replied to it than the Tsar had replied to his own petitions. Lenin's persistence in denouncing the dangers of Tolstoy's teaching and in making clear his unique relation to the Revolution prove what a widespread effect Tolstoy's principles and theories had on Russian thought, not only before the 1905 Revolution, but also preceding the one of 1917. His ideas pervaded the atmosphere. But he was upsetting; being neither in the revolution nor against it, he is part *of* the revolution.

Tolstoy's eightieth birthday was not only a national but a world event; Lenin pointed out the "hypocrisy of a double kind" it provoked, "official and liberal. The former is the crude hypocrisy of the venal hack who was ordered yesterday to hound Leo Tolstoy, and today to show that Tolstoy is a patriot, and to try to observe the decencies before the eyes of Europe," and the liberal hypocrisy is that which consists in "associating [oneself] with a popular name," and putting on Tolstoy's humanitarian ideas.[55]

Although Soviet Russia now presents Tolstoy as a revolutionary, that was impossible in 1908, not only on the ideological level but on the factual one as well. Everyone knew then that he had kept aloof from the 1905 Revolution and had "obviously failed to understand it," as Lenin said in reproaching him.[56]

Lenin was faced with a dilemma: he did not want Tolstoy for himself, but did not want him taken over by the bourgeoisie, either. The time bomb of Tolstoy's utopia was dangerous; it was primed, but no one knew in whose camp it would explode; the only sure thing was that it would do damage. Lenin's analysis was very adroit; it remains as accurate today as it was seventy years ago, and implies both a true understanding of the man and a knowledge of his works. An anecdote told by Gorky illustrates the fact: one day when visiting Lenin, he noticed a volume of *War and Peace* on the table, and Lenin greeted him with the words, "Yes, Tolstoy! I've been longing to re-read the hunting scene, but I remembered I had to write to a comrade." Then with his eyes half closed, he smiled and said, "What a rock, eh? What a formidable man! That fellow, my friend, was an artist! And do you know what's even more amazing? It's that before this Count came along there was no real mujik in literature!"[57]

Lenin chose to entitle his article "Leo Tolstoy as The Mirror of the Russian Revolution" even while observing in the second line that "to identify the great artist with the revolution . . . may at first sight seem strange."[58] The image of the mirror is "poetic" and misleadingly simple; its ambiguity renders accurately Tolstoy's ambivalent connection with the revolution, as well as that of the revolutionaries with Tolstoy: the revolution "looks at itself" in Tolstoy, but the use of a mirror implies a passive element: the mirror sends back an image, not a reality. So Tolstoy is not the revolution, he is only its reflection. This contradiction is the axis on which Lenin's demonstration revolves. And even today no Soviet specialist can talk about Tolstoy for five minutes without bringing up the fact that he was very "contradictory."

The balancing of praise and criticism in this article of Lenin's is regular and powerful like a pendulum: it is a steady singsong of "yes, but." Tolstoy is by turns "a great artist" and "a landlord obsessed with Christ"; capable of "forthright and sincere protest" *but* a "jaded, hysterical sniveller"; a "merciless critic of capitalist exploitation" *but* a "devout visionary"; expert at "unmasking" hypocrisies, *but* preaching "one of the most odious things on earth, namely religion."[59] For a final contradiction—and this is why Lenin thinks that Tolstoy must not be taken seriously—"he is laughable as a prophet who has discovered new nostrums for the salvation of mankind." But Lenin recognizes that he is "great as the spokesman for the ideas and sentiments that emerged among the millions of Russian peasants at the time the bourgeois revolution was approaching in Russia."[60]*

Thus Tolstoy receives at Lenin's hands the only title he had ever laid claim to, that of a Russian peasant. When he proclaimed himself the peasants' advocate, he was thinking of himself as the one-hundred-million-and-first among them. But for Lenin that label had quite another meaning; by conferring it on Tolstoy he was only asserting that Tolstoy represented but one class, the peasant class.† In Lenin's eyes only the proletariat counted, and it was precisely because Tolstoy neither "would" nor "could" admit its importance, that he put himself outside the revolutionary struggle.

* Lenin's text dates from September 1908. The letter to Stasov in which Tolstoy speaks of his "status of advocate for the 100 million people who work on the land" is dated October 18, 1905. Had Lenin some knowledge of the letter, or is it a coincidence?

† Lenin's sally—"the first mujik in literature"—implied that for him Tolstoy's contradictions and limitations were precisely those of the Russian peasantry as it was then.

In his peroration Lenin exhorted "the democratic masses of the peasantry" not to fall into "the historical sin of Tolstoyism,"[61] which would disable them. He wanted to make his voice heard right after Tolstoy's Jubilee, no doubt in the hope of blotting out all those who had spoken not only in Russia but all over the world, the echoes of which had already reached Yasnaya Polyana.

Lenin's second article, which he first thought of calling "The Importance of Tolstoy in the History of the Russian Revolution and Russian Socialism," came out nine days after the writer's death with the simple title "L. N. Tolstoy": the man dead was almost more dangerous than when alive; the emotions evoked by his passing might revive his harmful theories. Lenin did not want Tolstoy's "universal significance as an artist, his fame as a thinker and preacher" to give any warrant for the importance of the Tolstoyan credo, but only to serve as a witness to "the universal significance of the Russian revolution."[62]

He therefore set himself to prove that the attention paid to Tolstoy's death was due to the importance not of the writer but of the revolution. He fenced Tolstoy in between two dates, that of the abolition of serfdom and that of the revolution: 1861 and 1905. In Lenin's eyes Tolstoy had died in 1904, not in 1910: by not taking part in the revolution, he had crossed himself off the list of the living. True, Lenin credits him with the very great merit of having "fearlessly, frankly and ruthlessly posed the sorest and most vexatious problems of our day,"[63] but then he goes on to blame him for "raising them [only] in his writings" and failing to do more than merely identifying himself with "the strength and the weakness" of the first Russian revolution.

This second article, like the first, was built on the principle of "on the one hand, but on the other." Lenin recognized Tolstoy's "heated . . . protest against the state and the official church that was in alliance with the police . . . his unbending opposition to private property in land . . . his unremitting accusations against capitalism," but then changed tack, condemning Tolstoy's "lack of understanding of the crisis that overwhelmed Russia." Tolstoy's "dreamy, diffuse, and impotent lamentations"[64] could not supply the means to pull out of that crisis. He particularly fastened on Tolstoy's attempt—the most pernicious of all—to replace the official Church with "the preaching of a new, purified* religion, that is to say, of a new, refined, subtle poison for the oppressed masses."[65]

* A year earlier, in *The Attitude of the Workers' Party to Religion*, Lenin had written: "We must fight religion: this is the ABC of *all* materialism, and the starting point of Marxism." (V. Lénine, *Sur l'art et la littérature*, vol. 2, p. 237)

At the time of the Jubilee, Lenin had been tempted to put Tolstoy in the pantheon of the Revolution, where he undoubtedly belongs; he did not want the government, whose newspapers "now shed crocodile tears," or the liberals to put him in a counter-revolutionary niche. Lenin was willing that the Russian proletariat should accept and study the legacy of Tolstoy; it belongs to them by rights, but they should use it in a different way. They should not be content to curse capitalism, or to "confine themselves to self-improvement and yearnings for a godly life,"[66] as Tolstoy had done; they should "learn to utilize . . . the technical and social achievements of capitalism" so as to overthrow it and "create a new society in which the people will not be doomed to poverty, in which there will be no exploitation of man by man."[67]

If any doubt was left of the importance Tolstoy's thinking had assumed in Russian political and intellectual life, Lenin removes it. Only twelve days after publishing "L. N. Tolstoy," he wrote a third article; "L. N. Tolstoy and the Modern Labor Movement"[68] came out in a somewhat underground newsletter addressed to labor unions. Lenin at first had feared a takeover of Tolstoy by the Holy Synod or the liberals; now he feared that a section of the proletariat might be contaminated by some aspects of Tolstoyan doctrine. Already in May 1909 he had written that "an interest in everything connected with religion is undoubtedly being shown today by wide circles of 'society' and has penetrated into the ranks of intellectuals close to the working-class movement, as well as into certain circles of the workers."[69] He also knew that Tolstoy's passing had stirred up a great popular emotion.

> The Russian workers in practically all the large cities of Russia have already made their response in connection with the death of L. N. Tolstoy and, in one way or another, expressed their attitude to the writer who produced a number of most remarkable works of art that put him in the ranks of the great writers of the world, and to the thinker who with immense power, self-confidence and sincerity raised a number of questions concerning the basic features of the modern political and social system. All in all, this attitude was expressed in the telegram* printed in the newspapers, which was sent by the labour deputies in the Third Duma.[70]

Lenin subscribes to this homage but wishes to moderate the approval it implies by adding some reservations. He admits that although "by birth

* The telegram read: "The Social Democrat section of the State Duma, speaking for the Russian and international proletariat, expresses its profound grief at the death of the artist of genius, the intransigent and unconquered fighter, who opposed the official Church, was the enemy of arbitrary power and of slavery, and who raised his voice against the death penalty and was the friend of the persecuted." (Claude Prévost, *Littérature*, *Politique*, *Idéologie*, Paris: Editions Sociales, 1973, p. 14)

and education Tolstoy belonged to the highest landed nobility" in Russia, he "broke with all the customary views of this environment in his later works."[71] The "freshness, sincerity and fearlessness" of Tolstoy's criticism seemed to Lenin original and historically interesting, but its point of view being that of the "patriarchal, naive peasant, . . . [it] differs from the criticism of the same institutions by representatives of the modern labour movement."[72]

Tolstoy thus ceases to be the mirror of the revolution; he is now only the mirror of the mujiks, to whom the abolition of serfdom brought a false liberty; also he reflects "their naiveté . . . their alienation from political life, their mysticism . . . their impotent imprecations against capitalism and the 'power of money.' The protest of millions of peasants and their desperation—these were combined in Tolstoy's doctrine."[73] Now the contemporary workers movement knows "that they have plenty to protest against but nothing to despair about. Despair is typical of the classes which are perishing. . . ."[74] Lenin repeats that Tolstoy saw all the problems, but the solution he proposed was not the right one, the solution being exclusively in the hands of the contemporary industrial proletariat.

This warning mattered greatly to Lenin; less than a month later, he expressed identical ideas in a popular Bolshevik publication issued in Paris; the piece was dated December 18, 1910, and entitled "Tolstoy and the Proletarian Struggle."[75] In this fourth article, he no longer attacked the contradictions he found in the writer but those between Tolstoyism and the revolutionary struggle. He stresses the fact that in spite of Tolstoy's powerful indictment of the falsehood at the heart of all institutions, his "doctrine proved to be in complete contradiction to the life, work and struggle of . . . the proletariat."[76] Its only use is to make "the Russian people understand where their own weakness lies." Once again Lenin makes a point, as it were in passing, of the attempt at a rightist reform, because denouncing it gives him the opportunity of uttering a new condemnation of Tolstoy, indirect but clear. In the desire of the liberals "to utilise the anti-revolutionary aspect of Tolstoy's doctrine," he sees a proof that Tolstoy cannot be an intellectual mentor. Only the proletariat can teach the Russian people to fight and destroy "the old world which Tolstoy hated."[77]

It was also to fight these attempts at exploiting Tolstoy that Lenin replied in "Heroes of Reservation" to an article by Bazarov accusing the revolutionaries of bringing with them "a shapeless intellectual and moral mess." Unlike Trotsky and Plekhanov, who based their criticism of Tolstoy on his class origins, Lenin did not attack Tolstoy himself, but denounced instead the fallacious exploitation of his ideas. Bazarov had written that Tolstoy, "having passed through all the stages of demoralisation typical of modern educated man, succeeded in finding a synthesis." This last word infuriated Lenin, since he thought it was "the very thing that Tolstoy did not succeed in finding, or rather could not find."[78]

Lenin's irritation had been increased upon reading an article by the liberal critic Nevedomsky alluding to the homage paid to Tolstoy by the Chamber of Deputies in Paris. "All those European admirers . . . pay homage to the great integral man . . . the figure cast of a single pure metal."[79] Lenin was outraged by what he saw as a false interpretation of the work and of the man: "It is precisely not for his 'integrality,' but for his deviation from integrality, that 'all those' bourgeois admirers 'pay homage' to his memory."[80] Ideological criticism merges here with literary criticism, and even with psychological analysis, for if Tolstoy's doctrine did not in fact offer any synthesis, it was because it reflected not so much the contradictions of Russian society as it did his own.

A month later, Lenin found it necessary to issue another warning. In a sixth and last article, "Lev Tolstoy and His Epoch," he shut in Tolstoy once more within the period of 1861–1905, and stressed yet again that it was the transitional character of that time that "gave rise to all the distinguishing features of Tolstoy's works and of Tolstoyism."[81] To buttress his argument he leaned on none of the many more or less recent polemical pieces by Tolstoy, but chose a sentence from *Anna Karenina*, a novel that Tolstoy had written thirty-five years earlier, before his own "revolution." Lenin quotes Levin: "here today . . . everything has been turned upside down and is only just taking shape again." Though Lenin admits that "it is difficult to imagine a more apt characterisation of the period 1861–1905,"[82] he nevertheless puts Tolstoy in the populist camp, for "the novelist recognises only the standpoint of the 'eternal' principles of morality, the eternal truths of religion, failing to realise that this standpoint is merely the ideological reflection of the old order."[83] Lenin might have recalled another sentence in the book: "It [communism] is premature, but rational, and it has a future, as Christianity did in the first centuries."[84] So Nikolay had said to his brother, the same Levin that Lenin had quoted.

Thus it is no longer the first image of the revolution that the mirror gives back, nor even the second, the one-sided image of the peasants, but a third, execrable reflection, that of the Tsarist regime. Delving still further, Lenin quotes a passage from "Progress and the Definition of Education," published in 1862, in which Tolstoy rejected the meaning of history, and proclaimed: "There is no general law of human progress, and this is proved by the quiescence of the Oriental peoples."[85] Lenin leans heavily on this sentence to conclude that "Tolstoyism, in its real historical content, is an ideology of an Oriental, and Asiatic, order."[86] For him it is "precisely" because "the year 1905 marked the beginning of the end of 'Oriental' quiescence" that it also marks "the historical end of Tolstoyism."[87]

Lenin's criticism had hardened: the Holy Synod had not decreed excommunication against Tolstoy; they contented themselves with a Pastoral Letter. Nor would Lenin hurl major thunder at Tolstoy's head: he would simply exclude him from the revolutionary pantheon. He considered that "Tolstoy's doctrine is certainly utopian and in content reactionary in the most precise and most profound sense of the word. But that certainly does not mean that the doctrine was not socialistic or that it did not contain critical elements capable of providing valuable material for the enlightenment of the advanced classes."[88] The doctrine amounted to a "feudal socialism," and though it might "have been of some practical value a quarter of a century ago," it is no longer so, because "historical development has made considerable progress."[89] This is why "the most direct and most profound harm is caused by every attempt to idealise Tolstoy's doctrine, to justify or to mitigate his 'non-resistance,' his appeals to 'Spirit,' his exhortations for 'moral self-perfection,' his doctrine of 'conscience' and universal 'love,' his preaching of asceticism and quietism, and so forth."[90]

In the last analysis, then, it is not to the Historical Museum of the Revolution but to the Prehistorical that Lenin relegates Tolstoy.

III

After being combated by the governments of Alexander III and Nicholas II, and severely handled by Lenin, Tolstoy's doctrine is equally rejected today by the Soviets, though they place his literary and historical contribution very high.

Bulgakov declared in 1924: "The Soviet government wants none of Tolstoy as anarchist and religious thinker," and from 1920 on his theological works and articles on socialism had been on the list of books excluded from public libraries, a list based on the first "index" published by direction of N. Krupskaya. Nor have they been republished in Russia. Meanwhile, Russian children continue to read his *Popular Tales*, and young Soviet citizens fulfill a wish that was dear to Tolstoy by still learning their letters from his *Primers*. As for the novels, they are always sold out the minute they make their appearance in bookshops.*

The Russian commemoration in 1978 of the hundred and fiftieth anniversary of Tolstoy's birth was on a considerable scale: a visit to Yasnaya Polyana by Brezhnev, a formal session of the Academy, an exhibition at the Moscow Tolstoy Museum, lengthy articles in the daily and weekly press, and special numbers of literary periodicals.†

During his visit to Yasnaya Polyana the first secretary of the Russian Communist Party, Leonid Brezhnev, wrote in the Golden Book of the literary museum: "The characters of *War and Peace* are separated from us by 150 years, but what brings them close is the deep sentiment of patriotism and heroism, the same spirit of truth and justice, that inspires those who are ready to give their lives for the honor and independence of their country." By joining the patriotic virtues of Tolstoy's figures with those of the Soviet people, Brezhnev was defining the present official attitude toward Tolstoy; Professor Lumonov expounded it in the seminal article published in *Izvestia* during the Jubilee: "The Exploits of Genius."‡

During my stay in Moscow in November 1978, Lumonov explained to me how "while it retains its heroic and patriotic importance, *War and Peace* is understood today as a great work whose author speaks out against aggressive wars and those who cause them." He also dwelled on Tolstoy's concern with the peace movement, reminding me that as early as 1881 the "Union des Etudiants pour la Paix" in Paris had chosen Tolstoy as a patron. As "a partisan of peace" Tolstoy has particular importance today

* Statistics kindly provided by the cultural branch of the Russian Embassy in Paris suggest that by the beginning of the year 1980, 241,618,000 copies of the works of Tolstoy had been published in Russia, and that they were produced in 99 languages, including the 67 languages of the Soviet Union.

† *Novy Mir* devoted its whole issue of July 1978 to Tolstoy; a special television film was shot at Yasnaya Polyana; numerous theatrical productions were put on all over Russia (Tasganarov adapted *Strider, the Story of a Horse* in Leningrad); a very important combined publication appeared in *Tolstoy's World* (*Mir Tolstovo*), playing on the pun that in Russian *Mir* means both *peace* and *world*. This collection enjoyed a considerable success, since its lengthy articles treated Tolstoy not just ideologically but, more importantly, as a great artist: *Image of the Author in "War and Peace," Symbolism and Allegory in Tolstoy's Realism*, etc. There were also various giant calendars, postcards, and reproductions of portraits issued in 1978.

‡ The article stressed "the importance of Tolstoy's historical work," and discussed *Resurrection* as "a grand panorama" of Russian society in the nineteenth century." Since Tolstoy tried to eliminate the supernatural from the Gospels while retaining the fundamental teachings of Christ, Lumonov easily ignored the religious dimension of Tolstoy's works, without denying their spiritual message. "No one has conveyed so well as he the contents of life, its multiple colors and multiple sounds, the struggle of good and evil, and the dialectic of the soul linked to that struggle." (It was from the pre-revolutionary Marxist critic Chernychevsky that Tolstoy had borrowed this idea of the "dialectic of the soul," according to Lumonov.)

in the eyes of young Soviets, owing to the pacifist political line being followed by the U.S.S.R. Seventy years after Lenin's contribution, the reconsideration of Tolstoy on the occasion of his Jubilee in 1978 has therefore ended in making him, as it were, "a hero of the Soviet Union."

This official attitude contrasts with the less reverent one of some young intellectuals with whom I had a chance to talk during my trip. Vladimir Pozner's nephew Paul told me in perfect French: "Il n'y a rien de pire qu'une pute repentie." (There's nothing worse than a repentant whore.) He threw doubt, as many intellectuals of his generation do, on Tolstoy's sincerity. This aspect of "My lord Count's plow can be viewed just ahead" exasperated the modern critic, who was outraged that once upon a time travelers whose trains passed through Tula were informed at what time they might see Tolstoy working in the fields.

A young poet, Volgin,* with a doctorate in historical science and membership in the Union of Writers, confided to me that what he disliked most about Tolstoy was that everything he did was done in obedience to reason, to the cold intellect. He thought that every selfless gesture of Tolstoy's was spoiled by this error, whether his work for famine relief or his being faithful to his wife. "Evil" was not Tolstoy's forte, he continued; it was Dostoyevsky's: Dostoyevsky's concept of good and evil was less simplistic, less "rational"; he "loved his neighbor, while Tolstoy only loved humanity." Volgin also accused Tolstoy of "wanting to explain the inner motions of the spirit by reason, thus rejecting the poetic and mysterious side of the Bible." From these conversations and some others I was led to understand that part of the Soviet intelligentsia disbelieves in Tolstoy's sincerity and rejects him on that account.†

On the other hand, the writers and instructors who specialize in Tolstoy scholarship take part in the general Russian worship of him. Professor Makachin,‡ who teaches Russian literature in the University of Moscow, with whom I discussed the hidden continuity of Tolstoy's ideas, quoted to me the Russian proverb "as in the cradle so in the grave," and expressed the view that the reason Tolstoy kept himself at a distance from the Revolution grew out of his belief that politics could not show us how to live.

Professor Zinovyï Seriebrasky,§ a specialist on the Great Revolution,

* Volgin is now working on a new edition of Dostoyevsky's *Diary of a Writer.*

† On January 26, 1891, Sofia made almost the same accusation in her diary: "How much he puts on, not from the heart but the principle of it."

‡ He is deciphering and classifying for complete publication the thousands of notes taken by Dr. Makovitsky during the six years he remained with Tolstoy, from 1904 until Tolstoy's death.

§ Author of *History of the October Revolution* and *History of International Communism.*

was also much less critical of Tolstoy than his younger colleagues: he expressed much sympathy and understanding for Tolstoy's position after the 1905 Revolution and thought it must have been an "extremely difficult one to hold." Like all Soviet writers, Seriebrasky was emphatic concerning Tolstoy's contradictions, but he added that "although Tolstoy preached the necessity of loving one's enemy, he had understood that a revolution was necessary—there was no other solution." He also told me that when someone asked Tolstoy if he was for or against the Revolution, his answer was: "How can one be against the spring!"

IV

If Tolstoy remained "obviously aloof" from the 1905 Revolution, as Lenin puts it, he was at the same time equally distant from it physically. He did not leave Yasnaya Polyana; he tried to interpret the facts and find in them a different revolution, the one he was waiting for. The ups and downs of revolutionary violence came to his ears much attenuated. At the end of October 1905, Tatyana noted in her journal: "Slaughter on all sides, a bestial settlement of accounts between the 'black-hundred' men [the patriots] and the revolutionaries."[91] At Tula, she adds, "The Jewish question has also been mixed in"—forty people were said to have been killed, and the midwife who was supposed to look after Tatyana during her lying-in had been "lashed with a horse whip in the street."[92]

For Tolstoy all that matters by now is "to see and look for the spiritual content in everything."[93] His reaction to the two family afflictions that marked the year 1906—his wife's illness and the death of his daughter Masha—clearly show this resolve.

Sofia, who always complained of her nerves, had also suffered for quite a while from violent stomach pains. Suddenly, at the beginning of September, she had peritonitis and was at death's door. Tolstoy was amazed at her resignation and gentleness in the face of death: "She is touchingly sensible, truthful and good." They summoned a great surgeon, Dr. Snegirev, from Moscow with his staff and his equipment; Tolstoy was against the operation, much to his sons' indignation. Alexandra said later: "None of them understood that one thing mattered for father; that mother was living and 'unfolding.' "[94] The operation took place in the guest room. When the surgeon, exhausted and in a sweat, came out of the improvised theater, they threw warm clothes over his shoulders and poured him a glass of champagne. Tolstoy had gone into the woods to await the two strokes of the bell intended to let him know that all had gone well.[95] That evening he wrote in his diary: "They [Snegirev and his assistants] operated today. They say it's been successful. But it was very hard for her. This morning she was very well in herself."[96] This apparently uninvolved attitude is really deeply Christian, for what mattered to Tolstoy was the soul's health, not the body's. "Death is being revealed both to me and to her; and when she dies it will be completely revealed to her."[97] As he had felt before, at Masha's trepanning, Tolstoy was indignant to see how wealth permitted recourse to the utmost resources of medicine, the progress of science thus preventing the accomplishment of the divine law and holding back a soul ready to depart.

When Masha died three months later, at the age of thirty-five, carried off in a few days by congestion of the lungs, his attitude was the same. That very morning he wrote to Chertkov, "For me, selfishly, her death is neither terrible nor pitiful, although she is my best friend. . . ." Death had ceased to frighten him; it seemed "natural and necessary, not opposed to life but just as connected with it as the continuation of life."[98] Masha really *was* his best friend; he had written to her a year earlier: "With other people I am afraid to use the word 'God' but with you I know you will understand that I mean the highest spiritual thing which alone exists."[99] She had become "his spiritual confidante" as Alexandrine Tolstoy had been earlier.

With that self-distancing and attentive curiosity that are the mark of all great egoists, Tolstoy could write in his diary, a few moments after his daughter's death, "Just now . . . Masha died. A strange thing, I didn't feel horror or fear or the awareness of anything strange taking place, nor even pity or grief." He knew that his reaction was not normal and thought he had a duty to arouse in himself "a special feeling of emotion, of grief," and he succeeded. "But at the bottom of my heart" (he goes on) "I was more composed than I would have been in the case of another person's bad or improper behaviour—not to mention my own." It was not the physical aspect of death that interested him, but its mystery. "I watched her all the time she was dying: wonderfully calm. For me she was a creature experiencing revelation before my own revelation. I watched her revelation, and it made me glad."[100] It is a peculiar funeral speech for a father, and not unlike Luther's at his daughter's death: "I am sad in my flesh and happy in my soul."

Masha's passing gave Tolstoy another, more exact yardstick for measuring the emptiness of his communications with his sons. Seventeen years before, in a letter to Vasily Alexeyev, a teacher and friend, he had written: "Of my children only Masha is close to me in spirit. The others, poor things, are only oppressed by the fact that I am always around reminding them of what their conscience demands of them."[101] And he had recently admitted to Masha herself that he had lost his temper (something contrary to his nonviolent principles but part of his nature) "as a result of a conversation with Andrey and Lev, who argued that the death penalty is a good thing."[102] As for Sergey, this first-born son had published two articles in 1904 in *Modern Times* expressing complete opposition to his father's beliefs. Tolstoy had explained in a letter to Ilya how unhappy that situation made him: "With you, as with all my sons, I can't communicate sincerely. Probably I'm also to blame for this; nevertheless, this lack of communication, which will probably never change before I die, makes me very sad."[103]

TWENTY-FIVE

The Man with Black Gloves

IN 1907 CHERTKOV came back to Russia from ten years of exile. "His coming changed many things in our accustomed train of life," wrote Alexandra Lvovna, and she went on: "Life became more complicated with Chertkov's arrival."[1]

Sofia tried with all her might to keep the intruder out of Yasnaya Polyana, and particularly outside the private universe of her passion for Tolstoy. Not only did she fail, but Chertkov managed to create a new world, that of "the doctrine," into which Tolstoy at times slipped away, and from which Sofia was excluded.

From now on Chertkov's methodical takeover of people and things became more assured. Always wearing black gloves to hide the eczema on his hands, Chertkov must have had great powers of enticement, since in 1883 Sofia herself had looked kindly on his arrival and he had managed to win over all three of Tolstoy's daughters. When Chertkov was beginning to work for her father, Tatyana wrote: "My sister and I felt that in him we had gained an exceptional colleague."[2] When she visited Romain Rolland in Geneva in 1927, she said: "Chertkov's personality is singularly attractive and it is hard to resist him."[3]

Alexandra had been shocked by the way Chertkov was running the

Tolstoyan colony* set up in the imposing buildings he had built at Telyatinki, on land she had sold him; for she had imagined that within that enormous house, "built like a hotel" and the sight of which drew from Tolstoy the cry "I feel ill," there reigned perfect brotherhood and equality.[4] She was soon forced to conclude that things were otherwise. The places at table in the refectory were in themselves symbols of the artificiality that could lurk in Tolstoyism—at its worst it was a game played by the rich indulging in the luxury of being poor. Chertkov's family (his aged mother, his wife, and his son Dima) sat at the head of the table; halfway down came Tolstoyans and secretaries working on the Collection,† "and at the farther end sat the labourers, night watchmen, carpenters, herdsmen, and the like."[5] Still, for Alexandra, Chertkov was her father's friend and therefore perfect. She admitted later, "I forced myself not to see what I disliked; I loved him too, and I fell under his influence."

Tolstoy continued to feel toward Chertkov both deep friendship and high esteem: together they had founded *The Mediator*; his disciple had translated and published abroad works forbidden in Russia, taken an active part in the aid to the Dukhobors, and put his journal and archives in order. Moreover, Chertkov's merit in the master's eyes rested firmly on the fact that he had been persecuted and exiled for the propagation of those ideas that Tolstoy himself had done no more than express.

Chertkov abused his position; he would go into Tolstoy's study uninvited, which no member of the family had ever dared to do. Sofia used this brashness as a precedent for going in to her husband "to say good morning . . . before taking her coffee."[6]

Even Alexandra noticed that although at that time she was not paying much attention to Chertkov's authoritarian ways, she did remember he had made her father change his publisher for the fourth volume of *A Cycle of Reading for Each Day*, an incident that brought home to her the extent to which Chertkov was able to go against her father's wishes.[7] This power over her father's works made her angry. "Everything that came from father's pen Chertkov immediately read and criticized, sometimes asking father to change certain passages. . . . Chertkov insisted, and father did as requested."[8] Tatyana Lvovna confirmed this attitude when she spoke to Romain Rolland: "I admired him because he had renounced a brilliant

* Unable to live at Yasnaya Polyana, Chertkov put a succession of his own men in place there: Gussev, Tolstoy's secretary, paid by Chertkov and replaced (when arrested) by another of his fellow creatures, Bulgakov. Chertkov also had other friends living in the neighborhood, such as Goldenweiser, who informed him of everything that occurred at the house.

† Chertkov had begun assembling a collection, *The Thoughts of Tolstoy*, and had taken on a number of people to help. (A. Tolstoy, *The Tragedy of Tolstoy*, p. 176)

career out of a passion for my father," although she recognized that "the passion entailed jealousy of Countess Tolstoy." She went on: "The disciple wanted to have the master entirely to himself—not only the man but the ideas and the writings. He wasn't content to direct him into a . . . rigorous and narrow puritanism. He had the pretension to regiment even works of art."[9]

As early as the period when Tolstoy was writing *Resurrection*, Chertkov would send him a stream of reply-paid telegrams demanding that corrections be made. He no longer limited himself to being a steward of Tolstoy's writings, but exercised control over their very conception. Halperin-Kaminsky noted "the imperious will of an outsider dominating the aging and exhausted powers of an octogenarian."[10] Not satisfied with influencing the present, he extended his supervision over the early work as well, and thus, in a fashion, over Tolstoy's past. "Chertkov often looked through father's daily entries [in his diary]," says Alexandra, and Sofia who had never refrained from reading them decided that she "had as much if not more right than Chertkov to read the diaries."[11]

Tolstoy had long accepted as a necessity that his diary should be fair-copied, but he preferred not to know about it. "Take it when I'm not there [he had originally instructed Alexandra] so that I will not think about its being typed, because that would interfere with my writing it."[12] Victor Lebrun* records how every day Chertkov would turn up with a big suitcase "to take away the manuscripts."[13] Sofia was enraged that he sent them to England to keep them in his own files. She wanted to lodge them in the Moscow Museum of History. Alexandra, on her side, adds that her mother showed more nervousness than ever and tried "to wrest the manuscripts from Chertkov."[14]

There were certainly "two parties" at Yasnaya Polyana, as Biryukov said: "that of Chertkov, Alexandra, and her friend Varvara Feokritova; and that of Sofia and her sons." But within each of these coalitions there were shades of opinion. Thus the same Biryukov, a partisan in the Chertkov faction, nonetheless wrote "that it pained him to see Chertkov overbearing Tolstoy, and forcing him at times to commit certain actions that were not in accord with his way of thinking."[15] Alexandra reports that one day her father squashed a mosquito on the bald forehead of Vladimir Grigoryevich and burst out laughing. The disciple assumed a grave and disapproving air and rebuked his master for killing a living

* Son of a Frenchman employed on the Russian railways, died at Nice in August 1979. As a young man he had come under the spell of Tolstoy's ideas, went to see him several times at Yasnaya Polyana, and acted from time to time as his secretary.

creature. The story illustrates the naive and rather ridiculous aspect of the doctrine of nonviolence when pushed to extremes; it shows also to what an extent Chertkov had become the pharisee of Tolstoyism.

Chertkov's role was both beneficent and nefarious: he was a good secretary to the writer, but undoubtedly a bad angel to the man. Maxim Gorky was hard on him when he wrote to Romain Rolland fifteen years after Tolstoy's death: "In my view Chertkov was Tolstoy's parasite."[16]

Even today it is difficult to pass an objective judgment on Chertkov. On November 28, 1978, being in the library of the Tolstoy Museum in Moscow, I said to my interpreter: "Today we have to read *Tolstoy's Departure* by that horrible Chertkov." I had scarcely uttered the words before a lady rose briskly from her place and addressed me in perfect French. "Forgive my interrupting you, but I should like you to understand that Chertkov was not a monster. In France you think him Tolstoy's evil genius, and abominable things are said about him. I wish you would not do the same." I answered that I was sure he had been most useful to Tolstoy, or more exactly to his works, but that he seemed to me to bear a heavy responsibility for the bad relations between Tolstoy and his wife toward the end of their life together. I found it particularly hard to forgive him for pushing Tolstoy into signing, in front of two witnesses, a will he himself had secretly got his lawyer to draw up. The lady answered, "The lawyer, Muraviev, was my father." She thought Tolstoy was entirely right in acting as he did, and that he did so freely. The decision had come from him and not from Chertkov alone, she said, for Tolstoy was not a man to be influenced: "For him his convictions were the supreme law."* Muraviev's daughter, Madame Volkova, believed contrary to common opinion that Tolstoy was pushed to this extreme by his wife and family, who were torturing him. This is of course the thesis that Chertkov maintained in his book.

But Madame Volkova's last words provoked a reaction right then and there from Madame Rosanova, who is in charge of the complete edition of *Countess Tolstoy's Diary*, and who on that day was at work in the same room. She took up Sofia's defense with spirit. I therefore saw in battle before my eyes the upholders of those two clans that mangled one another around Tolstoy nearly a hundred years ago. The conversation was very earnest and vehement in tone—as if Tolstoy, Sofia, and Chertkov were still alive and their fate hung on our opinions.

* A phrasing very close to that of Tolstoy's daughter Tatyana, who said "the demands of his conscience were dearer to him than life itself." (T. Tolstoy, *Tolstoy Remembered*, London: Michael Joseph, 1977)

Yet another speaker suddenly broke into the debate, to declare in French in a stentorian voice: "Very negative, very negative, Chertkov!" It was an old gentleman* who could not resist uttering and arguing his view of the matter. He thought Chertkov was more conservative than his master, and worse, he was a Tolstoyan, which Tolstoy never was, because his mind "was wider than what was called Tolstoyism." Professor Seriebrasky even thought that Tolstoy was "probably against" Tolstoyism. He added that Chertkov's influence had had another very negative effect: "He tried to separate Tolstoy from his wife so as to be left the sole depositary of the Tolstoyan message."

Chertkov died in 1936, aged eighty-three, after working without cease on the Centenary Edition, a total of ninety volumes, of which Lenin had appointed him general editor.

* Professor Zinovyï Seriebrasky, the historian of the October Revolution.

TWENTY-SIX

Tolstoy, Starets of All the Russias

TOLSTOYS "unremitting accusations" and "heated protest,"[1] the importance of which Lenin himself acknowledged, had been an indirect but unquestionable influence on the first Russian revolution, that of 1905. It was to be even more indirect, but still undeniable, on the October Revolution of 1917. And yet the writer's political influence was small compared to the spiritual influence he had exercised at the turn of the century: two years before his death he was not only the Starets* of all Russia, but of the whole world.

Yasnaya Polyana had become a place of pilgrimage where sinners and wretches thronged in such great numbers that Tolstoy had to publish a letter in the newspapers to explain that he could not meet the numberless requests for "financial help"[2] that he received.

Peasants, workmen, revolutionaries, as well as princes, scholars, and international celebrities, rubbed shoulders with common pilgrims and with criminals. The criminologist Lombroso nearly drowned while

* The Starets played a considerable role in Russian life without an equivalent in Western Christianity. For all classes of Russian society, the Church meant the monastic institutions, not the village priests. The *Staretsi* were "masters of life"; "the elders," as they were called, whatever their age. They had dared to free themselves from the servitudes of the world, they were "men of God" who counseled and consoled. Some said they had the gift of clairvoyance and could perform miracles. Numerous writers, including Tolstoy and of course Gogol and Dostoyevsky, often went to consult them in their "deserts."

keeping Tolstoy company during his daily swim. Mechnikov, one of Pasteur's early coworkers, found himself cheek by jowl with the Dukhobor chief, who was back from exile to thank Tolstoy for his help. William Jennings Bryan, three times a candidate for the presidency of the United States, and Melchior de Vogüé, who introduced Russian literature into France, mingled with journalists of all nationalities. Anton Chekhov came to Yasnaya Polyana in 1891 and 1905; the ballet impresario Diaghilev, then editor of *World of Art*, paid a visit in 1904; Wanda Landowska made the journey from Poland toward the end of 1907, bringing with her, as usual, her harpsichord. Tatyana Lvovna remembered a Dane who had walked from Copenhagen and a prison-visiting priest about whom Tolstoy wondered whether he had come to convert or to spy on him.[3]

This uninterrupted procession of which Alexandra speaks made it necessary to sort people out, just as the flood of letters required selection. Tolstoy got as many as forty of these a day; some were addressed simply to Tolstoy, Russia, and yet reached him. He annotated the envelopes himself: N.A. (no answer); S.N.A. (silly, no answer); B.L. (begging letter).[4] (His own letters alone take up thirty of the ninety volumes of the Centenary Edition.) Tolstoy devoted a great deal of time to correspondence, which he deemed one of his sacred duties. He could not, of course, write to everyone himself, and he entrusted the task to Gussev rather than anybody else. But he looked over all the replies and a copy was kept.

Ever since his youth he had written abundantly to his brothers, his aunts, and especially to Tatyana Yergolskaya (Tante Toinette), Alexandrine Tolstoy,* and Valeriya Arsenyevna during their abortive engagement. Before and after his European travels he corresponded with Herzen, and in 1878 broke the silence with Turgenev, which had lasted since their quarrel of 1861. He wrote often to his wife and children and his near family—for example, to Tatyana Behrs-Kuzminskaya and to intimate friends such as Fet, Gay, Strakhov, and naturally Chertkov.

Like all writers, he had to correspond with his publishers,† translators, and biographers, and with the fashionable painters who were acquaintances, such as Kramskoy, Repin, and Leonid Pasternak; they all illustrated his writings and several projects of *The Mediator*. Besides, as we have seen, he addressed numerous letters to the Tsars and their

* One hundred and sixty-nine letters from Tolstoy survive, and sixty-nine from Alexandrine.

† One hundred and thirty-nine letters from Tolstoy to Fet have been published. Tolstoy's correspondence with Gay has been published separately. Thirty-three letters from Tolstoy to Nekrasov are extant.

brothers and uncles, and to various ministers and governors as well as to heads of foreign governments.* On top of this, he wrote to hundreds of unknowns.

This epistolary output took on a universal magnitude only in the last years of his life. References to himself rarely occur in it. He declined to give a British Museum librarian biographical information, on the ground that he did not know whether he would "be read after a hundred years or will be forgotten in a hundred days."[5]

Tolstoy's replies nearly always contained a general message; they were to him splendid opportunities to make clear his point of view, his doctrine. Thus in a letter of January 27, 1891, to Hamilton Campbell, a minister of the Church of Scotland, he expounded his ideas on miracles and on immortality.[6] Tolstoy always replied with the same care and the same earnestness to the most obscure correspondent as he did to the most illustrious. He will write at greater length to a young man of seventeen who has moral problems than he does to George Bernard Shaw.[7] On February 20, 1894, he wrote in French to a young Dutch medical student who had asked how he managed to feed himself on eighteen centimes a day: "My chief food is oat gruel which I eat hot twice a day with wheaten bread." He went on to mention cabbage soup, potatoes cooked in sunflower oil, and stewed prunes and apples. The letter stops just short of giving recipes.[8] To Rilke, whose visit to Yasnaya Polyana he valued, he sent only a few lines of thanks for a volume of his poetry,[9] but he wrote a long letter to an Indian army officer[10] who had accompanied the Dukhobors to Canada; he took pains to encourage the least important of Tolstoy societies, such as the one in Manchester,[11] and kept up with their like, scattered over the world, from India and Japan to the United States.

Tolstoy was always ready to use foreign newspapers to promote his views. When, in 1895, he wanted to bring the Dukhobor question before "the court of public opinion,"[12] he wrote to the *Times* of London, and it was to Italian correspondents in Paris that he uttered in 1901 his warning about the unfortunate Franco-Russian alliance.[13] On the eve of the 1905 Revolution, it was a Japanese journalist who received the statement of Tolstoy's position on socialism;[14] and the Revolution once over, he gave his definition of "genuine freedom" to a Chinese, Chan Chin Tun: liberty consists in "living without the need for a government and obeying nobody, only the supreme moral law."[15]

A few days after sending his pamphlet on autocracy to Nicholas II[16] he

* In an article published on the one hundred and fiftieth anniversary of Tolstoy's birth, Professor Lumonov points out that Theodore Roosevelt thought it necessary to reply in person to Tolstoy's article on lynching.

thanked (in French) a group of Swedish journalists who deplored the award of the Nobel Prize to the French poet Sully Prudhomme instead of to him, and explained that "it had saved me from the great embarrassment of having to dispose of all that money."[17]

On March 10, 1902, he wrote in German to the novelist Wilhlem von Polenz, whom he admired,* then again in French he reproached Octave Mirbeau, author of *Diary of a Chambermaid*, for the "excessive importance" he attached to the writings of Dostoyevsky and "especially to [my] own." Tolstoy attributes this partiality to "a particular pleasure" that his correspondent must feel "in discovering [his] ideals expressed in a new and unexpected way."[18]

Thanking Charles Wright, a London Library librarian, in 1904 for sending him Herbert Spencer's autobiography, Tolstoy remarked that "psychological facts of the highest degree of importance are often revealed in autobiographies, quite independently of their author's wills."[19]

This is a particularly interesting remark if one remembers that Tolstoy had just begun to write down for Biryukov his early recollections, which were to become the highly revealing *First Memories, Autobiographical Notes*.

Henryk Sienkiewicz, the author of *Quo Vadis*, had expressed to Tolstoy the disquiet he felt about the German policy of appropriating land in Poland. Tolstoy replied rather thoughtlessly that he was sorrier for the Germans than for the Poles, because he always found the hangman more pitiable than the victim. He added that if offered the alternative of being "a Prussian in solidarity with his government, or . . . a Pole driven out of his nest," he would not hesitate a moment to choose the latter.[20]

Bernard Shaw had sent him *Man and Superman* with its appendix, *The Revolutionist's Handbook*, and on August 17, 1908, Tolstoy thanked him. But with the thanks came reproaches for not being "sufficiently serious," and for distracting the reader's attention out of "a desire to surprise and astonish"[21]—which for Tolstoy was not far from being a definition of bad art. He was just as severe two years later about *The Shewing-Up of Blanco Posnet*, which Shaw had sent him with a letter ending rather provocatively: "Supposing the world is only a joke on the part of God, would you work any the less to make it a good joke instead of a bad?" Tolstoy enjoyed the epigram no more than the play, which he thought bad: "The reason of the failure," he said, "is that those who preach do not fulfill what they preach"; and he declared that "the problem about God and evil is too important to be spoken of in jest [original in English]."[22]

* In 1901 Tolstoy had written an introduction to Polenz's novel *Der Buttnerbauer*, reprinted later as *Art and Criticism*, in which he lambastes "the ignorance of the educated."

At the end of 1909, one year before his death, Tolstoy wrote in English to Gandhi, who wanted to publish Tolstoy's letter-essay to Tarakuatta Das, in which Tolstoy refuted the latter's theory that nonviolence could not be effective against the English in India because the "enslavement of the Indian peoples by the English" was due to the lack of a real religious spirit among the Hindus: they were prisoners by force precisely because they themselves had lived by force and not by love. After authorizing Gandhi to publish the letter, Tolstoy spoke of their common struggle—"that same struggle of the tender against what is hard, of meekness and love against pride and violence."[23]

Tolstoy also received letters from unknown people who were unable to understand how he could go on living on his lands. Alexandra called them "the censors." He was particularly sensitive to their criticisms, for he never ceased urging the same against himself. On March 22, 1906, he replied to a correspondent[24] who expressed amazement that Tolstoy could keep his estate while declaring that property was a sin. Tolstoy agreed that he had indeed come to that same conclusion twenty-five years before, and had then acted "as if he had died"* by distributing his goods at that time.

A certain Mutsenek was outraged that Tolstoy, who called himself a vegetarian, still wore boots and a leather belt. He answered: "In spite of the fact that I consider it would be better not to wear leather or fur, I am so far away from perfection in my own life . . . that I find it more important to direct my efforts toward improving my life in a moral sense than whether or not to use leather and fur objects for my clothing."[25]

Tolstoy's great fame gradually transformed the way of life at Yasnaya Polyana. The daughters who had taken over from their mother the duty of copying manuscripts were no longer enough, nor were the friends enlisted for the purpose, as at the time of *Resurrection*. Secretaries had to be engaged; Chertkov saw to it. Gussev, Lebrun, and then Biryukov were successively hired. The secretaries' office, known as "the Remington room" because the typewriter of that make bought by Tatyana Lvovna was enthroned there (it is still in position), was christened "the Chancery" by Tolstoy. That is indeed what it had become, being at the same time a propaganda center, a publisher's promotion office, and practically the cabinet of a political minister.

As a result, Tolstoy separated himself further from his wife. He was more and more detached from everything, and let himself be driven by Chertkov, a demanding impresario and a tyrannical literary editor. The

* This is still the illusion of *The Living Corpse* and the same refusal to admit the unconscious duplicity of his pretended renunciation.

author was now the heart of an industry managed by his disciple; postcards were printed so that Tolstoy could send autographs to his admirers; one of them reproduced his portrait by Repin, which Tolstoy did not like and refused to sign.

He was about to be eighty. A committee had been set up to make his birthday a world celebration. The idea was intolerable to him. The secretary of the committee was his friend M. A. Stakhovich.* Tolstoy wrote to him on February 28, 1908, that he would be eternally grateful if he would "put a stop to the preparation for this jubilee, which will cause me nothing but suffering, and worse than suffering—bad behaviour on my part."[26]

Nor did the government approve of the idea; some conservative circles were even scandalized by it. Princess Dondukova-Korsakova had written to Sofia that all the Orthodox would be "offended" by the celebration.[27] Tolstoy, who had not thought of this aspect of things, saw in it a new reason for canceling the glorification. He had quite a different idea of what this anniversary ought to be and mentioned it to Bodiansky, a landowner who had renounced his goods and gone to live with the Dukhobors in Canada: "The best and only way of celebrating my jubilee would be to put me in prison for writing those works, for distributing which you spent six months in prison, and for which so many, many people are now in prison." He goes on, "Nothing would satisfy me so much and give me so much joy, as actually being put in prison—a really good prison, stinking, cold and short of food."[28]

Any notion of glorification was foreign to him; his energies were centered entirely on his letters and on his compilation of *A Cycle of Reading*, for he saw in that work a sort of ecumenical summary that was more important than anything he had previously written. This belief was shared by the more militant of his disciples, some of whom, such as Gussev, had never been willing to read his novels.†

When Tolstoy thinks of humanity, his mind always turns to children uncorrupted by civilization; so he undertook *A Children's Cycle of Reading* and composed *The Teaching of Christ Retold for Children*. In the grip of his old pedagogical passion, he reopened his house to the little mujiks of Yasnaya Polyana village. Now it was not arithmetic or history that he wanted to teach them, but the meaning of life. But as a schoolmaster Tolstoy was no longer as lively and imposing as he used to be, and his preaching bored his audience. The experiment was short-lived. Sofia

* In 1886 Tolstoy had walked with him and Gay from Moscow to Tula.

† Alexandra put the three volumes of *War and Peace* into Gussev's suitcase when he went into exile in 1909, hoping he might end up reading them.

thought her husband was wasting his time. "It won't make any difference, they will grow up drunkards anyway."[29] Tolstoy was discouraged and so were the children. He heard one of them swearing and he wept, as Alexandra reports in her memoirs.[30] She also says that about this time "illiterate, stupid stewards irritated the peasants more and more. . . . Bitterness between the peasants and the estate grew."[31] Unpleasant incidents became more frequent; a row broke out between the gardener and the peasants, and Sofia asked for protection at Yasnaya Polyana: "The Tula authorities arrived in our village: the governor, the police chief, the inspector."[32] There were arrests and imprisonments.

Sofia had noticed that some trees had been stolen and she decided to prosecute, but Tolstoy refused. Another time, a gamekeeper found a mujik fishing and thrashed him; Tolstoy and Alexandra, as apostles of nonviolence, were in despair. Alexandra immediately appealed to the deputy-governor to have the guards withdrawn, but he showed her a letter from Sofia requesting that they be kept on duty. Back home, Alexandra had a violent argument with her mother, who was supported by the sons: they always took her side in incidents of this kind.

The presence of outsiders spying on everything that happened darkened the atmosphere of the house; intimates, secretaries, disciples, visitors, tutors—all were taking notes.* The most casual remark by Tolstoy was snapped up as if it were his last word. In truth, he was always on show and exasperated by these people, who "exerted themselves not to overlook anything that was happening in the house."[33] To avoid annoying him, Dr. Makovitsky had devised a most ingenious technique for the secret recording of his sayings; he took them down with a tiny pencil on little cards concealed inside his pocket. Alexandra often caught him at it and threatened to tell her father.

Of all these witnesses, Chertkov remained the most formidable. He was even more menacing since his return from exile, with his stiff imposing figure and ever-present black gloves. Sofia felt threatened—from outside by the peasants and the revolutionaries; from within by her husband's "friends" and her own daughters. For his part, Tolstoy was made unhappy by the suppressed violence and hatred all around him. One day he received a news clipping in which he was accused of hiring Cossacks to protect his woods from thefts. He replied to a man called Morov who had sent him the article, "Count Tolstoy's Workers," that he

* A. B. Goldenweiser, the pianist who came to live some four versts (2½ miles) from Yasnaya Polyana in 1909, wrote down, on Chertkov's instructions, every word that Sofia uttered, including her "hysterical outcries." He later put together a singularly unpleasant book (*Talks with Tolstoy*, London: The Hogarth Press, 1923) based on those notes.

had not owned anything for a long time; he had given everything to his heirs; and he repeated one more time that he had behaved "as though he were dead." He went on: "What the correspondent writes about the Cossacks being called in is completely untrue. . . . I am absolutely sure that even if there were any pretext for this, [my wife] would never do so."[34]

But Sofia did do it. She was obviously excusable, for Gorky reports how Leopold Sulerjitsky, "the most honest man in the world, a thoroughbred anarchist," judged her handling of the situation: "The Tolstoy family cannot have viewed with a very cheerful eye the mujiks carrying off little by little the belongings of Yasnaya Polyana and cutting down for wood the birch trees that Tolstoy had planted with his own hands. I think that he himself also missed that wood." According to this witness, everybody was pained, but no one dared to intervene; and although Sofia knew she would be blamed, "she took the risk. And for that I respect her." Sulerjitsky added that he was going to tell her one day, "I respect you!" because he felt that "they had silently forced her to act in just that way."[35]

The presence of guards at Yasnaya Polyana put Tolstoy, the enemy of all authority, in a ridiculous position in the eyes of the world. This predicament did not displease the police; they were delighted to "protect" him, after having had him "under surveillance" for so long. He was in despair at seeing "the law of force" reigning everywhere. In May 1908 twenty peasants were hanged after refusing to pay taxes. Tolstoy read the papers avidly; his friend Davydov sent him "photographs of execution by hanging."[36] It was too much. Tolstoy exploded. "I Cannot Be Silent!" he burst out in a piece so violent that it cost *Russkie Viedomosti* a thousand-ruble fine for printing it, and prison terms for the editors of various papers that reproduced it. Tolstoy demanded to die like those twenty mujiks: "I dare not even dream of such happiness . . . put on me, as on those twelve or twenty peasants, a shroud and a cap and push me also off the bench, so that by my own weight I may tighten the well-soaped noose round my old throat."[37] After this article "a Russian mother" sent him a rope with which to hang himself. It seems clear that to speak of "happiness" about an event that had cost twenty men their lives was offensive to many, and attitudes of this kind caused Gorky to remark: "His desire to suffer is repugnant." Perhaps it was, but it was also sincere: martyrdom and poverty had for Tolstoy the attraction of the unattainable.

The impunity he enjoyed was to him intolerable. He did not want to be the only one not paying the price for his convictions. Many of the young people who put his teaching into practice and refused military service had been imprisoned or deported; his secretaries were persecuted or exiled, his publishers prosecuted. Gussev fell into the hands of the police on two occasions, and Alexandra records that in August 1909 one of these arrests took place at Yasnaya Polyana: "It would have been impossible to invent a worse punishment for [my father]."[38] Marya Nikolayevna, Tolstoy's sister, who had found retreat in the Convent of Shamardino and did not share her brother's ideas, witnessed the incident, being on a visit at the time; she was so outraged that she spat ostentatiously at the police.

Tolstoy hoped that his "I Cannot Be Silent!" would bring "repressive measures"[39] against him, but the authorities continued to take no notice of his provocations. When Tatyana in 1904 had made efforts on behalf of "a doctor expelled from Russia for his revolutionary ideas," the director of police at St. Petersburg, whom she had known as a student, said to her: "It has been decided not to prosecute Tolstoyism."[40]*

The favors that the authorities allowed Tolstoy damaged his credibility. He had said to Gorky: "Were I to suffer for my ideas they would have a greater influence,"[41] and Gorky was certain that although he was still quite ill, Tolstoy would have been "really glad to be put in prison, to be banished—in a word, to embrace a martyr's crown."[42] He continually called for it. In June 1908, when Vladimir Molotchinov was sentenced to twelve months in prison for distributing some of the forbidden works, Tolstoy published an article entitled "Prosecute Me!," which claimed the punishment for himself: "the principal sinner, not just for the distribution of these books but for their very existence."[43] In an article written about the same time, "Christianity and Capital Punishment," he observed that "his position was unique in the midst of a population in which everybody else was gagged."[44] Romain Rolland was to say Tolstoy remained the only free man in Russia. People knew it. He had become the idol, apostle, and protector of the poor and persecuted; he was their voice. Alexandra noted that "the article 'I Cannot Be Silent' had made his popularity still greater."[45]

Tolstoy began to have fainting spells and in July 1908 came down with phlebitis. Against his wishes, doctors were summoned from Moscow. His leg was ordered kept in a raised position and packed with ice; he had to use the big wheelchair again. On August 28, his eightieth birthday, he had still not recovered. To the great relief of the authorities, Tolstoy had

* Although done for different reasons, this indulgence of the Tsar toward Tolstoy is not without similarity to that shown by Lenin toward Gorky, when, after the October Revolution, Gorky opposed certain measures taken by the new powers.

quashed any official celebration, but the spontaneous demonstrations were numerous. They took on a very "Tolstoyan" character; no doubt he was too tired to notice, though tears came to his eyes several times on the day he had so much feared.

Testimonials of admiration flowed in from all sides: more than one hundred letters on the day itself and six hundred telegrams, and during the next week the telegrams passed the two-thousand mark. His sons, "as always cheerful and sure of themselves,"[46] says their sister Alexandra, read him these messages, some of which made him cry. Professors at the St. Petersburg Polytechnic wished him long life, "that the power of darkness may be combated"; a Catholic priest sent "his greeting to a seeker of God"; a message signed by a group of English writers, including Wells, Kipling, and Shaw, arrived side by side with a telegram from a group of wheelwrights using "thee" and "thou": "God grant that thy life may last long, great sower of love and justice."[47]

Parcels also rained down. These presents* made a strange curiosity shop assembled by admiration and love: twenty bottles of Saint-Raphaël aperitif from France, boxes of candy with his portrait on the lid,[48] a samovar from the waiters of a St. Petersburg restaurant, while the greatest Russian painters of the day, Repin, Pasternak, and Levitan, sent him a collection of original drawings.

It was not just the telegrams and presents that invaded the house; people in droves crowded in; what had started as a family celebration ended up as a county fair. It was the day of the patron saint of the Russian people: cameramen shot newsreels, the local band played, the schoolchildren waved flags.

Tired and embarrassed, Tolstoy did not share in the gaiety. He submitted gently but without joy to the homespun celebration in his honor. "After dinner," wrote Alexandra, "the 'dark ones' surrounded father, sat down and looked at him, waiting for words to fall from his mouth. But he was tired and preferred a game of chess. And later, like a deliverance, came music—Goldenweiser played Chopin."[49] When she came to say goodnight to him, Tolstoy said to her quietly: " 'Depressing.' 'What—the fuss—the people?' 'Yes—rather the people. It's chiefly that there is so much insincerity!' "[50]

Still, in the end he found a kind of encouragement in these demonstra-

* The Ottoman Tobacco Company offered Tolstoy a box of cigarettes with his name and picture on each one. He thanked them, explaining that he had been warning people of "this bad habit" for more then twenty years, and though he was sending back the cigarettes, he would use the beautiful box to keep his papers in; he added that his wife had "taken one packet of cigarettes to put in the museum where she collects all the things that have to do with me." (*Tolstoy's Letters*, vol. II, p. 682)

tions; their scale surprised him and brought home to him that what Gorky called his "convict's hard labour"[51] had perhaps not been in vain.

On October 8, Tolstoy sent out a letter through several papers—there are five drafts of it—in which he addressed the people and institutions that had sent him good wishes on his eightieth birthday. He took great care not to forget anyone: "universities, town councils . . . academic institutions, societies, unions, groups of people, clubs . . . editorial boards of newspapers and journals," and, most particularly, "the clergy—although very few in number," whose marks of esteem he appreciated all the more for that.

What touched Tolstoy the most and what he found unexpected was not so much that people should agree with him as that they should agree "with the eternal truths which I have tried to express as best I could in my writings." He was especially delighted that among these people "there was a majority of peasants and workers";[52] for as he had written some months earlier to the Grand Duke Nikolay Mikhailovich, "What is most precious to me now is loving contact with all people, regardless of who they are: tsars or beggars."[53]

V

DEPARTURE

TWENTY-SEVEN

The Division of the Spoils

Tolstoy's notoriety was more and more embarrassing to the established powers; they still did not dare tackle him directly, but increased their attempts to neutralize his influence by indirect means. On January 20, 1909, the Bishop of Tula turned up at Yasnaya Polyana with a retinue of "six priests and policemen."[1] He got around Sofia, who found him "intelligent, simple and sweet" and noted that her husband "thanked him with tears in his eyes for having the courage to come and see him."[2] All the same, Tolstoy was much put out by this move, for he saw in it an intimation of the maneuver that the Church was preparing. He learned to his annoyance that the prelate had asked Sofia to let him know when Tolstoy was on the point of death. Fearing a scheme designed to spread the belief that he had "repented" before dying, he forestalled it: "I declare that all that may be said of my death-bed repentance and Communion is a lie. I repeat on this occasion that I ask to be buried without what they call divine service."[3]

The Church was not alone in worrying about what was to come after Tolstoy. Chertkov secured for himself and "for those to whom he would entrust the continuation of his task, the right to make free use of [Tolstoy's] private letters";* and Tolstoy was made to say explicitly that since he "does not recognize literary rights," he does not wish his letters to "become the property of the people to whom they are addressed."[4] If

* This is new, compared to the note of 1895.

this concern over inheritance is in the air, it is because Tolstoy's death looms closer and closer. He is "tired, feels ill," and in March suffers from phlebitis again.

Unbeknown to Sofia and his children; Tolstoy is living through an inner experience that isolates him from the world more than age or illness. He feels as if his self were divided in two in some peculiar way; he tells Chertkov: "I'll write to you, dear friend, about what has happened very recently to L. N. Tolstoy. . . . Somebody else has appeared who has completely taken possession of Tolstoy and allows him no freedom of movement." This double, as it were, often opposes his wishes: "This somebody, whom I call 'I,' decides things for himself, sometimes agrees, but usually, on the contrary, refuses permission to do what Tolstoy wants or tells him to do what Tolstoy doesn't want. . . . And the surprising thing is that ever since I've clearly understood that this 'I' is far more important than Tolstoy, . . . I immediately listen to him as soon as I hear his voice."[5]

In the spring, Chertkov was expelled once again from the Tula province and was forced to settle in Krekchino, near Moscow. Sofia's daily notes for March 6, 1909, read: "After Chertkov's new exile, Leo Nikolayevich is ill. His leg is not doing well. I have written a very harsh letter for the newspapers, not sent."[6] She gave herself the pleasure of taking up Chertkov's defense, even at the same time that she was "in out-and-out legal conflict with him over the possession of the diaries he had got hold of by surprise"—so Halperin-Kaminsky reports.[7] It was Halperin whom she finally asked to have her letter published in the press. "Chertkov's crime is manifest: it is his friendship for Tolstoy and his zeal in spreading Tolstoy's ideas. . . . I have always attentively observed the life and preaching of Chertkov, and although I do not share most of his ideas, or of Tolstoy's, notably their denial of the Church, I can state that Chertkov's efforts always had the purpose of spreading among men the love of their neighbors and the necessity for the moral improvement of mankind."[8] This move in favor of her "worst enemy" was not without *panache*, and it shows that in spite of her personal resentment, Sofia understood how useful he was to her husband.

Nonetheless, she kept on making scenes, more scenes than ever. She thought of Chertkov as a rival and was still aching after forty years from retrospective jealousy about Tolstoy's past, the same torture that his nostalgic words in *First Memories* about the peasant girl Aksinya had revived. ("I looked at my bare feet and remembered Aksinya . . .") Choking with rage, Sofia writes in her notes: "The same Aksinya with the glittering eyes comes back almost unconsciously at the age of eighty from the depth of his memories and sensations of earlier years!"

Husband and wife torment and destroy—and then console—one another. After one of their numerous quarrels, Tolstoy writes to his wife from "beyond the grave"*: "I have nothing to forgive you for, you were what your mother made you, a kind and faithful wife and a good mother." As before, he charged her with having stayed the same and not having made any effort to develop toward goodness and truth, clinging instead "with such obstinacy to all that was evil in my eyes and the opposite of all that was dear to me; you did a lot of harm to other people and sank lower and lower yourself and reached the pathological condition you are now in."[9] A year later he admitted it was not Sofia's will but her instinct that prevented her from changing.

In June they went together to spend some days on their daughter Tatyana's estate at Kotchevy. Tatyana found her father "alert and interested in everything." He told her in secret "that he intends to write another work on art."[10] Sofia had to leave rather early; Tolstoy stayed on, hoping that Chertkov would be allowed to live near Kotchevy, at Suvorovo, which did come to pass.

Tolstoy stretched out his visit until July 3. His daughter drove him back by troika to the railway station, and took advantage of having him to herself for a talk on something she had wanted to discuss for a long time. She consigned it to her diary six months later: "Why do you want your successors to renounce the property rights to your works and your land after your death? . . . I am afraid that your wish that my brothers should do something you have not done might give rise to ill feelings." His reply stated what at the time was true: "I really have not made it a condition. I have noted it as a desire. Legally that is not binding."

Tatyana persisted; she explained that by wanting to do good to some, one harms others, and so it would be if he wanted his sons "to give the land away to the peasants for the good of the peasants." Tolstoy protested. "Oh, no, no! It was, I must confess, to put myself in the right . . . though, what sort of putting right would it be?"[11] That answer is a twofold admission. Tolstoy admits an element of vanity among the motives that move him to put his heirs under a moral obligation to distribute his goods; at the same time, he admits his inability to make up his mind and do it himself. One fact remains certain: Tolstoy was *not able* to cut himself off from Yasnaya Polyana.

A short time later, it was Tatyana's turn to stay with her parents. Her

* The figure of speech turned out to be literal: this letter was given to Sofia only after her husband's death.

father complained again of the burden that "the possession of lands" put on him; she was amazed, and she reminded him that he had already given them away to his children. He evidently believed that Yasnaya Polyana still belonged to him. "Not at all," said she, "you gave it to your heirs at the same time as the rest." Perhaps Tolstoy had forgotten; or did he now see for the first time the kind of pretense inherent in *giving away* Yasnaya Polyana while *continuing to live there*?

Tolstoy had been invited to take part in the International Peace Conference in Stockholm. Under pressure from some of his disciples such as Lebrun, who thought "his attendance would be a world event,"[12] and urged by Alexandra, who always contradicted her mother, Tolstoy decided to go. Sofia, using common sense and fearing for her husband's health, tried to dissuade him. She showed less sense in her way of persuading him. To keep him at home, she made scene upon scene and went so far as to feign suicide by morphine. "Somebody had woken me up. Sofya Andreyevna hadn't slept all night. I went to see her. It was something quite mad," he notes on July 21, 1909. "I'm exhausted and at the end of my tether." But he gets his second wind. "Come, now, show your Christianity. *C'est le moment ou jamais.* [It's now or never.]"[13] He gave up the idea of the trip.

Incident followed incident. After the Stockholm affair came that of Chertkov's publication of *Three Deaths* and *Childhood*, works that presumably "belonged" to Sofia, since they had been written before 1881.

In September, "Lev Nikolayevich's preparations to visit Chertkov are very painful to me," wrote Sofia in her daily notes.[14] He left for Krekchino with Alexandra, Makovitsky, and Chertkov's son. They were recognized at the station, and "took refuge in a reserved compartment," much to Tolstoy's annoyance, as he always wanted to go third class.

Alexandra, who should have been in seventh heaven to find herself at Chertkov's with her father, disliked the atmosphere of the house—felt "ill at ease"—seeing the people around her father apparently "trying to snatch him from each other."[15] It was particularly unpleasant for her to note that on Tolstoy's daily walk, Chertkov trailed him "a hundred paces behind . . . but trying to escape notice."[16] Sofia in fact did the same thing at Yasnaya Polyana, probably for the same reason: they both feared that the old man might have a bad turn.

Sofia could not give up Tolstoy to her rival for very long. A week later she came to take her husband home. They were to go by way of Moscow. "Chertkov and mother willingly informed everybody of the day of father's departure," noted Alexandra.[17] Both Tolstoy's "guardian angels" liked to show him off; Gorky once remarked that "Countess Tolstoy made me think of a man exhibiting an old lion at the fair, who begins by startling the public, boasting of the animal's strength, and then asserts that he is the tamer, the only person the lion loves and obeys."[18]

The hermit of Yasnaya Polyana in Moscow was an event; he had not been there since 1902. The reporters arrived on tiptoe, "the telephone never stopped ringing."[19]

Tolstoy used the opportunity of his passage through the capital to have Alexandra take the will that Chertkov had succeeded in getting him to sign the night before to the lawyer Muraviev—who declared it invalid.

In spite of the confusion that reigned in Khamovnichesky Street, or maybe to escape it, Tolstoy, who felt rested after his stay at Krekchino, wanted to go to the ballet. The Bolshoi was closed, so he took his family and a group of friends, including the ever-present Chertkov and Goldenweiser, to the motion pictures. There again Tolstoy was recognized and cheered.[20]

The next day, September 19, Tolstoy and his entourage went in two hired carriages to the Kursk station. Scarcely had they stepped inside when a general saluted, with tears in his eyes. On the way, "cabmen stood up in their boxes and doffed their hats."[21] The arrival at the station was filmed.* "The crowd filled the whole square,"[22] and as he got down from the open carriage, Tolstoy for a moment disappeared from view amid the chaos. In the newsreel, one can make out Chertkov's white panama, the disciple trying to protect him. Tolstoy recorded: "Chertkov saved me. I was frightened for Sonya."[23] Hands stretched out, the faithful wanted to touch their icon, people ran along the platform and even on the rails; they waved flowers, climbed lampposts. Sofia was delighted by this idol worship. "A royal sendoff," she said to her husband when the train pulled out, and he replied, "A royal sendoff indeed . . . it means we're bad people."[24]

The frantic departure had exhausted Tolstoy; he had been manhandled and nearly stifled and was close to fainting. Once arrived at Yasnaya Polyana he lost consciousness. According to Alexandra, Sofia thought of only one thing—to get the keys of the chest containing the manuscripts. "What if he should die and they spirited away the manuscripts!"[25]

This fresh alarm showed the urgency of settling the question of the

* This is not the only film record extant. Earlier, Drukov had shot five scenes: Tolstoy on the steps of Yasnaya Polyana, in a sledge, on a horse, walking, and giving alms to the poor under their tree. Tolstoy's extraordinary vitality is of course much easier to see on these films than in photographs; he looks very old, but he walks with a quiet and light step, giving the impression of hardly setting foot on the ground, and doing it with the precision of an Arab thoroughbred. (There is also a newsreel of Tolstoy's funeral.)

will. The problem worried everyone, the sons, the daughters, but above all Chertkov. Even poor Marya Schmidt, quite detached as she was from material concerns, thought that Tolstoy "did not realize that when he died Sofia would take everything," and that she had "already [sold] all she could to the Moscow museums." At the same time, Sofia was convinced that Tolstoy would never agree to make an official will, which would mean submitting himself to authority.

In her innocence, Sofia noticed none of the maneuvers taking place. She did not know that Chertkov had sent Strakhov to Yasnaya Polyana with a *new* will, this one well and truly drafted by Muraviev. On November 1, two shadows slipped into the house after nightfall, without anyone's knowledge: Strakhov and Goldenweiser had come to make Tolstoy sign. From ethical considerations, Tolstoy began by questioning the very basis of the will, but in the end he yielded. Since he could not leave his copyrights to the Russian people, he would will them in their entirety to his daughter Alexandra.

TWENTY-EIGHT

The Last Days

In 1910 Yasnaya Polyana had become unlivable; it no longer deserved its name of "bright clearing." It was a house of suspicion: spying, dissembling, denunciation—everyone was intriguing and everyone was in pain. Tolstoy, who was so deeply attached to the place, would get away as often as he could. He was moreover less and less able to bear the conflict that had been tearing him apart since boyhood: "the disharmony between my life and my convictions." The old dream, of freeing himself "from the conditions of worldly life without breaking the ties of love,"[1] had not come true and he no longer believed in it.

The problem of identity that haunted his youth had never been resolved. He was still asking himself: "What is this self? Why is this self myself? And how could this self, which appeared in so inconceivable a manner from outside time, not disappear in a manner just as inconceivable, outside time?"[2] Though he does not yet possess the feeling of his unity, at least he now has the feeling of his continuity: "I had a vivid proof that I was aware of myself at eighty-one years exactly as I was aware of myself at five and six."[3]

His memory grew worse and worse. He might remember his childhood but no longer could recall recent events, as he complains at the end of January 1910: "I remembered nothing, to the extent of not recognizing the children."[4]* This old-age amnesia, which leaves ancient

* This often happened to him. Sofia noted on July 4, 1910, "He did not immediately recognize his grandson Ilyiushka." (L. and S. Tolstoy, *Journaux intimes*, Paris: Gallimard, 1940, p. 323)

memories intact but weakens the power to retain recent events was to get worse. It made Tolstoy more subject to influence, more vulnerable, while it also brought him liberation of a kind. He himself speaks of his "unforeseen freedom."* He had at last disentangled himself from the rules he used to set for himself, as well as those the Tolstoyans made for him, and he utters this prayer: "My God, help me to live outside human judgment, only before Thee, with Thee, and through Thee."[5]

He marveled still at the beauty of nature and kept up his riding.† "An insanely lovely spring. Each time I can't believe my eyes."[6] Alas, the moments of happiness were fleeting; he was "preoccupied with explaining" what he calls "my grief of living,"[7] and he continually blames himself for the sin of giving his fortune to his children.[8]

Tolstoy was working hard and remained active. The last pages of *A Cycle of Reading*[9] absorbed his attention. He attended the trial of a member of the revolutionary socialist party: his mere presence "acts as a defence of the accused, simply by his being there," said the Tula *Echo*.[10] He corresponded with sectarian protesters,[11] and talked with a factory worker who wanted to till the soil[12]—was this to atone for "the sin of refusing the request of a peasant woman who had come from a long way"[13] and whom he refused to see? Oddly enough, he also refused help to a girl who wanted to found a school; dismissed, she asked to be given something—"even if it's just a hair in memory of [you]."[14] In truth, he was withdrawing more and more from what for a long time had been his main "duty"—receiving the people who arrived endlessly to importune him with various requests.‡ To avoid them he goes to the length of having his meals served in his room.[15]

Religious meditation holds an even greater place in his life. Faith seemed to him "the spiritual structure on which the whole life of man rests."[16] He discovered an alternative to Christian revelation—a very gnostic outlook yet again: "We would never have arrived at the notion of God if it had not been gradually revealed to men by the efforts of thought of the greatest sages in the world."[17]

* When the future first president of Czechoslovakia Thomas Masaryk came to Yasnaya Polyana in May 1910, Tolstoy was embarrassed to drink a few drops of wine before his guest, which he did on the advice of Makovitsky when he had stomach pains. He resolved not to let himself be "embarrassed at being censured for drinking wine, playing cards, and living in luxury—but all of a sudden," he said, "I felt an unexpected freedom." (*Tolstoy's Diaries*, vol. II, pp. 651–52)

† One of his hagiographers has calculated that Tolstoy spent seven years of his life on horseback. He was still riding ten days before his death.

‡ People did not come to consult the oracle only at Yasnaya Polyana: when staying with Chertkov in June, during a walk Tolstoy was approached by a young man who asked him to foretell the future. The same day "a woman has come again to tell me the same thing as before, and complained to me about her husband." (*Journaux intimes*, p. 59)

"The folly of men" appears to him "more and more clearly,"[18] and he launches a formidable diatribe against materialism: "Machines, but for doing what? Telegraphs for transmitting what? Schools, universities, academies, for teaching what? Assemblies to deliberate on what? Books and papers to tell us what? Railways to carry whom? And where to? . . . Hospitals, doctors, chemists, to prolong life, to do what?"[19]*

Yet his temptation had not vanished for all that. After rereading some of his own works he noted: "I oughtn't to write any more. I think in this respect I've done all I can. But I want to, I terribly want to."[20]

The relations of the couple were about to become catastrophic. Sofia was continually complaining of her worries over the estate, the publication of the *Complete Works*, and the children. Goldenweiser reports that on one occasion Tolstoy answered her sighs with: "I don't understand you, Sonya, who's making you do all that? Give it all up! Take a journey, go away somewhere!"[21] She took this very badly, and after accusing her husband of trying to get rid of her, she ran off into the country. She was found in a ditch, and the coachman brought her home. Tolstoy's note reads: "A talk with Sonya. . . . I was afraid, but thank God, it turned out all right."[22]

These incidents grew more and more frequent; they often ended in tears and mutual forgiveness. It is clear that Sofia had lost all self-control. Tolstoy was well aware of it, but found it hard to stand, so hard that he wrote: "One must learn to love like learning to play the violin."[23] And that is virtually impossible when, as he admits, one succumbs so often to "self-pity."[24]

Everything that happened at Yasnaya Polyana had become misery to him. Returning from a walk, he found that the Circassian guard who had remained at Yasnaya Polyana by Sofia's will rather than his own (though it was perhaps more for her husband's security than hers) had arrested Prokofy, a former pupil of the Yasnaya Polyana school, for stealing a wooden beam. Violence in the name of the law to protect property seemed to him monstrous, and still more so when it was a matter of his own lands. "Felt terribly depressed and really thought of leaving."[25]

This event afflicted Tolstoy all the more in that it set him in contradiction with his own teaching, particularly "The Slavery of Our Times."† In despair he unburdened himself to Alexandra: "I have been doubting—am I right in keeping my silence and would it not be better

* As Malraux wrote fifty years later, "Why go to the moon if it's only to commit suicide there?"

† In the 1899 version Tolstoy had written that "one must not have recourse to government violence, either to guarantee landed property or one's personal security." (L. Tolstoï, *Les rayons de l'aube*, Paris: Gallimard [Pléiade], 1901, p. 369)

perhaps to go away, to disappear. . . . But I don't want to do this because it would be for my own sake, for the sake of getting rid of this life which has become poisoned on all sides. Yet it is my conviction that to suffer life, such as it is, is what I need."[26]

Just as he used to visit prisons and courtrooms in the past, Tolstoy now haunted lunatic asylums. There was one, the Mechtcherskoye, just six kilometers from Yasnaya Polyana near where Chertkov lived. Tolstoy went several times,* viewing also the weekly films designed for the insane.† He was particularly struck by what one of the inmates said, in front of whom he had used the phrase "the next world." The madman had retorted, "There's only one world."[27] This was bound to please Tolstoy, who had recently come to the same conclusion.

His interest in madness and psychiatry went a long way back. Thirty years before, on April 9, 1880, he had written to Kantor that "if people were to refuse, for their own safety, to lock up and kill these madmen and so-called criminals, they could concern themselves with seeing to it that more madmen and criminals are not created."[28] He always thought of the insane not as the enemies but the victims of society.

Tolstoy thought more and more often about the question of suicide—a temptation he himself had experienced while writing *Anna Karenina*—as well as about the enigma of insanity, which, according to Chestov, he had feared more than death during the night at Arzamas in 1869.[29] For Tolstoy the two are connected: he considers writing an article on the subject and explains to Bulgakov the thesis he wants to prove: it is the madness of our time that leads to suicide.[30] This renewed interest was partly due to the increasing number of suicides in Russia, but more particularly to Sofia's condition. She was always threatening to kill herself, and in fact tried several times to do it. Her love of Tolstoy, her morbid jealousy, and her justified resentment of Chertkov had driven her into a real persecution mania. She used it, moreover, to put pressure on Tolstoy, who was not fooled, but knew that she was seriously ill. "The

* On June 13, 1910, the day after he arrived at the Chertkovs', and again—this time taking Chertkov along—on the sixteenth.

† These visits worried Alexandra, who was frightened of the mad. She was amazed to observe her father wandering calmly among them and "giving the impression of not even suspecting the risk he was running." She remembered he had often said to her, "Insanity is egotism carried to its extreme: a person concentrates absolutely all his thoughts and interests on himself. . . . The more I look at them . . . the more I become convinced that, properly speaking, all people are abnormal, it is only a question of the degree . . . [but] a truly religious man who has a foundation in life never can lose his mind." (A. Tolstoï, *Ma vie avec mon père*, p. 272.) Was it his observation of mad people or the memory of his own experience at the time of writing *A Confession* that led Tolstoy to frame this "religious" conception of madness?

incoherence of her thought leaves me no hope,"[31] he noted in October.

To get away from abominable scenes with her, Tolstoy went to the Chertkovs' on June 12, with (as Sofia says) "his whole suite, doctor, secretaries, footman," and his daughter Alexandra.[32] Away from his wife, he thinks of her: "I want to try to win over Sonya consciously, by means of goodness and love. From a distance it seems possible. I'll try to do so when she's close by. . . ."[33] It was in this state of mind that he received a telegram from her. Unable to bear his absence and still less to support the knowledge that he is with Chertkov, she summoned him home.* " 'Entreat you to come 23rd.' I'll go," notes Tolstoy; "I'm glad of the chance to do my duty. God help me."[34]

Not understanding fully the pathological condition his wife was in, he replied—or perhaps Chertkov replied for him, as Sofia believed—that it would be "more convenient" for him not to come until the twenty-fourth. He wanted to hear the violinist Erdenko, who was to play on the twenty-third at Telyatinki, and the atmosphere was better there for his own work than it was at home. He had been able to finish the sixth chapter of *The Way of Life*, entitled "Sins, Temptation and Superstition," and was now proceeding with *The Wisdom of Children*.

But Sofia was sinking swiftly into madness. She was frightened, and her telegram was a true cry for help. Tolstoy's casual attitude brought fresh fuel to her mania and gave it new impetus.† For two days she "stays in her nightdress" and neither sleeps nor eats. She feels "spasms in the throat and a stabbing pain in the heart."[35] In her jealousy, now a disease, Sofia held Chertkov responsible for all the woes of her married life: "He is all that separates us. . . . I am uncontrollably jealous of [him]; . . . I feel that he has taken from me all I have lived on for forty-eight years, I have such a habit of loving Leo Nikolayevich, of taking care of him, of watching over his work! . . . And now I am completely left to one side, I am a burden on him."[36] Suicide seems to her the only solution. "No one will know I died of grief at losing my husband's love and of jealousy toward another man."[37] When Tolstoy did come home, he noted: "Found things worse than expected: hysterics and irritability. It's impossible to

* It is worth noting that this telegram arrived in the morning but was not given by Alexandra to Tolstoy until the evening: a noble concern not to disturb her father, but also, perhaps, the desire to oppose her mother, whom she did not get on with, and of whose behavior she disapproved.

† When she got the answer on June 23 she wrote a long piece from which the quotations in this paragraph are drawn. It was more or less intended for publication and entitled: "Another suicide (wanderings of a lunatic) written on the brink of the grave." Later, she admitted that "it is an insane person who wrote these outpourings"; and she ends her journal note by saying, "I wrote this under the influence of a violent attack of hysteria." (*Journaux intimes*, p. 333)

describe. I didn't behave very badly, but not very well either, not gently enough."[38]*

At Sofia's request Tolstoy gave her his diary, hoping it might pacify her. Unfortunately, on June 26 she discovered in reading it that her husband had been showing his diaries to Chertkov since 1900, "so that he could copy out extracts."[39] And the famous little remark "I want to struggle against Sonya with kindness and love" shattered her completely. She rushed in to her husband and made another scene. Tolstoy admitted in the end that he had turned over his journal to Chertkov. She bombarded him with questions. The diaries were in a bank, he told her. "Which bank?" Tolstoy wanted to know why she was so curious. "Because I am your wife, the person closest you." That was when he truly lost his temper. "Chertkov is the person closest to me!" he shouted.† "And I don't *know* where my diaries are!" Like one demented, Sofia ran from the house, and once again it was the coachman who brought her home.[40]

Possession of the diaries was to be at the center of nearly all the dramas that took place, with Tolstoy, Sofia, and Chertkov as actors. Those journals were something paramount to each of them and meant something different in each of their minds. For Tolstoy, his diary was a storehouse of ideas; he had told Chertkov so in 1904: "Frankly, I attach no importance to all these papers, except for my diaries of recent years. . . . These might have some importance, if only for the fragmentary thoughts expounded there. And so if you cut out from them all that is incidental, unclear and superfluous, their publication might be useful to people. . . ."[41] Thus Tolstoy felt rather detached about the full publication of the journals—perhaps he even rather favored it. For Chertkov, though, the diaries were possibly the outstanding work by Tolstoy, and he wanted to be their sole depositary even more than he wanted to be their owner. For Sofia, too, it was not material possession that mattered; these were the journals of the man she loved: "the holy of

* Varvara Feokritova witnessed this reunion. She had already alerted Tolstoy to his wife's condition by a telegram sent before Sofia's. "Violent nervous attack, pulse above 100, prostrate, tears, insomnia," which shows how alarming her condition was. "She wept and sobbed, and in a nervous crisis said she wanted to kill herself. She showed Leo Nikolayevich what she had written about that the day before. He seemed shattered, but remained tender and full of solicitude for her. . . . Their explanations went on till two in the morning." (*Journaux intimes*, p. 134)

† This sentence was terrible for Sofia; it is nearly word for word what her husband had written to her fourteen years earlier, on October 23, 1896, when they were both worried about their son Mikhail's wedding plans: "and who is closer to me than you?" (*Tolstoy's Letters*, vol. II, p. 549)

holies of his life . . . his soul's image, [they] must not be in the hands of any stranger."[42] If she lost hold of them she would be stripped of her past, her youth, her happiness—and threatened through the judgment that posterity had in store for her.

Tolstoy seemed to take his wife's hysterical fits quite calmly. "Yesterday she spoke about moving somewhere."[43] He read the famous Dr. Korsakov's *Psychiatry*—as usual, not so much to learn anything new as to stimulate his mind; he had conceived his own explanation of madness long since. He believed that just as the evils of the world are due to the sins of men, and not to economic causes, individual madness comes from "a moral weakening," not from organic causes. But it was probably his wife's disorder, rather than his reading Korsakov, that inspired the thought that "the insane always achieve ends better than those who are healthy in mind. This is because they know no moral obstacle; no shame, truth, conscience, or even fear."[44]

The Tolstoys went to spend two days with their son Sergey; there the interview took place that Chertkov had requested of Sofia when he got wind of her charges against him. On June 1 they had a violent altercation,* and a desperate haggling over the journals began. The next day Sofia obtained a written promise from Chertkov that he would give them back after making certain extracts. She was not appeased by the concession and thought of leaving her husband, as she confided to the good Marya Andreyevna Schmidt. Marya persuaded her that going to live somewhere else would be ridiculous. It was she who also tried to dissuade Tolstoy—the only one to do so—when he told her of his intention a few days before he ran away.

Home once more at Yasnaya Polyana, Tolstoy went nearly every day to see the man Sofia called his *idol*. The friendship between these two grew ever more unbearable to her; she harassed her husband, threatened him, watched him, cajoled him. It was absurd to try to keep him by scenes that, more than anything, made him eager to leave. On July 7 she went in to see him as he was going to bed. "Promise me you won't ever leave me on the sly, without telling me." He answered: "I wouldn't ever do such a thing—I promise I shall never leave you. I love you."[45] A few minutes later he came to her room and told her that he felt "very happy" after talking things over, and the two hugged and kissed.

* Chertkov lost his temper so far as to tell Sofia that for a long time he could easily have dragged "you and your family through the mud." And he went on with a snarl, "I can't understand a woman who spends her entire life murdering her husband." (*The Diaries of Sofia Tolstoy*, p. 502)

But everything proved a pretext for more scenes. Some days later, Tolstoy and Chertkov having gone riding in the woods, the disciple took some photographs of the master and lost his watch in a ditch. Everybody went looking for it. This show of good will toward Chertkov infuriated Sofia, who finally collapsed and spent the night on the balcony. Tolstoy complained that her groans kept him from sleeping; she fled into the garden; they found her two hours later, but she refused to return home if Tolstoy did not come and look for her himself—it was he who had "driven her out." Her third son rudely made his father go. "A terrible night. Until 4 o'clock, and Lev Lvovich was the worst of them all. . . . Sonya, poor woman, has calmed down. A cruel and depressing illness."[46] Once appeased, Sofia softened. "He looked so old and sad, lying with his face to the wall."[47] She kissed his hands. And once again they wept together.

The children would come frequently to Yasnaya Polyana, and take the side of one or the other parent. Sofia tells her troubles to anyone who will listen, and visitors leave horrified at the atmosphere of the house.* She complained even to Chertkov's own mother.† At times, pure chance complicated things. Filka, a servant sent to invite Goldenweiser to come riding with Tolstoy, got confused and gave the message to Chertkov. "I had a hysterical attack right there, in front of all the servants,"[48] Sofia confesses shamefacedly in her diary.

On July 14 Tolstoy yielded to his wife's urging and sent word to Chertkov by Alexandra asking for his journals back. That same day he composed a "letter of intent" for Sofia, but she was in such a state of excitement that she refused to read it. What he promised in the document was: not to give his "present diary to anyone" and "to take back the old diaries." He further reassured her about what "future biographers ill disposed [toward her] might write." The children called this part of the letter "mama's reference from her employer." It was true: Tolstoy was acknowledging the good and loyal services that his wife had rendered throughout their life together, and he concluded: "I have never ceased to love you and still love you, despite the various causes of coolness between us." He listed the reasons for this drifting apart: while he felt a growing

* Bulgakov, professor at the Moscow Conservatory, and a devout Tolstoyan, was shocked by what Sofia told him about Chertkov; he fled from Yasnaya Polyana in tears and rushed to Telyatinki. There he was still more astounded by the Chertkov household's stories of its brushes with Sofia. He left in despair at "the atmosphere of hate and malice that surrounded the great Tolstoy in the twilight of his life, Tolstoy who so needed rest." (*Journaux intimes*, p. 369)

† Chertkov's mother retorted: "And I have been so unhappy because your husband has taken my son from me!" (*The Diaries of Sofia Tolstoy*, p. 514)

revulsion concerning the "interests of worldly life," she on the other hand was unwilling to renounce them. He also lamented that her character was "more and more irritable, despotic, and uncontrolled." But "the chief cause was that fateful one"—and against it neither could do anything: "completely contrary views of the meaning and purpose of life."[49]

Tolstoy's letter asking Chertkov to return the diaries to his daughter had occasioned a huge commotion at Telyatinki. Bulgakov reports that the entire house immediately set about copying compromising bits about Sofia—in case she might manage later to suppress them—and that Chertkov made "with ludicrous solemnity" three quick signs of the cross on the bundle of journals as he handed them over to Alexandra.[50]

At Yasnaya Polyana, Chertkov's agent, Goldenweiser, scrupulously noted all that occurred. Lev Lvovich was keeping watch at the entrance to the estate; Sofia posted herself upstairs to keep an eye on the approach to the house. But Alexandra knew of all this in advance and took another road. She then handed the journals through the window to Varvara Feokritova, who passed them in turn to Tatyana. In the end, Sofia finally did get hold of the parcel, but after checking the contents, voluntarily turned it over.[51]

For once Tolstoy was firm. The journals would go into a safe in the State Bank: neither Chertkov nor his wife would have them in their keeping. Sofia accepted the compromise morosely.*

This partial defeat showed Chertkov the extent of the difficulties that awaited him after his master's death. Only an official document could confirm his role as editor of Tolstoy's works. Knowing that the will contained a fault in drafting, he asked his lawyer to make a new one and had it brought to Tolstoy for signature. Tolstoy, frightened of getting caught by Sofia, preferred to sign it outside the house; he went on horseback to a nearby clearing where he had made an appointment with Sergeyenko (Chertkov's secretary) and Goldenweiser. He dismounted, recopied and signed the new will, using a log for a table. He turned back at once, but not before remarking, "How painful this whole business is!" It went on tormenting him, and in his diary he mentioned it only in sibylline terms: "The writing in the woods."[52] On that same day (not surprisingly) Sofia had noted: "I stayed absolutely alone at home all day and worked on the proofs of the new edition."[53]

* Sofia wrote in her diary for July 16, 1910, "I went to Tula with Tanya and we deposited Lev Nikolayevich's seven notebooks. . . . I felt exactly as though my beloved lost child had been restored to me and [then] was taken away again." (*The Diaries of Sofia Tolstoy*, p. 520)

After the return of the journals, Sofia asked Chertkov to resume his visits,* because, in truth, she preferred an open relation to exchanges of notes or secret meetings between her husband and him. She does not know, though, if she will be able "to bear the sight of him."[54] When he returned to Yasnaya Polyana for the first time, she barely greeted him and demanded without mincing words the Jubilee telegrams which he had kept. She managed things so as not to leave the two men alone, but when Chertkov mentioned to Tolstoy the last letter received from him, Sofia sniffed out another secret. She was not wrong: the letter dealt with a codicil that Chertkov wanted to add to the will, and that would make him Tolstoy's true legatee through Alexandra's mediation. Sofia spent a sleepless night and decided once again to run away. She left a note for her husband that ended: "Be in good health and be happy with your Christian love of Chertkov and the whole human race, excepting of course your unhappy wife."[55] She also wrote a melodramatic article for the papers, beginning: "In peaceful Yasnaya Polyana an extraordinary event has taken place." A carriage bringing Andrey Lvovich from the station was arriving in the courtyard; she got into it, but her son guessed what she was up to and made her come back with him into the house. Contrary to her fears, when Tolstoy came to see her in her room, he said: "I realised that I simply could not live without you." He wept. "We are so close, we have grown so used to one another. . . ."[56]

Beginning on July 29, 1910, Tolstoy kept, in addition to his usual diary (referred to hereafter as the *Big Journal*), another one he called *Diary for Myself Alone*. This one he carefully hid, trying to escape from both Chertkov and Sofia, the two beings who loved him passionately—and effectively poisoned the last years of his life.

Sofia may have gained some points by getting Tolstoy to take back his journals from Chertkov, but Chertkov won a secret victory of special importance by getting himself made executor of Tolstoy's will. Needless to say, Tolstoy soon regretted having signed such a document. Less than a week afterward he wrote: "Chertkov has involved me in a struggle, and this struggle is both very depressing and very repugnant to me. I'll try to wage it with love."[57]

The disciple scented danger and intensified his campaign of denigration against Sofia. Tolstoy reacted sharply. "Not only do I wish to believe, but I do believe, the situation is not such as you make it out to

* Tolstoy notes on August 8: "Now she wants Chertkov to come back to our house." They had discussed the idea calmly and he had told her: "You're suggesting my seeing Chertkov again but I don't insist. All I want is to spend the last years of my life as peacefully as possible. The best for me would be to go to Tanya's for a week or so, and for us to separate and have some peace." (*Journaux intimes*, p. 257)

be," he informed Chertkov on July 28. And to Goldenweiser, who pretended that Sofia had duplicate keys made to open his desk, "In some irritable remarks [made by my wife] you suspect a whole covert program of action; but even if the facts prove you right, so much the better—I'll recover my freedom to act as I wish."[58] Makovitsky was certain that if Sofia ever discovered the existence of a will she would appeal to the Tsar.

Yet she was not surrounded solely by enemies. Biryukov reproached Tolstoy (who was upset by the criticism) for signing the document without the family's knowledge. "I've realised my mistake, very, very, clearly. I should have summoned all my heirs . . . and not kept it secret."[59] Then a fresh letter from Chertkov* accused Sofia of having "for many years planned, formed, and nurtured most prudently and with great skill and precautions the scheme that would permit her to possess herself of all her husband's writings after his death." It was enough to cause Tolstoy to recant once more. "I've been thinking about your letter of yesterday," he wrote Chertkov. "The conclusion I drew . . . is that Pavel Ivanovich [Biryukov] was wrong, and I was also wrong to agree with him; and I fully approve of your activity but am nevertheless dissatisfied with my own."[60]

That early August of 1910, Tolstoy was certainly not pleased with himself: the business of the will was really repugnant to him, first, because he wanted to stay outside legality,† and second, because he was sorry for Sofia,‡ and his double-dealing§ with her probably pained him greatly. On the practical level, his concern to entrust his works written after 1881 to someone who understood them, knew them, and was to some extent capable of extending the message,¶ was perfectly legitimate and reasonable. Chertkov had the required competence, whereas Sofia

* Sofia was right in suspecting the two friends of corresponding secretly; it was Biryukov who had conveyed the letter, dated August 18, 1910.

† Tatyana mentions in her journal a letter from her father to Chertkov that Biryukov told her about, in which Tolstoy said that all the good he had done or written in his life would probably never redeem the act he had committed in making a *legal* will. (T. Tolstoy, *Tolstoy Remembered*, p. 232.) The will took on great importance in Tolstoy's eyes because it brought him face to face with a new form of the problem of property, which he knew he had not resolved with his 1881 "renunciation."

‡ In a letter to Chertkov's wife Galya written then, Tolstoy said, "She is certainly ill, and one can suffer from her behavior, but it is impossible for me not to be sorry for her." (*Journaux intimes*, p. 116)

§ Lev Lvovich says in *The Truth About My Father*: "It was perhaps the first time in his life that he had hidden something from her"; he even saw the will as "the hidden yet main cause of the flight and death" of Tolstoy.

¶ Tolstoy could not imagine all the kinds of manipulation his disciple indulged in. They made Tatyana wonder six months after her father's death whether the manuscripts were any safer in Chertkov's hands than in her mother's. (T. Tolstoy, *Journal*, p. 288) had always maintained a negative and hostile attitude toward her husband's philosophic and religious thought. Tolstoy's patience was once again severely tested. A frightful scene occurred on August 3. "In the evening an insane note from Sofya Andreyevna. . . ."[61] She had copied out and put before her husband's eyes a passage from his diary for 1851 where he had written he had "never fallen for women," but had often "fallen for men." Sofia saw these lines as proof of a guilty relation* between him and Chertkov. "He turned white," and shouted, "Get out! Get out! I said I would leave you and I will."[62] Tolstoy locked himself in and sent Makovitsky to her. Bulgakov notes in his journal for the day: "The poor woman ran from one door to another."[63] These scenes always had their witnesses, their consolers, and their censorious observers.

The suicide threats, the flights, the cries, the continual spying on him† shattered and exhausted Tolstoy; his health was now precarious, and naturally those around him, wanting to spare him these shocks, urged him to leave. The same day he had noted once again that he considered going away and "leaving a letter," but he still hesitated, although he thought that "it would be better for her."[64]

Even so, Tolstoy gives evidence of great understanding; he feels that Sofia is afraid of going mad,[65] and he shares that fear. He was working on an article, "On Insanity," first entitled "On Suicide," and was full of his manual of psychiatry. "Read about 'paranoia' in Korsakov. It's as though it were copied from her."[66]‡ He took account of his own aging: "The work I have to do is very clear to me . . . but I don't seem to have the strength."[67] He observed that he had "many, many thoughts, but all scattered. Well, never mind. I pray and pray; help me!"[68]

* For two weeks Sofia had been certain that "Tolstoy was in love, in a repugnant and senile way, with Chertkov (falling for men was in line with his youth)." She also wondered if he was hiding his diary because he had been unfaithful to her. (*The Diaries of Sofia Tolstoy*, p. 522)

† She had always spied on him. On December 17, 1862, three months after their marriage, Sofia was already writing, "I feel incapable of really understanding him, that is why I spy on him so jealously." She justified herself in the same way now. On August 6, 1910, Tolstoy had met her in the grove and Alexandra hastened to explain to her father that her mother was not there by chance, but on purpose to spy on him. Varvara Feokritova also noted: "Now she gets to spy on him nearly every day," and it was true. On August 6, Sofia admits having "asked the children if the Count was alone," and two days later: "I went out, . . . wandered all over the woods and parks of Yasnaya." (*The Diaries of Sofia Tolstoy*, pp. 538–41.) She finally fell asleep exhausted on a bench.

‡ There is no doubt that Sofia had paranoid *tendencies* and suffered from persecution mania, but one cannot speak of paranoia, since that psychosis is irreversible; and after her husband's death she showed no more pathological symptoms: it was her love for Tolstoy that nourished the madness. Of course, she had no lack of reasons to think herself persecuted, but her jealousy was complicated—part morbid, part motivated and reactional; there was mania but there was also real persecution. Her sickness was grounded in numerous objective facts: Chertkov's appropriating the journals and manuscripts, the signing of a secret will, the campaign of denigration against her orchestrated by her husband's friends, whispers followed by silence when she entered the "Chancery."

The relative weakening of his physical and intellectual strength did not sadden him. On the contrary, he was aware that his "memory has gone, quite gone, and the astonishing thing is, I've not only not lost anything, but have actually gained a tremendous amount—in clarity and strength of consciousness."[69] It was the second reference to this decline since the new year 1910; they seem to have created a kind of serenity that helped him to put up with Sofia's scenes and cries and false departures. He told Chertkov's wife, who was annoyed with him for being so patient, that the closer he came to death the more clearly he saw that "to attain love of everyone, one must simply not act"; he no longer took account of anything in the world "but this one necessary task of life."[70]

With the summer, the usual visitors* reappeared at Yasnaya Polyana. "It's depressing with everyone [here]," wrote Tolstoy on August 11. He longed to go and spend a few days alone and in peace at Tatyana's. His wife wanted to go with him, and once more he gives in. The first day at Kotchevy went well, but in the evening, when Tolstoy asked Alexandra for his notebook, Sofia's suspicions reawakened; she was once more embattled. "This morning she hadn't slept again. They brought me a note from her saying that Sasha† was copying out my accusations against her from my diary, to give to Chertkov. Before dinner I tried to console her by telling her the truth, that Sasha was only copying out detached thoughts, and not my day-to-day impressions. She wants to be consoled and is much to be pitied. Something is going to happen, I cannot work. Perhaps it is useless."[71] Tolstoy only partly reassured Sofia, since the same day she noted: "The 'enemy' has come between us, as the peasants would say—i.e., an evil spirit."[72] Yet her mind kept relatively clear; speaking of the diaries she writes: "He hides them from me because I get upset, and I get upset because he hides them from me."[73]

The next day, the alert being over, Tolstoy rejoices. "A good day today. Sonya is quite well. It is good, too, because I felt anxious. And anguish expresses itself in prayer and trust."[74] This theme of the utility of anguish and suffering often recurs. He had already noted on August 10, "It's good to feel one is to blame, and I have this feeling." Having abandoned himself "to the natural wish to ask forgiveness" he had felt its "perfect joy."[75]‡

* Sofia mentions Boulanger, with whom she played whist, "Leva" and Tatyana, as well as Alexandra, Varvara Feokritova, Makovitsky, and Biryukov, who were almost permanent residents of Yasnaya Polyana.

† Tolstoy's youngest daughter Alexandra.

‡ In 1896 Tatyana noted: "Papa has definitely decided to give up bicycle riding. I am glad for his sake, because I know what pleasure it gives him to deprive himself of anything." (*The Tolstoy Home*, p. 271.) Gorky was exasperated by this cult of martyrdom. Tolstoy himself wrote: "The main thing is: I want to suffer, I want to shout out the truth which is burning me up." (*Tolstoy's Diaries*, vol. I, p. 327)

Sofia spent the day correcting *Childhood*, which would soon be ready for printing. She was doing a huge amount of work, despite the state of her nerves, for she wanted to beat Chertkov in the race to bring out a new edition of the works published before 1881—in case a will should in fact exist. Her proofreading appalls her; she is amazed to find "exactly the same traits of character in his youth as in his old age."[76] Rereading the chapter called "The Ivins," she is bent on seeing in it proof that "obsession and falling in love with a boy in childhood and with Chertkov—the wonderful idol—in old age, have one and the same origin."[77]

She urges Tolstoy to decide on a date for going back to Yasnaya Polyana. But he had no wish to return; he was happy at Kotchevy, glad to see his grandchildren, to play cards without shame, and above all to be quietly writing. Sofia explained his contentment: no one asked him to play the great man, and here "there are no petitioners, no beggars."[78] He answered crossly: "I'm not a soldier, and shan't be told how much leave I can take."[79]

Toward the end of this summer Chertkov changed tactics. He had always maintained that Sofia was not seriously ill and, like Alexandra and Makovitsky, took the view that she only feigned madness. Now he suggested "treatment." He listed for Tolstoy "the ways one must adopt with mental patients."[80] He made it clear that when the patient is married it is advisable not to give in or be present at the fits, lest one "set up between husband and wife a sort of specific and communicable nervousness." His formula defined rather well the relation that existed between Tolstoy and Sofia.

But soon Chertkov's influence exerted itself not only through letters and messengers.* Sofia had hoped that he would stay away from Yasnaya Polyana, but on August 18 she noted, "I read some terrible news in the papers today; the government has given Chertkov permission to stay at Telyatinki . . . my heart rate is 140."[81]† Tolstoy reports that when she heard the news she fell positively ill.[82] The next morning before she was up, Tolstoy came in to see how she was. He consoled her and confirmed all his promises. Sofia records in her diary that he is ready "(1) Never to

* Varvara Feokritova took part in the "smear" campaign. She heard about Sofia's plan to intervene with Stolypin, Minister of the Interior, so that Chertkov, who had just been allowed to stay at Telyatinki, would be expelled from the district; and she retailed this rumor to everybody.

In September Goldenweiser wrote Tolstoy a letter that "terrified" him. He imputed to Sofia the intention of proving after Tolstoy's death that he had written his will in a moment of mental collapse.

† The Tolstoy family had the odd habit of taking their pulse in moments of crisis. Tolstoy did it when he finally left Yasnaya Polyana.

see Chertkov again, (2) To give his diaries to no one, (3) To let neither Chertkov nor Tapsel take his photograph."* She had added this final provision because she "found it most distasteful that his idol should photograph him . . . like some old coquette."[83] Sofia was herself passionate about photography, and took umbrage at the intimacy created between Chertkov and her husband by their posing sessions. To keep the peace, Tolstoy now acceded to Sofia's demands. But on one point he did not yield: "I will keep writing to Chertkov, because he is useful to me in my practical affairs."

It was a good thing that Sofia did not know of the *Diary for Myself Alone*, because around this time Tolstoy wrote in it: "Today as I recalled my marriage I thought that there was something fateful about it. I was never even in love. But I could not not marry."† Those words would have depressed her all the more now that she acknowledged being haunted by an "idée fixe": "Lev Nik.'s intimacy with Chertkov."[84] The merest photograph of him shattered her, and she admitted: "the least mention of Chertkov . . . drives me into a frenzy."[85]

Tolstoy could see that Sofia was in agonies all the time but felt incapable of helping her.[86] Still, he tried. On the morning of August 25 he appeared "unexpectedly" at her door . . . he only wanted to know how she had slept; five minutes later he came back and said: "I thought you might be lonely all by yourself at night." She was "overcome with joy and this sustained me through the day."[87]

On his birthday, August 28, 1910, Tolstoy felt weary of his wife's everlasting recriminations. "It isn't love, but a demand for love that she projects." He was also beside himself at Makovitsky‡ and Alexandra's attitude of refusing "to recognize that [Sofia] is ill. They are wrong."[88]

That same evening, after his game of cards, Tolstoy went to see her. They bickered again, and she asked him "how they might recover their sense of intimacy." Tolstoy had a plan ready made: "Give away the copyrights, give away the lands, live in a hut." This sort of answer infuriated Sofia, who thought on the contrary that for his work Tolstoy

* Tapsel: English photographer, friend of Chertkov, who took numerous photos of Tolstoy. On August 27, Tolstoy speaks of his wife as being in "a terribly painful and pitiable state" (*Tolstoy's Diaries*, vol. II, p. 681), not knowing that her distress came from seeing fifty-seven photos of him taken by Chertkov. (*Journaux intimes*, p. 273)

† Written in his own hand, but at what date? Sofia added on the manuscript: "In his diary of the period of our engagement he wrote 'more in love than ever. I will shoot myself if she turns me down.' " (*Journaux intimes*, p. 122)

‡ Makovitsky, too, tried to indoctrinate Tolstoy. He says in his memoirs that he told Tolstoy "Sofia uses simulated madness to exert power." Tolstoy answered: "Where is the boundary of madness? Anyway, the mere fact that she behaves like that is abnormal." (*Journaux intimes*, p. 122, n. 34) Tolstoy knew perfectly well that she was ill.

needed a "comfortable, settled existence . . . he has lived all his life in these conditions—as though it were for my sake!"[89]* She was not entirely wrong. The curator of the Tolstoy House in Moscow told me that Countess Tolstoy said after her husband's death: "If I hadn't had my feet on the ground, he couldn't have had his head in the sky."

The tragic encounters became almost daily events. On August 29 she had not slept: "Yesterday morning was horrible. . . ." says Tolstoy. "She went into the garden and lay there. Then she calmed down. We had a good quiet talk. As she left† she touchingly begged forgiveness‡ . . . Sasha telegraphed that everything was well. What will happen next?"[90]

Two days later Tolstoy wrote her that he felt deeply touched by what she had said to him as she left, and he entreated her to conquer that feeling he "hardly knows how to call," which makes her torture herself.[91] Sofia knew perfectly well what to call it: jealousy. In her mania for "interpreting" everything, she went so far as to write to Tatyana that she saw in her husband's burst of affection "a bad intention and a claim of his right to see Chertkov again."[92] She would not retreat from her position. He had to choose between her, "his loving wife," and "that man, the present object of his insane preference."[93]

Their loving impulses did not coincide. On September 2, Tolstoy sent her a letter that came from his heart: "I never stop thinking of you and feel you near in spite of the distance. You take care of my physical well-being and I am grateful to you, while I on my side worry about your mental and spiritual condition. May God help you in the work that I know you are bent on accomplishing in your soul. . . . I want to act in such a way as may be agreeable to you." He knew that Sofia was struggling with her illness, but his letter crossed in the post "a very bad letter from her . . . the same demand for love, which would be comic if it wasn't so terrible and agonising for me."[94]

He was not aware that Sofia, on arriving at Yasnaya Polyana, had gone into his room, where "everything looked so different, as though some-

* As she put it a month earlier: "Who but he needs this luxury? There are doctors for his health, two typewriters and two copiers for his writings, Bulgakov for his correspondence, Ilya Vasilevich, the valet, to look after a weak old man, and a good cook for his weak stomach." (*The Diaries of Sofia Tolstoy*, p. 533)

† After this scene, Sofia had used the excuse of a telegram from her son Lev (telling her of a change of date for a trial that involved him) to return to Yasnaya Polyana. She did not like Kotchevy, where her room was "encircled by others full of people and noise, and where everyone thinks badly of me for daring to suffer so in soul and body." (*The Diaries of Sofia Tolstoy*, p. 558)

‡ Sofia also mentions the mutually tender feelings that overcame them at her leaving: "L.N. and I bade each other a tender and loving farewell; we both cried and asked one another's forgiveness. But the tears and the farewell were like the end of our former happiness and love." (*The Diaries of Sofia Tolstoy*, p. 558)

thing had been buried for good, and things would indeed be different from what they had been before."[95] Two days later she consigned to her diary an enigmatic note with the precise information: "I worked all day today, September 2nd, on *Resurrection* . . . and sent for a priest, who sprinkled holy water."[96]

What had happened? Varvara Feokritova tells the story in her memoirs. Sofia had taken down Chertkov's portraits in Tolstoy's room and sent for a priest "to sing a Te Deum and sprinkle holy water* in Leo Nikolayevich's room; otherwise the spirit of Chertkov would continue to reign there."[97]

It was just when Alexandra returned to Kotchevy, the next day, that she told her father about Sofia's strange behavior and that Sofia got Tolstoy's moving missive. She records "a very kind letter from my husband."[98] It was a complete turnabout in her feelings and the next day she wrote: "I am becoming increasingly impatient to see my husband."[99]† Back she goes to Kotchevy, hurrying to join Tolstoy, and also to snatch him away from Chertkov. But he was still vague as to the date of his coming home, and his shilly-shallying ruined Sofia's good mood: "She was hysterical all day; she ate nothing and wept. . . . She received a letter from Chertkov and answered it."[100] Chertkov was being generous with kind words, assuring her that she was wrong to fear that he was "getting hold of Tolstoy's manuscripts to deal with them [as he saw fit]."[101] Sofia found in this message a fresh proof of his baseness: "The purpose of your so-called good letter is perfectly clear but it is transparent: you want to resume your personal relations with Leo Nikolayevich." Chertkov's initiative failed of its hoped-for effect. "Sofia Andreyevna has eaten nothing for the second day." Tolstoy went himself "to ask her to come to dinner. Terrible scenes all evening."[102] For all the love and understanding that Tolstoy showed at that time, he could not help being incensed by Sofia's jealousy and frenzied suspicion. He shouted at her, "I shall never give in to you on anything ever again! I bitterly regret my promise never to see Chertkov. . . ."[103]

Challenging thus the terms of their agreement was a shock for Sofia. She lay prostrated on the divan in Tolstoy's room as he sat at his writing table. "Then he got up, and taking both my hands in his, he stared at me, smiled sweetly, then suddenly burst into tears." That was enough for her

* Already in 1895, her jealousy of Lyubov Gurevich had aroused in her fantasies of defilement; she thought then that "whoever touched the hand of Leo Nikolayevich was fated to perish." (*Journal de la comtesse Léon Tolstoï*, p. 138)

† In her diary for the sixties, Sofia called Tolstoy "Lyovochka," later "Leo Nikolayevich," now insistently "my husband," but at the time of his death she called him "Lyovochka" again.

to think that "he still has a glimmer of love for me in his soul."[104] But toward evening, it was more running out into the garden, more weeping and crying. "[She] ran off to hire a cart and go away at once." She called Chertkov a murderer and vowed she never would see him again. Tolstoy did not let himself be shaken. "When I lost control of myself and told her *son fait* [what I thought of her], she suddenly became well again and is still well today."[105]

Sofia left Kotchevy by herself the next day; they parted in a tender mood: "Lev Nik. suddenly came round to the other side of the carriage and said to me with tears in his eyes: 'Well, give me another kiss, then, and I'll be back very, very soon!' "[106] But Tolstoy lingered on with his daughter, and Sofia lamented: "He did not keep his promise and stayed another ten days in Kotchevy."[107]

Tolstoy was very tired; he was worried for her and also for himself; he felt weak but ready to do violence to his feelings: "I must remember that in my relations with Sofia Andreyevna the point is not my own pleasure or displeasure, but the fulfilment of the task of love in the difficult conditions in which she places me."[108] After a long meditation on the relation of the Self to Space and Time, Tolstoy tackled yet again the problem of the continuity of awareness, which he had already tried to clarify earlier in the year. He experienced again the feeling of being "always the same from eight to eighty-two." He was particularly aware of a state that he called "the zero distance," that is, of self-identity: "My self breaks free, a process of liberation is taking place in it . . . yes, the tearing away of veils which constitutes liberation happens doubtless in time, but my self is immovable all the same. . . . What constitutes my self independently of time is one always and exists certainly: it is the awareness of my unity with all things, with God."[109]

He pursued his meditation on evolution, on the progression of the world and the condition of the working class; then suddenly, in the tenth paragraph (he still loved to number them), the thought winds up in the dilemma of his relations with Sofia. "I can't get used to regarding her words as ranting madness. That's the cause of all my trouble." It is strange that Tolstoy, engrossed as he was in the fundamental problems of existence, should have transformed his wife's nervous condition into a calamity. He was sometimes aware of this paradox, as he had noted in his *Diary for Myself Alone*: "How comic is the contradiction in which I live, whereby, without false modesty, I am conceiving and giving expression to very important and significant ideas, and at the same time am involved in a woman's caprices and devoting a great part of my time to the struggle against them."[110]

He did not get home by Sofia's name day, but only on September 22, at midnight, for the forty-eighth anniversary of their marriage; it passes off without too many upsets. He had even agreed to let himself be photographed with his wife.* But as always the troublemakers were busy. Alexandra Lvovna thought that Tolstoy had betrayed Chertkov by yielding in this matter and not hanging up again in his study the pictures her mother had taken down. She criticized Sofia before her father, who flung out at her: "You are in danger of being like her."[111] Chertkov, on his side, writes letters† full of "reproaches and accusations." Tolstoy is once again reduced to wailing: "They are tearing me to pieces. I sometimes think I should go away from them all."[112]

Pressed by Alexandra, Tolstoy hung up the various pictures again on September 28. Sofia's reaction was immediate. "He can't bear to part with it [Cherkov's portrait] now he is not seeing Chertkov every day—so I took it down, tore it into little pieces and threw it down the lavatory." Tolstoy reacted equally fast: "Lev Nik. was furious of course, and quite rightly accused me of denying him his freedom. . . . I went to my room, found a toy pistol and tried to fire it, thinking that I would buy myself a real one. I fired it a second time when Lev Nik. returned from his ride but he didn't hear."[113]‡

The next day Tolstoy was amazed to find her "calm, as if nothing had happened."[114] Sofia showed him the pistol. "She is to be pitied but it is

* She had delegated this function to Bulgakov, but he was awkward. Sofia would have liked it done quickly, so as not to annoy her husband, who had just consented. The photos were bad and had to be retaken the next day. These snapshots assumed enormous importance for Sofia; in her eyes they "proved" to thousands of readers who saw them in the papers the "union" that reigned between her and her husband. She stuck one of them in the notebook she was keeping at the time, with the note: "Forty-eight years of married life, you are mine and I will not give you up to anyone." (*Journaux intimes*, p. 371)

† The "traffic in letters" that Sofia suspected had not stopped. Bulgakov brought one from Chertkov on September 26, in which he blamed Tolstoy for yielding to Sofia's demands. Tolstoy replied by return to Chertkov that his letter made a "painful impression. It all appears to me in a much more complicated light and seems to me harder to resolve than a friend as intimate as you can imagine. It is I alone who must resolve this question in my soul before God. And as I struggle to do it, any intervention from outside makes my work harder." (*Journaux intimes*, p. 371)

‡ Bulgakov gives a very detailed account of this tragicomic episode. He was with Marya Schmidt Schmidt in "the Chancery" when Sofia rushed in saying that she had burned the pictures. She came back a few minutes later with the torn pieces, then she left again and a shot was heard. "Sofia explained to [Marya] that she had fired." At what? She didn't say. Tolstoy comes in from his walk; his friends tell him what happened. He goes calmly into his room. Sofia fires again. Tolstoy doesn't stir. She runs off into the woods and won't come home till nightfall, when she gives in to entreaties from Marya Schmidt, who, distracted by the turn events are taking, sends a messenger with a note to Alexandra asking her to come at once from Toptykovo. Alexandra arrives with Varvara Feokritova. Sofia receives them gruffly (she calls them "the two garden pests") and dispatches her daughter's friend on the spot. Alexandra, in a rage, leaves as well. Tolstoy comments sadly on these events: "Everything leads towards the same ending."

very difficult"—still more so when he knew that she had followed him on his outing, "no doubt to spy on me," for on that day Tolstoy had gone out riding and Sofia had raced after him in a wild run of seventeen versts (eleven miles) in a dog cart.[115]

Yet the old affection would reappear between one scene and the next. On September 29 she sat beside her husband as he ate his breakfast. "It was wonderful to see the joy on his face when after asking who the pancakes were for I said, 'For you.'* . . . When other people are not here he is generally kind and affectionate to me, just as he used to be, and I feel he is mine again."[116] She was undoubtedly right, as Tolstoy remarked on the same occasion: "Today for the first time I saw the possibility of winning her over by kindness—by love. Oh, if only I could . . ."[117]

Endless quarrels and changeable health did not affect Tolstoy's desire to write. One afternoon, after a walk following "an agonizing talk with Sonya," he was struck coming home by the beauty of the flowers and the "healthy, bare-footed girls" sweeping the ground; and, moved by the brightness and excitement of the scene, he compared it with the sadness prevailing in his own house. In his diary he comments: "It would be good to write two [contrasting] scenes."†

On October 2, he came back to the idea of these two worlds, one the negative of the other. "Reading a story [*Une Vie*] by Maupassant yesterday made me wish to depict the vulgarity of life as I know it, and during the night it occurred to me to place in the midst of this vulgarity a person who is spiritually alive. Oh, how good! Perhaps something will come of it. . . ."[118] The same day he wrote in his *Diary for Myself Alone:* "I strongly felt the need to work at a literary creation, and yet I see I cannot work because of her,‡ because of the feeling that dogs me about her, because of my inward struggle"; and he tries to persuade himself that "this struggle and the possibility of victory in this struggle are more important than all possible works of art."[119]

If Tolstoy was spiritually alive, like the man he wanted to make the hero of his new book, physically he was very frail. After two days without entries in his *Big Diary* he took it up again on October 5: "I've been seriously ill . . . fainting spells and weakness";[120] and in his little

* On October 23 Sofia notes: "Later on he ate a delicious pear and brought one for me to share with him." (*The Diaries of Sofia Tolstoy*, p. 584)

† Chertkov interpreted this as indicating a project of Tolstoy's to write "what happens outside and what happens inside a house."

‡ Makovitsky reports that Tolstoy said: "If she could only go away just for a time . . . I should like to be able to be alone. I only have a few months, perhaps only a few days to live . . . while I'm waiting, I don't work." (*Journaux intimes*, p. 100)

Diary for Myself Alone he is even more explicit: "On the 3rd, following my nap after dinner, I lost consciousness."[121]

But he had again experienced what he called in his last letter to Alexandrine "the enlightenment that illness gives." It helped him to progress beyond a decisive phase. He had not yet managed to find the solution of his fundamental problem—harmonizing what he says with what he does—but he did contrive to restate the premises in a different way, explaining that when an intelligent man utters principles which his life contradicts, "this only shows that he is so sincere he cannot help expressing what exposes his weakness and that he is not doing what the majority of people do—tailoring his convictions to suit his weakness."[122]

Actually, Tolstoy just then nearly died.* "Convulsions in the face, terrible shuddering in the legs, unconsciousness, delirious, raving. Two or three men could not hold down his legs."[123] Thus notes Sofia on October 3. The illness reconciled her for a time with Alexandra, and appears for an instant to have drawn her closer to Chertkov. Tolstoy observed: "She is making an effort and has asked him to come here," but she could not prevent herself from requesting her husband not to kiss his friend. "How unworthy! She had a hysterical fit."[124] Sofia had the impression that her husband bore a grudge against her "for taking Chertkov's visit so hard."[125] The next morning Tolstoy came to see her and began by blaming her, but the conversation did not turn out badly. They were both aware of danger; she was afraid—"no reproaches . . . but there is something oppressing us."[126] Later she watched him through the balcony window writing at his desk: "gazing at his serious face with boundless love and the persistent fear that he would leave me, as he has so often threatened to do lately."[127] He wrote on the evening of the tenth: "It's quiet, but everything is unnatural and frightening. There's no tranquillity."[128]

But, as always, Sofia's fantasies soon overcame her good resolutions. Tolstoy noticed that she was again torn apart by worry over his supposed "secret interviews with Chertkov": "I'm very sorry for her, she is ill."[129] And in the *Diary for Myself Alone*: "This morning she was saying that I'd had a secret meeting with Chertkov yesterday. She hadn't slept all night. But thank goodness she is struggling with herself."[130] Vain hope. The

* Sofia in her fright had tied to her husband's bed the little icon with which Tante Toinette "had blessed her Lyovochka when he went off to war." (*The Diaries of Sofia Tolstoy*, p. 570.) This is the icon that had stopped a bullet on the chest of Tolstoy's grandfather—and on Prince Andrey's in *War and Peace*. Alexandra did not lose her wits; her brother Sergey writes in his memoirs: "Sasha took my father's little diary from his pocket and gave it to me." (*The Truth About My Father*.) As for Chertkov, he came secretly to Yasnaya Polyana, hid on the ground floor, and was constantly informed of Tolstoy's condition.

next day: "More talk this morning and a scene. It seems someone told her about a Will of mine bequeathing my diaries to Chertkov."[131]

No one had told her anything; she had simply found the *Diary for Myself Alone*, which Tolstoy had hidden in one of his boots.* She discovered there confirmation of the existence of a will, which she had suspected since July 24, and noticed with satisfaction that her husband insisted Chertkov had pushed him into an action he loathed. But the sentence in which Tolstoy declared that he had never been in love with her threw her once more into despair. Confronting him with these cruel words, she made her husband reread a page dating from the time of their engagement, in which he had written: "If she turns me down, I shall shoot myself."[132]

After reporting this painful episode in his journal, Tolstoy added that in the evening he read Dostoyevsky: "The descriptions are good, although certain little jokes, long-winded and not very funny, get in the way. But the conversations are impossible."[133] When he got further into *The Brothers Karamazov*, he became severer still: "How all this wants art."† Gorky had already observed in their conversations in the Crimea that Tolstoy spoke of Dostoyevsky only "reluctantly, constrainedly, evading or repressing something."[134]

On October 13, yet another quarrel. Sofia had "urged," even "begged," her husband to visit the Chertkovs; yet when he told her he was going that afternoon, "a stormy scene ensued; she ran out of the house and ran to Telyatinki."[135] Tolstoy then left for his daily ride and sent Makovitsky to let Sofia know he was giving up the visit. But she could not be found, having hidden "in the ditch near the gates leading to the Chertkovs' house."[136] She was discovered there toward six in the evening. She then blamed Tolstoy for not telling her clearly he was not going to see his friend. He got cross. "I want my freedom. . . . I'm 82 years old, not a little boy, I won't be tied to my wife's apron strings. . . . I take back all my promises. . . . I shall do whatever I want."[137] She twice tried to force his door and they made it up, but she knew he had an

* On October 13, 1910, Makovitsky noted: "Without telling him, she has read it and keeps it." (*Journaux intimes*, p. 128)

† In a letter of October 23, 1910 (*Tolstoy's Letters*, vol. II, p. 709), Tolstoy showed himself just as critical. "I can't get over my dislike of its anti-artistic nature, its frivolity, affectation, and unseemly attitude to important subjects." Sofia's comment four days earlier is quite amusing: "In the evening Leo Nikolayevich was enthusiastic over reading *The Brothers Karamazov*, and said 'Today I have understood why I love Dostoyevsky; it's because he always has beautiful thoughts'; then he began to criticize him, saying again that all the characters talk in Dostoyevsky's language." (*Journaux intimes*, p. 303.) The same day he had told Makovitsky: "His characters act continually in an original way, so that in the end one gets used to the originality, and it turns into banality." (*Journaux intimes*, p. 106)

idée fixe "about being 'free,' "[138] and he, on his side, wonders: "What is to come of it?"[139]

The next day Tolstoy notes that she behaved "gently and kindly. . . . she is very agitated and talks a lot," adding in the *Diary for Myself Alone*: "[She] seems to be repentant . . . she kisses my hands. She's very agitated and talks incessantly."[140] He found it painful "when she speaks in exaggerated tones about her love for me"; he was certain her behavior was deliberate, which was probably true, since she herself said: "Despite my jealousy of Chertkov, I surround [my husband] with love, care, and tenderness, and anyone else would appreciate it."[141]*

Tolstoy thought again of going to Tatyana's, but his wife's penitent attitude made him hesitate. He was unable to work, and kept Chertkov informed of the state of affairs. "Yesterday we had a really painful day. . . . I do not cease to pity her and am happy that I love her at times without any effort. . . . What's to be done if there are people to whom spiritual reality is inaccessible (besides, I think it's only a temporary impossibility)?"[142]

Sofia felt disturbed "both physically and emotionally."[143] During the night of October 19,† she went to Tolstoy's room and demanded the diaries. " 'There's another conspiracy against me.'—'What do you mean, what conspiracy?'—'Your diary has been given to Chertkov.' " Tolstoy replied, "It's not here. Sasha has it."[144] Knowing that her daughter had it pacified Sofia somewhat, but she felt humiliated by the diary's not being in her own hands.[145]

The next day she noted: "Some peasants came to see him—Novikov . . . who writes articles."[146] This Novikov, who to Sofia was but one visitor among the rest, appeared elsewise to Tolstoy, for he counted on the man to help him realize his hope of escape: Tolstoy had often promised to go and visit Novikov in his village. Now he said that at last he was going to keep his promise: "At present I am free." Seeing the peasant's skepticism, he added: "I've done my share at home, as people

* Montherlant, the French playwright and novelist, thought that Sofia was *femininity* at its fullest incarnation and he gave this analysis of the pair: "She clutches him in her tentacles; he cuts them off one by one; when her invincible love makes them grow again, he cuts them off again, one at a time, and he hardly feels their grip, owing to the blood that flows out of them. Indeed, he takes root in all this and, without gladness, raises himself higher. Make no mistake: he loved her too." Montherlant sees in the tragedy of their marriage a drama greater than they: "The guilty party was Tolstoy, but not in the drama, only in its genesis. And behind him, the guilt rests on marriage itself when it involves a man of genius." (H. de Montherlant, *Sur les femmes*, Paris: Sagittaire, 1942, p. 24)

† "Tolstoy was still awake," says Sofia, but "already asleep," according to Goldenweiser. (*Journaux intimes*, pp. 303, 130)

say, you understand? I've come out of the family circle. I'm *de trop* hereabouts."[147] And he elaborated: "I tell you in all sincerity, I'm not going to die at home, I've made up my mind to go to some unknown place, where nobody will know who I am. I might come straight to your cottage to die there."[148]

Novikov had retired to his room when he heard light steps outside.* It was Tolstoy coming back to try and explain to him—and explain to himself as well—why he had not gone away before this.† So it was to this self-taught peasant, who had learned to read in the army and had first come to see Tolstoy in Moscow in 1894, that Tolstoy chose to reveal the depths of his heart: "We have lived fifty years of love; we have each made the other into what we are. My wife has never deceived me. I could not go off somewhere just for my own sake and cause her grief. Only, when the children were grown up, I urged her to lead a simple life. But she feared more than anything this turn to simplicity. It wasn't her soul that fought against it, it was her instinct."[149]

Novikov responded to his confidences by telling him of a friend of his, who had patiently put up with his wife's drunkenness for thirty years, then one fine evening, beat her hard. From that day forward she stopped drinking. The story struck Tolstoy, who noted it down. It reminded him of what Ivan the coachman had said to Alexandra, which he had also recorded: "With us, things get fixed with the whip."[150] After talking with Novikov, Tolstoy slept badly. "During the night I thought about my departure."[151] Three days later, Tolstoy sent Novikov the letter he had said would come:‡ "Would you be able to find me a little hut in your village, no matter how small, so long as it is warm and standing by itself?"[152] He added that if he should send Novikov a telegram he would sign it "Nikolayev."

He had spoken of his intention not only to Novikov, but had let it out to Marya Schmidt and admitted it to his daughter Alexandra: "I keep dreaming, planning, how I shall go away."[153] He makes further reference

* Novikov, in his own account of "My Last Night at Yasnaya Polyana," says that Tolstoy's moving about made no noise. (C. Salomon, *Documents sur la mort de Tolstoï*, Paris: N.R.F., 1922, pp. 16 and 17.) Tolstoy had retained in old age a catlike agility, visible on the film of his eightieth birthday. Gorky spoke of "the short, light, quick step of a man accustomed to walk a great deal." (*Reminiscences of Tolstoy, Chekhov and Andreev*, p. 60)

† "This house is a hell in which I burn. But God has not given me the strength to break with my family. It is my weakness, maybe my sin, but I could not make my own suffer, even for my personal pleasure." (C. Salomon, *Documents sur la mort de Tolstoï*, p. 59)

‡ When the letter got to Novikov, Tolstoy was already ill at Astopovo. It remains a mystery that he never refers to it during his flight, and particularly so at a time when he was uncertain where to go.

to this conversation in a letter to Chertkov on October 17: "Sasha has spoken to you of my plan."[154] It was evidently an open secret. Alexandra later said: "We knew our father was leaving, but did not know when"; and Marya Nikolayevna confirmed to Sofia after Tolstoy's death that when she came to Yasnaya Polyana for the last time, her brother had spoken to her of his plan to leave. She had thought that "he simply wanted to settle somewhere and live just as he liked, without bother 'from anybody.' "[155]

On October 22 Tolstoy noted: "There's nothing hostile on her part, but this pretence on both sides depresses me."[156] As for Sofia, only one thing seemed to matter, for that same evening she wrote: "Thank God for another day when Lev Nik. hasn't been to see Chertkov."[157]

Dreadfully low spirits, a weariness with everything, appear in Tolstoy's last notes of October 1910. He speaks of an "agonizing wish to be alone."[158] He cannot work: "I've no wish even to write in my diary."[159] He complains for the third time that year that he has "lost his memory of everything, of nearly all the past," of all his writings. He records that "once I could never have imagined a state of mind in which I am conscious every minute of my spiritual self and its demands. I now live nearly always in such a state."[160] And the next day: "How can I not rejoice at the loss of my memory? . . . All of life is concentrated in the present, and how good that is."[161] Tolstoy had attained true detachment—detachment from the past, detachment from time.

Many among his near acquaintances or disciples said or wrote to him that he must "break with his family, go away, and live according to his principles."[162]* The only person who asked Tolstoy to stay at home was good old Marya Schmidt.† He went to see her and noted on his return: "I'm more and more oppressed by this life. Marya Alexandrovna tells me not to go away, and my conscience won't let me either."[163] Two days passed and he still "feels the same feeling of depression. Suspicion, spying. . . ." Tolstoy tried to persuade himself that going was a

* On October 22 Tolstoy records that Chertkov has sent a copy of his reply to one K. F. Dosev, who reproached Tolstoy for being a slave to his wife and not having given up his landowner's life. His disciple also submitted the plan of an announcement for the papers (which Tolstoy had asked him to draw up) to let it be known that the copyrights of his work were not for sale, intending to put an end to the rumors started by Alexandra that Sofia was arranging their sale for a million rubles. (*Tolstoy's Diaries*, vol. II, p. 687)

† Sukhotin, the husband of Tatyana Lvovna, told Chertkov in a letter of September 20, 1912, the story of this conversation, which he had direct from Tolstoy himself. "I intend to go away from Yasnaya," Tolstoy had confided, and Marya Schmidt cried out: "Leo Nikolayevich, my dear, you'll get over that, it's a momentary weakness." Tolstoy agreed with the old lady: "Yes, yes, I know it's my weakness, and I hope I get over it." (*Journaux intimes*, p. 132.) Another version has Tolstoy saying: "I will not get over it."

legitimate act of self-defense: ". . . desire on my part that she should give me an excuse to go away . . . and then I think of her situation, and I feel sorry for her and I can't do it."[164]*

Sofia may have been more Tolstoyan than her husband believed: she uses nearly the same words as his to express her own disgust: "endless excuses, lies, and evasions. . . . It's so sad." She can bear no more. "I am coming to the end of this terrible diary,† the history of all my sad sufferings, and I shall seal it up for a long, long time! Curses on Chertkov, curses on the person who was the cause of it all. Forgive me, Lord."[165]

On October 26, 1910, Tolstoy goes riding with Makovitsky. "Did a lot of writing, and read. It snowed." The day before, Sofia had already noted: "My soul is uneasy. What will happen?"[166]

* If Tolstoy blamed himself for his indecision, his disciples blamed him even more. On October 24 Tolstoy mentions receiving two letters that were "very disagreeable," one from a St. Petersburg student who says he is shocked by the contradiction between Tolstoy's doctrines and his actions, the other from one Albrecht of Breslau containing the same reproach. (*Journaux intimes*, p. 108)

† It is a fact that from October 26, 1910, onward, Sofia did no more than enter brief notes in what she called her "Daily Diary."

TWENTY-NINE

Escape

AT DAWN on October 28, 1910, like the wealthy prince in the *Russian Pilgrim*,* Tolstoy "left in secret the place of his birth."

He had yielded to the urgency that impels the perpetual wanderings of the Fools of God: "During the night of the 27–28 came the impetus which made me take this step."[1] Such is the laconic note in the *Diary for Myself Alone*. In the *Big Diary* he gave a very detailed account of the circumstances that caused him to run away and the conditions in which he did so. "As on previous nights [he] heard the opening of doors and footsteps." He saw Sofia go by, and without his knowing the reason, the occurrence aroused in him "indignation and uncontrollable revulsion." He saw "through the crack [in the door] a bright light in the study and heard rustling." He tossed in his bed for nearly an hour and in the end lit a candle. Whereupon "Sofia Andreyevna opened the door and came in, asking about 'my health' and expressing surprise at the light which she had seen in my room. My indignation and revulsion grew." He gasped for breath and took his pulse, which he noted was 97: "I couldn't go on lying there, and suddenly I took the final decision to leave."[2]

He began a letter to Sofia at once, a compromise with his pledge not to go away without telling her.

> October 28, 1910, 4 A.M. My departure will distress you. I am sorry about this . . . I couldn't do otherwise. . . . Apart from everything else, I can't

* *Stories of a Russian Pilgrim*, French edition (*Récits d'un pèlerin russe*, tr. by Jean Laloy, Paris: Seuil, 1974, p. 134)

> live any longer in these conditions of luxury in which I have been living, and I'm doing what old men of my age commonly do: leaving this worldly life in order to spend the last days of my life in peace and solitude. . . . I advise you to reconcile yourself to this new situation which my departure puts you in, and to have no unkind feelings towards me. If you want to let me know anything, tell Sasha; she will know where I am. . . .[3]

He signed it "Leo Tolstoy" and added as a postscript that he had asked his daughter to have his things and his manuscripts sent to him.

When his letter was finished, he went downstairs "in a dressing gown, barefoot in his slippers, with a candle in his hand"[4] to wake Makovitsky, "trembling at the thought that [Sofia] would hear."* For he feared what would happen then: "a scene, hysterics, and after that I wouldn't be able to leave."[5]

While Dushan, Sasha, and Varia† finished packing up the luggage, Tolstoy hastily gathered up his manuscripts and asked Alexandra "to put them somewhere safe." They left with "a trunk, a big bundle, a rug, a cloak, and a basket."[6] He went himself to order the horses harnessed, lost his way and also his cap in the dark, and came back to look for another and a pocket lamp. Once in the stables he got impatient with the coachman's slowness and pressed him to get a move on.

Tolstoy had made the great decision of his life: he was leaving Yasnaya Polyana. He took Dr. Makovitsky with him; Alexandra was to join them later. Escorted by Filia the groom, mounted and with a torch in his hand, the carriage started "but instead of passing by the house took the straight road which led through the apple orchard."[7] "Where to go? Where to go as far as possible?" Tolstoy wonders. The doctor suggested a distant retreat in Bessarabia, with a Tolstoyan friend of his called Gussarov. But they could not decide. Only when they reached Shchekino station was the question settled: the pair of fugitives would go to Optina-Pustyn. Tolstoy gave the coachman a note for Alexandra, telling her of his destination and asking her to confirm to Chertkov that, unless countermanded, "the statement to the papers" that Tolstoy had already approved should be sent out. He also asked her to let him know "how the

* It is indeed amazing that Sofia, on the watch "every night, ear to the keyhole," as she wrote in July (*Journaux intimes*, p. 345), and who had insisted only the previous night that he shouldn't lock his doors (*Tolstoy's Diaries*, vol. II, p. 675), heard nothing of the inevitable bustle of departure, that the sound of steps and the whispering of four people failed to reach her. Tolstoy's room was opposite his wife's and separated from it by a four or five foot corridor at the end of which was a storeroom where they had to go and look for the big trunk.

† Makovitsky, Alexandra, and Varvara Feokritova.

news about his departure was received, and everything else, the more details the better."[8]

The train would not be in for an hour: "every minute" Tolstoy expected his wife to appear.[9] Once settled in the train, "my fear passed, and pity for her rose up within me, but no doubt about having done what I had to do. Perhaps I'm mistaken in justifying myself, but I think it was not myself, not Lev Nikolayevich, that I was saving, but something that is sometimes, and if only to a very small extent, within me."[10] On the threshold of death, what he owed to humanity seemed more important than what he owed his wife. This belief was the central motive in his decision to leave.*

They had hardly left when Tolstoy felt like reading. He asked his traveling companion for the *Cycle of Reading*,† but the book had not been packed. Tolstoy "seemed very tired," Makovitsky noted, and though the old man was used to dictating while traveling, he "remained plunged in his own thoughts."[11] The doctor made coffee (Russian trains in those days always were equipped with a samovar containing boiling water), and Tolstoy asks himself out loud: "What can Sofia Andreyevna do now?" It was a complex, worrisome thought, made up of fear that she should find him and of anxiety for her—and the thought would never leave him.

They changed at Gorbachovo for the Sukhinitchi-Kozelsk train. "How good it is to be free,"‡ said Tolstoy, as he sat down in the crammed, smoky carriage: it was the worst and most cramped that Makovitsky had ever seen in Russia.[12] Shklovsky says that in those days they were jokingly called fourth-class carriages.[13] Tolstoy at first settled himself on the rear platform, then moved to the front one, where he stayed for an hour sitting on his shooting stick.§

It took more than six hours to cover 105 kilometers. Tolstoy makes no mention of these discomforts in his diary. He recalls from his adventure only his immersion in the folk. "The journey from Gorbachovo in a third-class carriage packed with working people was very edifying and

* Makovitsky oversimplifies in his report. Like Professor Makachin, he thought Tolstoy had decided to leave for fear of doing violence to his wife, which would have been intolerable to him. (*Tolstoï vu par lui-même et ses contemporains*, p. 384)

† During his stay at Optina-Pustyn, he borrowed it from his sister. These readings had become a need—his daily work of meditation. When he was in his last hours, he asked for passages to be read to him.

‡ According to Makovitsky, Tolstoy said: "How fine I feel, how free I am." (*Tolstoï vu par lui-même et ses contemporains*, p. 361)

§ The shooting stick is now in Tolstoy's room at Yasnaya Polyana; it appears in several of his photographs.

good, although I was too weak to take it in properly."[14] He had talked at first with a peasant from Dudino who complained of being unjustly accused of theft by his landowner, and Tolstoy leaned over to the doctor to whisper in his ear in German: "This is a typical peasant."[15] A surveyor joined the conversation and defended the landowner, who was a friend of his. He proved a good talker, "a liberal with scientific ideas," thought Tolstoy. The conversation soon turned to the single-tax theory of Henry George, to violence, then to Darwin and education, subjects dear to Tolstoy. He had come to be like "the strange, defiant old man, who denounced the authorities and was considered mad,"[16] of whom Nekhlyudov speaks in *Resurrection*.

According to Makovitsky's account of the journey in the review *Novy Mir* (July 1978), the coach was filled with "peasants, bourgeois, workers, intellectuals, two Jews, and a high-school girl who took notes and defended science when Tolstoy attacked it." Soon, all grew silent, and crowded into the middle of the carriage to listen to Tolstoy "standing up and holding the attention of the travellers." Shortly, he was the only one speaking.

During the stop at Belyor he had lunch in the second-class buffet, where the waiter and patrons recognized him. Back in the train, he asked the peasant from Dudino how to get to Optina-Pustyn. "Why don't you take the habit?" answered the mujik. Let worldly things drop away, and save your soul. Stay in the monastery."[17] Tolstoy had been right; the man was truly a "typical" peasant. "A worker sitting in a corner of the rear platform began playing an accordion and singing something. Leo Nikolayevich listened with pleasure and approval."

They reached Kozelsk toward five in the afternoon, with five kilometers still to go. Tolstoy, light on his feet, got down first and went himself to hire a two-horse carriage for Makovitsky and himself and another for the luggage. This journey was even more taxing than the long train ride. "We constantly had to duck to avoid the low branches of the willow trees."[18] Then they had to wait for a ferry.

At Optina-Pustyn, Tolstoy sent a telegram to Alexandra immediately; he signed it with his assumed name, Nikolayev, then wrote her a long letter. He gave both messages to the driver. In his letter he summed up the journey ("uncomfortable, but mentally very agreeable and instructive") and asked his daughter to send him the books he was studying when he left. "Montaigne, the 2nd volume of Dostoyevsky [*The Brothers Karamazov*] and [Maupassant's] *Une Vie*." He asked her to open his mail and gave her a message for Chertkov that described perfectly his own present state of mind: "Tell Vladimir Grigoryevich that I'm very glad and very afraid of what I've done. I'll try and write down the subjects I think about and the stories that are on the tip of my pen. I consider it better for the time being to refrain from seeing him. He will understand me as always."[19] In a postscript, he asked for a dressing gown, small scissors, and pencils. That done, he had tea and honey, and entered in his diary—in both diaries—the details of his departure and the incidents of his journey. He also finished an article on capital punishment.

Tolstoy lived just one day of freedom—a single day without Sofia and without Chertkov. As early as October 29, Sergeyenko, Chertkov's emissary, arrived: "The news he brought was horrible," notes Tolstoy—it was horrible, and also false in part.

It was true that Sofia really attempted suicide when Alexandra told her without kindness what she had feared for so long, that her beloved Lyovochka had left her. After reading the first lines of the letter her daughter handed her, Sofia ran toward the lake. Alexandra, Bulgakov, and two servants rushed in pursuit. "They could see Sofia Andreyevna's grey dress in the distance, appearing and disappearing between the trees." She stumbled, fell on the bridge, and slipped into deep water, whence the robust Alexandra promptly pulled her out. This attempt came closer to success than the previous ones. Sofia was taken to her room, and paper knives, pen knives, and opium were removed. But "hardly an hour had gone by when she was away again, heading for the lake."[20]

Chertkov's envoy also reported that Andrey, Tolstoy's sixth son and the one most attached to his mother, the one of whom she said, "He is mine, wholeheartedly mine,"[21] had arrived at Yasnaya Polyana. That also was true, but he added that Sofia had guessed where Tolstoy was hiding, and that was *not* true. He was lying.* The family knew nothing. But it was this lie, confirmed the next day by Alexandra, that pushed Tolstoy into taking the step that proved fatal to him—to leave Optina-Pustyn. Sofia and the children, who had rushed to Yasnaya Polyana at Alexandra's call,† learned only on November 1, in a telegram from Orlov, a journalist on *The Russian Word*, where the fugitives were.

In the afternoon, Tolstoy went to see his sister Marya,‡ a nun in the convent at Shamardino, thirteen kilometers from Optina. Recalling the visit, she said she did not believe that a starets or wise man could "offer

* Sergeyenko, Chertkov's devoted secretary, had not taken it on himself to give Tolstoy this false news. The decision had been deliberately made by Chertkov and Alexandra.

† Only Lev Lvovich, who was in Paris, did not join them.

‡ The year after her brother's death she recalled this meeting in a letter to Salomon (January 19, 1911) published in *Documents sur la mort de Tolstoï*, Paris: Gallimard, 1922.

any relief to the deep sorrow" of her brother; "his hurt was too complex." "He only wanted to regain serenity and to live in peaceful, spiritual surroundings."[22]

Marya Nikolayevna, Masha, loved her brother, but she also loved her sister-in-law. She had known them in the days of their happiness, and understood their tragedy: "The more Leo Nikolayevich rose with all his soul and all his mind toward heaven, the more she retreated into her beloved earth-bound life."[23] Masha put into proper perspective the oft-debated theory that Tolstoy would eventually have returned to the Church. Having chosen to end her days in a religious order, she could not fail to wish for his conversion: "I do not think he wanted to become Orthodox again, but I had hoped our Starets would bring out in him the feeling of spiritual humility which he did not as yet possess, but which he was not far from in his last days."[24] Tolstoy himself cherished the most radiant and consoling impression of his interview with "Mashenka."[25]

Sergeyenko's report had nearly driven him out of his mind. He felt "very depressed all day and physically weak besides"; he had not stopped thinking about "a way out of my situation and hers." His conclusion was that "there surely will be one, whether we want it or not, and it won't be the one we foresee."[26]

Sergeyenko was not only a messenger of true and false news, he also brought two letters, one from Alexandra and the other from Chertkov, who was in seventh heaven about Tolstoy's decisive act.* "I cannot find words to express to you my joy at knowing that you have left"; and he adds, "My wife saw in a dream last night that you were leaving."[27]

His envoy left Optina with a reply for Alexandra. Tolstoy confesses that he "can't help feeling a great burden" and admits that it is "a very difficult moment." "I haven't decided anything and don't want to. . . . I try to do only what I can't help doing, and not to do what I can help." There follows a skeptical comment on Sofia's suicide attempt, which Alexandra has told him about. "If somebody has to drown himself, it is I, not she, and I only want one thing—to be free of her, and of the falsehood, pretence, and malice which permeate her whole being."[28] Yet some hours earlier, speaking of her to his sister, he had said, "You can't imagine the state she is in. And really, now, just think, it's dreadful—in the water! . . ."[29] And he burst out crying.

On October 30, Tolstoy, who for many years had almost always begun his diary with the phrase "If I live," now notes: "Alive, but not entirely."

* Chertkov perhaps realized that his letter took too triumphant a tone, and was compromising, for he asked Tolstoy to return it to him by Makovitsky "at the first opportunity." He was also concerned to know if Tolstoy had given instructions for Alexandra to open his letters, and proposed to take over this task himself after she left. (*Journaux intimes*, p. 158 n.)

Still, he reads *The Relationship of Socialism to Religion in General and Christianity in Particular*, and dictates a letter to its author, Novosyolov, one of his old disciples.

That same day was notable for the arrival of Alexandra Lvovna and her faithful Varvara Feokritova. Tolstoy comments on it: "I was very glad, but also depressed."[30] For Alexandra had told him that Andrey entirely supported their mother and that Sergey suggested Tolstoy should take her to Moscow for treatment. Alexandra moreover tried to reassure her father by declaring that "Sofia Andreyevna was too selfish ever to attempt suicide seriously."[31]

In the morning Tolstoy had taken a step that shows his firm intention to stay at Optina. "Went to rent a hut in Shamardino."[32]* He decided to move in the next day and in the afternoon inquired of Makovitsky, "Has a woman come? Has she said anything about lodgings?"†

Alexandra had brought with her the dramatic atmosphere of Yasnaya Polyana,‡ and her words alarmed Tolstoy more than Sergeyenko's: her mother, she was sure, "was preparing to have him hunted down by journalists or by the mayor, surmising that he was at Shamardino; one must therefore expect that [she] and Andrey would arrive at any minute."§

Faced with this prospect, Alexandra suggested that Tolstoy should move on, to which he replied, "I must think about it; I am so comfortable here." "Then Varvara joined us [writes Makovitsky], and we talked a lot about Sofia Andreyevna's condition, and the anxiety that prevailed in Yasnaya Polyana. The two girls were in a panic of fear, they urged moving on as soon as possible and wanted to keep the coachman until the five o'clock train." Makovitsky adds what is probably the most interesting detail of this account: "Leo Nikolayevich did not want to leave; he was cold, he had put on a woollen cardigan, and after reading the letters he kept silent. Nor did [his sister] Marya Nikolayevna and her daughter Yelizaveta [who was visiting her mother in the convent at the time] want him to go away."[33]

Tolstoy retired to his room and replied to Sofia, to Chertkov, and to each of his children who had written to show their affection and their wish to help their parents. "With the exception of [our] eldest brother,

* It belonged to a widow who let it for three rubles a month.

† Marya Nikolayevna wrote to her sister-in-law after Tolstoy's death that when he came to see her, "he said he was there for a long time and thought of hiring an isba from a peasant and living here," that is, at Shamardino. (*La tragédie de Tolstoï et de sa femme*, p. 352)

‡ This was Tolstoy's sister's opinion: "Before Sasha [Alexandra] arrived, he had no intention of going any further." (ibid., p. 352)

§ Makovitsky's very detailed account of Tolstoy's last days was published in full for the first time in the July 1978 number of *Novy Mir*, for the one hundred fiftieth anniversary of Tolstoy's birth. The present chapter relies on it for much of the quoted material.

Sergey, all were of the opinion that father should come back," wrote Alexandra.[34] Sergey thought his parents should have separated long ago, and had concluded by saying that his father should not "reproach himself if anything were to happen."[35] Ilya, on the other hand, like the rest of his brothers and sisters, deplored the fact that his father had not had the courage to bear his cross to the end, and urged him not to break off relations with their mother—a recommendation Tolstoy followed by writing to Sofia. As for the letter from her, it was heart-rending. Calling her husband "my spiritual brother," she beseeched him to come home, to save her "from another suicide: All my children are here but they are no help to me in their confident despotism: I need only one thing, your affection, my friend, my dear, my beloved Lyovochka, forgive me, save me." Pathetically submissive, she implored him: "My friend, let me at least say goodbye to you, tell you one more time how I love you. . . . Goodbye Lyovochka, I do not stop looking for you, calling to you."[36]*

When he had finished reading the only one of her letters that he was to receive, Tolstoy asked to be left alone and wrote two replies. He sent the second, which was more affectionate than the first, and which left the door rather more open: ". . . so if your life changes and it seems to me possible to live with you, I will come home. But coming home now would be suicide."[37] It is a love letter much more than a letter of breaking off. The correspondence of the couple at this juncture is in fact an exchange of desperate love letters. They are particularly interesting, because in spite of fatigue Tolstoy is fully in control of his faculties; later he was ill and, as it were, the prisoner of his friends.

Tolstoy explained to Sofia that "a return 'now' " was "completely impossible," and he asked her to try to adjust to what was "temporarily a new position. . . . Don't think that I left you because I don't love you—I love you and pity you with all my soul—but I can't do otherwise than I am doing." And he went on: "To return to you when you are in this state would mean for me to renounce life, and I don't consider that I myself am entitled to do so."[38]

* Sofia wrote him four letters, but he got only the first; the others were intercepted by Alexandra and Chertkov. Had he read them, perhaps he would not only have agreed but asked to see his wife. The second (dated October 29) has not the same passionate tone; Sofia tried to explain why she was in her husband's room on the night of October 28. She asks him to forgive her "if her nervous malady annoyed him in his work" and tells him that the night before she had begun "an energetic cure . . . warm baths with cold compresses on the head." In a third letter (November 1), she voices the presentiment that they will never see each other again and tells him she is reconciled with Chertkov and has made confession to a priest for having attempted suicide. In a fourth letter she says that she *always knew* he would leave her. Sofia later collected these letters under the title *My Letters to Leo Nikolayevich at the Time of His Exodus* with the aim of justifying herself before posterity.

Alexandra left her father alone for twenty minutes, then went back to him. Makovitsky wondered, without clearing up this important detail, whether he called her or whether she went of her own accord. She found him "bareheaded before the open fanlight, which he refused to shut." She took his pulse; it was 90, but she said nothing to the doctor. The testimony of Tolstoy's niece Yelizaveta Obolenskaya completes Makovitsky's account: "Sasha insisted on staying alone with her father and they talked for quite a long time. She came away very thoughtful and said, 'I think papa almost regrets having left.' "[39]

Then Tolstoy came to join them. Around the samovar sat his sister, his niece, Makovitsky, Varvara Feokritova, and Alexandra. Maps were laid out on the table; they discussed possible places to go: "the Crimea, the Caucasus, Bessarabia," or a stay with a relation, Helena Sergueyevna Denisenko. Suddenly Tolstoy said: "Well that will do. . . . It is not necessary to make any plans, we'll see tomorrow."[40] Then he ate the eggs and dried mushrooms the girls had brought, and with a good appetite, but he said "his soul was heavy."[41]

Tolstoy had gone to bed undecided; at four in the morning of October 31 he woke Alexandra: he had already hired horses and engaged drivers. Before going he left a word for his sister, thanking her for her welcome and excusing himself for taking her copy of *A Cycle of Reading*. He had also mailed a letter to Chertkov telling him that he had written to Sofia and "was not refusing to return, but making it a first condition that she work on herself and calm down." He also asked Chertkov to send warning by telegram if Sofia discovered where he was. "A meeting with her would be terrible for me. Apprehending everything, we have decided to leave at once . . . but where to, we don't yet know."[42]

This departure proved as nerve-wracking as the first. The carriage for the girls was not at the rendezvous. Tolstoy and Makovitsky did not wait for them. Alexandra and Varvara caught up with them at the last minute and jumped on the train without tickets.[43] Tolstoy's companion noticed that the fugitive had hesitated at the station, and wondered later, "If I had put the question to Leo Nikolayevich, he might have said that he felt ill—that may be why he wanted to stop at the hotel."

Once in their compartment the travelers, who were still dithering over a destination, finally agreed to go as far as Volov and stop at Novotcherkaska, "where a niece of Leo Nikolayevich lived. They would spend a few days with her and decide there where to go next—the Caucasus, the Crimea, Bulgaria."[44]

At the first way station Tolstoy asked for newspapers. "Everything is known already,"[45] he laments. They had bought *Russkaya Slava*, in which the headline ran: "LEO TOLSTOY LEAVES YASNAYA POLYANA."[46]

During the journey the party was pursued by "journalists who sent telegrams to their editors," and spied upon by a policeman, now in civilian clothes and now in railway staff uniform, "who posted himself at the carriage window at every stop."

Toward four in the afternoon, though wearing a cloak and a rug, Tolstoy was shivering. His temperature was 100.6 degrees. In the evening his temperature rose to 103.1 degrees.[47] At the next stop, at Astopovo, Makovitsky got out and approached the stationmaster, Osolin, who could not believe that the great Tolstoy was on the train. When the conductor confirmed it, Osolin offered his house to receive him.[48] Meantime, at the station Tolstoy was put in the ladies' waiting room. As various women came in to fix their hats, they noticed him, made their excuses, and went out again.[49] He was shaking with fever.

Tolstoy's flight was front page news. He was recognized everywhere; the number one personality in Russia could not vanish like the hero of *The Living Corpse*. His leaving Yasnaya Polyana was a national event. A crowd gathered on the platform, and when he came out "all the men took off their hats."[50]

It was a very sick man, who "might lapse into unconsciousness at any moment,"[51] that Makovitsky and Alexandra undressed and put to bed in the stationmaster's narrow iron cot. According to the doctor, Tolstoy was afraid the sheets would be icy and refused at first to get in. "His left arm and leg began to twitch convulsively. At times, I could see the same twitching on the left side of his face."[52] He was given an enema and a glass of wine.

Tolstoy had escaped from the gilded cage of Yasnaya Polyana, where he was under Sofia's governorship. Now he was the prisoner of illness in the little red house of the stationmaster at Astopovo, which was swiftly surrounded by a triple protective cordon: the police, the Church (which had not given up hope of recapturing him), and a third, the most effective, which Chertkov soon had in position. In Chertkov's view, Tolstoy must die suitably to his legend, alone with his conscience. The State, the Church, and particularly Sofia must be kept at a distance.

The fever went down and the night was calm. When he woke on November 1, Tolstoy, still haunted by the idea of flight, of going farther away, asked Alexandra, "What do you think—can we go on tomorrow?" She had heard him muttering in his sleep ". . . to run away—to run away—they'll overtake . . ."[53] Osolin, who was suddenly the most famous stationmaster in the world,* came with his wife to apologize for the noise their children made. Tolstoy answered, "Oh those angel voices. It's nothing." They offered him hot tea, but he preferred Narzan† with red wine.[54]

Alexandra had promised to notify the family if her father was seriously ill. Tolstoy forbade it: "In no case let the family know of [my] whereabouts or [my] illness." Alexandra protested; Tolstoy was upset by this exchange and added: "I should like to see Chertkov."[55] He asked his daughter to send a wire: "Took ill yesterday. Passengers saw me leave train in weak condition. Afraid of publicity. Better today. Going on. Take measures. Keep me informed." It was signed, as agreed, "Nikolayev."[56]‡ Chertkov answered that he was arriving the next day.

Then Tolstoy asked Alexandra to note down for him "thoughts for his notebook."[57]

> God is the unlimited All of which man has the awareness of being a limited part.
>
> God alone exists truly. Man is his expression in matter, time, and space. The more God's expression in man unites with the expressions [lives] of other beings, the more that man exists. This union of one's life with the lives of other beings is achieved through love.
>
> God is not love, but the more love, the more man expresses God, and the more truly he exists.[58]

He then dictated a letter in which he addressed his son Sergey and daugther Tatyana together, telling them that Chertkov "occupies a special position in relation to me, having devoted his whole life to the service of the cause, which I have myself served for the last four years of my life." He called on Sergey to give up Darwinism, which "will not tell you the meaning of life," and ended his letter with a request: "Try to calm down your mother, for whom I have the most genuine feeling of compassion and love."[59]

Tolstoy did not know that Sofia was in a state of utter prostration, watched over by a psychiatrist and a woman medical student.§ "I haven't

* He was harassed by journalists and received, among other things, a wire plus a hundred rubles from *Russkaya Slava,* beseeching him to cable news.

† Sparkling mineral water.

‡ To confuse their trail, Tolstoy, Alexandra, and Chertkov called themselves Nikolayev, Batya, and Forlova.

§ The student had studied for three years with Dr. Korsakov, whose *Psychiatry* Tolstoy had been reading in recent months.

eaten or drunk anything for four days now," Sofia noted. She knew that Tolstoy's going had definitively broken something in each of them, so that even if he should come back, they could "never love one another as before," because they would now "always fear one another." She began to eat again next day to be able to "go to Lev Nik. should he fall ill."[60]*

Tolstoy then asked that *A Cycle of Reading* be read to him. "It was just then that he dictated one more thought about God," says Makovitsky.† That note is the last one in the *Diary for Myself Alone*: "If we want by the idea of God to clarify the phenomena of life, nothing solid or warranted is to be met with in this conception of God and of life—only vain arguments that lead to nothing. We know God only by becoming aware of his manifestation within us. All the decisions based on our conscience, as well as the conduct of life founded upon it, always give man complete satisfaction, both through a knowledge of God himself and through the conduct of life founded on that conscience."[61]

On November 2, at seven in the evening, Tolstoy's temperature was above 102 degrees. "Not good: it has gone up,"[62] he remarked. After observing that there were bedbugs in the room, Makovitsky reports that he felt apprehensive on noting Tolstoy's pain in his left side—it could easily turn into pneumonia. He also noted that "during the night he held his hands as if he wanted to pray; he dozed, woke readily, and repeated ceaselessly, in a weakening voice, 'Oh my God, Oh my God.' It was the first time, he adds, that he had heard Tolstoy use those words.[63]

At nine, Chertkov arrived with Sergeyenko: "They had not seen one another for two months. The meeting was touching," said Alexandra. She also noticed that her father asked his disciple at great length about Sofia.

The fever rose to 103.3 degrees, and caused some worsening of the patient's condition—the heartbeat was feeble and irregular. They made him drink champagne.

A secretariat was organized in the stationmaster's dining room, with

* To the dread Sofia felt at knowing that her husband had left was added the fear that he should fall ill away from her. She had written to her sister Tatyana on August 3, 1903, "I have lived with Lyovochka nearly 41 years and still am subject to an insane fear of his dying in my absence." (*La tragédie de Tolstoï et de sa femme*, p. 311)

† In his summing-up of November 1, Makovitsky said the time was 10:30 and Tolstoy's temperature 100.4 degrees. But in the diary, the note is dated October 31, which would not have been of particular importance in itself if it had not been the last in the *Diary for Myself Alone*. Tolstoy dictated on two occasions, according to Alexandra, but Makovitsky makes clear that when Tolstoy's temperature went up again, he said: "Perhaps it's death, but it's very good and very simple." Tatyana reports the same words but dates them November 5, the day before her father's death.

Sergeyenko in charge; postage alone cost twenty rubles a day. Tolstoy was living under a rule of semi-secrecy: his mail was censored before it reached him; Alexandra went through it first. She did not hand her father either the Metropolitan Anthonyi's telegram or Sofia's letters; visits were under the control of Chertkov. On the night of November 2–3, Makovitsky counted fourteen people in the house, doctors or friends.

When about three in the afternoon, Osolin announced that "a special train would arrive in the evening with the Countess,"* the news caused a panic. Alexandra later recorded, "It was plain to all of us that a meeting between father and mother might be fatal to him."[64] On his side, Makovitsky says: "We are afraid of her and have decided to bar her way. Osolin, who loves Tolstoy a great deal, is resolved not to let her through." Sergey had arrived at the end of the day and Tolstoy's guardians hesitated for a long while before they let him into his father's room. Tolstoy wept to see him, and his son kissed his hands. When he left the room, he too was convinced that they ought not let his mother in to see the patient. "It would cause him too much emotion."

The train that brought Sofia, with her nurse, her psychiatrist, her sons (Ilya, Andrey, and Mikhail), and Tatyana, came into the station at midnight. Makovitsky had been sent "to welcome them and charged with the duty of dissuading them from seeing the patient." He did not find in Sofia her "usual air of self-confidence"; she seemed to him "pale, undecided and timid."[65] Naturally she wanted to see her husband. When Makovitsky explained that it was impossible, she reproached him for not having awakened her on the night of October 28; for she was still convinced that she could have kept her husband from leaving. And she wondered again, probably for the thousandth time, "How I could have slept so soundly?" and added: "I put in too much salt," which is the Russian equivalent of "I went too far."

On the morning of November 3, Dr. Nikitin, the Tolstoy family doctor called in by Alexandra, stepped off the train. His arrival annoyed Tolstoy but reassured the others. One might say that the troupe of actors from Yasnaya Polyana had reassembled at Astopovo—only the scenery was different. It was no longer that of a pretty country house, but a sordid village station in the province of Riazan. There, parents, friends,

* When Sofia was told that Tolstoy was ill at Astopovo, 100 kilometers southeast of Tula, the only train of the day had already gone. Roused from the state of stupor in which her husband's departure had plunged her, she chartered a special train and left at once. Tatyana Tolstoy wrote: "Galvanized by febrile haste, my mother had thought of everything, arranged everything. She had brought everything with her my father might conceivably need; she had forgotten nothing. But despite the lucidity of her mind there was no charity in her heart." (*Tolstoy Remembered*, p. 240)

onlookers, spies, and journalists came thronging from all directions; the railway telephone lines were jammed.[66]

Sofia found herself "in the eyes of the world" placed in a ridiculous position, and all the more painfully so in that she was obsessed by the idea of what people would think of her. Hoping to put them off the scent and to explain why she was being held at a distance, she held virtual press conferences.* In the dining room everybody gathers for dinner—the Tolstoy family and the doctors at one table, the journalists at another.[67] That same day, Makovitsky noted that the special correspondents had talked with Sofia, and she had assured them that "Leo Nikolayevich had left home to get publicity." The next day, she told them that Tolstoy had left Shamardino because he thought he saw a spy below his windows.[68]

Chertkov got Alexandra to visit her mother, who was living with her party in the special railway carriage that had brought them, on a siding. "She found in [her mother] no sign of repentance; on the contrary, Sofia blamed them all,"[69] said Makovitsky. Depressed but furious, she admitted things to Alexandra that betrayed both her anger and her despair. She was ready to accept all of Tolstoy's terms, "she would go so far as to settle at Tula and come to Yasnaya Polyana only once a week, to get Tolstoy home. But if he went away she would follow him, and she was ready to pay . . . detectives to trail him."[70]† Being ill informed, Sofia did not realize how serious Tolstoy's condition was; her greatest concern seemed to be whether Tolstoy had mentioned her. Alexandra answered yes, but added that he had always been afraid and was still afraid of her coming.[71]

On that day "Sonya came to the house and Sergeyenko stopped her from entering," writes Makovitsky. According to all the witnesses, Tolstoy never knew that Sofia was at Astopovo; but one may wonder whether he had not some intuition of her presence; for, oddly enough, on that very evening, November 3, he noted: "Had a bad night, lay for two days in a fever. Chertkov came on the 2nd. They say that Sofia . . ." What *do* they say? The phrase ends up in the air. Did he suspect that she was there? If, on the one hand, it is astonishing that Sofia never heard Tolstoy leave, on the other it is equally amazing that Tolstoy, who was so shrewd and observant, never felt in the embarrassed answers of all those

* Although Sofia was the only one to know nothing, it was she who finally informed the journalists, who arrived in force and at speed, of everything that happened or was said at Astopovo. Alexandra pretended that that was why the news in the papers was not always accurate. Later the situation was reversed, and it was the family "who got news from the journalists," says Vladimir Pozner. (W. Pozner, *Tolstoï est mort*, Paris: Plon, 1949)

† Makovitsky also wrote to Tolstoy's sister Marya Nikolayevna that Sofia had assured him that if her husband went south or abroad, she would follow, and not hesitate "to pay 7,500 rubles to a detective who will watch him wherever he goes." (*The Tragedy of Tolstoy*, p. 284)

he questioned that something was being hidden from him. He noted again: "Seryozha came during the night, I was very much moved. Today, the 3rd, Nikitin and Tanya came, then Goldenweiser and Ivan Ivanovich [Gorbunov, publisher of *The Mediator*]. Now here is my plan. *Fais ce que dois, adv* . . .* And it's all for the good of the others and especially for me."[72] That is the last note of the *Big Journal*. Thereafter, Tolstoy's thoughts are no longer direct from him, but come to us distorted by other voices.

One detail nearly revealed to Tolstoy that his family were at Astopovo: among the things Sofia thought would be useful to her husband she had brought a cushion once embroidered by her, which always lay on Tolstoy's bed at Yasnaya Polyana (and has since been put back there). Makovitsky wanted it placed under the patient's head; Tolstoy would not have it, but was curious to know how the cushion had got there. Chertkov replied that Tanya had brought it. Tolstoy asked no further questions but sent for his daughter. Chertkov witnessed the interview and says it was "very touching, as much for the joy Leo Nikolayevich showed at seeing his eldest daughter, as for the affectionate concern he expressed in his questions about Sofia Andreyevna's condition"; but he adds: "Leo Nikolayevich did not utter a word that could lead one to think he would like to see Sofia Andreyevna."[73]

As for Alexandra, she reports that her father immediately questioned her sister about their mother: "Why don't you answer? Don't you understand how much I need to know?"[74] It is a fact that whenever an emissary came or was supposed to have come from Yasnaya Polyana, Tolstoy's first question was always about his wife's condition.

Tatyana, who as a good Tolstoyan hated lying, was relieved that her father's words to her had enabled her to reply, "without departing from the truth, that my mother was with my brothers and had a doctor and a nurse with her." But she admitted later that, faced with her reticence, Tolstoy had interrupted and cried out, "Go on, go on! What could be more important to me?"[75]

The conversation upset Tolstoy and soon afterward he brought up the same subject with Chertkov: "You understand . . . if she wants to see me, I shall be unable to refuse her, and yet meeting her would be fatal to me."[76]† Thereupon he dictated to Alexandra a telegram for his sons, who he thought were still at Yasnaya Polyana: "I beg you earnestly to keep

* The rest of the French proverb runs: *advienne que pourra*. The whole means: "Do what you must, no matter what follows."

† So it was rightly that the brothers, as Sergey reports, refused to go to their father: "for if they had gone, it would have been impossible to hold back my mother," and in particular, the fiction of her being at Yasnaya Polyana would have been shown up. (*Ma vie avec mon père*, p. 325)

mamma there. In my present weak state my heart would not withstand a meeting."[77]* It is obvious that Tolstoy still rejected the idea of seeing his wife again. Those around him, Chertkov and his friends, encouraged that attitude. Even Tatyana, whose "keenest desire was that he would ask [her] mother to come to him,"[78] thought it was clear that he feared a meeting. This feeling, together with filial respect, is doubtless the reason for the great opportunity lost of a reconciliation between Tolstoy and his wife. His elder daughter says that when she was on watch beside her father he murmured to her: " 'So many things are bearing down on Sonya' . . . The emotion I felt," she reports, "made me catch my breath. I tried to get him to repeat what he had said so that I could be sure I had heard correctly. I said: 'What was that, papa? So . . . what? Soda?' And he said again: 'Sonya, on Sonya, so many things bearing down on her.' I asked, 'Do you want to see her? Do you want to see Sofia?' But he had lost consciousness." She did not dare ask again. "I felt it would have been like blowing on a dying flame to say the words again."[79] Had Tolstoy heard his daughter's words? And what would he have said had she repeated her question?

The same evening Tolstoy weakened further and was unable to go to sleep. He had *The Voice of Moscow* read to him by Makovitsky, instructing him to leave out anything in the paper about his running away.† He interrupted oncc to ask thc doctor to "cut out an article on a triple suicide which interested him."[80]

"The night of the 3–4th was one of the hardest,"[81] Alexandra tells us. The care lavished on him and the presence of several doctors became unbearable to Tolstoy: they were going to have him die like the rich! He cried out with tears flowing, "And the peasants, the peasants—how do they die?"[82] He wanted to die like the mujik in *Three Deaths*.‡ Then he went into delirium and dictated numbers no one understood the meaning

* This telegram meant a great deal to Tolstoy. A few minutes later he made sure that Vavara Feokritova had sent it; it was delivered to Sofia in her compartment—only a few feet away from her husband. That evening Sofia wrote how Tolstoy "had himself sent for Chertkov by telegram," a fact that could only deepen the despair she felt upon reading the telegram addressed to her sons. She was all the more upset since she expected to be summoned at any moment by her husband. It was for that very reason that she had declined Tatyana's invitation to come and stay with her at Kotchevy.

† "One is not allowed to read him the least word about himself." (*Tolstoï est mort*, p. 18)

‡ A short story published in 1859, in which Tolstoy describes the deaths "of a lady, a peasant, and a tree." On May 1, 1858, he wrote at length to Alexandrine, who disliked the story, that she was "wrong to examine it from a Christian point of view"; what had interested him and what he wanted to show was that both the peasant and the tree died "in harmony with the whole world and not in discord as was the case of the spoiled rich lady." (*Tolstoy's Letters*, vol. I, p. 122)

of: 84, 85, 134, 135, 74, 75. They gave him a little champagne. He went on reciting numbers and uttered a few sentences, "some of which had meaning," says Makovitsky. What meaning? The doctor thought he understood: "Don't stop me. I don't want to."[83]

Alexandra had the idea of reading to her father passages from *A Cycle of Reading*, and that calmed him down. But he asked her where a glass door that was opposite his bed led to. "Into the corridor," replied Varvara Feokritova. Tolstoy persisted. "And what beyond that?" He wanted to know whether the farther door was properly shut. "It's strange—I saw very clearly two women's faces looking at me."[84] It is also most strange that Makovitsky noted on the same day, "At seven in the morning [Sofia] was wandering around the house. I was afraid she would call aloud to him. At eight she came to the door and had a long talk with [Dr.] Nikitin."[85] Sofia knew that Tolstoy was "growing worse: I wait in agony outside the little house where he is lying."[86] Pozner says that Sofia "did not sleep a wink all night. At dawn when the stationmaster's house began to wake, she tried to go to her husband. Four times she tried to get out of the railway coach, and four times she was prevented."[87]

It proved to be a fearful day. Tolstoy did not come out of delirium, no one understood what he said. From time to time some words could be made out. "To seek, to seek. . . ."[88] He had hallucinations. Varvara Feokritova entered the room and he took her for his daughter Masha, who had died in 1906. He tried to get up, to leave again; he was hard to restrain; he was dying.

Tolstoy knew nothing of the extraordinary wave of curiosity that his flight had occasioned, nor of the turmoil in the small station. Astopovo was invaded: the Governor of Riazan came in person; Meyer of Pathé News was already there; the Metropolitan Anthonyi sent telegrams; a building had to be requisitioned to accommodate all the journalists, the doctors, and the inquisitive. Beds and mattresses, lamps and provisions had to be ordered. Fresh doctors were summoned from Moscow. Since the day before, bulletins had been issued about Tolstoy's condition as for a head of state. The one for the evening of November 4 says: "The state of the affected lung is unchanged. The heart function gives rise to serious concern. He is conscious and lucid."[89]

The next morning, November 5, Tolstoy attempted to speak and rejected Makovitsky's attentions: "Leave me, my friend."[90] "He wanted complete rest and was cross at being disturbed,"[91] says Alexandra. Over a decade later, his son Lev (who was living in Paris in 1910) would write: "The only thing that could have prolonged his life would have been to let my mother in."[92]

In the afternoon Sofia "steps down with difficulty to the platform and goes toward the house. . . . The Countess enters the front garden . . . passes by the window where the sick man is lying, stops, raises her arm—and taps on the windowpane of the next room." She argues for five minutes with Alexandra. "The girl goes away and the door shuts behind her."[93] Tatyana, who felt "the ghastly horror of the situation,"[94] did not dare have her mother called. When he came to know about this, Lev Lvovich was indignant. "Had I been present I would have forced a passage with my fists to the one who loved her, and whom she loved more than anything in the world."[95] Chertkov and his clique remained adamant. The disciple and the wife had battled over Tolstoy's life and works and image, and now they were tearing apart his death.

Special trains crowded the line.* Visitors as varied as at Yasnaya Polyana poured in, including niece Yelizaveta, with two monks and Father Varsonofy, who talked with Sergey Lvovich, but whom the doctors refused to let see the patient. The priest, according to Pozner, tried to get into the house at night, but found the door locked.[96] Varsonofy, the Starets of the monastery of Optina-Pustyn, then tried another tactic, informing Alexandra in a letter that he wished to talk with her, but she answered with a definite refusal to receive him.† "We have unanimously decided" (a decision approved by the doctors) "not to propose anything to him or force his will."[97] The other members of the family were just as adamant with the clergy, which is to their credit, since most of them were fervently Orthodox.‡

Tolstoy had expressed his convictions very clearly the year before when Father Parfeny had come to Yasnaya Polyana.§ The next day Tolstoy wrote: "To return to the Church, to take communion before

* But the enginemen did not ply the whistles of their locomotives in or near Astopovo station.

† Varsonofy did not give up; he argued that Tolstoy, when in Optina, had told his sister Marya of his wish "to see us and talk with us for his soul's rest; he was deeply grieved that this wish could not be fulfilled." Catherina Lopatina, the sister of the philosopher Lev Lopatin, recounted a story from the monk who had opened the door to Tolstoy at Optina: "May I enter? I am Leo Tolstoy, maybe you won't want me to come in?" "My brother," answered the monk, and Tolstoy broke down and wept in his arms. (Y. Bounine, *La délivrance de Tolstoi*, Paris: Gallimard, 1939, p. 23.) In his letter, Father Varsonofy respectfully requested Alexandra "not to refuse to let the Count know of my presence in Astopovo." She never replied directly but only through intermediaries: "I could no longer think of such things," she writes. (*The Tragedy of Tolstoy*, p. 287)

‡ After Tolstoy's death, Father Parfeny, the Bishop of Tula, kept at Andrey Lvovich in order to know if Tolstoy while dying had not said any word that could make one believe he desired to return to the Church. Tolstoy's son replied that although he himself was a practicing Orthodox, or rather because he was, he could not lie and pretend that this had happened.

§ Sofia noted in her diary for January 20, 1909, "Everyone liked the bishop; he is an intelligent, simple, good man, Lev Nikolayevich thanked him with tears in his eyes . . . for his courage in coming to see us." (*The Diaries of Sofia Tolstoy*, p. 634) dying, is just as impossible for me as to utter obscene words or to look at obscene pictures before dying."*

According to Makovitsky† it was about two in the afternoon of November 6 that Tolstoy agreed to be moved into another room, so that they could air his own, and said in a clear voice, "This is the end! And it's nothing . . . *nitchevo*."[98] A little later, when Alexandra asked her father if his pillows needed adjusting: " 'No,' he said, stressing the word firmly and clearly. 'No, I only advise you to remember that there are many people in the world besides Lev Tolstoy and you are only looking after Lev.' "[99] These words, among the last Tolstoy ever spoke, echo the thought of the narrator of *Sevastopol in December* as he leaves the military hospital: "What do the death and the suffering of a contemptible worm like me matter in comparison with so many deaths and sufferings?"[100] What a strange, last link between the work and the life, the work and the death! Tolstoy, in the act of dying, puts his own agony at the center of mankind's, and it is by that act that he dies a Christian.

One can easily understand how Tolstoy's family and those close to him, wishing to respect the position he had taken, should have barred the clergy from him in his final moments; yet it remains a striking fact that in spite of his deeply religious disposition, his death was strangely secular. Between the concerns that Tolstoy had always expressed in his diary—and ever more openly at the end of his life—and the almost clinical attitude that reigned at Astopovo when he was at his last gasp, the contrast is flagrant. Those close to him seemed to regard his death as a purely physical phenomenon;‡ they were worried about his body and not his soul, whereas Tolstoy had considered death the great spiritual culmination of a lifetime. When in 1924 Romain Rolland came to read the reports written by the police at Astopovo, he was shocked to observe that "at the bedside of a great man, his *best friend*§ and the rest were busy playing out a petty scenario, while around him all one can see is a desert, a complete indifference on the part of *the people* to the death of their master, their spiritual guide."[101]

* In 1901 after his bout with pneumonia, Tolstoy had discussed this matter and expressed the wish to be asked as he was dying if he persisted in his beliefs; he would reply, he said, by moving his eyes if he was unable to speak. (See p. 286)

† Makovitsky's account in *Novy Mir* is particularly valuable, for it establishes from his daily notes a chronology that is sometimes faulty in Alexandra's and Tatyana's memories.

‡ Only Alexandra seems to have worried about it. When there was no more hope she felt that "the treatment—all those hypodermics, enemas, the oxygen—were useless and only disturbed the peace and that inner labour which entirely absorbed him in his preparations for death." (*The Tragedy of Tolstoy*, p. 284)

§ That is, Chertkov.

Tolstoy's condition was deteriorating. The pulse weakened, the breathing became difficult. The doctors multiplied their efforts. Tolstoy refused oxygen: "It's quite useless."[102] He was entirely conscious, and said with a kind of gentle humor to poor Nikitin, who was preparing a salt-water enema: "God will take care of everything."[103]

Sergey Lvovich records in his memoirs that a little later Tolstoy spoke again: "I cannot go to sleep. I am always composing. I write and it all links itself together like music." He adds a word about the "very disagreeable, indeed frightening moment when my father rose up in bed and said in a resounding, determined voice: 'Getting out! Must get the hell out!' "[104]

Tolstoy, extremely ill, sends for his son, who kneels by the bed. He utters with an effort what he thinks are probably his last words: "Seryozha . . . Truth—I love very much . . . How they . . ."[105] These unfinished sentences have been interpreted in diverse ways. According to Tatyana, Tolstoy said: "Sergei! I love Truth . . . very much . . . I love Truth."[106] Makovitsky thinks it: "Sergey . . . the truth I greatly love . . . all of them." As for Sergey himself, to whom the words were addressed, he admits: "He murmured a sentence that I could not make out,"[107] and he took it to be what Makovitsky thought he heard.

Translation increases the ambiguity of the testimonies, for Tolstoy used the word *istina*, which means factual, absolute, authentic truth, and not *pravda*, which is linked to the idea of justice. What is certain is that as he was dying Tolstoy uttered the word *truth*, the truth for love of which he had lived and written. Those words have long been thought to be the last Tolstoy spoke. According to Makovitsky's recently published account, "it is not so." We are to believe that Tolstoy went on to say, "one must live in God." He was suffocating and moaning; he was given a last injection of morphine. He is then supposed to have mumbled a few sentences from *Resurrection*, among which Makovitsky thought he heard: "I am going somewhere where no one will stop me," or "find me." But the doctor did not manage to hear all the words clearly. He only understood something like "must get away, escape somewhere."

"Sonya did not leave the coach for the whole day";[108] during the night, a little before four o'clock, she became aware of commotion and tried to get to the house, but she was repulsed. Chertkov and Alexandra* were

* Though Alexandra's attitude was heartless, it was perfectly logical. Since her father "himself, of his own free will, had severed relations with mother and left her, no one had the right to violate his will." She decided not to let Sofia in to see Tolstoy "unless father himself expressed his wish for it, even if the doctors and the family should find it possible to admit her." (*The Tragedy of Tolstoy*, p. 275.) Alexandra was a resolute young woman and she stuck to her decision, obviously encouraged by Chertkov.

cruelly determined to keep Sofia away from her husband while he lay dying.* The atrocious Calvary that Sofia was subjected to at Astopovo redeems all the sins that she may have committed against her husband.[109]

At five in the morning on November 7, Ilya dictated a health bulletin for the journalists: "Severe worsening of the heart function."[110] Sofia was finally allowed to see her husband: she can no longer kill him, he is already dead or nearly. Alexandra was in the room. "My mother was led in. He was already unconscious† . . . mother started to say something, lamenting. Someone asked her to keep quiet."[111]

Sitting at the bedside of the man she had loved since she was seventeen, Sofia murmured tender words. She asked him "to forgive her for all she had done wrong" (says Tatyana). "A few deep sighs were all the answer she got."[112] In her autobiography‡ Sofia recalled this scene. "The doctors let me see my husband when he was scarcely breathing and his eyes were shut. Very softly and gently I spoke into his ear hoping that he heard: 'I have been all the while here at Astopovo and I will love you to the end.' I don't remember what else I said to him. Two deep sighs were the answer to my words. And then he became very calm."[113]

What neither of the daughters says is told by Makovitsky: "She remained eight minutes, then they took her away."[114] The friends and the doctors thought Tolstoy might recover consciousness. Sergey Lvovich explains: "We feared he might come to and recognize her; she withdrew."[115]

After Sofia had left the room, Tolstoy answered again when Makovitsky called him loudly by name; then he turned away when a lighted candle was moved over his face. His faithful doctor and companion then offered him a glass of wine and he took a sip.

A little later his heart stopped.§

* The report of Militia General Lvov, which appeared in no. 4 of *Archives rouges*, mentions that Andrey Lvovich said in the course of a conversation with Captain Savitsky: "My father's isolation from his family and in particular his wife was the result of the pressure exercised by Chertkov on the doctors and on my sister Alexandra." Text quoted by Gorky, who always seeks to defend Sofia. (*Reminiscences of Tolstoy, Chekhov and Andreev*, p. 126)

† In her diary Sofia noted next day: "I was allowed in only as he drew his last breath. They would not even let me say farewell to my husband. Cruel people." (*The Diaries of Sofia Tolstoy*, p. 678)

‡ Published in Moscow in 1921 by Natchiala Press as *My Life*.

§ After Tolstoy's death, by his express wish and also because he was excommunicated, there was no religious service, but "at some point, nobody knew how, the rumor spread that shortly, during morning Mass, the priest would say the office of the dead for Tolstoy's soul." (*Tolstoï est mort*, p. 201.) The church was a hundred yards from the station; Sofia went in on her son Sergey's arm, and fainted.

THIRTY

The Outcome

TOLSTOY'S earliest memories were associated with the "contradictions" of his sensations, which he experienced as a torment since the very beginning of his conscious life. This archaic experience of anguish was rooted in his deepest self by the death of his mother, a wound never to be healed.

At the age of seventy-eight he wrote:

> All day a feeling of gloomy dread. Toward evening this state of wretchedness was transmuted into a feeling of deep tenderness, into a desire to be caressed, comforted. Like a child, I long to press myself against some loving, sympathizing being, to shed tears of love and affection, and to feel myself being consoled. But where is the being with whom I can find such a refuge? . . . Should I become a child again and hide my head against my mother as I picture her? Yes, you, mamma, you whose name I never spoke, because I was still too young to talk. . . . That is what my weary soul cries out for. You, mamma, you comfort me, console me. . . . All this is madness. . . . And yet it is true.[1]*

In spite of the indelible stamp that this tragic event left upon him, Tolstoy never ceased to marvel at his childhood, which he referred to as "a period of poetic and joyous innocence."[2]

* He set down these words not in his diary, which was read and copied day by day by zealous disciples, but on a mere scrap of paper for himself alone.

* * *

As for the early part of his adult life, Tolstoy characterized it as dreadful; he considered it his period of "gross depravity, ambition, vanity, and above all debauchery." The crisis of identity that every individual goes through in adolescence and youth took with Tolstoy not only an acute but also a permanent form, since it was never definitively resolved until the very end of his long life.*

In the Caucasus Tolstoy had had the feeling of being "a deer or a pheasant." It was his pantheist phase; at the same time he suffered from that fundamental and morbid loneliness that plagues adults who have lost their parents as children. He was to see his superego not only set itself up as judge and critic of his ego, but perhaps play in addition the roles of father and mother internalized. To the extent that each of us inherits from the superego of our parents cultural habits, family traditions, religious ideals, one may wonder whether for an orphan like Tolstoy this legacy was not all the harder to take on since the survivors had somehow increased the burden by presenting the child with an idealized, mythical image of his parents, an image that everyday reality would never tarnish. One may wonder whether as a young man he did not on this account find himself in the grip of a sort of super-superego.

Tolstoy was desperately alone; he said so over and over again; he wanted, and even felt compelled, in the neurotic desert that was his dwelling place, to find a personal solution to every problem and to solve it on his own.

He found himself caught in a total narcissism that invaded his sexual life, his intellectual life, and his spiritual life. Much later, after his crisis of the eighties, he said: "I'm every sort of onanist."[3] So far did this narcissism go that it was in himself he sought to discover God.

Tolstoy can tolerate only self-imposed disciplines; he rebels against the compromises and shams of society and the Church, what he was to call "falsifications." His passion for truth, which dates from this period, was the hope of rediscovering things in the original purity that they seemed to him to possess in his childhood. He rejected all teachings, retaining only those of his own making, and tried to give a kind of divine right to reason, so as to establish his own reason. From that early time on, his reforming

* In this he is the *homo religiosus* of whom Erikson speaks in connection with the young Luther. Writer and reformer both concentrated "precociously on the problem that others glimpse only after a lifetime: how to live and escape corruption, and how to find in death a way of giving meaning to life." (Erik H. Erikson, *Young Man Luther*, New York: W. W. Norton, 1958, Epiloque, part 3)

fervor was not limited to religion; he wanted to purify all human enterprises. At Sevastopol he had notions of reorganizing not only the army but the methods of agriculture, the institution of the nobility—and, of course, education.

Being incapable of putting order in his inner chaos, Tolstoy settled down amid his contradictions: he rejected the supernatural but recognized the presence of God in every man; he rejected mysteries but accepted the greatest of all, that of faith. He then tried to escape these dilemmas by drawing reassurance from two devices: he coupled the spiritual narcissism of moral perfection with the intellectual narcissism of tireless reasoning. The will to moral perfection, which is after all one of the fundamental demands of Orthodoxy, is centered on the ego, it is the desire to be perfect, to "do as one ought." As early as his university years, Tolstoy had divided people into those who were *comme il faut* (i.e., who did what "ought" to be done) and those who were not, a kind of narrow conformism that he did not get beyond until very late in life, when he began to seek perfection not to please himself but to please God. His narcissistic search was then transformed into a quest for the divine.

As for his rationalist obsession, it helped him to strengthen the defensive means of his ego, as well as to hide from himself his insoluble conflicts. An answer that does not come directly from him and has not passed under the steamroller of his reason is unacceptable to him; he denies whatever he does not understand and comes close to the obsession of the rationalist. Only the act of writing supplies him with a precarious identity and a temporary unity for his ego.

The keynote of Tolstoy's childhood and youth was solitude and self-love. He then moved on into a phase of sharing and mutual love—the time that stretches from his marriage in 1862 to the writing of *A Confession*, a period that, "from the worldly point of view, one might call moral."[4]

During that time he knew married happiness and family joys, a state of being that frightened him and that seemed to distract him from the problems of his ego rather than help him to resolve them. He even seemed to have forgotten what they were, for in June 1863 he wondered what had happened to his identity since marrying the woman he loved. ("Where is my self, the self I loved and knew? . . . I am petty and worthless. And what is worse . . . I am so since I married my wife whom I love.")

Tolstoy knew that happiness did not consist simply in a wife and children. He knew it already when as a boy he dreamed of love by the lake at Yasnaya Polyana. ("Something told me that SHE was far from being the sum of happiness . . .") Yet the inner peace that came with marriage and the equipoise he found in literary creation—not "a verbal cure" but a "scriptural cure"—seem for a time to have made him into an integrated man. It was then he used his memories of childhood and youth for *War and Peace*, and those of his more recent past for *Anna Karenina*. In this way he succeeded in reorganizing and remodeling the universe through which he had long drifted, making it into a new world under his control.

But one must not confuse writing with healing; they are not the same, only analogous. The work created has the power of transference and a therapeutic effect, but it brings no cure—or if it does, it is one without end.

* * *

Next came the crisis, the slow returning tide of unanswered questions that passion and art can no longer stem. There has been no real move into maturity, but on the contrary a return, a regression toward adolescence and youth. Tolstoy at fifty was still facing the problems he had already faced when he was twenty. The human condition, and his own in particular, still roused him to the same fury, a noble but in the end a sterile rebellion.

In 1880 came the fall into the abyss described in *A Confession*, then the illumination that suddenly snatched him out of the darkness of anguish. But it never became more than a foreshadowing. Tolstoy thought his "second birth" had taken place at that moment, but he was mistaken: it took him the rest of his life to bring about, painfully, the birth of his Self.

The crisis had destroyed everything except the fragile cover that sheltered him from his truth. Other people's religion did not suit him any more than their doctrines, so in the grip of his long-standing desire dating back to the Caucasus, he decided to found his own. Tolstoy meant to choose the best in each of the creeds—he looked everywhere and found what he wanted nowhere. He then embarked on a kind of rationalist gnosticism, rejecting revelation and tradition; in so doing he stayed within Christian ideology, but not within the faith. The psychological defense mechanisms that prevented Tolstoy from getting outside himself no doubt also blocked his spiritual development. His conversion was made up of negatives—in succession he repudiated, first, all sexuality in *The Kreutzer Sonata*, then art in all its forms in *What Is Art?*

* * *

The years 1890 to 1900 in Tolstoy's life belong under the rubric of love of humanity—what he later bitterly called the "abstract love of mankind." He had by then realized that he has powerless to bring about the Kingdom of God on earth; this love of others and his own religious dedication he lived in a mood of protest and rebellion also.

Tolstoy practiced the true Christian's renunciation but only by doing himself violence. For a long time he was unaware of the need for kindness, peace, and forgiveness in response to conflicts. He does follow the Gospel precepts, but particularly in what they contain that is negative and repressive; he condemns himself even more than he denies himself.* That is still the superego sitting as judge of the ego. He hates himself even more than he hates his life.† He puts himself outside his own family‡ to belabor it, and renounces his worldly goods§ while continuing to enjoy them.

The paradoxical promise of the Gospel, "he that loseth his life shall find it," was to be only half fulfilled in Tolstoy. He lost but did not find. He wanted to change not only his life but everyone else's. Befogged as he was by his battle with himself, he failed to understand that conversion is an individual experience, and that love of God, like human love, is not communicable to others. Unable to achieve unity within his own self, he tried to bring about that of the world. Unable to bear his own guilt, he projected it on all mankind and accused the universe: "governors and governed," masters and slaves together. He is "the man sent," he alone can save humanity. Having relapsed into the narcissistic, infantile dream of omnipotence, Tolstoy wished himself a messenger of love and becomes in fact a messenger of vengeance.

He had tried to escape from himself in literature; now he would run away from himself into action—famine relief, aid to the Dukhobors, defense of minorities and the persecuted. His tireless preaching marked the zenith of his passion for education; his "Christian teaching," a real handbook of spiritual guidance, was merely an enhanced form of his old "rules" for moral perfection.

The contradiction of contradictions was his effort to impose on mankind, almost by force, the Sermon on the Mount. Tolstoy willed himself to be on the side of the poor, the starving, those who mourn,

* Whosoever will come after me, let him deny himself. (Mark 8:34)

† He that hateth his life in this world shall keep it unto life eternal. (John 12:25)

‡ If any man come to me and hate not his father and mother and wife and children, and brethren and sisters, yea and his own life also, he cannot be my disciple. (Luke 14:26)

§ Whosoever he be of you that forsaketh not all that he hath, he cannot be my disciple. (Luke 14:33) those who hunger and thirst after righteousness, the peacemakers and the reviled, but his words are essentially contentious and violent.

Once excommunicated, he hurls his own anathema at the Church, which according to him has garbled the message of Christ, obscured his gospel of love, and distorted its meaning, thus committing the greatest sacrilege. It has become a new paganism, a parody of the Church of Christ. What the Church has been unable to accomplish, men can still succeed in doing, if they will only follow Tolstoy; he thereby substitutes his own aim for that of the Church. Similarly, he remained outside the Revolution, for he did not want it to be a mere change from one despotism to another, but rather "the application of divine law to things political."

He was convinced that without "works" faith is dead; it was only quite late in his life that he began to glimpse that works are nothing without love. Although he tried to practice a radical evangelical faith in his own conduct, he remained to the end much closer to the letter of the law than to the spirit; he never succeeded in putting his life in harmony with his doctrine; he was one of those who "say and act not."

This contradiction, which he found unbearable, was just as difficult for many of the Tolstoyans to accept. And even today many remain skeptical of Tolstoy's teaching, feeling that he "sounds the trumpet rather too much when he gives alms."

* * *

At the age of seventy-seven, Tolstoy called the most recent period of his life, begun (he thought) with his second birth in the 1880s, his "awakening to truth."[5] How would he have defined his final years? They stretch from 1905 to his death and bring him to the goal of his laborious march, where he recovers his original integrity and finds at last its true origin: "Somebody else has appeared, whom I call 'I.' "

The ego then ceases to obey the superego under the pressure of guilt and yields to love. Tolstoy leaves behind the "ascetic adventure" and enters that "ascesis" whose purpose is no longer the perfection and salvation he hoped for, but solely the love of God. His last mutation was to pass from *ego* to *I*, which leads him to discover his real identity, for the *I* that creates the new man consigns the *ego* to oblivion. Narcissus is delivered; by seeing the source of all things in God, he has found the center around which all things move in due order. His desperate "Who am I?" is heard no more.

In the last days of his life, Tolstoy stopped wondering where he came from and where he was going: he knew. Now that he no longer feared death, Tolstoy was no longer the slave of his "mortal self and *can* put [himself] at the service of the immortal, of God, from whom you came and to whom you go." It was at that point, and only at that point, that his second birth took place, since there could be no real conversion before the acceptance of oneself, and now Tolstoy accepted himself as part of God's plan.* It meant that he accepted himself as a writer as well: art was no longer a shameful habit but became a reason for existence.

Instead of the absolute disapproval of himself which formed the tragic inner core of his life, Tolstoy came to know the real love of oneself which merges with the divine love. The wound of Narcissus healed; the love of a woman and the love of humanity had not released him from the prison of his ego;† only the love of God was able to put an end to his solitude.

* * *

Since the end of the 1880s, writing had become to Tolstoy a pleasure that he forbade himself—like every other pleasure, more even than the others.‡ He had been "a bit ashamed" in 1889 of working for ten days on a comedy, *The Fruits of Enlightenment*, and in 1902 he confessed to Gorky that he had "suffered severely from temptation of the sin of writing," and that if he had expressed the wish to be put in jail, it was to lend his preaching the authority of martyrdom; but, as he admitted, it was with the secret hope of being able to write in peace.

Tolstoy's great refusal included art in general and his own in particular. For a writer, not writing is a self-inflicted wound. As Father Sergey (in the story of the same name) deliberately cuts off his finger, Tolstoy symbolically cut off the hand that held his pen. Dimitry Merezhkovsky spoke of "the incredible suicide of a genius," and Romain Rolland of "the sole example of a great artist in full creative power, and tormented by it, who resists it and sacrifices it to his God."

Tolstoy thus came to a true renunciation, not just a partial detachment, made up of snatching himself away from temptations and self-imposed

* In January 1901 he had written: "Life consists in acquiring more and more truth about what one is meant for and living more and more in accordance with that truth." (*Journaux et carnets*, p. 829)

† In 1902 he had written, "The only salvation is to carry one's ego out of oneself." (*Journaux et carnets*, vol. II, p. 887)

‡ Before leaving for the Crimea Tolstoy had finished "Notes for Soldiers" and "Notes for Officers." He still wanted to write "about religion and the lack of it, and a letter to Nicholas [II]." Then, he added, "I can relax over something literary." (*Tolstoy's Diaries*, vol. II, p. 496)

prohibitions. These went with guilt, which he had suffered until then; now it was the detachment of detachments, the acceptance of what is.

In truth, it was impossible for Tolstoy not to write. Even at the most militant times of his life, he always had a work of literature in hand. Like a painter, he would let "the background dry"; indeed, he compared his habit of dropping a work to take it up later with the various stages of making *khefir*.* Yet, he was no less sincere when he said: "This is it: I'm going to learn to live without writing; I can do it."[6] But he could not. In moments of "weakness" he yielded "to the uncontrollable itch of an incorrigible artist."[7]

The irresistible creative urge that he was trying to repress was probably, of all his drives, the hardest to hold back; the urge was still as potent, though different from what it had been in youth; then it was the gushing spring of the life force, now it was "a spiritual act" which dominated all others. The urge to write became more imperious than ever.

He had long believed that he would lose his soul if he wrote. Now, on the contrary, the act of writing had become the carrying out of the divine will. But this mission, the task God had chosen for him on earth, could not be fulfilled at Yasnaya Polyana. That is why he left.

His urge to write had grown more imperious than ever. A frantic patience, an inner turmoil, is very likely the underlying cause of Tolstoy's departure. This interpretation of Tolstoy's flight was not the basis of the present study, but its result. Of course, his misunderstandings with his wife played a large part in his decision. But it was much more because his wife prevented him from working, and thus obeying what was to him the divine plan, than because he no longer loved her, or could no longer bear her, that Tolstoy fled from Yasnaya Polyana. In this sense, and in this sense only, can it be said that "he left because of her."

In endeavoring to reconstruct the invisible "itinerary" that brought Tolstoy from his birth to his death, one comes upon clues—and sometimes symptoms—that in their convergence into a cluster of suggestive facts (not to say proofs) lead one to perceive what futurologists call a "directional scenario," one in which the data of the present make up a model already found in the past and thus permit the construction of a model for the future.

When Tolstoy left Yasnaya Polyana, one finds the same conjunction of elements as had preceded the production of every one of his most important works; those elements may be broadly stated as follows:

* Fermented mare's milk.

(a) an irresistible *desire to write*, having nothing to do with any humanitarian, social, or religious consideration; a kind of lust for creation takes hold of Tolstoy.*

(b) a deep preoccupation with a *problem of general concern*, though linked with personal problems, engrosses him completely—for example, that of property *and* his attempt to resolve it; or that of marriage *and* his attitude to his own.

(c) a *craving for reading*, the books read being more or less directly related to the theoretical question of the moment. He undertakes also a considerable amount of research for *documentation*, including *investigations on the spot*—what he calls "turning up the soil."

(d) lastly, a *chance encounter with an incident or a true story*. Stumbling on reality suddenly makes the three other elements fuse into a single scheme for the work, often radically different from his original conception.

This combination of foreshadowings may be seen every time Tolstoy enters a period of literary creation. When he began *War and Peace*, he declared that he had not "for a long time felt such a desire to write, such a strong, confident, definite desire." During the seven years that the composition of the novel took, Tolstoy read Stendhal, and a great deal of history.† He read deeply in the memoirs and letters of the time, questioned witnesses of the events he was recording, and went to Borodino. In this instance it was not just *one* incident that acted as catalyst, but a multitude of small facts and anecdotes borrowed from history or family tradition.

It was in the genesis of *Anna Karenina* that the same process appeared most clearly. Tolstoy was in a lethargic state and languid about writing. He had delved into Shakespeare, Molière, Goethe, Pushkin, and been meditating for three years about a Russian *Iliad*. He assembled for it a huge documentation on Peter the Great and his times. Then came the shock of the chance event: a certain Anna Stepanovna had killed herself from despair in love.‡ He rushed to see her body, and the idea that had

* Tolstoy himself speaks of an "overwhelming tension of the mind that demands expression." (*Journaux et carnets*, vol. II, p. 827)

† Tolstoy wrote to Fet in December 1866 that his conception of history complicated his work in an extraordinary way. (*Tolstoy's Letters*, vol. I, p. 208.) History for Tolstoy was no mere background for the characters and their drama. Isaiah Berlin gives a masterly account of what it was: "Tolstoy's concern with history springs from something more personal, a bitter inner conflict between his actual experience and his beliefs, between his vision of life, and his theory of what it, and he himself, ought to be, if the vision was to be bearable at all." (I. Berlin, *Russian Thinkers*, London: Hogarth Press, 1978)

‡ The young woman's suicide had spurred him into writing all the more strongly that Tolstoy himself had just been tempted to kill himself.

crossed his mind three years earlier, of taking a guilty but pitiable society woman as heroine, recurred to him and "almost in spite of himself, thanks to the divine Pushkin," he wrote the opening of *Anna Karenina*.

Each of his great works was born under conditions nearly the same. It was the death of a judge amid general indifference that incited Tolstoy to make *The Death of Ivan Ilych* an allegory of his own suffering at his family's lack of understanding about the inner sickness that afflicted him.

The Power of Darkness was inspired by the murder of a certain Loloskov, about whom his friend Davydov, state prosecutor at Tula, had told him. He went to see the accused in prison.

In just the same way for *The Kreutzer Sonata*, Tolstoy pinned his new ideas on marriage to a story Andreyev-Bulak told him, the actor having got it from the confidences of an anonymous railway traveler.

The starting point of *Resurrection* is the predicament of a juror who recognizes in the accused a woman he once seduced, and its secret source is Tolstoy's own affair with his aunt's maidservant. In the novel he also used the enormous research on prisons and courts he had done twenty years earlier when he had undertaken to write on the Decembrists.

When he began *Hadji Murad* in 1896, he drew inspiration from an anecdote he had mentioned as early as 1856 in a letter from the Caucasus to his brother Sergey.

* * *

The last year of Tolstoy's life, as we know it from his diaries and letters, shows the several forces that one finds at work in any of his creative periods. The evidence for this assertion appears from even the briefest review of facts:

The *desire to write* was not only strong but at last accepted. For two years Tolstoy had reconciled himself to the idea of doing literary work, as he noted in his journal for December 6, 1909: "I want to begin an artistic book. But I do not begin because it is not yet ripe. I write only when I cannot but write, as one marries when one cannot do otherwise."[8] What Tolstoy had in mind was not another polemic or religious work, but a real work of art. The purpose would not leave him alone; it tormented him. He resisted the "temptation" for a long time, rather out of fear of failure, it seems, than from virtue: "I *must* not write; I believe I have done all I can on that score. But I long to, terribly."* That note occurs in the journal for

* The expression "I long to, terribly" reappears several times in his diary and letters during the last months of his life.

May 1910. Some days later, when out walking, he suddenly "gets the clear idea of the way this work should be built up: 'none are guilty in this world'—and other things as well."[9]

It will be remembered that six months later, while walking to calm himself down after a scene with Sofia, Tolstoy had noticed "healthy, bare-footed girls" at work near the house, and thought at once of "writing two [contrasting] scenes,"[10] one of paradise, which would show the joy and health of the peasants, and the other of hell, depicting the sadness and quarrels of the rich.

In August 1910, when he got back from Kotchevy to find Sofia on the verge of madness, Tolstoy complained to Chertkov of no longer being able to do more than a little letter-writing. He had assured Chertkov that it was not the wish that was lacking: he "wants to write, and write something artistic"; but he wondered anxiously whether he would still be capable of it, "or whether a real egg will emerge. . . . If it is addled, it can't be helped."[11] In October Tolstoy reports his anxiety about his wife's behavior and the shackles it puts on his working. Hence his request to Novikov, ten days before he left Yasnaya Polyana, to find him a cottage, "a very small one, as long as it is warm and by itself." Tolstoy wanted to retire from the world, "make a desert"—but such lodgings would also make an excellent workroom. The wish to find a quiet, remote place where he could think and write was confirmed by the step he took in person on the afternoon of October 30 "to rent a hut in at Shamardino." Perhaps also the very choice of Optina-Pustyn as his first refuge answered the same purpose, for he remembered of course that in 1905 he had written there, in perfect peace, a large part of *Hadji Murad*.

Given this obsession during the last months of his life, one must not be surprised that on the first evening of his wild escapade, after talking with Alexandra and finishing an article on the death penalty, Tolstoy forced himself in spite of his fatigue, "to write down the subjects of [his] dreams and stories that are on the tip of [his] pen" nor that a few hours before his death he murmured in his delirium: "I keep on writing and everything comes together like music."

Intensive reading: at the end of 1910 Tolstoy was absorbed in reading two works, *Une Vie** and *The Brothers Karamazov*. In October he had

* He wrote in his 1894 introduction to the Russian translation of Maupassant: "*Une Vie* is excellent, not only incomparably the best of his novels, but perhaps the best French novel since Hugo's *Les Misérables*." It interested him particularly because, according to him, until then Maupassant had presented coarse animal sensuality as if it were the central feature of life, dominant over all else. "And in this book (for the first time) the author's whole sympathy is on the side of what is good." (*Ecrits sur l'art*, Paris: Gallimard, 1975, p. 79)

noted that "reading Maupassant" had made him long "to depict in literary form all the vulgarity of the life of the wealthy and bureaucratic classes and of the peasant workers, and to put in the midst of both groups at least one person who is spiritually alive." Then he added: "How it attracts me! What a great work it could be!"[12]

Tolstoy seemed to think his subject was in no way incompatible—quite the contrary—with the idea of the "two scenes" that he had conceived while out walking. He was also reading one of the masterpieces by the writer he doubtless thought of as his only rival, Dostoyevsky, who in spite of the reservations Tolstoy had about his artistry, aroused the old man's enthusiasm. He criticized Dostoyevsky's slipshod manner and complained of his "artificiality and fabrication."[13] Yet after finishing volume one on October 19, he noted: "There's much that's good in it, but it's so disorganised."[14]

One is reminded that volume two of *The Brothers Karamazov* was the book Tolstoy had left open on his desk the night he left Yasnaya Polyana.* When he got to Shamardino, he asked Alexandra to send it to him, together with Montaigne and Maupassant.

At the time of his flight, Tolstoy was also engaged in *pondering a general problem* and not thinking only of a literary project, since madness and suicide were once again at the center of his preoccupations. That he reverted to these two problems, which had always interested him,† was due to Sofia's really pathological condition: he was deeply worried by her repeated attempts to commit suicide; they revived the memory of his own feelings at the time he wrote *Anna Karenina*.

During the summer he had read Dr. Korsakov's *Psychiatry*, and—as was his habit—not content with research into theory, but wanting documentary evidence, he had gone several times to the asylum at Mechtcherskoye, where he had a number of conversations with the insane. He had even begun an article in which he hoped to prove that it is "the madness of our time that leads to suicide."

Finally, *the incident*, which is the cornerstone of every one of his works, came into his ken to complete the creative pattern: on the evening of November 3, 1910, less than four days before his death, Tolstoy asked

* That it was open at the chapter "Of hell, and of eternal fire—mystical considerations," at the page where Dostoyevsky defined hell as "the pain of being no longer able to love," loses any ominous or symbolic meaning one might read into it by being simply, prosaically, the place where Tolstoy stopped reading.

† Twenty years earlier he had written, "Suicide is waking up on purpose from a nightmare." (*Journaux et carnets*, vol. II, p. 130)

Makovitsky, who was reading aloud to him from *The Voice of Moscow*, to cut out for him an article on a triple suicide that he found interesting.

This last request was, for me, the revealing detail. It shows that Tolstoy, the indefatigable seeker after truth, was once again on the trail of a true story: once again, he wanted to lift from the web of life a living cell, out of which he could create new beings and a new world, as he had done in every one of his novels.

At any rate, this may well be the explanation of that enigmatic flight, at the beginning of a Russian winter, in the dawn of a freezing night, of a frail old man of eighty-two. He leaves his house secretly with thirty-nine rubles in his pocket, has himself led by torchlight to the local railway station, and sets out for an inaccessible destination, "the place where he wanted to be alone."*

In the end, then, Tolstoy accepted being what he was—neither a saint nor a reformer, but a writer who wanted to decipher the meaning of life and bequeath that meaning to mankind: he went away to write.

* From Tolstoy's last letter, dictated to Chertkov in English for Aylmer Maude, Tolstoy's English translator, at Astopovo on November 3, 1910.

Notes

I: THE DIFFICULTY OF BEING LEO TOLSTOY

1. Childhood

1. *Childhood, Boyhood and Youth* (Cent. Ed., vol. 3), p. 115.
2. *Childhood, Boyhood and Youth* (Cent. Ed., vol. 3), p. 107.
3. *Recollections and Essays* (Cent. Ed., vol. 21), p. 12.
4. *Childhood, Boyhood and Youth* (Cent. Ed., vol. 3), p. 14.
5. *Leo Tolstoy, His Life and Work*, p. 36.
6. *Childhood, Boyhood and Youth* (Cent. Ed., vol. 3), p. 58.
7. *Recollections and Essays* (Cent. Ed., vol. 21), p. 13.
8. *Souvenirs et récits*, p. 408.
9. *Tolstoy's Letters*, January 6, 1852, p. 20.
10. *Recollections and Essays* (Cent. Ed., vol. 21), p. 9.
11. *Leo Tolstoy, His Life and Work*, p. 17.
12. *Childhood, Boyhood and Youth* (Cent. Ed., vol. 3), p. 27.
13. *Leo Tolstoy, His Life and Work*.
14. *Childhood, Boyhood and Youth* (Cent. Ed., vol. 3), p. 229.
15. *Leo Tolstoy, His Life and Work*, p. 53.
16. *Leo Tolstoy, His Life and Work*, p. 35.
17. *Leo Tolstoy, His Life and Work*, p. 36.
18. *Leo Tolstoy, His Life and Work*, p. 36.
19. *Leo Tolstoy, His Life and Work*, p. 36.

2. *Boyhood*

1. *Childhood, Boyhood and Youth* (Cent. Ed., vol. 3), p. 144.
2. *Childhood, Boyhood and Youth* (Cent. Ed., vol. 3), p.150.
3. *Childhood, Boyhood and Youth* (Cent. Ed., vol. 3), pp. 194–195.
4. *Childhood, Boyhood and Youth* (Cent. Ed., vol. 3), p. 151.
5. *Childhood, Boyhood and Youth* (Cent. Ed., vol. 3), pp. 307–309.
6. *Childhood, Boyhood and Youth* (Cent. Ed., vol. 3), pp. 372–375.
7. *Childhood, Boyhood and Youth* (Cent. Ed., vol. 3), pp. 339–340.
8. *Childhood, Boyhood and Youth* (Cent. Ed., vol. 3), pp. 342–348.
9. *Childhood, Boyhood and Youth* (Cent. Ed., vol. 3), p. 342.
10. *Childhood, Boyhood and Youth* (Cent. Ed., vol. 3), p. 398.
11. *Childhood, Boyhood and Youth* (Cent. Ed., vol. 3), pp. 402–403.
12. *Resurrection*, pp. 140–141.
13. *Childhood, Boyhood and Youth* (Cent. Ed., vol. 3), p. 345.
14. *Childhood, Boyhood and Youth* (Cent. Ed., vol. 3), p. 348.
15. *Leo Tolstoy, His Life and Work*, p. 37.
16. *Childhood, Boyhood and Youth* (Cent. Ed., vol. 3), p. 326.
17. *Journaux et carnets*, vol. I, February 3, 1847, p. 40.

3. *Youth*

1. *Reminiscences of Tolstoy, Chekhov and Andreev*, p. 24.
2. *Tolstoy's Diaries*, April 17, 1847, vol. I, p. 11.
3. *Tolstoy's Letters*, February 13, 1849, vol. I, p. 6.
4. *Tolstoy's Letters*, May 1, 1848, vol. I, p. 7.
5. *Childhood, Boyhood and Youth* (Cent. Ed., vol. 3), p. 231.
6. *Tolstoï par Tolstoï*, March 8, 1851, p. 66.
7. *Tolstoy's Letters*, April 1858, vol. I, p. 120.

4. *The Caucasus and Sevastopol*

1. *Tolstoy's Letters*, May 30, 1852, vol. I, p. 25.
2. *Tolstoy's Diaries*, May 30, 1851, vol. I, p. 26.
3. *The Cossacks*, p. 276.
4. *The Cossacks*, p. 299.
5. *The Cossacks*, p. 181.
6. Saint Ignatius of Loyola, *The Spiritual Exercises*.
7. *Tolstoy's Diaries*, June 12, 1851, vol. I, p. 31.
8. *Tolstoy's Diaries*, August 10, 1851, vol. I, p. 35.
9. *The Cossacks*, p. 392.
10. *The Cossacks*, p. 215.
11. *Tolstoy's Diaries*, October 26, 1853, vol. I, p. 74.
12. *Tolstoy's Diaries*, April 3, 1851, vol. I, p. 27.
13. *Tolstoy's Diaries*, March 20, 1852, vol. I, p. 43.
14. *Tolstoy's Diaries*, March 20, 1852, vol. I, pp. 43–44.
15. *Tolstoy's Diaries*, March 20, 1852, vol. I, pp. 43–44.

16. *Tolstoy's Diaries*, March 20, 1852, vol. I, pp. 43–44.
17. *Tolstoy's Letters*, October 20, 1852, vol. I, p. 32.
18. *Tolstoy's Letters*, May 30, 1852, vol. I, p. 26.
19. *Tolstoy's Diaries*, August 28, 1852, vol. I, p. 60.
20. *Tolstoy's Diaries*, February 6, 1854, vol. I, p. 86.
21. *Tolstoy's Diaries*, October 26, 1853, vol. I, p. 74.
22. *Tolstoy's Diaries*, November 1, 1853, vol. I, p. 72.
23. *Tolstoy's Diaries*, November 1, 1853, vol. I, p. 76.
24. *Tolstoy's Diaries*, January 27, 1854, vol. I, p. 85.
25. *The Cossacks*, p. 170.
26. *Tolstoy's Diaries*, January 22–27, 1854, vol. I, p. 86.
27. *Tolstoy's Diaries*, July 7, 1854, vol. I, pp. 89–90.
28. *Tolstoy's Letters*, November 20, 1854, vol. I, p. 45.
29. *Tolstoy's Letters*, January 6, 1855, vol. I, p. 47.
30. *Tolstoï par Tolstoï*, 3 juillet 1855, p. 144.
31. *Tolstoï par Tolstoï*, 3 juillet 1855, p. 144.
32. *Sevastopol*, p. 22.
33. *Tolstoy's Diaries*, January 28, 1855, vol. I, p. 100.
34. *Tolstoy's Diaries*, March 2, 1855, vol. I, p. 101.
35. *Tolstoy's Diaries*, March 2–4, 1855, vol. I, p. 101.
36. *The Cossacks*, p. 171.
37. *Journal intime de Tolstoï*, 7 décembre 1895, pp. 24–27.
38. *Journal intime de Tolstoï*, 7 décembre 1895, pp. 24–27.
39. *Journal intime de Tolstoï*, 7 décembre 1895, pp. 24–27.
40. *Journal intime de Tolstoï*, 7 décembre 1895, pp. 24–27.
41. *Tolstoy's Diaries*, March 18, 1855, vol. I, p. 102.
42. *Sevastopol*, p. 9.
43. *Sevastopol*, p. 9.
44. *Tolstoy's Letters*, November 20, 1854, vol. I, p. 45.
45. *Tolstoy's Diaries*, April 3–7, 1855, vol. I, p. 103.
46. *Souvenirs et récits*, p. 473.
47. *Sevastopol*, pp. 71–72.
48. *Sevastopol*, pp. 71–72.
49. *Sevastopol*, pp. 71–72.
50. *Tolstoy's Diaries*, May 19, 1855, vol. I, p. 104.
51. *Tolstoy's Diaries*, June 5, 1855, vol. I, p. 104.
52. *Journaux et carnets*, tome I, 2 juin 1855, p. 306.
53. *Souvenirs et récits*, p. 471
54. *Tolstoy's Diaries*, August 1, 1855, vol. I, p. 106.
55. *Journaux et carnets*, tome I, 10 août 1855, p. 319.
56. *Tolstoy's Diaries*, September 2, 1855, vol. I, p. 107.
57. *Tolstoy's Diaries*, September 17, 1855, vol. I, p. 107.
58. *Tolstoy's Diaries*, October 10, 1855, vol. I, p. 108.
59. *Tolstoy's Letters*, May 1859, vol. I, p. 125.
60. *Tolstoy's Letters*, May 1859, vol. I, p. 126.
61. *A Confession* (Cent. Ed., vol. 11), pp. 6–7.
62. *Anna Karenina*, p. 191.
63. *A Confession* (Cent. Ed., vol. 11), p. 8.

5. Literary Life and Travels

1. *Tolstoy's Diaries*, May 8, 1856, vol. I, p. 112.
2. *A Confession* (Cent. Ed., vol. 11), p. 8.
3. *A Confession* (Cent. Ed., vol. 11), p. 8.
4. *Tolstoy's Diaries*, June 4, 1856, vol. I, p. 117.
5. *Anna Karenina*, p. 279.
6. *Anna Karenina*, p. 364.
7. *Tolstoy's Letters*, November 12–13, 1856, vol. I, p. 71.
8. Notes 8 through 19 in the text are all taken from: *Tolstoy's Diaries*, various entries for the months of June, July, and August 1856, vol. I, pp. 119–123. (It was thought simpler to handle it for the reader in this manner than to include twelve separate entries.)
20. *Tolstoy's Letters*, January 2, 1857, vol. I, p. 87.
21. *Tolstoy's Letters*, January 14, 1857, vol. I, p. 88.
22. *Tolstoy's Diaries*, January 12, 1857, vol. I, p. 129.
23. *Tolstoy's Diaries*, July 5, 1856, vol. I, p. 120.
24. *Tolstoy's Diaries*, November 22, 1856, vol. I, p. 125.
25. *Tolstoy's Diaries*, November 23, 1856, vol. I, p. 125.
26. *Tolstoï par Tolstoï*, 4 août 1857, p. 163.
27. *Tolstoy's Diaries*, February 23, 1857, vol. I, p. 130.
28. *Journaux et carnets*, tome I, 1 mars 1857, p. 408.
29. *Tolstoy's Diaries*, March 6, 1857, vol. I, p. 130.
30. *Tolstoy's Diaries*, March 8, 1857, vol. I, p. 131.
31. *Tolstoy's Diaries*, March 16, 1857, vol. I, p. 131.
32. *Tolstoy's Diaries*, March 16, 1857, vol. I, p. 131.
33. *Tolstoy's Diaries*, March 19, 1857, vol. I, p. 132.
34. *Journaux et carnets*, tome I, 21 mars 1857, p. 411.
35. *Tolstoy's Diaries*, March 27, 1857, vol. I, p. 132.
36. *Tolstoy's Diaries*, April 1, 1857, vol. I, p. 132.
37. *Journaux et carnets*, tome I, 5 avril 1857, p. 414.
38. *Tolstoy's Diaries*, April 6, 1857, vol. I, p. 133.
39. *Tolstoy's Diaries*, April 7, 1857, vol. I, p. 133.
40. *Tolstoy's Letters*, March 24–April 7, 1857, vol. I, pp. 95–96.
41. *Tolstoy's Diaries*, April 8, 1857, vol. I, p. 133.
42. *Tolstoy's Diaries*, April 17, 1857, vol. I, p. 133.
43. *Tolstoy's Diaries*, April 19, 1857, vol. I, p. 134.
44. *Journaux et carnets*, tome I, 21 juin 1857, p. 429.
45. *Journaux et carnets*, tome I, 2–3 juillet 1857, p. 431.
46. *Tolstoy's Diaries*, July 23, 1857, vol. I, p. 139.
47. *Journaux et carnets*, tome I, 30 juillet 1857, p. 440.
48. *Journaux et carnets*, tome I, 31 juillet 1857, p. 442.
49. *Tolstoy's Diaries*, August 6, 1857, vol. I, p. 140.
50. *Tolstoy's Letters*, August 18, 1857, vol. I, p. 63.
51. *Tolstoy's Diaries*, August 16, 1857, vol. I, p. 141.
52. *Tolstoy's Diaries*, August 13, 1857, vol. I, p. 141.
53. *Tolstoy's Diaries*, August 15, 1857, vol. I, p. 141.
54. *Journaux et carnets*, tome I, 28 août 1857, p. 446.
55. *Tolstoy's Diaries*, August 29, 1857, vol. I, p. 142.

56. *Tolstoy's Diaries*, October 21, 1857, vol. I, p. 143.
57. *Tolstoy's Diaries*, October 30, 1857, vol. I, p. 144.
58. *Journaux et carnets*, tome I, 9 décembre 1857, p. 459.
59. *Tolstoy's Diaries*, October 22, 1857, vol. I, p. 143.
60. *Journaux et carnets*, tome I, 14 janvier 1858, p. 482.
61. *Tolstoy's Diaries*, April 14, 1858, vol. I, p. 150.
62. *Tolstoy's Letters*, May 1, 1858, vol. I, p. 121.
63. *The Kreutzer Sonata, The Devil and Other Tales* (Cent. Ed., vol. 16), p. 243.
64. *Tolstoy's Diaries*, April 26, 1858, vol. I, p. 150.
65. *Journaux et carnets*, tome I, 4 mai 1858, p. 494.
66. *Journaux et carnets*, tome I, 9 mai 1858, p. 495.
67. *The Kreutzer Sonata, The Devil and Other Tales* (Cent. Ed., vol. 16), p. 246.
68. *Tolstoy's Diaries*, May 13, 1858, vol. I, p. 141.
69. *Tolstoy's Diaries*, June 15, 1858, vol. I, p. 151.
70. *Tolstoy's Diaries*, June 18–19, 1858, vol. I, p. 151.
71. *Tolstoy's Diaries*, September 15, 1858, vol. I, p. 152.
72. *Tolstoy's Diaries*, September 17, 1858, vol. I, p. 152.
73. *Tolstoy's Diaries*, November 27, 1858, vol. I, p. 152.
74. *Tolstoy's Diaries*, December 7–13, 1858, vol. I, p. 153.
75. *Ecrits sur l'art*, p. 68.
76. *Tolstoy's Letters*, May 3, 1859, vol. I, p. 127.
77. *Tolstoy's Letters*, May 3, 1859, vol. I, p. 126.
78. *Tolstoy's Diaries*, May 9, 1859, vol. I, p. 154.
79. *Tolstoy's Diaries*, May 9, 1859, vol. I, p. 154.
80. *Tolstoy's Diaries*, October 2, 1859, vol. I, p. 154.
81. *Tolstoy's Diaries*, October 11, 1859, vol. I, p. 155.
82. *Tolstoy's Diaries*, October 9, 1859, vol. I, p. 155.
83. *Journaux et carnets*, tome I, 12–13 octobre 1859, p. 509.
84. *Journaux et carnets*, tome I, 17 février 1860, p. 514.
85. *A Confession* (Cent. Ed., vol. 11), pp. 13–14.
86. *Tolstoy's Diaries*, February 1, 1860, vol. I, p. 156.
87. *Tolstoy's Diaries*, May 26, 1860, vol. I, p. 156.
88. *The Kreutzer Sonata, The Devil and Other Tales* (Cent. Ed., vol. 16), p. 289.
89. Léon Tolstoï, *Journal intime*.
90. *A Confession* (Cent. Ed., vol. 11), p. 14.
91. *Leo Tolstoy, His Life and Work*, p.273.
92. *Tolstoy's Diaries*, August 7, 1860, vol. I, p. 157.
93. *Tolstoy's Diaries*, July 17, 1860, vol. I, p. 157.
94. *Tolstoy's Diaries*, August 3, 1860, vol. I, p. 157.
95. *Tolstoy's Diaries*, August 5, 1860, vol. I, p. 157.
96. *Tolstoy's Letters*, October 17, 1860, vol. I, p. 141.
97. *Tolstoy's Diaries*, October 13–25, 1860, vol. I, p. 158.
98. *A Confession* (Cent. Ed., vol. 11), p. 13.
99. *Tolstoy's Diaries*, October 13–25, 1860, vol. I, p. 158.
100. *Tolstoï par Tolstoï*, 24 septembre 1860, p. 200.
101. *Tolstoy's Diaries*, October 13–20, 1860, vol. I, p. 158.
102. *Tolstoy on Education*, p. 80.
103. *Tolstoy's Diaries*, April 1–13, 1861, vol. I, p. 160.
104. Léon Tolstoï, *Journal intime*, p. 17.

105. *Tolstoy's Letters*, March 14, 1861, vol. I, p. 145.
106. *Tolstoy's Letters*, March 14, 1861, vol. I, p. 145.
107. Shklovsky, *Lev Tolstoy*.
108. *Tolstoy's Letters*, March 28–April 3, 1861, vol. I, p. 146.
109. *Journaux et carnets*, tome I, 20 avril 1861, p. 526.
110. *Tolstoy's Diaries*, May 6, 1861, vol. I, p. 161.
111. *The Diaries of Sofia Tolstoy*, p. 855.
112. *Leo Tolstoy, His Life and Work*, p. 300.
113. *The Diaries of Sofia Tolstoy*, p. 856.
114. *Tolstoy's Letters*, May 27, 1861, vol. I, p. 148.
115. *Tolstoy's Diaries*, June 25, 1861, vol. I, p. 162.
116. *Tolstoy's Diaries*, October 8, 1861, vol. I, p. 162.
117. *Tolstoy's Letters*, October 8, 1861, vol. I, p. 150.
118. *Tolstoy's Letters*, April 6, 1878, vol. I, p. 318.
119. *Tolstoy's Diaries*, September 4, 1858, vol. I, p. 153.
120. *Tolstoy's Diaries*, June 25, 1861, vol. I, p. 162.
121. *Journaux et carnets*, tome I, 16–28 mars 1861, p. 531.
122. *Tolstoy on Education*, p. 80.
123. *Tolstoy's Diaries*, September 22, 1861, vol. I, p. 162.
124. *Tolstoy's Diaries*, September 28, 1861, vol. I, p. 163.
125. *A Confession* (Cent. Ed., vol. 11), p. 14.
126. *A Confession* (Cent. Ed., vol. 11), p. 14.
127. *Tolstoy's Letters*, August 7, 1862, vol. I, p. 161.
128. *Tolstoy's Letters*, August 1862, vol. I, p. 158.
129. *Tolstoy's Letters*, August 1862, vol. I, p. 161.
130. *Tolstoy's Letters*, July 22, 1862, vol. I, p. 164.

II: THE TWO DROPS OF HONEY: LOVE AND ART

6. Engagement and Marriage

1. *A Confession* (Cent. Ed., vol. 11), p. 21.
2. *Anna Karenina*, p. 34.
3. *Anna Karenina*, p. 35.
4. *The Diaries of Sofia Tolstoy*, p. 828.
5. *The Diaries of Sofia Tolstoy*, pp. 828–829.
6. *The Diaries of Sofia Tolstoy*, p. 829.
7. *Tolstoy's Letters*, September 17, 1862, vol. I, p. 164.
8. *The Diaries of Sofia Tolstoy*, p. 831.
9. *The Diaries of Sofia Tolstoy*, p. 832.
10. *The Diaries of Sofia Tolstoy*, p. 832.
11. *The Diaries of Sofia Tolstoy*, p. 832.
12. *Tolstoy's Diaries*, August 23, 1862, vol. I, p. 164.
13. *The Diaries of Sofia Tolstoy*, August 17, 1863, p. 24.
14. *Tolstoy's Diaries*, August 26, 1862, vol. I, p. 164.
15. *Tolstoy's Diaries*, August 28, 1862, vol. I, p. 165.
16. *Tolstoy's Diaries*, August 28, 1862, vol. I, p. 165.

17. *Tolstoy's Diaries*, September 13, 1862, vol. I, p. 167.
18. *Tolstoy's Diaries*, September 3, 1862, vol. I, p. 165.
19. *Tolstoy's Diaries*, September 7, 1862, vol. I, p. 166.
20. *Tolstoy's Diaries*, September 7, 1862, vol. I, p. 166.
21. *Tolstoy's Diaries*, September 8, 1862, vol. I, p. 166.
22. *Tolstoy's Diaries*, September 9, 1862, vol. I, p. 166.
23. *Tolstoy's Diaries*, September 9, 1862, vol. I, p. 166.
24. *Tolstoy's Diaries*, September 12, 1862, vol. I, p. 167.
25. *Tolstoy's Diaries*, September 14, 1862, vol. I, p. 167.
26. *Tolstoy's Diaries*, September 15, 1862, vol. I, p. 167.
27. *The Diaries of Sofia Tolstoy*, p. 838.
28. *Tolstoy's Diaries*, September 16, 1862, vol. I, p. 167.
29. *Tolstoy's Diaries*, September 23, 1862, vol. I, p. 168.
30. *A Confession* (Cent. Ed., vol. 11), p. 21.
31. *Tolstoy's Diaries*, June 18, 1863, vol. I, p. 178.
32. *Monsieur le comte*, p. 108.
33. *The Diaries of Sofia Tolstoy*, December 16, 1862, p. 9.
34. *Journaux et carnets*, tome I, 6 janvier 1889, p. 893.
35. *The Diaries of Sofia Tolstoy*, October 17, 1863, p. 26.

7. Married Life

1. *Tolstoy's Diaries*, September 24, 1862, vol. I, p. 168.
2. *Tolstoy's Letters*, October 28, 1864, vol. I, p. 185.
3. *Tolstoy's Diaries*, August 5, 1863, vol. I, p. 179.
4. *Tolstoy's Diaries*, September 25, 1862, vol. I, p. 168.
5. *Tolstoy's Diaries*, September 26–30, 1862, vol. I, p. 168.
6. *Tolstoy's Letters*, September 28, 1862, vol. I, p. 169.
7. *The Diaries of Sofia Tolstoy*, October 8, 1862, p. 3.
8. *The Diaries of Sofia Tolstoy*, October 8, 1862, p. 3.
9. *The Diaries of Sofia Tolstoy*, October 8, 1862, pp. 3–4.
10. *Tolstoy's Diaries*, October 2–14, 1862, vol. I, p. 168.
11. *Tolstoy's Diaries*, October 15, 1862, vol. I, p. 168.
12. *Tolstoy's Diaries*, June 18, 1863, vol. I, p. 178.
13. *The Diaries of Sofia Tolstoy*, January 11, 1863, p. 11.
14. *The Diaries of Sofia Tolstoy*, October 8, 1862, p. 4.
15. *Journal intime*, p. 162.
16. *The Diaries of Sofia Tolstoy*, October 11, 1862, p. 6.
17. *The Diaries of Sofia Tolstoy*, October 9, 1862, p. 5.
18. *The Diaries of Sofia Tolstoy*, November 13, 1862, p. 7.
19. *The Diaries of Sofia Tolstoy*, October 9, 1862, p. 5.
20. *The Diaries of Sofia Tolstoy*, April 29, 1863, p. 18.
21. *Tolstoy's Diaries*, December 22, 1862, vol. I, p. 169.
22. *The Diaries of Sofia Tolstoy*, November 13, 1862, pp. 7–8.
23. *The Diaries of Sofia Tolstoy*, November 23, 1862, p. 8.
24. *Tolstoy's Letters*, October 5, vol. I, p. 172.
25. *Tolstoï par Tolstoï.*
26. *Tolstoy's Diaries*, December 27, 1862, vol. I, p. 169.

27. *The Diaries of Sofia Tolstoy*, January 11, 1863, p. 11.
28. *Tolstoy's Diaries*, December 27, 1862, vol. I, p. 169.
29. *The Diaries of Sofia Tolstoy*, January 15–17, 1863, p. 13.
30. *The Diaries of Sofia Tolstoy*, January 29, 1863, p. 14.
31. *Tolstoy's Diaries*, January 5, 1863, vol. I, p. 174.
32. *Tolstoy's Letters*, December 7, 1864, vol. I, p. 190.
33. *Tolstoy's Diaries*, January 23, 1863, vol. I, p. 175.
34. *Tolstoy's Diaries*, February 23, 1863, vol. I, p. 176.
35. *Tolstoy's Diaries*, January 23, 1863, vol. I, pp. 175–176.
36. *The Diaries of Sofia Tolstoy*, March 26, 1863, p. 15.
37. *Tolstoy's Letters*, March 23, 1863, vol. I, p. 176.
38. *Tolstoy's Letters*, March 23, 1863, vol. I, p. 179.
39. *Journaux et carnets*, tome I, 11 avril 1863, p. 550.
40. *The Diaries of Sofia Tolstoy*, May 8, 1863, p. 18.
41. *The Diaries of Sofia Tolstoy*, May 9, 1863, p. 19.
42. *The Diaries of Sofia Tolstoy*, June 7, 1863, p. 21.
43. *Tolstoy's Diaries*, June 18, 1863, vol. I, p. 178.
44. *Tolstoy's Diaries*, June 18, 1863, vol. I, p. 178.
45. *Tolstoy's Diaries*, June 18, 1863, vol. I, p. 178.
46. *Tolstoy's Diaries*, August 5, 1863, vol. I, p. 179.
47. *The Diaries of Sofia Tolstoy*, August 3, 1863, p. 23.
48. *Tolstoy Remembered.*
49. *The Diaries of Sofia Tolstoy*, August 3, 1863, p. 23.
50. *The Diaries of Sofia Tolstoy*, August 17, 1863, p. 23.
51. *The Diaries of Sofia Tolstoy*, August 17, 1863, p. 24.
52. *Tolstoy's Diaries*, March 1, 1863, vol. I, p. 176.
53. *Tolstoy's Diaries*, February 8, 1863, vol. I, p. 176.
54. *Tolstoy's Letters*, May 13, 1909, vol. II, p. 687.
55. *Tolstoy's Letters*, January 12, 1852, vol. I, p. 23.
56. *The Diaries of Sofia Tolstoy*, September 22, 1863, p. 25.
57. *The Diaries of Sofia Tolstoy*, October 17, 1863, pp. 25–26.
58. *The Diaries of Sofia Tolstoy*, October 28, 1863, p. 26.
59. *Tolstoy's Letters*, October 17–31, 1863, vol. I, p. 181.
60. *Tolstoy's Diaries*, October 6, 1863, vol. I, p. 180.

8. War and Peace

1. *Anna Karenina*, p. 506.
2. *The Diaries of Sofia Tolstoy*, July 23, 1863, p. 22.
3. *The Tragedy of Tolstoy*, p. 166.
4. *The Diaries of Sofia Tolstoy*, December 3, 1864, p. 30.
5. *Tolstoy's Letters*, December 7, 1864, vol. I, p. 189.
6. *Tolstoy's Diaries*, September 16, 1864, vol. I, p. 181.
7. *Tolstoy's Diaries*, March 7, 1865, vol. I, p. 182.
8. *The Diaries of Sofia Tolstoy*, February 25, 1865, p. 31.
9. *The Diaries of Sofia Tolstoy*, March 6, 1865, p. 31.
10. *The Diaries of Sofia Tolstoy*, March 7, 1865, p. 32.
11. *The Diaries of Sofia Tolstoy*, March 9, 10, 23, 1865, pp. 33–34.

12. *The Diaries of Sofia Tolstoy*, July 16, 1865, p. 37.
13. *Tolstoy's Letters*, December 7, 1864, vol. I, p. 190.
14. *The Diaries of Sofia Tolstoy*, March 26, 1865, p. 35.
15. *Tolstoy's Diaries*, March 23, 1865, vol. I, p. 183.
16. *Tolstoy's Diaries*, March 25, 1865, vol. I, p. 184.
17. *Journaux et carnets*, tome I, 10 avril 1865, p. 562.
18. *Tolstoy's Diaries*, August 13, 1865, vol. I, p. 184.
19. *Journaux et carnets*, tome I, mars 1866, p. 575.
20. *Guerre et Paix*, tome XIII, appendice.
21. *Guerre et Paix*, tome XIII, appendice.
22. Shklovsky, *Lev Tolstoy*, pp. 365–366.
23. *Tolstoy's Letters*, May 3, 1865, vol. I, p. 194.
24. *Tolstoy's Letters*, May 4, 1866, vol. I, p. 203.
25. *Tolstoy's Letters*, December 8, 1866, vol. I, p. 209.
26. *Tolstoy's Letters*, February 28, 1867, vol. I, p. 212.
27. Shklovsky, *Lev Tolstoy*, p. 372.
28. Shklovsky, *Lev Tolstoy*, p. 372.
29. *La délivrance de Tolstoï*, pp. 111–116.
30. *Sevastopol*, p. 70.
31. *Anna Karenina*, p. 522.
32. *Tolstoy's Diaries*, March 7, 1865, vol. I, p. 182.
33. *Tolstoy's Letters*, November 14, 1865, vol. I, p. 199.
34. *Tolstoy's Diaries*, March 19, 1865, vol. I, p. 182.
35. *The Diaries of Sofia Tolstoy*, May 3, 1865, p. 36.
36. *Tolstoy's Diaries*, September 24, 1865, vol. I, p. 184.
37. *Tolstoy's Diaries*, September 26, 1865, vol. I, p. 184.
38. *Tolstoy's Diaries*, October 15, 1865, vol. I, p. 185.
39. *Tolstoy's Diaries*, November 9, 1865, vol. I, p. 186.
40. *Tolstoy's Diaries*, November 10, 1865, vol. I, p. 186.
41. *Tolstoy's Letters*, January 3, 1865, vol. I, p. 191.
42. *War and Peace* (Cent. Ed., vol. 8), p. 538.
43. *Tolstoy's Letters*, November 17, 1870, vol. I, p. 230.
44. *Tolstoy's Letters*, May 10–20, 1866, vol. I, p. 206.
45. *Tolstoy's Letters*, January 18–23, 1865, vol. I, p. 192.
46. *Ecrits sur l'art*, p. 68.
47. *Tolstoy's Letters*, July–August 1865, vol. I, p. 196.
48. *Tolstoï par Tolstoï*, June 27, 1867, p. 296.
49. *The Diaries of Sofia Tolstoy*, April 28, 1866, p. 39.
50. *The Diaries of Sofia Tolstoy*, July 19, 1866, p. 39.
51. *The Diaries of Sofia Tolstoy*, August 10, 1866, p. 41.
52. *Anna Karenina*, p. 509.
53. *The Diaries of Sofia Tolstoy*, November 12, 1866, pp. 41–42.
54. *War and Peace* (Cent. Ed., vol. 8), p. 604.
55. *Reminiscences of Tolstoy, Chekhov and Andreev.*
56. *Reminiscences of Tolstoy, Chekhov and Andreev.*
57. *The Diaries of Sofia Tolstoy*, November 12, 1866, p. 42.
58. *The Diaries of Sofia Tolstoy*, January 12, 1867, p. 42.
59. *The Diaries of Sofia Tolstoy*, September 12, 1867, p. 43.
60. *Tolstoy's Letters*, September 27, 1867, pp. 215–216.

61. *Tolstoy's Letters*, September 27, 1867, pp. 215–216.
62. *The Diaries of Sofia Tolstoy*, July 31, 1868, p. 45.
63. *Tolstoï par Tolstoï*, pp. 298–299.
64. Shklovsky, *Lev Tolstoy*, p. 276.
65. *Reminiscences of Tolstoy, Chekhov and Andreev.*
66. *Tolstoy's Letters*, November 7, 1866, vol. I, p. 208.
67. *War and Peace* (Cent. Ed., vol. 8), p. 543.
68. *War and Peace* (Cent. Ed., vol. 8), p. 543.
69. *War and Peace*, p. 900.
70. *War and Peace*, p. 932.
71. *War and Peace*, p. 933.
72. *War and Peace*, p. 1404.
73. *War and Peace*, p. 1271.
74. *War and Peace*, p. 1405.
75. *War and Peace*, p. 1410.
76. *War and Peace*, p. 1407.
77. *War and Peace*, p. 1420.
78. *War and Peace*, p. 977.
79. *War and Peace*, p. 1426.
80. *War and Peace*, p. 1430.
81. *War and Peace*, p. 1440.
82. *War and Peace*, p. 1444.
83. *War and Peace*, p. 1431.
84. *War and Peace*, p. 326.
85. *War and Peace*, p. 968.
86. *War and Peace*, p. 1166.
87. *War and Peace*, p. 1237.
88. *War and Peace*, p. 1313.
89. *War and Peace*, p. 1150.
90. *War and Peace*, p. 1308.
91. *War and Peace*, p. 1311.
92. *War and Peace*, p. 886.
93. *War and Peace*, p. 1290.

9. *After* War and Peace

1. *Tolstoy's Letters*, May 10, 1869, vol. I, p. 220.
2. *The Diaries of Sofia Tolstoy*, February 14, 1870, p. 844.
3. *Tolstoy's Letters*, August 1869, vol. I, p. 221.
4. *Tolstoy's Letters*, September 1869, vol. I, p. 222.
5. *Ivan Ilych and Hadji Murad* (Cent. Ed., vol. 15), p. 211.
6. *Ivan Ilych and Hadji Murad* (Cent. Ed., vol. 15), p. 211–219.
7. *Oeuvres posthumes* (ed. Rencontre), p. 151.
8. *Ivan Ilych and Hadji Murad* (Cent. Ed., vol. 15), pp. 214–219.
9. *Ivan Ilych and Hadji Murad* (Cent. Ed., vol. 15), p. 219.
10. *Ivan Ilych and Hadji Murad* (Cent. Ed., vol. 15), p. 220.
11. *Ivan Ilych and Hadji Murad* (Cent. Ed., vol. 15), p. 217.
12. *Ivan Ilych and Hadji Murad* (Cent. Ed., vol. 15), p. 217.

13. *Ivan Ilych and Hadji Murad* (Cent. Ed., vol. 15), p. 218.
14. *Ivan Ilych and Hadji Murad* (Cent. Ed., vol. 15), p. 222.
15. *Ivan Ilych and Hadji Murad* (Cent. Ed., vol. 15), p. 223.
16. *Ivan Ilych and Hadji Murad* (Cent. Ed., vol. 15), p. 219.
17. *The Diaries of Sofia Tolstoy*, December 9, 1870, p. 846.
18. *Ivan Ilych and Hadji Murad* (Cent. Ed., vol. 15), p. 222.
19. *Ivan Ilych and Hadji Murad* (Cent. Ed., vol. 15), p. 224.
20. *Ivan Ilych and Hadji Murad* (Cent. Ed., vol. 15), p. 224.
21. *Ivan Ilych and Hadji Murad* (Cent. Ed., vol. 15), p. 224.
22. *Ivan Ilych and Hadji Murad* (Cent. Ed., vol. 15), p. 225.
23. *Ivan Ilych and Hadji Murad* (Cent. Ed., vol. 15), p. 210.
24. *La révélation de la mort*, pp. 163–164.
25. *The Diaries of Sofia Tolstoy*, February 14, 1870, p. 844.
26. *The Diaries of Sofia Tolstoy*, February 14, 1870, p. 844.
27. *The Diaries of Sofia Tolstoy*, February 15, 1870, p. 845.
28. *The Diaries of Sofia Tolstoy*, February 24, 1870, p. 845.
29. *Tolstoy's Letters*, February 16, 1870, vol. I, p. 225.
30. *Tolstoy's Letters*, May 11, 1870, vol. I, p. 229.
31. *Tolstoy's Letters*, November 17, 1870, vol. I, p. 230.
32. *The Diaries of Sofia Tolstoy*, March 27, 1871, p. 846.
33. *The Diaries of Sofia Tolstoy*, March 27, 1871, p. 846.
34. *Tolstoy's Letters*, May 4, 1871, vol. I, p. 233.
35. *Tolstoï par Tolstoï*, p. 309.
36. *The Diaries of Sofia Tolstoy*, August 18, 1871, p. 58.
37. *A Confession* (Cent. Ed., vol. 11), p. 58.
38. *Tolstoy's Letters*, June 18, 1871, vol. I, pp. 234–235.
39. *Tolstoï par Tolstoï*, 18 juillet 1871, p. 313.
40. *Journaux et carnets*, tome I, 25 juin, 26 juillet 1871, p. 614.
41. *Tolstoy's Letters*, September 13, 1871, vol. I, p. 239.
42. *Tolstoï par Tolstoï*, 20 février 1872, p. 318.
43. *Tolstoy's Letters*, November 1872, vol. I, p. 254.
44. *Anna Karénine* (Pléiade), p. 1663.
45. *Tolstoy's Letters*, November 1872, vol. I, p. 254.
46. *The Diaries of Sofia Tolstoy*, December 9, 1870, p. 846.
47. *Tolstoy's Letters*, March 1872, vol. I, p. 245.
48. *Tolstoy's Letters*, September 13, 1871, vol. I, p. 239.
49. *A Confession* (Cent. Ed., vol. 11), p. 18.
50. *A Confession* (Cent. Ed., vol. 11), p. 15.
51. *Tolstoy's Letters*, March 24, 1872, vol. I, p. 244.
52. *The Diaries of Sofia Tolstoy*, April 3, 1872, p. 47.
53. *Tolstoy's Letters*, September 1, 1872, vol. I, p. 247.
54. *Tolstoy's Letters*, September 15, 1872, vol. I, p. 247.
55. *The Diaries of Sofia Tolstoy*, January 16, 1873, p. 847.
56. *Tolstoy's Letters*, February 1873, vol. I, p. 357.
57. *The Diaries of Sofia Tolstoy*, January 16, 1873, p. 847.
58. *The Diaries of Sofia Tolstoy*, January 31, 1873, p. 847.
59. *Diary of a Writer*.
60. *Tolstoï par Tolstoï*, 12 novembre 1872, p. 346.
61. *Tolstoï par Tolstoï*, janvier 1873, p. 351.

62. *The Diaries of Sofia Tolstoy*, January 31, 1873, p. 847.
63. *The Diaries of Sofia Tolstoy*, March 19, 1873, p. 848.

10. Anna Karenina

1. *Anna Karénine* (Pléiade), p. 930.
2. *Tolstoy's Letters*, March 22, 1874, vol. I, p. 269.
3. *Tolstoy's Letters*, April 23–26, 1876, vol. I, p. 297.
4. *Tolstoy's Letters*, May 31, 1873, October 19, 1877, pp. 260–307.
5. *Tolstoy's Letters*, March 25, 1873, p. 258.
6. *The Diaries of Sofia Tolstoy*, October 4, 1873, p. 848.
7. *Tolstoy's Letters*, April 18–19, 1874, vol. I, p. 270.
8. *Tolstoy's Letters*, September 23–24, 1873, vol. I, p. 265.
9. *Tolstoï par Tolstoï*, 18 septembre 1873, p. 353.
10. Shklovsky, *Lev Tolstoy*, p. 450.
11. *Tolstoï par Tolstoï*, mars 1873, p. 354.
12. *Tolstoy's Letters*, June 23, 1874, vol. I, p. 270.
13. Shklovsky, *Lev Tolstoy*, p. 450.
14. *The Diaries of Sofia Tolstoy*, February 17, 1874, p. 51.
15. *The Diaries of Sofia Tolstoy*, August 27, 1866, p. 41.
16. *Anna Karenina*, p. 562.
17. *Tolstoy's Letters*, 1875, vol. I, p. 280.
18. *Anna Karénine* (Pléiade), p. 1662.
19. *Anna Karénine* (Pléiade), p. 973.
20. *Anna Karenina*, p. 532.
21. *Anna Karenina*, p. 533.
22. *Anna Karenina*, p. 749.
23. *Anna Karenina*, p. 802.
24. *Anna Karenina*, p. 827.
25. *Anna Karenina*, pp. 437–438.
26. *Anna Karenina*, p. 438.
27. *Anna Karenina*, p. 162.
28. *Anna Karenina*, p. 118.
29. *Anna Karenina*, p. 161.
30. *Anna Karenina*, p. 797.
31. *Anna Karenina*, p. 165.
32. *Anna Karenina*, p. 165.
33. *Anna Karenina*, p. 733.
34. *Anna Karenina*, p. 577.
35. *Anna Karenina*, p. 576.
36. *Anna Karenina*, p. 671.
37. *Tolstoy Remembered by His Son.*
38. *The Diaries of Sofia Tolstoy*, February 13, 1873, p. 50.
39. *The Diaries of Sofia Tolstoy*, October 12, 1875, p. 52.
40. *Anna Karenina*, pp. 432–433.
41. *Anna Karenina*, p. 433.
42. *Anna Karenina*, p. 583.
43. *A Confession* (Cent. Ed., vol. 11), p. 50.

44. *Anna Karenina*, p. 523.
45. *Anna Karenina*, p. 828.
46. *Anna Karenina*, p. 826.
47. *A Confession* (Cent. Ed., vol. 11), p. 15.
48. *Tolstoy's Letters*, August 26, 1875, vol. I, p. 280.
49. *Tolstoy's Letters*, March 1876, vol. I, p. 294.
50. Shklovsky, *Lev Tolstoy*, p. 452.
51. *Tolstoï par Tolstoï*, avril 1876, p. 373.
52. *Tolstoy's Letters*, April 1876, vol. I, p. 296.
53. *Tolstoy's Letters*, April 1876, vol. I, p. 296.
54. *Tolstoï et ses proches*.
55. *Tolstoy's Letters*, April 29, 1876, vol. I, p. 298.
56. *Anna Karenina*, p. 821.
57. *Anna Karenina*, p. 822.
58. *Anna Karenina*, p. 822.
59. *Tolstoy's Letters*, November 30, 1875, vol. I, p. 285.
60. *Tolstoy's Letters*, November 30, 1875, vol. I, p. 288.
61. *Anna Karenina*, p. 823.
62. *Anna Karenina*, p. 823.
63. *A Confession* (Cent. Ed., vol. 11), p. 18.
64. *Anna Karenina*, p. 825.
65. *Anna Karenina*, p. 272.
66. *Anna Karenina*, p. 828.
67. *Anna Karenina*, p. 829.
68. *Anna Karenina*, p. 829.
69. *Anna Karenina*, p. 832.
70. *Anna Karenina*, p. 835.
71. *Anna Karenina*, p. 853.
72. *Anna Karenina*, p. 853.
73. *Tolstoy's Letters*, April 15–17, 1876, vol. I, p. 295.
74. *The Diaries of Sofia Tolstoy*, November 20, 1876, p. 848.
75. *La tragédie de Tolstoï et de sa femme*, p. 11.
76. *The Diaries of Sofia Tolstoy*, September 17, 1876, p. 53.
77. *The Diaries of Sofia Tolstoy*, September 18, 1876, p. 54.
78. *La tragédie de Tolstoï et de sa femme*, p. 117.
79. *The Diaries of Sofia Tolstoy*, March 3, 1877, p. 850.
80. *The Diaries of Sofia Tolstoy*, March 3, 1877, p. 850.
81. *Tolstoy's Letters*, February 1877, vol. I, p. 303.
82. *Tolstoy's Letters*, February 1877, vol. I, p. 303.
83. *Tolstoy's Letters*, February 1877, vol. I, p. 303.
84. *The Diaries of Sofia Tolstoy*, August 25, 1877, p. 850.
85. *Tolstoy's Letters*, November 6, 1877, vol. I, p. 308.
86. *Tolstoy's Letters*, March 20, 1876, vol. I, p. 294.
87. *The Diaries of Sofia Tolstoy*, August 25, 1877, p. 850.
88. *Tolstoy's Letters*, November 1877, vol. I, p. 308.
89. *Anna Karenina*, p. 843.
90. *Anna Karenina*, p. 840.
91. *Diary of a Writer*, p. 661.
92. *Diary of a Writer*, p. 661.

93. *Diary of a Writer*, p. 662.
94. *Diary of a Writer*, p. 610.
95. *Diary of a Writer*, p. 610.
96. *Diary of a Writer*, p. 788.
97. *Diary of a Writer*, p. 812.
98. *Diary of a Writer*, p. 792.
99. *Diary of a Writer*, p. 812.
100. *Tolstoy's Letters*, June 10, 1877, vol. I, p. 306.
101. *Anna Karenina*, p. 346.
102. *Tolstoy's Letters*, August 10–11, 1877, vol. I, p. 306.
103. *The Diaries of Sofia Tolstoy*, September 12, 1877, p. 851.
104. *The Diaries of Sofia Tolstoy*, December 26, 1877, p. 58.
105. *Anna Karenina*, p. 900.

III: THE GREAT UNSETTLING

11. Moral Crisis or Rebirth? A Confession

1. *Tolstoï par Tolstoï*, août 1879, p. 407.
2. *The Diaries of Sofia Tolstoy*, March 1, 1878, p. 853.
3. *Évolution religieuse de Tolstoï*, p. 108.
4. *Évolution religieuse de Tolstoï*, p. 179.
5. *Tolstoy's Letters*, January 27, 1878, vol. I, p. 315.
6. *Tolstoy's Letters*, January 27, 1878, vol. I, p. 313.
7. *A Confession* (Cent. Ed., vol. 11), p. 62.
8. *The Diaries of Sofia Tolstoy*, January 8, 1878, p. 852.
9. *The Diaries of Sofia Tolstoy*, January 31, 1881, p. 853.
10. *The Diaries of Sofia Tolstoy*, January 31, 1881, p. 853.
11. *The Diaries of Sofia Tolstoy*, January 31, 1881, pp. 853–854.
12. *The Diaries of Sofia Tolstoy*, January 31, 1881, p. 854.
13. *The Diaries of Sofia Tolstoy*, June 1, 1881, p. 854.
14. *The Diaries of Sofia Tolstoy*, September 24, 1878, p. 55.
15. *The Diaries of Sofia Tolstoy*, September 25, 1878, p. 56.
16. *The Diaries of Sofia Tolstoy*, December 18, 1878, p. 69.
17. *The Diaries of Sofia Tolstoy*, October 9, 1878, p. 59.
18. *The Diaries of Sofia Tolstoy*, October 14, 1878, p. 59.
19. *The Diaries of Sofia Tolstoy*, October 18, 1878, p. 61.
20. *The Diaries of Sofia Tolstoy*, November 16, 1878, p. 67.
21. *Tolstoy's Letters*, April 8, 1878, vol. I, p. 321.
22. *Tolstoy's Letters*, April 6, 1878, vol. I, p. 320.
23. *A Confession* (Cent. Ed., vol. 11), pp. 18–19.
24. *A Confession* (Cent. Ed., vol. 11), p. 20.
25. *A Confession* (Cent. Ed., vol. 11), p. 21.
26. *A Confession* (Cent. Ed., vol. 11), p. 24.
27. *A Confession* (Cent. Ed., vol. 11), p. 23.
28. *A Confession* (Cent. Ed., vol. 11), p. 30.

29. *A Confession* (Cent. Ed., vol. 11), p. 31.
30. *Tolstoy's Letters*, November 26, 1877, vol. I, pp. 308–309.
31. *A Confession* (Cent. Ed., vol. 11), p. 40.
32. *Le meurtre du Christ.*
33. *A Confession* (Cent. Ed., vol. 11), p. 44.
34. *A Confession* (Cent. Ed., vol. 11), p. 45.
35. *A Confession* (Cent. Ed., vol. 11), p. 46.
36. *A Confession* (Cent. Ed., vol. 11), p. 47.
37. *A Confession* (Cent. Ed., vol. 11), p. 47.
38. *Evolution religieuse de Tolstoï*, p. 80.
39. *A Confession* (Cent. Ed., vol. 11), p. 49.
40. *A Confession* (Cent. Ed., vol. 11), pp. 50–51.
41. *A Confession* (Cent. Ed., vol. 11), p. 53.
42. *A Confession* (Cent. Ed., vol. 11), p. 55.
43. *A Confession* (Cent. Ed., vol. 11), p. 56.
44. *A Confession* (Cent. Ed., vol. 11), p. 57.
45. *A Confession* (Cent. Ed., vol. 11), p. 58.
46. *A Confession* (Cent. Ed., vol. 11), pp. 57–59.
47. *A Confession* (Cent. Ed., vol. 11), p. 60.
48. *A Confession* (Cent. Ed., vol. 11), p. 60.
49. *A Confession* (Cent. Ed., vol. 11), p. 62.
50. *Récits d'un pèlerin russe*, p. 130.
51. *A Confession* (Cent. Ed., vol. 11), p. 62.
52. *A Confession* (Cent. Ed., vol. 11), p. 62.
53. *A Confession* (Cent. Ed., vol. 11), p. 63.
54. *Journaux et carnets*, tome I, 24 mars 1879, p. 686.
55. *A Confession* (Cent. Ed., vol. 11), p. 63.
56. *A Confession* (Cent. Ed., vol. 11), p. 64.
57. *A Confession* (Cent. Ed., vol. 11), p. 63.
58. *A Confession* (Cent. Ed., vol. 11), p. 65.
59. *A Confession* (Cent. Ed., vol. 11), p. 66.
60. *Tolstoy's Letters*, March 8–15, 1881, vol. II, p. 345.
61. *A Confession* (Cent. Ed., vol. 11), pp. 67–69.
62. *A Confession* (Cent. Ed., vol. 11), p. 71.
63. *A Confession* (Cent. Ed., vol. 11), p. 71
64. *A Confession* (Cent. Ed., vol. 11), p. 71.
65. *A Confession* (Cent. Ed., vol. 11), p. 72.
66. *A Confession* (Cent. Ed., vol. 11), p. 73.
67. *A Confession* (Cent. Ed., vol. 11), p. 74.
68. *A Confession* (Cent. Ed., vol. 11), p. 73.
69. *A Confession* (Cent. Ed., vol. 11), p. 75.
70. *A Confession* (Cent. Ed., vol. 11), p. 80.
71. *A Confession* (Cent. Ed., vol. 11), p. 80.
72. *A Confession* (Cent. Ed., vol. 11), p. 80.
73. *A Confession* (Cent. Ed., vol. 11), p. 81.
74. *What Is Art? and Essays on Art* (Cent. Ed., vol. 18), p. 20.
75. *Evolution religieuse de Tolstoï*, p. 179.
76. *Tolstoy's Letters*, May 4, 1880, vol. II, p. 338.

77. *Tolstoy's Letters*, March 25, 1879, vol. I, p. 332.
78. *Tolstoy's Letters*, February 10, 1881, vol. II, p. 340.
79. *Tolstoy's Letters*, September 26, 1880, vol. II, p. 338.
80. *Tolstoy's Letters*, March 8–14, 1881, vol. II, pp. 341–347.
81. *Tolstoy's Letters*, March 8–15, 1881, vol. II, p. 347.
82. *La tragédie de Tolstoï et de sa femme*, 3 août 1881, p. 140.
83. *Diary of a Writer*, p. 621.
84. *Diary of a Writer*, p. 621.
85. *Diary of a Writer*, p. 621.
86. *Tolstoy's Diaries*, September 22, 1900, vol. II, p. 482.
87. *Tolstoy's Letters*, June 26–27, 1881, vol. II, p. 352.
88. *Tolstoy's Letters*, July 24, 1884, vol. II, p. 372.
89. *The Diaries of Sofia Tolstoy*, August 11, 1897, p. 229.
90. *A Confession* (Cent. Ed., vol. 11), p. 58.
91. *On Life and Essays on Religion* (Cent. Ed., vol. 12).
92. *Appels aux dirigeants*, p. 60.
93. *Souvenirs et récits* (Pléiade), p. 1274.
94. *Reminiscences of Tolstoy, Chekhov and Andreev*, p. 23.
95. *The Kingdom of God and Peace Essays* (Cent. Ed., vol. 20).
96. *Tolstoï par Tolstoï*, janvier 1873, p. 350.
97. *Documents sur la mort de Tolstoï*, p. 8.

12. Moscow

1. *Tolstoy's Letters*, March 1872, vol. I, p. 245.
2. *Tolstoy's Letters*, December 3–15, 1885, vol. II, p. 392.
3. *Journal de la comtesse Léon Tolstoï*, tome II, 7 février 1891, p. 9.
4. *Tolstoy's Letters*, December 15–18, 1885, vol. II, p. 393.
5. *The Tolstoy Home*.
6. *Tolstoy's Letters*, February 2, 1885, vol. II, p. 377.
7. *Tolstoy's Letters*, November 15–30, 1881, vol. II, p. 353.
8. *Evolution religieuse de Tolstoï*, p. 268.
9. *Tolstoy's Letters*, March 4, 1882, vol. II, p. 355.
10. *Tolstoy's Letters*, March 12, 1882, vol. II, p. 356.
11. *The Diaries of Sofia Tolstoy*, February 28, 1882, p. 71.
12. *Tolstoy's Letters*, December 20, 1882–January 20, 1883, vol. II, p. 362.
13. *Tolstoy's Letters*, November 15–30, 1881, vol. II, pp. 353–354.
14. *Tolstoy's Letters*, November 15–30, 1881, vol. II, p. 354.
15. *Tolstoy Remembered by His Son*.
16. *Tolstoy's Letters*, November 7–15, 1882, vol. II, p. 359.
17. *Tolstoy's Letters*, December 20, 1882, vol. II, p. 361.
18. *Tolstoy's Letters*, December 20, 1882–January 20, 1883, vol. II, p. 362.
19. *Tolstoy's Letters*, December 20, 1882–January 20, 1883, vol. II, p. 363.
20. *The Diaries of Sofia Tolstoy*, August 26, 1882, p. 71.
21. *The Diaries of Sofia Tolstoy*, August 26, 1882, p. 71.
22. *The Diaries of Sofia Tolstoy*, August 26, 1882, p. 72.
23. *The Diaries of Sofia Tolstoy*, March 5, 1883, pp. 72–73.
24. *Journaux et carnets*, tome I, juin 1884, p. 861.

13. *A New Way of Seeing*

1. A. Gide, *Journal*, 9 juillet 1932, p. 1139.
2. *A Confession* (Cent. Ed., vol. 11), p. 22.
3. *A Confession* (Cent. Ed., vol. 11), p. 22.
4. *Journal de la comtesse Léon Tolstoï*, p. vi.
5. *Tolstoy, His Life and Work*, p. xvii.
6. *La tragédie de Tolstoï et de sa femme*, 8 décembre 1884, p. 158.
7. *Tolstoy's Diaries*, March 31, 1884, vol. I, p. 207.
8. *Tolstoy's Letters*, December 13, 1884, vol. II, p. 374.
9. *Tolstoy's Diaries*, March 30, 1884, vol. I, p. 207.
10. *Tolstoy's Diaries*, March 27, 1884, vol. I, p. 206.
11. *Tolstoy's Diaries*, April 4, 1884, vol. I, p. 207.
12. *Tolstoy's Diaries*, April 24, 1884, vol. I, p. 212.
13. *Tolstoy's Diaries*, May 29, 1884, vol. I, p. 216.
14. *Journaux et carnets*, tome I, 16 août 1884, p. 853.
15. *La Tragédie de Tolstoï et de sa femme*, p. 152.
16. *Tolstoy's Diaries*, March 23, 1884, vol. I, p. 205.
17. *Tolstoy's Diaries*, May 21, 1884, vol. I, p. 215.
18. *Journaux et carnets*, tome I, 30 mai–11 juin 1884, p. 833.
19. *The Diaries of Sofia Tolstoy*, June 18, 1897, p. 201.
20. *Tolstoy's Diaries*, June 18–30, 1884, vol. I, p. 218.
21. *Europe*, juillet 1928, p. 427.
22. *Europe*, juillet 1928, p. 427.
23. *Journaux et carnets*, récapitulation: juillet, p. 380.
24. *Tolstoy's Letters*, July 24, 1884, vol. II, p. 373.
25. *Tolstoy's Letters*, May 22, 1886, vol. II, p. 404.
26. *Tolstoy, His Life and Work.*
27. *Tolstoy's Letters*, December 15–18, 1885, vol. II, p. 395.
28. *Tolstoy's Letters*, June 6–7, 1885, vol. II, pp. 383–384.
29. *Tolstoy's Diaries*, July 7–19, 1884, vol. I, p. 221.
30. *Tolstoy's Letters*, October 18, 1885, vol. II, p. 387.
31. *Tolstoy's Letters*, December 9–15, 1885, vol. II, p. 391.
32. *Tolstoy's Letters*, December 9–15, 1885, vol. II, p. 391.
33. *Tolstoy's Letters*, December 9–15, 1885, vol. II, p. 392.
34. *Tolstoy Remembered*, p. 210.
35. *Tolstoy Remembered*, pp. 210–211.
36. *Tolstoy's Letters*, December 15–18, 1885, vol. II, p. 399.
37. *Married to Tolstoy*, p. 125.
38. *Anna Karenina*, p. 853.
39. *A la recherche du temps perdu*, tome II, pp. 65–66.

14. The Death of Ivan Ilych

1. *Married to Tolstoy*, p. 126.
2. *The Cossacks (The Death of Ivan Ilyich)*, p. 106.
3. *The Cossacks (The Death of Ivan Ilyich)*, pp. 115–116.
4. *The Cossacks (The Death of Ivan Ilyich)*, p. 128.

5. *The Cossacks (The Death of Ivan Ilyich)*, p. 128.
6. *The Cossacks (The Death of Ivan Ilyich)*, p. 150.
7. *The Cossacks (The Death of Ivan Ilyich)*, p. 130.
8. *The Cossacks (The Death of Ivan Ilyich)*, p. 147.
9. *The Cossacks (The Death of Ivan Ilyich)*, p. 156.
10. *The Diaries of Sofia Tolstoy*, October 25, 1886, p. 76.
11. *The Cossacks (The Death of Ivan Ilyich)*, p. 131.
12. *The Cossacks (The Death of Ivan Ilyich)*, p. 144.
13. *The Cossacks (The Death of Ivan Ilyich)*, p. 117.
14. *The Cossacks (The Death of Ivan Ilyich)*, p. 118.
15. *The Cossacks (The Death of Ivan Ilyich)*, p. 121.
16. *The Cossacks (The Death of Ivan Ilyich)*, p. 117.
17. *The Cossacks (The Death of Ivan Ilyich)*, p. 132.
18. *The Cossacks (The Death of Ivan Ilyich)*, p. 160–161.
19. *The Diaries of Sofia Tolstoy*, August 4, 1887, p. 86.
20. *The Diaries of Sofia Tolstoy*, October 25, 1886, p. 75.
21. *The Diaries of Sofia Tolstoy*, October 25, 1886, p. 75.
22. *The Diaries of Sofia Tolstoy*, October 25, 1886, p. 75.
23. *The Diaries of Sofia Tolstoy*, October 25, 1886, p. 76.
24. *The Diaries of Sofia Tolstoy*, October 30, 1886, p. 77.

15. The Power of Darkness

1. *The Diaries of Sofia Tolstoy*, March 3, 1887, pp. 78–79.
2. *Tolstoy's Letters*, March 1, 1887, vol. II, p. 415.
3. *The Diaries of Sofia Tolstoy*, March 14, 1887, p. 80.
4. *Tolstoy's Letters*, March 5, 1887, vol. II, p. 416.
5. *Théâtre complet*, pp. 17–19.
6. *Théâtre complet*, p. 18.
7. *Tolstoy's Letters*, April 21, 1887, vol. II, p. 418.
8. *Tolstoy's Letters*, May 31, 1885, vol. II, p. 419.
9. *Tolstoy's Letters*, August 1887, vol. II, p. 421.
10. *Tolstoy's Letters*, October 1887, vol. II, p. 422.
11. *Tolstoy's Letters*, October 1887, vol. II, p. 422.
12. *Tolstoy's Letters*, October 1887, vol. II, p. 423.
13. *Tolstoy's Letters*, October 1887, vol. II, p. 427.
14. *The Diaries of Sofia Tolstoy*, June 18, 1887, p. 82.
15. *The Diaries of Sofia Tolstoy*, March 9, 1887, p. 80.
16. *The Diaries of Sofia Tolstoy*, March 9, 1887, p. 80.
17. *The Diaries of Sofia Tolstoy*, July 19, 1887, p. 85.
18. *The Diaries of Sofia Tolstoy*, July 19, 1887, p. 85.
19. *The Diaries of Sofia Tolstoy*, March 6, 1887, p. 79.
20. *The Diaries of Sofia Tolstoy*, June 18, 1887, p. 82.
21. *The Diaries of Sofia Tolstoy*, March 9, 1887, p. 79.
22. *The Diaries of Sofia Tolstoy*, June 18, 1887, p. 81.
23. *The Diaries of Sofia Tolstoy*, June 18, 1887, p. 82.
24. *The Diaries of Sofia Tolstoy*, June 18, 1887, p. 82.
25. *The Diaries of Sofia Tolstoy*, July 2, 1887, p. 84.
26. *The Diaries of Sofia Tolstoy*, July 2, 1887, p. 84.

27. *The Diaries of Sofia Tolstoy*, August 19, 1887, p. 86.
28. *The Diaries of Sofia Tolstoy*, August 25, 1887, p. 86.

16. The Kreutzer Sonata

1. *Tolstoy's Diaries*, March 21, 1889, vol. I, p. 244.
2. *Tolstoy's Diaries*, November 1, 1889, vol. I, p. 267.
3. *Tolstoy's Diaries*, December 1, 1889, vol. I, p. 271.
4. *Tolstoy's Diaries*, February 20, 1889, vol. I, p. 240.
5. *Tolstoy's Diaries*, March 27, 1889, vol. I, p. 244.
6. *Tolstoy's Letters*, March 29, 1889, vol. II, p. 443.
7. *Tolstoy's Diaries*, April 6, 1889, vol. I, p. 245.
8. *Journaux et carnets*, tome I, 6 avril 1889, p. 942.
9. *Journaux et carnets*, tome I, 31 mai 1889, p. 1097.
10. *Tolstoy's Diaries*, May 5, 1889, vol. I, p. 249.
11. *Journaux et carnets*, tome I, 15 mai 1889, p. 961.
12. *Journaux et carnets*, tome I, 3 juillet 1889, p. 985.
13. *Journaux et carnets*, tome I, 14 juillet 1889, p. 989.
14. *Tolstoy's Diaries*, July 4, 1889, vol. I, p. 254.
15. *Tolstoy's Diaries*, July 4, 1889, vol. I, p. 254.
16. *Tolstoy's Diaries*, July 24, 1889, vol. I, p. 257.
17. *Tolstoy's Letters*, August 22, 1889, vol. II, p. 446.
18. *Tolstoy's Diaries*, August 2, 1889, vol. I, p. 258.
19. *Journaux et carnets*, tome I, 21 juin 1889, p. 980.
20. *Tolstoy's Diaries*, September 21, 1889, vol. I, p. 264.
21. *Tolstoy's Diaries*, October 10, 1889, vol. I, p. 265.
22. *Tolstoy's Diaries*, August 29, 1889, vol. I, p. 261.
23. Shklovsky, *Lev Tolstoy*.
24. *The Kreutzer Sonata*, *The Devil and Other Tales* (Cent. Ed., vol. 16), p. 125.
25. *The Kreutzer Sonata*, *The Devil and Other Tales* (Cent. Ed., vol. 16), p. 131.
26. *The Kreutzer Sonata*, *The Devil and Other Tales* (Cent. Ed., vol. 16), p. 139.
27. *The Kreutzer Sonata*, *The Devil and Other Tales* (Cent. Ed., vol. 16), p. 140.
28. *What Then Must We Do?* (Cent. Ed., vol. 14), p. 351.
29. *What Then Must We Do?* (Cent. Ed., vol. 14), p. 354.
30. *What Is Art? and Essays on Art* (Cent. Ed., vol. 18), p. 326.
31. *The Kreutzer Sonata*, *The Devil and Other Tales* (Cent. Ed., vol. 16), p. 150.
32. *The Kreutzer Sonata*, *The Devil and Other Tales* (Cent. Ed., vol. 16), p. 170.
33. *The Kreutzer Sonata*, *The Devil and Other Tales* (Cent. Ed., vol. 16), p. 171.
34. *The Kreutzer Sonata*, *The Devil and Other Tales* (Cent. Ed., vol. 16), p. 162.
35. *Souvenirs et récits*, p. 1152.
36. *Souvenirs et récits*, p. 1149.
37. *The Kreutzer Sonata*, *The Devil and Other Tales* (Cent. Ed., vol. 16), p. 186.
38. *The Kreutzer Sonata*, *The Devil and Other Tales* (Cent. Ed., vol. 16), p. 208.
39. *Tolstoy's Letters*, April 15, 1891, vol. II, p. 478.
40. *Souvenirs et récits*, p. 1055.
41. *Journaux et carnets*, tome I, 2 novembre 1889, p. 1065.
42. *Tolstoy's Diaries*, December 6, 1889, vol. I, p. 272.
43. *Tolstoy's Letters*, January 15, 1890, vol. II, p. 451.
44. *Souvenirs et récits*, p. 1150.

45. *Tolstoy's Letters*, September 16, 1890, vol. II, p. 469.
46. *Souvenirs et récits*, p. 1160.
47. *Souvenirs et récits*, p. 1160.
48. *Tolstoy's Letters*, October 1887, vol. II, p. 434.

17. The Aftereffects of The Kreutzer

1. *Tolstoy's Diaries*, December 27, 1889, vol. I, p. 273.
2. *Tolstoy's Letters*, January 15, 1890, vol. II, p. 451.
3. *Journaux et carnets*, tome II, 4 janvier 1890, p. 5.
4. *Tolstoy's Diaries*, January 21, 1890, vol. I, p. 276.
5. *Journaux et carnets*, tome II, 21 janvier 1890, p. 10.
6. *Journaux et carnets*, tome II, 16 février 1890, p. 16.
7. *Journaux et carnets*, tome II, 21 janvier 1890, p. 10.
8. *Journaux et carnets*, tome II, 15 janvier 1890, p. 7.
9. *Journaux et carnets*, tome II, 15 janvier 1890, p. 7.
10. *Tolstoy's Diaries*, February 3, 1890, vol. I, p. 276.
11. *Tolstoy's Diaries*, February 5, 1890, vol. I, p. 276.
12. *Tolstoy's Diaries*, November 20, 1889, vol. I, p. 270.
13. *Tolstoy's Diaries*, February 27, 1890, vol. I, p. 278.
14. *Tolstoy's Diaries*, February 27, 1890, vol. I, p. 278.
15. *Tolstoy's Letters*, March 25, 1890, vol. II, p. 455.
16. *Tolstoy's Letters*, April 9, 1890, vol. II, p. 457.
17. *Tolstoy's Letters*, May 25–26, 1890, vol. II, p. 459.
18. *Tolstoy's Letters*, July 31, 1890, vol. II, p. 464.
19. *Tolstoy's Letters*, March 8, 1890, vol. II, p. 453.
20. *Tolstoy's Letters*, November 30, 1890, vol. II, p. 470.
21. *Journaux et carnets*, tome II, 10 mai 1890, p. 40.
22. *Tolstoy's Diaries*, May 9, 1890, vol. I, p. 283.
23. *Journaux et carnets*, tome II, 3 septembre 1890, pp. 88–89.
24. *Tolstoy's Diaries*, September 3, 1890, vol. I, p. 293.
25. *Tolstoy's Diaries*, July 15, 1890, vol. I, p. 289.
26. *Tolstoy's Diaries*, August 18, 1890, vol. I, p. 291.
27. *Journaux et carnets*, tome II, 19 août 1890, p. 81.
28. *Journaux et carnets*, tome II, 19 août 1890, p. 144.
29. *Journaux et carnets*, tome II, 19 août 1890, p. 81.
30. *Journaux et carnets*, tome II, 10 août 1890, p. 143.
31. *Tolstoy's Diaries*, March 18, 1890, vol. I, p. 279.
32. *Tolstoy's Diaries*, July 28, 1890, vol. I, p. 290.
33. *Tolstoy's Diaries*, August 20, 1890, vol. I, p. 291.
34. *Tolstoy's Diaries*, August 21, 1890, vol. I, p. 291.
35. *Tolstoy's Diaries*, November 21, 1890, vol. I, p. 297.
36. *Journaux et carnets*, tome II, 20 décembre 1890, p. 122.
37. *Tolstoy's Diaries*, October 31, 1890, vol. I, p. 296.
38. *Journaux et carnets*, tome II, 19 novembre 1890, p. 116.
39. *Journaux et carnets*, tome II, 27 novembre 1890, p. 150.
40. *Tolstoy's Diaries*, May 22, 1890, vol. I, p. 284.
41. *Tolstoy's Diaries*, December 31, 1890, vol. I, p. 299.

42. *The Diaries of Sofia Tolstoy*, November 20, 1890, p. 88.
43. *The Diaries of Sofia Tolstoy*, November 20, 1890, p. 88.
44. *Tolstoy's Diaries*, August 15, 1890, vol. I, p. 291.
45. *The Diaries of Sofia Tolstoy*, December 17, 1890, p. 95.
46. *The Diaries of Sofia Tolstoy*, November 20, 1890, p. 88.
47. *The Diaries of Sofia Tolstoy*, December 10, 1890, p. 91.
48. *The Diaries of Sofia Tolstoy*, December 10, 1890, p. 91.
49. *The Diaries of Sofia Tolstoy*, December 9, 1890, p. 90.
50. *Tolstoy's Diaries*, June 25, 1890, vol. I, p. 286.
51. *The Diaries of Sofia Tolstoy*, December 13, 1890, p. 93.
52. *The Diaries of Sofia Tolstoy*, December 16, 1890, p. 95.
53. *The Diaries of Sofia Tolstoy*, December 11, 1890, p. 92.
54. *The Diaries of Sofia Tolstoy*, December 11–16, 1890, pp. 92–94.
55. *The Diaries of Sofia Tolstoy*, December 16, 1890, p. 94.
56. *Tolstoy's Diaries*, June 18, 1890, vol. I, p. 285.
57. *Tolstoy's Diaries*, July 6, 1890, vol. I, p. 288.
58. *Tolstoy's Diaries*, July 20, 1890, vol. I, p. 289.
59. *The Diaries of Sofia Tolstoy*, December 16, 1890, p. 95.
60. *The Diaries of Sofia Tolstoy*, December 16, 1890, p. 95.
61. *The Diaries of Sofia Tolstoy*, December 14, 1890, p. 93.
62. *Journal de la comtesse Léon Tolstoï*, tome I, 25 décembre 1890, p. 228.
63. *The Diaries of Sofia Tolstoy*, December 27, 1890, p. 98.
64. *Journaux et carnets*, tome II, 27 décembre 1890, p. 124.
65. *The Diaries of Sofia Tolstoy*, January 18, 1891, p. 107.
66. *Tolstoy's Diaries*, February 14, 1891, vol. I, p. 301.
67. *The Diaries of Sofia Tolstoy*, February 15, 1891, p. 114.
68. *The Diaries of Sofia Tolstoy*, February 12, 1891, p. 114.
69. *Tolstoy's Letters*, April 15, 1891, vol. II, p. 478.
70. *Tolstoy's Diaries*, April 18, 1891, vol. I, p. 307.
71. *Tolstoy's Diaries*, March 5, 1891, vol. I, p. 304.
72. *Tolstoy's Diaries*, March 9, 1891, vol. I, p. 304.
73. *The Diaries of Sofia Tolstoy*, March 10, 1891, p. 120.
74. *The Diaries of Sofia Tolstoy*, March 10, 1891, p. 121.
75. *Tolstoy's Diaries*, March 9, 1891, vol. I, p. 304.
76. *The Diaries of Sofia Tolstoy*, August 15, 1891, p. 161.
77. *The Diaries of Sofia Tolstoy*, March 21, 1891, p. 123.
78. *The Diaries of Sofia Tolstoy*, March 10, 1891, p. 121.
79. *Journaux et carnets*, tome II, 5 janvier 1891, p. 159.
80. *The Diaries of Sofia Tolstoy*, March 10, 1891, p. 191.
81. *The Diaries of Sofia Tolstoy*, June 9, 1891, p. 148.
82. *Tolstoy's Letters*, January 27, 1891, vol. II, p. 475.
83. *Tolstoy's Diaries*, January 26, 1891, vol. I, pp. 300–301.
84. *Journaux et carnets*, tome II, 16 février 1891, p. 168.
85. *Tolstoy's Diaries*, February 17, 1891, vol. I, p. 303.
86. *Tolstoy's Diaries*, May 2, 1891, vol. I, p. 307.
87. *Tolstoy's Diaries*, February 11, 1891, vol. I, p. 301.
88. *Tolstoy's Diaries*, April 18, 1891, vol. I, p. 307.
89. *Tolstoy's Diaries*, April 18, 1891, vol. I, p. 307.
90. *Tolstoy's Diaries*, June 2, 1891, vol. I, p. 309.

91. *The Diaries of Sofia Tolstoy*, June 3, 1891, p. 144.
92. *Journaux et carnets*, tome II, 13 juillet 1891, p. 206.
93. *Journaux et carnets*, tome II, 13 septembre 1891, p. 213.
94. *Tolstoy's Diaries*, June 25, 1891, vol. I, p. 311.
95. *Tolstoy's Diaries*, June 25, 1891, vol. I, p. 312.
96. *Tolstoy's Diaries*, July 14, 1891, vol. I, p. 312.
97. *The Diaries of Sofia Tolstoy*, July 22, 1891, p. 155.
98. *The Diaries of Sofia Tolstoy*, July 22, 1891, p. 156.
99. *The Diaries of Sofia Tolstoy*, July 22, 1891, p. 157.
100. *The Diaries of Sofia Tolstoy*, July 27, 1891, p. 158.
101. *The Diaries of Sofia Tolstoy*, July 27, 1891, p. 159.
102. *The Diaries of Sofia Tolstoy*, August 12, 1891, p. 159.
103. *Tolstoy's Letters*, July 4, 1892, vol. II, pp. 480–481.
104. *Tolstoy's Diaries*, September 18, 1891, vol. I, p. 313.
105. *The Diaries of Sofia Tolstoy*, September 19, 1891, p. 164.
106. *Tolstoy's Diaries*, September 25, 1891, vol. I, p. 314.
107. *Journaux et carnets*, tome II, 25 septembre 1891, p. 218.
108. *Tolstoy's Diaries*, September 25, 1891, vol. I, p. 314.
109. *Tolstoy's Diaries*, October 24, 1891, vol. I, p. 315.
110. *Tolstoy's Diaries*, February 9, 1894, vol. I, p. 330.

IV: IMPATIENCE FOR THE KINGDOM OF GOD

18. Famine

1. *Tolstoy's Diaries*, April 29, 1898, vol. II, p. 458.
2. *The Diaries of Sofia Tolstoy*, October 8, 1891, p. 167.
3. *Tolstoy's Letters*, November 23, 1891, vol. II, p. 489.
4. *Tolstoy's Diaries*, November 26, 1891, vol. I, p. 316.
5. *Journaux et carnets*, tome II, 3 février 1892, p. 248.
6. *La Famine*. ("Une Question Terrible" is included in *La Famine*.)
7. *Tolstoy's Letters*, November 2, 1891, vol. II, p. 486.
8. *Tolstoy's Letters*, November 2, 1891, vol. II, p. 486.
9. *Tolstoy's Letters*, November 4, 1891, vol. II, p. 488.
10. *The Diaries of Sofia Tolstoy*, November 12, 1891, p. 170.
11. *Tolstoy's Diaries*, December 19, 1891, vol. I, p. 316.
12. *The Diaries of Sofia Tolstoy*, February 16, 1892, p. 171.
13. *The Diaries of Sofia Tolstoy*, February 16, 1892, p. 171.
14. *The Diaries of Sofia Tolstoy*, February 16, 1892, p. 172.
15. *The Diaries of Sofia Tolstoy*, February 16, 1892, p. 173.
16. *Tolstoy's Diaries*, February 3, 1892, vol. I, p. 317.
17. *The Diaries of Sofia Tolstoy*, February 16, 1892, p. 173.
18. Shklovsky, *Lev Tolstoy*, p. 628.
19. *Tolstoy's Letters*, September 14, 1891, vol. II, p. 483.
20. *The Kingdom of God and Peace Essays* (Cent. Ed., vol. 20), p. 82.
21. *Tolstoy's Diaries*, August 20, 1893, vol. I, p. 325.

22. *Tolstoy's Letters*, June 25, 1892, vol. II, p. 491.
23. *Tolstoy's Letters*, February 13, 1893, vol. II, p. 493.
24. *Tolstoy's Diaries*, May 26, 1892, vol. I, p. 318.
25. *Tolstoy's Diaries*, August 21, 1892, vol. I, p. 319.
26. *Tolstoy's Letters*, July 13, 1893, vol. II, p. 495.
27. *La Famine*, p. 113.
28. *La Famine*, p. 78.
29. *La Famine*, p. 95.
30. *Tolstoy's Diaries*, December 22, 1893, vol. I, p. 327.
31. *Tolstoy's Diaries*, December 22, 1893, vol. I, p. 327.

19. Master and Man

1. *Tolstoy's Diaries*, January 24, 1894, vol. I, p. 329.
2. *Tolstoy's Letters*, December 3, 1892, vol. II, p. 500.
3. *The Tolstoy Home*, p. 239.
4. *Tolstoy's Letters*, January 8, 1894, vol. II, p. 514.
5. *Tolstoy's Letters*, November 9, 1893, vol. II, p. 498.
6. *Tolstoy's Diaries*, March 23, 1894, vol. I, p. 330.
7. *Tolstoy's Letters*, March 12, 1895, vol. II, p. 515.
8. *Tolstoy's Diaries*, January 24, 1894, vol. I, p. 329.
9. *Tolstoy's Diaries*, January 24, 1894, vol. I, p. 329.
10. *Tolstoy's Diaries*, April 21, 1894, vol. I, p. 331.
11. *Tolstoy's Diaries*, January 24, 1894, vol. I, p. 329.
12. *Tolstoy's Diaries*, March 23, 1894, vol. I, p. 331.
13. *Journaux et carnets*, tome II, 24 janvier 1894, p. 324.
14. *Tolstoy's Diaries*, March 23, 1894, vol. I, p. 330.
15. *Tolstoy's Diaries*, July 19, 1894, vol. I, p. 336.
16. *Tolstoy's Diaries*, September 24, 1894, vol. I, p. 339.
17. *Journaux et carnets*, tome II, 18 août 1893, p. 349.
18. *Tolstoy's Diaries*, September 6, 1894, vol. I, p. 338.
19. *Ivan Ilych and Hadji Murad* (Cent, Ed., vol. 15).
20. *Ivan Ilych and Hadji Murad* (Cent. Ed., vol. 15).
21. *Tolstoy's Letters*,December 3, 1893, vol. II, p. 499.
22. *Tolstoy's Letters*, October 20, 1893, vol. II, p. 497.
23. *Tolstoy's Letters*, March 14, 1894, vol. II, p. 503.
24. *Journaux et carnets*, tome II, 25 septembre 1894, p. 361.
25. *Journaux et carnets*, tome II, 22 septembre 1894, p. 359.
26. *The Diaries of Sofia Tolstoy*, August 4, 1894, p. 175.
27. *The Diaries of Sofia Tolstoy*, November 7, 1894, p. 176.
28. *The Diaries of Sofia Tolstoy*, January 8, 1895, p. 179.
29. *The Diaries of Sofia Tolstoy*, August 2, 1893, p. 174.
30. *The Diaries of Sofia Tolstoy*, November 5, 1893, p. 174.
31. Tatyana Tolstoy, *Journal*, April 2, 1894, p. 214.
32. *The Diaries of Sofia Tolstoy*, February 21, 1895, p. 187.
33. *The Diaries of Sofia Tolstoy*, January 26, 1895, p. 185.
34. *Tolstoy's Diaries*, February 7, 1895, vol. II, p. 397.
35. *The Diaries of Sofia Tolstoy*, February 21, 1895, p. 188.

36. *The Diaries of Sofia Tolstoy*, February 5, 1895, p. 186.
37. *The Diaries of Sofia Tolstoy*, February 21, 1895, p. 188.
38. *The Diaries of Sofia Tolstoy*, February 21, 1895, p. 188.
39. *The Diaries of Sofia Tolstoy*, February 21, 1895, p. 189.
40. *Tolstoy's Diaries*, February 15, 1895, vol. II, p. 399.
41. *The Diaries of Sofia Tolstoy*, February 21, 1895, p. 189.
42. *The Diaries of Sofia Tolstoy*, February 21, 1895, p. 189.
43. *The Diaries of Sofia Tolstoy*, February 21, 1895, p. 190.
44. *The Diaries of Sofia Tolstoy*, February 21, 1895, p. 190.
45. *Tolstoy's Diaries*, February 15, 1895, vol. II, p. 400.
46. *Tolstoy's Letters*, February 14, 1895, vol. II, p. 514.
47. *The Diaries of Sofia Tolstoy*, February 23, 1895, p. 190.
48. *Tolstoy's Letters*, March 31, 1895, vol. II, p. 516.
49. *Married to Tolstoy*, p. 169.
50. *The Tragedy of Tolstoy*, p. 17.
51. *Ma vie avec mon père*, p. 46.
52. *Tolstoy's Letters*, March 31, 1895, vol. II, p. 516.
53. *The Tragedy of Tolstoy*, p. 20.
54. *Tolstoy's Letters*, March 31, 1895, vol. II, p. 517.
55. *Tolstoy's Diaries*, March 12, 1895, vol. II, p. 401.
56. *Tolstoy's Diaries*, February 26, 1895, vol. II, p. 401.
57. *Tolstoy's Letters*, March 31, 1895, vol. II, p. 517.
58. *Tolstoy's Diaries*, March 12, 1895, vol. II, p. 401.
59. *Tolstoy's Diaries*, March 12, 1895, vol. II, p. 401.
60. *Tolstoy's Letters*, March 31, 1895, vol. II, p. 516.
61. *Tolstoy's Diaries*, March 12, 1895, vol. II, p. 401.
62. *Tolstoy's Diaries*, March 27, 1895, vol. II, p. 403.
63. *Tolstoy's Diaries*, March 27, 1895, vol. II, p. 404.
64. *Tolstoy's Diaries*, April 10, 1895, vol. II, p. 405.
65. *Tolstoy's Letters*, April 26, 1895, vol. II, p. 517.
66. *Tolstoy's Diaries*, April 25, 1895, vol. II, p. 406.
67. *Journaux et carnets*, tome II, 26 avril 1895, p. 419.
68. *Journaux et carnets*, tome II, 7 septembre 1895, p. 448.
69. *Tolstoy's Diaries*, April 25, 1895, vol. II, p. 406.
70. *Journaux et carnets*, tome II, 5 janvier 1897, p. 568.
71. *Tolstoy's Letters*, September 10, 1895, vol. II, p. 522.
72. *Tolstoy's Letters*, September 10, 1895, vol. II, p. 522.
73. *Tolstoy's Diaries*, October 6, 1895, vol. II, p. 418.
74. *Tolstoy's Letters*, October 5, 1895, vol. II, p. 523.
75. *Tolstoy's Letters*, October 28, 1895, vol. II, p. 527.
76. *Tolstoy's Diaries*, November 5, 1895, vol. II, p. 420.
77. *Tolstoy's Diaries*, October 6, 1895, vol. II, p. 417.
78. *Tolstoy's Diaries*, November 7, 1895, vol. II, p. 420.
79. *Tolstoy's Letters*, October 16, 1895, vol. II, p. 524.
80. *Tolstoy's Letters*, October 27–30, 1895, vol. II, p. 527.
81. *Tolstoy's Letters*, December 18, 1896, vol. II, p. 552.
82. *Journaux et carnets*, tome II, 25 septembre 1895, p. 453.
83. *Journaux et carnets*, tome II, 7 décembe 1895, p. 471.

20. What Is Art?

1. *Tolstoy's Letters*, January 1896, vol. II, p. 533.
2. *Tolstoy's Diaries*, December 20, 1896, vol. II, p. 546.
3. *The Tolstoy Home*, p. 268.
4. *Tolstoy's Letters*, April 29, 1896, vol. II, p. 538.
5. *Tolstoy's Diaries*, February 27, 1896, vol. II, p. 424.
6. *Journaux et carnets*, tome II, 17 mai 1896, p. 513.
7. *Journaux et carnets*, tome II, 17 mai 1896, pp. 511–512.
8. *Journaux et carnets*, tome II, 3 mai 1896, p. 503.
9. *Tolstoy's Diaries*, May 17, 1896, vol. II, p. 426.
10. *Tolstoy's Diaries*, December 19–20, 1896, vol. II, p. 436.
11. *Tolstoy's Diaries*, May 17, 1896, vol. II, p. 427.
12. *Tolstoy's Diaries*, May 28, 1896, vol. II, p. 427.
13. *Tolstoy's Diaries*, June 19, 1896, vol. II, p. 428.
14. *Tolstoy's Diaries*, November 5, 1895, vol. II, p. 420.
15. *Tolstoy's Diaries*, May 5, 1896, vol. II, p. 425.
16. *Married to Tolstoy*, p. 175.
17. *Tolstoy's Diaries*, May 28, 1896, vol. II, p. 427.
18. *The Tolstoy Home*, p. 280.
19. *Tolstoy's Diaries*, July 19, 1896, vol. II, p. 429.
20. *Journaux et carnets*, tome II, 19 juillet 1896, pp. 520–521.
21. *Tolstoy's Diaries*, July 26, 1896, vol. II, p. 430.
22. *Tolstoy's Letters*, August 31, 1896, vol. II, p. 547.
23. *Tolstoy's Diaries*, July 26, 1896, vol. II, p. 430.
24. *Tolstoy's Diaries*, July 19, 1896, vol. II, p. 429.
25. *Tolstoy's Diaries*, July 19, 1896, vol. II, p. 429.
26. *Tolstoy's Diaries*, July 19, 1896, vol. II, p. 429.
27. Tolstoy, *His Life and Work*, p. 269.
28. *Tolstoy's Diaries*, July 31, 1896, vol. II, p. 430.
29. *Tolstoy's Diaries*, May 2, 1896, vol. II, p. 424.
30. *Tolstoy's Diaries*, June 6, 1896, vol. II, p. 428.
31. *Tolstoy's Diaries*, October 10, 1896, vol. II, p. 431.
32. *Tolstoy's Diaries*, November 17, 1896, vol. II, p. 434.
33. *Journaux et carnets*, tome II, 16 novembre 1896, p. 539.
34. *Tolstoy's Diaries*, November 17, 1896, vol. II, p. 434.
35. *Tolstoy's Diaries*, November 22, 1896, vol. II, p. 435.
36. *Journaux et carnets*, tome II, 25 novembre 1896, p. 543.
37. *Tolstoy's Letters*, November 13, 1896, vol. II, p. 551.
38. *Tolstoy's Diaries*, December 26, 1896, vol. II, p. 438.
39. *Tolstoy's Diaries*, December 21, 1896, vol. II, p. 438.
40. *Tolstoy's Diaries*, December 25, 1896, vol. II, p. 438.
41. *Journaux et carnets*, tome II, 26 décembre 1896, p. 550.
42. *Tolstoy's Diaries*, January 5–18, 1897, vol. II, p. 439.
43. *Tolstoy's Letters*, January 12, 1897, vol. II, p. 552.
44. *Tolstoy's Letters*, January 12, 1897, vol. II, p. 553.
45. *Tolstoy's Diaries*, January 6, 1897, vol. II, p. 439.
46. *Tolstoy's Letters*, February 1, 1897, vol. II, p. 555.

47. *Tolstoy's Letters*, February 1, 1897, vol. II, pp. 554–555.
48. *Tolstoy's Diaries*, February 4, 1897, vol. II, p. 440.
49. *Tolstoy's Diaries*, February 4, 1897, vol. II, p. 440.
50. *The Diaries of Sofia Tolstoy*, June 1, 1897, p. 191.
51. *Tolstoy's Diaries*, February 17, 1897, vol. II, p. 442.
52. *Tolstoy's Diaries*, February 4, 1897, vol. II, p. 441.
53. *Journaux et carnets*, tome II, 5 janvier 1897, p. 569.
54. *Journaux et carnets*, tome II, 25 février 1897, p. 580.
55. *Journaux et carnets*, tome II, 18 février 1897, p. 577.
56. *Journaux et carnets*, tome II, 25 février 1897, p. 578.
57. *Journaux et carnets*, tome II, 29 juillet 1897, p. 6.
58. *Journaux et carnets*, tome II, avril 1897, p. 624.
59. *Journaux et carnets*, tome II, 16 août 1897, p. 592.
60. *Tolstoy's Diaries*, May 16, 1897, vol. II, p. 444.
61. *Tolstoy's Letters*, May 12, 1897, vol. II, p. 557.
62. *Tolstoy's Diaries*, May 15, 1897, vol. II, p. 444.
63. *Tolstoy's Diaries*, May 18, 1897, vol. II, p. 444.
64. *Tolstoy's Letters*, May 19, 1897, vol. II, p. 558.
65. *Tolstoy's Letters*, May 19, 1897, vol. II, pp. 559–560.
66. *The Diaries of Sofia Tolstoy*, July 21, 1897, p. 217.
67. *The Diaries of Sofia Tolstoy*, June 5, 1897, p. 193.
68. *The Diaries of Sofia Tolstoy*, June 6, 1897, p. 194.
69. *The Diaries of Sofia Tolstoy*, July 21, 1897, p. 217.
70. *The Diaries of Sofia Tolstoy*, July 23, 1897, p. 219.
71. *The Diaries of Sofia Tolstoy*, June 6, 1897, p. 194.
72. *The Diaries of Sofia Tolstoy*, June 12, 1897, p. 198.
73. *The Diaries of Sofia Tolstoy*, June 21, 1897, p. 204.
74. *The Diaries of Sofia Tolstoy*, July 25, 1897, p. 221.
75. *The Diaries of Sofia Tolstoy*, July 3, 1897, p. 210.
76. *Tolstoy Remembered*, pp. 225–227.
77. *Tolstoy Remembered*, p. 227.
78. *Journaux et carnets*, tome II, 17 mai 1897, p. 586.
79. *Journaux et carnets*, tome II, fin de mai 1897, p. 587.
80. *Tolstoy's Diaries*, July 16, 1897, vol. II, pp. 444–445.
81. *Tolstoy's Diaries*, August 7, 1897, vol. II, p. 445.
82. *Tolstoy's Diaries*, August 25, 1897, vol. II, p. 446.
83. *Tolstoy's Diaries*, September 19, 1897, vol. II, p. 446.
84. *The Diaries of Sofia Tolstoy*, September 19, 1897, p. 244.
85. *Tolstoy's Diaries*, September 22, 1897, vol. II, p. 447.
86. *The Diaries of Sofia Tolstoy*, September 26, 1897, p. 245.
87. *The Diaries of Sofia Tolstoy*, October 6, 1897, p. 249.
88. *The Diaries of Sofia Tolstoy*, October 10, 1897, p. 250.
89. *Tolstoy's Diaries*, October 14, 1897, vol. II, p. 447.
90. *The Diaries of Sofia Tolstoy*, October 21, 1897, p. 253.
91. *The Diaries of Sofia Tolstoy*, October 23, 1897, p. 254.
92. *The Diaries of Sofia Tolstoy*, October 25, 1897, p. 254.
93. *Journaux et carnets*, tome II, 21 octobre 1897, p. 600.
94. *The Diaries of Sofia Tolstoy*, November 7, 1897, p. 258.
95. *Tolstoy's Diaries*, November 20, 1897, vol. II, p. 450.

96. *Tolstoy's Diaries*, December 2, 1897, vol. II, p. 451.
97. *Tolstoy's Diaries*, December 2, 1897, vol. II, p. 451; *Journaux et carnets*, tome II, 2 décembre 1897, p. 611.
98. *Journaux et carnets*, tome II, 28 novembre 1897, pp. 609–610.
99. *Tolstoy's Diaries*, December 7, 1897, vol. II, p. 542.
100. *Journaux et carnets*, tome II, 12 décembre 1897, p. 613.
101. *Tolstoy's Diaries*, December 3, 1897, vol. II, p. 452.
102. *Tolstoy's Letters*, October 17–29, 1860, vol. I, p. 142.
103. *Tolstoy's Letters*, May 28, 1889, vol. II, p. 445.
104. *Le Monde de Tolstoï.*
105. *What Is Art? and Essays on Art* (Cent. Ed., vol. 18), p. 120.
106. *What Is Art? and Essays on Art* (Cent. Ed., vol. 18), p. 124.
107. *What Is Art? and Essays on Art* (Cent. Ed., vol. 18), p. 124.
108. *What Is Art? and Essays on Art* (Cent. Ed., vol. 18), p. 125.
109. *What Is Art? and Essays on Art* (Cent. Ed., vol. 18), p. 129.
110. *What Is Art? and Essays on Art* (Cent. Ed., vol. 18), pp. 157–158.
111. *What Is Art? and Essays on Art* (Cent. Ed., vol. 18), p. 217.
112. *What Is Art? and Essays on Art* (Cent. Ed., vol. 18), p. 219.
113. *What Is Art? and Essays on Art* (Cent. Ed., vol. 18), p. 227.
114. *What Is Art? and Essays on Art* (Cent. Ed., vol. 18), p. 228.
115. *What Is Art? and Essays on Art* (Cent. Ed., vol. 18), p. 228.
116. *What Is Art? and Essays on Art* (Cent. Ed., vol. 18), p. 234.
117. *What Is Art? and Essays on Art* (Cent. Ed., vol. 18), p. 240.
118. *What Is Art? and Essays on Art* (Cent. Ed., vol. 18), p. 241.
119. *What Is Art? and Essays on Art* (Cent. Ed., vol. 18), p. 242.
120. *What Is Art? and Essays on Art* (Cent. Ed., vol. 18), p. 246.
121. André Suarès, *Léon Tolstoï*, p. 24.
122. *What Is Art? and Essays on Art* (Cent. Ed., vol. 18), p. 248.
123. *Tolstoy's Diaries*, December 19–20, 1896, vol. II, p. 437.
124. *What Is Art? and Essays on Art* (Cent. Ed., vol. 18), p. 264.
125. *What Is Art? and Essays on Art* (Cent. Ed., vol. 18), pp. 269–270.
126. *What Is Art? and Essays on Art* (Cent. Ed., vol. 18), p. 271.
127. *What Is Art? and Essays on Art* (Cent. Ed., vol. 18), pp. 277–279.
128. *What Is Art? and Essays on Art* (Cent. Ed., vol. 18), pp. 286–287.
129. *What Is Art? and Essays on Art* (Cent. Ed., vol. 18), p. 288.

21. Resurrection

1. *Tolstoy's Diaries*, March 21, 1898, vol. II, p. 456.
2. *Tolstoy's Diaries*, August 3, 1898, vol. II, p. 460.
3. *Tolstoy's Letters*, March 11, 1898, vol. II, p. 566.
4. *Tolstoy's Diaries*, December 29, 1897, vol. II, p. 453.
5. *Tolstoy's Diaries*, March 19, 1898, vol. II, p. 456.
6. *Tolstoy's Letters*, April 19, 1898, vol. II, p. 570.
7. *Tolstoy's Diaries*, April 27, 1898, vol. II, p. 457.
8. *Journaux et carnets*, tome II, 9 mai 1898, p. 654.
9. *Tolstoy's Diaries*, June 12, 1898, vol. II, p. 458.
10. *Journaux et carnets*, tome II, 11 mai 1898, p. 655.

11. *Tolstoy's Letters*, May 6, 1898, vol. II, p. 572.
12. *Journaux et carnets*, tome II, 19 février 1898, p. 641.
13. *Journaux et carnets*, tome II, 12 juin 1898, p. 659.
14. *Tolstoy's Diaries*, July 17, 1898, vol. II, p. 460.
15. *Tolstoy's Diaries*, July 17, 1898, vol. II, p. 460.
16. *Journaux et carnets*, tome II, 19 mars 1901, p. 838.
17. *Journaux et carnets*, tome II, 20 juillet 1898, p. 665.
18. *Tolstoy's Diaries*, July 28–29, 1898, vol. II, pp. 465–466.
19. *Tolstoy's Diaries*, July 28–29, 1898, vol. II, p. 464.
20. *Tolstoy's Diaries*, July 28–29, 1898, vol. II, p. 467.
21. *Tolstoy's Diaries*, July 28–29, 1898, vol. II, p. 467.
22. *Tolstoy's Letters*, July 14, 1898, vol. II, p. 573.
23. *The Diaries of Sofia Tolstoy*, August 26, 1897, p. 231.
24. *Tolstoy's Letters*, October 15, 1898, vol. II, p. 574.
25. *Tolstoy's Letters*, October 16, 1898, vol. II, p. 575.
26. *Tolstoy's Diaries*, November 2, 1898, vol. II, p. 462.
27. *The Tragedy of Tolstoy*, p. 78.
28. *Résurrection* (Pléiade), p. 1668.
29. *Europe*, July 1928, p. 113.
30. *Tolstoy's Diaries*, November 2, 1898, vol. II, p. 462.
31. *Tolstoy's Diaries*, June 26, 1899, vol. II, p. 469.
32. *Tolstoy's Diaries*, January 2, 1899, vol. II, p. 468.
33. *Tolstoy's Diaries*, March 19, 1901, vol. II, p. 492.
34. *Tolstoy's Diaries*, October 27, 1899, vol. II, p. 472.
35. *Tolstoy's Diaries*, December 18, 1899, vol. II, p. 472.
36. *Tolstoy's Diaries*, December 18, 1899, vol. II, p. 472.
37. *Résurrection* (Pléiade), p. 1666.
38. *Un cas de conscience*, p. 518.
39. *Tolstoy's Diaries*, June 19, 1896, vol. II, p. 428.
40. *Tolstoy's Diaries*, February 11, 1890, vol. I, p. 277.
41. *Tolstoy's Diaries*, June 14, 1890, vol. I, p. 285.
42. *Résurrection* (Pléiade), p. 1548.
43. *Résurrection* (Pléiade), p. 1574.
44. *Resurrection*, p. 80.
45. *Resurrection*, pp. 73–74.
46. Shklovsky, *Lev Tolstoy*, p. 639.
47. *Resurrection*, p. 43.
48. *Resurrection*, p. 45.
49. *Resurrection*, p. 76.
50. *Resurrection*, p. 22.
51. *Resurrection*, p. 219.
52. *Resurrection*, p. 218.
53. *Resurrection*, p. 201.
54. *Resurrection*, p. 200.
55. *Resurrection*, p. 220.
56. *Resurrection*, p. 397.
57. *Resurrection*, p. 398.
58. *Resurrection*, p. 561.
59. *Resurrection*, p. 475.

60. *Resurrection*, p. 519.
61. *Resurrection*, p. 519.
62. *Resurrection*, p. 552.
63. *Resurrection*, pp. 553–554.
64. *Resurrection*, p. 566.
65. *Tolstoy's Diaries*, January 8, 1900, vol. II, p. 474.
66. *Les rayons de l'aube*, p. 389.
67. *Tolstoy's Diaries*, January 16, 1900, vol. II, p. 475.
68. *Tolstoy's Diaries*, January 27, 1900, vol. II, p. 476.
69. *Plays* (Cent. Ed., vol. 17).
70. *Tolstoy's Diaries*, March 13, 1900, vol. II, p. 476.
71. *Tolstoy's Letters*, March 23, 1900, vol. II, p. 586.
72. *Tolstoy's Letters*, March 23, 1900, vol. II, p. 586.
73. *Tolstoy's Diaries*, March 24, 1900, vol. II, p. 477.
74. *Tolstoy's Diaries*, April 6–May 5, 1900, vol. II, pp. 477–478.
75. *Tolstoy's Diaries*, June 23, 1900, vol. II, p. 479.
76. *Journaux et carnets*, tome II, 12 juillet 1900, p. 759.
77. *Journaux et carnets*, tome II, 7 août 1900, p. 763.
78. *Journaux et carnets*, tome II, 13 mars 1900, p. 748.
79. *Journaux et carnets*, tome II, 26 novembre 1900, p. 792.
80. *Tolstoy's Diaries*, August 21, 1900, vol. II, p. 480.
81. *Tolstoy's Diaries*, August 21, 1900, vol. II, p. 480.
82. *Tolstoy's Letters*, February 9, 1900, vol. II, p. 586.
83. *Tolstoy's Diaries*, December 15, 1900, vol. II, p. 487.
84. *Tolstoy's Diaries*, December 19, 1900, vol. II, p. 487.
85. *Tolstoy's Diaries*, December 20, 1900, vol. II, p. 488.
86. *Journaux et carnets*, tome II, juillet 1900, p. 814.
87. *Tolstoy's Diaries*, November 14, 1900, vol. II, p. 485.
88. *Tolstoy's Diaries*, March 19–31, 1884, vol. I, p. 205.
89. *Tolstoy's Diaries*, November 23, 1900, vol. II, p. 485.
90. *Tolstoy's Diaries*, December 15, 1900, vol. II, p. 487.
91. *Tolstoy's Diaries*, December 19, 1900, vol. II, p. 487.

22. Excommunication

1. *Appel aux dirigeants*, pp. 226–229.
2. *Léon Tolstoï et ses contemporains*, p. 183.
3. *The Kingdom of God and Peace Essays* (Cent. Ed., vol. 20).
4. *Writings on Civil Disobedience and Non-Violence*, p. 135.
5. *Writings on Civil Disobedience and Non-Violence*, p. 135.
6. *Writings on Civil Disobedience and Non-Violence*, p. 153.
7. *Appel aux dirigeants*, p. 27.
8. *Appel aux dirigeants*, p. 226.
9. *The Truth About My Father*.
10. *Tolstoy's Diaries*, March 31, 1901, vol. II, p. 493.
11. *Appel aux dirigeants*, p. 232.
12. *Appel aux dirigeants*, p. 234.
13. *Appel aux dirigeants*, p. 239.

14. *Appel aux dirigeants*, p. 234.
15. *Tolstoy's Diaries*, March 19, 1901, vol. II, p. 492.
16. *Tolstoy's Diaries*, March 19, 1901, vol. II, p. 492.
17. *Evolution religieuse de Tolstoï.*
18. *Appel aux dirigeants*, p. 228.
19. *On Life and Essays on Religion* (Cent. Ed., vol. 12), p. 218.
20. *Appel aux dirigeants*, p. 228.
21. *On Life and Essays on Religion* (Cent. Ed., vol. 12), p. 219.
22. *A Confession*, p. 72.
23. *Sevastopol*, p. 75.
24. *On Life and Essays on Religion* (Cent. Ed., vol. 12), p. 225.
25. *Journaux et carnets*, tome II, 10 avril 1902, p. 896.
26. *Appel aux dirigeants*, p. 254.
27. *Appel aux dirigeants*, p. 254.
28. *Appel aux dirigeants*, p. 255.

23. The Crimea

1. *Tolstoy's Diaries*, July 16, 1901, vol. II, p. 496.
2. Shklovsky, *Lev Tolstoy*, p. 667.
3. *Tolstoy's Letters*, October 1901, vol. II, p. 605.
4. *Léon Tolstoï et ses contemporains*, p. 223.
5. *Tolstoy's Diaries*, November 29, 1901, vol. II, p. 497.
6. *Writings on Civil Disobedience and Non-Violence*, p. 39.
7. *Writings on Civil Disobedience and Non-Violence*, p. 46.
8. *Writings on Civil Disobedience and Non-Violence*, p. 37
9. *Tolstoy's Letters*, January 16, 1902, vol. II, p. 611.
10. *Tolstoy's Letters*, January 16, 1902, vol. II, p. 612.
11. *Tolstoy's Letters*, January 16, 1902, vol. II, p. 613.
12. *Tolstoy's Letters*, April 25, 1902, vol. II, p. 616.
13. *Tolstoy's Letters*, June 2, 1902, vol. II, p. 620.
14. Shklovsky, *Lev Tolstoy*, p. 676.
15. *Journaux et carnets*, tome II, p. 1342.
16. *Reminiscences of Tolstoy, Chekhov and Andreev.*
17. *The Tragedy of Tolstoy*, p. 53.
18. Tatiana Tolstoï, *Journal*, 9 décembre 1902, p. 265.
19. Shklovsky, *Lev Tolstoy*, p. 673.
20. *The Tragedy of Tolstoy*, p. 64.
21. *Journaux et carnets*, tome II, 22 janvier 1902, p. 886.
22. *Journaux et carnets*, tome II, 10 janvier 1902, p. 888.
23. *Journaux et carnets*, tome II, 22 janvier 1902, p. 886.
24. *Journaux et carnets*, tome II, 18 juin 1903, p. 993.
25. *Tolstoy's Diaries*, May 25–26–27, 1902, vol. II, p. 501.
26. *Journaux et carnets*, tome II, 31 janvier 1902, p. 890.
27. *The Tragedy of Tolstoy*, p. 62.
28. *Tolstoy's Diaries*, November 4, 1902, vol. II, p. 503.
29. *Tolstoy's Diaries*, March 21, 1898, vol. II, p. 457.
30. Shklovsky, *Lev Tolstoy*, p. 679.

31. *Tolstoy's Letters*, August 20, 1902, vol. II, p. 623.
32. *Tolstoy's Letters*, December 20, 1902, vol. II, p. 624.
33. *Tolstoy's Letters*, January 8, 1903, vol. II, p. 627.
34. *Tolstoy's Letters*, January 26, 1903, vol. II, p. 629.
35. *Tolstoy's Letters*, February 23, 1903, vol. II, p. 630.
36. *Journaux et carnets*, tome II, 29 juillet 1904, p. 1091.
37. *Tolstoy's Letters*, May 6, 1903, vol. II, p. 631.
38. *Tolstoy's Diaries*, June 18, 1903, vol. II, p. 509.
39. *Dernières paroles*, 27 avril 1903.
40. *Tolstoy's Letters*, October 9, 1903, vol. II, p. 633.
41. *Recollections and Essays* (Cent. Ed., vol. 21), p. 382.
42. *Recollections and Essays* (Cent. Ed., vol. 21), p. 382.
43. *Recollections and Essays* (Cent. Ed., vol. 21), p. 309.
44. *Recollections and Essays* (Cent. Ed., vol. 21), pp. 338–340.
45. *Recollections and Essays* (Cent. Ed., vol. 21), p. 349.
46. *Recollections and Essays* (Cent. Ed., vol. 21), p. 356.
47. *Recollections and Essays* (Cent. Ed., vol. 21), p. 374.
48. *Recollections and Essays* (Cent. Ed., vol. 21), p. 382.
49. *The Tolstoy Home*, pp. 314–315.
50. *Tolstoy's Diaries*, April 9, 1891, vol. I, p. 306.
51. *Tolstoy's Letters*, November 27, 1903, vol. II, p. 634.
52. *Tolstoy's Letters*, November 27, 1903, vol. II, p. 634.
53. *Tolstoy's Letters*, December 22, 1903 (note I), vol. II, p. 636.
54. *Tolstoy's Letters*, December 27, 1903, vol. II, p. 636.
55. *Tolstoy's Diaries*, April 5, 1904, vol. II, p. 519.
56. *Journaux et carnets*, tome II, 12 juillet 1904, p. 1086.
57. *Tolstoy's Diaries*, March 14, 1903, vol. II, p. 507.
58. *Tolstoy's Diaries*, April 14, 1903, vol. II, p. 507.
59. *Journaux et carnets*, tome II, 13 février 1903, p. 972.
60. *Journaux et carnets*, tome II, 19 février 1903, p. 972.
61. *Journaux et carnets*, tome II, 16 juillet 1903, p. 1001.
62. *Tolstoy's Diaries*, November 14, 1903, vol. II, p. 512.
63. *Journaux et carnets*, tome II, 18 août 1904, p. 1099.
64. *Tolstoy's Letters*, December 18–19, 1903, vol. II, p. 635.
65. *Anna Karénine* (Pléiade), p. 51.
66. *Tolstoy's Diaries*, February 23, 1904, vol. II, p. 518.
67. *Recollections and Essays* (Cent. Ed., vol. 21), p. 204.
68. *Recollections and Essays* (Cent. Ed., vol. 21), p. 205.
69. *Recollections and Essays* (Cent. Ed., vol. 21), p. 258.
70. *Tolstoy's Diaries*, December 31, 1904, vol. II, p. 531.
71. *Tolstoy's Diaries*, July 29, 1904, vol. II, p. 525.
72. *Journaux et carnets*, tome II, 12 février 1904, p. 971.
73. *Tolstoy's Diaries*, August 2, 1904, vol. II, p. 526.
74. *Journaux et carnets*, tome II, 29 juillet 1904, p. 1092.
75. *Journaux et carnets*, tome II, 18 janvier 1904, p. 1034.
76. *Tolstoy's Diaries*, January 3, 1904, vol. II, p. 515.
77. *Tolstoy's Letters*, May 13, 1902, vol. II, p. 642.
78. *Journaux et carnets*, tome II, 12 juillet 1904, p. 1085.
79. *Tolstoy's Diaries*, March 7, 1904, vol. II, p. 518.

80. *Tolstoy's Diaries*, July 18, 1904, vol. II, p. 525.
81. *Tolstoy's Diaries*, August 2, 1904, vol. II, p. 526.
82. *Journaux et carnets*, tome II, 17 juillet 1904, p. 1087.

24. Tolstoy and the Revolutionaries

1. *Adepts in Self-Portraiture*.
2. *Tolstoy's Letters*, July 6–19, 1905, vol. II, p. 648.
3. *Tolstoy's Letters*, October 15, 1905, vol. II, p. 650.
4. *Tolstoy's Letters*, October 15, 1905, vol. II, p. 650.
5. *Tolstoy's Diaries*, March 2–3–4, 1855, vol. I, p. 101.
6. *Tolstoy's Letters*, March 8–15, 1881, vol. II, p. 347.
7. *Adepts in Self-Portraiture*.
8. *Tolstoy's Letters*, April 25, 1892, vol. II, p. 491.
9. *Adepts in Self-Portraiture*.
10. *Souvenirs et récits*, p. 1153.
11. *Tolstoy's Letters*, October 23, 1904, vol. II, p. 645.
12. *Tolstoy's Letters*, October 18, 1905, vol. II, p. 652.
13. *Reminiscences of Tolstoy, Chekhov and Andreev*, p. 47.
14. *The Kingdom of God and Peace Essays* (Cent. Ed., vol. 20).
15. *Aux hommes politiques*, p. 115.
16. *Aux hommes politiques*, p. 121.
17. *Aux hommes politiques*, p. 124.
18. *Aux hommes politiques*, p. 124.
19. *Aux hommes politiques*, p. 125.
20. *Aux hommes politiques*, p. 20.
21. *Tolstoy's Diaries*, August 3, 1898, vol. II, p. 460.
22. *La révolution russe*, p. 70.
23. *Sur la révolution*, p. 311.
24. *Sur la révolution*, p. 312.
25. *Sur la révolution*, p. 314.
26. *Tolstoy's Letters*, September 20, 1906, vol. II, p. 659.
27. *Sur la révolution*, p. 336.
28. *Sur la révolution*, p. 320.
29. *Sur la révolution*, p. 325.
30. *Sur la révolution*, p. 332.
31. *Sur la révolution*, p. 321.
32. *Sur la révolution*, p. 333.
33. *Sur la révolution*, p. 316.
34. *Sur la révolution*, p. 337.
35. *Conseils aux dirigés*, p. 231.
36. *Conseils aux dirigés*, p. 222.
37. *Conseils aux dirigés*, p. 231.
38. *Diary of a Writer*.
39. Lenin, *Collected Works*, vol. 17, p. 119.
40. *La révolution russe*, p. 54.
41. *Tolstoy's Letters*, March 22, 1906, vol. II, p. 657.
42. *La révolution russe*, p. 76.

43. *La révolution russe*, p. 76.
44. *La révolution russe*, p. 90.
45. *Guerre russo-japonaise*, p. 39.
46. *Tolstoy's Letters*, April 12–25, 1906, vol. II, p. 657.
47. *Genghis Khan et le téléphone*, p. 539.
48. *Genghis Khan et le téléphone*, p. 541.
49. *Genghis Khan et le téléphone*, p. 542.
50. *Genghis Khan et le téléphone*, p. 542.
51. *Journaux et carnets*, tome II, 1er janvier 1901, p. 827.
52. *Journaux et carnets*, tome II, 22 décembre 1904, p. 1127.
53. *Journaux et carnets*, tome II, 11 décembre 1904, p. 1123.
54. Lenin, *Collected Works*, vol. 15, p. 208.
55. Lenin, *Collected Works*, vol. 15, pp. 204–205.
56. Lenin, *Collected Works*, vol. 15, p. 202.
57. Lénine, *Sur l'art et la littérature*, tome III, p. 71.
58. Lenin, *Collected Works*, vol. 15, p. 202.
59. Lenin, *Collected Works*, vol. 15, p. 205.
60. Lenin, *Collected Works*, vol. 15, p. 205.
61. Lenin, *Collected Works*, vol. 15, p. 209.
62. Lenin, *Collected Works*, vol. 16, p. 323.
63. Lenin, *Collected Works*, vol. 16, p. 326.
64. Lenin, *Collected Works*, vol. 16, pp. 324–325.
65. Lenin, *Collected Works*, vol. 16, p. 325.
66. Lenin, *Collected Works*, vol. 16, p. 327.
67. Lenin, *Collected Works*, vol. 16, p. 327.
68. Lenin, *Collected Works*, vol. 16, p. 330.
69. Lenin, *Collected Works*, vol. 15, p. 402.
70. Lenin, *Collected Works*, vol. 16, p. 330.
71. Lenin, *Collected Works*, vol. 16, p. 331.
72. Lenin, *Collected Works*, vol. 16, p. 332.
73. Lenin, *Collected Works*, vol. 16, p. 332.
74. Lenin, *Collected Works*, vol. 16, p. 332.
75. Lenin, *Collected Works*, vol. 16, p. 353.
76. Lenin, *Collected Works*, vol. 16, p. 353.
77. Lenin, *Collected Works*, vol. 16, p. 354.
78. Lenin, *Collected Works*, vol. 16, p. 369.
79. Lenin, *Collected Works*, vol. 16, pp. 371–372.
80. Lenin, *Collected Works*, vol. 16, p. 372.
81. Lenin, *Collected Works*, vol. 17, p. 49.
82. Lenin, *Collected Works*, vol. 17, p. 49.
83. Lenin, *Collected Works*, vol. 17, p. 50.
84. *Anna Karenina*, p. 376.
85. Lenin, *Collected Works*, vol. 17, p. 50.
86. Lenin, *Collected Works*, vol. 17, p. 51.
87. Lenin, *Collected Works*, vol. 17, p. 51.
88. Lenin, *Collected Works*, vol. 17, p. 52.
89. Lenin, *Collected Works*, vol. 17, p. 52.
90. Lenin, *Collected Works*, vol. 17, p. 53.
91. *The Tolstoy Home*, p. 327.

92. *The Tolstoy Home*, p. 327.
93. *Tolstoy's Letters*, December 24, 1905, vol. II, p. 655.
94. *The Tragedy of Tolstoy*, p. 113.
95. *The Tragedy of Tolstoy*, p. 113.
96. *Tolstoy's Diaries*, September 2, 1906, vol. II, p. 555.
97. *Tolstoy's Diaries*, September 2, 1906, vol. II, pp. 555–556.
98. *Tolstoy's Letters*, November 26, 1906, vol. II, p. 661.
99. *Tolstoy's Letters*, November 15, 1905, vol. II, p. 650.
100. *Tolstoy's Diaries*, November 27, 1906, vol. II, p. 561.
101. *Tolstoy's Letters*, August 22, 1889, vol. II, p. 445.
102. *Tolstoy's Letters*, July 14, 1906, vol. II, p. 658.
103. *Tolstoy's Letters*, December 21, 1906, vol. II, p. 663.

25. The Man with Black Gloves

1. *The Tragedy of Tolstoy*, pp. 177–179.
2. *Tolstoy Remembered*, p. 218.
3. *Monsieur le comte*, p. 161.
4. *The Tragedy of Tolstoy*, p. 227.
5. *The Tragedy of Tolstoy*, p. 228.
6. *The Tragedy of Tolstoy*, p. 230.
7. *The Tragedy of Tolstoy*, p. 231.
8. *The Tragedy of Tolstoy*, p. 229.
9. *Monsieur le comte.*
10. *La tragédie de Tolstoï et de sa femme.*
11. *The Tragedy of Tolstoy*, p. 178.
12. *The Tragedy of Tolstoy*, p. 123.
13. "Tolstoï vu par un témoin," *Europe*, 1960, p. 141.
14. *The Tragedy of Tolstoy*, p. 178.
15. *Tolstoï est mort*, p. 152.
16. *Monsieur le comte*, p. 146.

26. Tolstoy, Starets of All the Russias

1. Lenin, *Collected Works*, Lenin, vol. 16, p. 324.
2. *Tolstoy's Letters*, September 17, 1907, vol. II, p. 670.
3. *The Tolstoy Home*, p. 316.
4. *The Tragedy of Tolstoy*, p. 120.
5. *Tolstoy's Letters*, October 17, 1878, vol. II, p. 328.
6. *Tolstoy's Letters*, January 27, 1891, vol. II, p. 474.
7. *Tolstoy's Letters*, February 10, 1908, vol. II, p. 672.
8. *Tolstoy's Letters*, February 20, 1894, vol. II, p. 500.
9. *Tolstoy's Letters*, September 13–25, 1899, vol. II, p. 583.
10. *Tolstoy's Letters*, February 15, 1899, vol. II, p. 579.
11. *Tolstoy's Letters*, August 15, 1901, vol. II, p. 602.
12. *Tolstoy's Letters*, September 10, 1895, vol. II, p. 522.
13. *Tolstoy's Letters*, August 27, 1901, vol. II, p. 604.
14. *Tolstoy's Letters*, October 23, 1904, vol. II, p. 645.

15. *Tolstoy's Letters*, December 4, 1905, vol. II, p. 654.
16. *Tolstoy's Letters*, January 16, 1902, vol. II, p. 608.
17. *Tolstoy's Letters*, January 22, 1902, vol. II, p. 614.
18. *Tolstoy's Letters*, September 30, 1903, vol. II, p. 632.
19. *Tolstoy's Letters*, April 22, 1904, vol. II, p. 640.
20. *Tolstoy's Letters*, December 27, 1907, vol. II, p. 672.
21. *Tolstoy's Letters*, August 17, 1908, vol. II, p. 678.
22. *Tolstoy's Letters*, May 9, 1910, vol. II, p. 700.
23. *Tolstoy's Letters*, October 15, 1909, vol. II, pp. 691–692.
24. *Tolstoy's Letters*, March 22, 1906, vol. II, p. 656.
25. *Tolstoy's Letters*, November 6, 1909, vol. II, p. 692.
26. *Tolstoy's Letters*, February 28, 1908, vol. II, p. 674.
27. *Tolstoy's Letters*, February 28, 1908, vol. II, p. 675.
28. *Tolstoy's Letters*, March 12, 1908, vol. II, p. 675.
29. *The Tragedy of Tolstoy*, p. 159.
30. *The Tragedy of Tolstoy*, p. 158.
31. *The Tragedy of Tolstoy*, p. 161.
32. *The Tragedy of Tolstoy*, p. 162.
33. *The Tragedy of Tolstoy*, p. 125.
34. *Tolstoy's Letters*, March 22, 1906, vol. II, p. 656.
35. *Reminiscences of Tolstoy*, *Chekhov and Andreev*.
36. *The Tragedy of Tolstoy*, p. 180.
37. *Recollections and Essays* (Cent. Ed., vol. 21), p. 411.
38. *The Tragedy of Tolstoy*, p. 127.
39. *Recollections and Essays* (Cent. Ed., vol. 21), p. 411.
40. *The Tolstoy Home*, p. 321.
41. *Reminiscences of Tolstoy*, *Chekhov and Andreev*, p. 46.
42. *Reminiscences of Tolstoy*, *Chekhov and Andreev*, pp. 153–154.
43. *Ultimes paroles*, 1er juin 1898, p. 48.
44. *Ultimes paroles*, p. 119.
45. *The Tragedy of Tolstoy*, p. 181.
46. *The Tragedy of Tolstoy*, p. 183.
47. *The Tragedy of Tolstoy*, p. 184.
48. *The Tragedy of Tolstoy*, p. 184.
49. *The Tragedy of Tolstoy*, p. 185.
50. *The Tragedy of Tolstoy*, p. 185.
51. *Reminiscences of Tolstoy*, *Chekhov and Andreev*.
52. *Tolstoy's Letters*, October 5, 1908, vol. II, p. 683.
53. *Tolstoy's Letters*, February 28, 1908, vol. II, p. 674.

V: DEPARTURE

27. The Division of the Spoils

1. "Tolstoï vu par un témoin," *Europe*, 1960, p. 142.
2. *Novy Mir*, October 20, 1909.
3. "Tolstoï vu par un témoin," p. 143.

4. *Tolstoy's Letters*, January 30, 1909, vol. II, pp. 684–685.
5. *Tolstoy's Letters*, April 27, 1909, vol. II, p. 686.
6. *Novy Mir*, March 6, 1909.
7. *La tragédie de Tolstoï et de sa femme*, p. 320.
8. *La tragédie de Tolstoï et de sa femme*, p. 320.
9. *Tolstoy's Letters*, May 13, 1909, vol. II, p. 687.
10. *The Tolstoy Home*, p. 331.
11. *The Tolstoy Home*, pp. 331–332.
12. "Tolstoï vu par un témoin," p. 143.
13. *Tolstoy's Diaries*, July 21, 1909, vol. II, p. 621.
14. *The Diaries of Sofia Tolstoy*, September 2, 1909, p. 646.
15. *Ma vie avec mon père*, p. 253.
16. *The Tragedy of Tolstoy*, p. 195.
17. *The Tragedy of Tolstoy*, p. 196.
18. *Reminiscences of Tolstoy, Chekhov and Andreev.*
19. *The Tragedy of Tolstoy*, p. 197.
20. *The Tragedy of Tolstoy*, p. 196.
21. Shklovsky, *Lev Tolstoy*, p. 721.
22. *The Tragedy of Tolstoy*, p. 197.
23. Shklovsky, *Lev Tolstoy*, p. 722.
24. Shklovsky, *Lev Tolstoy*, p. 722.
25. "Tolstoï vu par un témoin," p. 142.

28. The Last Days

1. *Tolstoy's Letters*, March 11–13, 1898, vol. II, pp. 565–566.
2. *Journaux intimes*, 13 février 1910, p. 22.
3. *Journaux intimes*, 15 janvier 1910, p. 17.
4. *Journaux intimes*, 21 janvier 1910, p. 18.
5. *Journaux intimes*, 20 mai 1910, p. 50.
6. *Tolstoy's Diaries*, April 7, 1910, vol. II, p. 652.
7. *Journaux intimes*, 5 février 1910, p. 21.
8. *Tolstoy's Diaries*, April 10, 1910, vol. II, p. 652.
9. *Tolstoy's Diaries*, January 16, 1910, vol. II, p. 647.
10. *Journaux intimes*, 17 mars 1910, p. 29.
11. *Tolstoy's Diaries*, February 15, 1910, vol. II, p. 648.
12. *Tolstoy's Diaries*, February 15, 1910, vol. II, p. 648.
13. *Journaux intimes*, 12 janvier 1910, p. 15.
14. *Journaux intimes*, 7 avril 1910, p. 35.
15. *Journaux intimes*, 23 mai 1910, p. 52.
16. *Journaux intimes*, 27 mars 1910, p. 31.
17. *Journaux intimes*, 17 mars 1910, p. 29.
18. *Journaux intimes*, 10 mai 1910, p. 44.
19. *Journaux intimes*, 10 mai 1910, pp. 45–46.
20. *Tolstoy's Diaries*, April 14, 1910, vol. II, p. 653.
21. *Journaux intimes*, 29 mai 1910, p. 53.
22. *Tolstoy's Diaries*, May 29, 1910, vol. II, p. 658.

23. *Journaux intimes*, 5 juin 1910, p. 56.
24. *Tolstoy's Diaries*, June 5, 1910, vol. II, p. 659.
25. *Tolstoy's Diaries*, June 4, 1910, vol. II, p. 658.
26. *The Tragedy of Tolstoy*, p. 162.
27. *Tolstoy's Diaries*, June 14, 1910, vol. II, p. 659.
28. *Tolstoy's Letters*, April 9, 1880, vol. II, pp. 456–457.
29. *Les révélations de la mort*, p. 163.
30. *Journaux intimes*, 22 juin 1910, p. 61.
31. *Journaux intimes*, 26 octobre 1910, p. 132.
32. *Journaux intimes*, 23 juin 1910, p. 204.
33. *Tolstoy's Diaries*, June 20, 1910, vol. II, p. 660.
34. *Tolstoy's Diaries*, June 23, 1910, vol. II, p. 660.
35. *Journaux intimes*, 23 juin 1910, p. 204.
36. *Journaux intimes*, 23 juin 1910, p. 204.
37. *Journaux intimes*, 23 juin 1910, p. 206.
38. *Tolstoy's Diaries*, June 23, 1910, vol. II, p. 660.
39. *The Diaries of Sofia Tolstoy*, June 26, 1910, p. 498.
40. *The Diaries of Sofia Tolstoy*, June 26, 1910, p. 498.
41. *Tolstoy's Letters*, May 13–26, 1904, vol. II, p. 642.
42. *Journaux intimes*, 11–18 octobre 1910, p. 173.
43. *Tolstoy's Diaries*, June 27, 1910, vol. II, p. 661.
44. *Journaux intimes*, 27 juin 1910, p. 64.
45. *The Diaries of Sofia Tolstoy*, July 7, 1910, p. 508.
46. *Tolstoy's Diaries*, July 11, 1910, vol. II, p. 662.
47. *The Diaries of Sofia Tolstoy*, July 10, 1910, p. 513.
48. *The Diaries of Sofia Tolstoy*, July 12, 1910, p. 514.
49. *Tolstoy's Letters*, July 14, 1910, vol. II, p. 701.
50. *Journaux intimes*, 14 juillet 1910, p. 344.
51. *Tolstoy's Diaries*, July 14, 1910, vol. II, p. 662.
52. *Tolstoy's Diaries*, July 22, 1910, vol. II, p. 663.
53. *The Diaries of Sofia Tolstoy*, July 22, 1910, p. 525.
54. *The Diaries of Sofia Tolstoy*, August 1, 1910, p. 534.
55. *Journaux intimes*, 24–25 juillet 1910, p. 245.
56. *The Diaries of Sofia Tolstoy*, July 25, 1910, p. 529.
57. *Tolstoy's Diaries*, July 30, 1910, vol. II, p. 678.
58. *Journaux intimes*, 30 juillet 1910, p. 116.
59. *Tolstoy's Diaries*, August 2, 1910, vol. II, p. 675.
60. *Tolstoy's Letters*, August 12, 1910, vol. II, p. 704.
61. *Tolstoy's Diaries*, August 3, 1910, vol. II, p. 678.
62. *The Diaries of Sofia Tolstoy*, August 3, 1910, p. 536.
63. *Journaux intimes*, 3 août 1910, p. 354.
64. *Tolstoy's Diaries*, August 6, 1910, vol. II, p. 678.
65. *The Diaries of Sofia Tolstoy*, August 4, 1910, p. 537.
66. *Tolstoy's Diaries*, August 7, 1910, vol. II, p. 679.
67. *Tolstoy's Diaries*, August 7, 1910, vol. II, p. 679.
68. *Tolstoy's Diaries*, August 8, 1910, vol. II, p. 679.
69. *Tolstoy's Diaries*, August 8, 1910, vol. II, p. 679.

70. *Journaux intimes*, 10 août 1910, p. 119.
71. *Tolstoy's Diaries*, August 16, 1910, vol. II, p. 680.
72. *The Diaries of Sofia Tolstoy*, August 16, 1910, p. 545.
73. *The Diaries of Sofia Tolstoy*, August 16, 1910, p. 545.
74. *Tolstoy's Diaries*, August 17, 1910, vol. II, p. 680.
75. *Tolstoy's Diaries*, August 10, 1910, vol. II, p. 679.
76. *The Diaries of Sofia Tolstoy*, August 17, 1910, p. 546.
77. *Journaux intimes*, 21 août 1910, p. 268.
78. *The Diaries of Sofia Tolstoy*, September 4, 1910, p. 561.
79. *The Diaries of Sofia Tolstoy*, August 17, 1910, p. 547.
80. *Journaux intimes*, 17 août 1910, p. 167.
81. *The Diaries of Sofia Tolstoy*, August 18, 1910, p. 548.
82. *Tolstoy's Diaries*, August 18, 1910, vol. II, p. 680.
83. *The Diaries of Sofia Tolstoy*, August 19, 1910, p. 549.
84. *The Diaries of Sofia Tolstoy*, August 23, 1910, p. 552.
85. *The Diaries of Sofia Tolstoy*, August 20, 1910, p. 550.
86. *Tolstoy's Diaries*, August 23, 1910, vol. II, p. 681.
87. *The Diaries of Sofia Tolstoy*, August 25, 1910, p. 553.
88. *Tolstoy's Diaries*, August 28, 1910, vol. II, pp. 681–682.
89. *The Diaries of Sofia Tolstoy*, August 25–28, 1910, pp. 554–557.
90. *Tolstoy's Diaries*, August 30, 1910, vol. II, p. 682.
91. *Tolstoy Remembered*, p. 235.
92. *Journaux intimes*, 31 août 1910, p. 359.
93. *Journaux intimes*, 31 août 1910, p. 360.
94. *Tolstoy's Diaries*, September 2, 1910, vol. II, p. 682.
95. *The Diaries of Sofia Tolstoy*, August 30, 1910, p. 559.
96. *The Diaries of Sofia Tolstoy*, September 2, 1910, p. 560.
97. *Journaux intimes*, 2 septembre 1910, p. 123.
98. *The Diaries of Sofia Tolstoy*, September 3, 1910, p. 561.
99. *The Diaries of Sofia Tolstoy*, September 4, 1910, p. 561.
100. *Tolstoy's Diaries*, September 10, 1910, vol. II, p. 682.
101. *Journaux intimes*, 10 septembre 1910, p. 171.
102. *Tolstoy's Diaries*, September 10, 1910, vol. II, p. 668.
103. *The Diaries of Sofia Tolstoy*, September 10, 1910, p. 563.
104. *The Diaries of Sofia Tolstoy*, September 10, 1910, p. 563.
105. *Tolstoy's Diaries*, September 11, 1910, vol. II, p. 683.
106. *The Diaries of Sofia Tolstoy*, September 12, 1910, p. 564.
107. *The Diaries of Sofia Tolstoy*, September 12, 1910, p. 564.
108. *Tolstoy's Diaries*, September 14, 1910, vol. II, p. 668.
109. *Tolstoy's Diaries*, September 15, 1910, vol. II, p. 668; *Journaux intimes*, 15 septembre 1910, p. 94.
110. *Tolstoy's Diaries*, September 27, 1910, vol. II, p. 684.
111. *Journaux intimes*, 23 septembre 1910, p. 372.
112. *Tolstoy's Diaries*, September 24, 1910, p. 683.
113. *The Diaries of Sofia Tolstoy*, September 26, 1910, p. 567.
114. *Tolstoy's Diaries*, September 27, 1910, vol. II, p. 684.
115. *The Diaries of Sofia Tolstoy*, September 27, 1910, p. 568.
116. *The Diaries of Sofia Tolstoy*, September 29, 1910, p. 568.
117. *Tolstoy's Diaries*, September 29, 1910, vol. II, p. 684.

118. *Tolstoy's Diaries*, October 2, 1910, vol. II, p. 671.
119. *Tolstoy's Diaries*, October 2, 1910, vol. II, p. 684.
120. *Tolstoy's Diaries*, October 5, 1910, vol. II, p. 671.
121. *Tolstoy's Diaries*, October 5, 1910, vol. II, p. 685.
122. *Tolstoy's Diaries*, October 6, 1910, vol. II, p. 672.
123. *The Diaries of Sofia Tolstoy*, October 3, 1910, p. 569.
124. *Tolstoy's Diaries*, October 7, 1910, vol. II, p. 685.
125. *The Diaries of Sofia Tolstoy*, October 7, 1910, p. 572.
126. *The Diaries of Sofia Tolstoy*, October 9, 1910, p. 573.
127. *The Diaries of Sofia Tolstoy*, October 9, 1910, p. 573.
128. *Tolstoy's Diaries*, October 10, 1910, vol. II, p. 685.
129. *Tolstoy's Diaries*, October 11, 1910, vol. II, p. 672.
130. *Tolstoy's Diaries*, October 11, 1910, vol. II, p. 685.
131. *Tolstoy's Diaries*, October 12, 1910, vol. II, p. 685.
132. *The Diaries of Sofia Tolstoy*, October 12, 1910, p. 575.
133. *Tolstoy's Diaries*, October 12, 1910, vol. II, p. 673.
134. *Reminiscences of Tolstoy, Chekhov and Andreev*, p. 64.
135. *Tolstoy's Diaries*, October 16, 1910, vol. II, p. 673.
136. *The Diaries of Sofia Tolstoy*, October 16, 1910, p. 579.
137. *The Diaries of Sofia Tolstoy*, October 16, 1910, p. 580.
138. *The Diaries of Sofia Tolstoy*, October 16, 1910, p. 580.
139. *Tolstoy's Diaries*, October 16, 1910, vol. II, p. 673.
140. *Tolstoy's Diaries*, October 17, 1910, vol. II, p. 686.
141. *The Diaries of Sofia Tolstoy*, October 17, 1910, p. 581.
142. *Journaux intimes*, 17 octobre 1910, p. 179.
143. *The Diaries of Sofia Tolstoy*, October 18, 1910, p. 582.
144. *Tolstoy's Diaries*, October 19, 1910, vol. II, p. 674.
145. *The Diaries of Sofia Tolstoy*, October 19, 1910, p. 582.
146. *The Diaries of Sofia Tolstoy*, October 19, 1910, p. 583.
147. *Documents sur la mort de Tolstoï*, p. 15.
148. *Journaux intimes*, 20 octobre 1910, p. 380.
149. *Documents sur la mort de Tolstoï*, p. 19.
150. *Tolstoy's Diaries*, October 21, 1910, vol. II, p. 686.
151. *Tolstoy's Diaries*, October 20, 1910, vol. II, p. 686.
152. *Tolstoy's Letters*, October 20, 1910, vol. II, p. 710.
153. *The Tragedy of Tolstoy*, p. 248.
154. *Journaux intimes*, 17 octobre 1910, p. 152.
155. *La tragédie de Tolstoï et de sa femme*, p. 352.
156. *Tolstoy's Diaries*, October 22, 1910, vol. II, p. 687.
157. *The Diaries of Sofia Tolstoy*, October 21, 1910, p. 583.
158. *Journaux intimes*, 21 octobre 1910, p. 107.
159. *Tolstoy's Diaries*, October 22, 1910, vol. II, p. 674.
160. *Journaux intimes*, 23 octobre 1910, p. 107.
161. *Journaux intimes*, 24 octobre 1910, p. 108.
162. *Tolstoy Remembered.*
163. *Tolstoy's Diaries*, October 26, 1910, vol. II, p. 687.
164. *Tolstoy's Diaries*, October 25, 1910, vol. II, p. 687.
165. *The Diaries of Sofia Tolstoy*, October 25, 1910.
166. *The Diaries of Sofia Tolstoy*, October 27, 1910, p. 677.

29. Escape

1. *Tolstoy's Diaries*, October 28, 1910, vol. II, p. 687.
2. *Tolstoy's Diaries*, October 28, 1910, vol. II, pp. 675–676.
3. *Tolstoy's Letters*, October 28, 1910, vol. II, p. 710.
4. *Journaux intimes*, p. 153.
5. *Journaux intimes*, 28 octobre 1910, p. 110.
6. *Novy Mir*, Moscow, July 1978. (All other *Novy Mir* references in this chapter refer to same July 1978 issue.)
7. *The Tragedy of Tolstoy*, p. 253.
8. *Tolstoy's Letters*, October 28, 1910, p. 711.
9. *Tolstoy's Diaries*, October 28, 1910, vol. II, p. 676.
10. *Tolstoy's Diaries*, October 28, 1910, vol. II, p. 676.
11. *Journaux intimes*, 28 octobre 1910, p. 154.
12. Shlovsky, *Lev Tolstoy*, p. 746.
13. Shlovsky, *Lev Tolstoy*, p. 746.
14. *Tolstoy's Diaries*, October 28, 1910, vol. II, p. 676.
15. *Novy Mir*.
16. *Resurrection*, p. 561.
17. *Tolstoï par lui-même et ses contemporains*.
18. *Tolstoï par lui-même et ses contemporains*.
19. *Tolstoy's Letters*, October 28, 1910, vol. II, p. 712.
20. *Journaux intimes*, p. 182.
21. *The Diaries of Sofia Tolstoy*, October 28, 1910, p. 676.
22. *Documents sur la mort de Tolstoï*, p. 7.
23. *Documents sur la mort de Tolstoı*, p. 7.
24. *Documents sur la mort de Tolstoï*, pp. 7–8.
25. *Tolstoy's Diaries*, October 29, 1910, vol. II, p. 676.
26. *Tolstoy's Diaries*, October 29, 1910, vol. II, p. 676.
27. *Journaux intimes*, p. 158.
28. *Tolstoy's Letters*, October 29, 1910, pp. 712–713.
29. *Novy Mir*.
30. *Tolstoy's Diaries*, October 30, 1910, vol. II, p. 677.
31. *Novy Mir*.
32. *Tolstoy's Diaries*, October 30, 1910, vol. II, p. 677.
33. *Novy Mir*.
34. *The Tragedy of Tolstoy*, p. 257.
35. *Journaux intimes*, 29 octobre 1910, p. 113.
36. *Journaux intimes*, 29 octobre 1910, p. 325.
37. *Journaux intimes*, 2 novembre 1910.
38. *Tolstoy's Letters*, October 30, 1910, vol. II, pp. 713–714.
39. *La tragédie de Tolstoï et de sa femme*, p. 346.
40. *The Tragedy of Tolstoy*, p. 264.
41. *The Tragedy of Tolstoy*, p. 264.
42. *Tolstoy's Letters*, October 31, 1910, vol. II, p. 715.
43. *The Tragedy of Tolstoy*, p. 266.
44. *Novy Mir*.
45. *The Tragedy of Tolstoy*, p. 266.
46. *Novy Mir*.

47. *The Tragedy of Tolstoy*, p. 268.
48. *Novy Mir*.
49. *The Tragedy of Tolstoy*, p. 269.
50. *The Tragedy of Tolstoy*, p. 269.
51. *The Tragedy of Tolstoy*, p. 269.
52. *The Tragedy of Tolstoy*, p. 269.
53. *The Tragedy of Tolstoy*, p. 270.
54. *Novy Mir*.
55. *The Tragedy of Tolstoy*, p. 270.
56. *Tolstoy's Letters*, November 1, 1910, vol. II, p. 716.
57. *The Tragedy of Tolstoy*, p. 271.
58. *The Tragedy of Tolstoy*, p. 271.
59. *Tolstoy's Letters*, November 1, 1910, vol. II, pp. 716–717.
60. *The Diaries of Sofia Tolstoy*, November 1, 1910, pp. 677–678.
61. *Journaux intimes*, 31 octobre 1910, p. 133.
62. *The Tragedy of Tolstoy*, p. 273.
63. *Novy Mir*.
64. *The Tragedy of Tolstoy*, pp. 272–276.
65. *Novy Mir*.
66. *Tolstoï est mort*, p. 18.
67. *Tolstoï est mort*, p. 11.
68. *Tolstoï est mort*, p. 37.
69. *Novy Mir*.
70. *Novy Mir*.
71. *The Tragedy of Tolstoy*, p. 277.
72. *Tolstoy's Diaries*, November 3, 1910, vol. II, p. 677.
73. *Journaux intimes*, 3 novembre 1910, p. 114.
74. *The Tragedy of Tolstoy*, p. 278.
75. *Tolstoy Remembered*, p. 241.
76. *The Tragedy of Tolstoy*, p. 278.
77. *Tolstoy Remembered*, p. 241.
78. *Tolstoy Remembered*, p. 241.
79. *Tolstoy Remembered*, pp. 241–242.
80. *Novy Mir*.
81. *The Tragedy of Tolstoy*, p. 279.
82. *The Tragedy of Tolstoy*, p. 369.
83. *Novy Mir*.
84. *The Tragedy of Tolstoy*, p. 280.
85. *Novy Mir*.
86. *The Diaries of Sofia Tolstoy*, November 4, 1910, p. 678.
87. *Tolstoï est mort*, 4 novembre 1910, p. 28.
88. *The Tragedy of Tolstoy*, p. 281.
89. *Tolstoï est mort*, p. 61.
90. *Novy Mir*.
91. *The Tragedy of Tolstoy*, p. 283.
92. *Tolstoy Remembered by His Son*.
93. *Tolstoï est mort*, p. 77.
94. *Tolstoy Remembered*, p. 242.
95. *The Truth About My Father*.

96. *Tolstoï est mort*, p. 202.
97. *The Tragedy of Tolstoy*, p. 286.
98. *Novy Mir*.
99. *The Tragedy of Tolstoy*, pp. 285–286.
100. *Sevastopol*, p. 10.
101. *Monsieur le comte*, p. 221.
102. *The Tragedy of Tolstoy*, p. 286.
103. *The Tragedy of Tolstoy*, p. 287.
104. *Journaux intimes*, p. 160.
105. *The Tragedy of Tolstoy*, p. 287.
106. *Tolstoy Remembered*, p. 242.
107. *Journaux intimes*, p. 161.
108. *Tolstoï est mort*, p. 122.
109. *Tolstoï est mort*, p. 188.
110. *Tolstoï est mort*, p. 160.
111. *The Tragedy of Tolstoy*, p. 288.
112. *Tolstoy Remembered*, p. 243.
113. *Novy Mir*.
114. *Journaux intimes*, 7 novembre 1910, p. 390.
115. *Journaux intimes*, 7 novembre 1910, p. 390.

30. The Outcome

1. *Tolstoy Remembered*, pp. 147–148.
2. *Ultimes paroles*, p. 265.
3. *Tolstoy's Diaries*, July 28, 1884, vol. I, p. 223.
4. *Leo Tolstoy, His Life and Work*, p. xxv.
5. *Leo Tolstoy, His Life and Work*, p. xxv.
6. *Journaux et carnets*, tome II, 5 février 1898, p. 640.
7. *Tolstoï sans le tolstoïsme*, p. 34.
8. *Novy Mir*, Moscow, July 1978.
9. *Journaux intimes*, 10 mai 1910, p. 44.
10. *Tolstoy's Diaries*, June 24, 1910, vol. II, p. 660.
11. *Tolstoy's Letters*, August 14, 1910, vol. II, pp. 704–705.
12. *Tolstoy's Diaries*, October 2, 1910, vol. II, p. 671.
13. *Tolstoy's Diaries*, October 18, 1910, vol. II, p. 674.
14. *Tolstoy's Diaries*, October 19, 1910, vol. II, p. 674.

Bibliography

BOOKS IN ENGLISH

C. Asquith. *Married to Tolstoy*. London: Hutchinson, 1960.

I. Berlin. *Russian Thinkers*. London: Hogarth Press, 1978.

P. Biryukov. *Leo Tolstoy, His Life and Work*. London: Heinemann, 1906.

F. M. Dostoyevsky. *The Diary of a Writer*. Translated and annotated by Boris Brasol, 2 vols. New York: Scribners, 1949.

E. H. Erikson. *Young Man Luther*. New York: W. W. Norton, 1958.

M. Gorky. *Reminiscences of Tolstoy, Chekhov and Andreev*. Translated by Katherine Mansfield, S. S. Koteliansky, and Leonard Woolf. London: Hogarth Press, 1934.

A. Herzen. *My Past and Thoughts*. London: Chatto & Windus, 1979.

E. Kadloubovsky and G. E. H. Palmer, translators. *Writings from the Philokalia on Prayer of the Heart*. London: Faber and Faber, 1951.

V. I. Lenin. *Collected Works*. Translated by Dora Cox, edited by George Hanna. London: Lawrence and Wishart, 1963.

Loyola, Saint Ignatius. *The Spiritual Exercises*. Translated by L. J. Puhl, 1951.

V. Shklovsky. *Lev Tolstoy*. Translated by Olga Shartse. Moscow: Progress Publishers, 1978.

G. Steiner. *Tolstoy or Dostoevsky*. New York: Knopf, 1959.

A. Tolstoy. *The Tragedy of Tolstoy*. London: George Allen and Unwin, 1933.

L. N. Tolstoy: Quotations from Tolstoy's works are taken from the Centenary Edition published by Oxford University Press, translated by Aylmer Maude, except for *The Cossacks* (including *Happy Ever After* and *The Death of Ivan Ilyich*), *War and Peace*, *Anna Karenina*, and *Resurrection*, which are quoted in the Penguin Classics translation by Rosemary Edmonds.

Tolstoy's Diaries. Edited and translated by R. F. Christian. 2 vols. New York: Scribners, 1985.

Tolstoy's Letters. Edited and translated by R. F. Christian. 2 vols. New York: Scribners, 1978.

Tolstoy's Writings on Civil Disobedience and Non-Violence. London: Peter Owen, 1968.

S. A. Tolstoy. *The Diaries of Sofia Tolstoy.* Edited and translated by Cathy Porter. London: Jonathan Cape, 1985.

T. Tolstoy. *The Tolstoy Home, Diaries of Tatyana Sukhotin-Tolstoy.* Translated by Alec Brown. London: Harvill Press, 1950.

T. Tolstoy. *Tolstoy Remembered.* Translated by Derek Coltman. London: Michael Joseph, 1977.

L. L. Tolstoy. *The Truth About My Father.* London: John Murray, 1924.

S. L. Tolstoy. *Tolstoy Remembered by His Son.* Translated by Moura Budberg. London: Weidenfeld & Nicolson, 1961.

H. Troyat. *Tolstoy.* Translated by Nancy Amphoux. Harmondsworth: Penguin, 1970.

S. Zweig. *Adepts in Self-Portraiture,* New York: Viking, 1928.

BOOKS IN FRENCH

Y. Bounine. *La délivrance de Tolstoï.* Paris: Gallimard, 1939.

L. Chestov. *Les révélations de la mort.* Paris: Plon, 1923.

P. Claudel. *Journal,* tome II. Paris: Pléiade, Gallimard, 1969.

E. Erikson. *Luther avant Luther.* Paris: Flammarion, 1968.

Europe, no. 67, 15 juillet 1928, Paris: Rieder, 1928.

Europe, nos. 379–380, novembre–décembre 1960. Paris: Editeurs français réunis, 1960.

A. Gide. *Journal.* Paris: Pléiade, Gallimard, 1948.

N. Gourfinkel. *Tolstoï sans le tolstoïsme.* Paris: Seuil, 1946.

E. Halpérine-Kaminski. *La tragédie de Tolstoï et de sa femme.* Paris: Fayard, 1931.

S. Laffitte. *Léon Tolstoï et ses contemporains.* Paris: Seghers, 1960.

V. Lebrun. "Tolstoï vu par un témoin." *Europe,* nos. 379–380, novembre–décembre 1960.

V. I. Lénine. *Sur l'art et la littérature.* Paris: Gallimard [Collection 10/18], 1975.

D. Maroger. *Les Idées pédagogiques de Tolstoï.* Lausanne: Editions l'âge d'homme, 1974.

D. Merejkowski. *Tolstoï et Dostoïevski.* Paris: Perrin, 1903.

G. V. Plekhanov. *L'art et la vie sociale.* Paris: Editions sociales, 1949.

W. Pozner. *Tolstoï est mort.* Paris: Plon, 1935.

C. Prévost. *Littérature, politique et idéologie.* Paris: Editions sociales, 1973.

M. Proust. *A la recherche du temps perdu.* Paris: Gallimard, 1954.

W. Reich. *Le meurtre du Christ.* Paris: Champ Libre, 1975.

R. Rolland. *Monsieur le comte.* Cahiers, no. 24. Paris: Albin Michel, 1978.

C. Salomon. *Documents sur la mort de Tolstoï.* Paris: N.R.F., 1922.

A. Suarès. *Léon Tolstoï.* Paris: Union pour l'action morale, 1898.

A. Tolstoï. *Ma vie avec mon père.* Traduit par A. Pierre. Paris: Rieder, 1933.

L. N. Tolstoï (unless otherwise stated, references to L. Tolstoy's works are from Pléiade edition, published by Gallimard 1960–1985).

Appels aux dirigeants. Paris: Fasquelle, 1902.

Conseils aux dirigés. Paris: Fasquelle, 1903.
Dernières paroles. Paris: Mercure de France, 1905.
Ecrits sur l'art. Présenté par Radoyce. Paris: Gallimard, 1971.
Genghis Khan et le téléphone. Commentaires no. 4. Paris: Julliard, 1969 (first published in Russian in Paris in 1910, but never in Russia).
Journal intime. Traduction de J. Chuzeville et W. Pozner. Paris: Fasquelle, 1926.
Journal intime 1895–1899. Présenté par Birioukov. Genève: Flammarion, 1917.
La Famine. Paris: Perrin, 1893.
La révolution russe, sa portée mondiale. Paris: Fasquelle, 1907.
Les rayons de l'aube: Dernières études philosophiques. Paris: Stock, 1901.
Oeuvres posthumes. *Les mémoires d'un fou*. Traduit par G. d'Ostoya et G. Masson, Paris: Gallimard, 1926.
Oeuvres posthumes. *Notes d'un fou*. Traduit par Tougouchy. Genève: Editions Rencontre, 1962.
Paroles d'un homme libre. Paris: Perrin, 1901.
Propos anti-militaristes. Paris: La Chaux de Fonds, 1898.
Sur l'instruction publique. Oeuvres complètes, tome XIV. Paris: Stock, 1906.
Théâtre. Oeuvres complètes, tome XV. Genève: Editions Rencontre, 1963.
Ultimes paroles. Paris: Société des Editions et Publications Parisiennes, 1909.
Un cas de conscience. Paris: Stock, 1935 and 1979. (First version of *Resurrection*.)
L. and S. Tolstoï. *Journaux intimes de Léon Tolstoï et Sophie Tolstoï—1910*. Connaissance de soi. Paris: Gallimard, 1940.
S. A. Tolstoï. *Journal de la comtesse Léon Tolstoï*. Paris: Plon, 1930.
Journal intime, 3 vols. Paris: Albin Michel, 1980, 1981, 1982.
T. Tolstoï. *Journal*. Traduit par Banine. Paris: Plon, 1953.
N. Weisbein. *L'Evolution religieuse de Tolstoï*. Librairie des cinq continents, 1960.
Le monde de Tolstoï, "Comment travaillait Tolstoï." Ouvrage collectif. Moscou: Editions du Progrès, 1978.
Récits d'un pèlerin russe. Traduit par Jean Laloy. Paris: Seuil, 1974.
Tolstoï par Tolstoï, *Autobiographie épistolaire*. Paris: L'Edition moderne, 1912.
Tolstoï vu par lui-même et ses contemporains. Ouvrage collectif. Moscou: Editions du Progrès, 1977.

Index

Note: Titles of work not otherwise identified are by Leo Tolstoy.